THE
AUGUSTAN
ARISTOCRACY

Piso the Pontifex
(*see* p. 345)

THE
AUGUSTAN
ARISTOCRACY

RONALD SYME

CLARENDON PRESS · OXFORD

Oxford University Press, Walton Street, Oxford OX2 6DP

Oxford New York Toronto
Delhi Bombay Calcutta Madras Karachi
Kuala Lumpur Singapore Hong Kong Tokyo
Nairobi Dar es Salaam Cape Town
Melbourne Auckland Madrid
and associated companies in
Berlin Ibadan

Oxford is a trade mark of Oxford University Press

Published in the United States
by Oxford University Press Inc., New York

First published in hardback 1986
First issued in Clarendon Paperbacks (with corrections) 1989

British Library Cataloguing in Publication Data
Syme, Ronald, 1903–1989
The Augustan aristocracy.
1. Ancient Rome. Aristocracy, 1–68
I. Title
305.5'2'0937
ISBN 0-19-814731-7

3 5 7 9 10 8 6 4 2

Printed in Great Britain on acid-free paper at
The Alden Press, Oxford

PREFACE

The study of history has been pursued under a long preoccupation with the origins of Rome, laws and institutions, biography, and so on. Neglect attended upon an aristocracy unique in duration and predominance; and the better sort in the towns and peoples of Italy conveyed little appeal. Evidence there was, but miscellaneous and dispersed, infested with all manner of vexatious problems.

As always, material determines treatment, although it need not preclude variety. On a surface view the epoch of Caesar Augustus appears well documented. Narrations are built up around the person and actions of the ruler. Not enough is said about the *nobilitas* now renascent after civil war and tribulation. A proper enquiry into their families cannot be confined within narrow limits. Both ancestors and posterity come into the count.

A subject of this kind defies continuous exposition. The present volume comprises a sequence of studies (arranged not without care for coherence), each composed so as to be intelligible in itself and by itself. An original plan of ten chapters went on to fifteen, and, after changes and omissions, expanded to a portentous total. Much labour therefore and anxieties of selection for an author unable to emulate the easy people 'who write without fear or research'.

Since the same characters recur again and again in various contexts and combinations, repetition could not be avoided. Other constraints or defects will be evident, such as rigorous compression or scant regard for sundry aspects of a multifarious theme. When the annotation comes to be added in the course of the next twelve months, an attempt will be made to concentrate on the primary evidence. The execution may well turn out to baffle zeal for economy.

The thirty chapters were composed at different times in the course of the last decade. One essay for example, 'Nero's Aunts', coincided with a year which official declarations consecrated to the honouring of women. Seven others are likewise anterior to *History in Ovid* (which was completed in 1976).

Given the nature of the evidence, the present compilation carries conjecture and controversy in full measure. As a kind of incomplete work of reference it may be of use to students of literature as well as history.

Wolfson College   R. S.
30 September 1982

ADDENDUM TO PREFACE

Necessity ensued for genealogical tables. Hence labour and further delay. Out of the process emerged some admonitions. For example, a separate chapter should have been allotted to Paullus the Censor, a cardinal character in the alliances of the dynasty. As with other shortcomings in a long exposition, enough to recall what a historian said some two centuries ago: 'of what avail is this tardy knowledge? Where error is irretrievable, repentance is useless.'

For help with proofs (not for the first time) I am happy to render thanks to Eric Birley and to Anthony Birley; and the Index, arduous task, was neatly managed by Sonia Argyle.

Wolfson College   R. S.
1 May 1985

CONTENTS

I

The *Nobilitas*

The heir of Caesar celebrated his triumph in August of 29, rival in fame to Alexander as a world conqueror and also parading as the new Romulus. The last in the sequence of the monarchic faction-leaders terminated an epoch and confirmed autocratic government.

Senators and knights, the twin components of the propertied class, saw an end at last to disruption and turmoil. In 91 the allied peoples of Italia had seceded. On the Bellum Italicum, and blending with it, followed civil strife: in all a ten years' war. After Sulla the Dictator intervened three decades of precarious peace, broken when the proconsul of Gaul crossed the Rubicon, to issue in twenty years of violence or despotic rule.

From the young Caesar the two orders now expected security and recognition, change abated, the plebs and the armies curbed. For the *nobiles* (the consular families) the coming of the monarchy was the latest in a sequence of defeats. Bruised and diminished, though power lapsed, they might still hope to regain some of the resources of social prestige.

In the first place, as ancestry and 'dignitas' demanded, access to a consulship—and not submerged or extruded as recently by a mass of *novi homines*. Next, the major priesthoods, in the early time their monopoly and still tending to become hereditary in certain *gentes*. Third, governorships abroad, for pride and for profit even if not any more to refresh the laurels won by ancestors.

From 31 Imperator Caesar held the consulate each year for the full twelve months. The Triumvirate had obtruded numerous *suffecti*, as many as six in 33; and in 30 there were still three of them. For 29, only one. That was a promising sign. The next year more than confirmed.

The ruler handed over the twelve *fasces* to his colleague M. Vipsanius Agrippa.[1] The practice of the Republic thus returned: rotation month by month of the 'insignia imperii'. Normal government (it follows) was visibly heralded on February 1st of the year 28.[2] For certain civilian tasks the two consuls assumed censorial powers; and a single comprehensive decree annulled arbitrary or illegal enactments of the Triumvirs. In this

---

[1] Dio LIII. 1. 1. In the view of some scholars, following Mommsen, the ruler had hitherto carried twenty-four *fasces*, which were now divided. Dio's own comments were not helpful.
[2] This notion is accorded emphasis in *Tacitus* (1958), 365.

fashion the sixth consulship of Imperator Caesar established the new dispensation.[3]

On January 13th of 27 the Senate assembled to hear a proclamation. Caesar's heir resigned all his powers, transferring sovereignty where it belonged, to Senate and People. Senators adjured him not to abandon the 'res publica' which he had saved and preserved.[4] The Imperator was persuaded to accept a special mandate, namely the arduous charge of the principal military zones in the Roman dominion west and east, to be held for a period of ten years. Three days later, on the motion of a senior consular, the high assembly voted various honours and conferred the name 'Augustus'.

Caesar Augustus conceded that he had acquired supremacy, 'potitus rerum omnium'—but it was through a general consensus.[5] The new arrangement renounced less than instant gratitude assumed or the superficial fancied. Mere despotism was a crude and precarious form of government, repugnant to the traditions of a nation that had conquered the world through obedience to 'liberty and the laws'. Legalized authority enabled the ruler to circumvent rivalry, control the channels of patronage, and ultimately ensure a smooth transmission of the power. Against any questioning, Caesar would hardly require anxious thought or help from lawyers.[6] 'Potentia' now assumed the respectable name of 'auctoritas'.

The vast resources of the Princeps were in no way impaired: money and soldiers, the plebs of Rome, personal allegiance confirmed by the oath sworn in 32 by 'Tota Italia' and extended to take in cities and tribes, kings and princes and tetrarchs. 'Divi filius' was already worshipped as a king and a god in the eastern lands.[7]

The new form of government avowed its origin in the 'extraordinaria imperia' voted to the dynasts in the closing epoch of the Republic; and the autocratic rule of the Triumvirs was based upon a law of the Roman People. The Princeps duly went on to exploit the 'res publica', encroaching on the functions of Senate, of magistrates, of laws.

Nobiles had spoken of the 'res publica' as their own property.[8] It suited

---

[3] Tacitus, *Ann* III. 28.2: 'iura quis pace et principe uteremur'.

[4] Gibbon's exposition will be read with pleasure, and with profit, beginning with 'it would require the pen of Tacitus . . . to describe the various emotions of the senate' (Ch. III, p. 98, in the edition of 1802).

[5] *Res Gestae* 34, cf. below, p. 80.

[6] 'Staatsrecht' failed to excite the interest of Roman jurists. A paradoxical explanation was proffered by F. Schulz: 'because the last 150 years of the Republic were occupied by a continuous constitutional crisis' (*History of Roman Legal Science* (1946), 81).

[7] For the relevance of Hellenistic monarchies, E. Rawson, *JRS* LXV (1975), 148 ff.; for continuity between Triumvirate and Principate, F. Millar, *JRS* LXIII (1973), 50 ff.

[8] Thus Livius Drusus when aedile: 'Remmio collegae quaedam de utilitate rei publicae suggerenti, quid tibi, inquit, cum re publica nostra?' (*De vir. ill.* 66. 2).

their predominance admirably. It furnished a code of rules to conserve oligarchic equality through *leges annales* which regulated competition and thwarted youthful aspirations. It divided authority in the state and checked the rise of powerful individuals. Finally, the 'res publica' was a means to cajole and deceive through open elections, since the 'libertas populi Romani' tended to choose under guidance the known names.[9] To endure, the system depended on consent or docility—and further on cohesion, on restraint and public spirit in the governing class.

For the *nobilitas* as for the ruler, signal advantages at once became manifest. During the evil years the Senate had swollen to a total of over a thousand, admitting common soldiers, sons of freedmen, even foreigners. In 28 Caesar and Agrippa carried out a purge of the high assembly. They induced nearly two hundred undesirables to depart—persons falling short of the fortune requisite to maintain their station or deficient in loyalty and protection.

Defect of birth was no bar. Some of the great adventurers had perished, such as Ventidius and Canidius; and the magnate from Punic Gades, Cornelius Balbus, was no longer among the living. In the previous year his nephew had been accorded the rank of ex-consul.[10]

Triumviral Rome had seen partisans grasping the *fasces* far below the age of forty-two—and some scandalous, such as Agrippa, close coeval to Caesar's heir. Peace and order imported mitigation: the Republican norm, but for *novi homines*. The *nobiles* benefit from one of the gains of the Revolution. They get an advantage of ten years. As a necessary consequence, entry to the Senate by the quaestorship obtains at twenty-five instead of thirty. Missing direct record in the pages of history, these provisions may be assigned to the year of the census.[11]

As tradition ordained, provinces were disposed by lot or arrangement. An innovation of the year 52, devised with a political intent all too clear, was soon brought back into service.[12] It prescribed an interval of five years for praetors and consuls after the urban magistracy. Of the provinces, ex-consuls took Asia and Africa, as recently. Like Africa, Macedonia and Illyricum had garrisons of legions, but the contrast was visible and painful against the portion of Caesar: Spain, Gaul, and Syria.

Power receding, aristocrats looked to priesthoods for 'dignitas' and social

---

[9] Cicero shows up the vacuity of popular sovereignty: 'ferunt enim suffragia, mandant imperia magistratus, ambiuntur, rogantur, sed ea dant quae etiam si nolint, danda sunt' (*De r.p.* I. 47). Real power, he continues, is measured 'familiarum vetustatibus aut pecuniis'.

[10] Deduced from 'ex privato consularis' (Velleius II. 51. 3). Not in Dio, who presents two other names, viz. C. Cluvius and C. Furnius (LII. 42. 4).

[11] They emerge from privileges granted to Marcellus in 24 (Dio LIII. 23. 3 f.) and to the stepsons of the Princeps a little later.

[12] Dio LIII. 14. 2. The precise year is not on record.

eminence. The recent years witnessed a double phenomenon. While alien superstitions were rampant, ancient cults and ceremonies revived.[13] In January of 29 the Senate decreed that the Gates of War should be closed, to demonstrate warfare ceasing by land and sea; and the name of the victor was inscribed in the hymn of the *Salii*. The youthful priests of Mars had not been heard of for a long time, nor had the *Fetiales*, resurrected three years previously to declare a just war on the Queen of Egypt.[14]

It was from total obscurity that the *Sodales Titii* now emerged. The bare name was known to the learned Varro, who opined that they might have something to do with augury.[15] Nothing further is vouchsafed, except their antiquity. Romulus created the sodality, or better, the Sabine Titus Tatius.[16]

More important functions were designed for the fraternity of the *Arvales*, whose origin is explicit. Acca Larentia, the foster mother of Romulus, had twelve sons. When one of them died, Romulus was enlisted to complete the number.[17] Of both fraternities only Varro had shown awareness, and no annalist named a member.[18]

Imperator Caesar was advertising an affinity to Romulus in a variety of fashions. He wanted to take the name, so it is alleged.[19] Safer counsels prevailed. The Founder had a dubious repute, adored by plebs and army, but on one report an autocrat killed by senators. It was too close to Divus Julius whose temple was consecrated in 29, a few days after the triumph. With the old poet's 'augusto augurio', the new device and name evoked the birth of the city.[20]

The primeval aristocracy was the patriciate, long in decline but not to be neglected as 'decus ac robur' in a renascent Republic. Patrician themselves, both Sulla and Caesar showed them favour. New *gentes* were added in 29. Certain sacerdotal functions were confined to patricians, needed also to keep up a proportion in the major colleges.

Pontiffs, augurs, *quindecimviri sacris faciundis*, *septemviri epulonum*, these constituted the 'quattuor amplissima sacerdotia'.[21] For *nobiles* they were

[13] For the detail, K. Latte, *Römische Religionsgeschichte* (1960), 294 ff., with sombre conclusions about the Augustan religious revival (309 ff.), Observe likewise G. Dumézil, *Ancient Roman Religion* (Chicago, 1970), 533.

[14] Dio L.4.4.

[15] Varro, *De l.l.* V.95

[16] Tacitus, *Hist.* II. 95.1 (Romulus): *Ann.* I. 54.1 (T. Tatius).

[17] According to the jurist Masurius Sabinus, the source of Pliny (*NH* XVIII.6) and of Gellius (VII.7.8).

[18] Varro, *De l.l.* V.85: 'sacra publica faciunt ut fruges ferant arva'. Of which ritual, not a trace or sign in the ample *Acta* of the Brethren.

[19] Dio LIII. 16.7 (stating that the name was in fact offered).

[20] 'Augusto augurio post quam inclita condita Roma est' (Ennius, fr. 502 V: from Varro, *R.r.* III.1.2).

[21] For a full study, M. W. H. Lewis, *The Official Priests of Rome under the Julio-Claudians* (1955). Further, J. Scheid in *ANRW* II.6 (1978), 610 ff.

accessible even in extreme youth, well before the senatorial age. The colleges now received a marked augmentation, rising above twenty members for the first three. No senator could hold more than one. Many *nobiles* might thus aspire, even without especial claims on Caesar and the friends of Caesar.[22] By the same token they shared privilege with notable consulars among the *novi homines*—and Caesar Augustus belonged, supernumerary, to each college and fraternity (not excepting the inferior *Titii* and *Fetiales*).

In official precedence the *Arvales* of necessity took rank behind the 'quattuor amplissima'. Being twelve in number, they were highly select. The new Romulus was eager to promote and invest with prestige the invention of one of his antiquarian counsellors.[23] Messalla the Augur, still extant in 29, had recently been writing on congenial topics.[24] The first protocols of the Brethren are meagre. The earliest fragment (of 21/20) carries seven names, all but one consular.[25] It suitably exhibits the veteran Domitius Calvinus, the survivor of many campaigns, and the illustrious Messalla Corvinus. On the next document (in May of AD 14) occur among six names Piso the Pontifex, Lentulus the Augur, Paullus Fabius Maximus.[26]

Caesar Augustus put the state religion to various employ. What is called the Roman constitution was not a system of written ordinances. The 'res publica' had a dual nature (institutions and persons) and it functioned largely through precedent and religious prescriptions. That is, 'mos maiorum' and the 'auspicia'—each subject to manipulation on advice from senior statesmen.[27]

Augurs were valued and commended.[28] They proved useful for obstruction.[29] Excelling in 'auctoritas', the Princeps did not need their aid, and he possessed other devices. The *quindecimviri*, however, were custodians of the Sibylline oracles (soon to be purged and revised). Those experts might come in handy to interpret a text, improve a ritual, or change the date of a festival.

[22] He was careful to register a total of eighty-three priests: at Actium and subsequent accessions (*RG* 25).

[23] In 29, cf. J. Scheid, *Les Frères Arvales. Recrutement et origine sociale sous les Empereurs Julio-Claudiens* (1975), 335 f.

[24] Messalla was an augur for fifty-five years (Macrobius I.9.4). That is, recruited by Sulla. Varro died in 27, 'prope nonagenarius', according to Jerome (*Chron.* p. 164 H).

[25] *CIL* VI. 32338, cf. below, p. 46.

[26] *CIL* VI. 2023 = *ILS* 5026.

[27] C. Cethegus (notorious for intrigue) earned for his knowledge of the 'res publica' appreciation from another expert: 'totam enim tenebat eam penitusque cognoverat. itaque in senatu consularium auctoritatem adsequebatur' (*Brutus* 178).

[28] Cicero was moved to propose (in a renovated Republic) the death penalty for defiance of augurs (*De legibus* II.21).

[29] Even under a dictatorship, as demonstrated by Antonius in January of 44 (*Phil.* II.80).

The *nobilitas* had ceremonies of its own, notably the pomp of funerals with the images of ancestors high on show. They were now brigaded for public pageantry. Wearing their vestments and emblems the priests went on parade. They offered vows and sacrifices, inaugurated the monuments of war and peace, advertised the prince and the dynasty.

Through the ages aristocrats are shown amicably disposed towards ritual and ceremony. Rome offered few occasions for ostentation of attire. Even the military had to submit. The 'gens togata' which conquered an empire forbade the wearing of uniforms or decorations in the city.

To belong to an exclusive club confers value on a life devoid of talent or denied public recognition; and it is pure delight when membership brings arcane knowledge. After the end of the first dynasty the *Arvales* turned into a congregation of that kind, mediocrity no longer protected by birth and ancestors.[30]

Sacerdotal antiquities were the suitable predilection of patricians, to be surmised for Julius Caesar in his candidature for the office of *pontifex maximus*, and actively displayed in the political scene by the head of the *gens Claudia*, Ap. Pulcher.[31] In adversity those studies afforded refuge and comfort. The jurist Ser. Sulpicius Rufus imparted instruction in 'ius pontificium':[32] and old Messalla occupied the leisure of the Triumviral years with the treatise *De auspiciis*.[33]

Erudition and competition were stimulated to make useful discoveries. Janus attracted (earlier closings might be in controversy), the *Arvales*, and so on.[34] Inadvertent or popular writers were liable to miss some information about early Rome.[35]

There were limits to research, so it appears, and even to invention. No scholar explained Dea Dia, who was worshipped by the Brethren in the month of May, or produced a past *arvalis* (even not authentic).[36] On the other hand, ancient deities might suffer affront without imputation of sacrilege. To enlarge his mansion, the *pontifex* Domitius Calvinus demolished the shrine of the unimpeachable Mutunus Tutunus.[37]

[30] As shown in *Some Arval Brethren* (1980).

[31] For his doctrine about the *lex curiata*, *Ad fam*, I.9.25. He composed a *Liber auguralis*, dedicated to Cicero (*Ad fam*. III.4.1). His addiction to necromancy (*De div*. I, 137) was not a licit extension.

[32] *Brutus* 156 (at Samos, in 47).   [33] Quoted extensively in Gellius XIII, 14 ff.

[34] For problems about Janus, K. Latte, o.c. 132 f.: R. Syme, *AJP* C (1979), 188 ff.

[35] Both Livy and Dionysius ignore the Arval Brethren. Likewise the *lex curiata*: which, so it appears, was revived by Sulla.

[36] The Vestals were better served, the earliest being Gegania and Verenia (Plutarch, *Numa* 10). The second name should be corrected: an antiquarian writer called Veranius existed, to be presumed late Republican. For other Vestals of the early time see F. Münzer, *Philologus* XCII (1937), 47 ff.

[37] Festus p. 142 L: 'de quo aris sublatis balnearia sunt ⟨f⟩acta domus Cn. D⟨omitii⟩ Calvini, cum mansisset ab urbe condita ⟨ad pri⟩ncipatum Augusti.' For this old phallic deity, next encountered in the mockery of Christian writers, see K. Vahlert, *RE* XVI. 979 ff.; R. E. A. Palmer, *Roman Religion and Roman Empire* (1974), 187 ff.

The benefits that accrued to the aristocracy were clouded with distrust and suspicion. Caesar Augustus, abolishing proconsuls in Gaul, Spain, and Syria, took those regions as his 'provincia'. Precedents availed from the closing epoch of the Republic. In 59 Julius Caesar acquired both the Gauls together with Illyricum, to be held for a quinquennium. In the next year a *Lex Clodia* made provision for the consuls Piso and Gabinius: Macedonia and Syria, likewise for an extended tenure.[38] Then in 55 another law allocated the Spains to Pompeius, Syria to Crassus, with a prolongation for the proconsul of Gaul.

In 54 a vast portion of the imperial dominion had thus been segregated and removed from control by Senate and People. It was the habit of Cato to speak against 'extraordinariae potestates'.[39] They spelled ruin for the Republic. He was later to earn credit for prescience.[40]

Such 'imperia' were normally proconsular. Nothing prevented a consul from taking up his command before the end of his year. Caesar Augustus duly set out in the garb of war, making for Gaul in the summer of 27. At the same time, the Comitia elected him consul for the next year.

Some senators may have felt that they had been taken in several months previously. It was no consolation that precedents existed for fraud and flexibility. His consulship expiring, Pompeius refrained from going to Spain. A *Lex Cornelia* of Sulla the Dictator forbade a governor to wage war beyond the borders of his province. That he would never go there but take up his abode in the suburban vicinity had not been contemplated. Against which, no sign of protest, no prosecutor.

Magnus continued, 'cum imperio'. It was 'rei publicae causa'.[41] And Magnus was able to get elected consul for the third time in 52 without giving up the Spains and surrendering seven legions.

There was also Egypt. Pompeius and the dynasts in the sequel refused to annex the kingdom. They wished to keep the rich land intact, preserved from the avid intrusion of senators or bankers. Caesar Augustus ended the protectorate, ruling as a monarch in the place of the Ptolemies. The first of the viceroys, Cornelius Gallus (who had led the army of invasion from Cyrenaica), came to grief through ambition and imprudence—or from Caesar's need to discard an exorbitant partisan. Loyal men followed. Aelius Gallus was allowed to make an expedition across the Red Sea, in the direction of Arabia Felix; and P. Petronius marched a long way to the south into Ethiopia, as far as Napata, but not to Meroe.[42]

[38] The term is nowhere on record. Perhaps a triennium. If so, a 'legis dies', i.e. 'ad Kal. Ian. quartas'.   [39] *Pro Sestio* 68.

[40] *Ad Att.* XII.4.2. In Cato's verdict it was not the split between Pompeius and Caesar that doomed the Republic but their original alliance (Plutarch, *Pompeius* 47; *Caesar* 13).

[41] Caesar *BG* VI.1.1, cf. Dio XXXIX. 63. 3 f. For a diverse opinion later on, *BC* I. 85.8: 'in se novi generis imperia constitui' etc.

[42] Napata, 'cui proxima est Meroe' (*RG* 26). In fact 430 miles (Pliny, *NH* VI. 184 f.).

Senators tediously pent up in Italy envied the opportunities so richly enjoyed by the friends of Marcus Antonius. The Triumviral years enhanced the appeal of the remote or exotic: far lands or Arcadia and the Isles of the Blest, as well as Rome of the Kings. The new dispensation prevented any senator from visiting the land of Nile even as a tourist, 'cognoscendae antiquitatis'.

Asia allured, but it fell to few. Achaia or Sicily carried no compensation. Those petty and civilian provinces merely made visible and solid the inferiority of a proconsul in the face of the equestrian viceroy. Nor did a praetorian province attract a *nobilis*—and the five-year interval precluded, should he desire to be consul 'suo anno' or not long after.

For acquiring military renown (often easy under the Republic) Macedonia held out some prospect, left like Africa and Illyricum in the sphere of the Senate. In the past a 'provincia maxime triumphalis', Macedonia had recently been the scene of advantageous warfare, and the savage peoples of Thrace were a constant nuisance. Illyricum covered the north-eastern frontier of Italy, the Cisalpina being no longer a province. Enlarged, though not much, by campaigns in 35 and 34, Illyricum confronted Pannonians not yet subdued and recalcitrant Dalmatians of the interior beyond the Dinaric Alps. As concerned Africa, Juba the prince of Mauretania retained parts of his Numidian kingdom, affording protection against the nomads conveniently subsumed under the Gaetulian name.

For Caesar's mandate, the pretext was regions requiring garrisons or defence.[43] The three military provinces retained by proconsuls implied a specious yet honourable explanation that might have been adduced. They stood closest to Italy. Carthage and Macedon evoked the fears and memories of past history, whereas from Illyricum ran the route of invasion from Emona across the Julian Alps to Aquileia, a preoccupation on the eve of the war with Marcus Antonius.

Triumphs had recently been celebrated, from Africa by Autronius Paetus, from Macedonia by Licinius Crassus, from Gaul by Messalla Corvinus. The latest was Sex. Appuleius from Spain, in January of 26.[44] It might prove to be the last. Prospects were not promising. The army was now being reduced to a total force of twenty-six legions. Not more than five or six were conceded to the three proconsuls.[45]

To men who reflected on recent transactions, destiny ordained that total dominion should come to the last of the dynasts. It had to happen.

---

[43] Strabo XVII, p. 840; Dio LIII.12.2. Explaining and enumerating the original division, both writers neglect the fact that Illyricum and Macedonia were military provinces.

[44] For the detail, *Rom. Rev.* (1939), 302 f.

[45] Who in Illyricum and in Macedonia would tend to be praetorian in rank.

The *nobilitas* forfeited liberty and power. They had also to forgo some of the display and pageantry.

Rome of the Triumvirs witnessed lively competition between active partisans: triumphs, temples repaired, or new edifices for pleasure or public utility.[46] Conspicuous among them were *nobiles* like Domitius Calvinus who rebuilt the Regia, Marcius Philippus a shrine of Hercules. In the sequel the next constructions to commemorate a senator bore the names of *novi homines*: the amphitheatre of Statilius Taurus, completed in 29, and the theatre of Cornelius Balbus, in 13.[47]

At Rome the aristocracy demanded deference, and it was not denied, but their *clientelae* were lapsing to the *patronus* of the plebs, the dispenser of games and largesse. Abroad, Caesar anxiously watched any attempt to attach the soldiers. Towns and whole territories, kings, tetrarchs, and chieftains had once owed allegiance to the names of ancient power. Those traditions and habits were curbed by the cult of the ruler. After a time cities in the Greek lands cease to honour proconsuls with the title of 'saviour and benefactor'.[48]

Proconsuls now receive a stipend in lieu of free scope for integrity or for rapine. There was a further restriction: no senator permitted to visit a province (Sicily only excepted) save by leave of the Princeps.[49]

Something worse loomed ahead. Revival in religion was not confined to antiquarian innovation or fantasy. During the years of tribulation, disturbance and fear engendered feelings of guilt, and the pride of the nation was humiliated. When failure is ascribed to moral transgression and the decline of faith, a welcome path of redemption offers. A clamour arose for reform, at first spontaneous, then encouraged and directed. A measure was passed or at least promulgated in 28.[50] The full programme had to wait for a decade. Laws were then enacted to restrain licence, to protect marriage and the family—and adultery became a crime with penalties for men as well as women. That was a departure from the Roman tradition, most distasteful to the aristocracy.

Legislation to regulate the commerce of the sexes is not easy to enforce—or easy to assess by results.[51] There were techniques of evasion, and divorce did not abate, with signal examples among the highest in the land. Further, informers and prosecutions; and the ruler might interpret immoral conduct so as to support or cover charges of treason.

By contrast, luxury is a visible phenomenon. Sumptuary laws were an

[46] *Rom. Rev.* 241 f.; 292.
[47] Dio LI. 23.1; LIV. 25.2.
[48] G.W. Bowersock, *Augustus and the Greek World* (1965), 119, cf. 150 f.
[49] Perhaps not enforced from the outset.
[50] As indicated by Propertius II.7.
[51] For a candid and sombre assessment, P. A. Brunt, *Italian Manpower* (1971), 566.

old story at Rome, held undesirable as well as ineffectual.[52] After the War of Actium conspicuous expenditure spread and flourished for a century.[53]

Society in the aftermath of war and revolution presents unlovely features. An age of prosperity opened, much money came into circulation (the disbursement of Egyptian treasure contributing), the price of land rose rapidly. Those who benefited from the Proscriptions to acquire estates and mansions cheaply went on in confidence. Alert and rapacious partisans of the dynasts had amassed great fortunes. Hence rancour and envy in others of the upper order, or an intermittent affectation of antique parsimony.

History registers sporadically the opulence of *novi homines* such as Tarius Rufus or Marcus Lollius.[54] Less was said about the blameless aristocrats who had seen the better cause in time. Along with others not so percipient they took subsidy from Caesar. It is a pleasing notion that birth and breeding are largely indifferent to money and profit.[55]

If an aristocracy cannot retain military prowess and 'bonae artes' it risks becoming a plutocracy with a past.[56] Rebuking 'luxuria atque avaritia' in the governing class, Cato denounced those who devoted much care to houses and villas and paintings, less to the commonwealth.[57] In Augustan Rome the reign of wealth finds brief and pungent expression in a sociological discourse delivered to a poet by the god Janus:

> in pretio pretium nunc est. dat census honores
> census amicitias. pauper ubique iacet.[58]

Other dangers subsist. On one definition aristocracies run through three periods. Beginning in superiority they pass to privilege and decline into vanity.[59] Rome was familiar with contrasted types of deleterious noblemen, the empty and pretentious, the stupid and heavy. Palmary specimens of 'vani' and 'stolidi' among the patrician Manlii and Lentuli afford instruction and derision.[60]

---

[52] Observe the arguments of Hortensius in 55 (Dio XXXIX.37.3), echoed in an oration of Asinius Gallus (*Ann.* II.33.2).

[53] *Ann.* III.55.

[54] *Rom. Rev.* 381; below, p. 72.

[55] As stated by J. L. Hammond, 'aristocracies have their virtues, but the virtue of a magnificent disdain for money is not to be expected in a class which for generations has taken it as a matter of course that it should be maintained by the State' (*The Village Labourer 1760–1832* (1911), 329). Roman behaviour is illustrated by W. V. Harris, *War and Imperialism in Republican Rome* (1979), 87 ff.

[56] The phrase is taken from J. A. Spender, *The Comments of Bagshot* (1912), 114.

[57] Sallust, *Cat.* 52. 5.

[58] Ovid, *Fasti* I. 217 f.

[59] As declared somewhere by Chateaubriand.

[60] P. Manlius Vulso, one of three ambassadors in 149, was reputed 'the most stupid of the Romans' (Polybius XXXVII.6.2.). In a Livian *epitome* he is registered as 'Manlius Volso stolidus' (*P. Oxy.* 668, l. 113). With Lentulus Clodianus (*cos.* 72), Sallust achieved a double demolition: 'perincertum stolidior an vanior' (*Hist.* IV.1).

Protection of weaker members was a constant preoccupation, not now to diminish through a strong infusion of that 'industria et innocentia' so eloquently commended by publicists and accepted by historians. New senators conformed to normal habits of pomp and luxury, while the ancient houses spent their substance for ostentation or went into sullen retreat.

Ancestry and pedigree came to stand for more than in the last era of the Republic.[61] It issued in arrogance or torpor. Furthermore, whereas deference and docility in the lower classes earned approval, that comportment was now prescribed for men of rank, in voluntary or venal abasement before the Caesars.[62]

The dynasty of Julii and Claudii is an aristocratic faction, annexing certain of the great houses through congenial matrimony, resplendent and ominous. They went down in ruin together.

The *nobiles* have not spoken. Rome lived on imported talent, at first municipal until provincial Italy made its impact with energy and splendour. The new Romans from Transpadana, endowed with the patriotic virtue of a frontier zone, venerated the names of old renown, the builders of empire. The writers, belonging to the propertied class, were all for stability and concord, reconciling the memory of the Republic with unswerving allegiance to the monarchy.[63]

They came to maturity of age (and some of performance) during the twenty years of discomfort. The opening epoch of the 'novus status' saw the first instalment of Livy's enterprise. If those books reported outrageous behaviour in a patrician of remote antiquity, such was the tradition he followed or enhanced. No family in his own time conceived offence. The general exposition was innocuous and improving.

Parallel to the Patavine history, the Roman epic called up on parade the heroes of ancient days: 'nati melioribus annis'. Not to any excess of nostalgia. Virgil acclaimed a link with the present felicity, the martial fame of a Claudius Marcellus leading on to commemorate the nephew of Caesar Augustus. In this atmosphere and setting the comportment of Horace, a freedman's son from Venusia, occasions no surprise. Invective and satire to begin with (but not at the expense of birth or privilege), he went on to enjoin moral regeneration and ended by extolling the high aristocracy.

The surprise would be a contemporary indictment. Sallust in his first

---

[61] *Tacitus* (1958), 570 ff.

[62] As Saint Simon observed, 'l'excès dans l'orgueil et la bassesse s'accomodent presque toujours' (VI. 496, éd. Pléiade). And on courtiers at Versailles, 'on n'oseroit dire des valets' (II. 683).

[63] G. E. F. Chilver, *Cisalpine Gaul* (1949), 208 ff. When Thrasea Paetus (from Patavium) fell foul of Nero he was defending freedom of speech and a senator's dignity. He did not attack the monarchy or criticize imperial policy.

monograph (duly avoiding the word 'Optimates') attacked the *nobilitas*, arrogant and exclusive, but also corrupt and incompetent. The portrayal of individuals lent a sharper edge to animosity—Cornelius Sulla the author of evil and Sergius Catilina a predictable product of the Sullan restoration. For an annalistic exposition of his own time and memory, the Roman oligarchy was the theme, a government subverted by Pompeius Magnus, first as an enemy, then a false and fatal ally.

Sallust earned enormous admiration for an innovatory style combined with sentiments of conventional morality. Not all could approve the defamation of consuls and noblemen.

Compilations devoted to the history of Latin literature commonly lodge Sallust among late Republican writers. He belongs (it can be contended) to a 'Triumviral period' (from 43 to 28), embracing sundry other authors of lasting renown.[64] Sallust may be regarded as a precursor who heralds the censorious and negatory fashion of writing provoked by Rome of the Caesars.

To that Sallustian conception stands in contrast a casual and heterogeneous production, the opuscule of Velleius Paterculus which swells before the end into a panegyric of Tiberius Caesar. Revealing techniques of adulation, it furnishes precious details about consulars liked or disliked by the ruler.

Virgil and Horace were concordant. Writing a generation later, Ovid commends talent or integrity against birth; and he utters a warning against friendship with the 'potentes'.[65] Ovid ended in marked disillusion with the 'magna nomina' of Fabii and Messallae.

Otherwise the theme has to wait for Seneca. On a traditional topic, Seneca deprecates the display of grimy images of forebears or the long and many-branched family trees. The people who exhibit them are 'noti magis quam nobiles'.[66] Ancestors, he goes on to explain, cast radiance on obscure descendants and shield their failings.[67] Seneca was a man of the world, not afraid to specify a Fabius and an Aemilius in his own time and knowledge.[68] He could have said much more.

To Sallust, 'multa legenti, multa audienti', the truth was apparent that the greatness of the Populus Romanus had been achieved by the excellence of 'pauci cives'—and they were sparse enough in many seasons.[69] History is

---

[64] For this conception, *History in Ovid* (1978), 169 f.

[65] Ovid, *Met.* XIII. 140 f.; 'nam genus et proavos et quae non fecimus ipsi/vix ea nostra voco'. Further, *Ex P.* I 9. 39 f. And, for keeping away from the 'potentes', *Tr.* IV.4 (to an unnamed friend).

[66] Seneca, *De ben.* III. 28.2; *Epp.* 44.5. Cf. the 'commendatio fumosarum imaginum' (Cicero, *In Pisonem* 1).

[67] *De ben.* IV.30.4.

[68] *De ben.* II.21.5.

[69] Sallust, *Cat.* 53.2 ff.

close kin to epic. In Lucan's poem on the fall of *Libertas* the proconsul of Gaul declares a maxim to his army: the life of nations is carried on by a minority.[70]

Though the masses may count for weight and pressure in the revolutionary wars through the resources of the provinces and the demands of the troops (they wanted money and land, and they were sometimes able to prevent the generals from fighting), the writing of history does not well accord with bare abstractions or with appeal to the voiceless and anonymous.

On an extreme pronouncement, not fully honoured by its author, 'non omnia narratu sunt digna quae per squalidas transiere personas'.[71] Those who in any age compose the annals of Rome are moved towards 'clarorum virorum facta moresque'. They run a risk of dispraisal from adepts of recent fashions and doctrines, being condemned for prejudice or a narrow outlook.

Not that the writers themselves have been wholly inadvertent. For example, Tacitus happens to render admirably the behaviour of soldiers, mutinous for just grievances or breaking loose in civil war. Nor should a passing admonition from Edward Gibbon be neglected in this late season.[72]

In notable aspects the long reign of Caesar Augustus remains highly obscure. Whereas hitherto transactions of moment, although liable to distortion, had not defied ascertainment, the advent of centralized authority brought with it barriers and concealment, as suited the ruler and his allies in the power. Facts were either suppressed, or, if published, subject to disbelief.

Such was the diagnosis of Cassius Dio, a necessary prologue to his narration of imperial history.[73] Dio had recourse to a variety of sources. He has much of value to report, otherwise lost to knowledge. Nevertheless, although senator and consul, Dio missed significant names and persons when writing about the Augustan epoch at a distance of more than two centuries. Messalla Corvinus earns a stray and solitary mention, Fabius Maximus none at all.

Oligarchy is imposed as the guiding theme, the link from age to age whatever be the form and name of government. To comprehend the aristocracy entails what preceded and what followed: not only the period of the Triumvirs but the reign of Tiberius Caesar, for so much of the documentation derives from Cornelius Tacitus. Eighty years therefore, or

---

[70] Lucan V. 343: 'humanum paucis vivit genus'.

[71] Ammianus XXVIII.1.15.

[72] Only the decline of the Middle Ages 'gradually restored a soul and a substance to the most useful part of the community' (Ch. LXI, p. 294).

[73] Dio LIII. 1 ff.

even a century and a half. Men and families look backward to Sulla and forward to the fall of the dynasty.

Restriction is enjoined, and concentration. A number of consuls in the first decade of the reign, and in the last two, are only names on the *Fasti* or items of genealogy. Again, although the new men coming in, the pride and flower of municipal Italy (and some the progenitors of consular houses), are an essential component of social history, that whole class demands segregation—and most of the personal evidence concerns the *nobiles*.[74]

An economical recourse offers, namely the aristocratic consuls who adorn the single decade (16 to 7) that is of central value for estimating favourably the achievement of the reign. About some of them can be gleaned information sporadic and various yet fairly abundant. Piso the Pontifex might lay claim to a small monograph; and with good will or by artifice, something can be done with other characters such as Fabius Maximus and Quinctilius Varus—or even Lentulus the Augur.[75]

The subject deters an annalistic narration—which could not without effort be kept separate from the actions and policy of Caesar Augustus, whereas biographies of emperors are a menace and an impediment to the understanding of history in its structure and processes. A different approach may be worth trying: a sequence of interlocking essays.

In the summer of 17 the *Ludi Saeculares* announced a new era. By appropriate felicity the next year opens with P. Cornelius Scipio and L. Domitius Ahenobarbus and continues with a run of consuls from the high aristocracy. The great change was youth as well as ancestry. Born between 50 and 40 they benefited from the lowered consular age—and from the battles that thinned the ranks of the previous generation.

---

[74] None the less, they enter from time to time when appropriate, and they afford relief from the plethora of noble nomenclature—which lacks variety and can induce confusion or perplexities.

[75] Lentulus occupies four pages in *PIR*[2]—and Piso no fewer than six. Manifold problems adhere to both. Only Messalla Corvinus admits a kind of biography (Ch. XV): likewise infested with problems.

II

The Hazards of Life[1]

When arraigning the pretensions of a ruling class that now combined 'superbia' and 'socordia', C. Marius declared a pertinent appeal to their military origins: 'ex virtute nobilitas coepit'.[2] The long ordeal of the northern wars would soon be upon them. Against Cimbri and Teutones men of high birth served in the ranks, and casualties were heavy.

After a decade fecund in acrid contention, the strife of Roman factions involved the Italian allies, from Picenum all the way down to Lucania. They took up arms and fought for liberty and honour.[3] Murderous battles ensued. In the first year a consul fell in the field, in the second a consul and two legates of consular standing.[4] Before hostilities ceased everywhere, civil war erupted, with a general marching on Rome, and further, with sieges and capture of the city. The party of Marius and Cinna was able to establish a government, but Sulla overthrew it, returning as champion of the 'causa nobilium'.[5]

The Dictator enacted proscriptions. Not only for revenge or to weaken the opposition. He needed money, he confiscated property to enrich his adherents and fortify the oligarchy. Few *nobiles* are found among the victims. Their numbers had been thinned by warfare, with gaps of a generation manifest in many families of high distinction. As front and substance for a renovated order, the Dictator required not only dynastic houses of the plebian *nobilitas*, in the first place the Metelli and their kinsmen. The patriciate had to be resuscitated, especially to fill priesthoods. For Cornelius Sulla that was a congenial duty. He responded with effect.[6]

[1] In what follows much use is made of F. Münzer, *Römische Adelsparteien und Adelsfamilien* (1920): cited as *RA*. Likewise his entries in the *Real-Encyclopädie*. Further, reference to many facts, familiar or never in doubt, is obviated by *The Magistrates of the Roman Republic* of T. R. S. Broughton (1951 and 1952). For ages and stages in senatorial careers benefit accrues from G. V. Sumner, *The Orators in Cicero's Brutus. Prosopography and Chronology* (1973).

[2] Sallust, *Jug.* 85.17. For the military tradition and habits, W. V. Harris, *War and Imperialism in Republican Rome* (1979), 9 ff.

[3] As Ovid said of his own people, 'sua libertas ad honesta coegerat arma' (*Amores* III.15.9). The desire of the Italici for Roman citizenship tends to be over-estimated.

[4] viz. P. Rutilius Lupus (*cos.* 90), L. Porcius Cato (89), T. Didius (98), A. Postumius Albinus (99)—though Postumius is said to have perished in a mutiny (Orosius V.18.22).

[5] For definitions of 'nobilitas', Ch. IV.

[6] below, p. 54. Sulla's persecution of the young Julius Caesar has been much exaggerated, in act or intent. Sulla needed patricians and could no doubt offer a suitable bride (such as a Metella) in the place of Cinna's daughter.

Ruthless competition for office and honour had also exacted its toll. Since the practice of duelling was not condoned among citizens in this aristocracy, violence was liberated for language, and feuds were conducted through prosecution in the courts of law.[7] Signal mishaps in political life might consign a family or a whole group to obscurity for a generation, or for ever. No consular Sempronii Gracchi followed on the two ambitious tribunes, and no Fulvii. And in turn some enemies of that party dropped out, for example the Popilii.[8]

In a single year (109) no fewer than four consulars suffered condemnation and exile.[9] Five years later a lost battle in Gaul and the prosecution of Servilius Caepio (*cos.* 106) impaired and depressed an illustrious family of the patriciate.

For perpetuation, some lines hovered along a narrow margin. Scipio Africanus had one son only, who came to nothing, and the descendants of old Fabius Maximus were running out. For both houses recourse was had to Aemilii.[10] Paullus (*cos.* 182) surrendered without discomfort the two sons from his first wife, whom he had divorced. Hence Scipio Aemilianus (*cos.* 147) and Fabius Aemilianus (145); and a Servilius Caepio (142) had likewise become a Fabius.

In all, Aemilius Paullus had seven children. So had Metellus Macedonicus a generation later (*cos.* 143), his colleague Ap. Claudius Pulcher five.[11] Each of the four sons of Macedonicus became consuls, and the sons of a cousin brought in two more, all in the space of fifteen years (from 123 to 108).[12] Sheer numbers helped to confer that primacy which the Metelli took over from the Scipiones.

Admirable in conventional notions promulgated by the Romans, fecundity in aristocratic families may be considered a burden on the Republic.[13] Nor is mere fecundity a guarantee of success. The plebeian Aelii exaggerated: sixteen in one household—and impoverished, as a further commendation to sentimental posterity.[14]

[7] J. A. Crook, *JRS* LXVI (1976), 132 ff., with due attention to the judicial challenge or wager ('sponsio').

[8] In groups or families subsequent absence from the *Fasti*, or long intermission, may furnish clues to political allegiances.

[9] Cicero, *Brutus* 128: 'invidiosa lege C. Galbam sacerdotem et quattuor consularis, L. Bestiam, C. Catonem, Sp. Albinum civemque praestantissimum L. Opimium, Gracchi interfectorem . . . Gracchani iudices sustulerunt.'

[10] Ch. VIII.

[11] Following Pliny (*NH* VII. 59), and Münzer, Table I in *Rom. Rev.* shows two daughters for Macedonicus. Cicero in three places states three, all married. Cf. E. Badian, *Studies in Greek and Roman History* (1964), 66. For the stemma of the Claudii, *RE* III. 2666.

[12] Otherwise twelve consulates, censorships, triumphs in as many years (Velleius II.11.3). For their alliances, *Rom. Rev.* (1939), 20 ff.

[13] Thus Bacon in the essay *Of Seditions and Troubles*: 'take heed how their nobility and gentlemen do not multiply too fast.'

[14] Val. Max. IV.4.8.

An Aelius Tubero married a daughter of Aemilius Paullus. The son, although a nephew of Scipio Aemilianus, was not able to get further than a praetorship. Conspicuous frugality failed to endear him to any class at Rome.[15] Public life called for display and adequate disbursements.

A patrimony used in that exemplary fashion or forfeited through luxury and dissipation accelerated the decline of ancient families. A Fabius, the son of Allobrogicus (*cos.* 121), made his contribution.[16] Others lacked money or energy. For three generations the forebears of Aemilius Scaurus were out of the Senate.[17] His ascent to a consulship (in 115) had been arduous, but before long he emerged as a director of public policy, in alliance with the Metelli.[18] Another member of the decayed patriciate was the jurist Ser. Sulpicius Rufus: the grandfather of no consequence, the father only a Roman knight. His *nobilitas* was not verifiable save by historians and antiquarians, so it was asserted when in 63 he aspired to the consulate.[19]

The last epoch of the Republic still exhibited several large families. The redoubtable Ap. Claudius Pulcher (*cos.* 143) had two sons by a late marriage, the consuls of 92 and 79. The son of the latter (*cos.* 54) was left with two brothers and three sisters to provide for. He confessed to a strain on meagre resources.[20] Which comes as a surprise in the son of a Metella and a prince of the Optimates. By contrast, Cato. With five children (by two marriages), he amassed great wealth, benefiting no doubt from deaths and inheritance.[21]

Dearth of offspring is the normal phenomenon. Ap. Pulcher was blessed with two daughters. His colleague in the consulship, L. Domitius Ahenobarbus, the fifth of that line (son succeeding father), duly confirmed the 'artata numero felicitas' of that house with a single son.[22] The Metelli requited Sulla's alliance—four consuls after Metellus Pius, his colleague in 80. They could not keep it up: one son and two daughters surviving from all five.[23]

The phenomenon (there is plenty of other evidence) has not failed to engage curiosity. Appeal has been made to biology.[24] It is courting danger

[15] Cicero, *Pro Murena* 75 f.

[16] Cicero, *Tusc.* I.81.

[17] Asconius 20, with the comment 'itaque Scauro aeque ac novo homini laborandum fuit.'

[18] His second wife was a Metella, taken over on his decease by Sulla.

[19] *Pro Murena* 16.

[20] Varro, *R.r.* III.16.1 f.

[21] For his wealth, Seneca, *De vita beata* 21.3. Cato was left an orphan in infancy. His uncle Lucius (*cos.* 89) fell in battle. No issue known from him or from Marcus, of the other line (the son of a cousin of Cato's father). Praetor *c.*92, Marcus died during his governorship in Gaul (Gellius XIII.20.12).

[22] cf. Velleius II.10.2.

[23] below, p. 245.

[24] F. Galton, *Hereditary Genius* (1869), with remarks by H. M. Last, *JRS* XXXVII (1947), 153 f.

to espouse an heiress. By her very condition she is likely to derive from infertile stocks. A husband curtails his expectation of progeny.

Reasons more obvious explain limitation in aristocratic families. Noblemen were reluctant to split patrimony and estates, there being no primogeniture at Rome; and society women had no liking for repetitive pregnancy.

Families dwindled, but it is premature to accredit infecundity.[25] The analogy of aristocratic behaviour in other centuries dissuades. And it impels to a question: sons not acknowledged by their fathers.[26] At Rome the products of casual or illicit amours (freedwomen would attract) are doomed to disappear, submerged in the plebs; and nothing can be done for any bastard through a subsequent marriage.[27]

Adultery is another matter, not to be taken lightly by a student of high society, even if it eludes documentation through consequences other than dissidence or divorce. A singular silence obtains. Whereas Cicero in public invective can bring up murder or incest, he nowhere alleges that a son is not the son of his father.

Plain facts of scandal known to many at the time were covered up. What percolates is scanty, but enough to show young noblemen in the habit of making forays into households that harboured bold and emancipated women. Like others, Servilia was the mistress of Julius Caesar, and she was held by him in enduring affection.[28] That is clear enough. A fable of late date fancied him father to Marcus Brutus. It has earned credit with men of letters for sundry reasons, among them neglect of a plain fact: quaestor in 54, Brutus was born in 85.

In ancient times as in the recent, the tyrannicide and the fame of Philippi occluded another Brutus, namely the son of D. Junius Brutus, the consul of 77.[29] Decimus, four years junior to Marcus, enjoyed from the outset in Gaul conspicuous marks of favour and esteem. He took the name of a Postumius Albinus, the last of that ancient patrician house. In the year 63 the father of Decimus had the famous Sempronia for wife.[30] Rational conjecture points towards a Postumia as the mother of Decimus: sister therefore to the Postumia who married Ser. Sulpicius.[31]

---

[25] Caesar, thrice married, had no son. After begetting Julia, he lost the power of procreation, so it has been fancied. Thus J. P. V. D. Balsdon, *Historia* VII (1958), 86 f. Against which, *Historia* XXIX (1980), 422 ff. = *Roman Papers* III (1984), 1236 ff. Julia's birth was incautiously assigned to 83 (as by Münzer, *RE* X. 894). Better *c.* 75, cf. M. Gelzer, *Caesar*[6] (1960), 19. She was still unwed in 59.

[26] On which neglected topic, *Trans. Am. Phil. Soc.* CIV (1960), 323 ff. = *Roman Papers* (1979), 510 ff.

[27] Only through adoption. And a physical resemblance might arouse or confirm suspicions.

[28] Suetonius, *Divus Julius* 50.1: 'sed ante alias dilexit Marci Bruti matrem Serviliam.'

[29] On whom, F. Münzer, *RE Supp.* V. 369 ff.; R. Syme, *Historia* XXIX (1980), 426 ff. = *Roman Papers* III (1984), 1240 ff.   [30] Sallust, *Cat.* 40.5.

[31] For this conjecture, *Sallust* (1964), 134; *Historia* XXIX (1980), 429 = *RP* III (1984), 1243. Decimus was in fact a 'consobrinus' of the son (*Ad fam.* XI.7.1).

By hypothesis Caesar is equipped with a son who could not be directly installed as the heir. To be reduced to daughters was far from detrimental in the high aristocracy. Women are a prize or a weapon in the game of politics. Caesar's Julia was available at an opportune moment. Otherwise daughters served to retrieve influence for a family or extend a faction. Ap. Claudius Pulcher (*cos.* 54) consigned his three sisters to prominent members of the oligarchy: Marcius Rex, Metellus Celer, Licinius Lucullus.[32] In a similar fashion Servilia sagaciously annexed partners for the three daughters accruing from her second husband, D. Junius Silanus.[33] Not long after, her son Marcus Brutus married Claudia, a daughter of Ap. Pulcher. The other went to the elder son of Pompeius Magnus.

Facing impoverishment or decline, noble families turned for support to *novi homines* or new wealth.[34] Conscious of mixed origins (Latin, Oscan, Etruscan), the aristocracy of Rome in the past had not disdained propinquity with the better sort from other cities.[35] Recently a Calpurnius Piso had sought a bride in the Latin colony of Placentia, on the northern border;[36] and the mother of Manlius Torquatus (*cos.* 65) came from Asculum in Picenum.[37]

Despite pride in name and ancestry, and grief at the lapse of a male heir, that loss was repaired without discomfort or repining. As Scipiones and Fabii demonstrate, adoption compensated, from a house that stood on parity of splendour. Sons of the blood enjoyed no kind of organic or mystical preference. Even malice or folly would not induce an enemy to declare that Aemilianus fell short of an authentic Scipio.

Aemilianus left no male issue. Primacy passed to descendants of Scipio Nasica, a cousin of Africanus. Moreover, should the main line give out, minor branches of a *gens* might come in and preserve a name of ancient power. A reserve was available in families that for long ages had been absent from the consular *Fasti*.[38] As witness the Claudii Nerones.[39]

Finally, to abate in some measure the menace of extinction, matrimony at an early age. The Scipionic period can disclose youths in the high aristocracy taking a bride soon after they assume the toga of manhood.[40]

[32] *Rom. Rev.* 20.

[33] viz. P. Servilius Isauricus (*cos.* 48), M. Aemilius Lepidus (*cos.* 46), C. Cassius (*pr.* 44). The marriages occurred soon after the year 61. The son of Cassius assumed the *toga virilis* on the Ides of March, 44 (Plutarch, *Brutus* 14). For the operations and ambitions of Servilia, Münzer, *RA* 351 ff.

[34] T. P. Wiseman, *New Men in the Roman Senate 139 B.C.–A.D. 14* (1971), 53 ff.

[35] Münzer, *RA* 46 ff.; H. Galsterer, *Herrschaft und Verwaltung im Republikanischen Italien* (1976), 142 ff.

[36] Hence vituperation from Cicero, asserting that the maternal grandfather of L. Piso Caesoninus (*cos.* 58) was 'Insuber quidam . . . ., idem mercator et praeco' (*In Pisonem* fr. 11).

[37] *Pro Sulla* 25. For Alfidia, wife of M. Livius Drusus Claudianus, T. P. Wiseman, o.c. 57.

[38] Hence submerged aristocrats, mentioned seldom or never. More numerous than allowed for by Münzer, cf. C. and Ö. Wikander, *Opuscula Romana* XII (1979), 1 ff.

[39] No consul since 202.

[40] Münzer, *RA* 105 ff.; 267 f.

A pervasive and persistent habit in the senatorial order has thence been deduced.[41] With what justice, that is a question.

Evidence becomes fairly abundant in the closing years of the Republic, not without its problems. *Nobiles* might often marry when about twenty-two, as did Cato.[42] It happens to be the norm in the following epoch. In consonance therewith a man of forty or so is discovered with a son aged about fifteen. None the less, various reasons or pretexts counselled delay, among them military service and foreign travel. Some thus postponed until close on the quaestorship.[43] Marcus Brutus married Claudia about the year 54.[44] In 50 the son of Ser. Sulpicius is on show as an eligible bridegroom, along with Ti. Claudius Nero (elected quaestor the next year).[45]

For the bride the normal age was about fourteen or fifteen.[46] Young wives were under hazard of dying in childbirth; and children perished in masses or in a steady sequence. Of twelve born to Sempronius Gracchus and the daughter of Scipio Africanus, two sons and a daughter survived. The lost progeny of persons less conspicuous in Roman annals leave hardly a shadow or a vestige save in *Consolationes* to the bereaved.[47]

If a sole attested son first saw the light of day when a senator was about thirty-five or forty, a surmise becomes legitimate that others preceding had aggregated to the nameless nations of the dead. And by the same token, more wives than one. Not many eschewed matrimony (at least in the ancient families) until thirty, and even with them the evidence may be deceptive, ignoring a bride who had disappeared some years previously. The more that is known about any senator, the more consorts accrue.

Iterated matrimony is revealed by divergence in age between children or inferred from long intervals separating generations. The grandfather of Marcus Lepidus (*cos.* 78) had held his first consulship in 187; D. Brutus (*cos.* 77) was the son of Callaicus (*cos.* 138); and the son of old Aemilius Scaurus became praetor in 56.

Intervals during which a noble family misses the consulate avow a

---

[41] H. Humbert, *Le Remariage à Rome* (1972), 93: 'mariés à 16 ans ou moins'. Very early marriage (like marriages between cousins) may have been an especial feature of the patriciate.

[42] Cato was in competition *c.*73 with Scipio Nasica for the hand of an Aemilia Lepida (Plutarch, *Cato* 7). He consoled himself with an Atilia, of decayed plebeian nobility.

[43] Thus Publius, the younger son of M. Crassus, marrying the daughter of Metellus Scipio (below, p. 271).

[44] When he went out to Cilicia as quaestor to his father-in-law.

[45] Cicero was keen on both of them (*Ad fam.* V. 21.14; VI.6.1.). Terentia and Tullia prevailed, snapping up Dolabella. So far as known, Nero went without a wife for six or seven years, when he acquired Livia Drusilla. Ser. Sulpicius married a sister of Messalla Corvinus.

[46] M. K. Hopkins, *Population Studies* XVIII (1965), 309 ff.; P. Veyne, *Latomus* XXVI (1967), 750 ff.

[47] Münzer, *RA* 376 ff.

variety of hazards; and many boys or youths were carried off by 'atrox fortuna'. By contrast, a young widow who disdained remarriage, emulating the ancient renown of 'univirae', might endure until extreme senescence, to furnish precious instruction to those who composed *Consolationes* or took pleasure in genealogical pursuits.[48]

Funerals were noteworthy exhibitions: pageantry and pride not less than solemnity of mourning. And they were frequent in the insalubrious metropolis.[49] Maladies in any shape might prove mortal. Hence sudden deaths, sometimes with sinister imputations, as when Scipio Aemilianus perished in 129. When Scipio Nasica was cut short during his consulship in 111 and Livius Drusus two years later (while censor) grief and consternation attended upon their obsequies.[50]

Deaths of this order had political repercussions. In September of the year 91 the orator Licinius Crassus succumbed to a fever. It was the eve of the Bellum Italicum. In this memorable season two aristocrats of superior eminence fade out. After his praetorship (?93) the son of Scipio Nasica held a command in Spain. After which, no word.[51] And something should have been heard in peace or war of C. Claudius Pulcher, the consul of 92. Some remembered him for 'summam nobilitatem et singularem potentiam'.[52]

Disease and urban insalubrity were bad enough. Epidemics obtruded, some brought from distant parts by the legions of the imperial Republic.[53] The historian Livy supplied vivid and valuable accounts, the main facts going back ultimately to documentary record, such as deaths and ceremonies of ritual expiation. One pestilence broke out in 182 and lasted until 180. In the latter year a consul died and a praetor, and further, five priests.[54] A second visitation in 175 swept away six holders of priesthoods.[55]

Livy's narration lapses in 167, not long after the Macedonian triumph of Aemilius Paullus. During the week of that festival perished his two

---

[48] For the writings of Pomponius Atticus, below, p. 76.

[49] For mortality at Rome, P. A. Brunt, *Italian Manpower* (1971), 133 f.

[50] At least for Nasica's funeral (Pliny, *NH* XXI.10). Eulogies on both (from Posidonius) are reproduced in Diodorus XXXIV.33; XXXVII.10.1 Drusus (*cos.* 112) was married to a Cornelia (Seneca, *Ad Marciam* 16.4). Those deaths were rapid blows to the Scipionic faction.

[51] His decease (?90) emerges from *De oratore* III.8: son-in-law to L. Crassus.

[52] Cicero, *Brutus* 166. His father (*cos.* 143) split the Scipionic faction by annexing young Ti. Gracchus for his daughter. For the date, J. Briscoe, *JRS* LXIV (1974), 125 f.

[53] cf., for later ages, A. F. Prinzing, *Epidemics Resulting from War* (Oxford, 1916).

[54] Livy XL.37.1; 42. 6 ff. It was believed that the consul C. Piso had been poisoned by his wife.

[55] Livy XLI.21.5 ff. Then, between two censorships (174 to 169), not a single senator perished (Pliny, *NH* VII. 157).

young sons. Later writers deriving from Livy report famine and plague in 165, and again in 142.[56]

Evidence thereafter happens to be meagre. Between 142 and 22, only two pestilences on register, namely in 87 and in 43. Rome and Italy abode in prime health through a long tract of time, so it has been claimed.[57] Confidence was premature. It ignored the consequences of famine and warfare. There is no warrant for conditions changing. The ostensible record will have to be supplemented.

At the siege of Rome in 87, pestilence ravaged the opposing armies. It exacted seventeen thousand victims.[58] In no age or clime can contagion be confined to soldiers.[59] By the same token, not an isolated affliction during the Ten Years War.

Next, warfare during the following decade, notably the Spanish campaigns and the servile insurrection. A neglected item lends encouragement. In 68 died the consul L. Metellus, also the consul suffect.[60] It may afford passing instruction to evoke sporadic deaths in this season.[61] It is more significant if a man loses both his wife and his son. That happened to Sergius Catilina—to be incriminated by his enemies a few years later.[62] Catilina married the beautiful Orestilla, herself a widow and to be presumed a wealthy heiress, perhaps on a double count.[63]

Next, the year 54. Dire portents announced the seventh centenary of Rome: a flooding of the Tiber and a great conflagration.[64] Recourse to the sacred books of the Sibyl would be prescribed. They were being exploited assiduously for mundane matters.[65]

Moreover, the summer was atrociously hot, beyond all memory.[66] In October or November came heavy rains and inundations.[67] In that autumn a robust person is reported ill, namely Cato.[68]

The goddess Libitina claimed her due. A number of consulars could be mustered, extant in 57, but not heard of subsequent to 54. Two were still

---

[56] Obsequens 13 and 22. Of the latter visitation Orosius says 'iamque etiam magnae domus vacuae vivis plenae mortibus remanserunt: largissimae introrsum hereditates et multi penitus heredes' (V.4.8).

[57] T. P. Wiseman, *JRS* LIX (1969), 74: 'if then Rome and Italy were free from major epidemics for the unusually long period of 120 years' etc. And Brunt, discussing Wiseman's paper, states that 'the main factor was endemic disease' (*Roman Manpower* (1971), 707).

[58] Orosius V.19.8.

[59] Though suggested by Wiseman, o.c. 74.

[60] Dio XXXVI.4.1.

[61] Cicero mourned his cousin Lucius (*Ad Att.* I.5.1.), and the previous year carried off Caesar's wife.

[62] *In Cat.* I.14. Omitting the wife, Sallust registers the murder of the son (*Cat.* 15.2).

[63] Her father, Cn. Aufidius Orestes, is not on record after his consulship in 71.

[64] Dio has the flood (XXXIX.61.1 f.), Orosius, noting the anniversary, the great fire (VI.14.5).

[65] Dio XXXIX. 60.4: 61.3.

[66] *Ad Q. fr.* II.16.1; III.1.1.

[67] *Ad Q. fr.* III.5.8.

[68] *Ad Q. fr.* III.1.5; *Ad Att.* IV.17.4.

in their best years. Metellus Nepos (*cos.* 57), returning from a campaign in Spain, was one of the nine who spoke in defence of Aemilius Scaurus;[69] and Lentulus Marcellinus, active and vocal during his consulship (56), lapses from record thereafter.[70]

Extraneous evidence helps. No poem of Catullus indicates an event later than the previous year; the manuscript of Lucretius was now looking for an editor; and no device avails to prolong the life of young Licinius Calvus, a brilliant and active orator.

The Civil War duly conveyed pestilence. Thus in 46, 'hoc gravissimo et pestilentissimo anno'.[71] The express reference comes in Cassius Dio under 43: a violent plague at Rome and throughout Italy.[72]

So far casual and sporadic items spread over a century precisely, since 142. Brief inspection can pass to the reign of Caesar Augustus. Dio reports pestilence both in 23 and in 22, to the accompaniment of fire and floods and sundry other portents.[73] In the former year Claudius Marcellus succumbed, the nephew of the Princeps; and Dio, casually noting the decease of an aedile (not named), states that the victims were numerous.[74] Chance adds a second young man. The brother of Ovid, embarking on a senator's career, died at the age of twenty.[75]

Next, the year 12 brought calamity to ruler and government. Agrippa passed away, coeval with Caesar Augustus. The *Fasti* corroborate, with a consul dying early in the year and a consul suffect later on.[76]

Finally, the ominous overture to the last decade of the reign. In AD 5 Dio records famine, and it continued.[77] Dio says nothing of the normal concomitant. It is registered by Pliny when recounting the disasters that reduced the Princeps to despair.[78] Among them was the 'rebellio Illyrici', lasting from 6 to 9. The concentration of legions and levies, some from the eastern lands, was likely to foment epidemics. A solitary notice shows disease rampant. Not in the army, but among the insurgent Pannonians.[79]

---

[69] Asconius 24 (summer of 54).

[70] Older consulars disappearing can be registered by order of their latest mention as follows: M'. Glabrio (in 57), L. Lucullus (56), M. Lucullus (56), Gellius Poplicola (55), Manlius Torquatus (55), Metellus Creticus (54). Add perhaps two aristocrats not on record since their praetorships (in 59 and 57), viz. Cn. Lentulus Clodianus and P. Licinius Crassus Dives: in any event, a sign of high mortality prevalent at Rome.

[71] *Ad fam.* V.16.4.

[72] Dio XLV.17.8. The consul A. Hirtius, who fell in battle, was enfeebled through a long illness that began in the previous year (*Phil.* III.37; VII.12).

[73] Dio LIII.33.3; LIV.1.2. No historian happens to record another plague until that of the year 65 (*Ann.* XVI.13, a vivid account).

[74] Dio LIII.33.3 f.

[75] Ovid, *Tr.* IV.10.27 ff.

[76] below, p. 153.

[77] Dio LV.26.1, cf. 27.1; 31.3.

[78] Pliny, *NH* VII. 149.

[79] Dio LV.33.1.

At Rome one death only is certified, a consul of 7.[80] As in the two previous epidemics (one documented, the other to be assumed without discomfort), gaps in a generation find their explanation, or the disappearance of a young *nobilis* for whom a consulship could with some confidence be predicted. And by the same token, widows and remarriages to be surmised.

Livy opened the theme of pestilence, with express documentation. The excursus will suitably conclude with the author of imperial annals. A sequence of necrological notices sets in with the year 20, based in the main on the Senate's vote of public funerals. It furnishes precious detail about personages on high eminence in the previous reign. There is further benefit. By exception Tacitus admits a youth dying in 22, a grandson of Asinius Pollio.[81] The item offers guidance. In this season vanish several aristocrats in near expectation of the *fasces*.[82]

An epidemic emerges painlessly, or at the least a run of unhealthy years.[83] No need to appeal to sundry known facts. For example, at the beginning of 21 Tiberius Caesar went away to Campania, under pretext of health, and he stayed there for some twenty months.[84] In the same year Marcus Lepidus was able to bring up illness as an excuse for not going to Africa as proconsul.[85] Again, Drusus Caesar. They expected him to die in 21, and a clever poet composed a valedictory.[86] He perished in September of 23. Poison was alleged later, after a lapse of eight years.

The plague engenders alarming consequences in state and society. Fear arises, and anger. In 87 the Roman populace broke up the funeral of Pompeius Strabo.[87] Ruthless behaviour exacerbates enmity, rumour is rife, poison is credited. Tradition invokes ritual, and the lower orders surrender to foreign superstitions.

On a sober estimate, a cumulation of deaths (plague or coincidence of the normal distempers) disturbs the 'res publica'. A party is weakened or rivals fall out who served to maintain the system in equilibrium—since conflict was a saving element in Roman *Libertas*. Subsequent recollection is prone to call up the senior statesman who departed before the onset of tribulation, 'felix opportunitate mortis'. Thus the orator L. Crassus.[88]

[80] viz. A. Licinius Nerva Silianus (*cos*. 7), cf. Velleius II. 116.4 (under AD 9).
[81] *Ann*. III. 75.1.
[82] below, p. 126.
[83] See further *ZPE* 41 (1981), 126 ff. = *RP* III (1984), 1376 ff.
[84] *Ann*. III.31.2, cf. 64.1.
[85] III.35.2.
[86] III.45.1.
[87] Velleius II.21.4.
[88] Cicero, *De oratore* III.8: 'non vidit flagrantem bello Italiam, non ardentem invidia senatum, sceleris nefarii principes civitatis reos, non luctum filiae, non exsilium generi.'

The theme recurs. Consulars are duly congratulated who predeceased the war between Pompeius and Caesar.[89] Dying late in 50, Hortensius earned the most eloquent of tributes.[90]

It is a pleasing fancy (there subsumed or expressed) that the counsel and authority of certain consulars might have availed to prevent the fall of the old order. What is known about some of the most active falls short of conviction. The Optimates put their faith in the sagacity of Cato, as well as in the prestige of Pompeius Magnus and the force of his armies.

Continuity in government resided in a group (sometimes a nexus) of the ex-consuls, who direct policy by 'auctoritas'.[91] In stable epochs as many as twenty-five might be extant, not all of them vigorous or vocal. When Sulla assumed the dictatorship at the end of 82, war and disease and massacre had reduced to four the 'principes civitatis': two Valerii Flacci, L. Marcius Philippus, M. Perperna (the latter lapsing from political life). Hence the prominence devolving upon Philippus, who five years later impelled the Senate to take action against the insurgent Lepidus.

The total picked up during the first decade of the restored oligarchy— which, however, was not strong enough to resist the demands of two army commanders in the autumn of 71. They were not a collection of high quality or performance, some elderly and delayed in access to their consulships.

Twelve can be certified.[92] The Ten Years War had other and parallel consequences. Many political families lacked their head. Energetic women intervened to recapture 'dignitas' and influence. Servilia is the exemplar. Her mother Livia, sister to Drusus the tribune of 91, passed by divorce from Servilius Caepio (*pr.* 91) to a Porcius Cato.[93] She died shortly before the Bellum Italicum, so did her second husband, while Caepio fell in battle in 89. On Servilia reposed the task of rearing and guiding brothers and sisters from the two marriages, among them young Marcus Cato, half a dozen years her junior.[94] For herself, when her husband M. Brutus, an ally of Lepidus, was killed by Pompeius at Mutina (in 77), Servilia promptly

---

[89] Velleius II. 48.6: 'si prius gratulatus ero Q. Catulo, duobus Lucullis Metelloque et Hortensio.

[90] *Brutus* 1. 1 ff.

[91] For the nexus in the last epoch see *Rom. Rev.* 20 ff. In deprecation of that assumption, Chr. Meier, *Res Publica Amissa* (1966), 183 ff. In his view, for example, it is only 'ein seltener Zufall' that Catulus, Hortensius, and Domitius Ahenobarbus were related (ib. 186). For some criticism of Meier, E. W. Gray, *CR* XIX (1969), 825 ff.; K. Rauflaub, *Dignitatis Contentio* (1974), 39 f.; 159 f.

[92] viz. Metellus Pius (*cos.* 80), Servilius Vatia (79), Lutatius Catulus (78), Mam. Lepidus Livianus (77), D. Junius Brutus (77), Scribonius Curio (76), M. Cotta (75), L. Lucullus (74), M. Lucullus (73), C. Cassius (73), Lentulus Clodianus (72), Gellius Poplicola (72).

The survival of Mam. Lepidus Livianus is here admitted: argued by G. V. Sumner, *JRS* LIV (1964), 41 ff. For how long, that is a question, cf. M. T. Griffin, *JRS* LXIII (1973), 213.

[93] About 96, resulting from the fateful quarrel of Drusus and Caepio.

[94] Cato was born in 95. In 91 he is discovered in the house of Livius Drusus (Plutarch, *Cato* 2).

annexed a dull nobleman whom in due course she would bring to a consulship.[95]

Nor should Postumia be lost to view, likewise patrician, of a family verging to extinction. She married a patrician in manifest need of support, the jurist Ser. Sulpicius Rufus. A candidate in 63, he did not succeed until eleven years had elapsed.

The type of the political adventuress is delineated by the historian Sallust in the person of Sempronia, not only alert and elegant but a manager of intrigue, active and audacious. Her husband D. Junius Brutus (*cos.* 77) was no impediment, or her own age. Her extraction would be worth knowing. There may be a close link with the bold and ambitious Fulvia (also of a decayed family), whose mother was 'Sempronia Tuditani filia'.[96]

In the vicinity of these ladies are discovered young nobles whose careers they helped to promote. Postumia as well as Servilia belongs to the rubric concerning Caesar. The contest for power and honour was sharp and arduous: 'audacia largitio avaritia vigebant.'[97] A man born in the decade 100–90, coming to years of understanding in warfare and proscriptions, learned hard lessons, with nothing to contradict in the sequel; and he derived encouragement from the mediocrity of his seniors in the oligarchy.

When the proconsul of Gaul, circumvented by his enemies, faced an ultimatum, twenty-four ex-consuls were among the living (four of them in exile, three absent from Rome).[98] Along with men of principle, the more energetic or obtuse followed Magnus and the consuls across the sea to Macedonia. Six years later ten consulars present in his camp were commemorated in a fervid laudation. The list is variously instructive.[99] With the consuls added, it included, along with Metellus Scipio (unmatched for pedigree), two Lentuli, two Marcelli, two consulars related to Cato (Calpurnius Bibulus and Domitius Ahenobarbus), and Ap. Claudius Pulcher (potent and interlocking).

Of that company two survived, Cicero and Ser. Sulpicius. When Cicero in December of 44 announced a resurgence of the Republic and a programme of action against Marcus Antonius the proconsul of Gaul, the consulars were seventeen in number (six of them had accrued in the intervening years).[100] Not adequate in support of his policy, but feeble or

[95] D. Junius Silanus (*cos.* 62). He had never a chance for 64 (*Ad. Att.* I.1.2.).
[96] Asconius 35, cf. *Sallust* (1964), 135. The identity of Sempronia is amply discussed by T. J. Cadoux in *Humanitatis Vindex* (*Essays in Honour of J. H. Bishop*, 1980), 93 ff.
[97] The phrase of Sallust, *Cat.* 3.3.
[98] The exiles were C. Antonius (*cos.* 63), A. Gabinius (58), M. Valerius Messalla (53), Cn. Domitius Calvinus (53).
[99] *Phil.* XIII.28 f., cf. *Rom. Rev.* 44 f. For two of the ten, Cicero is not veracious, viz. M. Marcellus and Ser. Sulpicius (the consuls of 51). [100] *Rom. Rev.* 164.

disloyal, so the orator complained. On the other side, none able to curb his imperious eloquence and thwart the design of exploiting Caesar's heir to split the Caesarian party and destroy Antonius.

In the event, Cassius and Brutus won over the legions in the transmarine provinces. To the remnants of the Catonian faction aggregated many young *nobiles*. The field of Philippi annulled the cause of *libertas* and extinguished sons of Cato, of Hortensius, of Lucullus.[101] Among those who committed suicide was a Livius Drusus: a Claudius adopted in infancy by the tribune of 91.

Therefore not many consuls to issue in the future from those houses of the plebeian *nobilitas*. The recent accessions were a miscellaneous company.[102] The most vulnerable had in fact been the patrician P. Cornelius Dolabella, elected in 44 through favouritism when very young, yet by paradox not incriminated on that count by contemporary and hostile testimony.[103] It brings up dreadful things, in sanctimonious horror.[104]

The three Caesarian leaders brought back legalized autocracy in November of 43. Their first consuls, Ventidius and Carrinas, in brief tenure declared the resurgence of causes defeated fifty years before, namely confederate Italy and the party of Marius and Cinna. Not long after followed in 40 Asinius Pollio, whose grandfather fell in battle when leading the levies of the Marrucini. Also P. Canidius and the Gaditane Cornelius Balbus, lacking any disclosure of his secret operations for the space of four years.

The first calendar year of the Triumvirs (42) had opened with one of their number M. Lepidus (*cos.* 46), consul for the second time, sharing the *fasces* with Munatius Plancus. Colleagues for the following year were Lucius Antonius (the brother of Marcus) and P. Servilius Isauricus (*cos.* 48). Then, after three years each with a pair of *suffecti*, the list began to expand, in a progressive declension, with names never seen before at Rome: a Vipsanius, a Statilius, a Laronius.

A summary computation will afford precise and melancholy instruction. From 42 to 33 (not reckoning the dynasts, L. Antonius, and iterations) thirty-four consuls entered office.[105] Of that total, only twelve from consular families.[106] As follows:

[101] Velleius II. 71.1 f. For Roman writers a 'Romani bustum populi' (Lucan VII.862).

[102] For the Caesarian consuls see now H. Bruhns, *Caesar und die römische Oberschicht in den Jahren 49–44 v. Chr.* (1978), 141 ff. Out of nine (48–44), five were *nobiles*, three of them patrician.

[103] For the vexed problem of his age, perhaps thirty-five or even less, see *Historia* XXIX (1980), 432 f. = *RP* III (1984), 1245 f. Caesar's predilection for Dolabella is enigmatic.

[104] As exhibited by his former father-in-law (*Phil.* XI.9.) Having recently proposed an abatement of ten years for Caesar's heir (V.46), Cicero suppressed the age of Dolabella.

[105] The iterations are in 42–40: M. Lepidus, P. Servilius Isauricus, Cn. Domitius Calvinus.

[106] In due proportion it will be added that some of the others come from established praetorian families. Thus L. Caninius Gallus (*cos.* 37), L. Scribonius Libo (*cos.* 34), C. Fonteius Capito (*suff.* 33),

39 L. Marcius Censorinus
38 Ap. Claudius Pulcher : C. Norbanus Flaccus
   L. Cornelius Lentulus : L. Marcius Philippus
37
36 *cos.* L. Gellius Poplicola
35 Sex. Pompeius
   suff. P. Cornelius (?Scipio)
34 *suff.* L. Sempronius Atratinus : Paullus Aemilius Lepidus
33 L. Volcacius Tullus
   suff. M. Acilius Glabrio

Of those twelve, only six are dignified with the eponymate. In all, a variegated collection, youthful careerists matched with decorative nonentities. At the outset, men of birth and repute preferred Antonius; and a number of them threw in their lot with Antonius after Philippi. Some time elapsed before the young Caesar could enlist allies of distinction. The earliest are casually discovered in his company in 36, during the Bellum Siculum; namely Ap. Claudius Pulcher (nephew of the consul of 54) and Paullus Aemilius Lepidus (nephew of the Triumvir).[107] Both fairly youthful consuls, it is to be presumed. Of the other nine, two are also patrician. Nothing at all is known about L. Lentulus, while the identity and extraction of P. Scipio is a vexatious problem.[108]

Eight remain. The Marcii commanded ancestral prestige, barely conceding precedence to the patriciate.[109] Censorinus and Philippus stand in sharp contrast. The parent of Censorinus was one of Sulla's enemies.[110] Philippus, stepbrother to the young Caesar, had married Atia, his aunt.[111]

Like Censorinus, Norbanus Flaccus (his grandfather, consul in 83) recalled the Marian faction; and he was one of the Caesarian generals at Philippi.

Next, Gellius Poplicola, son of the elderly *novus homo* who acceded to the consulate in 72. He was step-brother to the illustrious Messalla Corvinus:[112] that is, a son of the first wife of M. Valerius Messalla (*cos.* 61).

As a consul in 35, Sextus Pompeius is only a name and a date and a

L. Autronius Paetus (*suff.* 33). And C. Memmius C.f. (*suff.* 34), son of the praetor of 58, was a grandson of Sulla, as his inscription proclaims (*Wiener Anzeiger* XCIX (1963), 48: see now *Inschr. Eph.* II. 403).

[107] *Rom. Rev.* 229; 237.
[108] Ch. XVIII.
[109] Münzer, *RE* XIV. 1535 ff.
[110] To be assumed one of the twelve outlawed when Sulla captured Rome in 88 (Appian, *BC* I.60.271.
[111] Further, the 'M]arcius' consul suffect in 36 might be his presumed cousin, viz. Q. Philippus, proconsul of Cilicia (*Ad fam.* XIII. 73 f.) in 47/6. On whom, *Anatolian Studies . . . Buckler* (1938), 317 f. = *RP* (1979), 135 f.
[112] Dio XLVIII.24:3. ff.

problem. On one view an obscure relic now aged about sixty, and further a nephew of Pompeius Strabo, hence first cousin to Magnus: mentioned once in boyhood and never again.[113] On another, a person of very remote kinship.[114] Thus in any event a nonentity, but with descendants.[115]

By contrast, Sempronius Atratinus who began an orator's career in fine style in 56 when seventeen.[116] Born a Calpurnius Bestia, he was adopted by an obscure Sempronius who laid claim to ancient lineage.[117] Finally, L. Volcacius Tullus, son of the *novus homo* consul in 66, and M. Acilius Glabrio: if a son of the consul of 67, on solitary attestation when a young man twenty years previously.[118]

Between some of them, alliances were forming. An inscription reveals Atratinus as husband to the sister or daughter of Marcius Censorinus;[119] and from another it can be argued that his sister married Paullus Aemilius Lepidus.[120] The wife of that remarkable person was a Cornelia, daughter of P. Cornelius (?Scipio, *suff*. 35), who is only a name and an item in genealogy.[121]

Among the twelve aristocrats four patricians are on show. They serve to cast into relief the absent *gentes*. No Valerius or Fabius, no Manlius or Sulpicius. More conspicuous the dearth of the 'magna nomina' of sundry houses in the plebeian *nobilitas*.

Of a notable group born between 90 and 80, already in the Senate when the War came, few survived in 33 apart from Antonius and Lepidus. A historian would be impelled to various reflections.[122] Philippi extended the devastation to young noblemen born during the next decade.

On the last day of 33 terminated the legal authority of the Triumvirs. Normal government came back with the consuls Cn. Domitius Ahenobarbus and C. Sosius, both partisans of Antonius. The young Caesar (now thirty) was ready for the emergency, not embarrassed but rather helped by resigning the name of Triumvir. He had recourse to a plebiscite of Tota Italia, he fought the war as consul, and he continued to hold the *fasces* for the full twelve months in the years that followed.[123]

[113] Plutarch, *Cato* 3. There is a hint of him in Seneca, *De ben.* IV.30.2. The parent, holding off public life, was a scholar and a jurist. See further *History in Ovid* (1978), 158.

[114] Going back to a cousin of Q. Pompeius (*cos.* 141). Thus G. V. Sumner, *Am. Journ. Anc. Hist.* II (1977), 20. For his stemma of the Pompeii, ib. 10.

[115] viz. his grandson, the consul of AD 14, and that consul's son (Seneca, *De tranq.* 11.10.).

[116] Jerome, *Chron.* p. 165 H.

[117] *ILS* 9461 (Hypata) discloses the real father: the 'L. Sempronius' eludes.

[118] Asconius 25 (at the trial of Scaurus).

[119] At Patrae, published by L. Moretti, *Riv. fil.* CVIII (1980), 450. Whence *SEG* XXX.433. To be added to *PIR*[2] M 223.

[120] *IG* II[2]. 5179, cf. below, p. 109. Another sister was the wife of Gellius Poplicola (*IG* II[2]. 4230 f.).

[121] Ch. XVIII.

[122] *Sallust* (1964), 21. Of ten coeval aristocrats there registered only two outlived him.

[123] The year 31, as printed in *Rom. Rev.* 527, needs to be corrected.

When the consuls went away to join Antonius, Caesar appointed a pair of aristocrats, L. Cornelius Cinna and M. Valerius Messalla. The former, married to the daughter of Pompeius Magnus, had left no trace in history for twenty years.[124] Messalla, at first sight only a name, can be identified as a son of Messalla Rufus (*cos.* 53), and now aged close on fifty.[125]

For the next year Caesar took for colleague a coeval, namely Messalla Corvinus, formerly a Republican and Antonian. Then, in the place of Corvinus, M. Titius, followed by Cn. Pompeius Q. f. The former had departed from Alexandria in the previous summer, along with his uncle, the smooth and agile Munatius Plancus, conveying useful information to the discredit of Marcus Antonius.[126] Titius had recently been able to acquire a Fabia for wife.[127]

Like Sex. Pompeius (*cos.* 35), Cn. Pompeius conveys vexation to students of genealogy. At first sight a son of Q. Pompeius Rufus, the turbulent tribune of 52, who was a grandson both of Pompeius Rufus (*cos.* 88) and of Sulla the Dictator.[128] Against which engaging notion, neither he nor his descendants carry 'Rufus' for cognomen. A chance subsists that kinship is distant indeed, that his line runs back to a cousin of the first Pompeius (*cos.* 141).[129]

Historic names returned to adorn the *Fasti*, and inconspicuous noblemen there consort with renegades. The youthful M. Licinius Crassus opens the next year, who had been with the son of Magnus in Sicily, and with Antonius.[130] As with others of the illustrious, the time and juncture of his transition would be worth knowing.

Three *suffecti* followed in turn. One of them was a new accession to the *nobilitas*, namely M. Tullius Cicero. In 29 Caesar's colleague was Sex. Appuleius, the son of his half-sister Octavia.[131] The year witnessed one *suffectus* only, Potitus Valerius Messalla. The degree of his relationship to Corvinus is not clear, neither are any previous occupations or allegiance.[132]

In the sequel to Ahenobarbus and Sosius, the consuls augment by

---

[124] The Cinna who married Pompeia (after the death of Faustus Sulla) had been identified as the praetor of 44. Thus *Rom. Rev.* 279, following Münzer, *RE* IV. 1287 f. and Groag, *PIR*² C 1339. Better, the homonymous quaestor of that year, cf. G. V. Sumner, *Phoenix* XXV (1971), 368 f. (with stemma). For the consul's son, below, p. 257.

[125] Since he was a *monetalis* in the year of his father's consulship: M. H. Crawford *RRC* I (1974), 457.

[126] Velleius II 83.1f.

[127] *IGR* IV. 1716 (Samos).

[128] Thus *Rom. Rev.* 279. This consul was styled 'Cn.f.' in *RE* XXI.2265.

[129] G. V. Sumner, *Am. Journ. Anc. Hist.* II. (1977), 20 f. He has for tribe the 'Arnensis', cf. J. Reynolds, *Aphrodisias and Rome* (1982), no. 8, l. 8.

[130] Dio LI.4.3. He had not held the praetorship.

[131] For the Appuleii, Ch. XXIII.

[132] Potitus is probably identical with the quaestor Manius Valerius Messalla Potitus on an inscription at Claros (*AE* 1956, 118), cf. *JRS* XLV (1955), 156 = *RP* (1979), 261 f.

eleven, seven of them aristocratic.[133] Nor did the war entail much wastage, so far as can be ascertained. Ahenobarbus died shortly after deserting Antonius, while after the battle Sosius was spared. Another admiral, Gellius Poplicola, may have benefited from close kinship to Messalla Corvinus.

In the words of a dishonest and mendacious writer, the victory of Italy's leader was 'clementissima': only those were executed who could not bear to ask for mercy.[134] A second allegation dispels the first. Canidius the marshal of Antonius failed to face death with constancy, so he says.[135] No mention would be expected of Scribonius Curio, the young son of Fulvia, or his half-brother Antullus. There were others.[136]

So far mortality and marriages, warfare, disease, and the plague. When in 28 Caesar and Agrippa revised the roll of the Senate, it included a block of consulars that defied precedent or forecast. Perhaps forty or more.[137]

Despite casualties in the wars, many *nobiles* survived, some after multiple hazards, others in retreat or dissidence, on sparse mention in Rome of the Triumvirs. As previously under Sulla, the proscriptions had not taken a heavy toll of birth and public excellence. Sons of consuls from the thirty years of precarious peace or descendants of defeated families might now begin to conceive hopes, if stable conditions returned, although access to the consulate would not prove easy against the favoured candidates of leader and party.

Expectations in the *nobilitas* were dashed. To their distress and rancour, few places became available during the absence of the ruler. Time and sundry vicissitudes had to intervene before certain families regained their 'dignitas'.

---

[133] Little is known about most of those seven—and wives for none save Corvinus.

[134] Velleius II.86.2.

[135] Velleius II.87.3.

[136] Along with Curio (stepson to Antonius) Cassius Dio cites the Aquillii Flori, father and son (LI.2.5 f.). For this rubric, *AJP* XCIX (1978), 51 f. = *RP* III (1984), 1095 f.

[137] Of the mass of senators who followed Italy's leader to victory, a total of eighty-three were consuls either already or subsequently (*RG* 25). For a computation, E. Groag, *Laureae Aquincenses* II (1941), 30 ff. He reached fifty-three down to the consuls of 17 BC, and finally seventy-eight. For twelve Antonians and renegades, ib. 36 f.

For details, A. E. Glauning, *Die Anhängerschaft des Antonius und des Octavian* (Diss. Leipzig, 1936).

III

Nobiles in Eclipse

It is expedient for an autocrat to go away for a season. Caesar the Dictator proposed to consign Rome to the care of the consuls Marcus Antonius and P. Dolabella, already at sharp variance; and the pair designated for the next year were nonentities. Caesar's heir, departing in the summer of 27, was in a more fortunate posture, with the end of the civil wars three years behind him, his powers regularized—and the great Agrippa continuing in the *fasces* to enforce stability and concord.

There was no call to wait for the Macedonian triumph of Marcus Crassus in the first week of July. On the contrary. That young aristocrat, grandson of the dynast and son of a Caecilia Metella, had provoked annoyance by excess of martial glory and by a demand for abnormal recognition most distasteful to Imperator Caesar.[1]

Cornelius Gallus had also been a cause of embarrassment. Left in charge of Egypt in 30, Gallus subjugated the Thebaid and carried the Roman arms southwards as far as the First Cataract of the Nile, exploits which he there advertised in pompous language on a victory monument.[2] Recalled in the sequel, Gallus found himself debarred from Caesar's 'amicitia' on various pretexts (base ingratitude and rash words alleged), but not carrying total conviction.[3]

The disgrace of Caesar's friend rendered him vulnerable to alert prosecutors. When the Senate took a hand, enjoining an indictment and even prescribing penalties, Gallus committed suicide.[4] Obscure in so many features, the transaction is narrated by Cassius Dio under the year 26, anecdotally and at great length. The end of Cornelius Gallus should be assigned to the second half of 27, subsequent to Caesar's departure to Gaul.[5]

---

[1] Ch. XX. A sharp political relevance of Crassus has been inferred. Thus *Rom. Rev.* (1939), 308 f. Much reduced however in *HSCP* LXIV (1959), 46 = *RP* (1979), 421. And see now E. Badian in *Romanitas–Christianitas* (*Festschrift J. Straub*, 1982), 18 ff; 38 ff.

[2] *ILS* 8895 (Philae: April of 29). The other memorial of Gallus is the obelisk commemorating the construction of a 'forum Iulium' at Alexandria (*AE* 1964, 255).

[3] Suetonius, *Divus Aug.* 66, 2: 'ob ingratum et malivolum animum.' Cf. Ovid, *Am.* III. 9.64: 'si falsum est temerati crimen amici'.

[4] Dio LIII.23.7. For definition of the Senate's procedure, W. Kunkel, *Kl. Schriften* (1974), 278 ff.

[5] Jerome (*Chron.* p. 164 H) has the date of his death, with 'XLIII aetatis anno'. That figure depends patently upon an assumed synchronism with the birth of Virgil, cf. the remarks in *CQ* XXXII (1938), 40 = *RP* (1979), 48 f.

For an ample discussion see L. J. Daly and W. L. Reiter in *Studies in Latin Literature and Roman History* (ed. C. Deroux, 1979), 289 ff.

Next to Agrippa among the marshals thrown up by the wars stood Statilius Taurus (*suff.* 37), and the electors suitably chose him as Caesar's next colleague. For 25 men may have expected a second consulate likewise for Calvisius Sabinus (*cos.* 39) whose long career of service had recently culminated in a triumph from Spain.

The earliest mention of Statilius Taurus declares him a close associate of Calvisius Sabinus: they formed a dual and fabulous monster.[6] When Sabinus held the *fasces* with Marcius Censorinus for colleague they advertised a signal reward for 'pietas' towards leader and party. These men (and no other senators) tried to protect the Dictator on the Ides of March.[7]

Instead of Sabinus a *nobilis* turns up to break the sequence, M. Junius Silanus: of no great prestige, and neither father nor grandfather came anywhere near a consulship. His past was variegated. First of all with M. Lepidus in 43, then joining Sextus Pompeius for a time and next an Antonian partisan, this Silanus made the transit in time to the better cause.[8] His emergence as consul is baffling.[9]

After that illustrious renegade, C. Norbanus Flaccus in 24 conveys a firm allegiance, the father (*cos.* 38) a Caesarian, a general in the campaign of Philippi and honoured with a triumph from Spain. Of the son no previous post is on record or subsequent employment. He married the daughter of a party magnate, the younger Cornelius Balbus.[10]

So far the first *nobiles* since Potitus Valerius Messalla, consul suffect in 29. At various times of emergency during the last sixty years the dearth of ex-consuls had been visible and painful. They were now numerous to excess. On a comforting view, senior statesmen lend dignity and authority to public transactions. They can also be a nuisance.

Of the Triumviral consuls it was not likely that many would find occupation abroad. Agility in changing sides impaired confidence for the future, and some of them had acquired bad habits or knew more than was healthy. To find a governor for distant Syria was an acute problem.[11]

---

[6] Cicero, *Ad fam.* XII.25.1: 'cum summo gaudio et offensione Minotauri, id est Calvisi et Tauri'. For the early career of Calvisius, with P. Ventidius for comparison, see *Latomus* XVII (1958), 73 ff. = *RP* (1979), 393 ff.

[7] Nicolaus, *Vita Caesaris* 96. Therefore Calvisius, not his son (as in *PIR*[2] C 353), claims the dedication to his 'pietas' (*ILS* 925: Spoletium). For converging evidence about his *patria*, *Historia* XIII (1964), 641 = *RP* (1979), 591.

[8] *PIR*[2] J 830. He left Alexandria in the company of the notorious Q. Dellius (Plutarch, *Antonius* 59).

[9] The Junii Silani are examined in Ch. XIV.   [10] *ILS* 7381, cf. *PIR*[2] C 1474.

[11] Tullius Cicero (*suff.* 30) had Syria (Appian, *BC* IV. 51.221): date uncertain, perhaps after Messalla Corvinus in 29 or 28. His aptitudes were 'urbanitas' and drink (Seneca, *Suas.* vii. 13; Pliny, *NH* XIV. 147).

Syria may well be the consular province of Potitus Messalla on *ILS* 8964 (incomplete), cf. the argument in *JRS* XLV (1955), 158 ff. = *RP* (1979), 266 ff. In 24 or 23 the governor was a praetorian called Varro (Josephus, *BJ* I. 398; *AJ* XV. 345).

For the more recent, Asia and Africa offered. Macedonia and Illyricum might appear to deserve consulars, it is true. The record of those two provinces happens to be sparse, almost void.[12] It would suit Caesar Augustus if the working of the lot produced ex-praetors of no known family. By the same token he preferred legates of that type—and, like Pompeius Magnus for Afranius and Gabinius, he would get them consulships.

Consulars retained a decorative function as 'principes civitatis' (which was all that some of them wanted, then and later), on show when the Senate heard despatches from Caesar, gave audience to embassies, and held earnest debate on miscellaneous matters. It was not intended that the high assembly should share in the shaping of imperial policy.

The Senate now paraded a good dozen 'viri triumphales', endowed with an experience of the Roman dominion west and east. By birth and past allegiances they were a variegated company. Apart from Taurus and Calvisius, the *novi homines* ranged from the veteran C. Sosius (*cos.* 32), the admiral of Antonius at Actium, to Sex. Appuleius (29), the latest to hold a triumph; and they included such persons of note and talent as Munatius Plancus (42) and Asinius Pollio (40).[13]

Although the war years had been inimical to birth and rank, *nobiles* exhibit a strong proportion, at least six still among the living. Beyond compare for his vicissitudes and his survival stood Domitius Calvinus, consul in 53 with Messalla Rufus (a pair lacking credit). He became a strong Caesarian, acceding to a second consulate in 40, and for three years thereafter governing the Spains.

Next came Marcius Censorinus (*cos.* 39) and the head of the Claudian house, Ap. Pulcher (38).[14] The youngest by far, and close coeval to Caesar Augustus, were Messalla Corvinus (31) and M. Crassus (30).

Corvinus recalled Philippi and Cassius his general with conscious pride. Some may have cast him for a political role, in opposition to the new order. The faction of Cato and the Liberators had been almost wiped out, Cato along with the consulars Domitius Ahenobarbus and Calpurnius Bibulus perishing in the first civil war, the younger men on the field of Philippi, while the survivors lapsed to Marcus Antonius. Their last leader had been Cato's nephew Ahenobarbus (*cos.* 32), who died soon after he deserted Antonius during the campaign of Actium.

For the present, malcontents saw little prospect, and some subsided into

---

[12] For Illyricum, none until P. Silius Nerva (*cos.* 20), proconsul in 16 (Dio LIV.20.1 f.; *ILS* 899: Aenona). For Macedonia the first after Crassus is the obscure M. Primus (Dio LIV. 3.2.), perhaps in 25/4. However, Paullus Aemilius Lepidus (*suff.* 34) may have been a proconsul (below, p. 110).
[13] Omitted, because not on mention after 27, are C. Carrinas (*suff.* 43), L. Cornificius (*cos.* 35), L. Autronius Paetus (*suff.* 33).
[14] L. Philippus (*suff.* 38) lacks attestation, but Norbanus Flaccus (*cos.* 38) should be added.

sullen retirement and the consolations of belonging to a minority.[15] They would have to wait and hope for accidents or a split in the government. At Rome Agrippa and Taurus kept order. The Praetorian Guard existed already, its pay augmented in January of 27; and private resources helped, such as the troop of Germans maintained by Taurus.[16]

Finally, in the background, Maecenas ever vigilant under the show of indolence, with his wife's brother, the sagacious Proculeius—and with Livia Drusilla, the consort of the absent Caesar.

Men recalled a recent admonition. In the autumn of 30, while Caesar was still at Alexandria, occurred the conspiracy of Aemilius Lepidus, the eldest son of the discarded Triumvir. It was taken seriously by the loyal historian Livy.[17] Velleius is explicit, in a copious exposition.[18] Young Lepidus proposed to assassinate Caesar when he returned to Italy.

Maecenas was resolute, and he went to work unobtrusively, 'per summam quietem et dissimulationem'. Pouncing on Lepidus with marvellous promptitude, he nipped in the bud a new civil war, without any perceptible perturbations. The rash youth paid the penalty of nefarious designs.

No ally or accomplice comes in, unless it be his mother Junia, the sister of Marcus Brutus.[19] Another account shows her in some embarrassment, being impugned by Maecenas, but the consul intervened with help and comfort.[20]

To detect a conspiracy is variously useful to governmental policy. In this instance a pawn or hostage was destroyed, no longer of value after victory. The action was also a deterrent, although none ignored the perils of high birth and a dynastic name.[21]

Rome was held under tight control, with no scope now for political eloquence, that fatal glory of the Republic. As under the Triumvirs, talent was diverted to diplomatic persuasion or exercised in the courts of law and schools of rhetoric. After the defeat of Sextus Pompeius in 36 Rome and Italy enjoyed a respite from civil warfare. Polite studies revived. One result of the violent distribution of property was to stimulate forensic

[15] Thus P. Servilius, the son of Isauricus (*cos.* II 41), after a praetorship in 25: 'ille praetorius, nulla alia re quam otio notus' (Seneca, *Epp.* 55.2).

[16] *ILS* 7448 f.

[17] Livy, *Per.* CXXXIII: 'coniuratione adversus Caesarem facta bellum moliens oppressus et occisus est.' Dio has a brief casual reference a dozen years later (LIV. 15.4).

[18] Velleius II.88.

[19] His wife Servilia committed suicide: to be identified as a daughter of Isauricus, hence his first cousin.

[20] Appian, *BC* iv. 50.215. Called 'Balbinus', this consul is L. Saenius, the concluding *suffectus* of 30.

[21] For the opposition now and during the next period see P. Sattler, *Augustus und der Senat. Untersuchungen zur römischen Innenpolitik zwischen 30 und 17 v. Christus* (1960), 24 ff.

activity. Casual testimony brings up Messalla Corvinus in this context, also a notable speaker generally obscured, the son of the patrician jurist Ser. Sulpicius Rufus.[22]

Poetry of various types was also in efflorescence, and even the writing of history. Despotism is not repressive everywhere. There are grounds for asserting a 'Triumviral period' in the annals of Latin literature, the fifteen years from 43 to 28.

The War of Actium intervened, not to interrupt but to furnish a new source of inspiration, avidly exploited. It is a question how far the high aristocracy was susceptible to fervour of any kind. They used religion and cult to impress or terrify the lower classes; and nationalistic zeal could be resigned to ordinary senators or the better sort in the towns of Italy.

Peace came, reinforced by order, and for some at least the emotions generated by peril and by victory would abate. Statesmen wrote their memoirs, salons opened, the social life of the aristocracy resumed its normal habits.

Betrothal and matrimony were a constant preoccupation, and political dissension produced notable disruptions. Sulla's return and his restoration of the *nobilitas* issued in several divorces.[23] For the breach between Caesar's heir and Antonius, the evidence happens to be defective, thwarting a legitimate curiosity.

Responsive to wealth and success, noblemen had recently surrendered their daughters or sisters to rank upstarts. They would not disdain advances from the usurper who had several nieces to dispose of. In the first place, four daughters of Octavia, brought up under her careful supervision, not without support from Livia Drusilla.[24] Aristocrats were ready to follow in the steps of Vipsanius Agrippa who, discarding in 28 his first wife, acquired the elder Marcella.[25] Her sister would become nubile about the year 25—when their brother, aged only seventeen, married Julia, the daughter of Caesar Augustus.

Next, the two daughters whom Octavia bore to Marcus Antonius. That does not exhaust the count of young females. Marcius Philippus (*suff.* 38) had married Atia, an aunt of the Princeps. Now perhaps deceased, he left no son, only a daughter: still a small child.[26]

[22] Horace, *Sat.* I.10.85 f. The orator Ser. Sulpicius has suffered from amalgamation with the parent, cf. CQ XXXI (1981), 421 ff. = *RP* III (1984), 1415 ff. And below, Ch. XV.

[23] viz. a Calpurnius Piso from Cinna's widow (Velleius II.41.2), Pompeius from Antistia, to marry Aemilia, daughter of Scaurus and Sulla's stepdaughter (Plutarch, *Pompeius* 4); while an alert Valeria, divorced recently, ensnared the Dictator, the fifth of his wives (*Sulla* 35).

[24] Plutarch, *Antonius* 87, cf. Ch. XI and Ch. XII.

[25] Dio LIII.1.2, with no mention of any preceding wife. That is, the daughter of Pomponius Atticus, incriminated for adultery with the scholar Q. Caecilius Epirota—who fled for protection to Cornelius Gallus: one of the 'gravissima crimina' brought against Gallus (Suetonius, *De gramm.* 16).

[26] Marcia, destined to marry Fabius Maximus (Ch. XXVIII).

A new family, the Appuleii, also belonged to the nexus. By an earlier marriage C. Octavius (*pr.* 61) had a daughter who went to Sex. Appuleius—an obscure person who however was made a patrician by Caesar the Dictator and benefited at the end by a public funeral.[27] Hence Sex. Appuleius, consul in 29 and proconsul of Spain. Marcus (*cos.* 20) is to be reckoned his brother. Sisters will be invoked to explain certain propinquities.[28]

By luck or by demography, several young aristocrats became available. First of all, a Domitius Ahenobarbus and a P. Scipio. Next L. Piso and M. Livius Drusus Libo. The latter, only a name on the *Fasti*, excites curiosity: a Scribonius Libo, it appears, taken in adoption by M. Livius Drusus Claudianus, who fell at Philippi. Therefore a stepbrother of Livia Drusilla.[29]

In this season the elder Antonia was consigned to Ahenobarbus, quaestor probably in 24. Her sister, three years younger, was kept in reserve by Livia (so it may be conjectured) for Nero Drusus, her second son (born in 38). The elder son would have to be content with a plebeian bride: Vipsania, the daughter of Agrippa and Caecilia Attica, betrothed when an infant.[30]

By methods traditional in the aristocracy, the principate of one man was thus annexing alliances that surpassed the various efforts of Pompeius Magnus (mainly intent on the Metellan connection); and Caesar the Dictator had few kinsfolk he could use apart from the grandnephew. These compacts foretold the lineaments and substance of a dynasty. Resources accrued—and the inherent menace of rivalry and discord.

A triennium passing in tranquillity and discretion, Rome awaited Caesar's return in the summer of 24. He had set out under the sign of war, Janus being opened, and he went from Gaul to Spain, to enter on his eighth consulship at Tarraco.

The design was to subjugate a vast zone of mountain territory, extending from northern Portugal to the Basque country.[31] It had been prepared by the operations of three proconsuls, namely Calvisius, Taurus, Appuleius. To succeed, it entailed the use of two armies in a concerted effort, the garrisons of Tarraconensis and of Lusitania (as they may conveniently be styled).

For the first campaign, Imperator Caesar himself took charge, attacking Cantabria with three columns of invasion. In the second, two legates dealt

---

[27] *ILS* 8963 (Carthage).
[28] The Appuleii are discussed under Quinctilius Varus (Ch. XXII).
[29] Ch. XIX.
[30] Nepos, *Vita Attici* 19.4.
[31] For the campaigns of 26 and 25, *AJP* LV (1934), 293 ff.: revised and expanded in *Legio VII Gemina* (León, 1970), 83 ff. = *RP* (1979), 825 ff.; W. Schmitthenner, *Historia* XI (1962), 29 ff.

with Asturia and Callaecia: Antistius Vetus, by exception a consular (*suff.* 30), and P. Carisius. Official language now proclaimed Spain conquered and pacified at last.[32] Janus was duly closed—but no triumph. Nothing could enhance the celebrations in August of 29.

Other preoccupations vexed the ruler, notably his health and survival. Ill in May of 27 before leaving Rome, and ill again on his return in June of 24, he had been prevented by a prolonged malady from taking the field in the second campaign.[33] He stayed behind at Tarraco, or visited salubrious resorts in the Pyrenees. Not yet forty, pride or despair now impelled Caesar to compose his autobiography.[34] The huge and regal monument constructed four years previously on the Campus Martius was waiting to receive his ashes, with a text perhaps already indited, to declare his 'res gestae'.

Only twenty years had elapsed since the tumultuous incineration of the Dictator in the Roman Forum; and old men still extant could recall the solemn obsequies accorded to Cornelius Sulla. Funerals conveyed delight to the upper order, and notably to the aged, ever prone to compare past and present. They contemplated the parade of *imagines* that exhibited ancient glories and family alliances, some now distant or otherwise forgotten, they appraised the senior consular chosen to deliver the oration, and the quality of his performance. Above all, the aristocracy seized the occasion to sharpen and reinforce verdicts normally confined to their clubs and conclaves. Reflection on chance and fate in the affairs of men led by an easy train to malice and detraction.

If Caesar now succumbed, there could be no doubt who should pronounce the laudation: the smooth and eloquent Munatius Plancus, who on January 16th three years before proposed the name 'Augustus'.[35]

His exposition would evoke comment—in the contrary sense. An ample indictment availed of violence and fraud, beginning with the private army raised by the young adventurer, the march on Rome not once but twice and the consulate seized at the age of nineteen. Then the Proscriptions, the 'vastitas Italiae', the wars continuing—and some might spare a word of regret for Lepidus circumvented and discarded, for the ruin of Marcus Antonius.

---

[32] cf. Livy XXVIII.12.12: 'nostra demum aetate ductu auspicioque Augusti Caesaris perdomita est.'

[33] The illnesses in 27 and 24 are documented by *Inscr. It.* XIII.1, p. 150.

[34] Suetonius, *Divus Aug.* 85.2: 'Cantabrico tenus bello nec ultra'. It is a question whether he narrated the second year of warfare. The accounts in Florus and Orosius yield explicit detail only for the first.

[35] Plancus, the most elegant and Ciceronian among the correspondents of Cicero, was a master in flattery: 'artifex ante Vitellium maximus' (Seneca, *NQ* IV, *praef.* 5). Character and style rendered Pollio doubly unsuitable.

Change and events moving so rapidly, much of that might seem ancient history now. The aftermath of victory was equivocal and disturbing. An autocrat is known by his choice of friends and agents. It was all to the good that he had rid himself of the arrogant Narbonensian, Cornelius Gallus. Others remained such as Vedius Pollio, the cruel and luxurious son of a freedman.[36] If Vedius might turn out deleterious, little chance offered of removing Maecenas, the alleged descendant of kings in Etruria, with multiple services to Caesar, among them the destruction of young Lepidus. Still less any abatement of the potent influences of Livia Drusilla—taken from her husband when pregnant.[37]

A golden shield hung in the Curia advertised to senators the cardinal virtues inherent in their Princeps: 'virtus', 'clementia', 'iustitia', 'pietas'. Clemency asserted after Actium and after the fall of Alexandria was refuted by names and facts. Gratitude for the preservation of an Aemilius Scaurus and a Cornelius Cinna was clouded by the fate of young Scribonius Curio.[38]

Nomenclature is revealing. By the Dictator's testament the grandson of a municipal banker annexed the *imagines* of the patrician Julii—he could show none of his own family, unless through fraud. Further, he had fabricated the style 'Imperator Caesar Divi f. Augustus', anomalous and exorbitant in each member. It was a travesty of any licences of nomenclature practised by the high aristocracy.[39] The military *praenomen* had in fact been taken in sequel to a defeat in naval warfare (in 38). To employ 'Caesar' in the place of a *gentilicium* could be conceded, but 'Augustus', being a name more than human, encouraged veneration and worship, which ensued—and 'Divi filius' carried a presumption of future consecration.[40] Furthermore, the Princeps was 'sacrosanctus' like the ten tribunes, with some of their prerogatives as ostensible protector of the common people. All of which denied the sovereignty of 'senatus magistratus leges'.[41]

Favourable comment would be short but cogent because obvious. Necessity imposed violence, success justifies—and no price is too high if it ensures Rome's dominion over the nations.[42]

---

[36] The corruption and lacuna in the text of Tacitus has defied solution: '† que tedii et Vedii Pollionis luxus' (I.10.5). It falls between 'abducta Neroni uxor' etc. and 'postremo Livia, gravis in rem publicam mater'. The linked themes are family and friends—perhaps reinforced by an allusion to the ruler's adultery with Terentia, the wife of Maecenas.

[37] For the marriage and the birth of Drusus, W. Suerbaum, *Chiron* X (1980), 337 ff. (a full account). Suspicion about the paternity of Drusus was inevitable (Suetonius, *Divus Claudius* 1.1).

[38] above, p. 31. For Scaurus, Dio LI.2.4. f.; for Cinna, Seneca, *De Clem.* I.9.11.

[39] *Historia* VII (1958), 172 ff. = *RP* (1979), 361 ff.

[40] When the order 'Augustus Caesar' occurs in writers ancient and modern it declares an allegiance.

[41] The brief definition of legitimate authority in *Ann.* I.2.1.

[42] Ch. XXX.

The near prospect of the ruler's decease inspired sombre forebodings in men of understanding, those 'prudentes' whose opinions, suitably conjured up at funerals, are elsewhere not beyond surmise. His testamentary dispositions could not fail to transmit name and possessions to an heir, to the nephew married to his daughter and destined four years from now to be elected consul at the age of twenty-two.[43]

Marcellus threatened to provoke conflict within the Caesarian party, unduly enlarged by taking in so many former adversaries. Dissidents or enemies of monarchy might cast about for a leader in the ranks of the aristocracy. If hopes fastened on Messalla Corvinus, they were fragile indeed. Though Messalla was patently 'capax imperii', having governed Syria and Gaul, and highly influential, he was not a prey to fierce ambitions. Messalla and other noblemen were coming to see where their interests lay.

Subversion would encounter Agrippa, whose favourite proverb enjoined 'concordia'.[44] Beside him stood Livia, capable, if her husband died, of converting an alliance (through the betrothal of their children) into a pact by matrimony.[45]

The following year enhanced fears and forecasts—another malady, much worse, and the Princeps was not expected to live. The emergency had been sharpened by a political crisis. It took its origin from a prosecution, a certain M. Primus being indicted for waging war without authority when proconsul of Macedonia.[46] When the Princeps decided to appear in court and denied that he gave sanction, Varro Murena who was defending Primus conceived offence. In the sequel Murena entered a conspiracy with the Republican Fannius Caepio, so it was alleged. Both were put to death.[47]

Manifold obscurity envelops the whole affair.[48] Identities add complication. The *Fasti Capitolini* show the consul Varro Murena dying or removed from office. If, as has seemed plausible, this man is the conspirator, the crisis was grave indeed. In any event one of the magnates of the Caesarian party came to ruin, brother to Terentia, the wife of Maecenas.[49]

[43] cf. Dio LIII.28.3.

[44] Seneca, *Epp.* 94.46. That is, 'nam concordia parvae res crescunt, discordia maxumae dilabuntur' (Sallust, *Jug.* 10.6.).

[45] To adduce a resemblance in active ambition to Servilia, the niece of Livius Drusus, one does not need the family affinity.

[46] Dio LIV.3.2 ff. (under the year 22).

[47] Velleius II.91.2. Fannius Caepio may be presumed a son of C. Fannius, a Republican among the last companions of Sex. Pompeius in 35 (Appian, *BC* V.139.579). The cognomen indicates the son of a Servilius—or perhaps of a Servilia.

[48] Here assumed to fall in 23. Date, details, and range are in sharp controversy. See Ch. XXVII.

[49] Dio LIV.3.5. And Caesar's friend C. Proculeius was half-brother to Varro Murena.

The Princeps now induced Cn. Piso to take the consulship, a Republican hitherto and recalcitrant. Finally, when restored to health, he proceeded at the end of June to modify the basis of power, giving up the consulate and acquiring compensation more than adequate.[50] The *imperium* Caesar retained, now redefined as 'maius', hence superior to that of proconsuls; and the ruler decided to put heavy emphasis on his *tribunicia potestas*.[51]

A further novelty, missing direct attestation in any source, is deduced from facts that emerge. Marcus Agrippa received a share in the proconsular *imperium* of the ruler, and he was at once despatched to the eastern lands.[52] Not long after (in 20 and 19) Agrippa is discovered in Gaul and in Spain, completing the pacification of the peninsula.

In the autumn of the year Marcellus died. A grievous blow to Caesar Augustus in his fervent desire to found a dynasty, it eliminated a previsible source of disquiet and friction—and it enhanced the predominance of Agrippa, to whom the young widow was consigned before two years elapsed. Anticipating a principate for a *novus homo*, the *nobiles* were not so happy.

When the Princeps resigned the *fasces* he handed them to L. Sestius, a Republican of a kind (he had been quaestor to Marcus Brutus), but less conspicuous on that count than his colleague Piso.[53] In the next year took office a Claudius Marcellus (namely Aeserninus), an old man now, and L. Arruntius, after a Pompeian past one of the Caesarian admirals at Actium.

Sundry measures followed, to confirm an iterated restoration of normal government. Censors were appointed, Paullus Aemilius Lepidus and Munatius Plancus: an ill-assorted pair who quarrelled and failed to complete any tasks. Further, the Princeps surrendered two small portions of his 'provincia', namely Narbonensis and Cyprus. More welcome, and a marked concession, two proconsuls of Africa before long celebrated triumphs, Sempronius Atratinus in 21, Cornelius Balbus in 19.[54]

The year was marked by dire portents, by a flood of the Tiber, by famine and pestilence continuing, with a popular clamour that the Princeps should take the dictatorship. Absence was a remedy—and it would teach senators a lesson. The ruler went to Sicily and proceeded on a tour of the eastern provinces.

The consular elections led to turmoil since one place had been kept

[50] It was already of urgency for Caesar, 'cos. XI', to surrender the consulate. The tenure by C. Marius (104 to 100) was a damaging precedent.

[51] On which, W. K. Lacey, *JRS* LXIX (1979), 29 ff.

[52] Agrippa's *imperium* is shown by his using legates (Dio LIII.32.1).

[53] For this Piso, Ch. XXVI.

[54] Not in Dio. Putting emphasis on the modesty of Agrippa (under the year 19), he states that others celebrated triumphs for trivial reasons, granted liberally by Augustus (LIV.12.1 f.)

vacant in the hope that Caesar would accept it. The next year thus opened with M. Lollius in sole charge of Rome. Two noblemen competing furiously, men of sober judgment wanted to bring the ruler back.[55] In the end Q. Lepidus prevailed over L. Silanus (a brother of Marcus, the consul of 25). For the next year M. Appuleius and P. Silius Nerva secured election without disturbance, so it appears, but 19 opened with a single consul, C. Sentius Saturninus. This energetic character, endowed with 'prisca virtus' and recalling consuls of the old time, had to deal with an undesirable candidate, the demagogue Egnatius Rufus.[56] He was thrown into prison and there executed. In the autumn the ruler on his return journey met in Campania a senatorial deputation and appointed one of its number as consul, Q. Lucretius Vespillo; and M. Vinicius took the place of the excellent Sentius.

Thus ended an interlude of *Libertas* at the capital. Agrippa had been there for a time, and Sentius Saturninus could count on support from the great Taurus.

By a decree of the grateful Senate the day of Augustus' advent (October 11th) was marked by an altar to Fortuna Redux. Glad tidings had gone before him. After negotiation, delay, and evasions the Parthian monarch surrendered the Roman standards. These trophies were to be housed in the shrine of Mars Ultor in a new forum now under construction. Caesar's heir had vowed that temple on the field of Philippi. Its purpose was modified by Caesar the Princeps, vengeance on the assassins of his parent being transmuted to revenge on the foreign enemy, and the national honour satisfied through operations of diplomacy. By the same token Janus and the theme of world peace came to be associated with Parthian submission.[57]

Caesar Augustus held authority abroad through *imperium* and the twelve *fasces* of a proconsul. He ought to have borne that title. No surprise that he disdained it, and no deception. Though the ruler had been permitted to retain his *extraordinarium imperium* within the sacred precinct of the city, he lacked any *insignia*, perhaps a cause of perplexity to earnest or superficial adherents. In this year (19) the twelve *fasces* were conceded.[58] The form of power which originated in provinces and armies was thus visibly domiciled at the seat of empire.[59] For civil government, however,

---

[55] Dio LIV.6.2 (οἱ ἔμφρονες).

[56] Velleius II. 91.3–92.5.

[57] *AJP* C (1979), 188 ff. = *RP* III (1984), 1179 ff.

[58] Dio LIV.10.5: τὴν δὲ τῶν ὑπάτων (sc. ἐξουσίαν) διὰ βίου ἔλαβεν, ὥστε καὶ ταῖς δώδεκα ῥάβδοις ἀεὶ καὶ πανταχοῦ χρῆσθαι. The word ὥστε should be taken as defining and restricting. Some assume a grant of *consulare imperium*. Thus A. H. M. Jones, *JRS* XLI (1951), 117 = *Studies in Roman Government and Law* (1960), 13.

[59] That the *imperium* of the Caesars was regarded as proconsular, retained in the City, emerges from Tacitus, *Ann.* XII.41.1; *HA, Marcus* 6.6.

the Princeps devised the tribunician power, vague and portentous—and deserving to be known in due course as the 'summi fastigii vocabulum'.[60] Plebs and army stand as the twin pillars of the 'novus status'.

What had happened to the consulate during the decade after it became normal and annual in 28 would provoke pertinent comment from the 'prudentes'. First of all, Caesar's monopoly and the iterations for Agrippa and for Taurus; and when it was liberated from Caesar's grasp, *novi homines* obtruded heavily.

In a total of fourteen consuls (with the *suffecti* of two years) six *nobiles* make a collection far from resplendent. Three of them were advanced in years. Cn. Piso was coeval with Aeserninus, who incurred disgrace when quaestor in Spain in 48.[61] Aeserninus had not been heard of until his consulship, nor had Q. Lepidus. The latter can hardly be supposed youthful, given the interval since his father's consulship (in 66). None of the three is on later record except Lepidus, who became proconsul of Asia.[62]

Of the eight *novi homines* neither Sestius nor Arruntius is likely to be under fifty. Lucretius Vespillo, a senator commanding troops for Pompeius in 49, had been among the proscribed.[63] Likewise Arruntius.[64] For age, the anomaly is M. Appuleius, the younger brother of Sextus (*cos.* 29)—and a nephew of Caesar Augustus.

The remaining four are characters of note and value. Marcus Lollius carried out the annexation of the Galatian kingdom after the death of Amyntas in 25;[65] and in the same year Vinicius won a victory over German invaders on the Rhine.[66] For Silius Nerva and for Sentius Saturninus merit earned in praetorian posts might be assumed. All four are subsequently found in consular commands.

Certain praetorian legates were not so fortunate. In 25 Terentius Varro subjugated the Salassi in Val d'Aosta, opening up communications to Gaul and to the upper Rhine through the St. Bernard passes.[67] Again a Varro is casually attested holding Syria in 24 or 23.[68] As for Spain, P. Carisius

---

[60] *Ann.* III. 56.2.

[61] Dio XLII.16.2.

[62] *IGR* IV.901 (Cibyra).

[63] Caesar, *BC* I.18.1.

[64] Arruntius returned to Rome in 39; and he commanded the left flank of the Caesarian fleet at Actium (Velleius II.77.3; 85.2.)

[65] Eutropius VII.10.2.

[66] Dio LIII.26.4.

[67] Strabo IV, p.206; Dio LIII. 25.3 f. Dio, it may be noted, places the action in 25—like the Spanish campaigns of 26 and 25. Further, this Terentius Varro is generally held identical with Varro Murena, the conspirator. The total of fourteen consuls (25–19) here discussed includes the consul of 23, reckoned among *nobiles*.

[68] Josephus, *BJ* I.398; *AJ* XV. 345. For problems about identities, 'M. Teren]tius M.f. Pap. Varro' comes in, attested in 25 by the *S.C. de Mytilenaeis* (*IGR* IV.33 = R. K. Sherk, *Roman Documents from the Greek East* (1969), 26, col. C, line 15).

continued in Lusitania for five years, with an early exploit to his credit. By
a rapid march he rescued the winter camp of the other army from a
surprise attack by the Asturians.[69] Victory in the field was exceptional in
those campaigns. The historian Dio describes Carisius as cruel and
luxurious.[70] No evil report would be likely to attend upon Aelius Lamia,
in Tarraconensis from 24 to 22; and his successor C. Furnius acceded to the
fasces in 17.[71]

Some of the military men came up from very low, and names never
seen at Rome invaded the *Fasti*, some by their shape acknowledging not
merely small towns but the territories of confederate Italia. Statilius
Taurus was Lucanian.[72] Taurus and others may derive from local
aristocracies, the class of 'domi nobiles'.

At Rome obscurity of birth was a normal label. It applied in propriety
to M. Vipsanius Agrippa. Even his parentage evaded scrutiny when it
became safe to publish. The *gentilicium* he did his best to suppress,
imitating the practice of aristocrats. It points to Venetia or Istria.[73]

By contrast, the four recent consuls noted above had respectable
origins. The term 'novus homo' covers a wide range. The families of Silius
and Vinicius were already senatorial, while Sentius Saturninus had for
great-grandfather a praetor, and a consular cousin, namely L. Scribonius
Libo (*cos.* 34).[74] His *patria* was Atina in Latium, and M. Vinicius (close kin
to L. Vinicius, *suff.* 33) came from Cales in Campania. Lollii, it is true, are
indistinctive, the *patria* of Marcus Lollius not verifiable, but perhaps
Ferentinum.[75] Lollius was able to acquire as his bride an Aurelia, sister to
the second wife of Messalla Corvinus.[76] Silius' wife was municipal, the
daughter of Coponius, a senator from Tibur.[77] The consorts of the other
two are not known.

While those names may help to redeem the *Fasti* from a continuance of
Triumviral iniquities, there was a parallel phenomenon. The shortage of
ex-consuls after 29 affected the proconsulates of Asia and Africa. Biennial

---

[69] Related in the sources (Florus, Orosius, Dio) at the end of 25, the episode probably belongs to
the beginning of 26.

[70] Dio LIV.5.1. Except for M. Lollius, such labels do not normally attach to Augustan generals.

[71] The Spanish legates from 26 to 17 are registered in *Legio VII Gemina* (1970), 86 f. = *RP* (1979),
829. They include P. Silius Nerva (?19–17). For the full detail, G. Alföldy, *Fasti Hispanienses* (1969),
3 ff.

[72] As argued in *Rom. Rev.* 237.

[73] M. Reinhold, *Marcus Agrippa* (1933), 8 f.; J. Untermann, *Die venetischen Personennamen* (1961),
136 ff.

[74] Deduced from *ILS* 8892. For the history of the Sentii, *Historia* XIII (1964), 156 ff. = *RP* (1979),
605 ff.

[75] M. Lollius and A. Hirtius were local censors there (*ILS* 5342). See however *Historia* XIII
(1964), 118 f. = *RP* (1979), 596 f.

[76] below, p. 178.

[77] Velleius II.83.3 (Coponius rebuking Munatius Plancus in 32: in fact his fellow townsman). For
the *patria* of the Coponii, Cicero, *Pro Balbo* 53; *ILS* 3700.

tenures in Asia happen to be on attestation for Sex. Appuleius and Potitus Messalla (consul and consul suffect in 29).[78] There may have been others. The evidence is meagre.[79] They are the only proconsuls registered subsequent to L. Vinicius (*suff.* 33), probably in 27/6, until the turn of Q. Lepidus (*cos.* 21). Likewise for Africa: after L. Autronius Paetus (*suff.* 33), in 29/8, only three for a dozen years and more, and those three were brought back by the government from consulars of the earlier epoch.[80] Biennial tenures, it may be conjectured, were quite common for a time and contemplated without dismay by Caesar Augustus.

Not long after his return the Princeps directed his attention to domestic reforms. In 18 the Senate was reduced to a total of six hundred by complicated methods; and the Julian Laws were enacted, not without protest and discontent. Further, the Princeps prolonged his *imperium* for a second decennium and associated Agrippa in the *tribunicia potestas*.

Rome being regenerated, with solid and enduring 'fundamenta rei publicae', it remained to crown the achievement and announce a New Age. The sacred books of the Sibyl were removed from the Capitol and lodged in the custody of Apollo on the Palatine.[81] Revised and purged (a plain necessity) the oracles were copied out by the *quindecimviri* in person.[82]

The college celebrated the *Ludi Saeculares* in June of 17, Augustus and Agrippa duly presiding. To justify the date chosen, a whole sequence of previous occasions, at intervals of a hundred and ten years, was fabricated.[83] Ateius Capito interpreted the oracle in the requisite sense, an expert in law both human and divine, though not a member of the college.[84]

After which, Agrippa departed to the East, his *imperium* now covering the 'provinciae transmarinae'.[85] This felicitous year further strengthened the dynasty. Julia had given birth to a son in 20, a second now followed. Augustus adopted them both. In the course of the next year he went away

---

[78] For Potitus, *ILS* 8964; for Appuleius an inscription at Claros (not yet published), cf. U. Weidemann, *Arch. Anzeiger* 1965, 463 f.

[79] For a list of proconsuls, D. Magie, *Roman Rule in Asia Minor* (1950), 1580: needing to be supplemented with L. Volcacius Tullus (?29/8) and L. Vinicius (?28/7): the latter to be held the '?L.]Vinicius' on the Latin letter of Caesar and Agrippa (*SEG* VIII. 555).

[80] B. E. Thomasson, *RE Supp.* XIII.1 f. That is, M. Acilius Glabrio (*suff.* 33), in 25; L. Sempronius Atratinus (*suff.* 34), ?21/20; L. Cornelius Balbus (consular in rank), 20/19. Then none until C. Sentius Saturninus (*cos.* 19), c.13.

[81] Already on the Palatine c.20, cf. Tibullus II.5.17 ff. Suetonius in error dates the transference to 12, enjoined by Augustus now *pontifex maximus* (*Divus Aug.* 31.1).

[82] Dio LIV.17.2 (in 18).

[83] K. Latte, *Römische Religionsgeschichte* (1960), 298 f.; P. Weiss, *R. Mitt.* LXXX (1973), 205 ff.

[84] Zosimus II.4. Ateius Capito was the grandson of a Sullan centurion (*Ann.* III. 75.1).

[85] Agrippa's *imperium* occurs on the fragment of the funeral oration delivered by the Princeps (*Kölner Pap.* I (1976), 10). For discussion see L. Koenen, *ZPE* 5 (1970), 217 ff.; E. W. Gray, ib. 6 (1970), 227 ff.; E. Badian, *CJ* LXXVI (1980), 97 ff.; M. W. Haslam, LXXV (1979), 193 ff.

to Gaul and Spain for another triennium, leaving Statilius Taurus as *praefectus urbi*, a novel post.[86] The strains of Caesar's alliance with Agrippa were alleviated, with concord easier since the pair were seldom together.

The inscribed *Acta* of the *Ludi Saeculares* enumerate ritual and ceremonies in copious variety, not without spurious archaisms; and the text of the hymn composed by Q. Horatius Flaccus survives. Hence manifold instruction.

Those *Acta* possess an adventitious value. As concerns men and families, the written sources for this epoch are sadly defective. Cassius Dio misses figures of consequence in state and society, he evinces slight interest in funerals and obituary notices.[87] Furthermore, compensation sought and elicited from the poets is liable to misconceptions.[88]

Inscriptions furnish remedy and supplement, though seldom enough. The first college of the *Arvales*, established in the year 29, would be worth having. The earliest piece extant belongs to 21 and 20.[89] It discloses seven names, two of them fragmentary. A recent and thorough discussion furnished a list.[90] It is here presented, according to rank:

Cn. Domitius Calvinus
Ap. Claudius Pulcher
L. Scribonius Libo
L. Cornelius Cinna
M. Valerius Messalla Corvinus
Cn. Pompeius Q. f.
M. Caecilius Cornutus

Five of the names call for curt annotation.

(1) Libo, the Pompeian partisan, the brother of Scribonia whom Caesar's heir discarded in 39 after she gave birth to Julia. An elderly person, he is not heard of subsequent to his consulship in 34. The document has ']s Libo'. There is a temptation to substitute M. Livius Drusus Libo (*cos.* 15).[91]

(2) Ap. Claudius Pulcher (*cos.* 38). To be taken as certain, although only 'A['.[92] The survival of this patrician 'triumphalis' is noteworthy.[93]

(3) Cinna, to be held identical with L. Cornelius, the consul suffect of

---

[86] below, p. 211.
[87] Under the year 19 Dio happens to note that Augustus honoured many of the eminent with public funerals (LIV.12.2). As later under Tiberius (LVIII.21.3), no names.
[88] Ch. XXVII.
[89] *CIL* VI. 32338.
[90] J. Scheid, *Les Frères Arvales* (1975), 13 ff.
[91] Not noted in *PIR*² L 295.
[92] J. Scheid, o.c. 27 ff. Not noted in *PIR*² C 982.
[93] His son is presumed M. Valerius Messalla Appianus (*cos.* 12). For daughters, Ch. XI.

32. That is, the Cinna attested as quaestor to P. Dolabella in 44.[94] From the nomenclature of his son (*cos.* AD 5) emerged a valuable fact: a grandson of Pompeius Magnus. The *suffectus* of 32 had therefore inherited Pompeia, the relict of Faustus Sulla.

(4) Cn. Pompeius Q. f. (*suff.* 31). At first sight a son of Rufus, the tribune of 52, who was a grandson of Sulla the Dictator.[95] The two consular appointments made in 32 and 31 after the breach with Antonius are of some significance.

(5) M. Caecilius Cornutus. His presence in this company is at first sight anomalous and enigmatic. The influence of Messalla Corvinus has been suitably adduced.[96] He was the patron of Tibullus, one of whose poems acclaims the marriage of a Cornutus.[97] This Cornutus might be identical with a historical writer of the name, all but unknown.[98] Further, the bride. She might even be the poetess Sulpicia. She was the daughter of the excellent orator, the patrician Ser. Sulpicius, who had married a Valeria, a sister of Corvinus.[99] A literary nexus is thus disclosed—also hereditary succession in priesthoods, for the son of Caecilius Cornutus became one of the Brethren.[100]

The seven names have encouraged speculation about the other five.[101] Thus Agrippa from the outset, young Marcellus in 25, to be replaced by the elder son of Livia Drusilla. More acceptable, Paullus Aemilius Lepidus (*suff.* 34) and Sex. Appuleius (*cos.* 29). Several of those persons are regarded as foundation members.

Since antiquarian erudition was at a premium, a preferential thought should have gone to Messalla Rufus (*cos.* 53). He survived until 26, having been an augur for fifty-five years.[102] And for that matter, the robust and venerable Varro was still among the living when the fraternity formed.

The *Acta* of the *quindecimviri* register the whole college: twenty-one names, Caesar and Agrippa at the head.[103] Apart from them, the entries reproduce the order of admission.[104] One list carries nineteen names; and two others are recorded on other portions of the document.

Omitting Caesar and Agrippa, the membership divides of itself into three sections, sharply. As follows:

[94] above, p. 30.
[95] above, p. 30.
[96] J. Scheid, o.c. 36 ff.
[97] Tibullus II.2.
[98] C. Cichorius, *Römische Studien* (1922), 261 ff.
[99] below, p. 206.
[100] *ILS* 5026, cf. *PIR*^{2} C 35.
[101] J. Scheid, o.c. 57 ff.
[102] below, p. 228.
[103] *CIL* VI. 32323. A piece carrying L. Marcius Censorinus and Cn. Pompeius Q.f. was omitted from *ILS* 5050.
[104] cf. M. W. H. Lewis, *The Official Priests of Rome under the Julio-Claudians* (1955), 86 ff.

A

L. Marcius Censorinus (*cos.* 39)
Q. Aemilius Lepidus (21)
Potitus Valerius Messalla (*suff.* 29)
Cn. Pompeius Q. f. (31)
C. Licinius Calvus Stolo
C. Mucius Scaevola
C. Sosius (*cos.* 32)
C. Norbanus Flaccus (38)
M. Cocceius Nerva (36)

B

M. Lollius (*cos.* 21)
C. Sentius Saturninus (19)
M. Fufius Strigo
L. Arruntius (22)

C

C. Asinius Gallus (8)
M. Claudius Marcellus
D. Laelius Balbus (6)
Q. Aelius Tubero (11)
C. Caninius Rebilus (*suff.* 12)
M. Valerius Messalla Messallinus (*cos.* 3)

The nine names in the first rubric represent the Triumviral intake. The sole Caesarian is Norbanus Flaccus, far from the earliest to enter.[105] On the other hand, three of Antonius' men who gained distinction in campaigns between 40 and 37. Marcius Censorinus and C. Sosius celebrated triumphs; and Cocceius Nerva had an imperatorial salutation.[106] The rest had escaped notice. Cn. Pompeius (also an *arvalis*) remains a decorative nonentity.[107] Of the two patricians, Potitus Messalla comes next after Q. Lepidus—who (it can be argued) was a much older man, coming late to his consulship.

Two members who crept into this congregation of the notables excite curiosity. Mucius Scaevola is the last member of a house of the plebeian *nobilitas* that earned renown for excellence in the law (five consuls between 175 and 95). The obscure Licinius by his two *cognomina* evokes the struggle of the Plebs for equality and their earliest consuls. The annalist Licinius Macer had contributed to embellish those transactions—and he equipped

[105] His son (*cos.* 24) was preferred by Groag, *RE* XVII. 933, cf. 1272.
[106] *ILS* 8780; *SEG* V. 604. Hence proconsul of Asia shortly before 36, cf. *PIR*² C 1224. His brother Lucius earned credit on diplomatic missions. A third brother may be C. Cocceius Balbus (*suff.* 39), like Marcus an 'imperator' (*IG* II². 4110).
[107] He lived on until AD 14 (*ILS* 5026).

his son with the *cognomen* 'Calvus'. That son, a poet and already an outstanding speaker, died before his prime in 54 or not long after. The *quindecimvir* might be a son of the orator or a kinsman—and like Mucius Scaevola acquiring a priesthood for interests remote from warfare or political life.

The next rubric comprises three prominent *novi homines* who joined the college during the first decade of the new dispensation—and M. Fufius M. f. Strigo. This fellow baffles any explanation. The *cognomen* is unique.[108]

Finally, separated by a wide gap of ages, six younger entrants, all except for Laelius Balbus of consular parentage or extraction.[109] At the end stands Messallinus the son of Corvinus, who benefited from special favour, co-opted in 21 when he assumed the *toga virilis*.[110] Of this company only one was to miss a consulship: Claudius Marcellus the son of Aeserninus (*cos*. 22).[111]

The nineteen names furnish instruction on the various counts of age and survival, rank and allegiance; and they offer a selection to illustrate the social life of the time.[112] Illustrious youths were found in the other three colleges—and also (given the totals of membership) a number of persons lost to fame.

Illness or absence abroad might add two or three names. Inscriptions reveal L. Aelius Lamia (Caesar's legate in Tarraconensis from 24 to 22).[113] Also M. Vinicius (*suff*. 19).[114] The latter may have had to wait, outdistanced by M. Lollius and Sentius Saturninus, his peers among the 'viri militares'.

Finally, the next members attested before the reign ended. Inscriptions at Lepcis yield two, viz. L. Caninius Gallus (*suff*. 2) and Cossus Cornelius Lentulus (*cos*. 1).[115] And there is the enigmatic Favonius, consul and proconsul of Asia.[116] Nor would it be fanciful to admit C. Ateius Capito (*suff*. 5) and L. Arruntius (*cos*. 6). In AD 15, when Asinius Gallus had proposed a consultation of the Sibylline Books (without success), they were chosen to investigate the flooding of the Tiber, a matter of signal religious import.[117]

[108] Apart from Calidius Strigo, a potter at Arretium (*CIL* XI.6700[149] etc.), and the graffito on the Bononia aqueduct, 'Strigones' (XI.739), of which the editors say 'si est nomen'.

[109] For the father, *PIR*[2] L 46. In 59 he was styled 'adulescens bonus, honesto loco natus' (*Pro Flacco* 18). Not therefore a descendant of C. Laelius (*cos*. 140).

[110] Tibullus II.5. (acclaiming his entrance).

[111] In *PIR*[2] C 926 the *quindecimvir* is assumed to be the parent.

[112] Albeit negatively. For the greater part they are absent from the written record.

[113] *AE* 1948, 93. Assigned to the consul of AD 3 by M. W. H. Lewis, o.c. 51.

[114] *ILS* 8965 (Tusculum). Assigned to P. Sulpicius Quirinius (ib. 51).   [115] *IRT* 521; 301.

[116] *ILS* 9483 (nr. Ipsus, in Phrygia). Favonius (*PIR*[2] F 121) is probably identical with one of the consuls in the last decade of the reign, cf. *JRS* LVI (1966), 60; *ZPE* 53 (1983), 198 ff. See further below, p 100.

[117] *Ann.* I. 76.1, cf. 79. The Arruntius of *ILS* 5349 should be the parent, cf. *PIR*[2] A 1129.

IV

Sixteen Aristocratic Consuls

When the consulate became annual in 28, the first results brought cruel disappointment; and after Caesar vacated the office, the *nobilitas* makes a poor showing. New names predominated, seven out of nine for the years 22–19, among them four with marked value for the future. By contrast, of *nobiles* only Marcellus Aeserninus and Q. Lepidus, a proportion recalling the rule of the Triumvirs.

In 18 the aristocracy seems to pick up with a pair of Cornelii Lentuli. The appearance is delusive. Neither avows a clear identity or can be proved youthful, and both revert to obscurity.[1]

The next year produced another aristocrat, C. Junius Silanus: of small consequence except that he is the third member of a family now coming to unexplained prominence, although this consul stands in no close relationship to Marcus (*cos.* 25) and his brother Lucius.[2] His colleague C. Furnius had been legate of Caesar in Tarraconensis. Like his father, Furnius earned fame as an orator—on a solitary item of attestation.[3] The father, surviving a long allegiance to Antonius, had been granted consular status in 29—which, on a lax or amicable interpretation, the son might be supposed to inherit.[4]

The word 'nobilis', not possessing or needing a legal definition, carries a clear connotation of social and political rank in the last epoch of the Republic. So potent is consular ancestry that the 'summa nobilitas' conceded to a member of the ancient patriciate can be deprecated as known only to historical research.[5] Hence a criterion that appeared satisfactory.[6] In certain respects the definition was vulnerable. Patricians cannot be excluded; and marginal cases occur, with families collateral or of ancient praetorian rank. Any curule office qualified, so it has been argued.[7]

---

[1] Ch. XXI   [2] Ch. XIV.

[3] Jerome, *Chron.* p. 159 H. He died before his father (*tr. pl.* 50).

[4] Dio LII.42.4 (the promotion of the parent).

[5] *Pro Murena* 16. And, by a negative token, the orator failed to assert 'nobilitas' for Licinius Murena.

[6] Introduced by M. Gelzer, *Die Nobilität der römischen Republik* (1912). That concise performance suffered long neglect, cf. remarks by R. Seager, in preface to his translation (*The Roman Nobility* (1969), XI f.). See also Chr. Meier in *Matthias Gelzer und die römische Geschichte* (1977), 29 ff.

[7] The view of Mommsen: restated with clear and careful arguments by P. A. Brunt, *JRS* LXXII (1982), 1 ff. For differing definitions of 'novus homo', ib. 5 f.

Nevertheless, the narrow definition will not seriously mislead when employed for senators in the years between Sulla and Caesar Augustus.

Subsequent usage has caused some perplexity. As employed by Tacitus and Pliny, the term 'nobilis' is confined to a small category, the descendants of the Republican aristocracy: 'illos ingentium virorum nepotes, illos posteros libertatis'.[8]

It remained to determine when the Republic be deemed to end. One comprehensive enquiry put the limit in 44 or 43, the last ancestor of a *nobilis* being Munatius Plancus, designated consul for 42 by Caesar the Dictator.[9] The notion was peculiar and vulnerable. It accords a kind of legitimacy to the Dictator, but denied to the Triumvirs, his heirs in autocracy.

Better, the descendants of Triumviral and Augustan consuls.[10] That respects the Roman proprieties. The birth of the Republic announced 'libertatem et consulatum'. Its demise was not declared until September of AD 14 when the elections were transferred from the People to the Senate.[11]

If needed, facts confirm. In the obituary notice on L. Volusius Saturninus (*suff*. 12) Tacitus was careful to state 'Volusio vetus familia, neque tamen praeturam egressa,' whereas the grandson is reckoned a *nobilis*.[12] Similarly C. Silius, a grandson of P. Silius Nerva (*cos*. 20).[13] Negative indications avail. To Aelius Lamia (*cos*. AD 3) is assigned only 'genus decorum'.[14] His father missed the consulate. The case of Rubellius Plautus, whose father married a princess, is highly instructive: 'cui nobilitas per matrem ex Iulia familia'.[15] The male parent, Rubellius Blandus (*suff*. AD 18), came too late to bequeath the label. Furthermore, women in the descent from Augustan consuls belong to the Roman *nobilitas*, as witness Lollia Paullina, the granddaughter of Marcus Lollius; and Poppaea Sabina, rebuking Nero, asserts that claim, though without the word.[16]

For the epoch of Caesar Augustus the question surpasses names and labels, pride or precedence. It embodies great political significance: rapid access to the *fasces*. A *nobilis* can now become consul at thirty-two, or not much later. The sons of new consuls share that advantage, as can be

---

[8] Pliny, *Pan*. 69.5, cf. *Epp*. V.17.6: 'nobiles nostri' (on a poetical Piso).

[9] M. Gelzer, *Hermes* L (1915), 395 ff.

[10] E. Stein, *Hermes* LII (1917), 264 ff. Not all have concurred. Thus E. Badian: 'where the limits were felt to lie hardly matters', and 'much unnecessary argument has been devoted as to whether the border was 44 or 31' (*JRS* LII (1967), 217, reviewing Gelzer, *Kl. Schriften*). For H. Hill, 'nobilis' had been used in a wide sense, and the process continued after AD 14 (*Historia* XVIII (1969), 230).

[11] cf. *Tacitus* (1958), 654: in support of E. Stein.

[12] *Ann*. III. 30.1; XIV. 46.2.

[13] XI.28.2. Adduced by T. D. Barnes, *Phoenix* XXVIII (1974), 444 ff.

[14] VI.27.2.

[15] XIV.22.1.

[16] XI.1.1.; XIV.1.2.

proved. The *triumviri monetales* hold their post in the early twenties.[17] C. Antistius Vetus and L. Vinicius were colleagues in 16, precisely.[18] Their consulships follow in 6 and 5.

Brief hesitation might intrude, whether the patriciate old or new made a difference. About the recent adlections (in 44 and 29) direct evidence is lacking, later indications have to be used. For example, attesting the Antistii Veteres.[19] And sundry other families may be surmised.[20] As a distinction, the patriciate mattered less than to be expected. It may be of some relevance that in the *Annales* the historian nowhere specifies any individual senator as a patrician. Before his time the word had become synonymous with aristocratic birth.[21]

None the less, some benefit would accrue to new patricians not of consular families. Sex. Appuleius (*cos.* 29) may not have had to wait until his forty-third year. The parent was adlected by Caesar the Dictator.[22] In AD 3 Aelius Lamia became consul, Publius, the eldest son of Silius Nerva, consul suffect. They had been *monetales* together in the same college, about 9 BC.[23] Lamia's father (it can be argued) acquired patrician status in 29.[24]

Monetales also contribute to another problem. A person taken in adoption undergoes a total change: nomenclature, filiation, status (patrician or plebeian), and tribe. But he could hardly abolish his ancestry. A Piso Frugi (*cos.* 61), adopted by the obscure M. Pupius, would count as a *nobilis*, one assumes. Now the second son of Silius Nerva, namely the consul of AD 7, stands on the *Fasti Capitolini* as 'A. Licinius A. f. A. n. Nerva Silianus'. He had been adopted by a non-consular Licinius.[25] That did not debar an early consulship. He had been *monetalis* in the same year as Messalla Volesus, consul in 5.[26]

Finally, a sporadic fact sums up and resolves the linked questions of *nobilitas* and the age differential. C. Caelius Rufus passed in four years from praetor to consul in AD 17.[27] More fortunate than Rubellius Blandus,

---

[17] Clear for L. Lentulus, the *flamen Martialis*, attested in 12, consul in 3 (*PIR*[2] C 1384). As previsible, five years earlier than to be postulated for the late Republic. For the social status of the forty-five Augustan *monetales* see T. P. Wiseman, *New Men in the Roman Senate* (1971), 150.

[18] *BMC R. Emp.* I. 19.

[19] *ILS* 948 (Gabii). Also the Domitii (Suetonius, *Nero* 1.2).

[20] H. C. Heiter, *De patriciis gentibus quae imp. R. saec. I, II, III fuerunt* (Diss. Berlin, 1909); H. H. Pistor, *Prinzeps und Patriziat in der Zeit von Augustus bis Commodus* (Diss. Freiburg, 1965).

[21] Lucan VII. 597; 761. The language of Statius (*Silvae* I.2.71) cannot prove that L. Arruntius Stella (*suff.* ?101) was patrician.

[22] Disclosed on *ILS* 8963 (Carthage).

[23] *BMC R. Emp.* I.40.

[24] His son, Ti. Plautius Silvanus Aelianus (*suff.* 45), retained patrician status when passing in some fashion into the Plautii (*ILS* 986: near Tibur). On whom, cf. *Epigrafia e Ordine Senatorio* I (1982), 406 f.

[25] *PIR*[2] L 224.

[26] *BMC R. Emp.* I. 45.

[27] *PIR*[2] C 141.

Caelius Rufus had a consular parent, albeit totally obscure (*suff.* 4 BC). The privilege, it is patent, was not restricted to the high aristocracy.

As concerns adoption, it was rapidly being replaced by a new device. Adoption by testament is not recognized or even mentioned by the Roman jurists. They were right. It is nothing other than the 'condicio nominis ferendi' imposed by the taking of an inheritance.[28] In this fashion a woman can transmit the name of her family. Some might wonder cursorily whether it was right and proper for a young *nobilis* to accept.[29]

To resign to a testament the naming of an heir carried manifest appeal. Men of property are loath to renounce before the end, the indecisive retained their options, while the malicious took pleasure in encouraging the hopes and the arts of 'captatores'.

Testamentary adoption provokes much discussion, most of it super-fluous. A plain fact stands. No man can thereby alter the *gens* of an heir or change his tribe. Caesar the Dictator could not transfer an Octavius to the patrician Julii, or ratify his passage from 'Scaptia' to 'Fabia'.[30] Status and tribe, those are the two criteria.[31] The consul of 52 has been a cause of some vexation. On a decree of the Senate he is styled 'Q. Caecilius Q. f. Fab. Metellus Pius Scipio'.[32] The 'Fabia', it follows, was the tribe of Scipio Nasica, his father. Metellus Macedonicus (*cos.* 143) was enrolled in 'Aniensis'.[33]

A third criterion, not always evident in the last epoch of the Republic, soon obtained: retention of the paternal filiation.[34] When polyonymy begins to proliferate in the aristocracy, with frequent adjunction of maternal ascendance (or even preference for it), these marks, if available, serve to determine a man's 'real name' and paternity.

The *Ludi Saeculares* inaugurated a run of youthful consuls elected from the high aristocracy. To men of the time they evoked the closing years of the 'res publica', but without premonition of any catastrophe.

Sulla conducted to victory the 'causa nobilium' and brought back deference to status and honour. Consul in 80 with Metellus Pius for colleague, he made provision for the immediate future with Ap. Claudius

---

[28] W. Schmitthenner, *Oktavian und das Testament Cäsars*[2] (1973), 39 ff.; E. J. Weinrib, *HSCP* LXXII (1968), 247 ff; D. R. Shackleton Bailey, *Two Studies in Roman Nomenclature* (1970), 79 ff.

[29] As when Dolabella inherited from a Livia (otherwise unknown). The amount was relevant, so Cicero observed (*Ad. Att.* VII.8.3). Young Claudius Nero took the inheritance of M. Gallius but dropped the name (Suetonius, *Tib.* 6.3).

[30] The heir retained an affection for 'Scaptia', cf. Suetonius, *Divus Aug.* 40.2.

[31] As firmly asserted, with later examples, in *Epigrafia e Ordine Senatorio* I (1982), 397 ff.

[32] *Ad fam.* VIII.8.5.

[33] *S.C. de agro Pergameno* (R. K. Sherk, *Roman Documents from the Greek East* (1969), 12, line 23).

[34] Thus 'C. Plinius L. f. Ouf. Caecilius Secundus' (*ILS* 2927): the starting point of Mommsen's valuable enquiry (*Ges. Schriften* IV (1906), 366 ff.). By contrast, M. Brutus becoming 'Q. Servilius Q. f. Caepio Brutus' (*AE* 1959, 248: Athens).

Pulcher and P. Servilius Vatia to follow, the one married to a Metella, the other a son. The next pair of consuls came to conflict, M. Aemilius Lepidus and Q. Lutatius Catulus; and Lepidus went on to foment a civil war.

The renovated oligarchy did not find it easy to produce energetic defenders—and foreign emergencies became exigent. Many of the ensuing consuls were dull and torpid, or advanced in age as a result of the Ten Years War.[35] Social distinction was also lacking: after 77 down to 66 only two patricians, both Cornelii Lentuli, who appear inevitable in such periods.[36] Sulla's efforts on behalf of young patricians then began to manifest some effects, with M'. Lepidus, L. Manlius Torquatus, and L. Julius Caesar in successive years.[37]

The *Fasti* from 57 to 49 consecrate the maturing of Sulla's predilections. The startling novelty emerges of a patrician in each year (apart from 55 with second consulships for Pompeius and Crassus): Q. Metellus Scipio claims that status, his adoption being only by testament, not plenary. The houses of the old plebeian *nobilitas* were also refulgent: Q. Metellus Nepos, L. Marcius Philippus, L. Domitius Ahenobarbus, Cn. Domitius Calvinus —and three Claudii Marcelli (no consul in their line since M. Marcellus, *cos. III* 152).

Such is the company and nexus which, with few exceptions, cast in their lot with Pompeius Magnus to provoke a civil war, not without credit and impulsion from Marcus Cato, to the ruin of the Republic—and few survived.[38]

The happy consuls of the decade 16 to 7 stand as follows:

16 L. Domitius Cn. f. Ahenobarbus:	P. Cornelius P. f. Scipio
	L. Tarius Rufus
15 M. Livius L. f. Drusus Libo:	L. Calpurnius L. f. Piso
14 M. Licinius M. f. Crassus Frugi:	Cn. Cornelius Cn. f. Lentulus
13 Ti. Claudius Ti. f. Nero:	P. Quinctilius Sex. f. Varus

---

[35] above, p. 25.

[36] Patrician, that is by birth (not reckoning Mam. Lepidus Livianus), viz. Clodianus (*cos.* 72) and Sura (71). The former has been assumed plebeian, the son of a Claudius Marcellus. Thus Münzer, *RE* IV. 1380. However, probably patrician, cf. *JRS* LIII (1963), 55 = *RP* (1979), 558; D. R. Shackleton Bailey, o.c. 88 f. The consuls from 80 to 49 are analysed by Chr. Meier, *Res Publica Amissa* (1980), 31; 308 f.

[37] For the decline of the patrician families see E. T. Salmon, *Rev. ét lat.* XLVII *bis* (1969), 321 ff. He employs two periods, viz. decline from 133 to 91, resurgence from 90 to 48.

One sign of Sulla's favour is a remission of two years in the *cursus*, divined from the ages or careers of Caesar, L. Paullus (*cos.* 50), and others, by E. Badian, *JRS* XLIX (1959), 81 ff. = *Studies in Greek and Roman History* (1964), 140 ff.

[38] Pollio, choosing for his inception the consulate of Metellus Celer and L. Afranius, enjoyed a marvellous opportunity for indicting the *nobilitas*; and he may have been able to resist the idealization of Cato, despite 'cuncta terrarum subacta/praeter atrocem animum Catonis' (Horace, *Odes* II.1.23 f.).

12	M. Valerius M. f. Messalla Appianus:	P. Sulpicius P. f. Quirinius
	C. Valgius C. f. Rufus	
	C. Caninius C. f. Rebilus:	L. Volusius Q. f. Saturninus
11	Q. Aelius Q. f. Tubero:	Paullus Fabius Q. f. Maximus
10	Africanus Fabius Maximus:	Iullus Antonius
9	Nero Claudius Drusus:	T. Quinctius T. f. Crispinus Sulpicianus
8	C. Marcius Censorinus:	C. Asinius Gallus
7	Ti. Claudius Nero II:	Cn. Calpurnius Cn. f. Piso

From the computation it is expedient to leave out two consulships held by stepsons of the Princeps, abnormal if only because each acceded when twenty-eight; and further, the iteration in 7. The Nerones belonged, it is true, to the inferior line of the Claudii, but would have secured admittance through the arts of Livia Drusilla (a worthy successor to Servilia), even if she had not annexed a Triumvir when she was nineteen. And on the decease of Ap. Pulcher (*cos.* 38) her elder son became head of the *gens Claudia*.

Likewise is to be segregated the *novus homo* Sulpicius Quirinius, consul in 12; and by a further convenience, the four consuls suffect from two years (the phenomenon is unique between 19 and 5).

Of Tarius Rufus (*suff.* 16) something will have to be said on miscellaneous counts.[39] Admiral in the naval operations that preceded Actium, 'militaris industria' promoted him, 'infima natalium humilitate'.[40] Perhaps from Picenum, where he went in for grandiose land speculation; perhaps even from a town in Liburnia across the Adriatic.[41] The *nomen* is Celtic or Illyrian.[42]

More prominence attends upon Sulpicius Quirinius. He impinges on a number of problems issuing from his governorships in Galatia and Syria.[43] Thirty years later Tiberius Caesar, when requesting the Senate to decree a state funeral, recounted his services and his personal allegiance.[44] The preface is noteworthy. Quirinius had nothing to do with the ancient and patrician Sulpicii: he came from the *municipium* of Lanuvium.

In the year 12 the colleague of Quirinius died almost at once, Messalla Appianus.[45] Valgius Rufus took his place. Valgius is eccentric to this

---

[39] below, p. 223. [40] Pliny, *NH* XVIII.37. As an admiral, Dio L. 14.1.

[41] G. Alföldy, *Epigraphische Studien* V (1968), 100 ff.; J. J. Wilkes, *Dalmatia* (1969), 330 f.

[42] *Danubian Papers* (1971), 119. Observe Tariates in the Sabine country and the river Tarus, an affluent of the Po (Pliny *NH* III. 107; 118). And, for that matter, Tariodunum (Zarten) in southern Germany. Silius Italicus, a writer from Transpadana, has a Tarius among the Italian allies of Rome (*Punica* IV.253).

[43] Ch. XXIV ('Piso the Pontifex'). [44] *Ann.* III.48.

[45] Before March 6, as shown by *RG* 10. For the order of the *suffecti*, A. Degrassi, *I fasti consulari* (1952), 4. Also Groag, *RE* IVA. 829.

company, well forward in years since named among poets as long ago as 35, and soon after (for his performance in epic) in the panegyric that celebrated the consulship of Messalla Corvinus.[46] The influence of Corvinus cannot fail to be surmised, or that of Claudius Nero (consul the year before). To the extraction and local origin of Valgius, no clue.[47] The name is not prepossessing.

Valgius ceded the *fasces* to Caninius Rebilus, ennobled through his father, the notorious one-day consul appointed at the end of 45 to succeed Fabius Maximus. The Caninii were an old praetorian family. Perhaps from Tusculum, so it can be argued.[48]

Then Caninius Rebilus succumbed. The closing *suffectus* of the year is the first consul of the Volusii, styled the 'primus adcumulator' of their great wealth.[49] Their *patria* may be Lucus Feroniae, near the western bank of the Tiber, not far from Rome.[50]

A stray notice brings up a Q. Volusius. That is, the parent, married to a sister of Ti. Claudius Nero (*pr.* 42).[51] Despite that attachment, L. Volusius was about fifty when he reached his consulship, as emerges from details concerning his son (*suff.* AD 3), the long-lived *praefectus urbi*.[52]

The consul had for wife Nonia Polla, daughter of another new consul, L. Nonius Asprenas (*suff.* 36).[53] The match furnished another link, both to Piso the Pontifex and to Quinctilius Varus, consul as colleague to Claudius Nero the year before.

The central theme is the sixteen aristocrats born between 50 and 40. Five of them justify separate chapters, viz. Piso the Pontifex, Lentulus the Augur, Quinctilius Varus, Fabius Maximus, Cn. Piso. Most of the others claim iterated mention, on a wide variety of counts. It will be of use to analyse the company and set forth the results under ten rubrics.[54]

(1) Ancestry. No fewer than seven derive from the patriciate, two of them

---

[46] Horace, *Sat.* I.10.82; *Pan. Mess.* 180.

[47] Q. Valgius, praetor before 129, is cited by T. P. Wiseman, *New Men in the Roman Senate* (1971), 269. Observe also 'A. Valgius, senatoris filius', a Caesarian (*Bell. Hisp.* 13.2.).

[48] *History in Ovid* (1978), 101 (on the Caninii Galli). A Caninius Rebilus held the office of aedile there, colleague of C. Caelius Rufus (*CIL* XIV.2622).

[49] *Ann.* III.30.1 (dying in AD 20).

[50] Where they owned a handsome estate, with important inscriptions emerging. On which W. Eck, *Hermes* C (1972), 461 ff., whence *AE* 1972, 174 ff. However, for Cingulum in Picenum, see T. P. Wiseman, o.c. 277 (citing *CIL* IX. 5680; VI. 7376 f.).

For other properties of the Volusii see J. H. D'Arms, *Commerce and Social Standing in Ancient Rome* (1981), 69 f.

[51] *Ad Att.* V.21.6, cf. *Rom. Rev.* 424.

[52] Pliny, *NH* VII. 62; Tacitus, *Ann.* XIII.30.2.

[53] *OGIS* 468 (Pergamum).

[54] Evidence for facts in the catalogues that follow will be discovered in later chapters entitled by consuls or by families, and by recourse to the Index. *PIR* and *RE* also avail. Annotation is therefore sparse.

doubly so. Messalla Appianus was by birth a Claudius Pulcher, son (or perhaps nephew) of Appius (*cos.* 38), taken in adoption by M. Messalla (*suff.* 32), who lacks discoverable issue. Next, T. Quinctius Sulpicianus, the consul of 9. The last Quinctius, a Flamininus, had graced the *fasces* in 123. Sulpicii, also decayed, were now fairly numerous.

Of the Plebeians, six represent ancient and recently powerful houses. For the rest, no Aelius had been consul since 167, and no Tubero ever. A question therefore arises about the consul of 11. However, Q. Aelius Tubero, the grandson of Aemilius Paullus, was styled a *nobilis* in public discourse.[55] The rank of Iullus Antonius went back to the great-grand-father, the renowned orator (*cos.* 99), while Asinius Gallus is the son of a Triumviral consul.

(2) Parentage. For the patricians, the parent of the two Fabii is clear and certified (the consul suffect of 45), and Ap. Pulcher may be presumed father to Messalla Appianus, P. Cornelius (?Scipio, *suff.* 35) to the consul of 16. The ascendance of the Augur Lentulus presents intricate problems and calls for separate treatment.

The Quinctius who took in adoption a Sulpicius is a total nonentity. He acquired in that fashion another son, T. Quinctius Crispinus Valerianus (*suff.* AD 2), so it may be supposed.[56] On another explanation the *cognomina* declare maternal ascendance, and two wives for the father.[57] Finally, Quinctilius Varus, of dim ancestry. His father (quaestor in 49) committed suicide at Philippi.

Of these seven patricians, only one avows a mother: P. Scipio, consul in 16, is a son of 'Scribonia Caesaris'. By contrast, the fathers of nine plebeian consuls had all been on some sort of prominence recently (all but two of them consuls), and wives can be discovered for most of them. As follows:

Cn. Domitius Ahenobarbus (*cos.* 32). An Aemilia Lepida and a Manlia.[58]

M. Livius Drusus Claudianus. An Aufidia, or rather an Alfidia.[59]

L. Calpurnius Piso Caesoninus (58).[60]

M. Licinius Crassus (30). Metella, daughter of Q. Creticus (*cos.* 69).

Q. Aelius Tubero, the historian. Sulpicia, daughter of Servius Sulpicius (*cos.* 51).

---

[55] *Pro Murena* 75. And so was the consul's grandfather (*Pro Ligario* 22). See further under 'Kinsmen of Seianus' (Ch. XXII).

[56] No statement about the relationship between Sulpicianus and Valerianus is proffered in the articles by R. Hanslik, *RE* XXIV.1106 ff. On the stemma the latter figures as a son of the former (995 f.)—whereas elsewhere he is taken to be a Valerius adopting a Quinctius (993).

[57] cf. Sex. Nonius Quinctilianus (*cos.* AD 8), the son of a Quinctilia.

[58] Ch. XII.

[59] For Alfidia, T. P. Wiseman, *Historia* XIV (1965), 333 f.

[60] For Rutilia, not the mother of Piso the Pontifex, see below, p. 330.

M. Antonius (44). Fulvia.
L. Marcius Censorinus (39).
C. Asinius Pollio (40). Quinctia, daughter of a senator.[61]
Cn. Calpurnius Piso (*suff.* 23). Popillia M.f.

A number of these men (it is no surprise) had fought for Pompeius, for the Republic, for Antonius. Over long periods the wives knew either absences or hazard. Ahenobarbus can seldom have seen Italy between 49 and his consulship. The identity of his first wife is an engaging problem.[62] When compiling the biography of the last Ahenobarbus, with much detail about the history of his line, Suetonius betrayed error and inadvertence, more than once. He missed the fact that the father of Ahenobarbus (*cos.* 54) married Cato's sister.

(3) Marriages. In this epoch a senator normally takes a wife about the time when he is a *monetalis*, two or three years before entering the high assembly as quaestor. Evidence from a century later confirms.[63] One incentive was the legislation that prescribed an advantage to the procreation of children. Some youths in the highest aristocracy may have entered matrimony a little earlier—and princes in the dynasty descend from nineteen to seventeen and even to fifteen.

The consorts of the sixteen consuls stand as follows:

P. Scipio.
Ahenobarbus. Antonia.
M. Drusus Libo.
L. Piso.
M. Licinius Crassus Frugi.
Cn. Lentulus.
Quinctilius Varus. A daughter of M. Agrippa; Claudia Pulchra.
Messalla Appianus. The younger Marcella.
Q. Aelius Tubero.
Paullus Fabius Maximus. Marcia, a cousin of the Princeps.
Africanus Fabius Maximus.
Iullus Antonius. The elder Marcella, transferred from M. Agrippa in 21.
Quinctius Sulpicianus.
Marcius Censorinus.
Asinius Gallus. 'Vipsania Ti. Neronis', transferred to him in 11.
Cn. Piso. A daughter (or granddaughter) of Munatius Plancus.

All of these ladies but one come on view and are a part of history

---

[61] On whom, *Historia* IV (1955), 67 f. = *RP* (1979), 287 f.
[62] Ch. XII.
[63] e.g. Pliny on Pedanius Fuscus and Ummidius Quadratus, consul and consul suffect in 118 (*Epp.* VI.26.1; VII.24.3).

because they belong to the dynastic nexus created by Caesar Augustus. Consorts fail for nine noblemen.[64] And, even if one wife stood on attestation for each of them, others who disappeared should not be left out of account. It is not likely that Asinius Gallus, of a robust stock, eschewed matrimony until he was thirty. For similar reasons a dearth of surviving offspring is no surprise.

(4) Children.

P. Scipio. Perhaps two sons, viz. the young man involved with Julia, and P. Cornelius Scipio, quaestor in Achaia *c.* AD 2.[65] A daughter may be 'Cornelia Scipionum gentis', wife of L. Volusius (*suff.* 3).[66]

Ahenobarbus. A son (*cos.* 32) and two daughters.[67]

M. Drusus Libo. A daughter is deduced, married to the renascent patrician M. Furius Camillus (*cos.* 8).

L. Piso. A daughter married L. Nonius Asprenas (*suff.* 6). His sons, that is an entertaining question, with ramifications in the history of Latin literature.

M. Licinius Crassus Frugi. A son (*cos.* 27), married to a Scribonia.

Cn. Lentulus. No surviving sons, as can be stated in confidence.

Quinctilius Varus. One son, late born by Claudia Pulchra.

Messalla Appianus. One son, who died before consular years (the first husband of Domitia Lepida); a daughter, Claudia Pulchra.

Q. Aelius Tubero. None, unless he be regarded as the father of L. Seius Tubero (*suff.* 18): hence adopted by the knight Seius Strabo.

Paullus Fabius Maximus. Persicus (*cos.* 34) and Fabia Numantina.

Africanus Fabius Maximus. None.

Iullus Antonius. Lucius, relegated in 2 BC; and another son, and possibly a daughter.

Quinctius Sulpicianus. None.

Marcius Censorinus. None.

Asinius Gallus. At least five sons, three of them consuls. No daughter on record.

Cn. Piso. Two sons, Lucius (*cos.* 27) and Marcus.

(5) Priesthoods. Of the senators on Caesar's side in the War of Actium, about one hundred and seventy held priesthoods, so he was careful to inform posterity.[68] As concerns the sixteen *nobiles*, a pair of assumptions will not deceive. Given augmented membership and the incidence of deaths, each of them had one of the 'quattuor amplissima sacerdotia',

---

[64] cf. the consuls of 32–29: wives only for Messalla Corvinus and for Sex. Appuleius.
[65] Recently revealed by *AE* 1967, 458 (Messene).
[66] Pliny, *NH* VII.62.
[67] For two earlier children, to be discovered on the *Ara Pacis*, see Ch. XII.
[68] *RG* 25.

although evidence is lacking for five of that company; and most of them acceded in early years.[69] The son of Messalla Corvinus came in with the *toga virilis*.

As concerns the Arval Brethren, Drusus Libo may have been a member in 21. After that year a long gap intervenes until May of AD 14, when the protocol exhibits Ahenobarbus, Piso, Cn. Lentulus, Fabius Maximus.[70] In December they were joined by Cn. Piso, and in the following summer by the boy Persicus, the son of Fabius Maximus.[71] As previously, hereditary claims could not be denied recognition.

(6) Early posts. They are seldom on direct record. The Princeps set great store by military service for young senators. The military tribunate was held at twenty, or less. Of those who took part with Claudius Nero in the Spanish campaigns of 26 and 25, one can be discovered: Cn. Piso, in the sequel his close and fatal friend.[72] The tribunate, like the minor magistracies at Rome, served as a social apprenticeship.

The pair of quaestors attached to Caesar were conspicuous by their function.[73] During his sojourn in the eastern provinces Varus and Fabius were with him.[74] By paradox the next on attestation (sparse indeed) are sons of Roman knights.[75] For others the brief sojourn in Achaia or Asia would hold out attractions.

Before or after the praetorship a senator might have charge of a legion. However, the post had not yet become regular and predictable. On inscriptions the earliest named legate of a named legion happens to occur in AD 22.[76] In fact, sporadic evidence suggests that a Roman knight, with the title 'pro legato', often had command of a legion. One such is attested who had been *tribunus militum* and *praefectus equitum* for twelve years.[77] Again, when Quinctilius Varus perished with three legions in Germany, the comportment of four subordinate commanders is described. Three of them were *praefecti castrorum*, whereas the fourth, a legate, escaped with the cavalry.[78]

Finally, the praetorian proconsulates.[79] A *nobilis* has generally reached

[69] Priesthoods are not attested for P. Scipio, Ahenobarbus, Drusus Libo, Messalla Appianus, Quinctius Sulpicianus. Those of Varus (*ILS* 88) and of Iullus Antonius (Velleius II. 100.4) cannot be specified. For the lists, M. W. H. Lewis, *The Official Priests of Rome under the Julio-Claudians* (1955).
[70] *ILS* 5026.   [71] *AE* 1947, 52.
[72] Deduced from 'quinque et quadraginta annorum obsequium' (*Ann.* III.16.4).
[73] M. Cébeillac, *Les Quaestores Principis et Candidati aux Ier et IIème siècles de l'Empire* (1973).
[74] *ILS* 8812; *IG.* II².4130.
[75] viz. Q. Vitellius (Suetonius, *Vit.* 1.2); Rubellius Blandus (*IRT* 330); Ummidius Quadratus (*ILS* 972).
[76] *ILS* 940; *Ann.* III. 74.2. (after the praetorship). For a quaestorian example, *ILS* 945.
[77] viz. T. Junius Montanus (*AE* 1938, 373: Emona).
[78] Velleius II. 119.4; 120.4. On which see remarks in *Germania* XVI (1932), 109 ff. The other two legions were under a consular legate, viz. Nonius Asprenas (120.3), no doubt at Moguntiacum.
[79] At this time eight, namely Baetica, Narbonensis, Sicily, Sardinia, Achaia, Bithynia-Pontus, Cyprus, Crete-Cyrene.

the *fasces* before the five years' interval has passed. For this reason it is not easy to suppose that Sex. Pompeius was a praetorian proconsul of Macedonia in AD 8, long anterior to his consulship in 14.[80]

(7) Consular commands. As has been shown, aristocratic ex-consuls are not to be expected among Caesar's legates during the first epoch of the new dispensation. An exception has turned up. The inscription of Potitus Valerius Messalla (*suff.* 29) discloses him, after the proconsulate of Asia, as legate in a province the name of which is missing. It may be Syria.[81] Perhaps therefore from 21 to 17, between the tenures of Marcus Agrippa.

The 'provincia' of Caesar Augustus developed into the system of the imperial provinces. When fifteen years had elapsed and the wars of conquest began in central Europe, five consular commands emerge: Tarraconensis, Gaul (with the legions now advanced to stations on the Rhine), Illyricum, taken from proconsuls, Syria, Galatia–Pamphylia (which still had an army).[82] Further, the Macedonian army was soon transferred in permanence to a legate.

Youthful aristocrats now came into use and prominence. Piso, called from Galatia to Thrace in 12, suppressed a great rebellion in three campaigns. The next legate in charge of the army 'in Thracia Macedoniaque' was Cn. Lentulus the Augur.[83] Crassus Frugi held Tarraconensis (?13–9), and after a time Syria fell to a *nobilis*, Varus, in 6. In that year a political crisis opened prospects for Ahenobarbus and for Fabius; and Censorinus may be one of the consular governors of Galatia (in AD 2); but Cn. Piso had to wait until 5 or 6 for Tarraconensis.

For the others, Messalla Appianus was dead, and no long survival may have been vouchsafed to Drusus Libo and Q. Tubero. Five remain. A military command was refused, it may be conjectured, to Iullus Antonius, husband to a princess, and to the ambitious Asinius Gallus (not likely to be approved by Claudius Nero). The others may have preferred the city to the camps and the chance of military renown: P. Scipio, Africanus Fabius Maximus, Quinctius Sulpicianus.

(8) Proconsulates. Piso, Crassus, and Lentulus enjoyed rapid advancement. For sundry reasons (some to be divined), the ruler might hesitate to entrust an army to others soon after their consulships. He needed them for Asia and Africa.

A dearth of consuls has been noted. There is also a dearth of information about the proconsuls over a number of years. For Asia after Q. Lepidus

---

[80] Often assumed (from Ovid, *Ex P.* IV.5.34), or even affirmed. Thus R. Hanslik, *RE* XXI. 2265. Against, *History in Ovid* (1978), 157.

[81] *ILS* 8964, cf. above, p. 229.

[82] For Galatia-Pamphylia, Ch. XXIV.

[83] For the problem of his date, Ch. XXI.

(*cos.* 21), there is only a mysterious Junius Silanus until 12, when the proconsul was assigned a tenure of two years: probably M. Vinicius (*suff.* 19).[84] Africa after the triumph of Cornelius Balbus in 19 is a blank until Ahenobarbus (in 13/12), apart from Sentius Saturninus (*cos.* 19).

Twelve from the group held proconsulates, in order of consular rank as follows:

Asia: Scipio, Piso, Lentulus, Fabius, Antonius, Gallus, Censorinus.
Africa: Ahenobarbus, Crassus, Varus, Africanus, Cn. Piso.

The order in tenure did not always conform to seniority.[85] In the event neither the quinquennial interval nor a regularity of sequence could be maintained. As is manifest in later periods, a variety of reasons operated to modify the working of the lot; and on discreet admonition from friends of Caesar a man might be persuaded to desist before or after the sortition.[86]

Contrasted phenomena occur. Fabius Maximus, an especial favourite of the Princeps, went out to Asia from his consulship. For Lentulus a dozen years elapsed. When his turn arrived he was on employ in an imperial command. In this season the shortage of available consuls had predictable effects. The causes were three consulships for the stepsons of the Princeps, Appianus dying, the survival of Drusus Libo and Q. Tubero being dubious. Quinctius Sulpicianus remains a potential proconsul.

In 6 Asinius Gallus went to Asia. An abridged interval may have held for other proconsuls in the next half-dozen years, such as Cn. Piso in Africa.

So far the sixteen *nobiles*. Volusius Saturninus (*suff.* 12) acceded to Africa, but there is no call to put in a plea for Valgius Rufus, the elderly man of letters. Quirinius is another matter. During seven years he was careful to keep up his attachment to Claudius Nero. For a part of the time he governed Galatia-Pamphylia. Asia is a painless supplement.[87]

(9) Survival. Messalla Appianus died during his consulship, while Drusus Libo leaves no trace after his, neither does Aelius Tubero. Again, not a word about Scipio, the younger Fabius Maximus, or Crassus Frugi, subsequent to their proconsulates. Deficiency in the written sources dissuades the notion that by 2 BC all five were no longer among the living. Some noblemen prefer to evade action or notoriety. Even in a well-documented sequence of senatorial annals an eminent consular may happen to leave no trace for long years.

In 2 BC Iullus Antonius and Quinctius Sulpicianus were involved in the

---

[84] Dio LIV. 30.3. For Vinicius, below, p. 405; for Silanus, p. 191.

[85] For the dating of these proconsulates see the lists below, p. 405 (Asia); p. 320 (Africa).

[86] The classic specimen is supplied by Tacitus, *Agr.* 42.1 f. Not so gentle the treatment of C. Sulpicius Galba (*cos.* 22): 'tristibus Caesaris litteris provinciam sortiri prohibitus' (*Ann.* VI.40.2).

[87] But not to be postulated.

catastrophe of the princess Julia. Then three years later Marcius Censorinus died in the eastern provinces; and Varus, called to the service of empire in Germany when aged about fifty-five, perished with an army, the victim of geography and native perfidy, the scapegoat to posterity of an ambitious design misconceived from the outset. Finally, the Roman summer of the year 14 was too much for Fabius Maximus.

Five were still among the living. Cn. Piso, arraigned on a valid charge of high treason, chose to take his own life. In 25 the historian seized with alacrity the opportunity to conjoin the obituary notices on Lentulus the Augur and Domitius Ahenobarbus, while Piso the Pontifex, after a long tenure as *praefectus urbi*, earned his due commemoration in 32. In the next year Rome mourned among various other deaths the passing of Asinius Gallus, voluntary or under constraint, in penal confinement. He was aged about seventy-three, close coeval to the ancient enemy, the recluse on the island Capreae.

(10) Direct descendants. Of the sixteen, as has been shown, only five were followed by consular sons. The extinction of noble families takes a large portion in the annals of Julii and Claudii. Among the earliest to acquire a close link was Ahenobarbus through his marriage to Antonia; and the aristocratic monarchy terminated with his grandson. The Fabii had already lapsed after Persicus (*cos.* 34). The grandson of Cn. Piso was the last of that line (consul in 57). The son of Crassus Frugi, marrying Scribonia, was progenitor of a large family and long descendance, whose Pompeian ancestry rendered them suspect to emperors. Yet they lasted into the second and third dynasties of Imperial Rome, equalled by the posterity of Asinius Gallus.

In the foregoing pages an age group has been segregated and inspected, not omitting women and children. The theme passes to the achievement of the decade (on brief and selective treatment), to urban occupations and habits of the aristocracy.[88]

---

[88] Certain aspects are more fully treated in Ch. XXV ('The Education of an Aristocrat').

V

Monarchy and Concord

In the course of this decade, war and conquest advertised the alliance between the ruler and the aristocracy. The Republic had evaded a necessary task of empire. While the great proconsuls went beyond Euphrates or crossed the channel that separates Britain from Gaul, they neglected Illyricum, the land mass behind which runs the route from Italy to the Balkans and to Byzantium, by Siscia, Sirmium, Serdica.

When Caesar the proconsul took up his command, three of his four legions stood at Aquileia, at the head of the Adriatic. The Helvetii and Ariovistus diverted his military ambitions, with 'Gallia omnis' more splendid and profitable than operations against Pannonians and Dalmatians. The Dictator proposed to embark on campaigns against Dacians and Parthians. Parthia engrossed notoriety at the time and in the sequel, for a variety of reasons, not one of them adequate for invasion, let alone conquest or annexations. The Parthians were not dangerous unless provoked, and seldom aggressive.

The Dacian monarch Burebistas, from his secure base in Transylvania, was extending his dominion in all directions, notably over the middle course of the Danube towards Noricum, the vassal state that protected north-eastern Italy. For the first stage (a march northwards) Caesar concentrated in Macedonia a force of six legions, the best in the whole army.

The imperial people thought in terms of roads and communications. The Aemilia before long was destined to bequeath its name to a region of Italy. Across the Adriatic the route of the Egnatia penetrated Macedonia and conducted the legions against the Seleucid; Cilicia for a season was the highway from Asia to the Gates of Syria; and Narbonensis is explained by the road into Spain which the ancestor of Domitius Ahenobarbus constructed.

The proconsul of Gaul knew about roads. Like others, including Marcus Agrippa, he would be aware of geopolitics, a term which had not yet been invented and abused. Facts of geography dictated. To hold together an empire strung out all the way from Gades to Antioch required an ample extension northwards. When divided between Caesar's heir and Marcus Antonius that empire threatened to split into two kingdoms, in consonance with geography, language, civilization. The boundary existed: the sea between Italy and Macedonia, the narrow strip of land at Scodra beneath the impassable mountains.[1]

Responsive to his mandate, Imperator Caesar had turned first to Spain. The long task of subjugation had to be completed by other generals, and in the end by Agrippa. In 16 Caesar went again to the western lands. Some expected war and a Sugambrian triumph.[2] Instead, under Caesar's supervision the two Claudii effected in the next summer the conquest of the eastern Alpine zone, the greater glory accruing to the younger brother.[3] Their combined action took the frontier as far as the upper reaches of the Danube, and Noricum was annexed.

In 13 Agrippa began the Bellum Pannonicum.[4] His decease in March of the following year meant no detriment to warfare—rather perhaps to counsel and restraint.

Claudius Nero took over the army of Illyricum. His first campaign overcame the Breuci, a large and bellicose tribe dwelling athwart the river Savus.[5] The road to Sirmium lay open. The strategic corollary was an advance from the south-east by the army of Macedonia.[6]

In the next year Claudius Nero dealt with the tribes in Bosnia, encircled now, and never accessible save from the north. He conducted further operations in 10 and 9. A pronouncement in the *Res Gestae* of the ruler, inserted (it is obvious) at a late stage in the composition of that document, and out of proper sequence, celebrates the achievement: Tiberius Nero conquered the nations of the Pannonians which no army of the Roman People had ever approached, and the bounds of Illyricum were advanced to the river Danube.[7]

Meanwhile, Germany. In 12 the younger Claudius dedicated at Lugdunum the altar of Rome and Augustus, convoking thither the notables of Tres Galliae (much use was to be made of their levies). Late in the year Drusus conducted operations against certain tribes, ending with a naval expedition. Then in 11 he was able to penetrate eastwards as far as

---

[1] *Rom. Rev.* (1939), 272; 290.

[2] Thus Propertius (IV.6.77) and Horace, in a Pindaric effusion to the address of Iullus Antonius (IV.2.34f.). Both Velleius (II.97.1) and Dio (LIV.20.4) attribute Augustus' departure to the defeat incurred by M. Lollius at the hands of the Sugambri; and most modern accounts assume a decisive change therefrom in imperial policy. Meanwhile, however, the Sugambri had come to terms with Lollius and delivered hostages (20.6).

Dio reported the affair in a resumptive chapter under the year 16. Better, the previous year, as in Obsequens 71—where there also occurs a portent which Dio assigns to 16 (19.7). See further *JRS* XXIII (1933), 17 ff.

[3] below, p. 300.

[4] Dio LIV. 28.1 f., cf. Velleius II 92.2 (with M. Vinicius, the last proconsul of Illyricum—or rather the first imperial legate).

[5] Suetonius, *Tib.* 9.2. For the conquest of Illyricum, *CAH* X (1934), 335 ff.; J. J. Wilkes, *Dalmatia* (1969), 63 ff.

[6] Ch. XXVII.

[7] *RG* 30.

the Weser, lucky because of dissidence between two powerful peoples, the Sugambri and the Chatti.[8]

There the enterprise might have found an expedient termination, profiting for the future from native rivalries to establish a pacified zone beyond the Rhine, to protect that frontier and the security of Gaul. In fact, the Senate voted in the winter of 11 that Janus be closed.[9] A comparison avails for the Danube. At a date not much later, an army crossed the river and 'compelled the nations of the Dacians to submit to the commands of the Roman People'.[10]

That modest outcome did not satisfy the designs of Caesar Augustus or the ambitions of the ardent prince; and it was never the habit of the proud Republic to renounce in the face of danger or initial discomfiture. In 9 Claudius Drusus drove forward as far as the Elbe. He died on the march back.[11]

To subjugate western Germany was a vast undertaking: forests and hills and marshes. And the distances to be traversed. Even a Greek writer could know. Strabo estimates three thousand stades from Rhine to Elbe—in a straight line, which (as he states) the nature of the country precluded.[12] A Roman officer, who had been on the Elbe, reckoned four hundred miles.[13]

The Romans are on frequent indictment for neglect of geography and for ignorance persisting. Some of the notions behind that verdict are shown invalid, if thought is given to the requirements of the military. Handbooks that happen to be extant retail information long obsolete and suitably garnished with archaic language. Historians equipped their narrations with digressions. The intent was to entertain the reader rather than to instruct.[14] The Porticus Vipsania now being built displayed a map of the world. Neither that map nor the *Commentarii* left by Agrippa gave a measure of his personal aptitudes or furnished guidance for those who planned campaigns.[15]

Roman generals suffered defeats in difficult country. Ignorance was not the cause. Rather pride and confidence, or the guile of the natives. About

[8] Dio LIV. 33.1 f.

[9] Dio LIV. 36.2. Not carried out because of a Dacian raid into Pannonia across the frozen Danube.

[10] *RG* 30. Both the date and the general evade precision.

[11] The purpose of these invasions (not explicit in ancient sources) is much in debate. For a discrete and minimal assessment, with emphasis on different phases, observe D. Timpe, *Saeculum* XVIII (1967), 286; *Monumentum Chiloniense* (*Festschrift E. Burck*, 1975), 141 ff. A full and clear account of controversy since Mommsen is furnished by K. Christ, *Chiron* VII (1977), 149 ff. For a brief statement, D. Kienast, *Augustus* (1982), 297 ff.

[12] Strabo VII, p. 292.   [13] Velleius II. 106.3.

[14] Livy deprecated 'deverticula amoena' (IX.17.1).

[15] Not only ignorance: boundless aspirations to world conquest have been adduced by P. A. Brunt, *JRS* LIII (1963), 170 ff.; C. M. Wells, *The German Policy of Augustus* (1972), 3 ff. For hesitations about planning and policy, F. Millar, *Britannia* XIII (1982), 1 ff. He also emphasizes the difficulty of obtaining useful information.

inner Germany a certain amount of information was available (practicable routes existed), though it would have to be supplemented.[16]

At the end of Drusus' first campaign he all but lost his navy: he was rescued by new allies, the Frisians. When he marched back from the second, the army barely avoided a catastrophe.[17]

Augustus was not deterred by these manifest hazards. His insistence owed not a little to the inordinate favour he bestowed on the younger stepson. To Drusus he allocated the larger part and the conspicuous role that evoked history and appealed to publicity. That is, vengeance at last on Cimbri and Teutones. To Tiberius the Princeps resigned the more arduous task, with no prospect of comparable fame. If Tiberius had deigned to accept 'Pannonicus', that appellation paled before 'Germanicus'.[18]

Posterity conformed to the dearest aspirations of the Princeps. When Cassius Dio narrated the campaigns of these four years, he accorded precedence and prominence to Drusus. The portion of Tiberius is reduced to the suppression of revolts. Dio was ignorant and impercipient.[19] Many expositions in the modern time concur. On a candid conclusion, primacy goes to Illyricum in the design of conquest.[20]

In the course of the year 8 Claudius Nero invaded Germany, but did not choose to penetrate far into the interior. He dealt with the Sugambri once and for all. The remnants of massacre were transplanted across the river, leaving a name to be exploited by poets until the last days.

At the outset of his second consulship Claudius Nero celebrated a triumph. The ruler was now 'imp. XIV'. No further salutation was registered until about eight years elapsed; and many legionaries were now released from service, with bounties in money instead of land.[21]

The previous year witnessed a ceremony suitable to engage interest, at least among antiquarians. Romulus when founding his city defined its limits by the *pomerium*. During the long sequence of centuries only Sulla and Augustus enlarged the sacred ambit, although other conquerors had subjugated great nations. Such is the declaration of a scrupulous historian, drawing on the best of sources.[22] On another doctrine, the 'priscus mos'

[16] In AD 6 the Romans were able to plan and conduct an invasion of Bohemia with two armies marching from widely distant bases (from Moguntiacum and from Carnuntum).

[17] Dio LIV. 32.2 f.; 33.3.

[18] It was offered on the occasion of his Pannonian triumph in AD 12 (Suetonius, *Tib.* 17.2).

[19] Perhaps misled by 'rebellio' and 'rebellare' in Latin sources.

[20] Thus *CAH* X (1934), 352 f., cf. 380 f. In this conception Germany is subsidiary. However, conquest as far as the Elbe admits an explanation: not so much a frontier as a shortening of communications to the Middle Danube. Bohemia thus comes in. Without Bohemia in ultimate prospect, annexation in north-western Germany looks peculiar.

[21] *RG* 16 (in every year but one from 7 to 2). That is, soldiers recruited in the years of peace—and before dismissal used in the wars of conquest. Cf. *JRS* XXIII (1933), 20 f.

[22] Tacitus, *Ann.* XII.23.2. He exploited, so it may be conjectured, the erudition of Claudius Caesar (sometimes idiosyncratic).

forbade any extension of the *pomerium* unless 'Italico agro adquisito'.[23] In fact, the boundary of Transpadane Italy was advanced into Istria during this period.[24]

Though zealous for the national antiquities, and a careful composer, the author of the *Res Gestae* omitted to publish a claim. Various explanations are canvassed. Perhaps even inadvertence, as can happen to a Caesar. Otherwise, he declined to advertise a distinction that fell short of the unique.

Finally, Janus. Augustus closed the Gates of War a third time. The year evades documentation.[25] Everything speaks of 8 or 7.[26] An epoch ended, with Germany seeming submissive, Illyricum extended to the Danube, the Thracians reduced and thinned by L. Piso in three fierce campaigns. A Roman peace obtained all the way from the German Ocean to the Euxine.

After the first pair of campaigns both stepsons acquired proconsular *imperium*.[27] They went on to take imperatorial salutations, and were duly voted ovations.[28] Tiberius celebrated his in January of 9, while Drusus had the posthumous honour of 'Germanicus'. Legates of Caesar in the Balkan command, Piso and Lentulus earned the *ornamenta triumphalia*.[29]

Proconsuls had to be content with that distinction. No more triumphs. For action in the field only Africa now offered, where disturbances recurred among the nomads on the western and southern edge of the province. A proconsul might still be acclaimed 'imperator' by the troops; and, in a solitary instance he was able to bequeath a triumphal appellation to his son. It was 'Gaetulicus'.[30] No Caesar would permit 'Africanus' for campaigns of this order.

Vassal princes, tetrarchs, and dynasts belonged to the portion of Caesar; and in the peaceful and opulent provinces he extended his *clientela* to the detriment of the aristocracy. Proconsuls in the past had given their names

[23] Seneca, *De brevitate vitae* 13.8. On which, M. T. Griffin, *JRS* LII (1962), 109 ff.; *Seneca* (1976), 401 ff.

[24] Strabo VII, p. 314; Pliny, *NH* III. 127. Dio in fact registers the extension of the *pomerium* under 8 BC (LV.6.6.). For the various rulers in controversy see a full discussion in *Bonner HAC* 1975/6 (1978), 217 ff. = *Historia Augusta Papers* (1983), 131 ff. Among them is Caesar the Dictator, expressly attested by Messalla the Augur (Gellius XIII.14.2).

[25] Not in Dio—who, it is worth recalling, missed the census and the *lustrum* held in 8 by the ruler, 'consulari cum imperio' (*RG* 8). Dio was aware of the abortive proposal in 11/10. This time he may have reserved the closure (after the summer of 6 there is a long gap in his text), possibly until the next opening (?1 BC).

[26] *AJP* C (1979), 201 ff. = *RP* III (1984), 1189 ff.

[27] Dio LIV. 33.5 (Drusus); 34.3 (Tiberius).

[28] For salutations from Actium onwards, T. D. Barnes, *JRS* LXIV (1974), 21 ff.; R. Syme, *Phoenix* XXXIII (1979), 308 ff. = *RP* III (1984), 1198 ff. For the date of Tiberius' *ovatio*, ib. 311 ff.; 329.

[29] The compensation had been devised in 12 for Tiberius (Dio LIV. 31.4). Being then a *legatus*, he was not qualified to take the title of 'imp.'

[30] From Cossus Lentulus (*cos.* 1 BC) to his son (AD 26).

to roads or cities, their persons had received extravagant honours. Restrictions set in. The last proconsuls to enjoy the title of 'saviour and founder', with a festival to carry their names, were Fabius Maximus and Marcius Censorinus.[31]

Generals of the Triumvirs adorned Rome with a variety of buildings from the proceeds of war booty. No new edifice now exhibited a name of ancient power; and to repair an ancestral construction might entail enormous expense.[32] For ruler and dynasty, a monopoly, and no limits. A huge theatre commemorated young Marcellus, while Livia and Octavia had their porticos.

So far display. It remains to ask what occupations were available to men of high birth, and attractive, in a well-ordered commonwealth. In the first place, eloquence.[33] Not needed in the Senate in Rome under the Triumvirs, it came in useful to quell or coax the legions, or from one diplomat to another in secret negotiations between the dynasts. The first epoch of the new dispensation imported scant amelioration. The high assembly heard embassies from cities or princes or far peoples; it approved statements about actions or intentions of the government; and a consul entering office would render thanks, in dignified effusions, to Caesar and the present felicity.[34]

It was not intended that the Senate should engage in debate about warfare and the armies, about foreign affairs. Domestic policy admitted discussion. Contention arose in 18 when the list of the Senate was revised and the *Leges Iuliae* were promulgated.

Under the Free State, prosecution opened the avenue for talent, eagerly entered in youth; for example by Servius Sulpicius after the elections in 63.[35] Before he took on the consular Ap. Pulcher in 50, P. Dolabella had already faced indictment on capital charges not once but twice.[36] Under despotic government a 'vastitas fori' is duly deplored.[37] It is not clear that such a desolation prevailed all the time under the Triumvirs. The years of peace promoted suits involving property.

The chance soon abated of exciting indictments for corruption or for

---

[31] *IGR* IV. 244 (Alexandria Troadis); *SEG* II. 549 (Mylasa).

[32] Repairing the Basilica Aemilia, Paullus (*suff.* 34) needed help from Augustus and from friends (Dio LIV. 23.3). On a later occasion his son offered to undertake the task at his own cost, but Caesar intervened (*Ann.* III. 72.1). As there emerges, no Pompeius was equal to the theatre carrying their name. That is, not even the millionaire Sex. Pompeius (*cos.* AD 14).

[33] Seneca, *Controv.* II, *praef.* 3: 'eloquentiae tantum studeas: facilis ab hac in omnes artes discursus est.'

[34] Sex. Pompeius (*cos.* AD 14) is the earliest on record (Ovid, *Ex P.* IV.4).

[35] *Pro Murena* 54, cf. 56. Assumed the son of the jurist. Thus Münzer, *RE* IVA. 860 f. Rather a young kinsman of the same name according to D. R. Shackleton Bailey, *HSCP* LXXXIII (1979), 257 f.

[36] *Ad fam.* III.10.5.

[37] *Brutus* 21.

misdemeanours in the provinces. When late in 24 or early in 23 a
proconsul of Macedonia stood on trial in the courts (he had transgressed
against Sulla's law *de maiestate* by embarking on warfare outside his
province), extreme embarrassment ensued, and worse, for the Princeps.[38]
For what it may be worth, the narration of Cassius Dio fails to register
other prosecutions of provincial governors. Later on, in 4 BC, the ruler
devised a procedure for dealing with charges of extortion (*repetundae*). By
making avowal and a pledge of restitution before a select committee, the
accused was dispensed from the graver penalties.[39]

Connivance is manifest between the Princeps and the governing class.
Spoliation of provincials was condoned, and it went on. One scandal late
in the reign could not be hushed up. Messalla Volesus (*cos.* 5), when
proconsul in Asia, passed from extortion to a murderous mass of
executions. Caesar was constrained to intervene and direct the course of
justice.[40] On the other hand, the cruel and rapacious Piso escaped
indictment for his conduct in Africa, or later in Tarraconensis. Caesar's
legates benefit from indulgence or protection.

Civil cases sometimes touched Caesar's friends or others among the
eminent. Not much is on record. Maecenas and the consular Sex.
Appuleius were roughly handled when giving testimony for the defence
against a charge of adultery.[41] About the same time occurred the
prosecution of Nonius Asprenas, married to a sister of Quinctilius Varus.
He held a splendid banquet, which wrought havoc among the guests.
They perished, to a total of a hundred and thirty. Poisoning was alleged.[42]
Cassius Severus prosecuted, while Asinius Pollio conducted the defence.
Posterity treasured their orations.[43]

Eloquence found refuge and exercise in the schools of rhetoric, which
flourished portentously. The senior magnates Pollio and Corvinus did not
disdain this recourse; and the voice of the *novus homo* Q. Haterius was
heard in voluble declamation on the theme of liberty.[44] Not many consuls
past or future frequented the numerous company. Fabius Maximus is
mentioned twice.[45]

Assiduity in the schools was not always a guarantee of forensic success.
Cassius Severus declaimed rarely. Nor would it lead to political honours.

---

[38] above, p. 40. And see further Ch. XXVII.

[39] *Cyrene Edicts* V carries the *senatus consultum* (*SEG* IX.8).

[40] *Ann.* III. 68.1. Alleged to have killed 300 persons in one day (Seneca, *De ira* II.5.5). After
which, 'graece proclamavit: o rem regiam'.

[41] Dio LIV.30.4.

[42] Pliny, *NH* XXXV. 164; Suetonius, *Divus Aug.* 56.3. Generally held identical with the consul
suffect of AD 6 (as in *PIR*[1] N 93). Rather his parent, cf. Groag, *RE* XVII. 866 ff.

[43] Quintilian X.1.22; XI.1.57.

[44] below, p. 145.

[45] Seneca, *Controv.* II. 4.9; 11 f. He is not the Fabius of X, *praef.* 13.

The surprise is the emergence of a consul, the elderly Vibius Rufus.[46] Furthermore, a nobleman risked encountering formidable rivals or persons of low degree, many of them vulgar and aggressive.

For excellence in the law this season knew no consular luminaries to recall the Mucii Scaevolae. The last of that name is not enrolled in any catalogue of the Roman jurists. Nor is Aelius Tubero (*cos.* 11), despite ancestry and an erudite parent.[47] Ateius Capito, styled a master of law both sacred and profane, interpreted the oracle that justified the year chosen for the Secular Games.[48] After Messalla Rufus, legal and antiquarian studies did not suffer neglect or dispraisal (and the religious policy of the government helped), but they were in danger of lapsing to scholars of lower estate.

During the evil years Tubero's father and a Sulpicius Galba sought consolation in ancient history;[49] and Sergius Plautus, a patrician, was now writing about the doctrines of the Stoics.[50] Neither pastime normally carried appeal to a young *nobilis*. His station permitted light or occasional verse. Some might have higher aspirations. Iullus Antonius emulated Pindar, a Sempronius Gracchus wrote tragedies.[51]

The Princeps had the best poets, seduced long since and embrigaded by Maecenas. Messalla Corvinus took a choice of the remainder. Next as a patron came Fabius Maximus; and in this season three young *nobiles* accepted odes from Caesar's poet, namely Fabius himself, Iullus, Censorinus.

Fashion tended more and more towards the fluent composers of elegiac verse, provoking veiled disapprobation. The trend was to be deplored, since Rome now possessed a national achievement to rival the Greeks, both splendid and salubrious.[52] Moreover, some aristocrats evinced a predilection for the poets of Alexandria (who had captivated the previous generation) or extended favour to contemporary writers of epigrams. The notable patron was Piso the Pontifex. And no assessment of education and taste in the epoch of Caesar Augustus will neglect the enigmatic Claudius Nero.[53] He is even disclosed before the end as an orator of unusual talent and power.

[46] On whom (*suff.* AD 16) see *History in Ovid* (1978), 84 ff.; *ZPE* 43 (1981), 365 ff. = *RP* III (1984), 1423 ff.

[47] For the parent (Q. Tubero L.f.), jurist and historian, see Ch. XXII.

[48] above, p. 45. On the Augustan jurists see further in Ch. XXV.

[49] Galba, father of the *suffectus* of 5 BC, composed a 'multiplicem nec incuriosam historiam' (Suetonius, *Galba* 3.3). It ranged widely, being cited by Plutarch, *Romulus* 17, and by Orosius for an item in the seventies (V.23.6).

[50] *PIR*[1] S 378. His inscription turned up at Urso in Baetica, of which he was *patronus* (*ILS* 2922).

[51] And the epic poet Camerinus (Ovid, *Ex P.* IV.16.19) might be Q. Sulpicius Camerinus (*cos.* AD 9), or a son.

[52] To be surmised as an unspoken motive in Horace, *Epp.* II.1 (to Caesar Augustus).

[53] Ch. XXV.

Under benevolent despotism an aristocracy debarred from useful occupations turns to hunting, racing, gambling.[54] Evidence is sparse.[55] Young Ahenobarbus was a skilled charioteer. He also liked putting on murderous contests of gladiators.[56]

In the last age of the Republic leaders of the Optimates like Lucullus and Hortensius devoted their leisure to game parks and to fish ponds. Their successor as a 'piscinarius' was Vedius Pollio, a friend of Caesar and a useful agent.[57] He threw living slaves to the *murenae*.[58] The Princeps, who inherited, demolished the Roman mansion and redeemed the site for the Portico of Livia.[59]

Agriculture commended esteem (enhanced by tradition or romance, by Cincinnatus or by Cato), although some found it beneath the attention and dignity of a gentleman.[60] The gains of good husbandry might be ample. A sagacious agronome accorded praise to the second consul of the Volusii.[61] In a different sphere, financial acumen may explain some of the riches accumulated by Lentulus the Augur.[62]

War and revolution engendered most of the great fortunes on show in this prosperous age, Caesar's bounty following the generosity of Marcus Antonius. The palace of Magnus, adorned with the beaks of vessels captured from the pirates, had been seized by Antonius. Messalla Corvinus now shared it with M. Agrippa.[63] Another famous mansion fell to Marcius Censorinus, on whose decease it passed to the Statilii.[64] Again, statues and paintings. As collectors none could compete with Agrippa, or with the refined taste of Claudius Nero. Finally, men of high birth acquired possessions of every kind bequeathed by testament from grateful or ostentatious persons of lower estate. Corvinus inherited from that Cestius who is commemorated by a pyramid at Rome.[65]

The riches of certain *novi homines* such as M. Lollius stand on scandalous record: not 'avitae opes', but the spoil of provinces.[66] For Quirinius and for

[54] For these and other recreations, P. Harvey, *Historia* XXVIII (1979), 329 ff. Versailles under Louis Quatorze offers comparisons.

[55] And sporadic, e.g. innocuous dicing by the Princeps along with P. Silius and M. Vinicius (Suetonius, *Divus Aug.* 71.2). Reckless gambling may explain the dissipation of some aristocratic fortunes.

[56] Suetonius, *Nero* 4.4.

[57] On whom, *JRS* LI (1961), 23 ff. = *RP* (1979), 518 ff. One will not omit the fact that he built a *Caesareum* (*ILS* 109: Beneventum).

[58] Stated in Dio's lengthy account (LIV.23), and elsewhere. Vedius owned the Pausilypon on the Bay of Naples.

[59] Ovid, *Fasti* VI.643 f.

[60] Sallust, *Cat.* 4.1: 'neque vero agrum colundo aut venando, servilibus officiis'.

[61] Columella I.7.3.

[62] Ch. XXI.

[63] Dio LIII.27.5.

[64] Velleius II.14.3 (Cicero's house on the Palatine).

[65] *ILS* 917a.

[66] Pliny, *NH* IX.117 (the pearls of Lollia Paullina).

others, wealth is briefly noted or to be assumed without discomfort. When Cornelius Balbus died he left a theatre for remembrance. His uncle had made a bequest of twenty-five *denarii* a head to the populace.[67]

Inheritance or marriage was a continuous source of profit and advancement. Periods well documented duly reveal fortune hunters. The avid and ambitious P. Dolabella needed money for a career likely to be hazardous and expensive. He married old Fabia.[68] Young Juventius Thalna, of a family in decay, is found paying court to 'Cornificiam, vetulam sane et multarum nuptiarum'.[69]

Warfare and proscriptions raised a crop of widows and heiresses, while shifts in political allegiance led to divorce. The 'Sullana tempora' bear witness, the Dictator himself ensnared by the arts of a Valeria recently parted from her husband. For the aftermath of Actium requisite testimony fails.

The upstart Titius had already possessed himself of Fabia, the sister of Maximus.[70] Lollius went on to acquire an Aurelia of the Cotta family now close to the end.[71] Quirinius married 'Claudia, Ap. f.', the sister of Messalla Appianus, his colleague in the consulship.[72] But no search has lit upon partners for Tarius Rufus or the great Statilius Taurus. The next and nearest that avails is for the grandson of Taurus.[73]

The aristocratic consuls between 16 and 7 might be expected to compensate. However, the consorts of nine are missing, as has been shown. In the new nobility the Volusii did not have to look for wealth in a wife. The son of L. Volusius was content with 'Cornelia Scipionum gentis'.[74] Others sought support in municipal families, to be presumed well endowed. Urgulania was the mother of Plautius Silvanus (*cos.* 2 BC), patently Etruscan. He chose to marry 'Lartia Cn. f.', whose origin and extraction defies ascertainment. No author discloses a senator of that name.[75]

The mausoleum of the Plautii near Tibur exhibits no other wife for Silvanus.[76] Marriage now made compulsory in the upper order failed to

[67] Dio XLVIII.42.2.

[68] Divorcing her to acquire Tullia. Fabia claimed to be only thirty. As Cicero said, 'verum est, nam hoc illam iam viginti annis audio' (Quintilian VI.3.73).

[69] *Ad Att.* XIII.28.4. She repulsed Thalna: too poor. His lineage went back to the sporadic consul of 163.

[70] *IGR* IV.1760 (Samos).

[71] below, p. 178.

[72] *CIL* VI. 15626.

[73] The wife of Sisenna Statilius Taurus (*cos.* 16) was a Cornelia (*PIR*[2] C 1477), presumably aristocratic. Yet her daughter, 'Cornelia Tauri f.', married the inconspicuous T. Axius (*CIL* XV. 7440).

[74] Pliny, *NH* VII.62.

[75] There is only 'L. Lartius L.f. Pap.', attested in 73 BC (*SIG*[3] 747: Oropus). The *nomen* is Etruscan, cf. Schulze, *LE* 84, citing *CIE* 1538 = *CIL* XI.2369 (Clusium).

[76] *ILS* 921.

entail continuance in monogamy.[77] Not long after the promulgation of
the Julian Laws Vistilia, a lady from Umbrian Iguvium, entered on a
career of matrimony that ran through six husbands spread along a tract of
about twenty years.[78] Given the incidence of mortality at Rome, it is harsh
and premature to tax Vistilia with at least five divorces; and she was
entitled to recognition from the author of family legislation since she
produced children from each husband. The student of fecundity and
demography will also applaud. Large families are not much in evidence
among the aristocracy at this juncture.[79]

While enjoining sexual morality, the government sought to restrict
luxury and ostentation. The household of the Princeps duly advertised
models of decorum and frugality. He was sober in habits himself and not
likely to indulge in banquets unless expedient.

Sumptuary legislation, that was an old story. Its effects could be seen
and measured. Firm testimony declares that luxury flourished unabated
for a century until the end of the dynasty, with many of the 'dites olim
familiae' brought to ruin through their 'studium magnificentiae'.[80]

It is not easy either to curb or to document the commerce of the sexes.
Society behaved as before, as predictable. The aristocracy could make
appeal to the 'clementia maiorum'. They resented penalty visited upon
mere adultery, 'culpam inter viros ac feminas vulgatam'.[81]

Since public life now offered little excitement, the bolder spirits,
disdaining sloth or futility, were impelled to active dissipation that might
prove perilous. They found ready accomplices in the other sex. In elegant
society the normal habits revived.[82] The doctrines of Epicurus, deprecated
or traduced by public men and other champions of morality, commanded
tacit assent.

The Princeps could neither avow the existence of a court nor conceal it.
There was a whole company of princesses along with their rivals for talent
or pedigree, avid for power and display. The monarchy brought out and
enhanced the political importance of women. Maternal ascendance
already conferred social parity. It now finds expression in nomenclature. A
Nonius Asprenas (*cos.* AD 8), of a new consular family, is 'Quinctilianus',
while Cornelius Cinna (*cos.* 5), the grandson of Pompeius, was conceded

---

[77] Seneca, *De ben.* III.28.2: 'inlustres quaedam ac nobiles feminae non consulum numero sed
maritorum annos suos computant.'

[78] Pliny, *NH* VII.39. First elucidated by C. Cichorius, *Römische Studien* (1922), 429 ff. For certain
modifications, *JRS* LX (1970), 27 ff. = *RP* (1979), 805 ff.

[79] Asinius Gallus made a notable contribution. Then the Junii Silani and Crassus Frugi (*cos.* 27).

[80] *Ann.* III. 55.

[81] *Ann.* III.24.2.

[82] J. Griffin, *JRS* LXVI (1976), 87 ff.; LXVII (1977), 17 ff. Ovid was disingenuous when asserting
that his precepts applied only to 'meretrices'.

the obtrusive 'Magnus' for *cognomen* on the *Fasti Capitolini*. After a time a man can reproduce a large piece from the maternal side or even take over a *cognomen* from his wife's family.[83]

Names convey potent significance in any aristocracy, and notably at Rome where oligarchic equality set a curb on the employment of titles. What was permitted or usurped cannot fail to instruct. Various devices are on show.[84]

In a man of birth the *gentilicium*, being so often indistinctive, tends to be suppressed, and the *cognomen* takes its place. Thus 'Q. Metellus'. The *praenomen* was of small consequence, but the ambitious and pretentious put emphasis on personality by using instead a *cognomen*, if it happened to be uncommon. Hence 'Faustus Sulla'; and the two young *nobiles* who completed the monument of Ap. Pulcher at Eleusis stand as 'Pulcher Claudius' and 'Rex Marcius'.[85]

Transferences then become exorbitant. A Valerius Messalla revives an ancient and forgotten *cognomen*, prefixing 'Potitus' to his style. More powerful was the distinction advertised by the two Fabii with 'Paullus' and 'Africanus', while 'Iullus' in the son of the Triumvir shows loyal attachment to the Julii.

Towns or villages of old Latium now come to life in *cognomina*. A Cornelius Lentulus is styled 'Maluginensis:' from Maluga, somewhere in the vicinity of Corioli. 'Mugillanus' appertained to the Papirii, but there had been none of that great patrician house for two centuries. However, a Sulpicius emerges as 'Camerinus': and a Furius Camillus calls his daughter 'Medullina'.

So far assertions of ancestry (not all perhaps valid), or products of antiquarian zeal.[86] A triumphal name would be better. The *novus homo* L. Mummius, the consul of 146, is frequently referred to as 'Achaicus', but he did not take that appellation—which did not prevent his obscure grandson from assuming it.[87] In this season his daughter, Mummia Achaica, married C. Sulpicius Galba (*suff.* 5). She was doubly illustrious, having Lutatia for mother, the daughter of Lutatius Catulus (*cos.* 78). Galba's son Servius (*cos.* AD 33), a fanatic for pedigree, was happy to parade that ancestry in his halls, along with others more remote, but no consul since 144.[88] His grandfather, the historian, had not gone further than the praetorship.

---

[83] Thus P. Clodius Thrasea (*suff.* 56), annexing 'Paetus'. In due course nomenclature from female ascendance can even extrude the father's name, as with C. Ummidius Quadratus (*suff.* 118), the grandson of Ummidia Quadratilla.

[84] *Historia* VII (1958), 172 ff. = *RP* (1979), 361 ff.   [85] *ILS* 4041.

[86] Ignorance had prevailed, at least in some quarters. Papirius Paetus was astonished when told about patrician Papirii (*Ad fam.* IX.21.2). His mentor drew profit from recent researches of Pomponius Atticus.   [87] Disclosed by *Inschr. v. Olympia* 331.

[88] Suetonius, *Galba* 3.4. The consul of 108 was not a linear ancestor.

Fable and fiction continued to attract, on steady augmentation from annalists, antiquarians, poets, although men became aware that the chronicle of the early Republic was infested with fraudulence—consulates and triumphs that never were, and plebeians alleged patrician to begin with.[89] On invitation from Brutus, Pomponius Atticus investigated and set forth the lineage of the Junii.[90] This astute person (both a banker and a publisher), although admitting scholarly dubitations, would not be impelled to discredit L. Junius, the founder of the Free State, or that Servilius who killed an aspirant to tyranny.

Requests followed from others in the *nobilitas*. Atticus extended his researches to the Fabii and Aemilii, also to the Claudii Marcelli. Than those productions, nothing could be more delightful.[91]

About the Marcii there was something peculiar, apart from the legend of Coriolanus, whom they were not able to insert in the consular *Fasti*. They claimed descent from two of the kings, from Numa Pompilius and from Ancus Marcius. Though plebeian, the Marcii stood next in prestige to patricians.[92]

Some plebeians arrived much too late to obtrude a consul. The Domitii explained their *cognomen* by an ancestor whose hair and beard turned ruddy when he met Castor and Pollux, announcing a great victory to the Roman People.[93] The facile explanation is a late product. It ignored philology. Their beard, like their face and their heart, was metallic, so the orator L. Crassus declared, in altercation with the consul of 96.[94]

The Calpurnii, who came later (their first consul in 180), descended from Calpus, a son of Numa.[95] No sign that the legend preoccupied Caesoninus, consul in 58, or his son the Pontifex. Nor did Marcus Antonius, parading heroic vigour, make anything of Anto, a companion of Hercules, so far as known.[96] For Licinii and Livii, legends and fabrications seem not in evidence; and Aelius Tubero had only the credit of a frugal ancestor, the grandson of Aemilius Paullus.

The patricians (it was asserted) went back to gods and kings, even to kings of Alba Longa, or to Trojan families.[97] In any age, the fraudulent

---

[89] Cicero, *Brutus* 62.

[90] Nepos, *Vita Attici* 18.3.

[91] ib. 18.4: 'quibus libris nihil potest esse dulcius iis qui aliquam cupidinem habent notitiae clarorum virorum.'

[92] Münzer, *RE* XIV. 1535 ff.

[93] Suetonius, *Nero* 1.1; Plutarch, *Aemilius Paulus* 25.

[94] Suetonius, *Nero* 2.2. Like the name 'Scenobarbus', the peculiar *cognomen* of the Domitii is Illyrian, pointing to an origin from the Abruzzi regions. Cf. *JRS* LX (1970), 34 = *RP* (1979), 816.

[95] Plutarch, *Numa* 21. Aristocratic legends are neatly examined by T. P. Wiseman, *Greece & Rome* XXI (1974), 153 ff.

[96] Plutarch, *Antonius* 4. 'Anto' supports a conjecture that the Antonii derive from Tibur.

[97] Trojan and Alban *gentes* are discussed by R. E. A. Palmer, *The Archaic Roman Religion* (1970), 133 ff.; 290 ff.

claim to be indigenous. The paradox of alien origin redeems Valerii and Claudii, immigrant from the Sabine country, faintly apparent in Valerii but proclaimed in pride by the Claudii.[98]

For the Aemilii erudite fantasy produced a daughter of Aeneas and Lavinia, a son of Numa, a son of Pythagoras.[99] The Fabii had shown some interest in Hercules as early as the Cunctator. The alert poet, the friend of Maximus, was suitably percipient.[100] Though never averse from advertisement and display, Fabii and Aemilii were not at pains to exploit these fables. They relied on the authentic memory of Carthage and Macedon and the epoch of the conquering Republic.

Like Atticus, and not much later, the old consular Messalla Rufus investigated family histories. Anger inspired him when observing what was on exhibit in the residence of a certain Scipio Pomponianus, who took his name, by 'adoptio testamentaria', from a person called Salvitto, of dubious extraction. Further, Messalla Corvinus raised loud indignation and refused to admit Valerii Laevini to his genealogical tree.[101]

On a gentle estimate, the delinquency of Salvitto and Pomponianus might deserve condonation as a tribute to public excellence acknowledged through the ages. In fact, the epoch of Caesar Augustus shows birth and pedigree on a higher rating and prestige than recently under the Free State. Women conformed. When Galba lost his Achaica, Livia Ocellina made advances to him, beautiful and wealthy as she was, and Galba both short in stature and deformed.[102]

Heavy emphasis reposes on patricians, since, whatever the value of any individual (in peace or war), that class is a necessary element and adornment in a 'res publica', as understood by other Romans. On some criterion or other, five of their *gentes* were reckoned 'maiores', namely Aemilii, Claudii, Cornelii, Fabii, Valerii.[103] The frequency of *nobiles* among the consuls of the last epoch of the Republic has already been observed. Of fifteen, no fewer than eight were patrician, of the *gentes maiores* only Fabii absent.[104] For parallel, the years 16–7 exhibit nine. The Fabii return, while Quinctilii and Quinctii are rescued from long obscurity.

Some were gone for good. Nothing could be done for the Servilii

---

[98] *Ann.* XI.24.1: 'maiores mei, quorum antiquissimus Clausus, origine Sabina'. As for the Valerii, Dion. Hal. II.46. Also the legend retailed by Valerius Maximus about 'Valesius, vir locuples rusticae vitae' (II.4.5). For the Claudii see T. P. Wiseman, *Clio's Cosmetics* (1979), 57 ff; with the comments of T. J. Cornell, *JRS* LXXII (1982), 205 f.

[99] Plutarch, *Aemilius Paulus* 1; *Romulus* 2; *Numa* 8. Cf. Festus, p. 22 L.

[100] *History in Ovid* (1978), 147.   [101] Pliny, *NH* XXXV.8.

[102] Suetonius, *Galba* 3.4: 'ditem admodum et pulchram, a qua tamen nobilitatis causa appetitus ultro existimatur, et aliquanto enixius'.

[103] Mommsen, *Römische Forschungen* I² (1864), 69 ff. He included the Manlii: disallowed by Münzer, *RA* (1920), 98 f.; 317.

[104] above, p. 54. That is, the consuls from 57 to 49.

Caepiones or the Postumii; and the Manlii now lapse, although they had been numerous enough.[105] Others were coming of age or awaiting their chance. For the ancient Sergii, the desperate ambition of Catilina had not availed; and Sergius Plautus, the adept of Stoicism, was not to succeed.[106]

Members of the renascent patriciate would soon have to face sharp competition. Not so much from the plebeian *nobilitas*, which had been sadly reduced in the recent age. Sons of partisans ennobled under the Triumvirate and in the early season of the new dispensation were pressing forward, with claims not to be denied: Statilii, Calvisii, Vinicii, Antistii, and others. And here and there a meritorious *novus homo* from some town of Italy.

The resplendent decade found its conclusion with the second consulship of Claudius Nero. The next year opened with D. Laelius Balbus and C. Antistius Vetus. To explain the former, it is enough to say that he had been one of the *quindecimviri* a dozen years previously. That fact itself renders this *novus homo* not a little enigmatic, but consecrates the value and significance of priesthoods as well as consulships.[107]

Claudius Nero when entering office in 7 at once announced the dedication of a temple to Concordia.[108] Monarchy and aristocracy abode in firm embrace, so it seemed, the *nobiles* having regained their inherited station and honour.

To the percipient or malicious, sundry phenomena cast a cloud on complacency. In foreign policy the recent success achieved by the government stood solid and unimpeachable, but most of the credit was engrossed by the Princeps and his stepsons, to the obscuration of some who had prepared or initiated the victorious campaigns.[109]

A monopoly of military glory could not be concealed.[110] It was paraded by pageantry and perpetuated on monuments. In any age the aristocracy of birth is prone to take delight in occasions for the display of vestimentary distinctions, not least if they had little else to show. They were now restricted to sacerdotal robes and emblems, some peculiar indeed, notably

[105] Even in the late Republic. A revised stemma is provided by J. F. Mitchell, *Historia* XV (1966), 30 f. For members of other *gentes* (more than allowed for by Münzer), see C. and Ö. Wikander, *Opuscula Romana* XII (1979), 7 ff. They also discuss plebeian *nobiles*.

[106] Probably to be identified as the 'Plaut.' who was praetor in AD 2 (*Inscr. It.* XIII.1, p. 297). On Sergius and his descendants see now *AJP* CIII (1982), 67 f.

[107] Duly included by Seneca in the rubric of ingratitude towards the bounty of Caesar: 'a me numerari voluit annum: sed deest mihi ad sacerdotium. cooptatus sum in collegium: sed cur in unum? consummavit dignitatem meam: sed patrimonio nihil contulit' (*De ira* III.31.2).

Compare Tacitus on those who benefit from evil times: 'sacerdotia et consulatus ut spolia adepti' (*Hist.* I.2.3).

[108] Dio LV.8.1 (in his name and in memory of his brother).

[109] Clearly P. Silius Nerva, by Alpine operations in 16 (Dio LIV.20.1).

[110] The diplomatic success of the year 20 was advertised by 'imp. IX' and the legends 'signis receptis' and 'Armen. capt.' (*BMC R. Emp.* I. 108 ff.).

those borne by the Arval Brethren (the plenary authenticity of which was not exempt from doubt). Ahenobarbus, it is true, stands prominent in a procession on the altar of *Pax Augusta*. He owed that to his wife, a niece of Caesar Augustus.[111]

The Forum, with the temple of Mars Ultor, was now nearing completion.[112] In that area stood the panoplied statues of ancient heroes and builders of empire, each with the inscribed record of his 'res gestae'. It was also in essence a dynastic evocation of the *gens Iulia*, beginning with Aeneas. The martial history of Rome culminated in Caesar Augustus, who had a unique and separate place in the Forum: a chariot and the catalogue of his conquests.[113]

The *nobilitas* recaptured the consulate. The prize fell to few. Individuals benefited, or small groups. Of any candidate thrusting forward against the disapprobation of Caesar, no sign now. Sundry techniques of pre-selection or of dissuasion were put to good employ. Their working in detail evades the scrutiny of a later time; and when the elections had been transferred from the Campus to the Senate, a careful historian who consulted the protocol avows his perplexity.[114]

In this season a certain modicum of competition was permitted, as a casual notice discloses. The consuls of 8 (Marcius Censorinus and Asinius Gallus) had resort to bribery. The Princeps declined to investigate, and he pretended to know nothing about it.[115] He was reluctant either to administer penalty or admit his public condonation.

Hence complicity, not the only example. And favouritism was elsewhere manifest. Not all of their coevals held Ahenobarbus or Fabius Maximus in esteem and affection; and the truculence of Cn. Piso invited enmities. Some saw that they had better renounce. Others were glad to be spared the cost of elections or of office. There was a further drawback: the chances of the ambitious diminished under competition since the praetorships rose from eight to twelve.

Discontent of another kind was provoked by the moral and social enactments of the year 18, most of all in the highest ranks of the Senate. They viewed with equanimity the reduction in membership to six hundred. *Nobiles* stood out anyhow.[116]

When the roll of the high assembly was revised, the Princeps insisted on

---

[111] Ahenobarus, Antonia, two small children; E. Simon, *Ara Pacis Augustae* (1967), 19, with pl. 15. On those children, Ch. XII.

[112] Below, p. 89 (in 2 BC).

[113] *RG* 35, elucidated through Velleius II.38.2. Augustus deliberately outdistanced other conquerors, cf. P. Frisch, *ZPE* 39 (1980), 91 ff.

[114] *Ann.* I. 81.

[115] Dio LV.5.3.

[116] For the *lectio* of 18, and for subsequent recruitment of the Senate, see A. Chastagnol in *Miscellanea . . . E. Manni* II (1980), 465 ff.

dragging from his retreat the failed Triumvir Lepidus, enjoining that he be asked his 'sententia' last of all the consulars. No aristocrat raised a voice in protest. The sole comment came from a senator of lower station.[117]

That year witnessed a notable consequence of the marriage legislation: nothing less than a definition of the 'senatorius ordo'. Senators were forbidden to marry freedwomen or daughters of actors—not only senators but lineal descendants to the third degree. A comparable interdict was imposed upon their womenfolk.[118]

In that fashion emerged a social class, on clear delimitation through penalty as well as privilege.[119] No concern likewise to the *nobilitas*, but an enhancement of public honour to the mass of senators, many of whom avowed recent equestrian extraction, and who, separated from Roman knights by the 'dignitas' of the governing class, none the less remained on social parity.

Not that a high barrier was thereby erected between the two orders. As in the last epoch of the Free State, it could easily be crossed by energy, influence, or wealth.

There subsisted a cause of distaste and annoyance to senators, whatever their rank. In the revolutionary wars, knights usurped great power as agents and ministers of the dynasts. In the secret counsels of the ruler, the sinister Maecenas was followed by Sallustius Crispus. Worse than that, the visible affront of Egypt. Senators were debarred. Caesar ruled the land of Nile as heir of the Ptolemies, his deputy (with an *imperium* perhaps not easy to define in legal terms) was a Roman knight. Prefects of Egypt, standing 'loco regum', looked down on proconsuls of Cyprus. In power and authority they surpassed most of the consulars.

For all that, a 'concordia' had now arrived between the two orders in state and society, 'dignitas' in harmony with wealth and in mutual support.[120] There also prevailed a consensus. Caesar Augustus, in acknowledging the supremacy he held at the time when he transferred the commonwealth to where it belonged, namely 'in senat]us populique Rom[ani a]rbitrium', inserted a parenthesis about the source of his predominance. It runs 'per consensum universorum [potitus reru]m omn]ium'.[121] The parenthesis is

---

[117] Dio LIV. 15.7 (the conservative jurist Antistius Labeo).

[118] By provisions of the *Lex Iulia de maritandis ordinibus* (*Dig.* XXIII.2.44) Observe the firm conclusions of M.-T. Raepsaet-Charlier, *Rev. int. des Droits de l'Antiquité* XXVIII (1981), 189 ff. The definition of the 'ordo senatorius' was put too late (under Caligula) by A. Chastagnol, *MÉFR* LXXXV (1973), 583 ff.

[119] Further confirmed by the *senatus consultum* found at Larinum (*AE* 1978, 145). It is directed against persons who appear on the stage 'contra dignitatem ordinis sui'. On this document see now B. Levick, *JRS* LXXXIII (1983), 97 ff.

[120] For 'concordia' as defence of the established order, cf. B. Levick in *Essays . . . C. H. V. Sutherland* (1978), 217 ff.

[121] *RG* 34.

balanced. It makes a concession ('potitus' is a strong word), matched with a firm assertion.[122] That is, power without limit, but everybody had wanted him to take it.

Consensus remained, and power changed into delegated authority. Aristocrats were not deceived by names and phrases, or by an ostensible antithesis. They knew the term 'principatus et dominatus',[123] and they refused legitimacy to the last of the dynasts. Fate or chance had produced him. Descendants of his rivals were extant.

Being 'Imperator Caesar divi f. Augustus', the ruler towered above them. They accepted him, for he was not one of themselves. The next Caesar might run into trouble.

Arrogant in comportment to those beneath, the *nobiles* showed deference to superior authority. The saving word is 'obseqium'. It was in danger of passing easily into 'adulatio'.

By 6 BC the historian who was close coeval to Caesar Augustus had advanced a long way forward in his vast enterprise. Assiduous industry in quiet Patavium may have now brought him to the fall of the Republic and the eruption of civil strife.[124] From arduous, the task became delicate or hazardous. Recent consuls had the War of Actium in vivid remembrance. Livy was saved by the existence of an official version.

Writers of contemporary history have to confront a problem, where to begin. They tend to move backwards, modifying the original point of inception. Livy was spared that anxiety, and the termination was clear.[125] A Greek writer would choose the fall of Alexandria.[126] For Livy, the triple triumph of Caesar's heir.

If life were vouchsafed, and no malady or sudden onset of senescence, the historian might resume, for all that the fame of a classic had been achieved. The year 9 offered campaigns to be recounted in ample narration, with for climax the martial renown of the two Nerones; or he could go on without discomfort to the second consulship of the elder brother. But not any further.

---

[122] Compare 'qui rerum potiuntur': Caelius' definition of Pompeius and Caesar (*Ad fam.* VIII.14.2). For 'potitus', 'potens' has been suggested by D. Krömer, *ZPE* 28 (1978), 127 ff. To be deprecated.

[123] Cicero, *Phil.* XI.36.

[124] Book CIX opened the Civil War. In CXX, Triumvirate and the Proscriptions.

[125] That is, with Book CXXXIV. It follows that the last nine books are an epilogue. For which conception, see the introduction to Ch. XXIX.

[126] i.e. Strabo for his continuation of Polybius. Not the year 27, as assumed by E. Honigmann, *RE* IVA. 89.

VI

Some Perturbations

After six years with the armies Claudius Nero had the right and the desire for some relief. Diversions at the capital appealed, both attractive and necessary: to hear the best orators and the new poets, to meet scholars or philosophers. Further, friendships to renew, and the *clientela* of the Claudii to be extended in all classes of Roman society.

For a 'bis consul' and 'vir triumphalis' who stood second only to Caesar, what further honours were desiderated? In the summer he was granted the *tribunicia potestas* for a period of five years: on June 26, so it is presumed.[1] The season was propitious, close on the plebeian festival of Fors Fortuna (a day of repose intervened).[2] The Claudii had ever been eager to solicit the favour and support of the urban populace. It was a novelty that this family now came out with a great general.

Claudius Nero thus entered into partnership in the supreme power: 'id summi fastigii vocabulum Augustus repperit.'[3] That the functions and the sacrosanctity of the ten tribunes could be assumed and concentrated in one person (or in two), that was an invention indeed. A Roman noble who venerated tradition might conceive genuine doubts or hesitations, for all the public and necessary profession of reluctance. It did not take a pedant or a jurist to see that the thing was an 'incivilis potestas'.[4]

That was not all. The Princeps proposed to send him abroad on a mission, to settle order in Armenia. Not good enough, that pretext for removing Tiberius from due prominence and influence at the 'caput imperii'. Fourteen years previously he had been sent to install Tigranes as ruler in Armenia. Not an arduous task, or even requiring force to supplement diplomacy. On that occasion glory accrued to Caesar Augustus, to whom the Parthians surrendered the emblems captured from Roman legions.[5]

Nor was there proof of any urgency. Rome was seldom able to keep firm control over the vassal princedom, or even anxious. The local barons were prone to anarchy and enjoyed that condition for long periods. It

---

[1] As nine years later, cf. the *Fasti* of Amiternum (*Inscr. It.* XIII.1, p. 218).

[2] Ovid, *Fasti* VI. 779 ff., cf. *History in Ovid* (1978), 33.

[3] *Ann.* III.56.2.

[4] As Messalla Corvinus styled the *praefectura urbis* (below, p. 211).

[5] Assigned to Tiberius by Suetonius, *Tib.* 9,1. The silence of Velleius contradicts, who magnifies his role and even his official functions (II.94.4).

would then be difficult to determine who, if anybody, was the ruler.[6] When Tigranes died (the date is quite uncertain) his son succeeded, and after a time proved unsatisfactory.

The author of the *Res Gestae*, referring to transactions about six years subsequent to 6 BC, described Armenia as 'desciscentem et rebellantem'.[7] The historian Tacitus in a succinct survey of eastern affairs adds a name and a valuable detail. Rome tried to impose as prince a certain Artavasdes, but to no purpose: he was 'non sine clade nostra deiectus'.[8] In how close vicinity to 6 BC occurred that mishap remains a question that may cheerfully be waived.

It mattered should the Parthians be tempted to intervene. That the Arsacid was not likely to do, save under grave provocation, insecure at home in his nominal suzerainty over vast territories. Four years previously he sent his four legitimate sons to Rome as hostages.[9]

Claudius Nero would no doubt subscribe to a Tacitean verdict on Parthia.[10] The Armenian mission was enough for him to take umbrage. Deeper reasons fermented, at the same time all too obvious.

Caesar Augustus was eager to promote rapidly the young inheritors, Agrippa's two sons whom he took in adoption a decade before. In 8 BC the boy Gaius, only twelve, was presented to the legions on the Rhine.[11] Two years later premature intriguers tried to get him elected consul. Which Augustus firmly deprecated.[12] But Augustus took the consulate for the next year, to induct Gaius into public life.

A consulship for Gaius when he reached nineteen was in sure prospect. That recalled all too sharply the provision made for Marcellus (to be elected when twenty-two). No protestations then availed to dispel the persuasion that Augustus intended to adopt his nephew.[13] He now had sons of his blood—on which he set passionate value, alien totally to the beliefs and the practice of the Roman aristocracy.

The head of the Claudian house took offence. The annals of empire exhibited Scipio and Flamininus consuls when not much over thirty—the

[6] Thus for most of the time between AD 4 and 14. As Tacitus says, 'magis sine domino quam in libertate' (II.4.2)

[7] *RG* 27.

[8] *Ann.* II.4.1. Not mentioned in *RG*.

[9] Strabo XVI, p. 748. Below, p. 321.

[10] *Germ.* 37.3: 'infra Ventidium deiectus Oriens'.

[11] Dio LV.6.4. To this year and occasion have been assigned coins with on the reverse C. Caesar on horseback and also military emblems. Thus, with conviction, C. H. V. Sutherland, *Coinage in Roman Imperial Policy* (1951), 68 f. Followed, e.g. by B. Levick, *Tiberius the Politician* (1976), 38; and not rejected by W. K. Lacey, *Antichthon* XIV (1980), 128. Not plausible.

[12] Dio LV.9.2 f.

[13] Recovering from his illness in 23, the Princeps recited the terms of his testament (Dio LIII.31.1). Nor would the audience have been convinced by the affirmation of H. U. Instinsky that the adoption was legally 'eine Unmöglichkeit' (*Hermes* XCIV (1966), 336 f.).

needs of warfare, personal ambition, or the rivalry of factions. He had been twenty-eight himself. That honour ensued after apprenticeship to the 'res publica', both military and civilian, crowned by a brilliant campaign. With C. Caesar consul at nineteen, a principate avowed visibly an authentic monarchy. Tiberius had no intention of going on to be exploited like Marcus Agrippa—and then perhaps edged out and discarded. He decided to secede and depart.

The truest explanation is declared in the pretext put out later on. Duty and loyalty determined what he did. He refused to stand in the way of the young princes. Thus Velleius.[14] The biographer confirms.[15]

Claudian pride was obdurate against all entreaty. Tiberius set out, leaving family and wife and a son (the son of Vipsania) now aged eight. About Julia, speculation could not fail to proliferate. Domestic discord had been sharp, not with much effort of concealment from the arrogant and outspoken princess. At a distance of four generations a historian was emboldened there to discover the main motive.[16] He was perhaps coming to form an excessive estimate of the role of women in the Palace. On sober reflection the lady recedes.

Tiberius rushed down in haste to Ostia and set sail for Rhodes. Of senatorial friends, only one chose to be his companion.[17] If the Senate had already voted proconsular *imperium*, it was void through refusal of the mandate. When he left he did not cross the *pomerium*, going out in the garb of war as 'paludatus'.[18]

It was not easy or expedient to divest tribunician powers. That abrupt and extreme act would blow away all comforting explanations, publish a political breach beyond repair, and preclude any return to power and honour.

Departing in protest (and more than that), Tiberius may have conceived an expectation that they would stand in need of him before long.[19] If so, in vain all through the self-imposed exile on the distant island. Five years later Tiberius brought himself to indite a private petition. He put forward two pleas. The princes had come to manhood and a share in government (no suspicion of rivalry now to be feared), and he wished to see his family again. A harsh and forbidding answer followed: 'dimitteret omnem curam suorum quos tam cupide reliquisset.'[20]

---

[14] Tiberius was moved 'mira quadam et incredibili atque inenarrabili pietate, cuius causae mox detectae sunt'. He insisted, 'ne fulgor suus orientium iuvenum obstaret initiis' (II.99.2).

[15] Suetonius, *Tib.* 10.2: 'quam causam et ipse, sed postea, reddidit'.

[16] *Ann.* I.53.1: 'nec alia tam intima Tiberio causa cur Rhodum abscederet'.

[17] viz. Lucilius Longus (*Ann.* IV.15.1).

[18] It has been maintained that Tiberius was in possession of proconsular *imperium* on Rhodes for a quinquennium. Thus B. Levick, *Latomus* XXXI (1972), 781 f.; *Tiberius the Politician* (1976), 39.

[19] Suetonius, *Tib.* 10.1: 'ut vitato assiduitatis fastidio auctoritatem absentia tueretur atque etiam augeret, si quando indiguisset sui resp.' In comment on these transactions the biographer discloses insight, as seldom elsewhere.   [20] Suetonius, *Tib.* 11.5.

When a split occurred in a party or a faction, the consequences were not always foreseen—or beyond remedy. Aristocrats asserted wide freedom of action in alliance or in feud. Enemies from long date could be persuaded on the plea of 'concordia' to forswear their 'inimicitiae' by public announcement, 'rei publicae causa'.[21]

That happy consummation seemed out of the question. It took an astrologer to foretell that Claudius Nero would come back. The prediction was uttered only in the last days on Rhodes.[22]

The angry Princeps was intent to demonstrate to Rome and to the whole world that his stepson had deserted the post of duty, that no one man is indispensable to the 'res publica'. A sagacious ruler aims at keeping a balance between parallel ambitions and competing groups. The primacy of Claudius Nero disturbed that equilibrium. Manifold prospects now beckoned to his peers and rivals. And some had close attachments to the 'domus regnatrix'.

An obscure decade sets in. The manuscript of Cassius Dio is marred by three gaps, each of two folia.[23] Important transactions are truncated or absent. Of Velleius, the habits are known or predictable. He leads off in fine style. When the 'custos urbis' departed, the whole world felt the shock. Germany took up arms again, and the Parthian laid hands on Armenia.[24]

Germany remained quiescent for the next six years, so far as known. As concerns Parthia, if the facts were secure, the pronouncement would be decisive, to a double and paradoxical conclusion: the Arsacid aggressive, the author veracious.

Caesar Augustus had to find legates for six military zones.[25] Some of the appointments patently derived from a change in high politics.

(a) Illyricum. In succession to Claudius Nero, Sex. Appuleius (Caesar's nephew), on casual and welcome attestation in 8.[26] Ahenobarbus took over several years later.

(b) Germany. There is a lacuna after Tiberius departed in 7. Perhaps an *Ignotus*, perhaps Sentius Saturninus, who left Syria in 7 or 6. Then Aheno-barbus, attested in AD 1.

(c) The Balkan command. No legate on record after Lentulus the

---

[21] For an edifying specimen, enjoined and confirmed by the oration of a senior statesman, consult Livy XL.45 f. For the political manoeuvres, Münzer, *RA* (1920), 200 ff.

[22] Suetonius, *Tib.* 14.4.

[23] viz. in 6–2 BC (LV.9.4 to 10.2); in 2 BC–AD 1 (10.15 to 10a.1); in AD 2–4 (11.2 to 13.2). See Boissevain, Vol. I, LXX. Late epitomators and excerptors furnish some valuable items.

[24] Velleius II. 100.1: 'nam et Parthus desciscens a societate Romana adiecit Armeniae manum et Germania aversis domitoris sui oculis rebellavit.'

[25] Evidence is registered and problems are discussed in later chapters concerning individuals; and recourse can be had to the Index.

[26] Cassiodorus, *Chron. Min.* II.135.

Augur (?10–6). The next, a few years later, are praetorian in rank. The army had been reduced to two legions, so it can be conjectured.[27]

(d) Tarraconensis. Fabius Maximus was there in 3. Who preceded and who followed, no sign.

(e) Syria. Quinctilius Varus succeeded Sentius Saturninus in 7 or 6. Then Piso the Pontifex in 4. After whom, a problem.

(f) Galatia-Pamphylia. In 5 and 4 Sulpicius Quirinius subjugated a mountain people, the Homonadenses.[28] Not all legates were consular in rank.

The vicinity of both Varus and Quirinius would prove congenial to Claudius Nero, had he consented to take up the eastern command. Not so Asinius Gallus, who two years from his consulship proceeded to Asia in the summer of 6: the sortition normally fell early in the year. Friction was likely to occur; and some may have discerned malice on the part of the Princeps.[29]

The Princeps had decided to confer emphasis on the ensuing year, consul for the thirteenth time (a long interval since 23). For colleague the election produced L. Sulla. The name was historic, but equivocally so. Men were put in mind of his grandfather P. Sulla (debarred from the consulate of 65), and a skilful oration purging him from charges of subversion. The more erudite recalled the fact that he had been the second husband of Pompeia, the sister of Magnus.[30]

Cinna Magnus, the grandson of the dynast, was now some distance beyond the 'suus annus'; and there may (or may not) have been a Memmius, son of C. Memmius (*suff.* 34), whose father married Fausta, the daughter of the Dictator.[31]

The choice of L. Sulla appears peculiar.[32] Not so another phenomenon of the year. *Suffecti* arrive, not seen since 12, and to a total of three. The government was alert to broaden its basis of support after the aristocratic decade; and the new nobility, the sons of Triumviral consuls, expected their due.

[27] below, p. 289.

[28] below, p. 333.

[29] Previous malice of the stepson has been divined by A. B. Bosworth *HSCP* LXXXVI (1982), 151 ff. The Princeps, so he argues, had altered the date of his first consulship in 43 from August 19 to September 23 (which date in fact stands in Velleius II. 65.2, and is not his own fabrication). During the ruler's absence in Gaul, Tiberius, among other things, had been responsible for the *senatus consultum* which introduced the new month name of August, 'huic imperio felicissimus' (Macrobius I.12.34). That showed up the fraud.

[30] Her first husband had been a (C.) Memmius, Pompeius' quaestor killed in Spain (Orosius V.23.12). In 54 P. Sulla had a stepson called Memmius (*Ad. Q. fratrem* III.3.2). Cf. *Sallust* (1964), 102.

[31] below, p. 265.

[32] It might be a question whether the elections occurred before or after the abrupt departure of Tiberius—who twenty years later expelled Sulla's son from the Senate (*Ann.* II.48.3).

The first consul suffect, L. Vinicius L. f., was one of them. He crops up as the 'clarus decorusque iuvenis' who disturbed the Princeps by assiduous attentions paid to Julia at Baiae.[33] For the student of Roman eloquence this Vinicius is redeemed by brilliant performance as an advocate, speaking impromptu.[34]

Next, Q. Haterius and C. Sulpicius Galba. The *novus homo*, an orator, was now verging on sixty. A dozen years previously he had been allocated for husband to a daughter of Marcus Agrippa.[35] Galba continues the renascence of the patriciate: no Galba in the consulate since 108.

The following year was introduced by C. Calvisius Sabinus and L. Passienus Rufus. The former is a son of the great Caesarian marshal, standing next behind Statilius Taurus. The parent of Passienus earned fame in the schools of rhetoric.[36] His son, solitary by equestrian parentage in the eponymate between Quirinius and Poppaeus Sabinus (*cos.* AD 9), arouses interest or perplexity. Men of the time would know or divine some link with Sallustius Crispus, who by testament was to adopt his son.

This year produced two *suffecti*. C. Caelius Rufus, not known otherwise, came from Tusculum;[37] whereas Galus Sulpicius turns up as a second patrician after Galba, asserting by the *praenomen* descent from the consul of 166.[38]

So far two years and eight consuls. Not a resplendent collection, but with a dubious merit of variety. The next year stands in double contrast: L. Lentulus with Messallinus (the son of Corvinus), and they held office the whole year through. Lentulus was a grandson of L. Lentulus, and like him *flamen Martialis*.[39] He may have laid claim to Scipionic descent. Two more Lentuli were to follow in quick succession, viz. Cossus (*cos.* 1 BC) and P. Lentulus Scipio (*suff.* AD 2).

After the pair of high aristocrats, Caesar Augustus again honoured the consulate. The colleague was Plautius Silvanus. On first inspection (and it seemed suitable), deriving from the ancient Plautii on high prominence in the plebeian aristocracy.[40] Second thoughts impart and confirm a strong doubt. The family is more recent, not even going back to M. Plautius Hypsaeus, consul in 125.[41] Silvanus emerging as colleague to the Princeps

[33] Suetonius, *Divus Aug.* 64.2.
[34] As the Princeps said, 'ingenium in numerato habet' (Seneca, *Controv.* II.5.20). Not heard of subsequent to his consulship.
[35] below, p. 145.
[36] Named by Cassius Severus along with Messalla and Pollio (Seneca, *Controv.* III, *praef.* 14).
[37] *CIL* XIV. 2622.
[38] Both *suffecti* are only names, first revealed in 1935 by the *Fasti Magistrorum Vici* (*Inscr. It.* XIII.1, p. 284).
[39] *PIR*[2] C 1384.
[40] Münzer, *RA* (1920), 43 f.
[41] These Plautii carry the tribe 'Aniensis' and come from Trebula Suffenas, as established by L. R. Taylor, *Mem. Am. Ac. Rome* XXIV (1956), 9 ff.

in this memorable year was far from evoking surprise. His mother Urgulania enjoyed the intimate friendship of Livia Drusilla.[42]

Like 5 BC, this year produced three consuls suffect.[43] The first, Caninius Gallus, held the *fasces* with the Princeps in the month of August.[44] Next Fufius Geminus, attested in the place of Caesar on September 18. His tenure was brief if not curtailed. On December 1 the colleague of Caninius Gallus is Q. Fabricius. Decease is perhaps the answer. A dark surmise might wonder whether Fufius Geminus was caught up in the trouble during the autumn of this year.[45] A delinquent consul could perhaps be persuaded to abdicate.

About Fufius and Fabricius, nothing can be ascertained. Caelius Rufus and the patrician Galus Sulpicius (*suffect* in 4) are also names and nonentities. So far the consuls of the reign have been registered year by year. *Suffecti* now supervening as a regular practice, with a plethora of names (some lacking labels of ready identity or any personal distinction, like certain of the recent specimens), deter detail of analysis and counsel a different approach. A number will find mention in the sequel, on various categories of birth, of merit, of documentation.

When Caesar Augustus again assumed the *fasces* it was to honour his second son's induction to public life, and he remained in office for about eight months. The ruler proposed to set his stamp on the year in other ways.

On February 5 they persuaded him to accept the title of 'pater patriae'. Spontaneous manifestations from the Roman plebs and the equestrian order gave the impulsion. In the Senate, acclamation and no need for a decree. The eloquent Messalla Corvinus chose (or was chosen) to express the proper sentiments.[46] His name and person evoked history but now reinforced civic harmony. Forty years had elapsed since the Battle of Philippi. Corvinus did not allow it to be forgotten that Cassius was his general.[47]

Philippi earned a more ample relevance in the pageantry ordained in the summer of the year when the new Forum was inaugurated and the temple

---

[42] below, p. 376. In the next year A. Plautius (?A.f.) emerges, consul suffect with A. Caecina Severus: to be presumed first cousin to Silvanus.

[43] For their order and tenures, A. Degrassi, *I fasti consolari* (1952), 5.

[44] Caninius Gallus has been assumed without doubt the son of the consul of 37. Thus *PIR*[2] C 390. Rather perhaps a grandson, cf. *History in Ovid* (1978), 100 f. The Caninii are an old praetorian family from Tusculum. A Caninius Rebilus was aedile there with C. Caelius Rufus (*CIL* XIV.2622); and observe a Taurus Caninius (2620).

[45] His name is erased on the *Fasti Magistrorum Vici*. The disgrace of his son (*cos.* AD 29) may be the reason. On whom, below, p. 430.

[46] Suetonius, *Divus Aug.* 58.2 (quoting both Corvinus and the response of the Princeps).

[47] *Ann.* IV.34.4: 'imperatorem suum Cassium praedicabat'.

of Mars Ultor.[48] The young Caesar had pronounced a solemn vow on the field of battle. Now accomplished, it was artfully diverted from the avenging of his parent to vengeance on the foreign enemy. The language of a contemporary poet is explicit.[49]

Parthia was indicated by another spectacle. Augustus organized a naval battle: Athenians against Persians, the former winning a predictable victory. Ovid in the *Ars Amatoria* inserted six lines alluding to the 'naumachia'.[50] He subjoined a long excursus, acclaiming the prince C. Caesar, a campaign in the Orient, a triumph to be celebrated over the Parthians.[51]

Janus symbolized war and the ending of war. The closure of the Gates of War had already been brought into relation with the submission of Parthia by Horace: more than once, in a fashion totally illicit.[52] Before that, Virgil, describing an observance of ancient Latium, turned his eyes to the present and described the unbarring of the Gates with a suitable prospect for a Roman consul,

> seu tendere ad Indos
> Auroramque sequi Parthosque reposcere signa.[53]

Closed for the second time after the Cantabrian War in 25 or 24, the Gates may have been opened a little later as a threat against the Parthians, to encourage them to surrender the Roman standards.[54]

Parthia was now on emphasis and in happy prospect. C. Caesar departed from Rome at the beginning of the next year, going first to the Danube, then to the eastern parts.[55] The time had arrived for a member of the dynasty to acquire advertisement or fame in the Orient—and, as previously, diplomacy would anticipate warfare. It is a fair conjecture that the opening of Janus announced the mission of the young prince.[56]

[48] The first day of August, that has been the accepted date. For May 12, see now the arguments of C. J. Simpson, *JRS* LXVII (1977), 91 ff. However, they are contested by F. Cassola, *Studi . . . in memoria di Fulvio Grosso* (1981), 106 ff.

[49] Ovid, *Fasti* V.579 ff.

[50] Ovid, *AA* I. 171–6.

[51] The two passages (in all 102 lines) patently interrupt the author's argument. To be regarded as an addition to an original *AA*, published half a dozen years earlier. For this thesis, *Bayerische S.-B.*, 1974, Heft 7, 16 f. = *RP* III (1984), 923; *History in Ovid* (1978), 13 ff.; 18 f.

[52] Horace, *Odes* IV.15.6 ff.; *Epp* II.1.255 f.

[53] *Aen.* VII. 605 f.

[54] Or rather for the benefit of some people at Rome. The edifice was very small, in a cramped location, the ceremonial not conspicuous.

[55] The departure of Gaius has been put before the end of the year by F. E. Romer, *TAPA* CVIII (1978), 187 ff. He argued from coins. Better, P. Herz, *ZPE* 39 (1980), 285 ff. That is, January 29 of 1 BC, by supplement to the *Fasti Praenestini*: 'C. Caesar princ. iuventut. ad provincias trans]/marina[s ordinand. missus est'.

[56] Proper meaning thus accrues to the words of Tacitus (from the *Historiae*), quoted by Orosius: 'sene Augusto Ianus patefactus' (VII.3.7.). Orosius' own notion of a closure of Janus in 2 BC precisely (the year of the Nativity) is examined and perhaps elucidated in *AJP* C (1979), 198 ff. = *RP* III (1984), 1187 ff.

In his *Res Gestae* the ruler allocated a separate paragraph to the 'naumachia', carefully enumerating ships and combatants;[57] and the exposition rises to its climax and proper ending with 'pater patriae'.[58] That year saw the all but final redaction of the document destined to be exhibited on pillars of bronze to the people of Rome.[59]

There was also the testament, consigned for custody to the sacred virgins of Vesta, and not in danger of being contested on his decease. The dispositions would include bequests to a number of the 'principes civitatis'.[60] What was said or not said about the most conspicuous of them, the absent stepson (whether expressing magnanimity or rancour), could not fail to excite curiosity.

Reaching the age of sixty on September 23 of the previous year, Caesar Augustus became a 'senex' in the full and official sense. For a long time he had craved release from his tasks and burdens, a 'vacatio rei publicae'. A letter to the Senate is quoted.[61] It would be pleasant to depart (the Princeps said) in a happy season, 'quoniam rerum laetitia moratur adhuc'. But he had to be content and consoled with a mere 'verborum dulcedo'.

The ruler abode at his post, hoping to survive until his young sons could succeed to that 'statio'. The grand climacteric would soon be upon him: the sixty-third year of life which in the persuasion of the educated class portended calamity or extinction.

Against the prospect of his decease, those who stood nearest to the power had a plain duty to make plans and provision for maintaining the dynasty. The situation entailed something like a council of regency—and with it perhaps a new husband for the mother of the princes. Hence hopes and fears, ambition and secret intrigue.

Trouble came sooner than expected. Hitherto Augustus had benefited largely from the connivance of Fortuna. But, as men knew, 'ut nihil extra lacessat aut quatiat, in se ipsa fortuna ruit'.[62] A sequence of disasters now set in. Before the year was out, scandal and worse convulsed palace and government.[63] The Princeps in a missive to the Senate denounced his

---

[57] *RG* 23.

[58] *RG* 35.

[59] The emphasis accorded to the two items fits this conjecture. The significant changes later are in 26 (Germany) and 30 (Illyricum).

[60] cf. *Ann.* I.8.1.: 'tertio gradu primores civitatis scripserat, plerosque invisos sibi sed iactantia gloriaque ad posteros.'

[61] Seneca, *De brevitate vitae* 4.3.

[62] Seneca, ib. 4.1.

[63] The catastrophe of Julia could not fail to engross scholarly attention. A catalogue of nearly fifty names (in order of the alphabet) was presented by E. Meise, *Untersuchungen zur Geschichte der julisch-claudischen Dynastie* (1969), 4.

The thesis here adopted goes back to E. Groag, *Wiener Studien* XLI (1919), 74 ff. For full exposition see *Bayerische S.-B.*, 1974, Heft 7, 18 ff. = *RP* III (1984), 923 ff.; *History in Ovid* (1978), 193 ff.

daughter for adultery and for flagrant misconduct on open exhibit. Indictments brought against other ladies duly confirmed a moral purge in high society and helped to cover up the political implications.

Of Julia's lovers, the prime delinquent does not baffle explanation. Antonius, attached to the dynastic nexus, was congenial to Julia through his age and through intellectual interests. If he aspired to her hand, nobody at the time would see an impediment in the fact that he was already married to a niece of the Princeps. He had acquired Marcella through a divorce two decades previously.

Iullus was executed or persuaded to commit suicide.[64] Next in the company, a coeval consular, the patrician Quinctius Sulpicianus (*cos.* 9), of whom nothing is perpetuated save the label 'unique depravity disguised by forbidding eyebrows'.[65] Three more names complete the list (but did not exhaust it), three of the younger *nobiles*: an Appius Claudius, a Sempronius Gracchus, a Scipio. This Scipio is taken to be a son of P. Scipio (*cos.* 16), who shared with Julia a common mother: namely 'Scribonia Caesaris', still among the living and of long survival thereafter.

The other patrician may be identified as son or nephew to the consul of 38. He is otherwise on record only as a *monetalis*.[66] About Gracchus, double testimony. He acquired fame as an author of tragedies.[67] Further, he carries the label 'sollers ingenio et prave facundus'.[68] It is borne out (if that is the word) by allegations that became current. Gracchus was a 'pervicax adulter', guilty long past with Julia when she was the spouse of Agrippa; and he composed the letter which Julia sent to her father, charged with complaints about Claudius Nero. Rational surmise will intervene and add something. In Gracchus is discerned a nobleman whose ambition and talents failed to earn recognition through a consulship.

Misconduct in a wilful princess (her husband far removed and of no account now) might have been condoned for reasons of state. Yet the Princeps was emboldened or compelled to confront a public scandal in the dynasty. Hence a valid suspicion. Something worse had to be covered up. Moral transgressions either disguise or aggravate a political offence.

That Julia with 'virilis audacia' was ready to assassinate her parent might be dismissed as a scandalous and trivial notion. He alleged it in public affirmation.[69] Treason wears various faces or masks. No monarch in

[64] In Dio's text, breaking off in the sentence (but continued by Xiphilinus), Iullus ὡς καὶ ἐπὶ τῇ μοναρχίᾳ τοῦτο πράξας ἀπέθανε μετ' ἄλλων τινῶν ἐπιφανῶν ἀνδρῶν (LV. 10. 16). No other names of the guilty. They are supplied by Velleius. [65] Velleius II. 100.5.

[66] *PIR*[2] C 985, cf. 982. For a new stemma of these Claudii (in part conjectural) see T. P. Wiseman, *HSCP* LXXIV (1970), 220.

[67] i.e. identical (nothing forbids) with the Gracchus of *Ex P.* IV.16.31. Otherwise only on record with two tragedies quoted by Priscian (cf. *PIR*[2] G 196). [68] *Ann.* I.56.3.

[69] Pliny, *NH* VII. 149. Believed by some, including J. Carcopino, *Passion et politique chez les Césars* (1958), 141.

the high season of his glory and success will view with equanimity plans or projects that concern his own supersession.

So far on brief statement the crisis of 2 BC.[70] Caesar Augustus acted in sudden anger, so it is reported, and he came to repent of it: the mishap would not have occurred if only Agrippa and Maecenas had lived. Thus Seneca, not without proper scepticism about monarchs and about ministers of state.[71]

The Princeps might have listened to advice from the subtle Sallustius Crispus. And there was a more potent influence, his consort Livia Drusilla, whose role in these transactions might tempt speculation or fiction but evades all estimate.

[70] The contrary thesis (morality, not politics) solicits recent advocates. Thus W. K. Lacey, *Antichthon* XIV (1980), 127 ff.; A. Ferrill in *Studies in Latin Literature and Roman History* II (ed. C. Deroux, 1980), 332 ff. And G. Williams was quite positive, *Change and Decline* (1978), 69. No question of sudden scandal. Indeed, the Princeps 'deliberately planned for his consulship the clean-up'.

[71] Seneca, *De ben.* VI.32.4: 'non est quod existimemus Agrippam et Maecenatem solitos illi vera dicere. qui si vixissent, inter dissimulantes fuissent.'

VII

Stability Restored

Ruler and government withstood the shock. No repercussion on provinces and armies, and foreign affairs behaved to perfection. On his sixty-third birthday the Princeps wrote a genial letter to Gaius, confident for his own part and happy that the young Caesars were responding to the duties of their eminent station.[1]

With Parthia careful negotiations were in course. The new king, recent on the throne after murdering his father, proved accommodating. In the spring of the next year he consented to meet the Roman prince on the Euphrates. The results were satisfactory and predictable.

'Atrox fortuna' now took a hand in the game. In August the younger brother, on his way to the army in Spain, died suddenly at Massilia. Gaius stayed on in the eastern lands. When laying siege to a small fort in Armenia he suffered a wound that refused to heal. The prince conceived a distaste for active employment of any sort, and wrote to the Princeps to that effect. Resigning his command, he took ship for Italy, and on February 21 of the year 4 passed away at a harbour town in Lycia.

Caesar Augustus saw his designs for Rome and for the dynasty abruptly shattered. For himself, although bodily health, once so precarious, had been adequate for a long time, he could not count upon five or ten years of duration. Next in the family circle stood Germanicus, the son of Drusus, whom the Princeps might with no delay marry to Agrippina, the younger of his two granddaughters. Julia, the elder, had been consigned to Aemilius Paullus about seven years previously.[2]

Germanicus was eighteen.[3] The recent disasters did not encourage hopes set on youthful Caesars. Yet a device had to be found for fitting Germanicus into the line of succession. Recourse to a reconciliation with Claudius Nero was embarrassing—and that man might refuse, unless persuaded that the needs of empire made the call of duty prevail over personal honour and resentment.

[1] Quoted in full in Gellius XV.7.3.

[2] Agrippina's birth falls at some time between 16 and 13 BC. Therefore, on any count, she could have been equipped with a husband before AD 4. That is of some significance. Julia (born in either 19 or 18) married L. Aemilius Paullus (cos. AD 1) c. 4: their grandson was born in AD 14 (Pliny, NH VII.58).

[3] Born in 15 BC, his cousin Drusus in 14. See the cogent arguments of G. V. Sumner, Latomus XXVI (1967), 413 ff. The birth of Germanicus' sister Livia Julia can be assigned to 14.

The wars in the North demanded a regent 'maturum annis, spectatum bello'.[4] In this season earnest or frivolous commentators on high policy and inner counsels may have been moved to speculate about the chances of eminent consulars. Ahenobarbus, who had just passed the age of fifty, was the husband of the elder Antonia and a 'vir triumphalis'. His personality, however, attracted enmities—and distrust or even dislike from the Princeps. Very different was Fabius Maximus, elegant, insinuating, deep in the confidence of the ruler—and married to Marcia, a cousin.

On June 26 Caesar Augustus announced his decision. He took in adoption Claudius Nero who, permitted to return to Rome two years previously, had been living since then in total seclusion, with no voice in public affairs.[5] Though the new Caesar had a son, Augustus had constrained him to adopt his nephew Germanicus, the son of Drusus— Drusus the much beloved, the husband of Antonia, and accorded favour on several counts at the expense of his brother. Moreover, to Germanicus he now assigned for wife his granddaughter, Agrippina.[6] As events soon showed, Germanicus was given marked preference over his cousin (and now brother), Drusus the son of Tiberius Caesar, although the elder by one year only.[7]

That did not complete the dynastic dispositions. Augustus also adopted the surviving son of Agrippa and Julia. Not, however, in the design of any rapid advancement. Despite his age (born in 12 BC) Agrippa Postumus did not put on the *toga virilis* until the next year.[8] And no trace of a remission in the future career of honours, which Germanicus received, his senior by three years. Before long Postumus began to show defects of temperament and eccentric behaviour, so it was alleged. He thus became an embarrassment. If Postumus seemed stupid and recalcitrant, young Claudius, the brother of Germanicus Caesar, was harmless but devoid of the social graces and held unfit for public life.

Absent from power and influence for nine years, the head of the Claudian house was intent, as earliest preoccupation, to build up his party again. The father can have had few kinsmen apart from the Volusii; and on the mother's side the nearest had been Libo Drusus, her stepbrother.[9] Some of

---

[4] The phrase of Tacitus, *Ann.* I.4.3.

[5] Suetonius, *Tib.* 15.1: 'statim e Carinis ac Pompeiana domo Esquilias in hortos Maecenatianos transmigravit totumque se ad quietem contulit.'

[6] There is no cause for delaying the marriage until the next year, as in *PIR*[2] J 221: 'anno ut videtur 5'. Nero, the eldest son, assumed the *toga virilis* and took a wife in 20 (*Ann.* III.29).

[7] No function for Drusus in any of the northern campaigns—and three years separate their consulships (12 and 15). His marriage to Livia Julia (the widow of C. Caesar) should be put in AD 4.

[8] Agrippa Postumus will occur in Ch. VIII and Ch. IX.

[9] Livia's father had been a Claudius Pulcher by birth. But nothing can be done with Livia C.f. Pulchra (*AE* 1969/70, 118: Formiae), or for that matter with Livia C.f. Livilla (*CIL* XIV.3796: Tibur). And there is no link with Livia L.f. Ocellina (*PIR*[2] L 305), the second wife of C. Sulpicius Galba (*suff.* 5 BC).

the personal following Tiberius acquired went back to the Spanish campaigns, coeval *tribuni laticlavii* in six or seven legions.[10] In the expedition to Armenia men of letters formed a congenial company.[11]

In Illyricum and on the Rhine the general had legates and a staff. With proconsular *imperium* for the last four campaigns, the assignment of a quaestor was appropriate, whom tradition assumed bound by a close tie to his proconsul. No quaestor or legate of Claudius Nero happens to be known. Some of them no doubt found a place in the long roll of subsequent consuls.

Eager scrutiny goes to the *Fasti*. The aristocratic sequence that ends with Cn. Piso has been discussed, also the consuls of 6, and L. Sulla, elected in the summer of that year. The notion is engaging, to search for consequences that issued from the secession and prolonged absence of Claudius Nero.

On curt statement, in the nine years from 5 BC to AD 4 (excluding L. Sulla), thirty-one consuls held office. Twenty-one are *nobiles* (eight of them patricians), with ten names new to the *Fasti*.

Comparison with other periods runs against a number of impediments.

(1) The large mass of names, with *suffecti*, sudden in the first year, now becoming normal. Hence some persons of no distinction, or retarded.

(2) The varying incidence of age groups and generations (as in the previous two decades).

(3) Of *nobiles*, ten are sons of Triumviral or early Augustan consuls, some benefiting from military excellence in the parent. First, C. Calvisius Sabinus (*cos.* 4), then P. Vinicius (AD 2), P. Silius (*suff.* 3), C. Sentius Saturninus (*cos.* 4), Cn. Sentius Saturninus (*suff.* 4).

(4) *Novi homines.* Like their predecessors, a number came from families already senatorial. Thus M. Plautius Silvanus (*cos.* 2 BC) and A. Plautius (*suff.* 1), while L. Aelius Lamia (*cos.* AD 3) had a praetorian father, not without merit and social distinction.

In passing, three features call for brief remark. First, although abating, the revival of the patriciate continues, with two Sulpicii (*suffecti* in 5 and 4); and a second Quinctius arrives, namely Valerianus (*suff.* AD 2). The other patricians are Messallinus (*cos.* 3 BC) and three Lentuli. The Aemilii now return with L. Paullus (*cos.* AD 1), the son of Paullus the Censor.

Second, the dearth of names from families in the old plebeian *nobilitas*. Many had now vanished for ever. In contrast to eight patricians, only three figure on this list, viz. L. Piso (*cos.* 1 BC), M. Servilius (AD 3), Sex. Aelius Catus (4). Servilius is noteworthy. His ancestry showed no consul

---

[10] Thus Cn. Piso (deduced from *Ann.* III.16.4). Perhaps also the *novus homo* A. Caecina Severus (*suff.* 1 BC), who in 15 had reached his 'quadragesimum stipendium' (*Ann.* I.64.4).

[11] Horace, *Epp.* I.3; 8 f.: no persons of name or rank, see further Ch. XXV.

since 202 BC.[12] He thus resembles a decayed patrician, but he managed better than the two Sulpicii by becoming *consul ordinarius*. Some had been moved to disparage the claims to nobility of these Servilii.[13]

Third, new names in the eponymate: Passienus Rufus, Plautius Silvanus, Aelius Lamia.

It is a variegated collection, and it fails to respond to the enquiry. For a plain reason, valid both before and after. Whatever the allegiance or deserts of an aristocrat, Caesar cannot deny him his birthright; and privilege extends to take in the new nobility.

During these nine years friends of Claudius Nero encountered disappointment and setback, could it be known. Cn. Piso, his firm ally may, or may not, have been able to extort from Caesar a rapid consulship for his brother Lucius (styled 'the Augur'). Both were notoriously difficult characters. Further, the excellent Volusius Saturninus, the son of Tiberius' cousin, reached the *fasces* in AD 3, when aged about forty, and then had to yield precedence as *suffectus* to Aelius Lamia and M. Servilius.[14]

The total of thirty-one consuls offers less than some might expect. A good dozen are mere names. Not only certain of the new men. That holds for nobles and patricians such as Galus Sulpicius (*suff.* 4), or the two *suffecti* of AD 2: P. Lentulus Scipio and T. Quinctius Valerianus.[15] As evident on so many other counts, this is an obscure decade.

In the summer of AD 4 a pair of patricians was elected: Volesus Messalla, the son of Potitus, and Cinna Magnus. These consuls gave their names to a law that prescribed a change in electoral procedure, namely a kind of pre-selection of candidates at the Comitia, entrusted to ten *centuriae* comprising senators and knights voting together.

Revealed by the chance find of a bronze tablet, the *Lex Valeria Cornelia* aroused abundant discussion, and unusual value was generally assigned.[16] What it signified for the understanding of Roman political life was not so clear. On an extreme view the measure rendered easier the election of *novi homines*. Such was the design of Caesar Augustus.[17]

The presuppositions are peculiar, namely wide freedom of choice permitted previously to the electors and fewer *novi homines* then elected than the ruler desired. Neither is borne out by the known facts. Whatever the system, a new man needs either Caesar or aristocratic patronage.[18]

---

[12] For these Servilii see *Hermes* XCII (1964), 408 ff. = *Ten Studies in Tacitus* (1970), 91 f. It is there assumed that M. Servilius married a Nonia. That he was himself a Nonius by birth is argued by H. Aigner, *Historia* XXI (1972) , 507 f. The *cognomen* 'Nonianus' was borne by his son (*cos.* 35), orator and historian. [13] Cicero, *De leg. agr.* II.19.

[14] Volusius was ninety-three when he died in 56 (*Ann.* XIII.30.2).

[15] Valerianus, however, was one of the *Arvales*: attested in 14 (*ILS* 5026).

[16] For the text of the *Tabula Hebana* see Ehrenberg and Jones, *Select Documents*[2] (1955), 94a.

[17] A. H. M. Jones, *JRS* XLV (1955). 9 ff. = *Studies in Roman Government and Law* (1960), 27 ff.

[18] For pertinent criticism, P. A. Brunt, *JRS* LI (1961), 71 ff.

On a sober estimate, the change had a social purpose.[19] As one more privilege for the upper class, it segregated them from plebeian voters. In short, 'concordia ordinum'. Should curiosity about the authorship of the new device extend to Ti. Caesar or to the agency of the loyal jurist Ateius Capito (consul suffect in this year), it can be quelled. By ordaining the ten *centuriae* 'quae C. et L. Caesar(um) adpellantur' the Princeps kept on show the memory of the sons he had lost.[20]

The consuls holding office in the ten years 5 to 14 are much more remunerative than those of the preceding nine. By a coincidence seldom vouchsafed to enumeration, they add up to thirty-one.[21] They further split in the identical fashion, twenty-one being *nobiles* old or recent. As follows:

A Patricians	L. Cassius Longinus (*suff.* 11)
L. Valerius Messalla Volesus (5)	Sex. Pompeius (14)
Cn. Cornelius Cinna Magnus (5)	
M. Aemilius Lepidus (6)	
M. Furius Camillus (8)	C Sons or grandsons of new
Q. Sulpicius Camerinus (9)	consuls
P. Cornelius Dolabella (10)	L. Arruntius (6)
Ser. Cornelius Lentulus Maluginensis	L. Nonius Asprenas (*suff.* 6)
(*suff.* 10)	A. Licinius Nerva Silianus (7)
M.' Aemilius Lepidus (11)	Sex. Nonius Quinctilianus (8)
	T. Statilius Taurus (11)
	C. Fonteius Capito (12)
B Plebeian *Nobilitas*	C. Silius P. f. A. Caecina Largus (13)[22]
Q. Caecilius Metellus Creticus Silanus (7)	L. Munatius Plancus (13)
C. Junius Silanus (10)	Sex. Appuleius (14)

It will be expedient to confine comment to the first twelve names. Of the patricians five lack a consular parent, and two of those five any verifiable ancestor for centuries, namely Furius Camillus and Sulpicius Camerinus. The line of the heroic Camillus soon lapsed from the *Fasti*. Which did not impede the proliferation of legend, or rather fable, recently

[19] P. A. Brunt, o.c. 78. For another matter, namely the conduct of elections in this period, see now A. J. Holladay, *Latomus* XXXVII (1978), 874 ff.

[20] The princes retain prominence on the coinage for a number of years, cf. C. H. V. Sutherland, *Coinage in Roman Imperial Policy* (1951), 73 ff. By contrast, no advertisement of the adoption of Ti. Caesar—and no coins with his name until AD 10.

[21] Two *suffecti* have been canvassed for the year 13, cf. A. Degrassi, *Epigraphica* VIII (1946), 34 ff.; *I fasti consolari* (1952), 5. First, Favonius, proconsul of Asia (*ILS* 9483). He should be identical with a consul of the previous decade: for a conjecture, below, n. 39.

Second, a son of M. Lollius: regarded as probable by P. A. Brunt, o.c. 81. For reasons against, below, p. 177.

Further, trouble has been caused by the nomenclature of the *ordinarius*, C. Silius P.f. A. Caecina Largus. The second member has been held a *suffectus*. Thus *JRS* LVI (1966), 55 ff., following A. E. and J. Gordon. However, a neglected inscription discloses 'L. Planco C. Caec. cos.' (*AE* 1966, 16), cf. S. Panciera, *Bull. Comm.* LXXIX (1963/4), 94 ff. No *suffecti*, he concludes, in the year 13.

[22] One person not two, cf. the preceding note. A problem subsists. If C. Silius (third son of P. Silius Nerva) was adopted by a Caecina Largus, the two pieces of nomenclature are in the wrong order. Otherwise, he has annexed the name of the maternal grandfather. For discussion, see *Epigrafia e Ordine Senatorio* I (1982), 408 ff.

rendered familiar and even exciting to contemporaries who saw Camillus paraded as the second Founder of Rome, linking Romulus to Caesar Augustus.[23] As concerns Camerinus, a close parallel: no consul since 345 BC. After Furius Camillus no further patrician *gentes* were rediscovered by the government.[24]

P. Dolabella is a grandson of the consul of 44. The father when a young man was in the company of Caesar's heir at Alexandria, entrusted with delicate negotiations with the Queen of Egypt.[25] The son (it is presumed) of a certain Fabia, he acquired for bride a sister of Quinctilius Varus.

By the archaic *cognomen*, Lentulus Maluginensis asserted a remote Scipionic ancestry.[26] Father and grandfather baffle identity. The father of Manius Lepidus was a son of the Triumvir, existing only as a necessary link in pedigree. For attested parentage or extraction those five thus stand in marked contrast to the other three: Messalla Volesus, Cinna Magnus, Marcus Lepidus.

Missing fathers, the same feature is manifest in the four consuls who represent the plebeian *nobilitas*.

(1) Creticus Silanus, son of a Q. Metellus. Two Metelli fought on opposing sides at the Battle of Actium. The son rescued the father.[27] That son has been discovered on a fragmentary inscription recording a proconsul of Sardinia.[28] Doubt is legitimate. To govern Sardinia is no compliment to any nobleman.

The consul of 7 is a Junius Silanus (not identifiable) taken in adoption by Q. Metellus M. f., a grandson of Creticus (*cos.* 69 BC).[29] The proud name adorns the *Fasti* for the last time.

(2) C. Silanus. The homonymous father is only a name. The nomenclature of descendants proves that he married an Appia Claudia.[30] A fact of prime importance.

(3) L. Cassius Longinus. He belonged to the family of the Liberator, but not as a lineal descendant. On the day of March 15, C. Cassius proposed to be present at the ceremony when his son put on the *toga virilis*.[31] That son disappears. The grandfather of the consul is L. Cassius (*tr. pl.* 44), killed at Philippi: cousin to C. Cassius.[32]

---

[23] Livy V.49.7: 'Romulus ac parens patriae conditorque alter urbis'.
[24] To recapitulate their renascence. Between 28 BC and AD 14, a total of twenty-eight patrician consuls (only one of them before 18). By *gentes* they stand as Cornelii (10), Aemilii (4), Valerii (3), Sulpicii (3), Claudii (2), Fabii (2), Quinctii (2), Quinctilii (1), Furii (1).
[25] Plutarch, *Antonius* 84.
[26] below, p. 252.
[27] Appian, *BC* IV.42.173.
[28] *CIL* X. 7581, cf. *PIR²* C 62.
[29] *PIR²* C 64.
[30] Ch. XIV.
[31] Plutarch, *Brutus* 14.
[32] Appian, *BC* IV.135.571. Rather than father as suggested ('fortasse') in *PIR²* C 502.

(4) Sex. Pompeius Sex. f. Given the space of years that separate him from the consul of 35 BC, a homonym is postulated in between.[33]

A generation missing the *fasces* (or even any record) in families of social eminence permits a variety of explanations.[34] First, disease and epidemics. Pestilence in 23/2 and also in 12 will be suitably recalled. Second, lack of money or talent, of friends or patronage. And some, from principle or resentment, refused to compete or collaborate. Third, certain groups (Republican and Pompeian) failed to win favour with the ruler and were kept at a distance.

As in the last epoch of the Free State, there subsisted a fairly large company of submerged *nobiles*, coming up on sporadic mention or never at all, and in political prospects falling far beneath numerous senators of equestrian extraction.

To separate and arrange consuls by antithetic categories is an imperfect procedure and often deceptive. Much depends on the periods chosen for examination or comparison.[35]

It has been supposed, for example, that during the final decade Caesar Augustus carefully promoted *novi homines*, whereas the aristocratic Tiberius Caesar was unable to satisfy his predilections, being absent with the armies.[36] That notion ignored, among other things, his visits to the capital, the use of letters and of confidential envoys.

The postulate is innocuous that Ti. Caesar had a powerful voice in the selection of consuls. Categories did not matter, but persons and personal allegiance, notably to one who set such value on 'amicitia' and 'fides'. The party that aggregates around a nobleman comprises adherents of merit as well as birth.[37]

The father Ti. Nero (*pr.* 42) fought against Caesar's heir in the War of Perusia, tried to enlist slaves for the cause of the Republic, and made his escape to Sicily. Then, not accorded proper honour by Sextus Pompeius, he joined Marcus Antonius and, after sundry vicissitudes, returned to

---

[33] Not however Sex. Pompeius Cn.f., adduced as a *suffectus* of 5 BC by R. Hanslik in *RE* XXI.2265 (cf. 2060, a double entry). Dessau's warning (*PIR*[1] P 449) was overlooked.

[34] Apart from various descendants of Sulla and Pompeius (Ch. XIX), additional sporadic instances may be cited. Thus Claudius Marcellus (*PIR*[2] C 927), son of Aeserninus and son-in-law to Pollio; Barbatus (Suetonius, *Divus Claud.* 26.2), the son of Messalla Appianus; two sons of Piso the Pontifex (discussed in Ch. XXVI).

Likewise the fathers of C. Silanus and M. Silanus, the consuls of 10 and 19 (*PIR*[2] J 824; 831), and the father of the enigmatic M. Acilius Memmius Glabrio, who is attested as a senator early in the reign of Tiberius (*ILS* 5893).

[35] The consuls of the late Augustan epoch have been examined by P. A. Brunt, *JRS* LI (1961), 80 f.; A. Ferrill, *Historia* XX (1971), 718 ff. While classifying, both were alert to hazards of interpretation.

[36] F. B. Marsh, *The Reign of Tiberius* (1931), 43 f., 67.

[37] As firmly stated in *Rom. Rev.* (1939), 434.

Rome in 39, bringing with him Livia Drusilla and an infant son. The 'pietas' of that son found expression in loyalty to defeated causes.

Among the consuls of the decade, a thought might go to Cinna Magnus, to the son by adoption of the last Metellus, to the grandson of the Triumvir Lepidus, to Cassius Longinus. Could they be shown to reach the *fasces* after retardation, that would help. Cinna Magnus was certainly far beyond the normal age (his life spared when a boy, after Actium). His consulship produced the fable of the conspirator rewarded on conversion from folly.[38]

Tiberius acknowledged a close attachment to Messalla Corvinus, continuing in signal favour towards the sons. It is not clear that it extended to Messalla Volesus. Tiberius discerned ever more clearly the failings of the *nobilitas* now brought back to wealth, prestige, and public honour. He disliked their luxury and conceit, neglect of 'bonae artes', subservience to power.

To use and promote *novi homines* was good Claudian tradition. They supplied what was often lacking in their social superiors, namely integrity and competence. And above all, loyalty. Lucilius Longus, the only senator to share the seven years of exile at Rhodes, received the consulship (*suff.* 7), and, with no commemoration of any public services, a state funeral.[39] That express and revealing tribute was accorded to Sulpicius Quirinius, who had maintained allegiance and respect during the Rhodian years.[40]

Ten new names appear on the *Fasti* of the decade. Several, one might assume, had been legates during the campaigns in Illyricum and Germany.[41] They now came into the seniority requisite in those without consular parentage (that is, not below forty).[42] Five of the ten are found in charge of consular armies at some time in the sequel.[43]

The abrupt turn taken by dynastic politics in the summer of 4 had repercussion on those commands. Committed beyond recall to a partner in the power (and before long a successor), the ruler would not run the risk of consigning legions to a rival or enemy of Ti. Caesar. The new appointments made either now or in the course of the next year or two carry a patient significance. They reveal adherents, some accruing

---

[38] Seneca, *De clem.* I. 9; Dio LV. 14 ff.

[39] *Ann.* IV.15.1. For a conjecture, namely identity with Favonius, proconsul of Asia (*ILS* 9483), see *ZPE* 53 (1983), 198 ff.

[40] *Ann.* III.48.

[41] Service by two younger men, viz. C. Pomponius Graecinus (*suff.* 16) and C. Vibius Rufinus (*suff.* 21 or 22) is indicated in Ovid, *Ex Ponto* I.6.1, cf. 10; III. 4.5, cf. 64). For identity and consulship of Rufinus see *ZPE* 43 (1981), 365 ff. = *RP* III (1984), 1423 ff.

[42] The standard age of about forty-two for *novi homines* emerges without effort from facts concerning Caecina Severus (*suff.* 1 BC). That is, reckoned from either service as a tribune (*Ann.* I.64.4) or from the quaestorship (III.33.1). Facts not exploited by recent commentators.

[43] viz. C. Vibius Postumus (*suff.* 5), L. Apronius (8), C. Poppaeus Sabinus (*cos.* 9), Q. Junius Blaesus (*suff.* 10), C. Visellius Varro (12).

recently, others to be presumed of long date, despite any dearth in precise documentation.

To the Rhine, in the place of his coeval M. Vinicius, the veteran Sentius Saturninus went at once.[44] Messallinus had Illyricum, attested two years later, as is the *novus homo* Caecina Severus (*suff.* 1 BC) in charge of Moesia (i.e. the Balkan army).[45] That command, now comprising three legions, was very important.[46] After the interval of fifteen years a renewed Thracian revolt might be feared. In Syria Volusius Saturninus is on attestation in 4/5.[47] On him followed Sulpicius Quirinius in 6.[48] As for Tarraconensis (which still kept a garrison of four legions), no legate is on record after Fabius Maximus until Cn. Piso (in 9/10).[49] For Piso nothing precludes a fairly long tenure.

It is no deception to carry the theme forward to the end of the decade and register the army commanders, now seven, in August of the year 14.[50] Four are *nobiles*, viz. C. Silius (Germania Superior), P. Dolabella (Dalmatia), Creticus Silanus (Syria), M. Lepidus (Tarraconensis). The others are Caecina Severus (Germania Inferior), Junius Blaesus (Pannonia), Poppaeus Sabinus (Moesia).

C. Silius (*cos.* 13) belonged to the new nobility, the third son of P. Silius Nerva (*cos.* 20 BC).[51] With Caecina Severus (*suff.* 1 BC) the great *gens* of Etruscan Volaterrae makes its first appearance among consuls. Poppaeus Sabinus (*cos.* 9) would be on subsequent mention, likewise Junius Blaesus (*suff.* 10), the maternal uncle of Aelius Seianus. For none of those four can any previous military occupations be discovered.

Of the seven army commanders all but Caecina Severus came to the consulate in the period 5–14. A brief epilogue (and negative testimony) will convey the value they possessed for Ti. Caesar. During the quinquennium from 15 to 19 seventeen consuls held office. Of them no fewer than ten are *novi homines*, a fact which might indicate an increasing favour extended to that class.[52] However, in that total of seventeen only one got a consular command from Ti. Caesar, and that not until fifteen years elapsed.[53] Whatever their claims of birth, merit, or allegiance, the ruler stood by his confidence in consuls of the previous decade.

So far an attempt, cursory and imperfect, to define and illustrate a large

---

[44] As Velleius says, 'qui iam legatus patris eius in Germania fuerat' (II.105.1). That justifies the conjecture of a previous command: between 6 and 1 BC., cf. above, p. 85. The notion was admitted in *Rom. Rev.* 401; 435.   [45] Dio LV.29.1 ff.

[46] For the distribution of the twenty-eight legions in AD 6 see *JRS* XXIII (1933), 25 ff.

[47] Attested only by coins, cf. *PIR*[1] V 660.

[48] Ch. XXIV.   [49] Ch. XXVIII and Ch. XXVI.   [50] For the detail, *Rom. Rev.* 437 f.

[51] The eldest, P. Silius, praetorian legate in Moesia (Velleius II. 101.3), is not heard of subsequent to his consulship (*suff.* 3), and the second died not long after his own in 7 (II.116.4).

[52] For analysis see *Historia* XXX (1981), 189 ff. = *RP* III (1984), 1350 ff.

[53] viz. L. Pomponius Flaccus (*cos.* 17), acceding to Syria when Aelius Lamia in 32 vacated his absentee tenure (*Ann.* VI.27.1 f.).

theme. Some confirmation can be drawn from the other sources. Velleius furnishes infallible testimony when he brings on persons either liked or disliked by Tiberius Caesar. Finally, his personal following took its origin in the camps, it was augmented and fortified by warfare. Of which there was to be more than they expected.

Soon after the adoption, and duly invested with proconsular *imperium*, Tiberius Caesar went with speed to the Rhine. It was expedient to win back the troops, who had not seen their general for a whole decade. His desires fell in with the convenience of the Princeps—and rendered more tolerable a recent and rapid reunion perhaps not infused with much cordiality.[54]

It was desirable to present the new partner as the sole and necessary 'custos vindexque imperii'. Three years previously Ahenobarbus, after his command in Illyricum, had run into trouble when intervening in the affairs of the Cherusci, but did not suffer a defeat in the field or engage on any further action.[55] His successor M. Vinicius fought a war which on one interpretation was crowned with incomplete success.[56] The evidence for a grave emergency fails to convince.

Tiberius invaded Germany, and in the next year a powerful campaign took the Roman arms to the river Elbe. If Germany could be subjugated and held, the time had come to achieve the ambitious design which explained and justified that conquest, begun fifteen years previously. Namely, to secure a shorter route of communication between Danube and Elbe. The design entailed Bohemia, the kingdom of Maroboduus. Launched in 6, the invasion was within a few days of success when the Pannonians and Dalmatians rose in rebellion.

The return of Tiberius to power and primacy announced a new era: stability and concord at home, to be completed with warfare and glory abroad. Measured forecast and pious hopes were quickly dashed.[57] Evil portents arrived in the next year, with great earthquakes, a solar eclipse, a flooding of the Tiber.[58] Then famine, which continued for three years, not without a pestilence. A concatenation of misfortunes ensued.[59] Abroad

---

[54] A few years later, confidence and affection in a letter which Suetonius quotes (*Divus Aug.* 21.4–7): perhaps shown to persons of judgement and influence.   [55] Dio LV. 10a.2.

[56] According to Velleius, 'immensum exarserat bellum. erat id ab eo quibusdam in locis gestum, quibusdam sustentatum feliciter' (II.104.2). To praise both Caesar and the grandfather of his patron, Velleius may be exaggerating the gravity of the emergency. Observe the double technique in reference to seven years of campaigning against Tacfarinas: 'magni etiam terroris bellum Africum'—but 'brevi sepultum est' (II.129.4).

[57] Velleius II.103.5: 'tum refulsit certa spes liberorum parentibus, viris matrimoniorum, dominis patrimonii, omnibus hominibus salutis quietis pacis tranquillitatis.'   [58] Dio LV.22.5 etc.

[59] For the difficulties of the government during these sombre years see T. Wiedemann, *CQ* XXV (1975), 264 ff.

native tribes revolted, the nomads in Africa made incursions, disorders broke out in the cities. With all Illyricum in arms, and the fear of other rebellions, it became difficult to find recruits. Hence extreme expedients and new taxation.

The great war in the North served to divert attention from discomfort and friction in the dynastic circle. The turn of events in the summer of the year 4 was sharp, and it seemed decisive. Some expectations were annulled, others enfeebled or deferred.

Aemilius Paullus (*cos.* AD 1), married to Julia (the elder granddaughter), had been passed over. Hope did not abandon them. Fortune by opportune deaths had been generous to other persons whom they now saw installed in the power.

Tiberius Caesar, at the seat of war, enjoyed robust health, long to defy the doctors and comfort his astrologer. Yet a variety of hazards threatened the survival of Tiberius and of others: battle and the plague, conspiracy or a casual assassin. Germanicus Caesar might perish in the field like his father. He went out to the war in 7, and in the next year he conducted arduous operations against mountain tribes.

Chance and usurpation conferred the supreme power, and the victor had to be aristocratic by name or by descent. If the campaign in Africa against Caesar the Dictator had gone otherwise, the world might have known a ruler with an appellation like 'Imp. Scipio Pius'. Scipiones and Aemilii were in close alliance at the time of the Hannibalic War, and their names thereafter occupy a large portion in Roman annals. The husband of Julia had Scipiones for ancestors.

VIII

The Resplendent Aemilii

In a martial nation defeat can ennoble no less than victory. The memory of Aemilius Paullus who fell at Cannae acquired embellishment. Much of that was due to allies and descendants. The young Scipio who defeated Hannibal married his daughter.[1]

The son of Paullus had no easy path to the *fasces*, which he reached in 182, nine years from the praetorship. Consul for the second time in 168, he won the battle of Pydna and put an end to the Macedonian kingdom. Paullus stood for discipline, harsh and cruel—and perhaps not reluctant to carry out the Senate's instructions which ordained the enslavement of seventy communities in Epirus. Of proved integrity in money matters and frugal in his habits, Paullus for his share of the booty got hold of the royal library, an action that may attest some affection for polite studies.

Through neither of his surviving sons was Paullus able to transmit the Aemilian name.[2] The one became a Fabius, to continue the line of the great Cunctator.[3] The other, adopted by the inconspicuous son of Scipio Africanus, reinforced the fame of his annexed grandfather by the destruction of Carthage.

The Scipionic connection ultimately earned for Aemilius Paullus a biography from Plutarch. Another Aemilius, coeval to a year, suffers obscuration. With his first consulship in 187, M. Lepidus got well ahead, and he later kept the lead, consul again in 175. Meanwhile an opportune death in 180 (there was a pestilence) enabled him to become *pontifex maximus*, and he was elected censor the year after. His success, signalized by a public scene of reconciliation with a bitter enemy, was the product of guile and secret compacts. An oration from a senior statesman proclaimed concord and the abatement of personal feuds for the sake of the common weal.[4]

When consul, Lepidus had not been eager for a military mandate; and, although he fought a campaign in Liguria, no triumph followed. He drove a great road across the new lands in the North. The other memorial to his

---

[1] For the continuing alliances between Aemilii and Scipiones see Münzer, *RA* (1920), *passim*. Familiar facts and dates will be found in *MRR*.

[2] Sons of Papiria, whom he divorced. The second wife (nowhere named) produced the two boys who died in the season of the Macedonian triumph.

[3] viz. Q. Fabius Aemilianus (*cos.* 145).

[4] Livy, XL.46. For the whole setting, Münzer, *RA* 200 ff.

name stood in the Roman Forum, the Basilica constructed during his censorship.

Dying in 152, Lepidus concluded an eminent station in the 'res publica'.[5] He had been *pontifex maximus* and *princeps senatus* for close on three decades. In that space of time, sacerdotal law was abating its rigour, ancient rituals and ceremonies lapsed. Aemilianus and his friends were not the only advocates of enlightenment.[6] Nor did the actions of popular tribunes contribute to the neglect of religious observances. The record is partial and imperfect. In his long tenure Lepidus the *pontifex maximus* might have been an agent of unobtrusive change or reform.

Only one of his sons became consul: M. Lepidus Porcina (*cos.* 137), who incurred a severe defeat in Spain and was recalled. He left orations, the earliest at Rome (so it is averred) to exhibit grace and elegance. That is, the 'levitas Graecorum' and an 'artifex stilus'.[7]

Between the epoch of Scipio Aemilianus and the dictatorship of Sulla sundry aristocratic houses are absent from the consular *Fasti*. Various reasons may be sought, among them the Gracchan sedition, the predominance of the Metelli, foreign wars and civil strife, the murderous Bellum Italicum. After Porcina a dearth of consular Lepidi obtains for fifty years, apart from M. Lepidus (*cos.* 126), who is only a name and a date. Two brothers of Porcina, viz. Quintus and Mamercus, belong to genealogy; and, from another branch (distant) the parent of Manius Lepidus, the consul of 66, is beyond recovery.[8]

The consul of 78, M. Lepidus Q. f., made a bid to bring the Aemilii back to a primacy more than traditional through methods that did nothing to recall his grandfather.[9] Like others who ended as adherents of Sulla when he vindicated 'dignitas' and the 'causa nobilium', he accrued from the other party.[10]

When consul, Lepidus came out with an attack on the ordinances of the Dictator, in the name of liberty, the Roman plebs, the dispossessed. He stands self-convicted in the oration composed by the historian Sallust, violent, vaunting, and fraudulent.[11] Nor did appeal to the 'bene facta gentis Aemiliae' avail when in the next year he passed to open insurgency.

[5] The injunction about his obsequies was remembered: 'non imaginum specie, non sumptibus nobilitari magnorum virorum funera solere' (Livy, *Per.* XLVIII).

[6] Posterity magnified the 'Scipionic Circle' in more ways than one. Cf. H. Strasburger, *Hermes* XCIV (1966), 60 ff. He speaks of 'poetische Fiktionen Ciceros' (ib. 61).

[7] Cicero, *Brutus* 95 f.

[8] That consul is 'M'.f.' (*Inscr. de Délos* 1659). In a long life he made little impact. In passing one should not omit Mam. Lepidus Livianus (*cos.* 77), by birth brother to Livius Drusus (*tr.pl.* 91). On whom, see the useful paper of G. V. Sumner, *JRS* LIV (1964), 41 ff.

[9] The relationship is affirmed by Cicero, *Phil.* XIII.15.

[10] On which theme, E. Badian, *JRS* LII (1962), 52 ff. = *Studies in Greek and Roman History* (1964), 206 ff.   [11] Sallust, *Hist.* I.77.

The identity of his wife has attracted interest—and premature certitudes.[12] A clue offers in the ancient and recurring affinity between Aemilii and Cornelii. To the faction of Marius and Cinna belongs L. Scipio Asiagenus (*cos.* 83), descended from the brother of Africanus, with no consul since. In the insurrection of Lepidus a certain 'Scipio Lepidi filius' met his end.[13] The formulation declares a son given in adoption to a Scipio. Another son may be an ephemeral Regillus, likewise on solitary attestation.[14] Those surviving are Lucius and Marcus. To the elder the consul assigned 'Paullus' for *cognomen* by a bold and urbane usurpation that none would bother to confute.

For splendour and success the sons of Lepidus were outshone by a coeval Scipio, in direct descent from Nasica (*cos.* 191), the cousin of Africanus. His adoption through the testament of Metellus Pius reinforced more recent alliances.

The fifties saw sharp competition in the parade of ancestors and pedigree. While Metellus Scipio set up statues on the Capitol, L. Paullus went in for an elaborate repair and embellishment of the Basilica Aemilia.[15] Like others he sought loan or subsidy from the proconsul of Gaul—after securing election as his enemy. A large sum is named.[16] Hence ambiguous behaviour in 50. In December he joined his colleague C. Marcellus who went to Campania and conferred a military mandate on Pompeius Magnus. That was illicit and provocative.[17]

However, when the war broke out Paullus declined to follow Magnus and the Republic. No action of his in the sequel, and no public attitudes until April of 43, when (a fact of some significance) the Senate charged him with an embassy to negotiate with Sextus Pompeius. Proscribed in November by the Triumvirs, he went away unharmed and ended his days at a city on the Ionian shore.[18]

His brother Marcus, barely heard of before his praetorship in 49, emerged as a pronounced Caesarian. Governing Hispania Citerior, he took the title of 'imperator'. So far as known, the achievement was diplomatic rather than military. After celebrating a triumph in 47 he acceded to the *fasces* the next year.

---

[12] An Appuleia was married to a M. Lepidus (Pliny, *NH* VII.122). Hence the notion (encouraged by Münzer, *RA* 308) that she was a daughter of L. Appuleius Saturninus (*tr. pl.* 103). Widely accepted. For reasons against the identities, below, p. 126.

[13] Orosius V.22.17.

[14] *Ad Att.* XII.42.2.

[15] *Ad Att.* IV.16.8 (in 55).

[16] Plutarch, *Caesar* 29, cf. Appian, *BC* II.26.103.

[17] For this episode, K. Rauflaub, *Dignitatis Contentio* (1974), 33 ff.

[18] Appian, *BC* IV.37.155. His wife is not known. One son only (*suff.* 34). Paullus has recently been described as 'a man motivated chiefly by devotion to the ideal of an aristocratic Republic' (R. D. Weigel, *Latomus* XXXVIII (1979), 637).

The Ides of March found Lepidus in a position of singular and strategic advantage. Deputy to the Dictator as *magister equitum* and about to depart for his provincial command (Hispania Citerior combined with Narbonensis), Lepidus had troops in the vicinity of Rome and the will to use them at need. He acted in full concert with the consul Antonius. Furthermore, family connections promised both now and later a role of mediation between the parties, his wife being a sister of Marcus Brutus. Another Junia was married to C. Cassius, the third to Servilius Isauricus (*cos.* 48), prominent among the Caesarians, though not perhaps averse to a shift in allegiance.

One result of Lepidus' talents soon became visible. It was convenient for Antonius to install him as *pontifex maximus*, through a procedure to be denounced as irregular.[19]

Another result was manifested in the autumn of the year. Lepidus induced Sextus Pompeius to abandon hostilities and come to terms. Antonius caused the Senate to pass an honorific decree. More followed when the enemies of Antonius gained control at Rome.[20] On January 3 the Senate on the motion of Cicero voted a gilded equestrian statue. Public gratitude was enjoined 'quod silentio bellum civile confecerat'.[21] Lepidus, it also emerges, had taken the title of 'imperator'—and a triumph was decreed.[22]

In the summer of the year the generals in the western provinces deserted the dubious cause of the Republic (ostensibly renascent through help of the army raised by the young adventurer, the heir of Caesar). Lepidus happens to publish their plea, less practised though he might be in eloquence and persuasion than his allies in dissidence, Asinius Pollio and Munatius Plancus. His despatch to the Senate is extant.[23] Personal feuds, he urged, should be abated for the Commonwealth—and the soldiers put pressure on him, refusing to shed the blood of citizens.

When the dictatorship returned as the compact of three rulers, Lepidus thus secured a place. He again celebrated a triumph and opened the year 42 as consul for the second time.

The predominant partners went eastwards to confront the Liberators. The third member or adjunct remained in Italy, careful not to show decision or energy in the disturbances that culminated in the War of Perusia. Assigned Africa, he went there in 39 and in the next year refused to help Caesar's heir in the naval war against Pompeius, who held Sicily. Lepidus waited. An alliance with Pompeius and with Antonius was not

---

[19] *RG* 10, cf. similar language in Livy, *Per.* CXVII; Velleius II.63.1.
[20] *Phil.* III.23 f.
[21] *Phil.* V.40 f.
[22] *Phil.* XIII.9.
[23] *Ad fam.* X.35.

beyond hope, or death as well as disaster on the sea. There was discord between the dynasts in 37, and a chance that the betrothal of Lepidus' elder son to a daughter of Antonius might ultimately issue in marriage.[24]

Meanwhile Lepidus consolidated his African dominion. The pretext for his third imperatorial acclamation eludes record, but he was able to build up a large army, no fewer than sixteen legions.[25] With twelve of them he disembarked in Sicily in the summer of 36 while Caesar and Agrippa were dealing with the fleets of Sextus. He conquered most of the island, and the eight Pompeian legions at Messana came over. At which point courage or fortune failed. The young military demagogue, uniting audacity and craft, seduced his army, stripped him of authority, and consigned him to seclusion at Circeii.

Such was the end of M. Lepidus, who equalled as *bis consul* and *pontifex maximus* the great ancestor—and surpassed him with two triumphs. When they wrote history, men of the time were put in mind of the calamitous parent.[26]

Disliked and distrusted by partisans eager for action or heroism, and failing to win approbation from sober senators who rated civil war the greatest of evils, or were prepared to recommend even 'inertissima consilia' in a dangerous conjuncture, Lepidus was duly arraigned for personal vanity, vain ambition, and persistent torpor.[27] Decimus Brutus, Caesarian and Republican, styled him 'homo ventosissimus'.[28] In the aftermath Cornelius Tacitus, responsive to the language and opinions of his predecessor, attached the Sallustian label of 'socordia'.[29]

The Aemilii Lepidi tended to evade battle and conquest: few triumphs and no triumphal *cognomina*. To primacy in oratory or in legal studies they felt no need to aspire; they leave no fame for patronage of arts and letters; and their daughters escape notice for praise or blame.[30]

Some ancient houses exhibited recurrent features, such as arrogance or vacuity. And some lacked dignity of presence or stature. To these Aemilii it would be premature to deny, along with luxury and display, the

---

[24] As desired by Antonius (Appian, *BC* V.93.391). He in fact married a Servilia.

[25] The acclamation was revealed by an inscription at Thabraca, where he established a colony (*AE* 1959, 77). For Lepidus' activities in Africa, F. Bertrandy, *Karthago* XIX (1980), 87 ff. In Tarraconensis he had founded 'colonia Iulia Victrix Lepida' at Celsa on the Ebro: an important strategic position (Strabo III, p. 161). For the coins, M. Grant, *FITA* (1946), 211 f.

[26] *Sallust* (1964), 220.

[27] The prudent Hirtius made a notable declaration in a letter: 'non medius fidius acerrimis consiliis plus quam etiam inertissimis, dum modo diligentibus, consequentur' (*Ad Att.* XV.6.3).

[28] *Ad fam.* IX.11.1. Six years before that, Cicero styled Lepidus 'iste omnium turpissimus et sordidissimus' (*Ad Att.* IX.9.1).

[29] *Ann.* I.9.4: 'postquam hic socordia senuerit'.

[30] That is, apart from the two Vestals of contrasted reputation (Propertius IV.11.53 f.; Livy, *Per.* LXIII).

elegance which their *cognomen* connoted—and arts of conciliation. And something else that courts and salons valued. When on embassy in youth to Philip of Macedon the *bis consul* extorted admiration for his demeanour and good looks;[31] and, to descend to an estimate perhaps conventional yet revealing, the son of the Triumvir is defined as 'iuvenis forma quam mente melior'.[32]

In political operations the Triumvir reflects a past age, exploiting birth and family connections. Hence tardy and obsolete, so some in stern condemnation opine.[33] Yet those claims proved not obsolete in the new order now taking shape. Lepidus showed the future path for the high aristocracy: to eschew violence, to acquiesce before superior power, to respond to alliance with the dynasty.

The Triumvir discarded, the hopes and fortunes of the Aemilian name reposed on his nephew. Put on the proscription lists along with his father, Paullus joined the Liberators. After Philippi some of the young *nobiles* came to terms with Marcus Antonius, in the forefront Messalla Corvinus. Others found their way to Domitius Ahenobarbus, whose fleet dominated the Adriatic, others again to Sicily. When Sextus Pompeius reached an agreement with the Triumvirs, some chose to return to Rome.[34]

Paullus happens not to be named in that context. He first turns up in the operations of 36, although not in a naval or military command. A stray anecdote discloses him in the company of Caesar's heir.[35] That Paullus had by now declared a new allegiance is by no means clear. Antonius had sent ships to help his ally in the invasion of Sicily, among his admirals being Messalla Corvinus and Sempronius Atratinus.[36]

Corvinus had not yet discerned the better cause, and Paullus may still have been an adherent of Antonius. In 34 he shared a suffect consulship with Atratinus. Not unsuitably, so it appears. Neglected testimony indicates a link between the two. A fragmentary inscription at Athens names the daughter of an Atratinus as wife of a Paullus.[37] A marriage to the daughter (or better, the sister) of the Antonian admiral is an attractive notion. Given the presumed age of Paullus, the match may have been contracted some years previously.

Sempronius Atratinus is one of the *nobiles* who abandoned the cause of Antonius before the end. Of most, a discreet silence envelops the season and the pretext of their transit. Of Paullus there is no clear trace after his

---

[31] Polybius XVI.18.3; Livy XXXI.18.3.
[32] Velleius II.88.1.
[33] Thus *Rom. Rev.* 230.
[34] Velleius II.77.3.
[35] Suetonius, *Divus Aug.* 16.3.
[36] *Rom. Rev.* 231. For Corvinus, Ch. XV.
[37] *IG* II². 5179 (cf. *SEG* XXIII.130): noted as *PIR*² A 327, but not assigned to Paullus in A 373.

consulship until he emerges to hold the censorship in 22, as colleague of Munatius Plancus, the astute *novus homo* whose changes of side are adequately documented.

Aristocratic renegades were a problem. To some the victor of Actium was at first unable to refuse military commands. Thus Marcus Crassus (*cos.* 30), with ambition and campaigns that proved vexatious. Corvinus, however, was regarded as trustworthy, proconsul of Gaul in 28/7.

Africa later yielded two triumphs, to Sempronius Atratinus and Cornelius Balbus (in 21 and 19). No more, however, from Macedonia after Crassus triumphed (in July of 27). There is a chance that his successor was none other than Paullus Aemilius Lepidus. An inscription at Athens awards him the title of proconsul.[38]

The last public appearance of Paullus is the censorship. His later life touches the question of his marriages and the identity of his offspring.[39]

As it happens, only one wife stands on clear and direct attestation. By paradox the poet who celebrates love and licence vouchsafes the revelation about marital concord. In Propertius' last poem Cornelia sends her husband a noble and melancholy message from beyond the grave. Cornelia proclaims Scipionic ancestry in the paternal line:

> testor maiorum cineres tibi, Roma, colendos
> 　　sub quorum titulis, Africa, tunsa iaces. (IV.11.37 f.)

The next couplet continues with a reference to Aemilius Paullus and the fall of Macedon, implying descent from Scipio Aemilianus.[40] Cornelia died during the consulship of her brother (65 f.). That is, P. Cornelius P. f. Scipio, consul in 16 BC with L. Domitius Ahenobarbus.

She also indicates (and embellishes) the other line:

> altera maternos exaequat turba Libones
> 　　et domus est titulis utraque fulta suis. (31 f.)

The mother is named, Scribonia (55); and Cornelia is therefore sister to Caesar's daughter.

Scribonia, united in brief matrimony to the young Caesar in 40 BC, had run through two previous husbands, so it is stated.[41] Hence several problems of identity and genealogy, to be waived in this place.[42]

[38] *IG* II².4115. PIR² A 373 suggests 'fortasse Asiae vel Macedoniae'.
[39] Ch. XI.
[40] Not in fact true.
[41] Suetonius, *Divus Aug.* 62.2: 'nuptam ante duobus consularibus'.
[42] Ch. XVIII.

Cornelia also addresses her two sons:

> tu, Lepide, et tu Paulle, meum post fata levamen. (63)

Of their identity, no doubt. And for a long time none about age and seniority: L. Aemilius Paullus, consul in AD 1, M. Aemilius Lepidus in 6. Questions should have been asked.[43] Cornelia commends them to their father: 'fungere maternis vicibus pater' (75). For sons who had reached and passed the age of puberty the request that the father should assume the function of their mother was a manifest impropriety. Neither son, it follows, had put on the *toga virilis* before 16 BC.

That is not the end of the count. Cornelia named Marcus in front of Lucius. Peculiar, if Lucius was the elder brother. The explanation is not far to seek. In 5 or 4 BC L. Paullus acquired as his bride Julia, the granddaughter of Caesar Augustus. She was born in 19 or 18, and the date of the match is given by the fact that the pair produced a daughter who gave birth to a son in the last year of the reign.[44] If L. Paullus became consul *suo anno*, he was born in 33 BC.

A neglected factor now intervenes. Marrying a princess, L. Paullus would be granted a remission of several years.[45] Probably the quinquennium, like the stepsons of the ruler. In that case his birth should fall in 28. Therefore Marcus (*cos.* AD 6) is the elder brother (as Cornelia indicated in the form of her address), born one year earlier, hardly more than two. This conclusion entails various corollaries, among them the date of Cornelia's marriage, to be put in the vicinity of the War of Actium.

The elegant and sagacious Cornelia was far from excluding a stepmother for her children; and there was a daughter, born in the year when Paullus was censor (67 f.). Cornelia proffered temperate advice (85 ff.).[46] Paullus (it appears) went on to acquire a Marcella.[47] A subsequent marriage is needed to explain without effort or discomfort a young man honoured as *patronus* of Saguntum, namely 'Paullus Aemilius Paulli f. Regillus'.[48] He was quaestor to Ti. Caesar, styled 'Augustus': hence born not earlier than 11 BC.

Paullus the Censor thus kept and reinforced his link with the ruling group. How long he survived, there is no clear sign. Towards 6 BC his son Marcus would be entering on matrimony, likewise the little sister. The turn of

[43] An answer was propounded in *Bayerische S.-B.* 1974, Heft 7, 30 = *RP* III (1984), 932. Reinforced in *History in Ovid* (1978), 140; 208.

[44] Pliny, *NH* VII.58.

[45] Assumed ('no doubt') in *JRS* XLV (1955), 24 = *Ten Studies in Tacitus* (1970), 34.

[46] For an unfriendly view of the lady, observe L. Richardson (in his *Commentary*, 1977), 48: 'a woman . . . who seems doubtful of the love of her husband. One even suspects that her own fidelity was not entirely assured, for she protests too much.'

[47] Ch. XI.

[48] *ILS* 949.

events in that year had various consequences for the high aristocracy, as has been indicated more than once.

Along with marriages, betrothals are significant, often contracted long in advance. In the palace or in its vicinity congregated a whole troop of children, supervised by Livia Drusilla, by Julia, by the young widow of Drusus. To wit the five children Julia bore to M. Agrippa, one son of Claudius Nero, two sons and a daughter of his brother Drusus.

In the forefront the two Caesars. For Gaius was destined Livia Julia, daughter of Drusus and Antonia.[49] For his brother Lucius a surprise, namely an Aemilia Lepida, whose extraction rewards curiosity. Lepidus the Triumvir had two sons by Junia, the sister of M. Brutus. Marcus resided at Rome during the War of Actium, perhaps kept as a hostage, to forfeit use and survival after the victory. In the following year the vigilant Maecenas detected and suppressed a conspiracy of M. Lepidus.[50]

His brother Quintus is not a character in recorded history (however fragmentary), only an item of genealogy, transmitted by M'. Aemilius Q. f. Lepidus (*cos.* AD 11), whose sister was betrothed to Lucius Caesar. A casual item concerning her ancestry permits (or rather imposes) the deduction that Q. Lepidus had married a Cornelia (likewise unattested), a daughter of Faustus Sulla and Pompeia.[51] Further, to judge by the putative ages of Manius Lepidus and his sister, Q. Lepidus was still alive as late as 13 BC. Not, however, admitted to the roll of consuls.

So far the ruler had kept at a distance the descendants of the dynasts Pompeius and Sulla, some of them friends of Claudius Nero who honoured a paternal loyalty to the cause of the Republic. Disturbed though not totally thwarted by the secession of his stepson, Augustus was now intent on conciliating the aristocracy and widening the ambit of his alliances. The situation is clear, the evidence largely missing or conjectural.[52]

Boy princes and an ageing autocrat entail all manner of hazards. Parallels offer in other epochs.[53] Political stability was requisite, and a sequence of tranquil years, immune from innovation at home or adventures abroad.

Paullus and wife escaped danger (or any mention) when Julia and her friends came to ruin. Interest fastens and concentrates on their persons or

---

[49] *PIR*[2] L 303. The marriage took place in 1 BC (Dio LV.10.18).

[50] above, p. 35.

[51] *Ann.* III.22.1 (below, p. 265). This Cornelia cannot have been born later than 46 BC.

[52] It would hardly have been disclosed by Dio, even were his text entire.

[53] Notably the concluding epoch of Louis Quatorze. In April of 1711 died the Dauphin (who had three sons); in February of 1712 the next heir, the Duc de Bourgogne (leaving two small boys); in April of 1714 the Duc de Berry, brother of the Duc de Bourgogne (the other son of the Dauphin had become Philip V, the King of Spain).

on their fate. If a genuine conspiracy was on foot, and some preparation for a seizure of power, the authors might give a thought to the army commanders, the arbiters soon or late when peril invests the city government.

Spain would play a role. Fabius Maximus (it is likely enough) was still holding that important command, but Julia's group could not expect help from Fabius, early or ever. Illyricum was central, with the nearest army to Italy. Ahenobarbus, himself the husband of a princess, had ambitions of his own—and a close link with the Aemilii.[54]

Not much more than a year elapsed after those transactions when Paullus assumed the *fasces*, colleague to his brother-in-law C. Caesar—who entered office in Syria. Therefore consul alone for six months. Not that he thereby acquired much accession of authority or a voice in public policy. His successor, likewise sole consul at Rome, was not a person of any consequence.[55] Caesar Augustus was imposing a tight regime. After the catastrophe of Julia he appointed for the first time commanders of the Praetorian Guard.[56]

The young consular was not assigned a military province or mission abroad, so far as known, whereas Lucius Caesar was on the way to Spain when he died in August of the year 2. Some may have expected Paullus to take his place or be permitted to visit one of the other armies. Like Claudius Nero, he got no advantage from the decease of the prince. Then, after the adoptions made in the summer of 4, Julia retained a link with the reigning group through her brother Agrippa Postumus. Yet the boy Postumus, although now a son of Caesar Augustus, was neither shown to the armies nor promised a bride.

The link was soon broken. Two years later the Princeps was impelled to take harsh measures against Postumus. He cut him off from the family, relegating him to seclusion at Surrentum.[57] After a year, character and habits showing no improvement, a decree of the Senate consigned Postumus to banishment, to be kept under military custody on the island Planasia.[58]

For Caesar Augustus, Paullus and Julia had likewise become super-fluous—and perhaps a nuisance, a cancer to be excised ruthlessly. It was not clear that they would survive long enough to enter Roman annals as

[54] Ch. XII. His mother is to be presumed a Lepida, and probably a sister of Paullus the Censor.

[55] viz. M. Herennius Picens, son of the consul suffect of 34.

[56] Dated after the pageantry and anterior to the catastrophe by Dio (LV.10.10). Surely in error. Another mistake is the conferment of the title 'pater patriae' (ib.)—which fell on February 5.

[57] Suetonius, *Divus Aug.* 65.1. With Degrassi's supplement, the *Fasti Ostienses* of AD 6 yielded 'Agrippa Caesar [abdicatus est' (*Inscr. It.* XIII.1, p. 183). Accepted by B. Levick, *Tiberius the Politician* (1976), 57; and cf. *History in Ovid* (1978), 206, n. 2. Better, a local magistracy. Thus L. Vidman, in his *Fasti Ostienses*[2] (1982).

[58] For the date, Velleius II.112.7; Dio LV.32.2 (conflating the two stages). The *senatus consultum* is registered by *Ann.* I.6.1; Suetonius, *Divus Aug.* 65.4.

the 'primum facinus novi principatus'. Nobody expected that Ti. Caesar would have to wait for a decade since the adoption: Augustus in AD 8 celebrated his seventieth birthday.

Deriving some consolation from public calamities and from a chance of opportune deaths, the pair ran into trouble and came to grief. By accident or by design, notable transactions are obscured to posterity. The fate of Paullus is a problem, while the banishment of his wife is not properly documented (or even dated) except by a curt notice in the pages of a historian writing over a century later.

His *Annales* remain the essential source for investigating and for illustrating the Augustan *nobilitas*. Ample recourse is enjoined. The episode concerning Julia declares the insight of Tacitus as well as his skill in artful composition.[59]

---

[59] Peculiar notions about Tacitus persist among adepts of Latin literature. Thus K. Quinn, *Texts and Contexts* (1979), 236: 'the structural problems of historical narrative do not interest him'.

IX

The End of L. Aemilius Paullus

When composing the Tiberian books Tacitus soon came upon a number of transactions that echoed back to the previous reign and excited his lively curiosity. One small but significant item even elicited from this reticent writer a personal avowal: he hoped one day to be able to deal with the epoch of Caesar Augustus.[1] The whole context repays inspection.[2]

In the year 20 the high assembly sat in judgement on Aemilia Lepida, the sister of Manius (*cos.* 11), of illustrious lineage (she counted Sulla and Pompeius among her ancestors) and evil life. Along with adultery, poisoning, and consultation of astrologers, this lady was charged with falsely alleging that she had borne a child to P. Sulpicius Quirinius, her former husband. The case is fully narrated. The historian does not neglect to register the fact that Lepida had been betrothed to Lucius Caesar, on whose decease she was transferred to the elderly *novus homo* (*cos.* 12 BC).

After the condemnation of Lepida the neat transition of 'inlustrium domuum adversa' leads on to another scene in the Senate, bringing up another calamity in high places. M. Junius Silanus (*suff.* 15), a nobleman of great eloquence and 'potentia', rendered thanks because his brother Decimus had been allowed to come back to Rome. The response of Tiberius Caesar was amicable—and tinged with that irony which had so strong an appeal to the historian. He too, he said, was gratified that D. Silanus should return from a pilgrimage in far lands; that was in order, since Silanus had not been condemned under any law or by decree of the Senate; but he was bound to respect the resentment of Augustus and endorse the dispositions taken by his predecessor.

Tacitus furnishes elucidation. Though guilty of adultery with the granddaughter of Augustus, Silanus had managed to evade penalty by going into voluntary exile when the Princeps annulled his 'amicitia'. That action remained valid in the eyes of Tiberius Caesar.

The next item in senatorial business was a proposal to relax the provisions of the *Lex Papia Poppaea* enacted by Augustus 'in order to intensify the penalization of celibacy and enrich the treasury', with imperfect success, and with certain deleterious consequences. Laws, so Tacitus comments, had now become a burden more grievous than crime.

[1] *Ann.* III.24.2.   [2] III.22–30.

With this encouragement, the historian embarks on a long digression about legislation, couched in choice Sallustian language.[3] Beginning in primordial times, it comes down to the turbulent years with Sulla and the consulship of Lepidus (the exordium of Sallust's *Historiae*); then by way of tribunes' laws it passes quickly to Pompeius Magnus ('gravior remediis quam delicta erant'), to terminate after the twenty years of anarchy with the sixth consulship of Caesar Augustus when he ordained the regulations to govern the new dispensation.

Narration suitably takes up again with measures designed to abate abuses engendered by the *Lex Papia Poppaea*. Then follow privileges which the Princeps requested on behalf of Nero, the eldest son of Germanicus Caesar (who now assumed the *toga virilis*), notably the quaestorship five years in advance of the legal term. Tiberius made appeal to what had been done for himself and for his brother. Which evokes unfriendly comment from the historian.[4] Next came the nuptials of Nero and Julia (the daughter of Drusus Caesar), which augmented the public joy, with by contrast disapprobation when the betrothal of the son of Claudius was announced: he was to marry a daughter of Aelius Seianus. That was sheer profanation.[5]

At the end of the year died two men of high distinction. The consular L. Volusius Saturninus (*suff.* 12 BC) came of an old family that had not got beyond praetorships, and there was not much to be said about him. Space and emphasis is allotted to the other man, for more reasons than one.

Only a knight by station, Sallustius Crispus in 'potentia' excelled many consulars and holders of the *ornamenta triumphalia*. Tacitus seizes the opportunity with alacrity and puts it to double employ. Crispus was the grand-nephew of the historian, here styled by an author who normally eschews the superlative as 'rerum Romanarum florentissimus auctor'. On a surface view, the formulation looks conventional, resembling the laudatory labels affected by Velleius. Therein lies the historian's irony. Tacitus meant what he said.

Crispus was also the peer of the great Maecenas, and his successor as the minister and custodian of the 'secreta imperatorum', and like Maecenas disguising decision behind the mask of indolence. His agency in the elimination of Agrippa Postumus in the first days of the reign is suitably recalled, and the historian concludes with a maxim in the classic manner of Sallust about the favour of princes and its impermanence: 'fato potentiae raro sempiternae'.

Such is the earliest necrological notice in the *Annales*. Though he was not one of the consular worthies who were honoured with a state funeral

---

[3] III.26.1–28.2.
[4] III.29.2: 'sed neque tum fuisse dubitaverim qui eius modi preces taciti inluderent.'
[5] III.29.4: 'polluisse nobilitatem familiae videbatur'.

(and hence a mention in the *acta senatus*), Sallustius Crispus gains admittance to the rubric. The deaths of illustrious survivors brought back past history, with sundry revelations and paradoxes. They were welcome as structural devices—and they disclose not a little about the author's tastes and predilections.

This section of the work exhibits to perfection what could be done with the annual record by a master of architecture and suggestion. The choice and arrangement of material, subtly and tightly interwoven, reveals his dominant preoccupations. Not only Princeps and Senate or the politics of the dynasty but the general themes of morality, legislation, and power.

The incident of D. Silanus was charged with sharp relevance, in more directions than one. Silanus departed 'non senatus consulto non lege pulsus'. Thus Tacitus, reporting the firm and correct statement of Tiberius Caesar.[6] The phrase and the situation could not fail to evoke in the minds of senators the thought of what had happened to the poet Ovid in the same season (he had died at Tomis only two or three years previously): Ovid who departed likewise under no legal injunction, but by command of the angry emperor.[7]

Tiberius cherished the aristocratic ideal of free speech, he was hostile to social regimentation, and in the course of a long despatch to the Senate he even expressed doubts about the moral and sumptuary legislation of Caesar Augustus.[8] Whatever his own sentiments, or those of Ovid's aristocratic patrons, the ruler did nothing to alleviate the lot of the exile. The dispositions of his predecessor had to stand.

Some would be impelled to draw a damaging contrast: the young *nobilis* permitted to go as and where he chose and the poet relegated to the end of the world. If there were any justice, the offence of Ovid was a transgression much more serious than adultery with a princess.

The subtle historian was aware of the parallel and of its implications, so it may be assumed without discomfort. His senatorial annals did not comport extraneous items of literary interest.[9]

Tacitus exploits the episode of Silanus in order to pass judgement on Caesar Augustus himself. By interpreting adultery as *maiestas*, the Princeps went against a tolerant tradition and exceeded the letter of his own legislation. In this place Tacitus affirms that Augustus punished with death or exile the lovers of his daughter and his granddaughter. Silanus in fact went unscathed. He was able to benefit from the 'clementia maiorum'.

---

[6] III.24.4.

[7] Ovid, *Tristia* II.131 f.: 'nec mea decreto damnasti facta senatus/nec mea selecto iudice iussa fuga est.' See further in Ch. XXVIII ('Fabius Maximus').

[8] *Ann.* III.54.2.

[9] No reference to writings of Petronius (XVI.18). The tragedies composed by a consular general (Pomponius Secundus) are another matter (XII.28.2).

His attention whetted by Silanus, and recently reminded of Iullus Antonius, the author would be alert for particulars concerning Julia—or her mother.[10] Other paramours are lost to knowledge. The vagaries of several princesses as related in the missing books may have revived, by a name or an incident, the memory of ancient scandals.

In the year 25 died two 'viri triumphales' who recalled the expansive period of the Augustan wars, namely Lentulus the Augur and Domitius Ahenobarbus.[11] Tacitus pays the homage due to birth and achievement. Further, he subjoins remarks about the son of Iullus Antonius, who passed away at Massilia in the obscurity of a private station. The Senate decreed that the remains of L. Antonius should be admitted to the Mausoleum of Augustus. These notices are normally arranged in pairs and restricted to eminent consulars.

There was no public record or ceremony when in 28 Julia ended her days on a barren island off the coast of Apulia. Augustus had banished her for adultery twenty years previously.[12] That item gives the date of the catastrophe, otherwise not registered but plausibly assigned to AD 8 because of the large gap in the text of Cassius Dio.[13]

In two references to Iullus Antonius, the historian observes that he committed adultery with the daughter of the Princeps.[14] Similarly, a clear statement about the offence of the younger Julia: 'adulterii convictam'.[15] He nowhere indicates or suggests a political background to their transgressions. And nowhere does he name L. Aemilius Paullus, despite an interest in conspirators.

Again Suetonius. The emphasis is on immorality, with concentration on the two Julias and abundance of detail: Iullus he omits. He states that Augustus relegated the younger Julia for scandalous conduct; ordered the infant born to her in exile to be exposed; demolished her luxurious country house; debarred her by his testament from the Mausoleum.[16] Suetonius brings in the name of her husband in neutral language when registering the grandchildren of Augustus: 'Iuliam L. Paullo censoris filio ... collocavit'.[17] In another place, however, the biographer includes L. Paullus, styled 'progener' of Augustus, in a list of conspirators.[18] That is

---

[10] The name of Iullus 'qui domum Augusti violasset' had cropped up early in the year (III.18.1).
[11] *Ann.* IV.44.   [12] IV.71.4.
[13] Among other things the great battle at the river Bathinus in Pannonia has fallen out. Probably on August 3, cf. the entry in the *Fasti Antiates* (*Inscr. It.* XIII.1, p. 328).
[14] III.18.1; IV.44.3.
[15] IV.71.4, cf. Pliny, *NH* VII.149: 'aliud in nepte adulterium'. Whereas 'adulter' in Tacitus has a wide meaning (e.g. VI.25.2), 'adulterium' is precise. The word has been adduced to show that Julia's husband was still among the living in AD 8. Thus *History in Ovid* (1978), 208; 220.
[16] Suetonius, *Divus Aug.* 65.1; 65.4; 101.3.
[17] ib. 65.1.   [18] ib. 19.1.

to say, husband and wife are not linked by Suetonius in a common incrimination.

The dearth of evidence about this man is remarkable. He might be expected to earn a mention somewhere from Seneca, who was a prominent figure in high society in the days of Caligula when the last Aemilius came to ruin through conspiracy—and who was banished by Claudius for alleged adultery with a princess (Julia Livilla, the youngest daughter of Germanicus). Not so.[19] Apart from the notices in Suetonius and the *scholium* on Juvenal VI.158, there is no testimony to the actions or to the fate of L. Aemilius Paullus.[20]

The *scholia* on Latin poets, often adduced incautiously and without proper regard for context, call for careful scrutiny. In truth, harsh scrutiny. When facts of history are in question the scholiasts betray gross ignorance and confident imbecilities. Servius and the commentators on Juvenal offer palmary specimens of folly as well as error.[21] The most notorious instance is the elucidation of the Fourth Eclogue which produced a son of Pollio named Saloninus who duly smiled on his parents in the hour of birth and passed away soon after, most conveniently; and it will be suitably recalled that the scholiast on Horace amalgamates Sallust the historian with the Augustan minister of state.[22]

Taken as a whole, the Juvenalian *scholia* are poor stuff, with a limited range of information. There is no sign, for example, that they used the *Annales* of Tacitus or the poems of Martial. None the less, authentic and valuable items can turn up in the most unlikely places. In comment on 'Crispi iucunda senectus' (IV. 81) the scholiast, not knowing about Q. Vibius Crispus, the eloquent courtier of Domitian, delivers a handsome piece of annotation about Passienus Crispus (*cos. II* 44), the son by adoption of Sallustius Crispus: a wit and orator and husband of two princesses. The notice derives from a lost work of Suetonius, the *De oratoribus*.[23]

The reference to L. Aemilius Paullus occurs in another piece of erroneous attribution. The poet mentions the diamond ring given to Berenice by King Agrippa: 'dedit hunc Agrippa sorori' (VI. 158). The comment runs as follows:

[19] Some modern editors introduced 'Paullusque' instead of the first word in 'plusque et iterum timenda cum Antonio mulier' (*De brevitate vitae* 4.6). Thus E. Hermes (Teubner, 1905); R. W. Basore (Loeb, 1932); L. Castiglioni (1946). H. Dahlmann (1949) and P. Grimal (1969) retained 'plusque'. However, 'Iullusque' (R. Waltz) was the remedy: adopted by L. D. Reynolds (OCT, 1977).

[20] Elsewhere Paullus as a person occurs only in Propertius IV.11.3. The rubric in *PIR*[2] A 391 is therefore meagre.

[21] For specimens from both, *Ammianus and the Historia Augusta* (1968), 86.

[22] Pseudo-Acro on *Odes* II.2.

[23] Suetonius, ed. Roth, p. 290.

Iuliam neptem Augusti significat quae nupta Aemilio Paulo cum is maiestatis crimine perisset ab avo relegata est, post revocata, cum semet vitiis addixisset perpetui exilii damnata est supplicio. huius Agrippa frater propter morum feritatem in Siciliam ab Augusto relegatus est.

The passage asseverates two facts of signal importance, if facts they are. Namely the execution of L. Paullus for high treason and two banishments of his wife. At first sight not easy to impugn, and the information has generally been held authentic and valid. The standard repertorium for imperial Rome quotes the *scholium* without any sign of doubt or even disquiet.[24] The time was ripe for a rigorous examination.

That Julia, after being relegated, was allowed to return and then consigned to perpetual exile is not easy to credit. What Suetonius reports, not vaguely but with several particulars, looks like the single act of an angry autocrat: as in the case of her mother, imperious and savage and not revocable without public discredit of the ruler, especially since, as with the elder Julia and with Agrippa Postumus, that act had the sanction of the Senate's decree. The location of an exile might be modified, it is true, for better or for worse.

The daughter of the Princeps got a slight alleviation five years after the catastrophe, being transferred from Pandateria to the city of Rhegium, at the extreme end of Italy. There had arisen popular clamour more than once that she be allowed to come back to Rome. The autocrat was unbending. He made his meaning clear in a public speech, 'tales filias talesque coniuges pro contione imprecatus'.[25]

A change in the political atmosphere or a new ruler and the influence of Caesar's friends might encourage hopes in a victim of political justice or fraudulent charges. The high-born Junia Calvina was permitted to return after the murder of her enemy Agrippina.[26] And D. Silanus came back; but Silanus had not undergone condemnation by any law or by decree of the Roman Senate.

The chance thus emerges, and something more than a chance, that the scholiast is in error, having conflated the exiles of mother and daughter.[27] Confusion between the two has been known to occur in writers of a later age and higher competence.[28]

---

[24] *PIR*[2] J 635. No need to cite anything else.

[25] Suetonius, *Divus Aug.* 63.5.

[26] *Ann.* XIV.3.1.

[27] As suggested in *Ammianus and the Historia Augusta* (1968), 86. The double banishment of Julia is also rejected by E. Meise, *Untersuchungen zur Geschichte der julisch-claudischen Dynastie* (1969), 40 ff. Not all have accepted this explanation. It is deprecated, as showing 'incredible ineptitude' on the part of the scholiast, by B. Levick, *Latomus* XXXIV (1976), 309.

[28] It appears to be subsumed in the sentence about 'his daughter Julia' and 'the poet Ovid' in *CAH* X (1934), 395. Compare G. Highet on 'the bad daughter Julia' and 'her accomplice Ovid' (*Juvenal the Satirist* (1954), 30). Sidonius Apollinaris had gone further, identifying Julia as Ovid's Corinna (*Carm.* XXIII.158 ff.).

So far Julia. The problem of L. Aemilius Paullus subsists. Suetonius, as has been shown, omits him from the context of Julia's misconduct and brings him in separately as a conspirator. Otherwise only the scholiast records his treason.

Faced with embarrassment, the holders of power in any age remove damaging facts from their nexus and context, often deceiving posterity, unless historians are on guard. Artful writers who defend a ruler adopt the same practice. Velleius was careful to segregate the fate of Agrippa Postumus from the accession of Tiberius Caesar. He alludes to his end in veiled language under the year 7, as having occurred subsequently.[29]

On the evidence furnished by Suetonius and the scholiast it seemed possible to disjoin the misdemeanours of husband and wife and even put the 'conspiracy' of Paullus a number of years earlier than the banishment of Julia in AD 8. On one estimate it fell in AD 1, precisely: the year of the grand climacteric in Augustus' life which he was so happy to have survived.[30]

That hypothesis possessed a double advantage. It explained the absence of all mention of Paullus subsequent to his consulship—and the text of Dio is defective at this point. However, there is an objection that cannot be gainsaid. A notice in another biography of Suetonius had often been overlooked. Young Claudius, the brother of Germanicus, was as unlucky in his intended brides as later in his marriages. First of all he had to forfeit his betrothed Aemilia Lepida 'quod parentes eius Augustum offenderant'. At the time Claudius was 'admodum adulescens'.[31] Quite so. His seventeenth birthday fell on the first day of August, in the year 8.

This disjunction therefore lapses. Julia and her husband were brought to ruin together in that year.[32] As nine years previously, moral delinquency was invoked and advertised in order to cover up something of graver import.[33] That expedient device was reinforced by the relegation of Ovid. His was a double offence—'duo crimina, carmen et error'. The poem is the *Ars Amatoria*, composed long ago when he was a 'iuvenis', so he affirms—but republished a year or two after the disgrace of the elder Julia, so it can be contended.[34] The 'error' about which he is studiously vague

---

[29] Velleius II.112.7: 'hoc fere tempore Agrippa qui . . . iam ante biennium qualis esset apparere coeperat, mira pravitate in praecipitia conversus patris atque eiusdem avi sui animum alienavit sibi, moxque crescentibus in dies vitiis dignum furore suo habuit exitum.' That the last phrase refers, not to Agrippa's death in 14, but to his banishment in 7, has been argued by A. J. Woodman, *CQ* XXV (1975), 305, cf. his *Commentary* (1977) ad loc. The run of the sentence ('alienavit' referring to 'hoc fere tempore') tells against this interpretation.

[30] E. Hohl, *Klio* XXX (1937), 337 ff.

[31] Suetonius, *Divus Claudius* 36.1. Not adduced by the author of *Rom. Rev.*, or by some others.

[32] *Rom. Rev.* (1939), 432; *History in Ovid* (1978), 206 ff; 219 f.

[33] E. Meise, o.c. 35 ff. For the contrary view, G. Williams, *Decline and Fall* (1978), 60. The Princeps, he assumes, was operating a moral purge, preliminary to the *Lex Papia Poppaea* of AD 9.

[34] Thus, briefly, in *Bayerische S.-B.* 1974, Heft 7, 16 f. = *RP* III (1984), 923.

did not consist in any action. It was a negative offence, but it touched the ruler at a sore point. One concludes that Ovid's mistake was linked in some fashion however tenuous with the behaviour of Paullus and Julia.[35]

The manner and the measure of their guilt defies all enquiry. The turn of fortune that destined Tiberius for the imperial succession was a blow to the pair. Hence discontent, and various exacerbations. Paullus, so far as is known, was not permitted to command an army, whereas his brother Marcus served as a legate under Tiberius in Illyricum in 8, if not earlier.[36] Young Germanicus (at the age of twenty-two) also earned laurels in the field. The talk went at Rome that Tiberius was prolonging the war needlessly, for his own advantage.[37] Paullus and his friends may have been vocal in criticism of the strategy—and conspicuous luxury in a season of warfare, plague, and famine would render them vulnerable.

There was another grievance, Julia's last surviving brother disinherited and sent away to an island the year before. Several attempts were made to rescue Agrippa Postumus from Planasia, so Suetonius reports.[38] If Julia's offence did not go beyond angry words or illicit communication with her brother, that was enough to stimulate informers and excite the suspicious resentment of the Princeps. For what it is worth may be mentioned the fact that Ovid was on Elba (not far from Planasia) when the message arrived notifying the displeasure of Caesar Augustus.[39]

Speculation is baffled about the delinquency of Paullus and Julia. Treason, the truism will be reiterated, can cover almost anything. Suetonius happens to prefix his list of the conspiracies against Augustus with a judicious and revealing remark about their discovery: 'prius quam invalescerent indicio detectas'.[40] The main purpose of the present disquisition is to emphasize the singular dearth of information—and to offer compensation (by its nature inconclusive) for deficiencies in historians both ancient and modern.[41]

A document of sharp relevance is not always cited in the present context. It is an edict issued in the second half of the year 8. For ascertaining the truth about 'capitalia et atrociora maleficia' it is necessary to put slaves to torture, so the Princeps declared.[42]

[35] From Ovid's own avowals it is clear that he had been present on some scandalous occasion. For the doxography, J. C. Thibault, *The Mystery of Ovid's Exile* (1964).

[36] Ch. X.

[37] Dio LV.31.1 (under the year 7).

[38] Suetonius, *Divus Aug*. 19.2.

[39] *Ex P.* II.3.84 ff. (to Cotta Maximus). Not to be regarded as Ovid's 'error'.

[40] Suetonius, *Divus Aug*. 19.1.

[41] Julia seems to be absent from *CAH* X (1934); and a solitary item in the Index conflates Paullus with M. Lepidus, the eldest son of the Triumvir. Paullus was left out even by R. Seager, *Tiberius* (1972). By contrast, ample compensation in B. Levick, *Tiberius the Politician* (1976) 58 ff.

[42] *Dig*. XLVIII.18.8, cf. A. Ehrhardt, *RE* VIA. 1787.

The language announces something more than adultery. It therefore becomes difficult to maintain that Paullus encountered punishment and death previously, in 6 or in 7.[43] In the former year, so Dio reports, subversive pamphlets were in circulation, with a certain Publius Rufus alleged the author.[44] No other names, and no sign of any penalties or prosecutions. The person is presumed identical with Plautius Rufus, in Suetonius the accomplice in a plot of L. Paullus.[45] No clear warrant, however, for assigning their alleged conspiracy to the year 6.[46]

The biographer registers Paullus as a conspirator; it was reasonable to assume that he was put to death; and the *scholium* on Juvenal, the only other testimony to his treason, states that he perished for *maiestas*. Hence the universal and unquestioned belief that L. Aemilius Paullus underwent the penalty of death.

In these obscure transactions, recognition of a single fact may be enough to dissipate the consensus of scholarship. Paullus, it appears, was not executed but sent away to confinement in some city or penal island. The protocol of the Arval Brethren shows him surviving the catastrophe.

On May 12 in the last year of Caesar Augustus they chose Drusus Caesar 'in locum L. [Aemili] Paulli'.[47] The identity of the man who died is a question. Not the husband of Julia, not possibly, so it has been decreed. He must be a young son of the guilty pair.[48]

There is something else. The same man has been detected on a fragmentary inscription found in the Basilica Aemilia: three incomplete names only. The supplement proposed is: '[M. A]grippa[e L. Aemilius P]aulli [f. Paulli n. Paullu]s av[o . . .'.[49] On this showing, he is identified as a son of L. Aemilius Paullus (*cos.* AD 1), as a grandson of Paullus Aemilius Lepidus the Censor. Since he honours Agrippa as his grandfather, he must be a son of L. Aemilius Paullus and the younger Julia.

Such is the standard view.[50] Julia's marriage should be put in 5 or 4. At first sight, no objection to a son of L. Paullus and Julia old enough to become *arvalis* by the last year of the reign.

A young aristocrat of exceptional lineage could be enrolled in a sacerdotal college or fraternity when assuming the *toga virilis*—which was normally in the vicinity of the fifteenth birthday. There are clear cases.

[43] As recently B. Levick, o.c. 59, with Julia 'now a widow' (ib. 60).

[44] Dio LV.27.2.

[45] Suetonius, *Divus Aug.* 19.1: 'Plauti Rufi Lucique Paulli progeneri sui'.

[46] *History in Ovid* (1978), 212. The activities of Rufus in that year may have been brought up later, to aggravate charges against Paullus.

[47] *ILS* 5026.

[48] *PIR*[1] A 269; *PIR*[2] A 392. E. Meise was positive (o.c. 45). And observe recently R. Weigel, *RE* Supp. XV. 4; T. Wiedemann, CQ XXV (1975), 268. The *arvalis* found no mention in *Rom. Rev.*

[49] *CIL* VI.36907.

[50] *PIR*[2] A 392.

Valerius Messallinus (*cos.* 3 BC), the elder son of Messalla Corvinus, was a *quindecimvir sacris faciundis* about 21 BC.[51] That accords with birth in 36, deduced from the year of his consulship. Again, Paullus Fabius Persicus was co-opted among the *Arvales*, taking the place of his father Maximus in June of 15.[52] Maximus, as is notorious, perished a year earlier, in the summer of 14, soon after his alleged visit to Agrippa Postumus on the island Planasia. They were waiting, it may be surmised until the boy Persicus should reach the suitable age. If so, he was born in 1 BC or AD 1, which suits his consulship in 34.

Now Paullus the *arvalis*, if a son of Julia, cannot have been born before 4 BC. It would be just possible for him to join the *Arvales* by AD 14. A big obstacle has been left out of account. He could hardly have been co-opted after the year when his parents were punished for grave misdemeanours. The resentment of Caesar Augustus was signally and sharply manifested.

Innocent sons, it is true, might benefit from the clemency of Caesar and escape penalty for a parent's treason. Thus Furius Scribonianus, the son of Arruntius Camillus (*cos.* AD 32), who when legate of Dalmatia had made a proclamation against Claudius Caesar.[53] But it passes belief that Augustus at any time in the last six years of his reign would have permitted a young son of L. Paullus and Julia to be enrolled among the *Arvales*, a body enjoying high prestige, as the detail of its membership demonstrates. The son of Iullus Antonius, 'admodum adulescentulus', was not only debarred from public life but relegated. Not, it is true, sent to a penal island, but to the university city of Massilia, 'ubi specie studiorum nomen exilii tegeretur'.[54]

Facts and dates speak against the assumption that L. Aemilius Paullus the *arvalis* was a son of Julia. Who then can he have been? A neglected item of sacerdotal law furnishes the clue. As is known, an exclusive privilege appertained to augurs: crime or exile could not impair their office, only death could take it away.[55] The same distinction, it appears, was conferred by Augustus on his Arval Brethren. According to the elder Pliny, the *arvalis* goes on to his life's end, albeit an exile or a prisoner of war.[56]

On this showing, the husband of Julia prolonged his existence until late 13 or early 14.[57] The extinction of Paullus was a convenience for the

---

[51] Tibullus II.5.
[52] *AE* 1947, 52.
[53] *Ann.* XII.5.21 f.
[54] IV.44.3.
[55] Pliny, *Epp.* IV.8.1., Plutarch, *Quaest. Rom.* 99.
[56] Pliny, *NH* XVIII.6.
[57] J. Scheid, *Les Frères Arvales* (1975), 91 f.; R. Syme, *History in Ovid* (1978), 211. The new fact produces further repercussions. See now T. D. Barnes, *Phoenix* XXXV (1981), 362 f. He puts emphasis on Julia's child, whom the Princeps 'adgnosci alique vetuit' (Suetonius, *Divus Aug.* 65.4). That is, patently the fruit of adultery: Paullus, he argues, had been banished in AD 6. On that showing the punishment of husband and wife can be disjoined.

ruler—and it may have been accelerated. For removing such encumbrances the annals of the dynasty reveal that the sword of a centurion, obedient to a tribune's order emanating from some higher authority, was not the only method. Inhuman treatment would be applied, slow starvation, and various incentives to suicide. Like the end of Julia fourteen years later, the event would not attract publicity, and it might well elude the less alert among the historians.

The *arvalis* disposed of, another problem of identity subsists. The dedication in the Basilica Aemilia disclosed a Lepidus who was a grandson of Agrippa. It follows that his mother was a Vipsania. That is, deriving from Agrippa's marriage (his second) to Marcella, the elder Marcella.[58] Since Suetonius mentions children from that marriage, it would be permissible and helpful to postulate another Vipsania who survived childhood and became a wife and mother—that is, apart from the Vipsania recently revealed as the wife of Quinctilius Varus in 12 BC.[59] The birth of this postulated Vipsania must fall between the limits of 28 and 21.[60]

Two explanations are available. First, this Vipsania might have been for a time the wife of L. Aemilius Paullus (*cos.* AD 1) before he married the granddaughter of the Princeps. If consul *suo anno* and therefore born in 33 BC, Paullus might have produced a son adult and *arvalis* before the catastrophe.[61] However, another question of ages now intervenes. L. Paullus, it is argued, when marrying Julia, got a remission of age for his consulship and hence was presumably born as late as 28 BC.[62] If this is so, Julia was the first and only wife of L. Paullus, who acquired her when he reached the suitable and normal age for matrimony.

Second and preferable (and perhaps unavoidable), a Vipsania as wife to the other son of Paullus the Censor: Marcus Lepidus (*cos.* AD 6). As the language of a poet indicates, or rather proves, Marcus was the elder brother, born in or about 30 BC.

The dedicant at the Basilica Aemilia was assumed to be a son of L. Paullus (*cos.* AD 1), by name '[L. Aemilius P]aulli [f. Paulli n. Paullus]'. In that case, however, the proper style would perhaps have been 'L. f.', not 'Paulli f.'. The inscription can with equal right be supplemented to show a son of Marcus and 'Vipsania Marcella'. That is to say, either '[L. Aemilius M. f. P]aulli [n. Paullu]s', or '[M. Aemilius M. f. P]aulli [n. Lepidu]s'.

---

[58] Referring to the divorce (in 21), Suetonius states 'nam tunc Agrippa alteram Marcellarum habebat et ex ea liberos' (*Divus Aug.* 63.1).
[59] *Kölner Pap.* I (1976), 10 (Augustus' funeral oration on Agrippa). For Varus' wives, Ch. XI and Ch. XXIII.
[60] Agrippa divorced Marcella in 21.
[61] In fact E. Bayer suggested that the *arvalis* was a son of Paullus, from a marriage to the younger Marcella contracted in 12 BC (*Historia* XVII (1968), 118 ff.).
[62] Ch. VIII.

For Marcus Lepidus no consort could hitherto be discovered or surmised. In which respect he follows the majority among the aristocrats who held the *fasces* between 16 and 7 BC, including his uncle P. Scipio, who leads the illustrious sequence. In the year 21 Marcus Lepidus had young children and a 'nubilis filia'.[63] He was then about fifty. They issue from a late marriage.

On the hypothesis thus emerging, the first of his two wives is 'Vipsania Marcella', who disappeared by the time her husband became consul. Their son (Marcus or Lucius) died either as a youth or when in sight of his consulship. That fate overtook Regillus the late-born son of Paullus the Censor, quaestor to Ti. Caesar Augustus;[64] and also Barbatus, the son of Messalla Appianus (*cos.* 12 BC).[65] No emperor could have denied them honour. Furthermore, Aeserninus, the last of the Claudii Marcelli, leaves no trace after his praetorship in 19. By his mother a grandson of Asinius Pollio, Aeserninus stood already among the foremost for eloquence.[66] Sporadic but convergent evidence points to a sequence of unhealthy seasons in the vicinity of the year 22, or even a pestilence that escaped the notice of the Roman annalists, preoccupied by the decease of elderly consulars in normal recurrence.[67]

A stray anecdote may redeem from oblivion the grandson of Paullus the Censor and Agrippa. Among instances of unusual affection Pliny records M. Lepidus who died from grief when divorced by his wife Appuleia.[68] Date and identities have not failed to excite curiosity. A popular view enjoying weighty sponsors and wide assent detects the ill-starred consul of 78 BC and a daughter of the tribune Saturninus: hence premature certitudes about his political affinities.[69] Others may be drawn to a later season, to the newly ennobled Appuleii, to the family of Sextus and Marcus (the consuls of 29 and 20), nephews of Caesar Augustus through his half-sister Octavia.

In AD 17 Appuleia Varilla was prosecuted for adultery and sent into exile, a grandniece of Augustus, as Tacitus duly indicates.[70] Perhaps the lady who had previously discarded the unfortunate M. Lepidus. Better perhaps, she was a sister, a cousin, a niece of Varilla. Other missing links in this family are surmised.[71]

[63] *Ann.* III.35.2.
[64] *ILS* 949 (Saguntum).
[65] *PIR*[1] V 88. On whom, below, p. 147.
[66] On prominence in *Ann.* XI.6.2, among 'ad summa provectos'. Whence assumed a consul suffect under Tiberius. Thus *PIR*[2] C 928. Against, A. Degrassi, *Epigraphica* VIII (1946), 38.
[67] *ZPE* 41 (1981), 128 f. = *RP* III (1984), 1377 f.; cf. above, p. 24.
[68] Pliny, *NH* VII.122; 186.
[69] Münzer, *RA* 308. Followed, at least with 'probably', by H. M. Last in *CAH* IX (1932), 314; and accepted by E. Badian, *JRS* LII (1962), 53 = *Studies in Greek and Roman History* (1965), 218.
[70] *Ann.* II.50.1.
[71] Ch. XXIII.

An Appuleia would be a suitable bride for a putative son of Marcus Lepidus and 'Vipsania Marcella', dying in youth or at least before he reached consular years. The language of Pliny can be taken to preclude a consul of any period.[72]

Whatever may be thought of this construction, the objections that attend upon the standard assumption about the parentage of L. Aemilius Paullus the *arvalis* appear to be insuperable. Instead, the argument holds that the deceased *arvalis* is none other than the husband of Julia. Furthermore, the only surviving child of that pair is the Aemilia Lepida whom young Claudius had to forfeit.

Lepida in due course was consigned to a tranquil and innocuous nobleman—by good fortune not at wide disparity of age, namely M. Silanus M. f. He begot a son in the last year of Caesar Augustus and acceded to the *fasces* in 19. This Silanus leaves scant trace in Roman annals—apart from sons whom ancestry doomed to peril and extinction.[73]

Meanwhile the brother of Paullus sustained the credit of the Aemilii in war and peace, in a fashion still permitted to the high aristocracy, and better than most.

[72] As shown by the second passage: 'M. Lepidus nobilissimae stirpis, quem divorti anxietate diximus mortuum' (VII.186). For the consul of 78 the label is inept. Observe that this Lepidus was registered by Groag as *PIR*[2] A 370. He cited Hirschfeld's opinion: the husband of Appuleia Varilla.
[73] Ch. XIV.

X

Marcus Lepidus

High command and military renown introduce Marcus Lepidus. When the Pannonians and Dalmatians rose in rebellion, little could be achieved in the first year. Patience was rewarded in the next when two consular legates, coming up with five legions from the Balkans, won a victory to the north-west of Sirmium and made their way to join Ti. Caesar at Siscia.[1] As in the conquest of Illyricum two decades previously, control of the central route was the prime need of strategy.

Success ensued in the summer of 8 when the Pannonians laid down their arms after defeat at the River Bathinus. Next, the Bellum Delmaticum. Lepidus, after having sole charge of the winter camp at Siscia, led out the army and marched southwards across the mountains of Bosnia, effecting a junction with Tiberius in the Dalmatian hinterland. By birth and esteem, if not also in capacity, Lepidus far outshone the other legates who earned the *ornamenta triumphalia*, being indeed 'vir nomini ac fortunae Caesarum proximus'.[2]

The Dalmatian insurgents being reduced in that year, Illyricum was divided.[3] Lepidus stayed behind as a governor (of either Dalmatia or Pannonia), or soon acceded to the post.[4] On the accession of Tiberius he is discovered in Spain, holding Tarraconensis and preserving the army immune from the disturbances that infected the legions in Pannonia and on the Rhine. The town of Uxama honoured him with a dedication; and a young man styled 'Paullus Aemilius Paulli f. Pal. Regillus' became *patronus* of Saguntum.[5]

In that occupation M. Lepidus succeeded Cn. Piso (*cos.* 7 BC), whose name stood on a large and impressive monument erected on the Asturian coast, with the date registered (9/10).[6] The duration of Piso's tenure before

---

[1] viz. Caecina Severus (legate of Moesia) and Plautius Silvanus (Velleius II.112.4). In 6, Valerius Messallinus was governor of Illyricum. Other consular legates in service under Tiberius were M. Lepidus, C. Vibius Postumus, L. Apronius.

[2] Velleius II. 114.5. Dio mentions him in 9 (LVI.12.2): his sole reference to Lepidus anywhere.

[3] The first governor of Dalmatia was Vibius Postumus (Velleius II.116.2).

[4] Pannonia is generally awarded preference over Dalmatia. Observe, however, the fragment 'Aemi]lio [Le]pido', in fine letters (*CIL* III. 13885: Gradac). Duly adduced by Groag in *PIR*[2] A 369.

[5] *CIL* II. 2820; 3837 = *ILS* 949. When discussing Velleius II.125.5, a disturbed text, A. J. Woodman in his *Commentary* (1977) stated that it is 'irresponsible' to assign Tarraconensis to Marcus Lepidus.

[6] *CIL* II. 2703, cf. Ch. XXVI.

or after is uncertain. The years of emergency saw governors prolonged, both in 6 and in 9.[7]

Tiberius Caesar earned bad repute for keeping governors in office for inordinate periods, some to the end of their days. Various reasons were canvassed. The most extreme cases fall late in the reign extending even to the proconsuls of Asia and Africa. The practice had an early origin. For example, P. Dolabella (*cos.* 10), in Dalmatia in 14, may have stayed there until 19 or 20, to be succeeded by L. Volusius Saturninus (*suff.* 3) who continued into the reign of Caligula.[8]

M. Lepidus had an amicable mention from the Princeps in the course of 17.[9] That does not quite prove his presence in the Senate. He may not have come back from Spain until two more years had elapsed.

When Cn. Piso faced prosecution early in 20, whereas five advocates declined to act for the defence, M. Lepidus was one of the three consulars who undertook the delicate task.[10]

In the pages of Tacitus, Marcus Lepidus and Manius have caused some perplexity, not through any fault of the author, who was at pains to obviate confusion between homonyms in the aristocracy. A dogma formed, promulgated in the beginning by Justus Lipsius, with long and loyal posterity. The operation entailed eight changes of the abridged *praenomen*, to read 'M'.' instead of 'M.' in the manuscript. The result amplified and exalted the consul of 11, while Marcus dwindles—although evidence external to Tacitus declared him a 'vir triumphalis' and governor of Tarraconensis.[11]

Quiet inspection of one passage only should have sufficed, and one emendation, namely 'Marcum' to 'Manium'.[12] A drastic revision was called for.[13] Marcus comes out with a total of eleven entries.[14]

Manius is cut down to two. First, the prosecution of Aemilia Lepida in 20, 'defendente ream Manio fratre'.[15] Second, an episode early in 21, when the proconsulates came into discussion.[16] A despatch from Caesar pointed

---

[7] Dio LV.28.2; Suetonius, *Divus Aug.* 23.1.

[8] *CIL* III. 2822 (Corinium). A new inscription shows Volusius already there in 23 (*AE* 1980, 693: Varvaria).

[9] *Ann.* II.48.1.

[10] III.11.2.

[11] Hence Marcus was patently the 'capax imperii' of *Ann.* I.13.2. Assumed in *Rom. Rev.* (1939), 433 and reiterated in *JRS* XXXIX (1949), 7 (review of the text of H. Fuchs). Little heed was paid in the sequel.

[12] In *Ann.* III.32.2.

[13] *JRS* XLV (1955), 22 ff. = *Ten Studies in Tacitus* (1970), 30 ff.

[14] The consensus of scholarship had acquiesced in eight alterations of the *Codex Mediceus*, viz. I.13.2; III.11.2; 35.1; 50.1; IV.20.2; 56.3; VI.5.1; 27.4. The revision modifies *PIR*[2] A 363; 369. It has been accepted by recent editors (E. Koestermann and F. R. D. Goodyear).

[15] III.22.1.

[16] III.32.

out that renewed trouble in Africa called for a governor 'corpore validum et bello suffecturum'. Whereupon Sextus Pompeius (*cos.* 14), seizing the chance to make an attack on Manius Lepidus, demanded that he be debarred from the sortition for Asia: Manius was impoverished and slothful, a disgrace to his ancestors. Senators then intervened to protect Manius, pleading 'nobilitatem sine probro actam', and Manius went to Asia.[17]

Declared innocuous and deserving, M'. Lepidus forfeits renown. He also loses some children and a wife (anonymous).

No son is discoverable, only a daughter who married Ser. Sulpicius Galba (*cos.* 33). A stray anecdote discloses Galba embarking on matrimony in the year 20.[18] He was then at the suitable age of twenty-two.[19] To the rapacious Galba a family suffering under 'paternae angustiae' carried no appeal, but he was a fanatic for pedigree, while descent from Sulla and Pompeius did not yet appear perilous.

Two decades later Galba was a widower, having lost at some time his Lepida along with two young sons. He ventured on no further experiment, although under urgent solicitation (like his ugly father) from ladies of high birth.[20]

Of the consulars put on frequent show in the *Annales*, Asinius Gallus, M. Lepidus, and L. Arruntius annex the most numerous entries. No estimate of their role in history will safely neglect the personality and predilections of Cornelius Tacitus. A great orator himself, he contributed a chronicle of Roman eloquence under the first dynasty, through various devices, in the first place fabricated speeches.

Lepidus and Arruntius had gone on different paths since their consulship in 6, the former absent for long years. Arruntius makes an early entrance, speaking along with Gallus at the first meeting of the Senate, when the funeral procedure was ordained, and at the second, when the consuls introduced the motion 'de re publica' to which the new Princeps had to offer a predictable response.[21]

In the sequel Gallus stands for recalcitrance, of necessity subdued; and he came out with specious and insidious proposals, not deceiving Tiberius

---

[17] That is, as successor to C. Junius Silanus (*cos.* 10). The Tiberian proconsuls are discussed in *ZPE* 53 (1983), 191 ff.

[18] Dio LVII.19.4. (not naming the bride). Suetonius supplies Lepida (*Galba* 5.1).

[19] About Galba's age, ancient dates or estimates are discordant. Two facts are decisive. Galba was born on December 24, 3 BC, by the consular date (Suetonius, *Galba* 4.1); and he assumed the *toga virilis* on January 1 of AD 14 (Dio LVI.29.5). Therefore sixty-nine when he made his proclamation.

[20] One is named, viz. Agrippina, now a widow on the decease of Ahenobarbus (*cos.* 32): so insistent 'ut in conventu matronarum correpta iurgio atque etiam manu pulsata sit a matre Lepidae' (Suetonius, *Galba* 5.1).

[21] *Ann.* I.8.3; 13.1.

Caesar.[22] Like others, Gallus took a parent for model—and he was in his own right a powerful orator.[23] The historian had thus an easy and congenial task. For Arruntius, no recourse to the parent. Tacitus declared him 'divitem promptum artibus egregiis et pari fama publice'. Despite the frequent evocations (but no speech on any state occasion), Arruntius lacks colour and relief. He only comes alive, albeit with point and vigour, on his late and deliberate exit.[24]

Consular orators reproduce 'quaedam imago rei publicae', they diversify the annalistic record of senatorial business, they prevent Roman history from degenerating into the biography of the Caesars. On public policy, not much influence: at the best, intermittent or casual. The lesson was read, the maxim obtained: 'neque alia re Romana quam si unus imperitet.'[25]

A larger role was prescribed for Marcus Lepidus, a subtler admonition. Five episodes combine to build up his quality and performance.

Concluding the discussion about the proconsulates in 21, the Senate resigned to Caesar the nomination for Africa, and the next meeting discussed two names: M. Lepidus and Junius Blaesus. Lepidus drew back, on a plea of health and domestic impediments. What he did not say, the audience understood. Junius Blaesus was the uncle of Aelius Seianus.[26]

Later in the same year an informer denounced a certain Clutorius Priscus whom an illness of Drusus Caesar had induced to display his talent by composing and reciting a poem in premature valedictory. In the Senate the consul designate opined for the death penalty. It was decreed and carried out, only one of the ex-consuls voting against, apart from Marcus Lepidus, who delivered a powerful and temperate discourse.[27]

In the following year Lepidus asked the Senate for permission to repair the monument of his ancestors, the Basilica Aemilia, at his own expense.[28] As the historian observes, with allusions to three buildings of the previous reign, 'publica munificentia' of that kind was still current. As for the theatre of Pompeius (damaged by a fire), Caesar himself undertook the reconstruction, none of that family possessing the means.

[22] After the inundation of the Tiber Gallus proposed that the Sibylline Books be consulted: 'renuit Tiberius' (I.76.1). For Tacitus' account of Gallus, described as 'opaque and baffling', observe A. B. Bosworth, *Am. Journ. Anc. Hist.* II (1977), 173 ff.

[23] Seneca, *Controv.* IV, *praef.* 4; 'magnum oratorem, nisi illum, quod semper evenit, magnitudo parentis non produceret sed obrueret.' Gallus in a pamphlet perpetuated Pollio's strictures on Cicero (Quintilian XII.1.22).

[24] VI.48.1 ff.

[25] IV.33.2.

[26] III.35.2.

[27] III.50.

[28] III.72.1. His father had completed the edifice during his consulship (Dio XLIX.42.2). It needed attention in 14 (LIV.24.3). For the history and function of the Basilica, G. Fuchs, *Röm. Mitt.* LXIII (1956), 14 ff.

Of Sextus Pompeius (*cos.* 14) it happens to be known that he owned vast estates in Campania, in Sicily, in Macedonia.[29] Whole rivers, they said, rose and ended within the compass of his domains—which before long were taken by the Caesars.[30] This Pompeius (their last consul) may have been reluctant to disburse.

The generous Lepidus had a modest fortune, 'modicus pecuniae', and Tiberius Caesar had already found an honourable way of according help.[31] Standards of wealth and display, often relative, were now exorbitant, and the houses of ancient opulence in the aristocracy had not yet spent their substance.

Marcus Lepidus comes next on the scene in 24, when Seianus instigated an attack on the friends of Germanicus Caesar and the faction grouped around Agrippina. C. Silius (*cos.* 13), indicted for high treason, anticipated the verdict by suicide. His wife, Sosia Galla, was associated in guilt. Lepidus intervened to abate some of the penalty.[32]

In 26 a casual notice reveals that the province Asia had been allotted to Lepidus.[33] Twenty years from his consulship, that was an abnormal seniority. A ready explanation avails: absence in another employment (Tarraconensis) when his year arrived for the sortition.[34] In that season Vibius Postumus (*suff.* 5) had Asia, Nonius Asprenas (*suff.* 6) Africa.[35]

The item has further value. An inscription shows him proconsul for two years.[36] A third is not excluded—no proconsul has so far turned up to occupy the tenure 28/9. More evidence therefore to confirm the ruler's confidence and illustrate his policy. When P. Petronius (*suff.* 19) went to Asia in 29 he was kept there for a sexennium.[37]

Meanwhile Ti. Caesar in 26 departed to Campania and established his residence on Capreae the year after. Not a new project, and annoyances multiplied. Among them the widow of Germanicus, avid for power and importance. She had asked him to find her a husband.[38]

Whom Agrippina had in mind for consort and for guardian for her children (six in number) would not escape the 'sagacissimus senex'. Men of the time, even the less percipient, might be impelled to wonder about Asinius Gallus, a widower since the decease of Vipsania in 20. His children were cousins to the offspring of Germanicus and Agrippina; and young

---

[29] Ovid, *Ex P.* IV.15.15 ff.
[30] Seneca, *De tranq.* 11.10 (referring to the son, whom Caligula put to death).
[31] II.48.1.
[32] IV.20.2.
[33] IV.56.2.
[34] For parallels, *JRS* XLV (1955), 30 = *Ten Studies in Tacitus* (1970), 43 f.
[35] *OGIS* 469 (Samos); *IRT* 346 (Lepcis). Each for the triennium 12–15.
[36] *AE* 1934, 87 (Cos). Registered in *PIR*[2], Vol. III, p. XI.
[37] For the tenures (29–35) of P. Petronius in Asia, M. Silanus (*cos.* 19) in Africa, see now *Historia* XXX (1981), 196 f. = *RP* III (1984), 1357 f.
[38] IV.53 (in 26).

Saloninus, who died in 22, had been betrothed to one of the daughters.[39] Gallus had at least four other sons, two of them by now of consular standing.[40] The match would produce a combination formidable to the ruler, who had sundry reasons for disliking Gallus, one of long date and personal (namely Vipsania), others arising from confrontations in the Senate.

A posthumous echo is instructive. When it was reported that Agrippina had died in prison (in 33), the Princeps asserted that she was a woman of immoral character—and he impugned Asinius Gallus.[41]

If not daring to hope for Gallus (his years, coeval with Ti. Caesar, were not the impediment), the princess may have had her eye on some younger consular already possessing a link with the dynasty. Hardly Haterius Agrippa, about her own age (she was now forty): the granddaughter of *Divus Augustus* would hold him in proper disdain.[42]

Better and beyond compare, Marcus Lepidus, in fact her cousin. About this time Agrippina secured his daughter as bride for Drusus, her second son.[43] The youth was born in 7 or 8: he assumed the *toga virilis* early in 23.[44]

In 24 Seianus set out on his campaign against that family, the first results a visible warning in the prosecution of C. Silius and Sosia Galla.[45] That Lepidus none the less reinforced an attachment to a dynasty riven by discord seems to belie the sagacity for which he earns express commendation, many times. Perhaps Lepidus could not withstand the imperious widow—or Tiberius Caesar enjoined the match. But again, an early betrothal not decently to be repudiated might be taken into account, and Lepidus was out of reach or pressure, proconsul in Asia from 26 to 28 or 29.

Book V of the *Annales* breaks off at the beginning of 29 with the indictment of Agrippina and Nero, her eldest son. Like Gallus and Arruntius, M. Lepidus found mention at least once in the missing portion.

The years marked by the rapid ascension of Aelius Seianus and his abrupt catastrophe carried hazards or complications that few could evade. In 30 Asinius Gallus was taken into custody, likewise Drusus Caesar. Even Arruntius incurred danger in the course of the next year, to be rescued only by the intervention of a consular deep in the counsels of Ti. Caesar.[46]

---

[39] III.75.1. The notion of an alliance with Agrippina is discounted by A. B. Bosworth, o.c. 179.

[40] viz. Asinius Pollio (*cos.* 23), Asinius Agrippa (25). No daughter is on record.

[41] VI.25.2.

[42] Agrippa (*cos.* 22) was the son of the elderly *novus homo* Q. Haterius, who had married a daughter of M. Agrippa. Hence related to Germanicus Caesar (II.51.1). See further Ch. XI.

[43] The marriage had been referred to somewhere in Book V, cf. VI.40.3.

[44] IV.4.1. For the season compare Nero, the eldest son, taking the *toga virilis* and a bride (Julia, the daughter of Drusus Caesar) in 20 (III.29.4).

[45] C. Silius (*cos.* 13) had been a legate of Germanicus on the Rhine and his wife was 'caritate Agrippinae invisa principi' (IV.19.1).

[46] viz. Cossus Lentulus (below, p. 268).

The discreet Lepidus may somewhere have had a useful and honourable role.

Both Lepidus and Arruntius emerged unscathed, their influence unimpaired. In 32 Cotta Messallinus was moved to complain about the 'potentia' they exercised in the Senate.[47] That man (*cos.* 20), much disliked and with reason, was now in trouble, but preserved by Caesar, being an especial and privileged favourite. There is no sign that either Lepidus or Arruntius forfeited his approbation.

In 33 Marcus Lepidus passed away. The historian chose to register his decease as the last item of the annual chronicle with a fitting tribute to that 'moderatio atque sapientia' which his previous books had adequately documented.[48]

The next year saw the end of another Aemilius, diverse in character and attainments, namely the eloquent Scaurus, 'insignis nobilitate et orandi validus, vita probrosus'. Under prosecution, not through friendship with Seianus but through the enmity of the next commander of the Guard, Scaurus elected to take his own life, 'ut dignum veteribus Aemiliis'.[49]

Marcus Lepidus is built up as a significant figure by various devices. Of all the consular orators not even the elder son of Messalla Corvinus was conceded a speech in direct discourse. If Lepidus possessed talent in keeping therewith, the evidence has escaped notice from other writers.[50]

His speech carries at least one echo of Sallust, and no reader in any age could miss the comment subjoined to the case of Sosia Galla: 'hunc ego Lepidum temporibus illis gravem et sapientem virum fuisse comperior.'[51] The historian goes on to make his testimony explicit, and draw the moral from the encouraging example offered by Lepidus. Not all things are perhaps determined 'fato et sorte nascendi'. In dealings with princes, a man may be able to steer a path safely between the extremes of abrupt defiance and degrading servility.

Cornelius Tacitus was intent to assert the freedom of human decision against the decrees of fate and the science of the Chaldeans. As he pronounced long since in his first monograph, there can still be great men under bad emperors.[52] His Marcus Lepidus shows the senator how to

---

[47] VI.5.1.

[48] VI.27.4.

[49] VI.29.3f.

[50] A M. Lepidus is on mention, declaiming 'novissime' along with Scaurus (Seneca, *Controv.* X, *praef.* 3). There is also a Lepidus, quoted and called 'Neronis praeceptor' (II.3.23), held identical with the consular by M. Winterbottom in the Index to his text (Loeb, 1974). That might be doubted; and nothing can be done with 'Lepidus, vir egregius' (IX, *praef.* 5) with whom begins a broken sentence.

[51] IV.20.2. Cf. Sallust, *Jug.* 45.1: 'Metellum . . . magnum et sapientem virum fuisse comperior.' Tacitus nowhere else uses the deponent form of the verb.

[52] *Agr.* 42.4.

preserve honour under despotism—even if not much can be achieved. The lesson does not stop there. It adumbrates an august theme. Lepidus is endowed with capacities that Rome looked for in a ruler.

With so much on exhibit to the credit of Marcus Lepidus, certain omissions may cause disquiet. That he was 'gnarus militiae' is implied when claims to the African proconsulate came up, but there is no word of the *ornamenta triumphalia*. In fact, the historian happens nowhere to mention military distinction earned by any consulars in the wars that marked the last decade of Augustus' reign—and the great rebellion in Illyricum is absent from his pages, although it might suitably have been adduced by the men of understanding in their comments at the funeral.[53]

Again, no allusion to Scipionic descent or close propinquity to the 'domus regnatrix'. Tacitus might have said something in the missing Book V when the marriage of a daughter was recorded. He was not under call to name her mother.

When Lepidus in the year 21 gave a reason (not the most potent) for declining the proconsulate of Africa, he adduced young children, and also a 'nubilis filia'.[54] That is, late progeny. He was now close on fifty. Lepidus, so one would opine, had been equipped with a wife long since, when about twenty-two.

For other aristocrats in this age an unattested previous marriage, with or without surviving offspring, can be usefully surmised. In 12 BC Quinctilius Varus (*cos.* 13 BC) was the husband of a Vipsania. Given his age (and hers), he may have acquired a wife a decade earlier.[55] Further, one would like to know who had been the wife of Asinius Gallus (*cos.* 8 BC) before he took over 'Vipsania Ti. Neronis'. Cassius Dio reports the marriage of Tiberius and Julia at a late stage in the transactions of 11, episodically, the context being the death of Octavia.[56] It might have occurred early in the year, or even before the end of 12. According to Suetonius, Claudius Nero was compelled by Augustus to marry Julia 'confestim', giving up Vipsania although she was pregnant.[57] The matter concerns the eldest known son of Gallus, namely C. Asinius Pollio, praetor in 20, consul in 23. On no account can he have been born later than 11 BC. The second son was M. Asinius Agrippa (*cos.* 25), whose *cognomen* advertises the grandfather on the maternal side.

What then follows? M. Lepidus (*cos.* AD 6) may have married a 'Vipsania M. f. Marcella' *c.*6 BC, as his first wife, the second marriage

[53] They were content to evoke 'Lollianas Varianasque clades' (I.10.4). One more sign perhaps to indicate that the historian had not given sufficient thought to the last decade of the reign.
[54] III.35.2.
[55] Ch. XXIII.
[56] Dio LIV. 35.4.
[57] Suetonius, *Tib.* 7.2.

falling a decade later. That first wife, it will be recalled, is deduced from the dedication at the Basilica made by a Lepidus who was a grandson of Agrippa.[58] He might be styled 'M. Aemilius M. f. Paulli n. Lepidus'. Marcus Lepidus was more closely linked 'nomini ac fortunae Caesarum' than had been fancied, and not merely through his mother Cornelia (the half-sister of Julia) and through the marriage of his brother Lucius to a princess.[59]

After much speculation about the unverifiable, tedious perhaps as well as intricate, yet not to be avoided, it will be a relief to conclude with brief remarks about the known progeny of Marcus Lepidus and his unnamed wife (i.e. second wife). First, the daughter described as nubile in the year 21. She married Drusus, the second son of Germanicus. Lepida came to an evil fate, discordant with her husband, worked upon by the artful Seianus—and at the end, incriminated for intercourse with a slave, she took her own life.[60]

Second, a young son, Marcus: the friend and favourite of Caligula who gave him the hand of his sister Julia Drusilla, breaking the marriage which she had contracted in 33 with L. Cassius Longinus (*cos.* 30). Caligula, it is said, promised him the succession, and accorded the privilege of acceding to the *fasces* five years before the normal age.[61] Since M. Lepidus perished in 39, involved, along with two princesses (Julia Agrippina and Julia Livilla), in the mysterious conspiracy of Lentulus Gaetulicus, before that privilege became operative, he was born not earlier than 12 (the birth year of Caligula). Hence at least five years younger than his sister, and a small boy in 21 when the children of M. Lepidus came into public mention.[62]

Such was the end of the Aemilii, close to the supreme power more than once but frustrated by ambition urged to excess, by accident or by untimely deaths. Registering the decease of the exemplary Marcus Lepidus, the historian pronounced the verdict on the various destiny of their line: 'quippe Aemilium genus fecundum bonorum civium, et qui eadem familia corruptis moribus inlustri tamen fortuna egere.'[63]

When the first dynasty collapsed the power went to Sulpicius Galba in the seventieth year of his age, fulfilling the prediction uttered long since by a

[58] above, p. 125, with the further conjecture that a son, Marcus, married an Appuleia.

[59] At Aphrodisias a marble base carries his name: like that which honours the mother of Augustus. Cf. J. Reynolds, *Proc. Camb. Phil. Soc.* XXVI (1980), 81, no. 15: adducing now strong reasons for preferring his son, the friend of Caligula. The text is on register as *SEG* XXX. 1251; *AE* 1980, 876.

[60] IV.60.2; VI.40.3.

[61] Dio LIX.22.6 f. Cf. below, p. 179.

[62] III.35.2. There should have been at least one more child. Perhaps the Paulla Aemilia on a fragment at Emporiae in Tarraconensis (*CIL* II. 4623).

[63] VI.27.4.

Caesar who knew the science of the stars—and abruptly confuting forecasts about a patrician who abnormally had military merit to commend him: 'omnium consensu capax imperii nisi imperasset.'[64]

The seductive theme of 'capax imperii' makes an early emergence in the *Annales*. On September 17 of the year 14, with Caesar Augustus expeditely enrolled among the gods of the Roman State, a necessary ceremony ensued without delay, the heir and successor being under constraint to expound and deprecate the burden of empire: 'tanta moles' was too much for one man's capacity. After which, a loyal and sagacious assembly would persuade the ruler to continue in his powers and authority. The alternative was abdication. A principate of Ti. Caesar already existed.[65]

In the debate a collaborative function fell to senior statesmen. Asinius Gallus, however, came out with an awkward interrogation.[66] And L. Arruntius (it is implied) failed to prove helpful.

The historian adds documentation. Gallus, he explains, inherited the 'ferocia' of his parent Pollio—and he had married Vipsania. Of personal resentment against Arruntius, no precise grounds are alleged: only an eminence of active distinction that excited distrust in the suspicious Caesar.

At this point the author chose to subjoin a digression.[67] Caesar Augustus in his last hours canvassed the quality and ambitions of three consulars. Gallus, he opined, was eager for the supreme station, and not good enough; Arruntius, not unworthy, might make a bid; whereas Marcus Lepidus did not want it, 'capax sed aspernans'. Further, a variant report: some had Cn. Piso instead of Arruntius. Finally, all except Lepidus were brought to ruin in due course by the device and intent of the Emperor: 'variis mox criminibus struente Tiberio circumventi'.

The digression is portentous and vulnerable. It interrupts the course and exposition of a debate in the Senate, since on Gallus and Arruntius followed two other orators of rank and repute, namely Mam. Aemilius Scaurus and Q. Haterius. It betrays a further and cumulative defect of artistry.[68] Whereas Gallus and Arruntius had previously entered the narration and were now defined when intervening in the debate, two characters are obtruded (M. Lepidus and Cn. Piso) with no label of

---

[64] Tacitus, *Hist.* I.49.4.

[65] Ti. Caesar possessed *tribunicia potestas* and *imperium*, the legal basis of authority. Furthermore, an oath of allegiance had been taken (I.7.2).

[66] I.12.2: 'interrogo, Caesar quam partem rei publicae mandari tibi velis.' On this passage, below, p. 449.

[67] I.13.2 f.

[68] Not all perceive or concede defects of this character. Thus F. R. D. Goodyear in his *Commentary* (1972), 182: 'it is hard to establish any artistic objection to this digression, indeed even to call it such is scarcely justifiable.'

identity. The anecdote, it appears, is an insertion, added by Cornelius Tacitus to his basic text: added at the moment of composition or subsequently when a new and novel source came to his notice, who shall say?

That is not the worst. As later specimens confirm, the man designated 'capax imperii' is doomed thereby—and a paradox if he happens to survive.[69] The dubious anecdote duly serves up three illustrious persons of consular rank destroyed by Ti. Caesar: discrepant with the facts set forth in the subsequent narration, except for the fate of Asinius Gallus.

In 30, that hazardous year, the elderly Gallus was indicted in absence while banqueting with Ti. Caesar on Capreae and taken off to prison.[70] He remained there for three years and perished through starvation, whether by his own decision, not ascertained.[71] Piso however was loyal until death towards the friend of his youth. The failed mission, aggravated by atrocious behaviour and the quarrel with Germanicus Caesar, issued in the levying of war and condemned him for manifest high treason. Suicide was the only exit, a relief to the Princeps but at the same time personal distress: a victim in one sense, but a victim to the bad judgement of the ruler.[72]

Arruntius prolonged his life into the last weeks of the reign, when he foresaw a more evil tyranny. In the words of the historian, the sequel demonstrated that Arruntius put death to good employ.[73]

Worse still, an anecdote about 'capaces imperii' is idle and misleading in the context of the year 14: the transmission of the power had been decided ten years previously, and none of the consulars could now be reckoned a rival to Tiberius Caesar.

Both Gallus and Arruntius are ruled out. Neither, so far as known, had ever governed one of the armed provinces in the portion of Caesar, even in a tranquil season, and their parents originated their nobility. Later events, some much later, gave them enhancement.

In the year of Seianus, Gallus was under custody and Arruntius never possessed the resources to make a bid for the power. But speculation might make play with the name of Marcus Lepidus.

However that may be, the theme of 'capax imperii' emerged to sharp relevance when the dynastic successsion was again in peril after the assassination of Caligula, sundry candidates putting up a claim until the Praetorian Guard discovered and imposed a forgotten Caesar, the brother of Germanicus. In the next year Arruntius Camillus the legate of

---

[69] *Tacitus* (1958), 485 f.
[70] Dio LVIII.3.3.
[71] VI.23.1.
[72] Ch. XXVI.
[73] VI.48 3.: 'documento sequentia erunt bene Arruntium morte usum.' Condemned as an interpolation by H. Fuchs in his edition (1946).

Dalmatia, made an armed proclamation. His ascendance went back to Pompeius and Sulla.[74] That fact explains how L. Arruntius came into the rubric.

On inspection the true and solitary 'capax imperii' turns out to be Marcus Lepidus: ancient lineage, propinquity to the dynasty and military renown. Yet even Lepidus' presence may owe something to the role and ambitions of his son, who might have succeeded Caligula.

Not all stories about the last days or hours of a despot are fiction, whether amicable or malicious, whether disseminated at the time or the patent product of later transactions. Suetonius furnishes a full account of Augustus' journey in Campania down to the scene at Nola on the nineteenth of August. The moribund ruler invited his friends to the bedchamber and asked them whether he had played well his part in the comedy of life.[75] The biographer vouchsafes no further topics of conversation, but Cassius Dio supplies an additional item: the city of Rome transformed from brick to marble.[76]

Dio had a propensity to anecdote. A senator writing in the age of the Severi would not miss an emperor's verdict naming candidates worthy to hold the power. He duly has Trajan bring up the engaging theme at a symposium.[77]

Dio went back to the annalistic historians who wrote under Caligula and Claudius, hostile in the presentation of Tiberius, and some of them credulous as well as malevolent. For the events of the year 14 one of them was a source also used by Tacitus. Now the dubious anecdote is a patent insertion in the debate of September 17. Tacitus got it from some subsidiary source not known to Dio, or, for that matter, to Suetonius.

The methods used by Cornelius Tacitus in the first hexad do not defy rational analysis. Context and structure indicate a frequent and constant consultation of the *Acta Senatus*.[78] Various negative signs are in accord, notably items concerning the tastes and habits of the ruler. His addiction to astrology does not come up before Book VI (the prediction about Galba); and it was Capreae, so it can be supposed, that revealed to Tacitus the significance of the retreat to Rhodes—and suggested a small addition to Book I.[79]

In Book IV he adduced a valuable item, 'a scriptoribus annalium non

[74] Ch. XIX.
[75] Suetonius, *Divus Aug.* 99.1.
[76] Dio LVI.30.3.
[77] Dio LXIX.17.3 (in the version of Zonaras). Cf. *Tacitus* (1958), 486.
[78] As argued in *Tacitus* (1958), 278 ff. Further, *Historiographia Antiqua* (1977), 235 f. = *RP* III (1984), 1018 f.; *JRS* LXXII (1982), 73 ff. The thesis fails to find favour with scholars who assume that Tacitus normally followed a single source.
[79] In I.4.2, cf. IV.57.2 (itself perhaps an addition).

traditum'. The widow of Germanicus begged Tiberius to find her a husband. That was related by her daughter, who consigned to writing 'vitam suam et casus suorum'.[80]

The recluse on Capreae had also composed an account of his life, in expedient brevity. He was impelled to punish Seianus, he explained, on ascertaining his murderous feud against the sons of Germanicus.[81] The purpose of the younger Agrippina may be divined: to refute any apologia, and to bring up anything she could find to discredit the enemy of her parents and her brothers. To invoke the death-bed testimony of her great-grandfather served to demonstrate that Tiberius was not the sole 'capax imperii' or the predestined and inevitable successor. Other traces of the curious and damaging document may be sought rather than verified in the pages of Tacitus.[82]

In anger with her son, Julia Agrippina proclaimed that she was ready to publish the most recent scandals of the family.[83] It is a pleasing thought that the ruthless Augusta, when extruded from power and influence, soon took to authorship for consolation and revenge. High standards of talent and cultivation prevailed, no bar to unbridled behaviour. Habits of court life came in with the monarchy, despite disapprobation from the ruler, the domestic example advertised by Livia Drusilla, and all the legislation designed to enforce sobriety and chastity. Some of the princesses conformed or were not found out, others rebelled.

[80] IV.53.2.

[81] Suetonius, *Tib.* 61.1: 'ausus est scribere Seianum se punisse quod comperisset furere adversus liberos Germanici filii sui: quorum ipse alterum suspecto iam, alterum oppresso demum Seiano, interemit.'

[82] Perhaps Seianus' petition in 25 for the hand of Livia, the widow of Drusus Caesar (IV.39.1). More than was useful or credible was evoked by B. R. Motzo, *Studi Cagliaritani* I (1927), 19 ff. An abundance of scandal and malice was already current: in historians who wrote soon after the decease of Tiberius Caesar.

[83] XIII.14.2: 'non abnuere se quin cuncta infelicis domus mala patefierent, suae in primis nuptiae, suum veneficium.'

XI

Two Nieces of Augustus

In default of a son or a nephew, quite a lot can be done with nieces. Caesar Augustus was well equipped. His sister Octavia, twice married, furnished two of them each time. From her marriage to C. Claudius Marcellus (*cos.* 50 BC) came two daughters as well as the son who died in 23, the young and short-lived husband of Julia. The second marriage, contracted in the autumn of 40, was a potent element in the Pact of Brundisium, concluded between Caesar's heir and Marcus Antonius. Octavia, left a recent widow by the opportune death of C. Marcellus, was consigned in matrimony to Antonius. The consulship of Asinius Pollio might therefore anticipate and herald the birth of a son from this match, destined to be a ruler of the world.[1] In the event, Rome and the nations saw only two daughters, born in 39 and 36.[2]

The daughters of the Triumvir Antonius engross attention, for various reasons. Both had emperors in their descendance. The elder was married to L. Domitius Ahenobarbus (*cos.* 16 BC), the younger to Drusus, the stepson of the Princeps. Each had one husband only, which was not usual in the political schemes of the dynasty. The younger enjoyed length of days, surviving to acquire the appellation of 'Augusta' in the first year of Caligula's reign (her grandson); and she benefits from abundant and varied testimony, all to her credit because or although she commanded much influence and patronage in the last years of Tiberius Caesar.

The elder Antonia is baffling. Little more than a name, and even her decease went unchronicled. No actions adhere to her name, and the long principate of Augustus discloses no trace of her existence save the birth of her children. Her son Cn. Domitius Ahenobarbus (*cos.* 32) was born *c.*2 BC. If nothing else, his marriage in 28 to Julia Agrippina would surely convey him to the consulate *suo anno*. A little earlier, that would not be excluded, but in this instance there is no cause to surmise a remission of the age limit. The nephew of Tiberius' own brother, it is true. Yet Tiberius Caesar had betrayed no sign hitherto that he cherished this side of the family. He no doubt disliked the parent, legate of Caesar Augustus in Illyricum and in Germany during the period of his own eclipse.

---

[1] The thesis of W. W. Tarn, *JRS* XXII (1932), 135 ff. The poem looks like an epithalamium.
[2] *PIR*² A 884 f.

So far no problems about the daughters of Marcus Antonius. By contrast, the issue of the consul Claudius Marcellus. Their marriages raise a number of questions important for political and social history. Investigations into this territory are impeded by dearth of evidence, and sometimes precluded. As has already been shown, many essential facts and relationships are missing. For example, the wives of nine out of sixteen aristocratic *consules ordinarii* in the decade 16 to 7 BC inclusive.[3] Further, for men of eminent station or long life more marriages than one tend to emerge or have to be postulated. They are the result of deaths in childbirth—or of divorce, which was frequent on personal grounds as well as for reasons of high politics: some ladies of proud lineage were violent, litigious, or morose. Late offspring that accrued to a nobleman after his consulship may well excite the suspicion that he had an earlier wife, or wives. Again, pestilence or malady carried off sons of the *nobilitas* whom ancestry, apart from any talent or promise, designated for public honour without effort.

Finally, many men and women in the high aristocracy, lacking direct attestation, are only recoverable through descendants or through items of nomenclature. For some connections, the gravestones of slaves or freedmen furnish the necessary clues. Each and all of these factors will come up somehow in the course of the present enquiry. Even when a firm conclusion remains elusive, something of general value and relevance may subsist.

The ancient evidence concerning a man of rank and consequence may be sadly defective. His significance therefore fails to be recognized. Thus patently L. Aemilius Paulli f. Paullus, the husband of the younger Julia, explicitly named by only three authors, and summarily at that.[4] The evidence may also be erroneous. Suetonius asserts that Gnaeus, the son of L. Domitius Ahenobarbus, was a *comes* on the staff of C. Caesar in the eastern lands.[5] Which is manifestly impossible: this Ahenobarbus was an infant at the time.[6]

It will come as no surprise that some statements in modern works of reference, whether confident or conjectural (and elsewhere propagated without independent inspection of the evidence), turn out to be shaky or untenable. They need to be either corroborated or discarded. By the same token, when conventional doctrines are under revision, a new hypothesis should be formulated with sharp clarity—and also in due caution.

Multiple hazards encumber and infest the path of enquiry, especially

---

[3] Ch. IV.

[4] Ch. IX.

[5] Suetonius, *Nero* 5.1.

[6] An explanation avails. The biographer amalgamated Gnaeus with an elder brother (?Lucius), who died. See further Ch. XII.

when it leads towards, or has to invoke, persons who are never named (and might never have existed). Alternative solutions have to be envisaged, with intricate lines, or convolutions, of argument. One palmary example may be adduced: L. Arruntius, one of the three consulars deemed 'capax imperii' in the notorious anecdote. An excellent man, but his connections with descendants of Sulla and Pompeius (not there disclosed by Tacitus, but perhaps to emerge in the sequel) determined much of his importance. Hence speculation (not to be avoided or deprecated) about his wife and about his mother. One theory assigned him for wife a Cornelia of unattested parentage, only a genealogical item. A recent and exhaustive enquiry, balancing many alternatives, suggests that she was an Aemilia. That is, an Aemilia Q. f. Lepida, a sister of Manius Lepidus (*cos.* AD 11).[7]

Investigation also operates on the basis of certain assumptions, such as the age to be held normal in the aristocracy both for taking a wife and for the consulship. Hence conclusions no better than probable, or arguments of a circular nature. No impediment, if recognized as such.

First of all therefore the elder Marcella.[8] She is the more easily disposed of. The marriage of C. Marcellus and Octavia may have taken place about 54 BC. There is no direct evidence, only the abortive proposal made early in 52 that, to maintain a political alliance, the wife of Marcellus might be transferred to Pompeius Magnus.[9] As for her children, the son was born in 42, the younger daughter in 39: Octavia, so it is reported, was pregnant when assigned for wife to Marcus Antonius.[10]

The elder Marcella, it should seem, is close by age to her brother and her sister. That is, born about 43. No evidence contradicts, and something speaks for it. Her earliest attestation is in 28 when Cassius Dio states incidentally that Augustus, as a sign of his trust in Agrippa, gave him his niece (not named) in matrimony.[11] That year may be the actual date of the match. It finds independent confirmation.

Agrippa's first wife was Caecilia Attica, the daughter of Cicero's friend. From the account in Cornelius Nepos, it appears that the marriage was contracted in 37.[12] It subsisted until about 28, as a stray notice indicates. The scholarly freedman Q. Caecilius Epirota was impugned for excessive familiarity (if nothing more) with Attica. Whereupon he went away and took refuge with Cornelius Gallus (the Prefect of Egypt, soon himself to suffer incrimination).[13] Something nasty may be surmised—the divorce of

---

[7] E. J. Weinrib, *HSCP* LXXII (1968), 247 ff. (with stemma, 274.). Further, Ch. XIX.
[8] *PIR*[2] C 1102.
[9] Suetonius, *Divus Julius* 27.1.
[10] Dio XLVIII.31.3.
[11] Dio LIII.1.2.
[12] Nepos, *Vita Attici* 12.1 f.
[13] Suetonius, *De gramm.* 16.

the rich heiress Caecilia Attica, discarded when something better offered. That is, the niece of Caesar Augustus, being now providentially ready for wedlock (if born *c.*43).

Marcella passed seven years as consort of M. Agrippa. In 21, under impulsion from Augustus, Agrippa took over his daughter Julia, divorcing the niece. Thus Cassius Dio, again not naming her.[14] Nor does Plutarch, when he states that a niece of Augustus married Iullus Antonius.[15] Her identity emerges from two notices about the fate of her second husband. Iullus, so Velleius says, had been honoured by Augustus 'matrimonio sororis suae filiae'; and Tacitus, recording the decease at Massilia of the son of Iullus, shows due awareness when stating that Augustus banished 'sororis nepotem'.[16]

Plutarch proclaims that the son of Marcus Antonius stood next in honour and esteem to the sons of Agrippa and the sons of Livia. That estimate (complimentary to the generous clemency of the victor) passes over Domitius Ahenobarbus. Iullus Antonius reached the consulate *suo anno* in 10, it is true, and became proconsul of Asia.[17] Yet, so far as is known, he was not permitted to govern one of the armed provinces. Literary tastes or lack of experience in the field was not always a bar to those commands.

Iullus Antonius married Marcella at the suitable season when about twenty-two. He left a son who was 'admodum adulescentulus' when his father perished in 2 BC—and who presumably had been already betrothed to some girl of high birth. Iullus and Marcella had also a daughter.[18] She might (or might not) be invoked to explain the Antonian ancestry of an aristocrat in a later generation.[19]

Subsidiary questions now impinge. Relating the marriage of Agrippa to Julia, Suetonius states that he had several children from one of the two Marcellae.[20] It is worth the effort to look for them, however little may emerge. At the same time, attention goes to the first marriage of Agrippa, of which the only directly attested issue is the Vipsania who was betrothed in infancy to Ti. Claudius Nero.[21] In the sequel it was largely that alliance which preserved the memory of Agrippa's first and broken marriage—and may have obscured the existence of other daughters of Caecilia Attica.

[14] Dio LIV. 6.5.
[15] Plutarch, *Antonius* 87. He attributes her divorce to her mother's initiative.
[16] Velleius II. 100.4; Tacitus, *Ann.* IV.44.3.
[17] *PIR*² A 800.
[18] Deduced from a freedman (*CIL* VI. 11959).
[19] That of a Junius Blaesus (Tacitus, *Hist.* III.38.3). G. V. Sumner suggested descent from the son of Iullus (*Phoenix* XIX (1965), 143 f.). Against which, below, p. 163.
[20] Suetonius, *Divus Aug.* 63.1.
[21] Nepos, *Vita Attici* 19.4.

There is no trace of a son anywhere. But, apart from 'Vipsania Ti. Neronis', two daughters have come to light in different and contrasted ways (and there may have been others).

First, the mother of D. Haterius Agrippa (*cos.* 22). When a praetor died in the course of the year 17, with keen competition for the vacant place, this man had strong family support: he is described as a relative of Germanicus Caesar.[22] Further, the *cognomen* indicates the maternal grandfather. Observe for the close parallel M. Asinius Agrippa (*cos.* 25), the son of C. Asinius Gallus and Vipsania, the ex-wife of Tiberius.

Therefore a Vipsania had been given in matrimony to the *novus homo* Q. Haterius (*suff.* 5 BC), an elderly man who was born about 63.[23] On the standard assumption, she was a daughter of Agrippa and Marcella.[24] The age of her son, however, renders Marcella the less likely mother. Haterius Agrippa was tribune of the plebs in 15 and (it is a rational conjecture) either eligible for a praetorship in 18, or already one of the candidates, when elected in the previous year. If that is so, his birth may be assigned to 13 BC.

Next, his mother Vipsania. Difficult, if a daughter of Marcella, hence born between 27 and 21 BC. Better, the wife of Q. Haterius was a daughter of Agrippa and Caecilia Attica.[25] Thus the disparity in age, striking enough through not without parallel, would be a little attenuated.[26] Likewise the social disproportion. Who was Haterius that he should deserve the grand-niece of Caesar Augustus?

Despite the connection, which was formed not later than 14 (as is shown by the age of Haterius Agrippa), the consulship of Q. Haterius was long deferred: he was in his fifties when consul suffect.

What Ti. Claudius Nero thought of this brother-in-law would be an entertaining topic for speculation. Not that the patrician would be hostile to the claims of *novi homines* showing excellence in the arts of war and peace or loyal attachment to the bonds of political and family allegiance. Tiberius, estranged in many ways from his own class, was noted for his advancement of *novi homines* at different times in his life.

Haterius acquired great celebrity as an orator, fluent and voluble, imitating Cicero to excess. Augustus took no pleasure from his manner, as a caustic comment reveals.[27] Nor can it have been congenial to Tiberius who adopted Messalla Corvinus for his model (at least with imperfect

---

[22] *Ann.* II.51.1.

[23] Jerome, *Chron.* p. 172 H.

[24] Thus F. R. D. Goodyear in his *Commentary* (1981) on *Ann.* II.51.1. *PIR²* H 24 has 'fortasse filia M. Agrippae et Marcellae maioris'.

[25] Although the phrase of Tacitus, 'ut propinquum Germanici' suits better a daughter of Marcella.

[26] For parallel, observe Sulpicius Quirinius and Aemilia Q.f. Lepida.

[27] Seneca, *Controv.* IV. *praef.* 7: 'Haterius noster sufflaminandus est'. Not cited in *PIR²* H 24.

success, according to Suetonius), and who, as the renderings in Tacitus declare, spoke with vigour and concentration.[28]

In the debate of September 17, AD 14, Haterius incurred the displeasure of Tiberius Caesar by an ejaculation beginning with 'quo usque patieris, Caesar?'; and his subsequent attempt to make atonement produced an embarrassing scene.[29] On a later occasion Haterius proposed that certain decrees of the Senate should be inscribed in letters of gold. Which produced mockery. He was a 'senex foedissimae adulationis'.[30]

That label should have been enough to damn Haterius for ever. None the less, Tacitus drives home his disapprobation by according an obituary notice. The item deserves to be singled out. It illustrates the subtle technique of his discourse, the accuracy of his information about men and families—and one of his paramount interests, namely the annals of eloquence in Rome of the Caesars.

Two men of note died at the end of the year 26.[31] First Asinius Agrippa, briefly described as 'claris maioribus quam vetustis vitaque non degener'. This is the consul of the previous year, otherwise only a date in the pages of the *Annales*. He is praised by Tacitus, though no word or action of his was put on show. But M. Asinius Agrippa was a grandson of Asinius Pollio, and Tacitus elsewhere evinces a keen interst in the Asinii, who endured down to his own time. Asinius Agrippa was also in fact related to Q. Haterius, being the son of a Vipsania and grandson of M. Agrippa (which Tacitus did not need to specify). Next, Q. Haterius himself, who earns a longer entry. In choice language Tacitus defines and condemns his fashion of oratory. It died with him, whereas 'aliorum cura et meditatio in posterum valescit.'

Second, a Vipsania as wife of P. Quinctilius Varus (*cos.* 13). The papyrus fragment of Augustus' oration delivered at the funeral of Agrippa early in 12 discloses a small fact of some interest: Varus as well as Tiberius was a son-in-law of Agrippa.[32] If this Vipsania was a daughter of Marcella, she must have been born in the period 27–21. Hence a recent bride indeed.[33] A daughter of Caecilia Attica is not excluded.

In any event, it will be added, Vipsania was probably not the first wife of Quinctilius Varus. One would expect him to find a bride by the time of his quaestorship (he was *quaestor Augusti c.*21).[34]

[28] For Suetonius' verdict, *Tib.* 70.1. And see Ch. XXV.

[29] *Ann.* I.13.6: 'cum deprecandi causa Palatium introisset ambulantisque Tiberii genua advolveretur' etc.

[30] III.57.2.

[31] IV.61.

[32] *Kölner Pap.* I (1976), no. 10.

[33] Assumed by L. Koenen, *ZPE* 5 (1970), 237. The parentage of the mother is relevant to the wife of Q. Haterius.

[34] *OGIS* 463 (Tenos).

Third, to justify Suetonius' statement about children of a Marcella—or rather to give body to some combination or other—it may be expedient to conjure up at least one more daughter.[35] Agrippa's next performance in matrimony engendered no fewer than five children in the space of eight years (20–12).

The real perplexities begin with the younger Marcella.[36] She is not on separate named record in any ancient author. Identity and relationship are established in two ways. First, by inference and construction. About the year 39 Claudius married Valeria Messallina, described as 'Barbati Messallae consobrini sui filiam'.[37] This Barbatus is clearly a son of M. Valerius Messalla Appianus (*cos.* 12 BC), himself by birth an Appius Claudius Pulcher, adopted by a M. Messalla.[38] Now Claudius was the son of one niece of Augustus (Antonia), Barbatus his cousin likewise the son of another. That is, of the younger Marcella. Further, Claudia Pulchra (the widow of Quinctilius Varus), prosecuted and condemned for adultery in AD 26, is styled a 'sobrina' of Agrippina (daughter of M. Agrippa and Julia).[39] Therefore Claudia Pulchra must be the daughter of a niece of Augustus.[40]

Second, inscriptions. The *columbarium* for Marcella's household was dedicated in AD 10 by 'C. Claudius Marcellae minoris l. Phasis'.[41] It housed a mass of urns of slaves and freedmen. They include her own and those of relatives, attesting by nomenclature several connections.[42] Even 'Antonia Domiti' and 'Antonia Drusi' are represented (once each), and the otherwise unattested 'Lepida Servili'.[43] The Valerii are in highest frequency, with M. Messalla, Valeria, and Valeria Messallina.

For purposes of the present enquiry most notable are five *liberti* of Paullus Aemilius Lepidus (carrying the praenomen 'Marcus'), two of L. Aemilius Paullus (with erasure of the name, thus indicating the unfortunate consul of AD 1), and four of Regillus.

From this converging testimony the great pioneer Borghesi long ago established two marriages for Marcella Minor. As follows. First, to Paullus

---

[35] That is, a first wife for M. Aemilius Lepidus (*cos.* AD 6), cf. above, p. 126.

[36] *PIR*[2] C 1103.

[37] Suetonius, *Divus Claudius* 26.2.

[38] On Borghesi's view, the adopting parent is the consul of 53. Which 'muss richtig sein' according to R. Hanslik, *RE* VIIIA. 130. Better, his son (*suff.* 32), cf. *JRS* XLV (1955), 157 = *RP* (1979), 264 f. The consul of 12 is styled 'Barbatus': only on the list of consuls prefixed to Dio, Book LIV.

[39] *Ann.* IV. 52.1.

[40] Thus Borghesi. Doubts were expressed by Stein in *PIR*[2] C 1103, by Groag in 1116.

[41] *CIL* VI. 7895 = *ILS* 7879.

[42] For annotation on the various names, *CIL* VI, p. 909.

[43] *CIL* VI. 4694, registered as *PIR*[2] A 417. No attempt has been made to identify the husband, even by Münzer (*RA* 371). Conceivably a son of P. Servilius Isauricus (*cos. II* 41).

Aemilius Lepidus, consul suffect in 34 BC, censor in 22. Paullus lost his wife Cornelia, precisely in 16, as the poem of Propertius reveals.[44] Apart from the evidence of the *columbarium*, two inscriptions register the existence of a lady called 'Marcella Paulli'.[45] The son of this match, so Borghesi surmised, is the young senator Paullus Aemilius Paulli f. Regillus, attested by the inscription at Saguntum.[46]

Second, when Paullus died soon after, Marcella married Messalla Appianus, the consul of 12 BC, who perished early in his year of office. The children are Barbatus, the cousin of Claudius Caesar, and Claudia Pulchra.

The construction was vulnerable on several counts, obvious but not all recognized in the sequel. First, Marcella, born in 39, should have been given a husband long before 16 or 15. Second, Regillus was quaestor of Tiberius Caesar. That is, not earlier than AD 15. Therefore his birth falls in 11 BC at the earliest.[47]

None the less, Borghesi's construction was generally accepted and propagated.[48] Recently two attempts have been made to subvert it and put up something better. Each in its own fashion confronts and seeks to get over the difficulty of two marriages for Marcella, with three children born within the narrow limits of 15 and 12 BC. Either one husband is argued out, or one child.

First, the elimination of Paullus the Censor. Instead, his son L. Aemilius Paullus (*cos.* AD 1) as a husband of Marcella Minor.[49] He married her in 12, after the decease of the consul Messalla Appianus, but later divorced her in order to acquire Julia, the granddaughter of the Princeps. That match was consummated in 5 or 4.

That notion overlooked a vital fact. If L. Paullus acceded to the consulate *suo anno*, he was born in 33 BC. No example is to hand in this epoch of a young *nobilis* aged about twenty-one marrying a lady some seven years his senior. There is abundant evidence in the contrary sense. The bride is normally about seven years younger.

And there is something more. L. Paullus, singled out to marry a princess (for such is Julia to be styled in the accelerating evolution from ostensible principate to real monarchy), surely benefited from a remission in his promotion to the consulate. If so, he was born about 29 BC.[50]

Second, as an alternative, the firm elimination of Claudia Pulchra.

[44] Propertius IV.11.
[45] *CIL* VI. 900; X. 5981.
[46] *ILS* 949.
[47] The objection was not recognized in *PIR*[2] A 372; 396.
[48] *PIR*[2] C 1103 (apart from hesitations about Claudia Pulchra); A 373. Duly followed in *Rom. Rev.* 378; 422.
[49] E. Bayer, *Historia* XVII (1968), 118 ff. (with a stemma, 123). Regillus is assumed a son of this marriage—and Paullus the *arvalis* a son of Paullus and Julia.
[50] Ch. VIII.

A different parentage of this lady has now been evoked.[51] There was a son of P. Clodius Pulcher and Fulvia, in 52 a small boy, in 44 described by his stepfather M. Antonius as 'in optima spe puer repositus'.[52] The inscription on an alabaster vase shows that P. Claudius Pulcher answered fair prospects as far as becoming praetor and augur.[53] Further, he is furnished by conjecture with a wife, none other than the elder Marcella, and with a daughter, Claudia Pulchra. Which would explain the fact that Claudia Pulchra was a cousin of Agrippina. It follows that P. Claudius Pulcher was the husband of Marcella Maior for a time before she married M. Agrippa (in 28). It is therefore suggested that Marcella might have been born as early as 53.[54]

On this notion four observations are pertinent. First, no evidence indicates that the elder Marcella was born before 43; and it is an attractive assumption that she was given in marriage to Agrippa as soon as she reached the appropriate age. Second, the son of P. Clodius may easily have acquired a praetorship—under the Triumvirs, when one year saw sixty-seven praetors, also a boy among the quaestors.[55] Hardly, however, the hand of the senior niece of Caesar's heir. Further, an anecdote related by Valerius Maximus shows a wasted youth and a discreditable end.[56]

Third, if Marcella Maior saw the light of day as early as 53, she would be a decade older than Iullus Antonius, to whom she was transferred in matrimony in 21. Fourth, the age of Claudia Pulchra. If a daughter of P. Claudius Pulcher, she was not less than fifty-three when prosecuted for adultery in AD 26. No impediment, it is true. But observe the fact that her son by Quinctilius Varus was betrothed when a boy to a daughter of Germanicus Caesar:[57] presumably the youngest, Julia Livilla, who was born in AD 18.[58]

Therefore there is no reason to deny that Claudia Pulchra was the daughter of Messalla Appianus (*cos.* 12 BC) and of Marcella Minor (hence born not later than 12). Messalla was the son of Ap. Claudius Pulcher (*cos.* 38), or perhaps a nephew. Claudia Pulchra duly inherits that *cognomen*, which served to distinguish her from her (presumed) aunt, namely the Appia Claudia who married Sulpicius Quirinius, colleague of Messalla Appianus in the consulate.[59]

Borghesi and his critics having been put under scrutiny, a firm link

---

[51] T. P. Wiseman, *HSCP* LXXIV (1970), 207 ff. (with stemma, 220).
[52] *Ad Att.* XIV. 13a.2.
[53] *ILS* 882.
[54] T. P. Wiseman, o.c. 216 f.
[55] Dio XLVIII.43.2.
[56] Val. Max. III.5.3.
[57] Seneca, *Controv.* I.3.10.
[58] *PIR*² J 674. She found a husband in 33 (*Ann.* VI.15.1).
[59] *CIL* VI. 15626.

between Marcella Minor and the Aemilii Lepidi still subsists. As has been shown, the notion that she married the youthful L. Paullus, the son of Paullus the Censor, is debilitated if not demolished by disparity of age.

A solution offers. Let it be conjectured that Paullus the Censor took over the widow of Messalla Appianus. No question of ages renders such a match awkward or implausible. To judge by his consular year (34), Paullus (son of the consul of 50) would still be in his middle fifties, whereas Marcella was on the better side of thirty.

It was premature to suppose that Paullus was no longer among the living in 12. Borghesi's theory entailed his decease in 15 or 14. Under the latter year Cassius Dio reports that the Basilica of Paullus was destroyed by fire; and it was subsequently restored, nominally by Aemilius, the descendant of the man who built it, but in fact by Augustus and by the friends of Paullus. This notice is far from furnishing an indication that Paullus was dead.[60] The expense of total restoration might well tax the resources of the family.[61]

This solution (Paullus marrying the widow) is advantageous on another count. It permits retention and defence of the belief that Paullus Aemilius Paulli f. Regillus was a product of this match. Therefore he is a little brother to the sons of Cornelia, namely M. Lepidus and L. Paullus. Wide discrepancy of age between sons from different wives is no surprise. Thus the two sons of Messalla Corvinus: Messallinus (*cos.* 3 BC) and M. Aurelius Cotta (AD 20).

In any case, the dedication honouring Regillus at Saguntum has a ready and welcome reason. M. Lepidus is on attestation as legate of Tarraconensis in the last year of the reign. The youth Regillus may have been with him for a time in Spain before becoming a senator, and the people of Saguntum subsequently paid him honour, perhaps in the precise year when he became quaestor, in 15 or not long after.

Regillus, it may be concluded, was carried off before his consulship, which if *suo anno* would fall in 23 at the earliest. The years from 20 to 23 were unhealthy, as sporadic evidence shows.[62] To take two examples. Young Asinius Saloninus, betrothed to a daughter of Germanicus, died in 22.[63] M. Claudius Marcellus Aeserninus, a grandson of Asinius Pollio, and himself an orator of great fame, was praetor in 19: no sign that he ever became consul.[64] Similarly, it can be added, the high-born Messalla Barbatus, the cousin of Claudius Caesar. He ought to have been consul at the latest by 23.

---

[60] Dio LIV. 24.3.
[61] above, p. 131.
[62] above, p. 24.
[63] *Ann.* III.75.1.
[64] Despite PIR[2] C 928.

To sum up. The following brief statement about the husbands of Marcella Minor may now be presented. Perhaps three rather than two.

(1) *Ignotus*. Since Marcella was born in 39 she may well have been allocated a husband as early as 25. It is not easy to find girls in the dynasty left unwedded as late as seventeen or eighteen. Hence no certainty that Messalla Appianus (*cos.* 12 BC) was her first husband. Analogy would introduce some son of a family already linked to the 'domus Augusta'. Perhaps, for example, a son of L. Marcius Philippus (*suff.* 38), who like other young *nobiles* escaped all record, being cut off before he reached a predictable consulship.[65] Or again, M. Appuleius Sex. f. (*cos.* 20), whose father had married Octavia, a half-sister of the Princeps.[66] This man is not heard of after his consulship.

(2) M. Valerius Messalla Appianus (*cos.* 12 BC). No critic so far has had qualms about his marriage to the younger Marcella. As issue, first Messalla Barbatus, who died before he could attain to the *fasces*, but not before marrying Domitia Lepida (the second daughter of Ahenobarbus). Second, as argued above, Claudia Pulchra the second (or perhaps rather the third) wife of P. Quinctilius Varus.

(3) Paullus Aemilius Lepidus (*suff.* 34), by a small but necessary modification of Borghesi's theory. Let it now be assumed that Paullus the Censor married Marcella after the decease of Messalla Appianus. Nothing precludes his being the father of Paullus Aemilius Regillus, quaestor to Ti. Caesar Augustus. To repeat, Regillus is half-brother to the two sons of Cornelia—and to her daughter, who tends to be ignored in modern works of reference. She was born in the year of her father's censorship.[67]

So far sporadic items and combinations requiring support from epigraphy. Brief recourse is now enjoined to testimony of a different order. When Caesar Augustus, from his three years' sojourn in Gaul and Spain, returned to Rome in the summer of 13, the Senate decreed an altar in commemoration of *Pax Augusta*. The *Ara* was 'constituta' on July 4, dedicated in the year 9, on January 30.[68]

Extolling the legendary origin of the *gens Iulia* and the achievement of the Princeps, the *Ara Pacis* conveys various instruction and appeal, not least to those who in the recent time have been drawn to eager or congenial appraisal of government policy in its monumental advertisement.[69] Nor have parallels in the poets suffered neglect. For present

[65] Philippus' wife was an aunt of Caesar Augustus (*ILS* 8811: Paphos). That is, Atia. Only a daughter, Marcia, is on attestation.

[66] i.e. the daughter of C. Octavius and Ancharia.

[67] Propertius IV.11.67.

[68] The evidence for the two dates is on convenient register in J. Gagé, *Res Gestae Divi Augusti* (1935), 174; 167.

[69] As in the lavish and elaborate edition of G. Moretti, *Ara Pacis Augustae* (1948).

purposes it must suffice to cast a glance at one part of the procession on the southern frieze.

Some identities confronted long doubts or perplexity, and hazardous notions were promulgated. About the figures on highest prominence, a fairly wide consensus seems now to emerge.[70] For the rest, engaging problems subsist, not all of them resolved, and several not suspected.

Augustus can be recognized. Four *flamines* follow. Three are youthful.[71] The other is an elderly man, with distinctive features.[72] Then Marcus Agrippa, next to whom stand Livia and her elder son. Finally, two married couples: Antonia (with a small boy) and Drusus, and in due sequence, the other Antonia and Ahenobarbus, accompanied by two children.[73]

Drusus has a military cloak and sandals: at the time he was abroad with the armies in Gaul and on the Rhine. The boy appears to be aged about two or three. That is, the future Germanicus, born on May 24 of the year 15.[74] The item is cogent: a ceremonial put on show in 13, whether actual or ideal.

Between that date and the completion of the reliefs, death, divorce, and remarriage had intervened. Hence a question, how and where was the daughter of the Princeps to be lodged? Julia is discovered on a much damaged fragment belonging to the other procession, on the northern frieze.[75] It also presents two of her children, along with a matron (Octavia) and a male figure. The boy looks about seven, and in features he resembles Gaius.[76] The girl (a little smaller) is therefore Julia, born either in 19 or in 18. The male figure, whose hand is gently poised on the girl's head, is none other than Iullus Antonius, so it is claimed.[77] Certain other aristocrats attached to the 'domus Augusta', such as Paullus the Censor, or sundry wives and daughters of relevance, cannot be discussed in this place.[78]

When the *Ara Pacis Augustae* was decreed, the vulgar or the impercipient of better condition might expect a closing of Janus and a cessation of warfare throughout the world.[79] Agrippa, back from the eastern lands, and

[70] E. Simon, *Ara Pacis Augustae* (1967), 17 ff. with plates 10–15.

[71] The first should be the *flamen Dialis*. None was in fact appointed until 11 BC (*Ann.* III.53.2; Dio LIV. 36.1). The second can be identified as the *flamen Martialis*: L. Lentulus, the consul of 3 BC (*PIR*[2] C 1384).

[72] Sex. Appuleius, the *flamen Iulialis* (*ILS* 8963; Carthage). Or possibly his son (*cos.* 29)

[73] On whom, Ch. XII. The boy has generally been identified as Nero's father, consul in AD 32. Doubt, or rather denial, comes late.

[74] *PIR*[2] J 221.   [75] E. Simon, o.c. 21, with pl. 16.1.

[76] Compare the head at Mainz published and discussed by E. Simon, *Mainzer Zeitschrift* LVIII (1963), 1 ff.

[77] E. Simon, o.c. 21. And the veiled woman close to the girl is taken to be Marcella, his wife.

[78] See further 'Neglected Children on the *Ara Pacis*', *AJA* LXXXVIII (1984), 583 ff.

[79] Several scholars have recently argued for a closing of Janus, cf. *History in Ovid* (1978), 170; *AJP* C (1979), 201 f. = *RP* III (1984), 1190. They were under influence from Horace, *Odes* IV.15.8 f.; *Epp.* II.1.155 f.

his *imperium* now redefined, went to Illyricum and fought a winter campaign against the Pannonians, the prelude to ambitious designs of conquest in the North.

On his return, he fell ill in Campania and died about the middle of March, some ten or twelve days subsequent to the induction of Augustus as *pontifex maximus*. At the funeral the Princeps spoke the laudation on his partner in the supreme power.[80] The reception would be mixed and predictable—generous recognition of services to Empire, while the *nobiles* recalled an enemy to birth and privilege not mollified by success.

Conspicuous at the ceremony were two aristocratic sons-in-law, the consuls of the previous year: Ti. Claudius Nero and P. Quinctilius Varus. The obscure Q. Haterius would also be there, a coeval of Agrippa. Along with them, the dynastic group made up an impressive assembly. Drusus, the husband of Antonia, had been left behind in Gaul;[81] and his brother-in-law Ahenobarbus was also absent.[82] But Iullus Antonius (married to Agrippa's second wife, the elder Marcella), was available. Then Sex. Appuleius (*cos.* 29), a nephew of the Princeps; but his brother Marcus (*cos.* 20) may no longer have been among the living. Nor had there been any recent trace of L. Marcius Philippus (*suff.* 38), husband of Atia. However, the father of the Appuleii was still extant, likewise Paullus the Censor; and Fabius Maximus (*cos.* 11) should not be lost to sight. Unmarried when Horace dedicated an ode to him, he had by now celebrated the wedding for which the poet Ovid composed the epithalamium.[83] The bride was Marcia, a cousin of the Princeps.

The consuls superintended the obsequies of Marcus Agrippa, it may be supposed. Messalla Appianus and P. Sulpicius Quirinius had opened the year, but the former was already dead (before March 6).[84] This year became peculiar (and anomalous since 30), for it exhibits three suffect consuls: C. Valgius Rufus, C. Caninius Rebilus, L. Volusius Saturninus. The second of those suffects also died in office—and the *novus homo* Valgius may have had no long survival thereafter.

The months of August and September were notoriously unhealthy at Rome. Something else is suggested by the coincidence of deaths among the notables, two of them early in the year. The robust frame of Agrippa may (or may not) have been undermined by long years of warfare and travel in diverse climes from Gaul and Spain to the Pontus, to be finally

---

[80] *Kölner Pap.* I. no. 10. For comment, L. Koenen, *ZPE* 5 (1970), 217 ff.; E. W. Gray, il. 6 (1970), 227 ff. And above, p. 45 n. 85.

[81] Dio LIV.25.1.

[82] Ahenobarbus was proconsul in Africa for the tenure 13/12 (*ILS* 6095).

[83] Horace, *Odes* IV.1; Ovid, *Ex P.* I.2.131 f. (Ch. XXVIII).

[84] *RG* 10 (Augustus' election as *pontifex maximus*, on that day, cf. Ovid, *Fasti* III. 419 ff.).

shattered by a Pannonian winter. The two aristocratic consuls, however, were junior by about twenty years.[85]

Some pestilence or contagious distemper had been taking its toll, perhaps brought by the military and propagated by the crowd, numerous beyond all precedent, that flocked to Rome to witness the august ceremony of March 6.[86] It had further consequences, of high political import: new husbands for Julia and for her coeval cousin, the younger Marcella.

[85] M. Livius Drusus Libo (*cos.* 15) and some other aristocrats who fade out may also have succumbed. The nature of the evidence deters speculation. Many consulars survive without a trace in better documented periods.

[86] For the great concourse, *RG* 10.

XII

Nero's Aunts

Late progeny often excite the valid surmise that an aristocrat had made an earlier match which left no traces. Divorce was rampant in high society, wives succumbed in childbirth, a mass of infants perished without name or record, as did even adult sons of the *nobilitas* before they could confirm the rank of the family in the career of honours.

There are exceptions, such as the three children of L. Domitius Ahenobarbus (*cos.* 16 BC) and Antonia. She married him, it will be assumed without discomfort, at the suitable season, in 25 or 24: compare the marriage of her cousin Julia to C. Marcellus. Ahenobarbus would accede to the *fasces* at the age now standard for a *nobilis*, hence born in 49.

Likewise his son Gnaeus, to be supposed born about 2 BC since consul in AD 32. Of the two daughters, Domitia and Domitia Lepida, the elder precedes him, but nothing encourages a date for her birth earlier than 6. That is to say, Domitia is the first child, so far as known, issuing from a marriage that had been contracted some twenty years previously.

Extraneous evidence now intervenes, at first sight disturbing. The procession on the *Ara Pacis Augustae* presents on the south frieze a pair of married couples whose identity finds general acceptance. First, Antonia and Drusus, with a boy, very small. That is, Germanicus, who was born in 15. Next, the other Antonia and Ahenobarbus. They are equipped with two children. The boy, robust and heavy, is suitably linked to Drusus by clasping his cloak. The boy looks six or seven, his slender sister about ten (a slight distortion might be allowed for, to differentiate these children). They are identified as Domitius (i.e. Gnaeus, the future consul of AD 32) and Domitia.[1]

Hesitation (and more than that) should have been conceived. By age the two children concord with the presumed season of their parents' marriage (*c.*24). They conflict with other indications, with the consular year of Gnaeus (not to be fancied in long retardation), and with Domitia, older than her enemy Julia Agrippina (who was born in AD 15), but not older by close on forty years, and not an octogenarian when she met her end.

An easy solution can be proffered.[2] The boy, coeval with Gaius Caesar, is in fact the youth whom Suetonius amalgamated with Gnaeus, assuming

---

[1] One need only cite E. Simon, *Ara Pacis Augustae* (1967), 19, with pl. 15.
[2] See 'Neglected Children on the *Ara Pacis*', *AJA* LXXXVIII (1984), 583 ff.

him a *comes* on the eastern expedition.[3] He might have been called 'Lucius'—and have perished in the near sequel. The sister may not have survived the year that carried off two consuls. Hence added testimony on a familiar theme: the ravages of disease or pestilence.

The Domitii invite scrutiny on manifold counts. Writing in 30, Velleius in his tribute reports a sequence of seven consuls, son following father.[4] Suetonius furnished a copious exposition—which needs to be corrected and supplemented.[5]

To begin for convenience with the consul of 122. Victorious in Gaul, he celebrated a triumph over the Arverni, but was content to waive a *cognomen*, unlike Fabius Maximus (*cos.* 121) who annexed 'Allobrogicus'. Instead, he left his name to the road that led into Spain.[6] His son, after an active tribunate in 104, got himself elected *pontifex maximus*. Consul in 96 and censor in 92, he did not survive to win laurels in warfare against confederate Italy.[7]

Next Lucius, consul with Ap. Pulcher in 54. On ample show (and most of it damaging) as the enemy of Pompeius and of Caesar, he met his end at the battle in Thessaly.

He had married a sister of Marcus Cato. From this match issued Gnaeus, born towards 70, destined to many vicissitudes, and to renown as admiral of the Republic. The *Lex Pedia* proscribed him, ostensibly one of the assassins, although he had no share in the conspiracy. Going eastwards with Cassius and Brutus, he had command of a large fleet during the campaign of Philippi and, master of the Adriatic, acceded to Antonius two years later.[8]

Trouble came with the consulship in 32. He went back to join Antonius, standing next to Antonius in the leadership, but he abandoned the cause on the eve of Actium and died a few days later.[9] The Queen of Egypt supplied the reason or pretext. Beyond any doubt the best of the Domitii, in the opinion of the biographer—and he offered a suitable subject for a Roman tragedy composed by a senator.[10]

[3] *Nero* 5.1. That Gnaeus was with Germanicus Caesar (nearly twenty years later) is the standard view. Thus Dessau, *PIR*[1] D 109; Groag, *RE* IV. 1331; K. R. Bradley in his *Commentary* on the *Nero* (1978), 42, cf. 43.

In *PIR*[2] D 127 Groag admitted possible confusion with 'fratre maiore eius aliunde sane ignoto'. No hint, however, of the two children on the *Ara Pacis*—whose ages tend to be ignored by students of the monument.

[4] Velleius II.10.2. That is, preceding Gnaeus, 'hunc nobilissimae simplicitatis iuvenem'. The boy on the *Ara Pacis* would now be about fifty.

[5] *Nero* 1–5. [6] One of his milestones has turned up (*AE* 1952, 38).

[7] The biographer amalgamated him with his father and omitted *pontifex maximus*. He also assigned two triumphs to the Domitii.

[8] In 37 he betrothed his son to the daughter of Antonius (Dio XLVIII.54.4).

[9] Velleius II.84.2; Plutarch, *Antonius* 63; Suetonius, *Nero* 3.2; Dio L.13.6.

[10] i.e. the *Domitius* of Curiatius Maternus (Tacitus, *Dial.* 3.4.), cf. Wissowa, *RE* IV. 1833. Add the fact that the theme had a sharp relevance: Titus and Berenice.

Apart from the admiral, the Ahenobarbi ran true to form. In a notorious altercation with the consul of 96, the orator L. Crassus brought up 'os ferreum, cor plumbeum'. That was sharply to the point, alluding to the proper and metallic derivative of the peculiar *cognomen*.[11] The legend made play with an inferior notion: the ancestor whose beard turned red when he encountered Castor and Pollux.

The consul of 54 was arrogant in demeanour, obstinate, and savage; and some held him stupid. As for the husband of Antonia, 'arrogans, profusus, immitis'. When aedile in 22 he ordered the censor Plancus to give way before him; and his display of gladiators was so murderous that Caesar Augustus, after vain intercession in private, had to publish an edict. Next therefore the husband of Agrippina, 'omni parte vitae detestabilis'.

Generations in the *nobilitas* transmitted patterns of behaviour.[12] Thus 'ferocia' in one branch of the Pisones.[13] There may also be resemblances of physique. A coin struck by Ahenobarbus the admiral presents on the obverse a heavy-jowled head.[14] Palpably his father—who fell in battle at the age of fifty. He looks like an authentic 'stolidus'.

This consul commanded various resources of power and influence. At Rome 'urbana gratia' inherited from the parent, in Narbonensis a *clientela* enhanced by the eclipse of the Fabii but now passing (to his anger and resentment) to Caesar. Wealth had accrued from the Sullan proscriptions.[15] The estates in the Abruzzi country, however, were probably ancestral.[16] There and on the Etrurian coast near Cosa he was able to recruit troops from tenants and clients.[17]

In the sequel the Domitii benefited from the dynastic alliance and from advantageous marriages. Casual evidence refers to properties owned by Domitia and by Domitia Lepida.[18] To Lepida belonged also a granary at Puteoli, in the 'praedia Barbatiana', the name usefully recalling the husband she lost before she was twenty.[19]

Ahenobarbus, the admiral of the Republic, was a nephew of Cato. The selection of a wife could hardly fail to be determined by family or faction. A Manlia happens to be on epigraphic record, married to a Cn. Domitius Ahenobarbus.[20]

[11] For detailed remarks see *JRS* LX (1970), 33 f. = *RP* (1979), 815 f.
[12] Not much is to be got from E. Bethe, *Ahnenbild und Familiengeschichte bei Römern und Griechen* (1935).   [13] Ch. XXVI.
[14] J. M. C. Toynbee, *Roman Historical Portraits* (1978), 60, no. 83.
[15] Dio XLI.11.2. For his possessions, P. A. Brunt, *Latomus* XXXIV (1975), 619 ff.
[16] To be claimed as the regional origin of the Domitii—and 'Ahenobarbus' as Illyrian, cf. *JRS* LX (1970), 34 = *RP* (1979), 815 f.
[17] Caesar, *BC* I.17.4; 34.2; 56.3.
[18] For Domitia, below, p. 161. For Domitia Lepida, ranches in Calabria (*Ann.* XII.65.1).
[19] J. H. D'Arms, *Commerce and Social Standing in Ancient Rome* (1981), 76, n. 17.
[20] *CIL* VI. 31735, cf. the stemma in *PIR*², Pars III, p. 30.

The name of Manlia should have engaged interest. This house of the ancient patriciate missed the consulate between 164 and 65. The Valerii Messallae show a similar gap (161 to 61), but, renewing their splendour, go on to show three consuls in the epoch of Actium. Of the Manlii, however, no consul after 65, and the last of them is Torquatus, the friend of Horace.[21]

When registering the decease of Junia, sister to Brutus and widow of Cassius, at the end of AD 22 the historian Tacitus states that the *imagines* of twenty illustrious houses were paraded at her obsequies: 'Manlii Quinctiique aliaque eiusdem nobilitatis nomina'.[22] The selection of names is peculiar and calls for annotation.

One would expect Servilii and Livii, conveying more historic relevance. The mother of Marcus Brutus was a daughter of Q. Servilius Caepio (*pr.* 91) and Livia, sister to M. Livius Drusus. As for the relations of Junii with Manlii, the only known link is remote and tenuous.[23]

Even more enigmatic seem the Quinctii, likewise decayed patricians, with no consul since 123 until Augustus resuscitated the family—and none in the sequel. T. Quinctius Sulpicianus (*cos.* 9) came to grief as an ally of Iullus Antonius, banished if not put to death. That disaster did not impair the prospects of his brother, T. Quinctius Valerianus, who, praetor precisely in 2 BC, duly became consul in AD 2. The Quinctius who adopted these two men has escaped all record, and no conjecture can hope to establish which Sulpicii and Valerii they came from.[24]

From the notice of Quinctii and Manlii it is clear that the historian was in command of exact information. Preoccupied with the decline of the *nobilitas*, he has chosen names that evoked the glories of the ancient Republic, not the turbulent annals of its last epoch.

Manlii belong to the ascendance of Marcus Brutus, and a Manlia is a plausible wife for his cousin Cn. Domitius Ahenobarbus. A daughter perhaps of L. Manlius Torquatus (*cos.* 65), or of his coeval, T. Torquatus, who might have secured election to a consulship but for the prevalence of corrupt practices.[25]

A Manlia does not close the rubric. The younger daughter of Ahenobarbus and Antonia carries the nomenclature 'Domitia Lepida'. That is significant. 'Lepida' reproduces a *cognomen* from the maternal side, that of the mother or the grandmother. Compare, for both phenomena, Junia Calvina and Junia Lepida, the daughters of M. Silanus (*cos.* AD 19).[26]

On that showing, an Aemilia Lepida is discovered as one grandmother

[21] Ch. XXVII.
[22] *Ann.* III.76.2.
[23] Ch. XIV.
[24] For the Quinctii, above, p. 57.
[25] Cicero, *Brutus* 245.
[26] *PIR*² J 856; 861, cf. Ch. XIV.

of Domitia Lepida (the other being Porcia). Hence the first wife of Ahenobarbus the admiral, Manlia to be his second (acquired from a congenial family during the war years).

On computation of ages, the marriage should fall between 52 and 50. Of relevance therefore to transactions between the third consulship of Magnus and the outbreak of war. In the summer of 51 L. Aemilius Paullus secured election as consul, being hostile to the proconsul of Gaul. A daughter might be available (none happens to be certified). That is, a young sister of Paullus, consul suffect in 34. Less attractive would be a daughter of M'. Lepidus (*cos.* 66), from the inferior line. Manius, an inconspicuous consular, was still alive in 49 when he declined to follow Magnus and the cause of the Republic across the seas.[27]

So far the mother of Ahenobarbus (*cos.* 16). The link with the Aemilii may have retained value in the decade of his own high prominence (6 BC–AD 4). On the hypothesis admitted above, he was first cousin to L. Paullus, the husband of Julia. However, propinquity can also be a cause of competition and enmity.

It is time to turn to his two daughters. According to Suetonius his son was under indictment shortly before the death of Tiberius, on grave charges, including incest 'cum sorore Lepida'; and she is twice named a little further on.[28] In another place the biographer reports the death of Nero's aunt (not named) at an advanced age. He has not made it clear that there were two of them.[29]

First, Domitia. Her earliest attestation shows this fierce and contentious lady in litigation with her brother. The suit concerned money, and she was defended by her husband Passienus Crispus. The orator's pertinent comment on both parties cannot have been to her liking: 'nihil vobis minus deest quam de quo contenditis.'[30]

Their divorce is no surprise. If not due to natural causes (Domitia's temperament), it was accelerated by the machinations of Julia Agrippina, whose husband, none other than Domitia's brother, had died in 40, leaving a son three years old. Agrippina, brought back from exile the next year by Claudius Caesar, was on the lookout for a new husband. She solicited, so it is recorded, the aristocratic Sulpicius Galba.[31]

Her choice then fell on an older man, Passienus Crispus (*suff.* 27), by his full style C. Sallustius Crispus Passienus. A son of the *novus homo* L. Passienus Rufus (*cos.* 4 BC), he had been adopted by the great minister of

[27] The last of this line was his son Q. Lepidus (*cos.* 21).

[28] Suetonius, *Nero* 5.2 (not in Tacitus); 6.3; 7.1.

[29] *Nero* 34.5 (i.e. Domitia). For inadvertence, omissions, or errors in this scholar when he deals with men and families, cf. *Mus. Helv.* XXXVII (1980), 125 = *RP* III (1984), 1272.

[30] Quintilian VI.1.50.

[31] Suetonius, *Galba* 5.1 (above, p. 130).

state, the opulent Sallustius Crispus. Passienus Crispus, an orator of mark, a man of fashion, and consul for the second time in 44, has scant mention in the historical sources for the period. Suetonius (who like Dio ignores his adoptive father) names him once, as the husband of Agrippina; and Tacitus in the last Tiberian book transmits one of his witticisms.[32] Stray notices help to build up his personality and attainments. Above all, a *scholium* on Juvenal, which among other things relates that he was poisoned by Agrippina, greedy for the rich inheritance that would go to her son.[33]

His first wife Domitia earns her first entry in the *Annales* as extant in the year 55. The episode, to which Tacitus devotes a copious narration, is highly instructive for political and social history.[34]

After the murder of Britannicus the influence of Nero's mother declined sharply. Nothing, says Tacitus, is more instable and transient than 'potentia' without substance. Nobody would console or visit Agrippina save a few society ladies, and from mixed motives: 'amore an odio incertas'. Among them was Junia Silana, once very dear to her, but now in savage estrangement: Agrippina had deterred a youthful nobleman, Sextius Africanus, from marrying her. Eager for revenge, Silana now thought of a way to bring Agrippina to ruin.

She invented a plot, alleging that Agrippina was going to overthrow Nero and elevate in his place the young Rubellius Plautus, whom she would take as her consort (Plautus belonged to the dynasty, his father having married Julia, the daughter of Drusus Caesar). Silana chose as agents a pair of clients, who got into touch with the actor Paris, a freedman of Domitia. There was a long and bitter feud between Nero's aunt and Nero's mother.

Paris reported the matter to Nero at a nocturnal banquet. Panic ensued, Nero proposing to kill his mother and Rubellius Plautus forthwith, and even to demote Afranius Burrus, the Guard Prefect. Then he made Burrus promise to have Agrippina killed, but Burrus insisted that she be first given a chance to clear herself.

Agrippina, 'ferociae memor', took a firm and aggressive line. She denounced Silana for promiscuity and lack of maternal feeling (Silana had never borne a child). As for Domitia, all she had done was to vaunt the

---

[32] Suetonius, *Nero* 6.3; Tacitus, *Ann.* VI.20.1. Seneca paid a noteworthy tribute: 'quo ego nil subtilius novi' (*NQ* IV, *praef.* 6).

[33] *Schol. Juv.* IV.81 = Suetonius, ed. Roth (1898), p. 290. From Suetonius, *De vir. ill.*

The decease of Passienus was assigned to 48 by R. Hanslik, *RE* XVIII.2097. It surely occurred before early 47, otherwise there would be extant an obituary notice from Tacitus (cf. *Tacitus* (1958), 328 n. 12). With appeal to *CIL* VI. 10399, death quite early in the year of his second consulship is argued by P. R. C. Weaver, *Epigraphische Studien* XI (1976), 215 f.

[34] *Ann.* XIII. 19–21.

attractions of her villa at Baiae while Agrippina took the necessary steps to secure the throne for Nero.

Agrippina prevailed, and Silana was sent into exile, also her two clients. Domitia now fades from the pages of Tacitus, apart from a notice about Paris: Nero secured possession of him by a piece of legal trickery.[35]

After the murder of Agrippina in March of the year 59, the episode of Junia Silana was recalled by measures Nero took to incriminate her memory and advertise his own clemency, victims of her enmity being rehabilitated.[36] Junia Calvina was allowed to return, likewise Calpurnia, a lady whose beauty Claudius had incautiously praised. Lollia Paullina had been killed in exile: her ashes were brought back. Even the two clients of Junia Silana were pardoned. Death had overtaken that lady at Tarentum on the way back from her distant place of exile, her journey begun because Agrippina's power was slipping—or her resentment abated.

The name of Silana might have evoked that of her ally Domitia, who managed to outlive Agrippina and died soon after, in 59. Her end was hastened by Nero, so it is alleged. In the account of Suetonius, Nero urged the doctors to give his aged aunt rough treatment, he seized her possessions before she passed away, and he suppressed her testament.[37] The version of Dio has poison, Nero not waiting for the course of nature but avid to lay hands on her properties at Baiae and at Ravenna.[38] Domitia was a wealthy woman. Her gardens across the Tiber are on subsequent record.[39] She was also mean and sordid, as shown by her altercation with a certain Junius Bassus. He had alleged, so she said, that she sold old shoes. Not so, was his retort: she bought them.[40]

It is strange that Tacitus should have omitted to register the decease of this potent female. It was not his habit to lose sight of characters that excited his interest; the women of the dynasty are accorded lavish treatment and narration; and Domitia must have cropped up previously, more than once. Various phenomena in the later books of the *Annales* suggest that the work did not benefit from a final revision. Among them are omissions. The historian, confident of survival when in Book III he proclaimed the intention of going back and dealing with the Augustan times, may not have lived long enough to complete his present task.[41]

When extinguished, Domitia was 'grandis natu'.[42] Surely over sixty.

---

[35] XIII.27.3.
[36] XIV.12.3.
[37] Suetonius, *Nero* 34.5.
[38] Dio LXI.17.1 f. She is amalgamated with Domitia Lepida by J. H. D'Arms, *Romans on the Bay of Naples* (1970), 212, cf. the Index.
[39] cf. *PIR*[2] D 171.
[40] Quintilian VI.3.74.
[41] *Ann.* III.24.3, cf. *Tacitus* (1958), 742 ff.
[42] Suetonius, *Nero* 34.5.

She may have seen the light of day several years before her brother, the consul of 32. Her husband was a son of L. Passienus Rufus, consul in 4 BC and proconsul of Africa when for an unrecorded war he earned the *ornamenta triumphalia*.[43] An inscription shows the people of Thugga recalling 'amicitia' with him when they paid honour to his son, military tribune in the legion XII Fulminata.[44] This Passienus Rufus is probably the man subsequently taken in adoption by Sallustius Crispus. His service in that legion may fall at the time of the Bellum Gaetulicum waged by Cossus Cornelius Lentulus. It is recorded by Cassius Dio under AD 6.[45] What is known of the distribution of the legions makes it a plausible assumption that the province Africa at this time had XII Fulminata as well as III Augusta.[46]

If the tribune is identical with the husband of Domitia, his accession to the *fasces* in 27 occurred later than might have been expected; and he was *suffectus*, not one of the *ordinarii*. The 'potentia' of Sallustius Crispus, on the wane well before his decease in 20, so Tacitus is careful to record, may not have been effective beyond the grave.[47] Yet Crispus had annexed influential connections. The inscription of a freedman discloses a Sallustia Calvina.[48] Hence descent from Domitius Calvinus—and also a link with one branch of the Junii Silani.[49] Nor will one neglect a high equestrian official.[50]

No other husband is attested for Domitia. Something of an anomaly among the great ladies of the epoch. Her sister Lepida had at least three (see below). Domitia may therefore be put to good employ in order to elucidate obscure links in genealogy.

First, Q. Haterius Antoninus, the consul of 53 with for colleague a descendant of Augustus, namely D. Junius Silanus Torquatus, one of the three sons of M. Silanus and Aemilia Lepida. His father was D. Haterius Agrippa (*cos.* 22), described as a relative of the imperial prince Germanicus Caesar. The relationship is explained by postulating the marriage of the *novus homo* Q. Haterius to a daughter of Marcus Agrippa.[51]

---

[43] Velleius II.116.2; *ILS* 120.

[44] *ILS* 8966.

[45] Dio LV.28.4.

[46] As suggested in *JRS* XXIII (1933), 25.

[47] *Ann.* III.30.4.

[48] *CIL* VI. 23601 exhibits C. Sallustius Calvinae l. Utilis, son of P. Ostorius Scapulae l. Pharnaces. Discussed in *Historia* XVII (1968), 79 = *RP* (1979), 666. As was there deduced, either Sallustius Crispus or Passienus Crispus had married a descendant of Domitius Calvinus.

[49] *PIR*² D 173, cf. J 876.

[50] His daughter had married P. Ostorius Scapula, a Prefect of Egypt under Augustus. Thus A. E. Hanson, *ZPE* 47 (1982), 247 (in a full discussion of the Ostorii, including Q. Ostorius Scapula, Guard Prefect in 2 BC).

[51] Ch. XI.

The *cognomen* 'Antoninus' which Haterius Agrippa bestowed on his son permits a conjecture. Namely that he married a daughter of Ahenobarbus and Antonia. If so, he acquired a fresh link with the dynasty. Haterius Agrippa is last heard of in 32.[52]

Cornelius Tacitus had no good to report of old Q. Haterius, an overvalued orator. Haterius Agrippa was a savage prosecutor of evil life, 'somno aut libidinosis vigiliis marcidus' (such is the heavily stylized label), Haterius Antoninus, with whom the line ended, a mere spendthrift.[53]

Next, Junius Blaesus, to whom Tacitus assigns 'claritudinem natalium et elegantiam morum', a man of integrity as well as style, legate of Lugdunensis in 69 when Vitellius was proclaimed by the armies of the Rhine. He died not long after at Rome, from poison so it was said. The brother of Vitellius denounced him as a menace to security through his pride of birth: 'hostem Iunios Antoniosque avos iactantem'.[54]

Few attempts have been made to indagate the Antonian ancestry of Junius Blaesus. Some might wonder about a daughter of Iullus Antonius, it is true. But the sole sign of any daughter is faint indeed. There is something better, a Domitia.[55]

On that hypothesis Domitia married one of the 'duo Blaesi' who committed suicide in 36, anticipating the condemnation implied when Tiberius transferred to others their destined priesthoods.[56] Their father was the *novus homo* Q. Junius Blaesus (*suff.* 10), the uncle of Aelius Seianus and the only man of consular rank fatally involved in his destruction. The elder of the two brothers was Q. Junius Blaesus, consul suffect in 26.[57] By reason of age and standing perhaps the better candidate for the hand of Domitia.[58]

To equip Nero's aunt with two husbands anterior to Passienus Crispus is not an operation to strain belief. Given her character, there are no grounds for fancying that matrimony with Passienus had been blessed with either concord or long duration when Agrippina snatched him.

To proceed with the hypothesis. Going by the consular year of Haterius Antoninus, Domitia was still married to Haterius Agrippa (*cos.* 22) in 20. If she was born a little before 2 BC, the nuptials would belong in a suitable season for a first marriage of both partners. Divorce in the sequel and marriage to Junius Blaesus would find an easy explanation in the mounting power of Aelius Seianus.

[52] *Ann.* VI.4.4.
[53] VI.4.4.; XII.34.2.
[54] *Hist.* III.38.3. No suggestion was offered in *PIR*² J 737.
[55] For this conjecture, *Antichthon* IX (1975), 62.
[56] *Ann.* VI.40.2.
[57] *PIR*² J 739.
[58] Space happens to be available for his brother, and for Q. Sanquinius Maximus (*suff. II* 39), in the year 28. Cf. *ZPE* 43 (1981), 373 = *RP* III (1984), 1432. That is, despite the presentation of the year in Degrassi, *I fasti consolari* (1952).

The hypothesis here ventured unites two enigmatic relationships in an economical fashion. If one or the other of the marriages conjectured for Nero's aunt is rejected, or if both are held not valid, the best recourse is to invent a third sister who did not live long enough to come into prominence under Caligula and Claudius. Suetonius, it may be recalled, does not happen to register the separate existence of Domitia and Domitia Lepida. However, the Domitii were notoriously a non-prolific family. For the consul of 54 BC and his descendants only one son is certified in each generation; and there is no Domitia on show during the last epoch of the Republic or the reign of Caesar Augustus.[59]

Next, Domitia Lepida, the mother of Valeria Messallina. In a careful account of what befell Claudius in the search for a wife (two betrothals failing and two marriages), Suetonius defines the third wife as 'Barbati Messalae consobrini sui filiam'.[60] That discloses the husband of Lepida, not named in any other author. His parents were Messalla Appianus and the younger Marcella. Since his father died quite early in his consulship, the birth year of Barbatus is 12 at the latest. Further, his lineage would have indicated a consulship by AD 23.

The date of the marriage of Barbatus and Lepida is bound up with that of her next marriage, with Lepida's own age, and with the age of her daughter.

The identity of her second husband, namely Faustus Cornelius Sulla (*suff.* 31), is revealed by a notice in Zonaras which states that his son was a half-brother of Messallina.[61] At first sight the date of Lepida's marriage to Faustus would appear to be not later than 18, given the consulship of her son, Faustus Sulla (*cos.* 52). However, reflection will suggest that he acceded to the *fasces* several years in advance.[62] In 46 or 47 he married Antonia, the elder daughter of Claudius Caesar, made available by the execution of the young Pompeius Magnus, who had been given a remission of five years when he took her in 41.[63]

There is no evidence to define the duration of this second marriage or its termination, whether by death or divorce. Faustus is not heard of after 31.

In the early months of his reign Claudius Caesar was impelled to make various matrimonial arrangements. One of them was a husband for his wife's mother (he had married Messallina about two years previously). For this purpose the Emperor summoned to Rome from his governorship of Tarraconensis the aristocratic C. Appius Junius Silanus (*cos.* 28), who had Claudian blood through his maternal grandmother.[64]

---

[59] The *Ara Pacis* however can now counter that established persuasion. That is, two forgotten children.

[60] Suetonius, *Divus Claudius* 26.2.

[61] Zonaras XI.9.

[62] *PIR*² C 1464: 'ante tempus legitimum, ut opinor'.

[63] Dio LX.5.8.

[64] Dio LX.14.3. On whom, see further Ch. XIV.

A suitable match, it should seem. If acceptable to Domitia Lepida (who can tell?), it was not to the liking of Messallina, and Ap. Silanus fell victim to her intrigues in the course of the next year. The imperial freedman Narcissus reported to Claudius a dream in which he had seen the Emperor slain by the hand of Silanus; Messallina had had a similar vision.[65] Claudius lent credence, and Silanus was put to death.

At her first entry in the *Annales*, Lepida exhibits compassion and fortitude. Although 'florenti filiae haud concors', she was with Messallina at the end, urging upon her the argument of honour in firm and noble language.[66] Messallina was not responsive: 'animo per libidines corrupto nihil honestum inerat.' In irresolute panic she had to be finished by the sword of a tribune.

After this there happens to be nothing until the last year of Claudius Caesar (and her sister Domitia does not emerge until 55). They were not women of a discreet and retiring nature—and they remained on bad terms with their cousin Agrippina all through, perhaps from the day she married their brother.

In 54 it was alleged that Lepida had been employing magical arts against Agrippina; and she had also failed to keep in order the armies of slaves on her vast estates in Calabria.[67] She was condemned and put to death.

Equal in their vices (each was 'impudica, infamis, violenta'), equal also in pride of lineage, Lepida and Agrippina had been in bitter competition for influence over Nero. Lepida tried to win him by gifts and by acts of kindness, whereas Agrippina was 'trux ac minax' in her demeanour, domineering, and masterful.[68] Lepida in fact had taken care of the boy when his father died in 40: on this occasion he testified against her.[69]

When alluding to the family and ancestry of Domitia Lepida, Tacitus calls her a daughter of the younger Antonia; and that Antonia was also named in the obituary notice of Lepida's father.[70] The error was easy to make. Tacitus assumed that the elder niece of Caesar Augustus went to his stepson Drusus. Inadvertence of this kind can deceive the most diligent of enquirers. Tacitus made another assumption about Lepida. Matching her with Agrippina, the historian states that they were more or less of an age: 'nec forma aetas opes multum distabant'.[71] Commentators have failed to see that that can hardly be. Agrippina was born in 15. Now Lepida

---

[65] Suetonius, *Divus Claudius* 37.2.
[66] *Ann.* XI.37.3.
[67] XII.65.1.
[68] XII.64.3.
[69] Suetonius, *Nero* 6.3; 7.1.
[70] *Ann.* XII.54.2; IV.44.2.
[71] XII.64.3.

married Messalla Barbatus in that season; and she further had a son by her second marriage not long after (Faustus Sulla, the consul of 52).[72] Lepida might therefore be as much as a dozen years older than Agrippina (but still younger than her brother and her sister).

As has been observed, Antonia stands on meagre record.[73] Some may have suspected that she passed away in the last decade of the reign, not long after giving birth to Domitia Lepida. An isolated item dispels the notion and endows her with length of days.

The elder Seneca, sparse in allusion to events or persons in the next reign, mentions 'Domitium, nobilissimum virum'. After having constructed when consul a bath house in his mansion overlooking the Via Sacra, Domitius took to frequenting the schools of declamation. That was in the right order, said the witty *rhetor* Asilius Sabinus, making comment to his mother, who had complained about sloth in her son.[74]

The present enquiry has conjured up a wife for Ahenobarbus the admiral, two husbands for Domitia antecedent to Passienus Crispus. A different operation retrieves from erudite negligence the two children of Ahenobarbus and Antonia on the monument of *Pax Augusta*.

Another figure in their immediate proximity solicits brief inspection. Between Antonia and her husband, in the background, is the head of an elderly man bowed towards the right (they and the girl occlude his body).[75] About identity, not much speculation. On one notion, perhaps Maecenas.[76] Or even the poet Horace.[77]

For either to parade in an aristocratic gallery is exorbitant. Why not a consular attached to the 'domus Augusta'? That is, Paullus the Censor. He had lost his Cornelia three years previously, but was soon to take over the younger Marcella when the consul Messalla Appianus died.[78] Furthermore, here lodged in suitable vicinity to Ahenobarbus if the assumption be cogent that the mother of Ahenobarbus was an Aemilia Lepida, none other than a sister of Paullus.

Children of Ahenobarbus and Antonia augmented the dynastic group in an early season, parallel to the progeny of Agrippa and Julia. The girl,

---

[72] These facts are relevant to the age of Valeria Messallina, cf. below, p. 178.

[73] Observe *PIR*² A 884 in contrast to A 885 (the widow of Drusus).

[74] Seneca, *Controv.* IX.4.18. Cited in *PIR*² D 127, but not in A 884. In the Index to the Loeb edition (1974) Domitius is described as an 'unidentified nobleman', and 'perhaps the consul of 32 BC.'

[75] E. Simon, *Ara Pacis Augustae* (1967), p. 15.

[76] G. Moretti, *Ara Pacis Augustae* (1948), 231, cf. 256.

[77] E. Simon, o.c. 19 f.

[78] As argued in Ch. XI. The female figure standing on the *Ara* between Drusus and the wife of Ahenobarbus has sometimes been supposed a Vipsania. Thus Moretti, o.c. 231. The younger Marcella is not excluded.

one surmises, enjoyed no long survival—yet by all analogy already betrothed to some illustrious youth.[79] Curiosity also attends upon her coeval (and presumed cousin), namely the daughter whom Cornelia bore to Paullus in 22. No trace, save in the poem of Propertius.[80]

Next, the robust boy, who may be called 'Lucius', close in age to Gaius Caesar. When a young man he accompanied the prince to the Orient and there behaved atrociously. He killed one of his freedmen 'quod potare quantum iubebatur recusarat', and in consequence he was expelled from the 'cohors amicorum'.[81]

Nevertheless, Lucius might expect a bride and a priesthood in the near sequel. Further, if he survived much longer, he might hope to derive benefit, like others, from opportune deaths—or else, regarded as a nuisance, find himself consigned to seclusion on some penal island, like the cousin who bears the label 'robore corporis stolide ferox'.[82]

---

[79] Not that an early decease (perhaps in 12) can with confidence be assumed. Observe how scanty is the written evidence about her mother—or about the younger Marcella.

[80] Propertius IV.11.67. Not named, this Lepida was denied an entry in *PIR*[2]. Likewise Julia, the niece of Hadrian.

[81] Suetonius, *Nero* 5.1.

[82] *Ann.* I.3.4.

XIII

Princesses and Court Ladies

Women have their uses for historians. They offer relief from warfare, legislation, and the history of ideas; and they enrich the central theme of social history, if and when enough evidence is available. Ladies of rank under the first imperial dynasty are a seductive topic. In the first place, betrothal and marriage, adultery and divorce. Next, licence and luxury, kinship and discord. Finally, the enormous wealth accruing to a widow or a daughter in families ancient or recent that had benefited from civil war and the bounty of the victor: the palaces at Rome, the villas in the Italian countryside, the wide estates, the hordes of slaves. The testimony is casual and sporadic. The historian Tacitus has a keen eye for wealth and inheritance, but he seldom specifies the origin and nature of a great fortune: he is generally content with the plain but ample word 'opes'.[1]

Court life rose and flourished with the coming of the monarchy. Not all of its manifestations were approved by Caesar Augustus, or by his spouse. Two princesses in turn brought annoyance. Disasters abroad and repression at home darkened the last decade of that long reign. The sombre successor also disliked luxury and display. A bleak season supervened even before he went away to Capreae.

On the accession of young Caligula, life picks up sharply, and liberation, with vivid and predictable results through three decades until Nero's end. A whole group now emerged: the three sisters of Caligula, the daughter of Drusus Caesar, Nero's aunts on the paternal side, and half a dozen women of beauty, ambition, and high spirits, from families in the kinship or entourage of the dynasty. Their vicissitudes prove instructive on various counts.

Tiberius took no pleasure in feminine society. His aversion, it appears, was not confined to disapprobation of women active in politics. To share and comfort the long years on Rhodes and on Capreae he chose philosophers and astrologers, scholars and poets. Of the scandalous stories adhering to Capreae, only one brings in a woman. A certain Mallonia repulsed obscene advances and was put to death.[2]

[1] The words 'opes' and 'pecunia' each take up nearly five columns in the *Lexikon* of Gerber–Greef.
[2] Suetonius, *Tib.* 45.

Nor is there any hint of an illicit son, apart from L. Salvius Otho (*suff.* 33). There was a close physical resemblance, and Tiberius liked him.[3] Otho's father, of ancient stock among the notables of Etruria, had in fact been brought up in the household of Livia, who got for him the rank of senator and a bride from an illustrious house (the biographer does not say who she was). Illegitimacy in the Roman governing class is a subject not lacking in appeal—and in perplexities, given the rarity of the allegation.[4]

After Julia, Tiberius was not disposed to essay another experiment in matrimony. Augustus, when adopting Tiberius, had his own strong views and precise plans about the way the succession should go. In the first place Germanicus Caesar (the son of his niece Antonia), now marrying Agrippina, then Drusus, the son of Tiberius.

A wife for Tiberius Caesar would import various complications (even had Tiberius been willing and appetent), either in the near sequel or later on, if children ensued. Society ladies abated their hopes or fears.

In 22 Tiberius Caesar passed unscathed through the sixty-third year of his life. The next year brought with it a predicament, Drusus perishing so soon after Germanicus. The ruler was left with boy princes, much as Augustus had once been; and he was encompassed by four widows.

Tiberius seems to have been on good terms with Antonia, his brother's relict, but he now had much to suffer from the domineering nature of his mother, the old Augusta. The urgent menace and preoccupation came from Agrippina and Livia Julia, discordant and soon to be clamouring for husbands. Livia (the wife of Drusus) had been seduced by Aelius Seianus, and Seianus now used his arts to inflame the Emperor's suspicions about Agrippina (who was ambitious, outspoken, and indiscreet).

Tiberius was eager to make his escape from a noxious atmosphere, a perilous environment. In 26 he went to Campania, and the next year saw him installed in his island citadel, never to enter Rome again. The ruler's decision to retire did not need much encouragement from the artful persuasions of his favourite and minister. Seianus, as Tacitus saw, was an explanation all too obvious and superficial.[5]

For building up an account of the principate of Tiberius Caesar that should not degenerate into the biography of the ruler, Tacitus had constant recourse to the *Acta* of the Roman Senate, as is evident from many indications and notably from the choice and disposition of matter in Book III.[6] After a time he became aware of factors and episodes in private or secret history.

---

[3] Suetonius, *Otho* 1.2: 'tam carus tamque non absimilis facie Tiberio principi fuit ut plerique procreatum ex eo crederent.' He might have been born as late as 6 BC.

[4] *Proc. Am. Phil. Soc.* CIV (1960), 323 ff. = *RP* (1979), 510 ff.

[5] *Ann.* IV.57.1: 'plerumque permoveor num ad ipsum referri verius sit.'

[6] *Historiographia Antiqua* (Louvain, 1977), 247 ff. = *RP* III (1984), 1028 ff.

Under the year 26 he reports a pertinent item.[7] Not from any of the annalists. He found it in the memoirs of Agrippina's daughter. Agrippina formally entreated Tiberius to assign her a husband. Tiberius left her without an answer.

Whom Agrippina had in mind as a consort and guardian of her six children might seem 'a question above antiquarism, not to be resolved by men or even by spirits'. Men of the time might have been impelled to wonder about Asinius Gallus, a widower since the death of Vipsania.[8]

Annoyed by Agrippina's request, the Princeps had already shown reticence about the matrimonial prospects of Livia Julia. The historian produces an interchange of letters between Seianus and Tiberius the year before.[9] The minister asked for the hand of Livia as a recompense for his loyal devotion. The Emperor in a long and carefully reasoned reply enlarged upon sundry impediments, and, after asseverating that he would not stand in the way, ended with a vague hint of intentions for the future benefit of Seianus: no elevation was too high for his virtues and devotion, as would be announced in due course either in the Senate or before the people.[10]

The pair of letters exhibits the historian's inventive art to deadly perfection. To impersonate Tiberius Caesar was tempting and congenial, and he had the model, a number of orations and despatches. Not so for Seianus.[11]

The closing words of Tiberius are intended (there can hardly be a doubt) to foreshadow what happened in the Senate when the 'verbosa et grandis epistula' was read out on October 18 of the year 31, conveying the doom of Aelius Seianus.[12]

The 'conspiracy of Seianus' is beset with many problems. At the least it should appear that the minister was not plotting to murder Caesar and reign in his stead. Dynastic loyalty had struck its roots too deep for that. Rather was it his design to act as regent for the boy Ti. Gemellus, the grandson of the Emperor. To that end the hand of a princess was desirable.

In the course of the year 31, Seianus had managed to get betrothed to a lady of the dynasty. Her identity is one of the obscure points. Various reasons speak for Livia Julia, the mother of Ti. Gemellus.[13] Rather perhaps

---

[7] *Ann.* IV.53.

[8] Ch. X.

[9] *Ann.* IV.39 f.

[10] IV.40.7.

[11] Some assume a basis in genuine documents (somehow felicitously preserved). Thus R. Seager, *Tiberius* (1972), 196. For comparison, one observes the antiphonal orations of Seneca and Nero (XIV.53 ff.).

[12] Juvenal X.71. From brief indications in Dio (LVIII.10.1), Ben Jonson was able to construct a convincing version (*Sejanus*, Act IV, Scene IX).

[13] For her nomenclature, *PIR*[2] L 303. Tacitus calls her 'Livia' (ten times), cf. Pliny, *NH* XXIX.

her daughter Julia, aged about twenty-five:[14] now available since Nero her husband (the eldest son of Germanicus) had been arrested in 29 and put to death the year after.[15] Livia (originally married to C. Caesar), was now about forty-three.

Livia committed suicide a few days after the fall of Seianus. Apicata, whom Seianus had divorced in 23, alleged that Seianus and Livia poisoned Drusus Caesar. Which was held to be confirmed by confessions elicited through torture from a doctor and a eunuch.[16]

That was not the end of problems about princesses. Tacitus opens the year 33 with that theme. Tiberius Caesar, who hated making decisions, could no longer put off the selection of husbands for two daughters of Germanicus, namely Julia Drusilla and Julia Livilla.[17] The eldest, Agrippina, had been consigned five years earlier to Domitius Ahenobarbus (*cos.* 32).

Early marriages ensued from the dynastic schemes of Caesar Augustus. The family produced princes as well as princesses, with habits appropriate to monarchy in any age. In the year 20 Nero, the eldest son of Germanicus Caesar, both assumed the *toga virilis* and was united in matrimony to Julia, the daughter of Drusus Caesar.[18]

The recluse of Capreae was now seventy-three. His years, if nothing else, set him firmly against the pretensions of young men who stood in promising or dangerous proximity to the power. Alert observers, noting his choice of Ahenobarbus, might speculate on existing relationships, especially where the Princeps approved of ancestry or parentage. The excellent M. Lepidus had a son, close coeval and friend of Caligula. And there was M. Junius Silanus, born in the last year of Augustus: his father had married Aemilia Lepida (the daughter of L. Paullus and the younger Julia).

If youth was a bar, and kinship perhaps to be avoided (the recent match between Ahenobarbus and Agrippina was not a good idea), high birth seemed requisite. Several patricians of consular years might offer for

20, and the epigraphic evidence. In both Suetonius (three times) and in Dio (twice) she is styled 'Livilla'. Hence confusions or defects in some modern accounts.

That Seianus secured betrothal to Livia is assumed by recent writers, e.g. E. Meise, *Untersuchungen zur Geschichte der julisch-claudischen Dynastie* (1969), 57 ff.; R. Seager, *Tiberius* (1972), 213; B. Levick, *Tiberius the Politician* (1976), 170; D. Hennig, *L. Aelius Seianus* (1975), 78.

[14] As in Dio LVIII.3.9. Assumed with no mention of alternative in *PIR*[2] J 636.

[15] Their marriage took place in 20 (*Ann.* III.29.3). Julia's birth is put *c.*AD 3 in *PIR*[2] J 636. Surely two or three years too early.

Livia's marriage to C. Caesar is registered by Dio under 1 BC (LV.10.18). Perhaps a year too soon. In *PIR*[2] L 303 her birth is put 'inter annos 14 et 11 a. Chr.'

[16] *Ann.* IV.11.2.

[17] VI.15.1.

[18] III.29.

inspection. Thus two descendants of Sulla the Dictator in the direct line, Faustus (*suff.* 31) and Sulla Felix (*cos.* 33). Faustus had acquired a link with the dynastic group by marrying Domitia Lepida, the sister of Aheno-barbus. There is no sign how long the match endured. Next to nothing is known about the younger brother, apart from brief wedlock seven years later, casually emerging on a provincial inscription.[19] Again, Paullus Fabius Persicus (*cos.* 34), whose father had married Marcia, a cousin of Caesar Augustus. But the father had been a rival and enemy of Tiberius.

No reproach could attach to Ser. Sulpicius Galba, high in prestige though he had not yet acquired his principal and delusory claims, high also in the esteem of Tiberius. A curious anecdote brings Galba, consul in this same year, into the dynastic context. Tiberius summoned Galba to an interview and after a probing conversation dismissed him with the remark 'tu quoque, Galba, quandoque degustabis imperium'. Tiberius through the science of the Chaldaeans had cognisance of this man's imperial destiny: 'seram et brevem potentiam'.[20]

However that may be, the head of the *gens Claudia* turned aside from patricians; he distrusted the conceit and ambition of youth; he was responsive to ability, but not eager for too much of it; and he would look for stable character among aristocrats already mature, or even perhaps approaching the middle years of life.

There was a further, and limiting, factor if the Princeps wished to avoid a consequence all too often entailed by dynastic matches (and painfully familiar to himself), namely the disruption of a marriage. At Rome it was not easy to discover an aristocrat still a bachelor in his late twenties. However, liberation from a wife through death or divorce may sometimes have come opportunely to further the ambitions of a *nobilis*.

Tiberius Caesar gave the matter long and anxious thought, after his fashion.[21] The historian has not chosen to enlarge on the ruler's motives—which would not escape the kind of reader he has in mind. But he furnishes indirect illumination through the brief comments he appends on the selected husbands, whom Tiberius in his missive presented 'levi cum honore' (such was his manner). They turned out to be the consular pair of the year 30, L. Cassius Longinus and M. Vinicius. Drusilla went to Cassius, Julia Livilla to Vinicius.

[19] *AE* 1927, 172 (Pisidian Antioch), which styles him 'gener [German]ici Caesar[is.' After the death of Ahenobarbus (in 40) Agrippina married him, before acquiring Passienus Crispus. Thus Groag in *PIR²* C 1465.

[20] *Ann.* VI.20.2. Dio assigns the anecdote to the year 20, when Galba was taking a wife (LVII.19.4). In Suetonius, Augustus is the author of the prediction (*Galba* 4.1).

[21] *Ann.* VI.15.1: 'diu quaesito.' Neglect of this significant phrase leads to aberration. Thus G. V. Sumner, exalting Vinicius, puts the betrothal of Julia Livilla a number of years before his consulship (*HSCP* LXXIV (1970), 295). Observe further J. Humphrey, *Am. Journ. Anc. Hist.* IV (1979), 131: 'in fact two betrothals of Germanicus' daughters seem to have been settled well before Agrippina's marriage to Ahenobarbus.'

Cassius Longinus belonged to the old plebeian *nobilitas*. Though brought up by a strict parent, he failed to reproduce the family type, being an easy-going fellow: 'facilitate saepius quam industria commendabatur'.

The ultimate extraction of M. Vinicius was municipal, from Cales in Campania, the father and grandfather consular. He was an elegant orator and gentle in disposition: 'mitis ingenio et comptae facundiae'.

For convenience, for artistry, or perhaps for some other reasons, Tacitus segregates the marriage of another princess, that of Julia (the daughter of Drusus Caesar) to Rubellius Blandus. It is recorded at a later point in the year.[22] In between he had narrated a sequence of deaths (among them the state criminals Gallus, Drusus, and Agrippina).[23]

Tacitus goes on to proclaim that this marriage was one of the reasons for grief at Rome in this deplorable year. Julia had once been the wife of Nero, the son of Germanicus, whereas Blandus (men remembered) had for grandfather a Roman knight from Tibur. Rubellius, consul suffect in 18, may now have been about fifty-five.

This was in fact the first time that a *novus homo* had been honoured by alliance with the reigning house since the nuptials of Q. Haterius and a Vipsania nearly fifty years previously. Curiosity is excited. The grandfather of Rubellius Blandus had been a famous teacher of rhetoric at Rome.[24] Tiberius Caesar may have been intending to pay homage to polite studies as well as good character.

To Tiberius' sagacious disposition concerning those princesses a later epoch furnishes an engaging parallel, namely the principles followed by Marcus Aurelius in providing for a whole collection of daughters.[25]

The four princesses escape notice for the rest of the reign of Tiberius, but the historian keeps their husbands in view by an unobtrusive device. In 36 they were chosen to form the committee that estimated the damage caused by a conflagration at Rome.[26]

All of them managed to evade peril, except for Ahenobarbus. Early in the next year a loose lady called Albucilla, 'multorum amoribus famosa', was indicted for high treason, Ahenobarbus and two senior consulars (L. Arruntius and Vibius Marsus) being implicated.[27] There may have been

---

[22] *Ann.* VI.27.1. For this marriage, and for the family of Blandus, see *AJP* CIII (1982), 62 ff. Dio registered it together with the other two (LVIII.21.1). For Dio's arrangement of events in 33, *Athenaeum* LXI (1983), 5 ff.

[23] There is a chance that it fell in the summer of the year, when Tiberius, departing from the vicinity of Rome, provided Caligula with a wife (VI.20.1): Claudia, daughter of M. Silanus (*suff.* 15).

[24] Seneca, *Controv.* II, *praef.* 5.

[25] For the detail, H.-G. Pflaum, *Journal des Savants* 1961, 28 ff.

[26] *Ann.* VI. 45.

[27] VI.47.2.

other charges against Ahenobarbus. At least Suetonius adds incest with his sister Lepida.[28]

Arruntius elected to die, for he saw a worse tyranny on the way. Whatever their guilt or their danger, Ahenobarbus and Marsus were rescued by the death of Tiberius.

Under Tiberius Caesar the texture and emphasis of the history begins to change. Despite all his efforts, the position of the ruler grew ever more autocratic—and no less when he was absent from Rome. Under his successors it is patently monarchic. Instead of senatorial annals and the relations between Princeps and Senate, the Palace now occupies the centre of interest, with dominant roles for women, for courtiers, and for the imperial freedmen. Palace politics accelerate the decline of the dynasty and the ruin of the ancient families.

The enquiry may now go forward and take in eight ladies not named in the Tiberian books, but presumably brought on in the missing portion, as prominent figures in the brilliant and pernicious court life under Caligula, and then in the first half of the reign of Claudius (which might be styled the epoch of Valeria Messallina).

The problems attendant upon Nero's aunts were such as to entail and deserve a separate treatment.[29] Enough to repeat the fact that Domitia was now the wife of the elegant Passienus (she may previously have run through two husbands). As for Domitia Lepida, bereaved of Messalla Barbatus towards the year 20, her status at the death of Tiberius is not clear. There is no word of her second husband Faustus Sulla subsequent to his consulship in 31.

After the daughters of Antonia may follow Junia Calvina and Junia Lepida, by reason of their lineage.[30] The parents were M. Junius Silanus (*cos.* 19) and Aemilia Lepida (the descendant of Caesar Augustus). They had three brothers, Marcus (*cos.* 46), Decimus (*cos.* 53), and Lucius (*pr.* 48), betrothed to Octavia, the daughter of Claudius Caesar. The sisters were born between 15 and 28, those limits being given by the ages of Marcus (born in 14) and of Lucius, who was about fifteen when honoured for his presence at the campaign in Britain.[31]

Junia Calvina first comes on record at the end of 48, in relation to charges against her brother Lucius. The historian there discloses the fact that she had recently separated from her husband, the younger son of the potent L. Vitellius, the friend and minister of Claudius Caesar.[32] Of her

---

[28] Suetonius, *Nero* 5.2.

[29] Ch. XII.

[30] For the Junii Silani, Ch. XIV.

[31] Still only a boy (Dio LX.21.5; Suetonius, *Divus Claudius* 24.3, cf. 'an]n. XVII' on *ILS* 957). Groag observed 'modo sit recte suppletus' (*PIR*[2] J 829).

[32] *Ann.* XII.4.1.

sister Junia Lepida, the first mention is late indeed, in the year 65.[33] She was then the wife of the eminent jurist C. Cassius Longinus (*suff.* 30), the brother of the husband chosen for Julia Drusilla in 33. No sign indicates when this marriage may have been contracted, and it was perhaps not the first marriage of either partner. Lepida escaped notoriety for long years. The austere discipline of her husband may have kept her safe from the perils of illustrious ancestry and the seductions of high society.

Next, Junia Silana, from another branch of that prolific family. Her identity is a question. Clearly not a daughter of M. Silanus (*cos.* 19). Rather perhaps of his homonym (consul suffect in 15), so it is generally held.[34] Junia Silana happens to turn up for the first time, briefly, in the context of Messallina and C. Silius in 48. The impetuous Messallina had broken their marriage.[35] She makes her next appearance in conflict with her erstwhile friend Agrippina in the second year of Nero's reign.

Agrippina, intervening to block her marriage to a young nobleman, denounced her as 'impudicam et vergentem annis'.[36] The imputation of unchastity may be accepted without disquiet. The graver charge is her age. By how much was she older than Agrippina, who was born in 15? Agrippina was not prone to understatement. However, to render the accusation plausible, Silana has to be older than Agrippina, were it by as little as half a dozen years. That is, waiving the validity of Tacitus' dramatic presentation. Yet he may have known more about Silana than is here disclosed.

The behaviour of Junia Silana is of clear interest for the student of Roman society. In discussing the Roman aristocracy in the time of Caesar Augustus it has been assumed that a young *nobilis* would normally marry in his early twenties, taking for his bride a girl about seven years his junior. In that period it would not be easy to discover a wife older than her husband.

That norm would continue to obtain, at least for first marriages.[37] It would, however, be overridden from time to time by the superior charms of some older lady, or by her ample possessions. And with the caprice of rulers anything can happen. Nero was at least six years younger than the beautiful Poppaea Sabina, while Caligula had taken as his fourth wife a certain Milonia Caesonia, 'neque facie insigni neque aetate integra'.[38]

On any count, the opulent Silana must have been older than C. Silius (consul designate in 48), whom Messallina took from her, 'iuventutis

---

[33] XVI.8.2.

[34] *PIR²* J 864.

[35] *Ann.* XI.12.2.

[36] XIII.19.2.

[37] Evidence from the epoch of Trajan is in conformity. Thus the marriages of Pedanius Fuscus and Ummidius Quadratus, consul and consul suffect in 118 (Pliny, *Epp.* VI.26.1; VII.24.3).

[38] Suetonius, *Cal.* 25.3.

Romanae pulcherrimum'.[39] Worse was to follow. Willing to marry her in
55, the young Sextius Africanus was frightened off by Agrippina. Not
that she wanted him for herself. Her motive was 'ne opibus et orbitate
Silanae maritus poteretur'.[40] Silana may easily have been as much as fifteen
years senior to Sextius Africanus (who became consul in 59). His ancient
family had missed distinction in the recent age; and Silius lost much of his
inheritance when his father was condemned after his proconsulate of
Asia.[41]

Fortune-hunters cannot have been lacking in the age of Augustus
among families that failed to come back from long obscurity or had
recently suffered defeat and impoverishment in the civil wars. This
depressed class of *nobiles* tends to be overlooked, as is natural. Most of the
evidence adheres to the alert and successful: consulships, priesthoods,
decorative marriages, the favour of the dynasty. Their enrichment can be
taken for granted. Such were the rewards accruing to loyalty—or quite
often to changes of allegiance.

In comment on the moral and sumptuary legislation of Caesar
Augustus, Tacitus is at pains to point out that luxury and extravagance
flourished unabated from the War of Actium to the fall of the dynasty.[42] In
consequence, houses of ancient opulence went to ruin through competi-
tive expenditure and display. In this exemplary digression the historian
does not have much to say about the victims of ambition or political
justice, plundered by the Caesars and by their agents. His whole narration
documents the process.

Impoverished for one reason or another, the descendants of old families
were reduced to all manner of expedients, but seldom to commerce or
industry. Venal noblemen were induced by Nero to perform on the stage.
Tacitus refrains from registering their names: the men were dead, and
their forebears called for deference.[43]

So far reflections suggested by Junia Silana. The great Agrippa became an
ancestor of emperors, and with the efflux of time ladies descended from
other *novi homines* occupy the front ranks of society and become eligible
consorts for the rulers.

Lollia Paullina was the granddaughter of the notorious M. Lollius (*cos.*
21 BC), singled out by Horace for integrity, by Velleius for craft and
corruption—and a bitter enemy of Tiberius.[44] For a time Lollia was the
wife of the excellent Memmius Regulus who as consul performed loyal

[39] *Ann.* XI.12.2.
[40] XIII.19.2.
[41] IV.20.1.
[42] III.55.
[43] XIV.14.3.
[44] below, p. 401.

service to Tiberius in the demolition of Aelius Seianus. Later, when governor of Moesia, Memmius agreed to surrender his wife to the importunacies of Caligula, who had heard tell of the beauty of her grandmother.[45] However, Lollia's charms lacked efficacy, and Caligula discarded her, but would not let anybody else possess her.

Memmius lived on for long years, but Lollia did not revert to him, so it appears. She was available in 48 for the hand of Claudius Caesar: 'maxime ambigebatur inter Lolliam Paullinam M. Lollii consularis et Iuliam Agrippinam Germanico genitam'.[46]

On the basis of this text a number of scholars have supposed that the great Lollius had a son who reached the consulate; and some would even have him a consul suffect of the year 13.[47] That is not likely, given the disgrace of M. Lollius in AD 2—and the enmity nourished by Tiberius for long years thereafter. When requesting the Senate to honour Sulpicius Quirinius with a public funeral and recounting his merits and his loyalty, the Princeps was put in mind of the Rhodian years and could not suppress harsh words about Lollius.[48]

However that may be, the expression 'M. Lollii consularis', taken to indicate filiation, is incorrect as well as without parallel in the usage of Tacitus.[49] The text requires amendment. The best solution is probably to add the word 'neptem'.[50] With which, the son of M. Lollius remains a cipher.[51]

The next notice about Lollia, a little further down, also carries a problem. Claudius Caesar, announcing to the Senate her banishment, prefaced his sentence (there had been no trial) with copious annotation about her pedigree: 'multa de claritudine eius praefatus'.[52] Her mother, he said, was a sister of L. Volusius, her 'patruus maior' Cotta Messallinus. Further, he mentioned her marriage to Memmius Regulus but kept quiet about Caligula.

The nowhere named son of the consular M. Lollius had married a sister of L. Volusius Saturninus (*suff.* 3).[53] This man, the second consul of that remarkable family, happens not to find a mention in the *Annales* before the notice of his decease in 56 at the age of ninety-three.[54] As for Cotta

---

[45] Suetonius, *Cal.* 25.2; Dio LIX.12.1.   [46] *Ann.* XII.1.1.

[47] The son was registered, below the line, with a query, by Degrassi, *I fasti consolari* (1952). A consulship is regarded as certain, and probably in 13, by P. A. Brunt, *JRS* LI (1961), 81. For reasons against, *Tacitus* (1958), 748; *JRS* LVI (1966), 59: reasons accepted in *PIR*² L 312.

[48] *Ann.* III. 48.2: 'quem auctorem C. Caesari pravitatis et discordiarum arguebat'.

[49] No doubts were disclosed by H. Fuchs (Ed. Helv., 1949) or by E. Koestermann (Teubner, 1965).

[50] The remedy of Ritter. Better than the insertion of 'filio', cf. *Tacitus* (1958), 748.

[51] For the Lollius in Horace (*Epp.* I.2.1; 18.1), cf. *JRS* LVI (1966), 50; and further, Ch. XXVII.

[52] *Ann.* XII.22.2. As the context shows, clearly from the *acta senatus*.

[53] Hence Lollia Saturnina (*PIR*² L 329), sister to Paullina—and the wife of Valerius Asiaticus (*suff.* 35).   [54] *Ann.* XIII.30.

Messallinus, the great-uncle of Lollia, the clue lies somewhere in the history of the Aurelii Cottae: most obscure for the time of Augustus, and no consul since 65 BC. It is necessary to recall that Cotta Messallinus, otherwise M. Aurelius Cotta (*cos.* 20), was the younger of the two consular sons of Messalla Corvinus, by his second wife, an Aurelia; and he was adopted by an uncle on the maternal side.[55]

How much further can one go? M. Lollius, it has been supposed, was himself an Aurelius Cotta by birth, adopted by a Lollius.[56] This explanation tends to be repeated, or at least not contested. It is not very plausible. The consular would have every reason to retain and advertise the aristocratic and distinctive *cognomen* of his line.

A different solution may be worth canvassing. That is, M. Lollius marrying an Aurelia, a sister of the postulated and unattested Aurelius Cotta who adopted the younger son of Messalla Corvinus. Cotta Messallinus would thus be a nephew through adoption of that Aurelia, hence great-uncle to Lollia Paullina. Furthermore, for what it may be worth, the grandmother, the report of whose beauty excited Caligula, now acquires a name: Aurelia.

It will be suitable to register at this point another illustrious lady from a new family: Poppaea Sabina, whose fame and follies have been all but extinguished by her homonymous daughter. The mother comes into the *Annales* at the beginning of Book XI where the text resumes after the long gap.[57] At that time she was the erring wife of P. Lentulus Scipio (*suff.* 24). Both had been married previously. Poppaea had once been the wife of T. Ollius, an obscure person from Picenum, who came to grief in 31, one of the adherents of Seianus.[58] Her father was C. Poppaeus Sabinus (*cos.* 9), the exemplary *novus homo* who governed Moesia for the space of twenty-four years. Poppaea lacks commemoration save in Tacitus who, when introducing her daughter, was careful to note that she surpassed in beauty all the women of her time.[59]

Finally, to complete to perfection the catalogue, there stands Valeria Messallina. Among the youngest in the whole collection, yet perhaps several years senior to Junia Lepida and Junia Calvina. As though to extenuate the enormities of her conduct, the notion has been promulgated that she was only fifteen years old when in 39 she was given in matrimony to Claudius, then close on fifty.[60] That should be doubted. Her father

[55] Ch. XVII.
[56] Thus Groag, *RE* XIII. 1378.
[57] *Ann.* XI.1.1, cf. 2.1. She was accused of adultery with Valerius Asiaticus.
[58] XIII.45.1. For his origin, *CIL* I². 1919 (Cupra Maritima).
[59] XIII.45.2.
[60] Thus M. P. Charlesworth, *CAH* X (1934), 672; V. Scramuzza, *The Emperor Claudius* (1940), 90. According to R. Hanslik, Messallina was born *c.*25 (*RE* VIIIA. 246). Cf. *OCD*² (1970), 675: 'married at 14'.

Messalla Barbatus was dead by 20 at the latest, so it can be argued.[61] Messallina may already have had the benefit of matrimony or divorce.

The missing portion of the *Annales* must have had a lot to tell about these ladies. The historian made a generous allocation to Caligula and to the first epoch of Claudius: two books for each, so it may be assumed, Book X ending with the end of 46.[62] The 800th anniversary of Rome made the next year attractive for the beginning of a book (XI, of which about one third is lost). By contrast, the rest of Claudius' reign where a single book carries the story from late in 48 down to October of 54.

With Caligula the dynastic succession had come to the line of Germanicus. Caligula paid exorbitant honour to his sisters. Their husbands, it should seem, would not escape notoriety or hazard. Yet there is no word of Ahenobarbus before his decease in 40, or of M. Vinicius (*cos.* 30), the husband of Julia Livilla, until the last day of Caligula's life. Neither is named in Suetonius' biography of Caligula. Julia Drusilla was married to L. Cassius Longinus, a man of no conspicuous talent or energy. At the instance of Caligula he gave her over to M. Aemilius Lepidus, the son of Marcus Lepidus, the man deemed 'capax imperii'.[63]

Drusilla died in the summer of 38, extravagantly mourned by her brother, and deified. No setback for Lepidus, an intimate friend of the prince (there were nasty imputations), and close to him in age (Caligula was twenty-four when he came to the power). Caligula now promised Lepidus the succession and gave him a five years' remission for the consulate.[64]

Ambition, intrigue, or mischance consigned Lepidus to destruction in the autumn of the next year, dynastic politics involving one of the army commanders. This was Cn. Lentulus Gaetulicus (*cos.* 26). Appointed legate of Germania Superior in 29, by his long tenure and popularity with the troops he had built up a strong and even menacing position—and he had betrothed his daughter to a son of Aelius Seianus. Hence an engaging report. Gaetulicus intimated to Tiberius that he would not cause trouble unless himself molested.[65]

The whole affair is mysterious, the evidence disconnected and fragmentary. After expatiating on Drusilla, but failing to register the essential fact that she had been the wife of M. Lepidus, Suetonius states that the other sisters were condemned by Caligula 'in causa Aemili Lepidi' for

[61] above, p. 150. Messallina cannot have been born later than 20, cf. C. Ehrhardt, *Antichthon* XII (1978), 55.

[62] *Tacitus* (1958), 256, cf. 260. Three books are assigned to Caligula by K. P. Seif, *Die Claudiusbücher in den Annalen des Tacitus* (Diss. Mainz, 1973), 9.

[63] Suetonius, *Cal.* 24.1, cf. Dio LIX.11.1.

[64] Dio LIX.22.6.

[65] *Ann.* VI.30.2.

adultery and complicity in a plot against his life.[66] No indication of time or place. In the next biography one learns that Claudius was among the envoys despatched from Rome 'in Germaniam' after the conspiracy of Lepidus and Gaetulicus had been discovered.[67]

Suetonius comes off badly. The full narration of the historian Cassius Dio promised something better. It happens to be confused. After cursorily mentioning expeditions of Caligula beyond the Rhine and to the edge of the Ocean, it passes to games and pageantry at Lugdunum and the spoliation of wealthy Gauls, all copiously related.[68] After noting the execution of a certain Julius Sacerdos, Dio states that of the others who perished he will name only those deserving historical mention. First, Lentulus Gaetulicus, who had been governor of Germania for ten years, killed because he had won the affections of the soldiers. Then Lepidus, with relevant particulars; and Caligula banished his sisters for adultery with Lepidus.[69]

Dio is vague in chronology, he implies that Gaetulicus and Lepidus were killed at Lugdunum—and he does not link them in treason or in a plot. It is fortunate indeed that a date happens to be available. On October 27 of the year 39 the Arval Brethren rendered thanksgivings because the 'nefaria consilia' of Lentulus Gaetulicus had been detected.[70]

The essential facts are as follows, briefly. In September Caligula left Rome and went to Moguntiacum. The legate Gaetulicus was suppressed. Along with his sisters, Caligula had taken Lepidus with him. Lepidus was killed by a tribune, while Agrippina and Livilla were sent into exile on the island of Pontia.

Nothing is said of the whereabouts of their husbands at this juncture, and other eminent persons might excite curiosity. When four years later Claudius Caesar went on a journey to Gaul and Britain, mixed motives dictated the selection of the illustrious company: precaution as well as esteem and confidence. The list is instructive.[71] On this occasion it is only a stray notice that furnishes one of the *comites*: Passienus Crispus (the husband of Domitia), crossing the Alps with Caligula.[72] Both Domitia and her sister Lepida escape mention in this season.

To take the place of Gaetulicus on the upper Rhine Caligula chose not some unpretentious *novus homo* but another aristocrat of patrician lineage, Ser. Galba, a friend and favourite of the dynasty, whose austere manner

---

[66] Suetonius, *Cal.* 24.3.
[67] *Divus Claudius* 9.1.
[68] Dio LXIX.21.3–22.4.
[69] Dio LXIX.22.8.
[70] *CIL* VI.2029
[71] *CQ* XXVII (1933), 143 = *Danubian Papers* (1971), 27 f.
[72] *Schol. Juv.* IV.81.

and passion for military discipline earned prestige greater than his talents.[73] At the lowest, he was counted safe and sagacious; and he resisted solicitations to make a bid for the power after the assassination of Caligula, so it is alleged.[74] Claudius took Galba with him to Britain in 43.

One conspiracy can carry the seeds of another. Of the authors of the plot to which Caligula succumbed some sixteen months later, the most eminent was the enigmatic L. Annius Vinicianus. He was impelled, it is said, by the will to avenge his friend Lepidus.[75] And, on the day after the deed (Claudius having been already proclaimed in the camp of the Praetorians), when there was debate in the Senate about the selection of a new ruler, Vinicianus advocated the claims of M. Vinicius.[76] They were close relatives, nephew and uncle, so it is presumed.[77] Vinicianus was soon to be heard of again, in treason against Claudius.[78]

The new ruler could not forget those two days of eventful hazard, and he did his best to cover up their memory. The reign began under the name and auspices of amnesty. The men of rank who had been active participants went unscathed. Further, in the policy of conciliation Claudius (or his counsellors) devised clever stratagems to satisfy or abate rival pretensions.

In the first place there were kinsfolk of the dynasty to be thought of, the three sons of M. Silanus (*cos.* 19) and Aemilia Lepida. Claudius at once betrothed his infant daughter Octavia to L. Silanus, investing the youth with special privileges. And, a small token perhaps, a few years later when his eldest brother M. Silanus became consul in 46, at the age of thirty-one, he was allowed to hold the *fasces* for the whole twelve months.

At the same time Claudius did not neglect the descendants of the dynasts Sulla, Pompeius, and Crassus who hitherto for the most part had been denied the honour and spared the perils of propinquity (the exceptions are the Aemilia Lepida once betrothed to Lucius Caesar and Faustus Sulla, the second husband of Domitia Lepida). For his daughter Antonia (by Aelia Paetina, his second wife) Claudius selected the young Cn. Pompeius Magnus, a son of M. Licinius Crassus Frugi (*cos.* 27) and Scribonia. Like L. Silanus, Pompeius was accorded the remission of five years for the consulship.[79] Further, and not to be predicted, Claudius assigned to Crassus Frugi a military command in Mauretania, with the *ornamenta triumphalia* as his reward, an honour to be iterated most anomalously for his share in the British campaign.[80]

[73] Suetonius, *Galba* 6.2 f.   [74] *Galba* 7.1.
[75] Josephus, *AJ* XVIII.20, cf. 49. For a careful analysis, M. Swan, *AJP* XCI (1970), 149 ff.
[76] *AJ* XVIII.251.
[77] *PIR*² A 701. Vinicianus was a son of Annius Pollio (A 677).
[78] In the proclamation of Arruntius Camillus Scribonianus (below, p. 278).
[79] Dio LX.5.8.   [80] below, p. 277.

Claudius, though not lacking in craft and not as dull as he often seemed, was prone to suspicion and fear, an easy prey to women and freedmen. Valeria Messallina soon showed her paces, avid, envious and vindictive. She exploited her domination through intrigue and crime, her chief agents being Narcissus, the imperial freedman *ab epistulis* and P. Suillius Rufus (*suff.* ?41) a prosecutor of savage eloquence whose career had suffered vicissitudes since the time when he had been quaestor to Germanicus Caesar.[81]

The first year of the reign was signalized by the first victim of the Empress, namely Julia Livilla, who along with Agrippina had come back from exile. Agrippina, a recent widow with a small son, was attracted by the wealth of Passienus. She promptly took him from Domitia, whence a long feud.

Agrippina was more than a match for Messallina, but her sister succumbed. Livilla's beauty and her influence with her uncle aroused ferocious jealousy in Messallina. Accused of adultery, she was sent away to an island (this time Pandateria) and put to death soon after.[82] Of her lovers real or alleged, history preserves the name of only one: Annaeus Seneca, a brilliant orator and man of fashion. He was relegated to Corsica.

In the next year the Empress contrived the destruction of C. Appius Silanus (*cos.* 28), who had recently married her mother Domitia Lepida, by injunction of Claudius. This crime had momentous consequences, if Cassius Dio be accorded credence. It aroused the indignation of Annius Vinicianus who instigated Arruntius Camillus, the legate of Dalmatia, to make a proclamation.[83] The pretext was liberty and the Republic, as might be expected. The soldiers showed no alacrity, and the revolt collapsed within five days.[84] In himself the pretender was a formidable menace through his illustrious lineage, also by the quality of some of his allies.[85] Sympathizers at Rome were duly punished, and the affair was exploited by Messallina and the freedmen to involve many who were innocent.

The next princess to incur the anger of Messallina was Julia, the daughter of Drusus Caesar. She was put to death in 43, immoral conduct being alleged, the accuser Suillius Rufus.[86] Of her husband Rubellius Blandus, nothing is on record subsequent to the year 38. He may have died soon after. There was a son of this match, the impeccable and ill-starred Rubellius Plautus.

Meanwhile M. Vinicius, the husband of Julia Livilla, lived on, despite

---

[81] For his earlier career, *JRS* LX (1970), 27 f. = *RP* (1979), 806 f. For his consular year, P.A. Gallivan, *CQ* XXVIII (1978), 419.

[82] Dio LX.8.4 f.

[83] Dio LX.15.1 f.

[84] Suetonius *Divus Claudius* 13.2; Dio LX.15.2 ff.

[85] Ch. XX.

[86] Dio LX.18.4, cf. *Ann.* XIII. 43.2.

his perilous prominence in 41, the fate of his wife and the treason of his nephew Annius Vinicianus. He was preserved by discretion and his 'mite ingenium.' And Claudius in 45 conferred a high and abnormal distinction.

The man who enjoyed the implicit trust of the ruler was the able and artful L. Vitellius (*cos.* 34). In 43 Claudius made him consul for the second time, an honour confined since 26 BC to members of the 'domus regnatrix'.[87] That year in fact opened a notable and in some ways peculiar sequence of second consulates: Passienus Crispus (44), M. Vinicius (45), Valerius Asiaticus (46), and then no more (not even Fabius Persicus, *cos.* 34). Passienus was the husband of the Emperor's sole surviving niece. The like honour for Vinicius and Asiaticus advertised generosity and confidence on the part of the ruler—and oblivion covering the transactions of January 24 and 25 of the year 41.

Vitellius went on to hold a third consulate in 47. None of the other three had a long survival. Vinicius died in 46 and received a state funeral. He was poisoned by Messallina, whose advances he repulsed—and who feared that he might be meditating revenge for Julia Livilla, so at least Dio avers.[88] Death also overtook Passienus.[89] Poison again, administered by his wife who wanted the ample inheritance for her son. However, she was cheated of the gardens of Sallustius Crispus, for that part of the estate had previously passed into imperial possession.[90]

In the same year fell the conspiracy of two aristocrats of conspicuous ancestry, T. Statilius Corvinus (*cos.* 45) and Asinius Gallus: grandsons of the orators Messalla and Pollio.[91] A mysterious affair, which may not have been serious, or even authentic. Gallus, a small ugly man, incurred contempt and ridicule. He was exiled. There is no record of the fate of Statilius Corvinus, the last consul in the line of the great Taurus.

The notable catastrophe in this season (46 or early 47) was the killing of young Pompeius Magnus for alleged conspiracy, by agency of Messallina.[92] Being married to Antonia, Magnus was an obstacle to the prospects of her own son Britannicus. Antonia was transferred to Messallina's half-brother Faustus Sulla (*cos.* 52). Along with Magnus perished his father and his mother. Crassus Frugi would be little more than a name if Seneca had not said that he had the makings of an emperor: he was such a fool.[93]

Tacitus would have been well served by fortune if chronology allowed him to terminate Book X effectively with the doom of Frugi and

---

[87] Apart from Q. Sanquinius Maximus, succeeding Caligula in 39. This enigmatic character was *praefectus urbi*.
[88] Dio LX.27.4.
[89] above, p. 160.
[90] *ILS* 1795. That is, bequeathed to Ti. Caesar.
[91] Dio LX.27.5.
[92] Dio LX.31.7. By inadvertence Messallina was exculpated in *Tacitus* (1958), 259.
[93] Seneca, *Apocol.*11.2. For the family and its history, Ch. XX.

Magnus.[94] When the text of the *Annales* resumes, it carries a reference to Poppaea Sabina. Messallina believed that Valerius Asiaticus had once been her lover—and she was eager to lay hands on the gardens of Lucullus, which were in his possession.[95]

This bold and spirited man was in fact highly vulnerable. In a public speech after the assassination of Caligula he proclaimed that he would gladly have done the deed himself.[96] From which it was a short step to alleged complicity in the plot. The case was heard in the imperial bedchamber, Messallina being present. The indictment, launched by Suillius without much success, was taken over by Vitellius and concluded with a plea for mercy, namely that Asiaticus be permitted to choose freely the manner of his death. Then Claudius spoke, 'in eandem clementiam'.[97]

In the meantime Messallina by her threats had driven Poppaea to suicide. One reason for their enmity is disclosed: rivalry for the favours of the dancer Mnester.[98]

The next year saw the end of Valeria Messallina, whose outrageous conduct culminated in a nuptial ceremony celebrated with C. Silius. Her removal at last opened the path to power for a woman whose concentrated ambition would stop at nothing. Learning of a prediction about her son, she exclaimed 'occidat dum imperet!'[99]

Sharp competition arose for the vacant place, each of the three great imperial freedmen pressing the claims of birth, beauty, and opulence while Claudius adjudicated and wavered.[100] Narcissus spoke for Aelia Paetina (the divorced wife who had born him Antonia); and Lollia Paullina was supported by Callistus. Agrippina prevailed, thanks to alliance with Pallas and her own arts.

Her first thought was to secure Octavia for her own son, Nero. This meant action against L. Silanus, who was accused of incest with Junia Calvina.[101] Then in the next year the nuptials of uncle and niece were duly celebrated, by sanction of the Roman Senate after an elegant and hortatory address by L. Vitellius.[102] Silanus committed suicide, and his sister was relegated.

Before that year was out Agrippina wrought vengeance on her rival Lollia Paullina. She was accused of dabbling in magic and astrology, and of a suspicious consultation of an oracle. Claudius decreed that she should

[94] Otherwise he could perhaps use the public funeral of M. Vinicius.

[95] *Ann.* XI.1.1.

[96] XI.1.2, cf. Josephus, *AJ* XVIII. 159 ff. His candidature was frustrated by Annius Vinicianus (ib. 252).

[97] XI.3.1.

[98] XI.4.1.

[99] XIV.9.3.

[100] XII.1 f.

[101] XII.4.

[102] XII.5 f. For the technique and art of the oration, *Tacitus* (1958), 330 f.

forfeit her fortune and be banished from Italy. She was killed by a tribune of the Guard.[103]

Other bitter feuds subsisted, although nothing emerges until the last year of Claudius when Agrippina contrived the execution of Domitia Lepida.[104] Early in the next reign, old enmities again revived when Agrippina, her influence waning, was still able to counter the elaborate plot staged by Junia Silana with due encouragement from old Domitia.[105]

Such in brief statement are the vicissitudes of twelve court ladies. Along with Julia, the daughter of Drusus, the three sisters of Caligula may without impropriety be styled princesses. Domitia and Domitia Lepida are not far behind them in rank, while the blood of Augustus was transmitted to Junia Lepida and Junia Calvina.

Of the twelve, only Drusilla was spared either banishment or violent end. It is a portentous story of ambition and crime, or folly and misfortune. The evidence is imperfect. Only Tacitus reveals the existence of Junia Silana, Junia Lepida, and Poppaea Sabina.

The lost books of the *Annales* would no doubt have conveyed much elucidation. Yet many facts and relationships were gone beyond recall, the families having perished long since. Allowance has to be made for persons unattested yet divined from pedigrees.

The evidence is also partial and prejudiced. For example, Valeria Messallina bears the main burden for most of the crimes that diversified the first half of Claudius' reign; and it does not have to be believed that Nero's greed and impatience hastened the demise of old Domitia by maltreatment or by poisoning. Imputations of incest often lacked due warrant, and conspiracies tend to be suspect unless they succeed. Astrology and magic is another matter. All too plausible, even when not invoked to prove designs against the reigning house.

To extenuate evil habits in the daughters of Germanicus, their earlier experiences might be adduced. In 28 Agrippina at the age of thirteen had been given to Ahenobarbus, a nasty fellow with a pair of domineering and intolerable sisters. In 29 Drusilla and Livilla, still young girls, saw their mother and their brother Nero carted off to prison; and Drusus was likewise put under arrest in the course of the next year. Then in 33 Tiberius selected husbands, consulting himself, not them: the bridegrooms were senior by about eighteen years.

In the autumn of that same year their mother died, and also Drusus (or were encouraged to die). In a despatch to the Senate announcing the end of Agrippina, Tiberius Caesar declared that she was lucky not to have been

[103] XII.22.2 f. Paullina had been conceded only a small portion of 'immensae opes'.
[104] above, p. 165.
[105] above, p. 160.

strangled by the public hangman; and he proclaimed a happy coincidence, the anniversary of the fall of Aelius Seianus.[106] The Senate decreed that the day should be celebrated by solemn and public thanksgiving.

Dire hazards and humiliations reinforced ties of affection in the last surviving members of a doomed family. According to Suetonius, Caligula committed incest with each of his sisters; and, after taking Drusilla from Cassius Longinus, 'in modum iustae uxoris propalam habuit.'[107] Then in October of 39 he turned sharply against them. He published documentary evidence to demonstrate their complicity with Lepidus; and he dedicated in the temple of Mars Ultor the three daggers destined for his murder.[108]

If more were known, Julia the daughter of Drusus Caesar might deserve redemption from the general depravity.[109] Nothing incriminates Lollia Paullina except for wealth, ostentation, and pretensions. One may also conceive regrets for the lovely Junia Calvina whom Seneca labelled 'festivissimam omnium puellarum'.[110] Tacitus gently discounts the charge of incest with her brother.[111] Nor does anything stand to the discredit of Junia Lepida. The prosecutors alleged magical practices and incest with her nephew, the youthful L. Silanus.[112] A convenient allegation, to aggravate the false charge of treason brought against her husband, the jurist C. Cassius Longinus. Cassius and Silanus were consigned to exile— and Silanus was killed on the way by a centurion. The historian omits to relate what happened to Lepida.

Unlike most of the other ladies, Calvina and Lepida may each have been married once only: at least, only one husband is on attestation. They appear to be the youngest in the collection, the oldest being Domitia and Domitia Lepida. Offspring are not in high frequency. None of the twelve can show more than two children. It is expressly stated that neither Junia Silana nor Lollia Paullina had any; and none is recorded for Drusilla, Livilla, Junia Lepida, and Junia Calvina.

The Tacitean narration conveys various and valuable information about society ladies under the first dynasty. The portrayal has not failed to incur

---

[106] *Ann.* VI.25.3. Not on emphasis in apologists. Thus F. B. Marsh, *The Reign of Tiberius* (1931), 223: 'there is nothing in the record to prove that he was implacable or vindictive.'

[107] *Cal.* 24.1.

[108] *Cal.* 24.3.

[109] Her melancholy memory abode with Pomponia Graecina for forty years (*Ann.* XIII. 32.3): a casual indication of the author's personal knowledge.

However, so he stated, Julia transmitted to her mother hostile reports about her husband Nero (IV.60.2).

[110] Seneca, *Apocol.* 8.2.

[111] *Ann.* XII.4.2. Calvina was 'sane decora et procax'.

[112] XVI.8.2.

distrust as well as disapprobation. Nero's mother is the conspicuous instance.[113]

On the contrary, to be held authentic and convincing, especially in view of the peers and rivals she surpassed. Women as well as men in the high aristocracy exhibit stubborn pride: Agrippina inherited 'ferocia' from her formidable mother;[114] and she is not only 'ferox' but 'atrox'.[115] In enmity unrelenting, avid and ruthless in her designs, she achieved domination in government and imposed tight control: 'adductum et quasi virile servitium'.[116]

Late survivors from a lurid epoch attracted eager attention. Notably Junia Calvina.[117] And Statilia Messallina may have lived on, who in sequence to four husbands had annexed Nero after the decease of Poppaea Sabina.[118]

Younger and less amiable specimens recalled by tastes and behaviour the 'luxuriam imperii veterem'.[119] Early in the reign of Vespasian his younger son took Domitia Longina from her husband. Not for enduring concord or any comfort. Like Nero's aunt, and like Messallina, Longina, when becoming the Augusta, succumbed to infatuation with an actor and dancer. Domitian broke with his consort and sent her away for a season.[120]

Domitia Longina was arrogant, perhaps advertising maternal lineage and the pride of the Cassii.[121] Also bold and shameless on her own avowal when discounting adultery with Titus.[122] The notion is not idle that Longina lent confidence as well as colour when the historian depicted Julia Agrippina.[123]

---

[113] Thus, alleging distortion in Tacitus, M. L. W. Laistner, *The Greater Roman Historians* (1947), 132. 'No parallel in all history' (he said) to Messallina and Agrippina.

[114] *Ann.* XIII.2.2; 21.2, cf. II.72.1 (the last injunction of Germanicus).

[115] XII.22.1; XIII.13.3.

[116] XII.7.3.

[117] Suetonius, *Divus Vesp.* 23.4 (below, p. 197).

[118] For this accomplished lady (*PIR*¹ S 625), see below, p. 240.

[119] Juvenal IV.137.

[120] *PIR*² D 181.

[121] That is, Longina's mother was a daughter of either L. Cassius (*cos.* 30) or his brother the jurist by otherwise unattested marriages: for the former, after the death of Drusilla, for the latter, anterior to Junia Lepida. For this conjecture, *JRS* LX (1970), 36 f. = *RP* (1979), 820.

[122] Suetonius, *Divus Titus* 10.2: 'persancte Domitia iurabat, haud negatura, si qua omnino fuisset, immo etiam gloriatura, quod illi promptissimum erat in omnibus probris'. On which, *Tacitus* (1958), 780. She was still alive in the year 126.

[123] For aspects of Tacitus in relation to women see further *Greece & Rome* XXVIII (1981), 40 ff. = *RP* III (1984), 1364 ff.

XIV

The Junii Silani

When a princess by her mere existence becomes an embarrassment, autocracy in any age employs alternative methods of disposal: seclusion or a safe husband. Several penal islands offered along the shores of Italy. Julia, the daughter of Drusus Caesar, after sundry vicissitudes, was perhaps fortunate in being consigned to the elderly and unpretentious Rubellius Blandus, by whom she had several children.

To the girl Aemilia Lepida no reproach adhered save the disgrace of her parents Paullus and Julia. Forfeiting her betrothed (Claudius, the brother of Germanicus), she passed as soon as nubile to a young *nobilis*: M. Junius M. f. Silanus, who acceded to the *fasces* in 19.[1]

Lepida bore him five children, whom descent from Divus Augustus foredoomed to splendour and tribulation. The annals of the dynasty exhibit a parallel line of Junii Silani, likewise prolific. Hence annoyance for a reader, whether innocent or studious, when confronted by homonyms or by tedious instruction about names and nonentities.[2]

Few Silani ever made an impact through personality or talent, or from any action. Yet they lasted for a long time, far outliving other branches of the once numerous Junii. Equity demands that the Silani be put on review in a survey that takes life and substance from noblemen whom excellence or infamy commemorated.

While the first Junius to bear that *cognomen* goes back to a praetor during the War of Hannibal, the first tangible is the praetor of 141, by birth a patrician, a Manlius.[3] To create ancestors, adoptions were invented, or passage into the plebs in the primeval time.[4] The present case happens to be the earliest such adoption on authentication.

The father was T. Torquatus, the consul of 165, who had an elder son, also a brother, for whom he was able to gain a consulship the year after. No deficiency of Manlii therefore, although they cannot enforce another consul until a century elapses.

With a decent interval after the extinction of the Manlii (but not very

---

[1] Suetonius, *Divus Claudius* 26.1; Pliny, *NH* VII.58. Apart from the first item she is nowhere on named record.

[2] For the stemma, *PIR*², *Pars* IV, p. 351.

[3] For Junii of the Republic, consult Münzer, *RE* X. 1085 ff.; Broughton, *MRR*.

[4] Cicero, *Brutus* 62.

long) the Silani in the imperial epoch revived their *cognomen*.[5] A link with another patrician house is discoverable, the Quinctii (now passing rapidly from prominence).[6]

The son of Silanus Manlianus was elected consul for 109 along with Q. Metellus. While Metellus went to Numidia, there to earn a triumph and a *cognomen*, Silanus had to fight against the Cimbri in southern Gaul. He suffered a signal defeat. Four year later he had to face prosecution, but was acquitted.[7]

When his son Decimus came within reach of the *fasces* in the middle sixties, expert appraisers did not rate him very high. Not a good candidate for 64, since he lacked friends and reputation; and an obscure or industrious *novus homo* could beat him, so they opined.[8]

That estimate ignored potent influences that became apparent in 63. From a memorable contest, two members of decayed patrician houses succumbing (Sergius Catilina and Ser. Sulpicius), the victors came out as D. Silanus and Licinius Murena. When both were indicted for electoral bribery, the formidable Cato protected Silanus (being half-brother to his wife) and joined forces with Ser. Sulpicius to prosecute Murena.

The artful defence of Murena extols military experience and deprecates legal studies. Eloquence is subsumed by the orator; and elsewhere it is conceded that the jurist Ser. Sulpicius possessed enough of it for a consul.[9] Of claims for Murena's colleague, the advocate did well to say nothing.[10]

When the consul requested the Senate to pronounce on the associates of Catilina, it fell to Silanus to open the debate. He proposed the death penalty. The consulars concurred. Then, shaken by the speech of C. Caesar (praetor designate), Silanus changed his mind, and at a later stage he proffered an elucidation: he had not really meant to advocate a sentence of death.[11]

From transient notoriety, D. Silanus fades out after his consulship.[12] For history it is his wife Servilia who counts. Not merely as the mistress and political ally of Caesar, who supported as candidates her husband and Ser. Sulpicius.[13] In this season Servilia had in mind prospects for her three daughters. Before long they are disclosed: P. Servilius Isauricus (*cos.* 48), M. Lepidus (46), C. Cassius (*pr.* 44). Those names open a significant chapter in political vicissitudes.[14]

[5] *PIR*[2] J 838; 866.

[6] *Ann.* III. 76.2 ('imagines' of Manlii and Quinctii at the funeral of Junia). Above, p. 158.

[7] For the detail, *RE* X. 1093 ff.

[8] *Ad Att.* I.1.2.

[9] Cicero, *Brutus* 155. On which, *CQ* XXXI (1981), 421 ff. = *RP* III (1984), 1415 ff.

[10] He got named only once (*Pro Murena* 82). A subdued tribute was duly furnished in *Brutus* 240.

[11] Sallust, *Cat.* 50.4; Plutarch, *Cato* 21.

[12] He would have liked a province (*In Pisonem* 56).

[13] As argued in *Sallust* (1964), 70.

[14] See above all Münzer, *RA* (1920), 328 ff.

Discreetly receding, the consul D. Silanus M. f. left no son. As a close
kinsman can be enlisted M. Silanus D. f., praetor in 77, then proconsul in
Asia without subsequent record.[15] On the standard stemma all later Silani
descend from this person, except for C. Silanus C. f. (*cos.* 17).

The reign of Caesar Augustus shows two other consuls (25 and AD 10),
not to mention Creticus Silanus (AD 7), taken in adoption by the last of the
Metelli.[16] His extraction is not verifiable. Perhaps a son of C. Silanus, the
otherwise isolated consul of 17. For some of the others enquiry is
hazardous, entailing names nowhere documented as persons. Furthermore, speculation to account for the anomalous success of the family.

The earliest in the collection is certified as M. Junius M. f. D. n. Silanus,
the consul of 25. The filiation declares him son to the proconsul of Asia. At
once a problem of identities obtrudes. A Marcus Silanus served as legate to
the proconsul of Gaul in 54, and a homonym was with M. Lepidus in 43.[17]
They are generally held to be the same.[18] An argument avails against.
Caesar sometimes entrusted large forces in the field to young men, namely
P. Crassus and D. Brutus. Each is labelled 'adulescens'.[19] That is, not yet of
senatorial rank. M. Silanus, however, is one of three legates charged with
raising new legions in the winter of 54. Therefore, at the lowest, born in
86—which may not accord well with the consul of 25.

The earliest appearance of that consul is when he took a detachment
from Gaul to Antonius, fighting for him at Mutina, an action which
Lepidus disavowed when the outcome of the battle became known.[20]
Silanus then joined Sextus Pompeius in Sicily, and along with other
persons of note, returned to Rome in 39. He is later found in Greece in the
service of Antonius; and from Antonius he was able to make his departure
in time, disapproving of the Queen of Egypt, so it was said.[21]

After these vicissitudes the happy renegade, following on two
consulships of Agrippa and one of Taurus, held the *fasces* as colleague of
Caesar Augustus. Since he was the son of a praetor of 77, M. Silanus may
have passed the normal age, as had some other aristocrats in the first epoch
of the new dispensation.

Inscriptions in Greece equip him with Sempronia for mother, Crispina
for wife.[22] The former defies any identity.[23] The latter might be a Quinctia,
patrician. Between the last consul of the Quinctii (in 123), and the pair of

---

[15] *MRR* II.94, cf. 64.
[16] below, p. 253.
[17] *BG* VI.1.1; Dio XLVI.38.6 (cf. below, n. 20).
[18] *PIR*² J 830. For difficulties, Münzer, *RE* X. 1095 f.; Broughton, *MRR, Supp.* (1960), 32.
[19] *BG* III.11.3; VII.9.1.
[20] Dio XLVI.38.6, cf. *Ad fam.* X.30.1; 34.2.
[21] Plutarch, *Antonius* 59.
[22] *IG* VII. 1851 f. (Thespiae).
[23] One might wonder about a sister of the Antonian Sempronius Atratinus (*suff.* 34). For his
female relatives, above, p. 29.

Augustan consuls, the sole link is T. Quinctius Crispinus, on casual mention as a quaestor in 69.[24]

Although in clear possession of great influence, Marcus the consul of 25 was not able to get a consulship for his brother Lucius. In the course of 22 M. Lollius secured election, but a sharp contest for the other place arose between L. Silanus and Q. Lepidus, so much so that men of sober judgement wanted Caesar to return from Sicily.[25] In the end Lepidus prevailed (a son of Manius, *cos.* 66). Of L. Silanus nothing further is heard, and no son is on attestation.[26] Marcus may be the Silanus revealed as proconsul of Asia when Agrippa was in the eastern lands.[27]

On the other hand, a Silanus not closely related turns up: C. Silanus consul in 17. Of whom all that can be said is 'C. f.'.[28] Nor can descendants be identified.

Since the grandson of Marcus, namely the consul of AD 19, is 'M. f.', a homonymous son is a necessary postulate. From the name of Junia Calvina two generations later Mommsen divined his wife: the daughter and heiress of the great Domitius Calvinus (*cos. II* 40), still extant as late as 21. Which confirms the success attendant upon the parent. The son should have become consul. He was still among the living about the year 15, to judge by the presumed age of his own son, the consul of AD 19.

This was the man chosen to marry Aemilia Lepida. Despite the dynastic connection, M. Silanus M. f. appears to be absent from the *Annales* as extant. At first sight a surprise. A prudent disposition in Lepida's husband might explain it, averse from publicity or hazard in the Senate.

Nevertheless, M. Silanus comes into history and into a historical problem. Briefly as follows. The ageing ruler fell into the habit of proroguing the proconsuls of Asia and Africa until both reached a six year term.[29] To P. Petronius (*suff.* 19) is assigned the tenure of Asia from 29 to 35.[30] For M. Silanus an inscription indicates a sexennium in Africa.[31] The terminal year is clear. Rubellius Blandus (*suff.* 18) went there in 35.[32]

[24] Cicero, *Pro Fonteio* 1.1.
[25] Dio LIV.6.2.
[26] L. Silanus, consul suffect in AD 28, is attached to him with a query on the stemma in PIR², *Pars* III, p. 351. Better, a grandson. If so, one more *Ignotus.*
[27] Josephus, *AJ* XVI. 168. This view is held dubious in PIR² J 830. For C. Silanus (*cos.* 17) as a praetorian governor, K. M. T. Atkinson, *Historia* VII (1958), 303. To be deprecated for more reasons than one.
[28] On the stemma in PIR², C. Silanus appears as a conjectured cousin of Marcus (*cos.* 25).
[29] It happens to be registered under 33 by Dio, without names (LVIII.23.5).
[30] cf., for both Petronius and Silanus, *JRS* XLV (1955), 30 = *Ten Studies in Tacitus* (1970), 44.
[31] *ILS* 6236 (Tibur).
[32] *IRT* 330 f. (Lepcis) None the less, by overriding Dio and explaining away *ILS* 6236, some scholars have argued that M. Silanus was proconsul from 36 to 39. Thus B. E. Thomasson, *Eranos* LXVII (1969), 179 ff.; *RE Supp.* XIII (1973), 2; *ANRW* X.2 (1982), 16.

A statement made by Tacitus in the *Historiae* has caused some trouble. Caligula removed the legion in Africa from the proconsul, 'Marcum Silanum obtinentem Africam metuens'.[33] In a parallel account Cassius Dio names L. Piso (i.e. the consul of 27)[34] For once, he wins the preference.[35] For a good reason. Cornelius Tacitus was alluding to a period he had not yet investigated.[36]

In the year 36, when a great conflagration laid waste the Aventine, Caesar provided a generous relief fund, with four consular husbands of princesses to administer it, and P. Petronius added on the nomination of the consuls.[37] They did not call upon M. Silanus. Not a sufficient reason, however, for presuming decease close upon his return from Africa. He may have found a mention in the next reign when the family politics of the dynasty took on a lively aspect.

The ruler's prorogation of proconsuls in 30 and in the sequel kept Silanus and Lepida out of harm.[38] Of his three sons, the fate of the youngest (Lucius) has already been told, betrothed to Octavia and brought to ruin by Agrippina. From the resentment of the eldest (*cos.* 46) she had little to fear. His was a sluggish nature, earning from Caligula the label 'the golden sheep'.[39] Yet before the year 54 was out, Agrippina had him poisoned (he was then proconsul of Asia). Imperial lineage, suitable years of life, and an unblemished character spoke for Silanus against the claims of a boy installed by crime in the supreme power. Thus did 'prima novo principatu mors' echo the end of Agrippa Postumus (the brother of his grandmother).

The remaining brother, D. Junius Torquatus, had acceded to the consulate in 53. He went on unscathed for twelve years until, facing condemnation on flimsy allegations, he chose to commit suicide—without waiting to experience Nero's clemency, so Nero said.[40] Finally, in the aftermath of Piso's conspiracy, Lucius, the young son of M. Silanus (*cos.* 46) was sentenced to exile (the charges were 'inania et falsa') along with old Cassius Longinus, the husband of his aunt Lepida. A centurion killed him.[41]

It is time to turn to the other line of Junii Silani, likewise destined to long

---

[33] *Hist.* IV. 48.1.

[34] Dio LIX.20.7.

[35] cf. *Historia* XXX (1981), 197 = *RP* III (1984), 1357 f., where the whole problem is briefly set out.

[36] He knew about M. Silanus C. f. (*suff.* 15): because of the fate of Agricola's father, ordered to prosecute Silanus by Caligula (*Agr.* 4.1).

[37] *Ann.* VI.45.2.

[38] Lepida was still among the living in 28, to judge by the age of her son L. Silanus in 43.

[39] *Ann.* XIII.1.1. In Dio the label is attached to M. Silanus C. f. (*suff.*15) who was on high public fame. The error is not noted in *PIR*² J 832.

[40] XV. 35.3.   [41] XVI. 7.

duration and involvement with the dynasty. At the head stands a C. Silanus whom genealogy retrieves from oblivion.[42] The filiation of his eldest son (*cos.* AD 10) establishes him as 'M. f.'. Furthermore, his daughter Junia Torquata reveals by her *cognomen* close kinship with other Silani, in descent from a Manlius. Identity is a question. Perhaps a son of that isolated M. Silanus, the legate in Gaul. Perhaps rather a third brother of M. Silanus, the consul of 25.[43]

That does not exhaust the count. From the nomenclature of two grandchildren (see below) emerges the fact that this C. Silanus married an Appia Claudia.[44] Once again, one presumes, a daughter of Ap. Pulcher (*cos.* 38).[45] If so, C. Silanus was brother-in-law to Messalla Appianus (*cos.* 12). The potency of Junii Silani in this period (exhibited already in a marriage to a daughter of Domitius Calvinus), becomes more and more explicable. With these connections, it would be difficult to debar C. Silanus from a consulship—if he survived. He was still among the living about the year 18, so it can be argued (from the age of his third son, consul suffect in AD 15).

C. Silanus thus acquires an identity. He had three sons. The eldest and homonymous, consul in AD 10, underwent indictment in 22 after his proconsulate of Asia.[46] The trial, on full narration, carries features of some interest, among them Mam. Aemilius Scaurus, consular and noble, leading the prosecution. It showed Silanus guilty beyond doubt 'saevitiae captarumque rerum'. To justify condign punishment, Caesar himself took a hand, ordering to be read out in the Senate the documents concerning the case of Volesus Messalla a dozen years previously. Piso the Pontifex formulated the penalty. At the end Lentulus the Augur (likewise a close friend of the ruler) proposed an abatement: 'separanda Silani materna bona, quippe alia parente geniti'.[47] Under the word 'alia' of the manuscript lurks the mother of C. Silanus. Hence a vexatious problem. Grotius opted for 'Manlia', Madvig for 'Atia'. That finds support in a consensus of recent editors.[48]

Sundry consequences follow.[49] The name evokes Atia, the mother of Caesar Augustus and her younger sister Atia, who married Marcius Philippus (*suff.* 38 BC), whence Marcia, a cousin of the Princeps. If Philippus died *c.*30, the widow would be available for a second husband.

[42] *PIR*[2] J 824.
[43] As conjecturally on the stemma in *PIR*[2].
[44] Groag by inadvertence assumed C. Silanus C. f., the consul of 17 (*PIR*[2] C 1058).
[45] Or of his brother, on attestation in 25 (*PIR*[2] C 983).
[46] *Ann.* III. 66 ff.
[47] III.68.2.
[48] H. Fuchs (*Ed. Helv.* 1949), E. Koestermann (Teubner, 1965).
[49] Seldom drawn save by E. Hohl, *RE* X. 1088.

A third Atia can now be conjured up. Coins disclose M. Atius Balbus, proconsul of Sardinia in the epoch of the Triumvirs.[50] A daughter would supply a wife for C. Silanus, the postulated father of C. Silanus (*cos.* AD 10).[51] On that showing, the Claudian link still has to be explained. That is, Atius Balbus marrying a Claudia.

A more attractive solution is the emendation of 'alia' to 'Appia'.[52] It appears adequate. And it serves to elucidate both nomenclature and the prominence of this branch of the Junii Silani.[53]

The son of C. Silanus C. f., the criminal proconsul, is C. Appius Junius Silanus (*cos.* 28), who in 41 married Domitia Lepida and was destroyed the next year by her daughter Messallina.[54] No earlier wife is attested. A son had been discovered in the person of M. Silanus, consul suffect in probably 54 (hence born about 20), who escapes other notice.[55] He may have had a peaceful end. After Torquatus (*cos.* 53), he is the last consul of the Silani.

The second brother of the proconsul is Decimus who, involved in the disgrace of the younger Julia, saw that he had to leave.[56] Allowed to come back in 20, he discreetly eschewed the career of public honours. A son and a grandson can be evoked.

They are revealed by the gravestone of a polyonymous youth who died at twenty.[57] He is styled a grandson of Lentulus Gaetulicus. From it emerges as his father D. Silanus Gaetulicus. He is assumed a son of Lentulus (*cos.* 26), taken in adoption by the lover of Julia.[58] That is by no means certain. Advertisement of maternal ascendance by the *cognomen* cannot be ruled out. On that hypothesis, D. Silanus married a daughter of the consular. Either way, an adoption or a marriage, the attachment excites interest.

The deceased youth had the item 'Lutatius Catulus' appended to his nomenclature. His mother was therefore a Lutatia. Apart from the mother of the Mummia Achaica who married C. Galba (*suff.* 5 BC), that is the sole and last trace of a name long illustrious in the plebeian aristocracy.[59] Everything gone, except pedigree and ancestral portraits.

[50] M. Grant, *FITA* (1946), 150 ff.

[51] *JRS* XXXIX (1949), 9 = *Ten Studies in Tacitus* (1970), 63.

[52] U. Weidemann, *Acta Classica* VI (1963), 638 ff. Approved in *PIR*[2] J 824—and now accepted by H. Heubner (Teubner, 1983).

[53] Doubts have been voiced by T. P. Wiseman, *HSCP* LXXIV (1970), 212, n. 32; C. Ehrhardt, *Antichthon* XII (1978), 59.

[54] above, p. 165.

[55] *PIR*[2] J 834, cf. below, p. 196. From the nomenclature of a freedman (*CIL* VI. 7611) Mommsen deduced a 'M. Ap. Iunius Silanus' (*PIR*[1] J 542). Not with safety to be followed.

[56] *Ann.* III.24.3: 'exilium sibi demonstrari intellexit.'

[57] *ILS* 959.

[58] Thus in *PIR*[2] J 835.

[59] above, p. 75 (Mummia Achaica).

Finally, the third brother, M. Silanus C. f. He held the *fasces* in 15, as consul suffect, but sharing them with Drusus Caesar for the second half of the year. Only a *suffectus*, that might occasion surprise, since Ti. Caesar held him in especial esteem.[60] Swift promotion may have compensated for the eponymate. On his first introduction, Silanus is credited with 'potentia', and further, 'per insignem nobilitatem et eloquentiam praecellebat.'[61]

His request on behalf of his brother Decimus would not be made public without previous consultation of Caesar, who inherited the affront to the dynasty. That was hardly the case when in 22, tribunician powers being conferred on Drusus Caesar, with an opportunity for 'quaesitior adulatio' from the eminent, Silanus proposed that the holders of those powers be added to the consuls in dating both private and public documents.[62] Silanus escapes without express and personal censure from the historian, while Q. Haterius, the sponsor of another notion on that day, is derided and denounced.[63]

The author would show up the comportment of M. Silanus in a hostile enumeration later on: 'Scipiones haec et Silani et Cassii . . . censebant.'[64]

The name of M. Silanus comes into a story which Tacitus chose to narrate with much detail. Late in the year 31 Poppaeus Sabinus (governing Moesia along with Macedonia and Achaia) embarked on a long journey in pursuit of a youth who passed himself off as Drusus Caesar, then imprisoned in a dungeon in the Palace.[65] The trail led Sabinus as far as Nicopolis of Epirus, where the impostor had taken ship for Italy, after admitting that he was a son of M. Silanus. Sabinus duly made report to the Emperor, but the historian could ascertain nothing further. A physical resemblance to the prince had given support to the imposture, so one presumes.[66]

At the beginning of the year 33 the ruler issued from his island retreat and lurked for several months in the near vicinity of Rome. After announcing to the Senate husbands for the two daughters of Germanicus, he went back in the summer. He took with him Caligula, now provided with a wife: Claudia, a daughter of M. Silanus.[67]

[60] Dio LIX. 8.5. Friendship perhaps went back a long way, to the man's youth. Tiberius had been absent from Rome during most of the previous decade.

[61] *Ann.* III.24.1.

[62] III.57.1.

[63] III.57.2.

[64] VI.2.2.

[65] V.10. Dio has this item, at the end of the year 34 (LVIII.25.1). Under avowed wish to jettison Tacitus' date, sundry speculations are furnished by B. Levick, *Tiberius the Politician* (1976), 211 ff.

[66] Koestermann in his *Commentary* (1965), ad loc., goes on to assume an authentic son of the consular.

[67] *Ann.* VI.20.1. In Suetonius, 'Iunia Claudilla' (*Cal.* 12.1). Suetonius puts the marriage anterior to the fall of Seianus, while Dio reports it at the beginning of 35, with Antium the place (LVIII.25.2).

Claudia died in childbirth a few years later. When Caligula acceded to the power, he set out to humble her father. For example, he was no longer to be asked his opinion first in the Senate.[68] In unabating resentment, Caligula set on foot an indictment for treason the next year.[69] Silanus was driven to suicide. On May 24 the Arval Brethren replaced him with C. Piso.[70] He had probably been a member since early in the reign of Tiberius.[71]

So far the descendants of the obscure C. Silanus M. f., the husband of an Appia Claudia. Two women wait for brief mention. First, the famous and ferocious Junia Silana, generally held a sister to the young bride of Caligula.[72] The discrepancy in their ages should be noted, but is not itself a bar.[73] Some difficulty for Silana resides rather in the father's age (*suff.* 15), not a retarded consul. Second, Claudia's aunt, Junia C. f. Torquata, presiding over the virgins of Vesta.[74]

The Junii Silani, of slight account previously (and only one of them on record during twenty years of civil war), attained to abnormal prominence during the reign of Caesar Augustus with three consuls—not counting Creticus Silanus, the legate of Syria, who (it is significant) managed to betroth his daughter to Nero the eldest son of Germanicus Caesar.[75] Four more followed under Tiberius and two under Claudius. Then their last, he only a *suffectus*, probably in 54.[76] This man, a Marcus Silanus, has been claimed a son of the illustrious Ap. Silanus (*cos.* 28). He leaves one other trace, albeit faint.[77]

Ever and again a generation missing in a noble family arouses attention. The parents of two Silani, the consuls of 10 and 19 (C. Silanus and M. Silanus) have rewarded curiosity in ample measure. The phenomenon also attracts students of demography, or of disease and pestilence—who will be well advised to reckon with a pertinent and limiting factor. Until

---

[68] Dio LIX.8.4 ff. (with the aberration that Claudia was still his wife).

[69] *Agr.* 4.1. In comment on which, Ogilvie and Richmond in their edition (1967) suggested that this M. Silanus might be the consul of 19, proconsul of Africa 'probably A.D. 33–38'.

[70] *CIL* VI. 2028.

[71] Replacing Sex. Appuleius (*cos.* 14), according to J. Scheid, *Les Frères Arvales* (1975), 161. That scholar adopted the notion that Silanus did not become consul until about fifty (ib. 203).

[72] Thus in *PIR²* J 804.

[73] For Silana's age in relation to that of Agrippina, above, p. 175. The wife or wives of M. Silanus (*suff.* 15) would be worth knowing about: clearly illustrious.

[74] *PIR²* J 866.

[75] *Ann.* II. 432., cf. *ILS* 184 (her gravestone). The girl, deceased in or before the year 20, has missed an entry in *PIR²*.

[76] Disclosed by *CIL* XIV.3471 (shortly before 56). The colleague, 'A.[' has now been identified as A. Ducenius Geminus. Rather A. Pompeius Paullinus, cf. now W. Eck, *ZPE* 42 (1981), 229.

[77] A Scipio and a M. Silanus were involved in a property transaction with C. Caesius Bassus (*CIL* XIV. 3471: territory of Tibur). That is , the known poet, cf. *PIR²* C 192. The item (concerning also other Tiburtine Caesii) should be added to *PIR²* J 834. See further *AJP* CIII (1982), 73.

suffecti became a regular practice, Silani were too numerous to enjoy each and all the favour of Caesar.

Their abundance recalls the Metelli in a past epoch or the contemporary Cornelii Lentuli, whose distinction was social, not deriving from talent or achievement. Junii Silani cast into sharp relief the dearth obtaining for other families in the old plebeian *nobilitas*. The figures for the consuls in the last Augustan decade are instructive.[78] Apart from a Silanus, only L. Cassius Longinus and Sex. Pompeius (and Pompeii did not go back very far). By contrast, vitality in the patriciate. No fewer than ten, among them a Furius Camillus emergent after a gap of more than three centuries. Patricians, as has been shown, tend to evade, or at least survive, warfare and proscriptions.

Twenty years of civil strife reduced or extinguished noble houses dominant in the last age of the Republic. After restoration in alliance with the monarchy ensued the peaceful years of the Caesars, destroying their rivals, the descendants of the dynasts Sulla, Crassus, and Pompeius, and fatal to so many other aristocrats, whatever their quality. The decline and fall of Julii and Claudii emerges as a dual and interlocking theme.

A young man entering on public life in the early years of the second dynasty would witness and remember the funeral of Cassius Longinus, who had been the husband of Junia Lepida.[79] Nor could Rome ignore the passing of her sister Junia Calvina, the last in the blood of Divus Augustus, announced when the doors of the Mausoleum sprang open.[80]

Manifold paradoxes of fame and duration are on exhibit. The Silani went on and prospered—but no more Junii Bruti. In the son of Servilia men of the time might have discerned not only strong conservative sentiments but even a future adherent of Julius Caesar.[81] Or at least no inclination towards Pompeius Magnus, who had killed his father in the insurrection of Lepidus.[82]

Setting himself apart from other young *nobiles*, Marcus Brutus disdained to seek renown as prosecutor. His earliest production is literary. In the year 52 Brutus composed an oration for Annius Milo (after the event) and a pamphlet in which, protesting against the domination of Magnus, he came out with a firm declaration: empire is not worth it if a man has to submit to autocracy.[83]

Cato carried Brutus into the camp of Magnus. Though he gave up the

---

[78] Ch. VII.

[79] The jurist returned under Vespasian (*Dig.* I.2.47).

[80] Suetonius, *Divus Vesp.* 23.4.

[81] Through his mother's ambitions.

[82] Before the outbreak of the Civil War he refused even to speak to Pompeius (Plutarch, *Brutus* 4).

[83] Asconius 36; Quintilian IX.3.95.

cause after the battle in Thessaly, and accepted a province from Caesar, Cato's end at Utica rendered Brutus susceptible to feelings of honour and remorse, to a family feud as well as tradition and principle. In the following year he divorced his wife Claudia (the daughter of Ap. Pulcher) in order to marry Porcia, left a widow by the decease of Calpurnius Bibulus.

No great resistance therefore when Cassius solicited him to join the conspiracy. To posterity, Brutus obscured and extruded the fame of his ally. Benefiting from the close nexus with Cato, he became a hero of the educated class. Philosophers added their powerful contribution, above all those of the Stoic persuasion, with many earnest or eager adepts. In any verdict on men and motives, the modest fact will not escape notice that C. Cassius, the military man, was an Epicurean.[84]

Another Brutus suffered early occlusion. Without winning over Decimus and other Caesarians, Cassius might have lacked prospects of success. From 56 (if not earlier) D. Brutus had spent long years in Gaul with the proconsul; and in the ensuing campaigns, although in several high commands, he was never put under the necessity of fighting against fellow citizens.[85] That was not the only mark of special favour. Four years younger than Marcus Brutus, Decimus was designated to hold the consulate in 42. As a conspirator, Marcus is anything but a mystery. No proper estimate of those transactions will neglect Decimus. In him reside many unknowns, one of them being his mother, by valid conjecture a Postumia.[86] The father (*cos.* 77) was elderly and inconspicuous.

Sundry political ladies emerging in the late Republic were alert for action as well as intrigue, notably daughters of families that had missed the consulate. And for some, such as Servilia, dullness in a husband furnished incentives. Less is known about the elegant Postumia, the wife of the jurist Servius Sulpicius, a patrician like her—and not acceding easily to the *fasces*.[87]

At a party conference in the summer of 44, Servilia, arrogating precedence before a consular, assumed the role of chairman and undertook to have a decree of the Senate modified in the interests of Brutus and Cassius.[88] From that it was a short step when the energetic Fulvia took action on behalf of Marcus Antonius and stirred up a civil war in Italy.

The artful Sallust, familiar no doubt with more specimens than one of the female politician, came out with a full-length portrait of Sempronia,

---

[84] *Ad fam.* XV. 16–19.
[85] As emphasized by Münzer, *RE Supp.* V. 373.
[86] above, p. 18.
[87] Münzer, *RE* XXII. 959 f. For her convivial habits, Catullus 27.3.
[88] *Ad Att.* XV.11.

who lent her mansion for a meeting of conspirators.[89] She was bold and shameless, with nothing to deter her from crime: 'saepe virilis audaciae facinora fecerat.' Not only brains and resolution—Sempronia had wit and charm, with all the accomplishments of a polished education.

Females less obtrusive or ferocious attract and detain the student of Roman society when he casts a glance backwards or forwards. Before the epoch of the Scipiones verged to its end, women were acquiring education, and attractive examples came on show. In the sequel it was held sheer delight to converse with old ladies. Their language conveyed an archaic purity and charm.[90]

Other benefits accrued. Potent from their marriage in early years, and precious sources of political intelligence, women of the *nobilitas* survived to become repositories of facts and history.

Amiable and astute, Pomponius Atticus was assiduous in cultivation of Servilia. His essays on Roman families brought him to Junii and Servilii soon after the Battle of Pharsalus.[91] For that design it was not too late to consult a great-aunt of Servilia, deceased at the age of ninety-seven.[92] That is, Livia, the relict of Rutilius Rufus (*cos.* 105), also aunt to Livius Drusus, tribune of the plebs in 91. Some who had met Rutilius Rufus in his exile at Smyrna derived or asserted reminiscences of the 'Scipionic circle'.[93] No appeal was ever acknowledged to old Livia.

Livia by her long survival furnished a link between that age and the closing epoch of the Free State. Livia Drusilla, whose father had been a Claudius adopted by the famous and ill-starred tribune, reached the age of eighty-six, dying when her son, born in the year of Philippi, entered upon his seventieth year.

The Republic had earned a sad and solemn commemoration seven years previously. In 22 Junia Tertia passed away, the widow of C. Cassius, aged about ninety-five. Her funeral paraded the emblems of twenty noble houses, the germane being not there: 'praefulgebant Cassius atque Brutus eo ipso quod effigies eorum non visebantur.'[94]

[89] *Cat.* 25 (above, p. 26). Sempronia was at that time the wife of D. Brutus (*cos.* 77). For conjectures about her extraction, *Sallust* (1964), 134 f.

[90] Cicero, *De or.* III.45; *Brutus* 211.

[91] For his researches, Münzer, *Hermes* XL (1905), 50 ff.

[92] Pliny, *NH* VII. 158.

[93] Cicero, *De r.p.* I.13; *De natura deorum* III.80. For value or veracity concerning the 'circle', H. Strasburger, *Hermes* XCIV (1966), 60 ff.

[94] *Ann.* III.76.2.

XV

Messalla Corvinus

'Eadem magistratuum vocabula'. The names abode but the substance was gone. The survival of men and families embodies the authentic continuity, with notable specimens extant to recall the Republic—or to inspire paradox and melancholy in a historian when in his turn he cast his eyes backwards and composed the annals of Rome under the first dynasty.

Asinius Pollio and Messalla Corvinus stood out as the shining glories of Augustan eloquence, each lasting into the last decade of the reign; and their posterity went on for a long time. Pollio came of local stock, his grandfather one of the leaders of confederate Italy, and he advertised a fierce independence (not always borne out by the facts), whereas Corvinus accepted the new order gracefully, in his own person enhancing ancient lineage with the credit for excellence in the arts of peace and of warfare.

The evidence for the life and career of Messalla Corvinus is heterogeneous and often enigmatic. The documentation varies inordinately from writer to writer. Some episodes find full treatment, but others are absent where they might be expected to occur, as in the copious narratives of Appian and Cassius Dio. Several important particulars are only on casual or sporadic record. Modern reconstructions are much more composite and vulnerable than the reader might suspect.

That is not all. Orator, poet, and patron of letters, Corvinus is involved with Tibullus in questions of chronology and interpretation. Worse, that peculiar miscellany, the *Corpus Tibullianum*.

The birth and fame of Messalla solicited devout celebration from two versifiers who have remained anonymous (the quality of their products is enough to justify modest reticence). The first, included in that *Corpus*, is the *Panegyricus Messallae*, in honour of the consulship he held as colleague of the young Caesar in 31. Some scholars have suspected a later date. However, certain features of the poem indicate that it was in fact written, as it purports, in that year.[1]

Next, the ninth poem in another collection, the 'Virgilian' *Catalepton*. It is addressed to a Messalla, acclaims his triumph and welcomes the prospect of further laurels in far lands. Messalla, proconsul in Gaul, held his triumph on September 25 of 27. This poem likewise has come under suspicion.

[1] below, p. 203.

Questions of date and attribution often concern literary studies rather than history; and the *Corpus Tibullianum* has engrossed an enormous mass of writing. The *Panegyricus* calls for brief attention, since it furnishes several place names and is the sole source to reveal the fact that Messalla participated in the campaigns in Illyricum (35 and 34).

There are genuine problems enough, various and some of them intricate. A monograph exists, of sober merit.[2] Meanwhile, although no fresh knowledge has accrued, a different approach might be essayed, the more so since the latest comprehensive treatment of Messalla Corvinus needs to be corrected as well as modified.[3] The following remarks do not present a biography, albeit brief. They deal with a select series of defined problems, in a spirit of severe economy.

The Date of Birth. Jerome in his Chronicle puts it in 59.[4] Various reasons tell against, and long ago the sagacious Borghesi proposed the vicinity of 64.[5] Indeed, that precise year has been explained as well as advocated. Instead of 'Caesare et Bibulo', Jerome should have written 'Caesare et Figulo'.[6] The demonstration took some time to percolate. It now enjoys a fairly wide acceptance.[7]

There is a corollary of some interest. Jerome places Corvinus and Livy in the same bracket. Therefore let Livy also be put back five years.[8] Nothing impedes. However, not all show awareness; and not all are prepared to concede that Livy, said by Jerome to have died at the age of seventy-five, passed away in AD 12 (or thereabouts), not in 17.[9] The new dating carries consequences for the rhythm of his writing.

Messalla Corvinus at Philippi. Plutarch's biography of Brutus has a lavish account, with vivid personal detail. No surprise, for it derives in the main from the memoirs of Messalla. His name occurs in five chapters.[10]

Corvinus related what Cassius said on the eve of the first battle. Cassius, against his habit, was silent and preoccupied, but he told Corvinus that, like Pompeius Magnus, he was under constraint to risk all in a single

---

[2] J. Hammer, *Prolegomena to an Edition of the Panegyricus Messallae* (New York, 1925).

[3] R. Hanslik, *RE* VIIIA (1955), 131 ff. That scholar states that he differs from Hammer in most controversial matters.

[4] Jerome, p. 170 H.

[5] cf. Dessau in *PIR*[1] V 90.

[6] H. Schulz, *De M. Valerii Messallae aetate* (Prog. Stettin, 1886), 6.

[7] The consequent lowering of his decease to AD 8 was not so easy. See Ch. XVI.

[8] G. M. Hirst, *Collected Classical Papers* (1938), 12 ff. There is no awareness of the problem in *PIR*[2] L 292.

[9] The latter year was incautiously accepted in *Tacitus* (1958), 337. For the full argument for AD 12, see *HSCP* LXIV (1959) = *RP* (1979), 412 ff. R. M. Ogilvie leans towards the five years' lowering in his *Commentary on Livy* I–V(1965), 1. In *OCD*[2] (1970) A. H. McD(onald) is agnostic.

[10] Plutarch, *Brutus* 40–2; 45; 53.

contest; yet he was in good spirits since it is right to trust Fortuna, even after an unwise decision. Brutus had been eager for battle, and he insisted on taking charge of the right wing. That would have been more appropriate to the military experience of Cassius, who gave way and assigned to Brutus some of the best legions, along with Corvinus.

Those are the more significant items. In the ensuing battle the right wing was victorious, capturing three eagles, so Corvinus reported. But Cassius despaired too soon and took his own life. Finally, the biography has nothing to tell of any word or deed of Corvinus before, during or after the second battle, which occurred twenty days later.

To turn to the other narratives. Appian and Dio, in ample accounts, fail to mention the name of Messalla Corvinus. Appian, it is true, furnishes two incidental pieces of information in other sections of his work, the one when Corvinus was proscribed, the other as annotation on the Bellum Siculum: the survivors of the Republican party chose Corvinus as their leader, but, instead of prosecuting the struggle, he came to terms with Marcus Antonius.[11]

The Bellum Siculum. By contrast, Corvinus finds mention in no fewer than seven chapters of Appian's narration of the last campaign, in 36.[12] He had probably brought a squadron from Antonius, a portion of the hundred and twenty ships based at Tarentum under Statilius Taurus.[13] At his first mention Corvinus (so Appian states) was holding a command in the absence of Agrippa.[14] Yet, in the sequel, although charged with sundry missions (mainly on land), Corvinus fights in no action, and he fades out well before the Battle of Naulochus.

Which is peculiar. Nor does Dio's account disclose his name. He comes in a little later, after the victory honours voted to the young Caesar: Corvinus is made an augur (supernumerary, since the college was full).[15]

In Illyricum. Caesar's heir undertook two campaigns against Pannonians and Dalmatians (35 and 34). In the first he subjugated the Iapodes and reached Siscia on the river Save, a place of notable strategic value. The second found him operating on or close to the coast of Dalmatia (there is no sign that he crossed the Dinaric Alps). There is a detailed account in the *Illyrike* of Appian, deriving from the autobiography of Caesar Augustus who (as the compiler notes) recounted his own military exploits, not those of others;[16] and there is Cassius Dio, fairly full on the first campaign, but compressed on the second.[17]

[11] Appian, *BC* IV.38.162; V.113.471.   [12] *BC* V.102 f.; 105.; 109 f.; 112 f.;
[13] *BC* V.98.404.   [14] *BC* V.102.425.   [15] Dio XLIX.16.1.
[16] Appian, *Ill.* 15.   [17] Dio XLIX.36 f; 38.2–4.

One of the Iapodian *oppida* was called Arupium;[18] and the Arupini are named in the *Panegyricus*,

> at non per dubias errant mea carmina laudes
> nam bellis experta cano. testis mihi victae
> fortis Iapydiae miles, testis quoque fallax
> Pannonius, gelidas passim deiectus in Alpes
> testis Arupinis et pauper natus in arvis. (106 ff.)

The precision is uncommon in a poet (he might have been an officer in the campaign of 35), and highly welcome to those who stand by the ostensible date. Doubt has often been expressed, it is true, and even the notion that the poem celebrates Messallinus, the elder son of Corvinus, consular legate in Illyricum in AD 6.[19]

To counter which, a subtle argument has been produced.[20] The poet contemplates further exploits for his hero. Not Gaul or Spain, but distant, to the world's end, in the Orient (exotic rivers are named, Choaspes, Araxes, Tanais), finally in the far West:

> te manet invictus Romano Marte Britannus. (149)

The passage is significant. It touches the intention of Caesar's heir (published but hardly credible) of invading the island. Cassius Dio records that intention three times, in 34, in 27, in 26.[21] Poets loyally took the hint and kept Britain on show for some years.[22]

The author of the *Panegyricus* waives Gaul, where Corvinus was in fact to go in 28. But he mentions Britain. That was hardly to be contemplated as a field of military glory for anybody else after Caesar Augustus had renounced. Hence, failing anything better, a firm indication that the poem is what it professes to be.

It may be relevant at this point to adduce the other poetical product, *Catalepton* IX. The author acclaims 'magni magnum decus ecce triumphi' (line 3);[23] and he also evokes further regions for warfare, namely Africa, the golden stream of Tagus, and even the world's end:

> nunc aliam ex alia bellando quaerere gentem
> vincere et Oceani finibus ulterius. (53 f.)[24]

The exuberant vaticination may (or may not) appear to echo the

---

[18] Appian, *Ill.*16; Strabo IV, p. 207; VII, p. 314.
[19] D. Van Berchem, *Mus. Helv.* II (1945), 33 ff.
[20] A. Momigliano, *JRS* XL (1950), 39 ff.
[21] Dio XLIX.38.2; LIII.22.5; 25.2.
[22] Ch. XXVII.
[23] Strangely taken to refer to the triple triumph of 29 by R. Hanslik, o.c. 150.
[24] Because of the mention of 'celeres Afros' (l.51) and the river Tagus, Hanslik assumes that Messalla was at Alexandria; and also, 'unzweifelhaft', in Spain at the time of his Gallic command (o.c. 148; 150). Alexandria (it need not be said) was not in Africa in the conception of the ancients.

Panegyricus. It gives a hint of Britain, without naming the island. This is no place to worry about the problems of *Catalepton* IX; but one keeps in mind the sometimes over-valued predictions about world conquest in which the poets indulged.[25]

To resume. On the evidence of the *Panegyricus*, Corvinus participated in the campaign of 35, perhaps briefly, and in a modest role. Not but that some scholars have denied it, for various reasons. The mere absence of other testimony is no bar, given the caprice of the tradition about the actions of Messalla, already evident in the accounts of Philippi and the Bellum Siculum, and to be demonstrated more than once in the sequel.

Messalla and the Salassi. This recalcitrant people, occupying Val d'Aosta, had been an annoyance and an obstacle since they commanded the two St. Bernard passes. They defied Roman generals until subjugated and all but extirpated by Terentius Varro, in 26 or 25.[26] By an anomaly in the evidence, no fewer than three authors bring Messalla into relation with the Salassi: all discordant.[27]

According to Dio's summary report of the Dalmatian campaign in 34, Messalla subdued the Salassi and other rebellious tribes. In Strabo, Messalla, while in winter quarters, had to purchase firewood from the Salassi. In Appian, Messalla reduced them by famine, a date subsequent to Actium being implied.

At first sight it is not easy to go against Dio, an annalistic historian, and (adding the testimony of Strabo) refuse to admit that Messalla (who had been active in the campaign of 35) had charge of troops in a winter, facing Val d'Aosta. Nevertheless, most scholars assume Dio in error. They assign these transactions to his governership in Gaul, in 28/7.[28]

Controversy has been abundant, even introducing the aberrant notion of an Illyrian tribe of Salassi.[29] For present purposes let it be enough to subjoin three statements. First, no sign that Messalla achieved anything at any time. Second, once again marked discrepancy about Messalla. Third, the testimony of Appian. He did not go on to record the conquest of the

---

[25] For this theme of debate, as concerns the ambitions of Caesar Augustus, see *History in Ovid* (1978), Ch. IV, and below, Ch. XXVII.

[26] Dio LIII. 25.1: recorded under 25, along with the Spanish campaigns of 26 and 25. The 'standard date' is 25. Terentius Varro is also named by Strabo IV, p. 206.

[27] Strabo IV, p. 205; Appian, *Ill.* 17; Dio XLIX. 38.3.

[28] e.g. *MRR* II. 411. An argument to dispose of Dio can be adduced. When an author abridges drastically he is liable to produce a false suture through omissions. Dio omitted the campaigns of Antistius Vetus against the Salassi, which took two years according to Appian, *Ill.* 17: probably 35 and 34.

[29] J. Carcopino, *Rev. phil.* LXXII (1946), 108 ff., cf. 116. The article, questionable in other assertions, was styled 'brilliant' by A. Momigliano, o.c. 40. Against 'Illyrian Salassi', W. Schmitthenner, *Historia* VII (1958), 207 ff.

Salassi by Terentius Varro. Messalla gets the credit (for a slow operation). Caesar Augustus, contrary to his normal practice in the Autobiography, may have introduced a flattering reference to Messalla Corvinus.

The Change of Allegiance. In a conversation with Caesar's heir subsequent to the battle of Actium, Messalla intimated that he had always followed the better and juster cause.[30] A plea no doubt urged by others, and the formulation 'meliora et utiliora' could apply.[31] Whatever the personal apologia, the action was liable to be glossed over or embellished through deference or deceit.

Two items are instructive. According to Velleius, this 'fulgentissimus iuvenis', standing next in 'auctoritas' to Brutus and Cassius, preferred, instead of going on with a doubtful contest, to have his life saved 'beneficio Caesaris'. The victor deemed this the happiest of all his victories; and Corvinus requited him in loyal gratitude, an 'exemplum hominis grati ac pii'.[32]

That is to say, no sign in Velleius that Corvinus had ever been a partisan of Marcus Antonius. In fact, he capitulated to Antonius after the Battle of Philippi—and, in the company of the Republicans, Calpurnius Bibulus may have stood higher in rank.[33]

Next, Appian. He states that Corvinus remained with Antonius until the Triumvir fell totally under the domination of Cleopatra.[34] Like the choice of the better cause, that notion represents a process rather than a single act. It eludes precision.[35]

Messalla was active in the Sicilian War of 36. That is not enough to prove him already a declared partisan, as were two other aristocrats a little his senior, namely Ap. Claudius Pulcher and Paullus Aemilius Lepidus.[36] Nor is his presence at Rome in 36 or 35. A poem of Horace shows him in a congregation of men of letters, highly heterogeneous. In the first place are named Vergilius, Maecenas, and others. There follows a different group:

> Pollio, te, Messalla, tuo cum fratre, simulque
> vos, Bibule et Servi, simul his te, candide Furni.
> (*Sat.* I. 10.85 f.)

The names are instructive. Asinius Pollio was by now neutral between the dynasts. Servius is Ser. Sulpicius Rufus, the son of the consular jurist,

---

[30] Plutarch, *Brutus* 53.
[31] Velleius II.85.2 (the treachery of Amyntas the Galatian).
[32] Velleius II.71.1.
[33] Appian, *BC* IV.38.162.
[34] ib. 161.
[35] According to Hammer, 'the date of Messalla's transfer of allegiance to Octavian can be fixed' (o.c. 25). He put it in 40.
[36] It was incautiously so assumed in *Rom. Rev.* (1939), 237.

and close coeval to his cousin D. Brutus.[37] He had been able to evade action or hazard during the war of Pompeius and Caesar; and he was present at Rome in February of 43 when the Senate paid honour to his deceased parent.[38] Some have been disposed to believe that he perished in the Proscriptions.[39]

When the text of Quintilian is put under proper scrutiny, a startling fact comes up. No fewer than eight passages, so it appears, have been wrongly assigned to the illustrious parent.[40] The young Servius emerges as an orator who always improvised, whose only type of 'exercitatio' was translating Greek verse.[41] He won signal rank through three speeches.[42] Finally, a place in the rubric of classical orators, after Licinius Calvus and M. Brutus, preceding Cassius Severus of the Augustan time.[43] Hence new light on Roman eloquence under the Triumvirs.

Ser. Sulpicius had for a wife a sister of Messalla Corvinus.[44] The poetess Sulpicia is their daughter.[45] Another relative happens to occur in an earlier passage of the poem, namely a certain Pedius, a speaker in the courts of law: he is here named in the company of Messalla.[46] This is the obscure Q. Pedius (*q.* 41). His father, a nephew of Caesar the Dictator, had shared the *fasces* with Caesar's heir in August of 43: he was also the husband of a Valeria, a sister of Messalla.[47] The younger Pedius, like Ser. Sulpicius, is not heard of in the sequel.

There remain three firm partisans of Marcus Antonius. L. Calpurnius Bibulus had fought for the Republic at Philippi. He became governor of Syria and died there in 32.[48] Next, the brother of Messalla referred to without the name. He is the stepbrother, L. Gellius Poplicola (*cos.* 36), previously of some notoriety in the social life of the capital.[49] Finally, C. Furnius, who had recently been proconsul of Asia (in 36/5).[50] Through the

---

[37] *Ad fam.* XI.7.1.

[38] *Phil.* IX.12, cf. *Historia* IV (1955), 70 = *RP* (1979), 289 f.

[39] Münzer, *RE* IVA. 862. Cf. Shackleton Bailey on *Ad Att.* V.4.1 ('probably').

[40] As argued in *CQ* XXXI (1981), 421 ff. = *RP* III (1984), 1415 ff.

[41] Quintilian X.5.4.

[42] X.1.116.

[43] XII.10.11, cf. X.1.116.

[44] Jerome, *Adv. Iovin.* I.46 (from Seneca, *De matrimonio*).

[45] 'Tibullus' III.16.4: 'Servi filia Sulpicia'. Another Sulpicia Ser. f. married a Cassius (*ILS* 3103). Perhaps her sister, and not a daughter of the jurist (as Münzer, *RE* IVA. 878 f.).

[46] The name 'Pedius' in *Sat.* I.10.28 goes with 'Poplicola' in the same line, according to E. Fraenkel, *Horace* (1957), 134: against Münzer, *RE* XIX. 40.

[47] As emerges from Pliny, *NH* XXXV.21.

[48] Appian, *BC* IV.48.162. Messalla may have been related to Bibulus by marriage, cf. below, p. 232. Not the son of Bibulus (*cos.* 59) and Porcia, as incorrectly assumed in *History in Ovid* (1978), 119 f.: instead, a son by an earlier marriage.

[49] The son of the homonymous consul of 72. The *cognomen* may suggest an earlier relationship with the patrician Valerii.

[50] Appian, *BC* V.137.567; Dio XLIX.17.5.

intercession of his son he was saved after Actium—and in fact adlected to consular rank in 29.[51]

After warfare by sea and land, and various peregrinations, these men no doubt had embraced eagerly the chance to see the capital again, to enjoy the diversions of polite society—oratory among them—and meet some of the new school of poets. Messalla, it can be argued, saw Antonius and the eastern lands again before the breach between the dynasts. His diplomatic offices may well have been in demand in the course of the year 33.

Perhaps it was not until then that Messalla Corvinus abandoned Antonius. Such is the thesis expounded in an erudite disquisition, which may have deceived the ingenuous.[52] Devices more than questionable are brought into the game, apart from devious arguments.

Brief reflection submits a painless answer. The heir of the patrician Valerii enjoyed a wide licence of manoeuvre. By contrast, the *novus homo* was bound to his patron and leader, not free to lapse without damage or discredit. Very different the *nobilis* in the ambit of 'amicitia': an equal, not a client. Metellus Celer, legate under Pompeius Magnus in the eastern wars, expected his help to acquire the consulate. No sooner elected than he turned against Magnus. No blame ensued.

As long as the alliance of the Triumvirs subsisted, Messalla benefited from a patent advantage: to be courted and solicited by both dynasts. To have been with Cassius and Brutus enhanced credit, not least in the eyes of the Caesarians; and the Republicans preferred Marcus Antonius to the upstart Caesar. Calpurnius Bibulus (it will be recalled) was an Antonian; and Domitius Ahenobarbus, the nephew of Cato, remained loyal for long years.

Messalla Corvinus may have been able to maintain his independence until late in 33, or even in the early weeks of 32, when the crisis broke and the consuls Ahenobarbus and Sosius departed to Alexandria. Messalla's choice was signalized by his consulship in the next year.

Messalla was now able to justify his accession to the better cause by publishing revelations about the conduct of his former friend, based on what he had seen or learned not so long ago at Alexandria. He issued some pamphlets. More perhaps than was necessary to get his consulship or material gain in the sequel, namely to share with Agrippa the mansion of Antonius on the Palatine.[53]

Three pamphlets happen to be attested by a grammarian of late date.[54] First, *De Antonii statuis*. This product of the high-minded aristocrat blamed and mocked (it is to be presumed) a practice of which neither

---

[51] Seneca, *De ben.* II.25.1; Dio LII.42.4.
[52] J. Carcopino, *Rev. Phil.* LXXII (1946), 96 ff.
[53] Dio LIII.27.5.
[54] Charisius, *GL* 104.18; 146.34; 129.7.

dynast had the monopoly. Statues or images of Roman magistrates in the Greek lands among the subject peoples, that was no novelty or scandal. After the Bellum Siculum the loyal cities of Italy consecrated images of the 'Divi filius' in the temples of the gods.

Next, *De vectigalium Asiae constitutione*. This piece, it may be surmised, brought up for discredit eccentricities such as are recorded by Strabo: Antonius assigned a flute player to collect the revenues of four cities in the province.[55] It is not clear, by the way, that the agents appointed by the victor of Actium were above reproach. The unspeakable Vedius Pollio was given high authority in Asia.[56]

Finally, *Contra Antonii litteras*: either a personal defence or something to refute scandalous allegations against Italy's leader.[57] The tract may have been drawn on by the elder Pliny, who reports evidence about luxury at Alexandria, for example vessels of gold used for domestic and intimate purposes:[58] well calculated to anger the victims of taxation and repression in impoverished Italy.

Something better was brought from Alexandria by the consular Munatius Plancus and his nephew M. Titius in the summer of 32: information about the testament of Marcus Antonius, kept in the custody of the sacred virgins of Vesta. Likewise no doubt the report of various frolics. For example, the fable of the pearl dissolved in vinegar, Plancus adjudicating the wager between Antonius and the Queen of Egypt. The versatile Plancus himself performed at court pageants, dressed (or rather stripped) as a god of the sea, so Velleius alleged.[59]

Plancus before long was enlisted to sponsor the name 'Augustus' on another ceremonial occasion; and Messalla Corvinus, twenty-five years later, came out with 'pater patriae'.

At Actium. Once again a matter of fragmentary evidence. According to Plutarch, Caesar's heir praised Messalla for the zeal he displayed at Actium; and Appian in a piece of annotation states that he was one of the admirals.[60] But no account of the battle names Messalla Corvinus. As in an earlier season of naval warfare, his function appears to be largely decorative.

On the other side, Gellius Poplicola commanded the right wing, Sosius the left.[61] According to Velleius, a 'victoria clementissima'.[62] Sosius was

[55] Strabo XIV, p. 648.
[56] His 'constitutio' is mentioned in *CIL* III.7124 (Ephesus), and coins of Tralles carry his name and portrait, cf. M. Grant, *FITA* (1946), 382. On this person see further *JRS* LI (1961), 23 ff. = *RP* (1979), 518 ff.
[57] For the detail of the mutual charges, K. Scott, *Mem. Am. Ac. Rome* XI (1933), 7 ff.
[58] Pliny, *NH* XXXIII. 50.
[59] Velleius II.83.2. The story about the pearl comes from Pliny, *NH* IX.119 f.
[60] Plutarch, *Brutus* 53; Appian, *BC* IV.38.162.
[61] Velleius II.85.2. For the admirals on each side, *Rom. Rev.* (1939), 296 f. [62] Velleius II.86.2.

preserved by the intercession of L. Arruntius and by Caesar's clemency. Of Gellius Poplicola, the stepbrother of Messalla, no word now or in the sequel. On an earlier occasion when Gellius was with the Liberators in Asia (in 43), he came under suspicion of treachery, but Brutus let him go unharmed, out of regard for Messalla.[63] The ties of family or friendship prove often valid in times of civil war.

In Syria. The direct evidence comes from Cassius Dio.[64] He recounts the vicissitudes of a school of gladiators maintained by Antonius at Cyzicus. Apprised of the disaster at Actium these loyal swordsmen tried to break through to Egypt by land. On the way they had to fight against some of the vassal princes who had deserted Antonius, and, reaching Syria, they came into contact with the governor, Q. Didius. He persuaded them to give up the enterprise and establish themselves at Daphne, the suburb of Antioch, awaiting the decision of the victor. Subsequently the gladiators were deceived by Messalla, dispersed on pretext of service in the legions —and conveniently destroyed.[65]

Didius may have been despatched quickly from Actium to occupy Syria. Rather perhaps an Antonian, prompt to abandon his leader.[66] Messalla, it appears, was the next governor of Syria. The period of his tenure is in question, either 30/29 or 29/8. The former is preferable.[67] M. Tullius Cicero (*suff.* 30) may be his immediate successor.[68]

The occupations and the journeys of Messalla in these years are not easy to establish with precision.[69] Complications arise from two passages in Tibullus.[70] First,

Ibitis Aegeas sine me, Messalla, per undas
o utinam memores ipse cohorsque mei! (I.3.1 f.)

The poet had fallen ill at Corcyra and was unable to proceed. On which

[63] Livy, *Per.* CXXII; Dio XLVII.24.5.
[64] Dio LI.7.2–7.
[65] Dio LI.7.7.
[66] As assumed in *Rom. Rev.* (1939), 267. For the governors of Syria see now E. Schürer, *The History of the Jewish People in the Age of Jesus Christ* (1973, in the revised edition of G. Vermes and F. Millar), 253 ff.
[67] A biennial tenure is not excluded by any known facts. Messalla's presence at the triple triumph in August of 29, would, it is true, have been useful and decorative.
[68] Attested by Appian, *BC* IV.51.221. The only evidence, but *CIL* X.704* (Rocca d'Arce, between Arpinum and Aquinum) may be genuine, as suggested in *JRS* XLV (1955), 160 = *RP* (1979), 270. The date is uncertain, cf. *Rom. Rev.* (1939), 303: 'the period 29–27 B.C. is attractive, but 27–25 is not excluded.'
[69] For a long doxology, see Hammer, o.c. 48 ff.
[70] According to Hanslik, the poems have 'die erste Rolle' (o.c. 148). That scholar's interpretations of Tibullus (and of *Catalepton* IX) import intolerable confusion. He puts the Gallic campaign soon after Actium, and asserts that Messalla must have been in Syria in 28 because Cicero was proconsul in 27 (o.c. 152); and Messalla's Gallic triumph had to be delayed because he was in the Orient in 28 (o.c. 153 f., cf. 150).

journey, and with whom? There is no clear solution—but much debate, fruitless.

One possibility tends to be ignored. In the winter following Actium the victor crossed the stormy seas to Brundisium; and after less than a month he returned to spend the rest of the winter in Asia.[71] Messalla may have gone with him to Italy, and set out again for the East in the spring of 30, to take up his Syrian command—or, better, to go with the young Caesar to Egypt. Another poem of Tibullus (I.7) is further in cause (see below).

In Gaul. This governorship, not noted by Cassius Dio, is casually alluded to in Appian, with an implication that it fell shortly after Actium.[72] The *Acta Triumphalia*, with September 25 of the year 27 indicate the tenure 28/7, which should never have been doubted. He may be presumed the successor of C. Carrinas (*suff.* 43), who held his triumph in 28, on June 28.

Again Tibullus comes in, to engender confusion (at least in the minds of some scholars). The poet (who was in Messalla's company) acclaims his exploits in Aquitania,

> non sine me est tibi partus honos: Tarbella Pyrene
> testis et Oceani litora Santonici
> testis Arar Rhodanusque celer magnusque Garunna
> Carnutis et flavi caerula lympha Liger. (I.7.9 ff.)[73]

After which Tibullus goes on at once to the Cilician river ('an te, Cydne, canam?'), and the mountain of Taurus; and he proceeds by way of Tyre to the land of Nile, with a long digression on Osiris and Bacchus before the conclusion, which mentions Messalla's repair of the Via Latina after his triumph (7.57 ff.) and then reverts to the birthday (63 f.), proclaimed in the opening line of the poem.

The sequence adopted by the poet has impelled certain scholars to argue that Messalla held a governorship in Gaul and fought a campaign there shortly after the Battle of Actium: he went to Syria subsequently.[74]

There is nothing in it. Prosaic minds have neglected the structure and purpose of the poem as a whole.[75] Therefore Syria before Gaul (as everything else indicates). As concerns Syria, Cydnus and Taurus are in place. When the great province of Cilicia, governed by three consulars from 56 to 50, was dismantled in the sequel, Cilicia Pedias was assigned to Syria, probably as early as 44.[76]

---

[71] Dio LI.4.3.

[72] Appian, *BC* IV.38.161.

[73] The *Vita* attached to MSS of the poet states 'cuius et contubernalis Aquitanico bello militaribus donis donatus est'.

[74] Thus, after others, R. Hanslik, o.c. 148 ff.

[75] For which see now R. J. Ball, *Latomus* XXXIV (1975), 729 ff.; F. Cairns, *Tibullus* (1979), 80 ff., who, however, omits the actual governorship in Syria.

[76] *Anatolian Studies . . . Buckler* (1938), 323 = *RP* (1979), 140.

Finally, it may be suitable to adduce at this point a neglected Greek inscription. The people of Mallus in Pedias honour a 'Valerius M. f.' as benefactor, saviour, and patron.[77] But this might be another Messalla.[78]

The *Praefectura Urbis*. Having proclaimed the return of normal government and acquired a *cognomen*, the ruler went to Gaul in the summer of 27, where he spent some time, carrying out a census among other measures; and he may there have benefited from the company of the retiring proconsul. Caesar Augustus then proceeded to Spain, with the design of conquering the Cantabri and the Astures; and he entered upon his eighth consulship at Tarraco.

About this time occurred at Rome a most peculiar transaction. Messalla Corvinus assumed the post of *praefectus urbi*—and gave it up almost at once. Tacitus records it in the excursus he subjoined on the decease of L. Piso, who had been *praefectus urbi* for twenty years. Tacitus states the plea of Corvinus: he did not see what his function was—'quasi nescius exercendi'.[79] Which is by no means implausible.

Jerome in his Chronicle adds something: a tenure of six days and Messalla's objection, 'incivilem esse potestatem contestans'.[80] There is no other evidence.

A mysterious incident, but not beyond divination. If the Princeps (or his expert advisers) adduced precedents such as those to be found in the Tacitean excursus (they went back to Romulus), Messalla Corvinus could have reason for doubts and distrust. He might observe the recent proliferation of antiquarian lore as manifested in the creation of the *Arvales* or the argument about the *spolia opima* which ruled out the youthful and ambitious proconsul of Macedonia, M. Licinius Crassus.[81]

Moreover, what was the point in having yet another magistrate or rather official (appointed, not elected), when one of the consuls was present in Rome? Statilius Taurus was consul in 26: behind him stood the great Agrippa and the influence of Maecenas. How could a man compete with both 'imperium' and 'potentia'?

The novel post could be described as verily 'incivilis', recalling (if it meant anything) the power without title exercised over Rome and Italy by Maecenas during the War of Actium. After noting the alleged precedents for a *praefectura urbis* the careful and sceptical historian brought in Maecenas, thus subverting the case.

The situation thus clarifies. After consenting to hold office, Corvinus

---

[77] Published by Heberdey and Wilhelm, 'Reisen in Kilikien', *Wiener Denkschriften* XLIV (1896), no. 20. Said to be at Adana, found at Karataş.
[78] That is, possibly M. Messalla (*suff.* 32) or Potitus (*suff.* 29). On whom see Ch. XVII.
[79] *Ann.* VI.11.3.
[80] Jerome, p. 164 H.
[81] Ch. XX.

quickly saw his error—and detected an artful device. His name and repute were being inveigled into visible and vulnerable approbation of the new regime; and he could claim that the thing was illicit, even in terms of an ostensible 'res publica'. Furthermore, prompt withdrawal served to advertise an attitude of independence, laudable and innocuous.

Jerome gives 26 BC as the date, and the first six days of January may be accepted. Otherwise one might have wondered about the previous summer, when Caesar Augustus departed from Rome. The next *praefectus urbi* was Statilius Taurus, appointed in 16, when the ruler again went away to the western provinces.[82] But there is a potent factor against—Corvinus held the *imperium* of a proconsul, hence debarred from entering the city before his triumph in September of 27.

This odd item seems to have been ignored by the main historical tradition. Jerome got it from one of the writings of a scholarly researcher, from the *De viris illustribus* of Suetonius Tranquillus. What then of Tacitus?

The sources of his antiquarian digressions are an entertaining topic. Some have assumed the use of a single handbook. That is not likely. In a number of instances one may suspect orations in which Claudius Caesar expounded his erudition to the Roman Senate.[83] Unique items and variants from the standard tradition about early Rome are a clue, for example in Tacitus' digression on the history of the quaestorship.[84]

Now Tacitus on the *praefectura urbis* produces two names from the age of the kings, nowhere else on attestation, viz. Denter Romulius and Numa Marcius. Claudius, when appointing early in his reign L. Volusius Saturninus, may have seized the opportunity to deliver a lecture. Volusius lasted until his decease in 56 at the age of ninety-three, earning from Tacitus a brief obituary notice which strangely omits the prefecture.[85]

Tacitus, it appears, was familiar with Claudian orations well before he approached the reign of that emperor.[86] Otherwise, Suetonius might be the source: no problem of chronology impedes. However that may be, the digression, not wholly antiquarian in content and purpose, is one of the many signs that reveal his growing preoccupation with the epoch of Caesar Augustus.

The Testimony of Dio. After the abortive prefecture of 26, and the charge of the Via Latina, no office or action of Messalla Corvinus is on record

---

[82] Dio LIV.19.6.

[83] *Tacitus* (1958), 703 ff.

[84] *Ann.* XI.22.

[85] *Ann.* XIII.30.2. The only witness to attest his prefecture is Pliny, *NH* VII.62; XI.223. Tacitus, who has a keen interest in the Volusii, had surely noted the office earlier.

[86] Thus in his digression on the Mons Caelius (IV.65), cf. *Tacitus* (1958), 709.

until 11, when Augustus put him in charge of the aqueducts of Rome.[87] He continued in that function until his death. Then an interval again, and the year arrived which the ruler designed for inordinate emphasis. On February 5, 2 BC, Corvinus initiated the solemnities by proposing that the Princeps be invested with the title 'pater patriae'.[88]

For the second half of a long existence, that is not much. Once again the caprice of the evidence obtrudes and clamours for elucidation. After Messalla's cajoling of the gladiators in Syria Cassius Dio has nothing to offer except the notice that when his mansion burned down in 25 the Princeps gave him money in compensation: a minor item, coming at the end of miscellaneous annotation on Marcus Agrippa.[89]

Dio's treatment of the reign of Augustus is peculiar and highly individual.[90] His main concern rests with ruler and dynasty, with administration and warfare. He happens to furnish information, not elsewhere to be found, about sundry wars and campaigns, which points to the use of an annalistic source.[91] Again, for the chronicle of the first two years of Tiberius Caesar, he furnishes a number of items not in Tacitus.[92] At the same time, some sections are treated very briefly, for example the years AD 11 and 12. And there are sundry strange omissions.

Dio contributes a variety of anecdotal material, often inserted out of the historical context.[93] And, although he supplies information of this kind when reporting, for instance, the deaths of Vedius Pollio and of Maecenas,[94] he failed to learn from Cornelius Tacitus the art of the obituary notice. That historian himself did not hit upon the device until he reached the year 20.[95] Various reasons then impelled him: a personal interest in Sallustius Crispus, the minister of state, and in the family of the Volusii; and also perhaps the discovery of notable deaths and public funerals in the following years. And, paramount, the insistence that his annals be senatorial, deprecating the biography of the Princeps.

Dio, it is clear, was deficient in concern for personages other than the ruler, his family, his closest associates. Furthermore, a double accident may help to explain the eclipse of Messalla Corvinus after his governorship in Syria.

[87] Frontinus, *De aquis* 99. He was assigned two senators as assistants, viz. Postumius Sulpicius and L. Cominius: the former a relative, though not close.

[88] above, p. 88.

[89] Dio LIII.27.5.

[90] For analysis and appraisal, F. Millar, *A Study of Cassius Dio* (1964), 83 ff.

[91] below, p. 291.

[92] *Tacitus* (1958), 691; *ZPE* 43 (1981), 366 = *RP* III (1984), 1424 f.

[93] For the anecdotal material, F. Millar, o.c. 86 ff. But it is not necessary to suggest 'perhaps that no adequate chronological source was available' (ib. 91). There was the Roman annalist Cremutius Cordus (ib. 85).

[94] Dio LIV.23.1–6; LV.7.1–6. For anecdotal material in the Tiberian books see *Tacitus* (1958), 388, *Athenæum* LXI (1983), 6.　　　　　　　　　　　　　　　　　　　[95] *Ann.* III.30.

First, in his lavish exposition devoted to the pageantry staged by Augustus in 2 BC Dio did not miss 'pater patriae'.[96] But he ought to have named the sponsor of the motion, with some anecdotal matter, after his fashion.

Next, the large gap in AD 8.[97] To this place may be assigned a great scandal in the dynasty, the catastrophe of L. Aemilius Paullus and his wife Julia. Also perhaps the death of Messalla. Whether the Greek historian would have known or cared about the relegation of a Latin poet is another matter.

As has been demonstrated, the evidence for the earlier career of Messalla is fragmentary and capricious. Plutarch and Appian against Dio, the contrast is sharp and striking. Dio allows Messalla no role at Philippi, in the Bellum Siculum, or at Actium. That is strange if, as has been widely believed, Livy was Dio's main source down to 30 or 29.[98] Livy was an innocuous 'Pompeianus', he usefully combined admiration for the Republic with a happy acquiescence in the new order; and he was generous in tribute to persons of eminence.[99]

Bias might therefore be invoked in one of Dio's sources, or deliberate silence. Perhaps there was a historian of pertinacious Republican or Pompeian allegiance who suspected that the exploits of Messalla Corvinus had been rated above their proper value (especially if he read the memoirs of that aristocrat). Observe how Messalla's behaviour towards the gladiators in Syria is rendered: he cheated them.

Epilogue. Such are the multiple hazards that confront any who might essay to recount the life and actions of Messalla Corvinus: 'fulgentissimus iuvenis', mature statesman, orator and friend of the poets. Literature contributes a large measure of his fame, in part through various poems, bad as well as good.

A candid but rational assessment might inspire some dubitation. Comment from the less fortunate would be worth having. Not all survivors from the defeated cause of Cato and Brutus or former friends of Marcus Antonius would relish the conventional apologia of the renegade aristocrat or approve his pamphlets. Messalla made himself vulnerable by coining a phrase which made Q. Dellius proverbial for changes of side: 'desultor bellorum civilium'.[100] Worse could be said about some people. According to Velleius, Munatius Plancus had not been moved by good sense to choose the right course, or by devotion to the 'res publica' and to

---

[96] Dio LV.2.10
[97] Between LV.32.2 and 34.1.
[98] E. Schwartz, *RE* III. 1697 ff.
[99] Seneca, *Suas.*VI.22: 'candidissimus omnium magnorum ingeniorum aestimator'.
[100] Seneca, *Suas.*I.7.

Caesar. No: treason abode in him like a disease, he was 'morbo proditor'.[101]

Asinius Pollio stood in proud eminence as the sole neutral in the war of the dynasts. On the score of mutual 'beneficia' Antonius had been the gainer, so he asserted.[102] But Pollio took up the pen to write against his erstwhile leader, though not without provocation: *Contra Antonii maledicta*, so was the product styled.[103] And indeed, both Pollio and Messalla could be reckoned profiteers from the wars, as the historian Tacitus indicates in an invented oration: 'inter Antonium et Augustum bellorum praemiis refertos'.[104]

Messalla continued to proclaim that Cassius had been his general.[105] Which caused no harm anywhere; and Augustus bore no malice for the refusal to collaborate as *praefectus urbi*. Nor should Messalla incur harsh words for consenting in old age to honour the Princeps forty years after the Republic went down at Philippi. He merely accommodated himself to the spirit of the times. However, deference towards government might glide into adulation of the ruler, as was manifest in the comportment of Messalla's sons.[106]

To Messalla's talent as an orator there is adequate and varied testimony. He acquired distinction when very young, as is shown by Cicero in a letter sent to Brutus in July of 43. Cicero extols his elegance, skill, and judgement 'in verissimo genere dicendi'.[107] And Messalla, it will be recalled, was taken for model by the young Claudius Nero some twenty years later.[108]

Messalla had exacting taste, he devoted much care to the choice of words:[109] he even wrote on niceties of grammar and orthography, perhaps something of a pedant.[110] The grace of his style does not fail to be commended. Messalla is twice called 'nitidus' by Quintilian.[111] At the same time, the critic detected a certain lack of vigour.[112] Both Quintilian and Tacitus were moved to complain about the feebleness of his 'exordia':

[101] Velleius II.83.1.
[102] Velleius II.86.3.
[103] Charisius, *GL* I.80.2.
[104] *Ann.*XI.6.2.
[105] IV.34.4 (in the oration of Cremutius Cordus).
[106] Ch. XVII.
[107] *Ad M. Brutum* I.15 (XXIII, ed. Watt), 1.
[108] Suetonius, *Tib.* 70.1.
[109] Seneca, *Controv.* II.4.8: 'exactissimi ingenii quidem in omni studiorum parte, Latini utique sermonis observator diligentissimus'.
[110] Quintilian I.7.35.
[111] I.7.35; X.1.113. Ovid refers to 'nitor ille domesticus' in an epistle to the elder son (*Ex P.* II.2.49).
[112] X.I.113: 'Messalla nitidus et candidus et quodam modo praeferens in dicendo nobilitatem suam, viribus minor'.

Messalla was in the habit of making excuses, he was not ready, his health was in a poor condition.[113]

The fame of Messalla Corvinus abides, but a certain ambiguity attends upon the quality of the classic orator no less than upon the behaviour of the general and politician. The same might be said about Asinius Pollio.[114]

Fortuna and sound judgement guided them safely through the turbulent years. Ambition was satisfied, and ambition was not to be deprecated in a Roman of the governing order.[115] The eminent consulars could now exhibit oratory in the Senate, in the courts of law, and in the schools of rhetoric. They were also in a position to parade airs of independence and look down on young *nobiles* who had benefited from an easier passage to the *fasces*.

Not only achievement and pride. For one reason or another many of the successful *novi homines* failed to perpetuate a sequence of consuls.[116] Pollio had one consular son, Gallus; and a daughter married the son of the last consul of the Marcelli.[117] Gallus by his marriage to Vipsania acquired a propinquity with the dynasty that proved fatal. However, descendants of Pollio were still on show in the time of Trajan.[118]

Messalla aided his kinsmen in renewing the splendour of the patrician Valerii; and although the direct line ended under Nero, the female side produced descendants of some consequence.[119]

[113] IV.1.8; Tacitus, *Dial.* 20.1.

[114] For avowed reasons, Pollio received favourable treatment in *Rom. Rev.* For the other side see now A. B. Bosworth, *Historia* XXI (1972), 441 ff.

[115] Sallust, *Cat.*11.1: 'quod tamen vitium propius virtutem erat.' It was 'ambitio mala' that had kept him from the better path, the writing of history (4.2).

[116] *Rom. Rev.* (1939), 498 f.

[117] viz. Aeserninus (*cos.* 22 BC). The grandson (*pr.* AD 19) was an orator of note (*PIR*² C 928). Only death could have forestalled his consulship.

[118] viz. M. Asinius Marcellus (*cos.* 104) and Quintus (*suff. ann. inc.*). The historian evinces a keen interest in the descendants of Pollio. For the stemma, J. H. Oliver, *AJP* LXVIII (1947), 147 ff.

[119] Ch. XVII.

XVI

The Decease of Messalla

The problem has been in sharp debate: AD 8 or 13.[1] The first thing is to look at what Ovid says. From early youth he enjoyed the favour and esteem of Messalla Corvinus. Making his first appeal to the family, the poet addresses the elder son. The parent's eloquence was supreme in the forum at Rome, it lives on in Messallinus:

> cuius in ingenio est patriae facundia linguae
> qua prior in Latio non fuit ulla foro. (*Tristia* IV.4.4 f.)

A little lower down Ovid exhorts the son to call to mind how the parent used to approve the poet's 'ingenium' and would recite his verses:

> nam tuus est primis cultus mihi semper ab annis
> (hoc certe noli dissimulare) pater
> ingeniumque meum (potes hoc meminisse) probabat
> plus etiam quam me iudice dignus eram
> deque meis illo referebat versibus ore
> in quo pars magnae nobilitatis erat. (4.27 ff.)

The appeal is to the past. No sign that Corvinus is still an Ovid-fancier, despite a certain catastrophe. The tone and language implies that Corvinus is no longer among the living. No need to insist, the words are there (and the tenses of verbs). And finally, no hint of a recent bereavement.

The poem admits a fairly close dating, to the year 11. In Book IV of the *Tristia*, two autumns have passed in Pontus, the sun has returned twice after the chill of winter (6.9; 7.1). Book IV indicates spring or summer of 11, while in Book V, the winter of 11/12 is registered (V.10.1).

The next epistle to the address of Messallinus is *Ex Ponto* I.7. It contains the reference to the funeral of Corvinus on which controversy revolves (7.29 f.). The whole context calls for exact scrutiny.

Ovid puts in a plea to justify his approach. He is no intruder now. Enough if Messallinus concedes that the family mansion had opened its doors to the poet:

> nec tamen inrumpo quo non licet ire, satisque
> atria si nobis non patuisse negas. (7.23 f.)

---

[1] Compare the brief but firm argument in *History in Ovid* (1978), 122–5. The present chapter was written several years previously.

One will compare in the former poem 'me domus ista recepit' (*Tristia* IV.4.33). The poet is clearly alluding to a period of friendship, with an open house, that went far back into the past.

Next, Ovid adduces the parent, who inspired and encouraged the poems, and did not disavow the poet:

> nec tuus est genitor nos infitiatus amicos
> hortator studii causaque faxque mei. (7.27 f.)

How interpret 'nec . . . infitiatus'? To what period or situation do the words refer? Those who argue that Corvinus did not die in the course of the year 8 put it thus: before Ovid's catastrophe in the autumn there was no reason for Corvinus to disavow him, therefore Corvinus was still among the living when the storm broke and Caesar published his edict of banishment.[2]

The contrary has been firmly asserted.[3] Ovid is not referring to any recent comportment of Messalla Corvinus, he merely makes the mild and inoffensive statement that Corvinus never went back on him (that is, not at any time in a long past). Compare, in the first passage of this poem, quoted above, what Ovid modestly expects Messallinus not to be able to deny: 'atria . . . patuisse'.

That is to say, the reference is to a long period antecedent to Ovid's transgression. It would be strange indeed if the great mansion on the Palatine admitted the criminal who had offended Caesar so grievously. And Ovid did not make that claim. Nor did he venture to approach the elder son of Corvinus until three years had elapsed. It was done with diffidence (although overplayed).

Finally, the obsequies of Messalla Corvinus:

> cui nos et lacrimas, supremum in funere munus
> et dedimus medio scripta canenda foro. (29 f.)

Ovid, it appears, was present at the public funeral, or in the near vicinity, since he supplied a dirge to be recited.

Not so, it has been argued by those who wish to prolong the life of Corvinus by five years. The tears he shed do not prove Ovid's presence at the funeral, and he sent the text from Tomis.

If Ovid was on the Pontic strand when Corvinus died, factors of time and distance for the transmission of news and the despatch of a dirge will properly be invoked—without any need or temptation to adduce Ovid when he speaks of a whole year and tactfully suggests that a widower might be able to acquire a new wife in the interval.[4]

---

[2] Thus F. Marx, *Wiener Studien* XIX (1897), 150 ff. Accepted in *PIR*[1] V 90.

[3] e.g. J. Hammer, *Prolegomena to an Edition of the Panegyricus Messallae* (New York, 1925), 8 f.; Schanz–Hosius, *Gesch. der r. Lit. II*[4] (1935), 23. They could appeal to the powerful witness of Nipperdey, *Rh. Mus.* XIX (1864), 283.   [4] *Ex. P.* IV.11.16; 21 f. (to Junius Gallio).

Chronology intervenes when appeal is made to this letter in the first book of the *Epistulae ex Ponto*.[5] The first three books disclose a unit (the same person having the first poem and the last), and they were published in the course of 13. As for Book I, the fourth autumn is registered (8.28) and the fourth winter (1.26). Nothing brings any poem of this book out of 12 and into 13. Reference to the Pannonian triumph of Tiberius (in October of 12) does not arrive until the next book (II.1), and that event is prominent in the next poem, addressed to Messallinus (namely II.2).[6]

To sum up. *Tristia* IV.4 alludes to Messalla Corvinus as a character who belongs in the past, deceased some time before the year 11; *Ex Ponto* I.7, written in 12, shows that his obsequies antedated the departure of Ovid for the shore of Pontus; and he is described as an 'umbra' in the autumn of 12 (II.2.98).

Therefore, let the orator die in the course of the year 8. In favour of which, but merely on the flank, may be mentioned the large gap in the text of Cassius Dio—supposing him to have registered the death and state funeral of that eminent citizen.[7] The signal victory over the Pannonians at the river Bathinus occurred on August 3 of that year.[8] It has fallen out of Dio's very full narration of the war. Corvinus' death might be put in the summer of this year. According to the notice in Jerome, he had lost his memory two years before, and he ended his life by starvation.

For clarity of exposition, the testimony of Jerome has been postponed until this point. It ought not to be introduced without a warning. Jerome's Chronicle is a hasty and careless piece of compilation. He described it himself in the preface as a 'tumultuarium opus'. The erudite and disingenuous monk was truthful in this instance—there was no cause or plea needing to be supported by mendacity.

Many of the items touching literary annals which he added while translating Eusebius are shown to be false when independent evidence avails. Furthermore, his figures, even if accurately transcribed from his source (Suetonius in the main), were liable to be corrupted. Hence variants in the manuscripts—and licence for the modern scholar in his ambition to extract precision at any cost.

All in all, it might be a useful economy, satisfying the needs of history and of good sense, to waive Jerome, to assume that Messalla was a fairly close coeval of Cicero's son (who was born in 65), that Messalla died in AD 8 (on the witness of Ovid), when aged about seventy-two.

---

[5] For the chronology, *History in Ovid* (1978), 39 ff.

[6] As is natural, for Messallinus was among the 'viri triumphales' in the happy procession. Hence the *terminus ante quem* for I.7, which mentions the funeral of Messalla.

[7] The gap (four folia) extends from LV.33.2 to 34.1.

[8] Where the *Fasti Praenestini* register 'Ti.Aug. ⟨in⟩ Inlyrico vic(it)'.

However, let the matter be stated briefly. Under the year 11 the chronicler mentions Messalla's collapse two years before his death and goes on to say that he died when aged 'LXXII annos' (at least according to some manuscripts).[9] The total of years, be it observed, is in agreement with Jerome's date for the birth of the orator, namely 59 BC. That gives AD 13 for his decease.[10]

That turns out not to be decisive. As has been demonstrated, Jerome puts Messalla's birth too late, by five years.[11] Most scholars now accept 64. Therefore not 13 but 8 ought to emerge as the date of his death.

However, other and indeed better manuscripts offer other figures for the age of Messalla.[12] Therefore the span of his life could be taken to extend from 59 BC to AD 13. Indeed, that result is acclaimed as 'firm and clear'.[13]

That pronouncement is undermined and blown up by a straightforward interpretation of Ovid. It shows Messalla already dead, not merely in 12 (*Ex Ponto* I.7), but in 11 (*Tristia* IV.4)[14]

Why was that ignored or traversed? It is not good to go against primary sources. Confidence in 13 for the death of Messalla Corvinus relied upon an extraneous adjuvant.

The prepotent factor may now be disclosed. Nothing less than a document. Placed by the Emperor Nerva in charge of the aqueducts of Rome, the senior consular Julius Frontinus at once composed a treatise on the subject. It carries a list of the *curatores aquarum* from Messalla Corvinus (appointed in 11 BC) down to his own taking office in the course of the year 97.

Each entry is equipped with a consular date. At the outset 'Messallae successit Planco et Silio consulibus Ateius Capito'. That is, the year 13. Now Messalla died in 8, if one stands by Ovid and the interpretation recommended above. What is to be done? The only recourse was to suppose that the post was left vacant for five years. That was Borghesi's explanation.[15]

Not all are prepared to concur. The office occupied by Messalla appears important no less than honorific, with eager aspirants among the

---

[9] Jerome, p. 170 H.

[10] Thus *PIR*[1] V 90—and a number of scholars in the sequel.

[11] above, p. 201.

[12] For the MSS evidence, R. Hanslik, *RE* VIIIA. 135 f.

[13] R. Hanslik, o.c. 136 'eindeutig'. Error or confusion about Messalla's death had an early origin, observe Tacitus, *Dial.* 17.6: 'nam Corvinus in medium usque Augusti principatum, Asinius paene ad extremum duravit'. No comments.

[14] The important testimony of *Tristia* IV.4 (to Messallinus, though he is not named) seems to have been neglected in the dispute about *Ex Ponto* I.7. For example, not cited by Marx (o.c. 150 ff.), by Hammer (o.c. 8), or by Hanslik (o.c. 136 f.). For the inordinate bibliography of the whole controversy, see the last two authors; also Schanz–Hosius, o.c. 22 f.

[15] Accepted and supported by J. Hammer, o.c. 9.

consulars, with Caesar Augustus or Ti. Caesar not loath to reward active merit or a long allegiance.

Reflection will suggest a doubt. In any age public office entails less of exertion or ability than the ingenuous opine. Some of the administrative boards set up by Augustus had a double purpose. Not merely work to be done or civic duty inculcated, but occupations far from arduous for senators.[16] To take a parallel from the second order in Roman society: Pliny, wishing to enhance the 'dignitas' of a friend who had chosen not to enter the Senate, asks a high official to provide something 'quod sit splendidum nec molestum'.[17]

A suspicion arises that some posts came close to the ideal of 'something to live for and nothing to do'. Inertia or even absence might not be detrimental. The *cura aquarum* happens to offer a pair of clear instances. Cocceius Nerva, appointed in 24, left Rome with Tiberius Caesar two years later and abode with him in the island seclusion until the day of his death in 33.[18]

Next, Didius Gallus, holding the office for eleven years (38–49). In the middle of his tenure he was legate of Moesia, from 44, for several years.[19] The claims of the metropolitan post cannot furnish a reason for abridging that governorship.[20] Didius Gallus, it appears, could be dispensed with, precisely in the season when Claudius Caesar was devoting zealous attention to the aqueducts. The Emperor no doubt preferred the help and agency of minor bureaucrats or genuine experts: knights or freedmen.

The *cura aquarum* was less important and (as will emerge) lower in prestige than might have been fancied. No strain therefore on belief should it lack a tenant from 8 to 13. And the government had grave preoccupations in that period, both abroad and at home.

If that solution be denied, another path opens, of extreme hazard, and an alarming prospect. Frontinus produces a document: who would refuse assent to statements of this consular? The treatise *De aquis* declares an author who liked facts. Frontinus had wide experience, and he had probably known service as an equestrian officer before being admitted to the senatorial order. For all their care and scruple, those who deal with facts and dates and names of senators can succumb to error or inadvertence. The accurate Cornelius Tacitus shows that—and great scholars in the recent age.[21]

It will be useful to set out Frontinus' list, from Ateius Capito to Domitius Afer (*De aquis* 102):

---

[16] *Some Arval Brethren* (1980), 100 f.   [17] Pliny, *Epp.* II.2.5 (to Vibius Maximus).

[18] *Ann.* IV.58.1; VI.26.1.   [19] *PIR*² D 70.

[20] As by A. Stein, *Die Legaten von Moesien* (1940), 26.

[21] L. Saenius (*suff.* 30 BC) was omitted by Degrassi from his *Fasti consolari* (1952).

AD 13 C. Ateius Capito   (*suff.* AD 5)
  23 L. Tarius Rufus   (16 BC)
  24 M. Cocceius Nerva (AD 21 or 22)
  34 C. Octavius Laenas   (33)
  38 M. Porcius Cato   (36)
     A. Didius Gallus   (39)
  49 Cn. Domitius Afer   (39)

With so many names (a consular pair and *two curatores* in each year of transfer), the text of Frontinus may have been modified or mutilated in the transmission. In fact, it omits one consul in 23: 'C. Asinio Pollione' has fallen out.

Further, there is a disturbance and a lacuna in 38, between the names of Porcius Cato and Didius Gallus, where editors have adopted 'post ⟨mensem⟩', or 'post ⟨menses quattuor⟩'.[22] That is, a brief tenure indeed for Cato. It has a ready explanation. Cato belonged to the group of four senators who devised the ruin of Titius Sabinus, a knight who had been a friend of Germanicus. After a full account of the disgraceful affair, Tacitus foretells the doom awaiting them all.[23] Cato therefore came to grief in the second half of the year 38—by anomaly the text here registers not the *ordinarii* of the year but the *suffecti* who entered office on July 1, viz. Ser. Asinius Celer and Sex. Nonius Quinctilianus.[24]

There is a further possibility touching this year. It was assumed that A. Didius Gallus was suffect consul in 36, as colleague of M. Porcius Cato. New evidence now shows him holding the *fasces* with Cn. Domitius Afer in September of 39.[25] Now the *curatores* are without exception of consular rank. It has therefore to be supposed that Didius got the post when consul-designate.[26] He was in fact a highly ambitious person, and very successful. There might be a different explanation: a larger lacuna in the text and another *curator* before Didius.

These disturbing phenomena lend some encouragement. They might permit a conjecture: namely that after the words 'Messallae successit' the original text had the names of the consuls of 8 and the name of a *curator*, preceding Ateius Capito. That would be a solution. The trouble may lie deeper.

First of all, brief comment on the list is expedient, for more reasons than

---

[22] The former was Nipperdey's suggestion. P. Grimal has the latter (from Hülsen) in his edition (Budé, 1944). C. Kunderewicz (Teubner, 1973) has nothing to offer.

[23] *Ann.* IV.71.1.

[24] In the condition of the text, Mommsen once considered whether Asinius Celer did not become *curator*, cf. Groag in *PIR²* A 1225: 'nescio num recte'. But see on the passage L. Vidman, *Fasti Ostienses* (Prague, 1957), 39 f.

[25] *AE* 1973, 138.

[26] Thus L. Vidman, *Listy fil.* XCVI (1973), 16 ff. That Didius Gallus did not acquire the post until 46 is suggested by R. H. Rodgers, *HSCP* LXXVI (1982), 175.

one. The preponderance of recent consuls is notable. Some of them were already past their prime. Ateius Capito, the jurist subservient to power, came into note as a sacerdotal expert as early as 17 BC, when he interpreted a Sibylline oracle to support Augustus' choice of a date for the *Ludi Saeculares*.[27] And the other jurist, Cocceius Nerva, may be the son, not the grandson, of the man who inaugurated the rank of his family.[28] If so, close coeval to his friend the Emperor Tiberius.

Next, not only some elderly men. The *curatores* tend to remain in office to the end of their days. Thus Capito, Nerva, and Afer, whose deaths are registered by Tacitus.[29] Finally, a lack of social distinction. Without exception they are *consules suffecti*; and the only *nobilis* is Cocceius Nerva.[30]

To complete and conclude this rubric. Nothing shows that the post enjoyed high estimation, at least in this season; and it happens to be absent from Tacitean annotation on consulars dead or alive. The historian was always alert to Prefects of the City. That office carried authority as well as prestige.

Attention can now concentrate on the eccentric entry, L. Tarius Rufus. Caesarian admiral long ago in the campaign of Actium, this *novus homo* attained at last to a suffect consulship in 16 after a governorship of Macedonia and operations against invaders on the lower course of the river Danube.[31]

Appointed to the *cura aquarum* in AD 23 when fifty-three years had elapsed since Actium, Tarius Rufus must have been well over eighty. Anything can happen in Rome of the Caesars, as the favour or caprice of the ruler dictates. Exceptional honour accrues to the elderly or a tenure of office prolonged beyond the normal term of human existence. Thus L. Piso ended his days as Prefect of the City at seventy-nine, L. Volusius Saturninus at ninety-three.[32]

None the less, Tarius Rufus arouses disquiet. One asks how and why emerged this sudden honour for an octogenarian. An incident in his earlier life aroused the interest of Seneca, who recounts it at some length.[33] Tarius had some reason to believe that his son was plotting his murder. Summoning a *consilium* in his house, he pronounced a sentence of

---

[27] Zosimus II.4.

[28] In *PIR²* C 1225 a son of the consul of 36 BC.

[29] *Ann.* III.75; VI.26.1; XIV.19.

[30] It is not safe to assume this Porcius Cato a descendant of the consular house, as in *RE* XXII.219: 'zweifellos'.

[31] *PIR¹* T 14. Add Ritterling's emendation in Dio LIV.20.3 (operations recorded under 16 BC), and the inscription found at Amphipolis (*AE* 1936, 18). For his position (proconsul or imperial legate), *Danubian Papers* (1971), 68. Tarius had perhaps been proconsul of Cyprus, cf. *IGR* III.952 (Paphos), with the remarks of Groag, *RE* IVA. 2821.

[32] *Ann.* VI.10.3; XIII.30.

[33] *De clem.* I.15.2–7.

relegation (Caesar Augustus was present, but did not speak). The youth was sent away to comfortable seclusion at Massilia.

According to Seneca, the father's action and comportment earned general approbation.[34] Now Tarius Rufus was an upstart, 'infima natalium humilitate'.[35] He owned great riches, deriving in large part (it may be assumed) from war booty and the bounty of the ruler. Not a person likely to enjoy esteem in Roman society: one is put in mind of Sulpicius Quirinius.[36] And some might have asked what it was that turned the young man against his parent.

None the less, the name of Tarius stands in the list of the *curatores aquarum*. Is the reason to be sought in some eccentricity of Tiberius Caesar, or a debt of ancient gratitude?

On the showing of the document, Tarius was appointed in 23 and died in 24. Unlike Sulpicius Quirinius, he escaped an obituary notice from Cornelius Tacitus, who from the year 20 onwards devoted alert attention to the deaths of consular survivors. Tacitus records for example the death in 24 of Lucilius Longus (*suff.* 7), a person not named by any other author—but the sole senator to accompany Tiberius to Rhodes twenty-nine years previously.[37] Tarius was worth noting, on more counts than one, if he survived into the twenties.

Disquiet does not diminish.[38] The time has come to ask whether the order of *curatores* in Frontinus is correct, whether there may not be a displacement as well as a lacuna. That is to say, Tarius might have been appointed to succeed Messalla in 8, holding the office until 13. If so, his age becomes acceptable and the order of seniority is preserved—but his appointment will still be a paradox, deserving emphasis and inspiring curiosity.

That hypothesis would entail three modifications in the text of Frontinus. First, a lacuna into which must go the consuls of 8. Second, transference of Tarius Rufus to that place, after those consuls. Third, a lacuna after the consuls of 23, with an *Ignotus* to step in between Capito and Nerva for a brief tenure terminated by death.[39]

---

[34] *De clem.* I.15.2: 'Tarium qui filium deprehensum in parricidio exilio damnavit causa cognita nemo non suspexit'.

[35] Pliny, *NH* XVIII.37 (on his grandiose land speculations in Picenum). That Tarius Rufus was Dalmatian by origin has been argued by G. Alföldy, *Epigraphische Studien* V (1968), 100 ff.; J. J. Wilkes, *Dalmatia* (1969), 330 f. For strong doubts, *Danubian Papers* (1971), 119. Cf. above, p. 55.

[36] Observe a demonstration in the theatre provoked by his ex-wife Aemilia Lepida: 'tantum misericordiae permovit ut effusi in lacrimas saeva et detestanda Quirinio clamitarent' (*Ann*.III.23.1). [37] *Ann*.IV.15.1.

[38] Dessau long ago was moved to ask whether the *curator* might not be a son of the old consular (*PIR*[1] T 14). His doubts were not noticed by any who in the sequel discussed the list of Frontinus.

[39] Thus, exempli gratia, something like this: 'Messallae successit ⟨Furio et Nonio consulibus Tarius Rufus, Tario⟩ Planco et Silio consulibus Ateius Capito, Capitoni ⟨C. Asinio Pollione⟩ et C. Antistio Vetere consulibus ⟨Vibius Rufus, Vibio⟩ Servio Cornelio Cethego L. Visellio Varrone consulibus M. Cocceius Nerva.'

The common *cognomen* 'Rufus' might well have been a cause of confusion. Therefore another Rufus can be conjured up and allocated to the year 23. Perhaps the enigmatic *consul ordinarius* of 17, C. Caelius Rufus.[40] But C. Vibius Rufus is a more suitable candidate, consul suffect in 16 and president not long after of the *curatores* of the Tiber.[41] After a severe inundation (in 15) the board was set up, although not in direct sequence to the report which L. Arruntius and Ateius Capito submitted.[42]

Rufus is not merely an adjunct to the dull annals of administration. Assiduous in the schools of declamation, he is on frequent show (nearly thirty times) in the pages of Seneca. In his performance Rufus followed the 'antiquum genus dicendi'; he went in for 'cotidiana verba'; he did not eschew coarse or crude expressions.[43] Not but that competent critics accorded praise.[44]

As though to enhance his eloquence, Vibius Rufus annexed for wife a relict of Cicero.[45] Not, to be sure, the harsh and coriaceous Terentia, who lived to 103.[46] It was Publilia, the girl (in fact his ward) whom the orator married in 46. Inscriptions of a freedman found at Tusculum confirm the matrimonial pair Vibius Rufus and Publilia M. f.[47]

Rufus also acquired the curule chair of Caesar the Dictator, without incurring suspicion from Ti. Caesar.[48] Instead, the consulate, and at an advanced age. The *Fasti* of this season repay inspection.[49] For example, Rubellius Blandus (*suff.* 18), the grandson of the Tiburtine *rhetor*. Both Blandus and Rufus suggest personal ties with the ruler, of some kind or other.

The son of old Rufus proceeded without delay to a consulship. To 21 or 22 should be assigned the pair M. Cocceius Nerva and C. Vibius Rufinus.[50] Rufinus, it will be noted, figures among those on parade at the martial pageantry of October 23 in the year 12.[51]

To sum up. Three solutions have been presented:

[40] Son of the obscure C. Caelius (*suff.* 4 BC).

[41] *ILS* 5925: president of the second board, not of the first, as by error in *Rom. Rev.* (1939), 403.

[42] *Ann.* I.79. Tacitus chose to omit the creation of this board. For the chronology, *ZPE* 43 (1981), 369 ff. = *RP* III (1984), 1428 ff.

[43] Seneca, *Controv.* IX.2.25; I.2.23; 25.

[44] *Controv.* IX.2.25 (Pollio); 19 (Votienus Montanus).

[45] Dio LVII.15.6.

[46] Pliny, *NH* VII.158.

[47] *CIL* XIV. 2556; *AE* 1907, 78 (of AD 33). Cf. *CQ* XXVIII (1978), 293 f. = *RP* III (1984), 1087.

[48] Dio LVII.15.7.

[49] *Historia* XXX (1981), 189 ff. = *RP* III (1984), 1350 ff.

[50] *ILS* 1795, cf. Groag in *PIR²* C 1225. Borghesi had suggested 21. Others, among them Degrassi, have preferred the vicinity of the year 40.

[51] Ovid, *Ex. P.* III.4.5, cf. 64 ('duce ... tuo'). The articles on Rufus and Rufinus in *RE* VIIIA. 1979 ff. are variously deficient. For 36/7 as the date of Rufinus' proconsulate in Asia, see *History in Ovid* (1978), 85 f.; *ZPE* 43 (1981), 374, with the *Addendum* (376) = *RP* III (1984), 1433; 1435.

(1) The *cura aquarum* was in fact left vacant after the decease of Messalla in 8.

(2) A lacuna in the text of Frontinus, an *Ignotus* occupying the years 8–13.

(3) The same lacuna, but with Tarius Rufus transferred from 23/4 to 8, an *Ignotus* taking his place between Capito and Nerva: perhaps Vibius Rufus.

If the text is to be tampered with, the second solution is the simpler, but it leaves unanswered the problem of Tarius Rufus. The third is complicated, hazardous, and vulnerable. One must know and declare what one is doing. The intrusion of Tarius as *curator aquarum* from 8 to 13 has a justification of its own.[52] At the same time the intention (that is clear) is to support the thesis that Messalla Corvinus died in 8. That thesis takes its inception and incentive from the language of Ovid, a poet of singular and pellucid clarity—and it stands by Ovid.[53]

[52] The problem of Tarius Rufus as *curator aquarum* engaged my attention long years ago, when a portion of this chapter was in fact written.

[53] In *Rom. Rev.* 512 the authority of Frontinus and Dessau (in *PIR*[1] V 90) was followed, to the neglect of Ovid. That defect was firmly compensated in *HSCP* LXIV (1959), 41 = *RP* (1979), 415. However, in an *addendum* in that place, the editor expressed disagreement, citing F. Marx: that is, Messalla still alive when Ovid fell into disgrace.

XVII

The Posterity of Messalla

War produces widows, civil war brings divorce into the bargain (the term is appropriate), alliances being dissolved for advantage or under constraint. Sulla the Dictator benefited from the divorce that liberated a Valeria. At the games celebrating his victory she plucked a thread from his robe, for good luck. Matrimony ensued.[1] This alert girl was a niece of the orator Hortensius and sister of the Messalla who was present in court along with other young *nobiles* when Cicero delivered his speech in defence of Sex. Roscius.[2]

Without that felicitous initiative, the Valerii Messallae now stood in clear prospect of resurgence. Sulla's victory vindicated the 'causa nobilitatis', as Cicero asseverated, truthfully.[3] Belonging himself to a branch of the patriciate long in eclipse, the Dictator, urgent to reinvigorate the traditional 'res publica', required patricians who would lend both substance and adornment. In the first place, young men to fill certain priesthoods, with consulships in the sequel. The results duly emerge in the sixties.[4] Before long arrives M. Messalla in 61. He was unofficially styled 'Niger' to distinguish him from the homonymous and coeval 'Rufus'.[5] The latter, candidate in 63 for the praetorship, suffered retardation and did not reach the *fasces* until 53 (after scandalous electoral pacts and corruption).

The destiny of the two cousins was paradoxical. The successful Niger, censor in 55, passed away before the outbreak of the Civil War. He had been an orator of merit, sharp and diligent rather than brilliant.[6] Rufus encountered vicissitudes. Prosecuted for bribery in 51, he succumbed, despite the advocacy of his uncle Hortensius—almost the last of his orations, and among the best.[7]

Rufus came back with Caesar; and, with no sign hitherto of military

---

[1] Plutarch, *Sulla* 35.
[2] Cicero, *Pro Sex. Roscio Amerino* 149.
[3] ib. 135.
[4] above, p. 54.
[5] The filiation of Rufus being unattested, it was convenient to assume 'M'.f.' However, 'Marcus' now emerges, cf. J. Reynolds, *Aphrodisias and Rome* (1982), 67 f.
[6] *Brutus* 246.
[7] ib. 328. For the relationship to Hortensius, see Val. Max. V.9.2.

prowess, was active in the field, commanding cavalry in the African campaign.[8] Clearly a vigorous old fellow: he earned praise from Varro in the treatise *Messalla de valetudine*.[9] Unlike his consular colleague Domitius Calvinus, Rufus passed the bleak Triumviral years in tranquillity, suitably occupied with the study of family history and Roman antiquities: his views on the *pomerium* and on *auspicia* have been preserved.[10] He was an augur for fifty-five years.[11] That carries him from 81 into the new dispensation, as far as 26.

Corvinus, the son of Niger, signalizes the renascent glory of the house, consul with Caesar's heir in 31, taking the place of Marcus Antonius. The Valerii show two other consuls in the vicinity of the War of Actium. For a time their identity was a troublesome problem. Clarification is now to hand.[12]

First, M. Valerius Messalla, consul suffect in 32. Nothing precludes a son of Rufus. That is, he is the Messalla whose coins declare him a *monetalis* in the year of his parent's consulship.[13] He was thus born about 80. Identity has been denied, to be sure.[14] That can only proceed from a baseless and culpable aversion to elderly consuls. Along with opportunist young aristocrats, the period can show a number of consuls aged fifty or more.[15] Nothing is known about this Messalla apart from his consulship. He probably took in adoption a Claudius, i.e. M. Valerius Appianus (*cos.* 12).[16]

Second, Potitus Valerius Messalla (*suff.* 29). Like other *nobiles* in this age, he followed the new fashion of parading a *cognomen* in the place of a *praenomen*.[17] There is a chance that he might have been a Manius Messalla to begin with.[18] The general assumption has him a son of Rufus, hence younger brother of the foregoing (the *suffectus* of 32).

[8] *Bell. Afr.* 28.2; 86.3; 88.7. Cicero denounced him as a war profiteer. After naming three notorious centurions he passes on to persons of better standing: 'scripsi de Censorino, de Messalla, de Planco, de Postumo, de genere toto' (*Ad Att.* XIV. 10.2).

[9] C. Cichorius, *Römische Studien* (1922), 233 ff. Cichorius also adduces Servius on *Aen.* VIII.310: a dialogue of Maecenas in which Messalla expounded the praises of wine.

[10] Gellius XIII.14 f. For his work *De familiis,* Pliny, *NH* VII.143; XXXIV.137; XXXV.8. Also ten items from Festus, cf. H. J. Bäumerich, *Über die Bedeutung der Genealogie in der r. Lit.* (Diss. Köln, 1964), 17 ff.

[11] Macrobius I.9.4.

[12] A. E. Gordon, 'Potitus Valerius Messalla, Consul Suffect 29 BC' (*U. of Cal. Pub. in Class. Arch.* III.2 (1954)), discussed in *JRS* XLV (1955), 155 f. = *RP* (1979), 260 ff.

[13] Crawford, *RRC* I (1974), 457.

[14] R. Hanslik, *RE* VIIIA. 169.

[15] Such as, on various grounds, L. Caninius Gallus (37), Sex. Pompeius (35), L. Scribonius Libo (34).

[16] R. Hanslik declares Rufus the adopting parent, it 'muss richtig sein' (o.c. 130). Nor was there anything in the notion that the consul was 'perhaps an adopted son of Corvinus', *Rom. Rev.* (1939), 423.

[17] For the emergence of this fashion, *Historia* VII (1958), 172 ff. = *RP* (1979), 361 ff.

[18] That is, the quaestor M'. Valerius Messalla Potitus, revealed by an inscription at Claros. But he might be a son of Potitus. For the problems, *JRS* XLV (1955), 156 = *RP* (1979), 261 f.

Potitus enjoyed high favour with the ruler; and he did not decline useful occupations. The stone carrying his epitaph shows him proconsul in Asia for two years.[19] Also legate of Caesar Augustus in a province. It may well have been Syria.[20] In the first decade after 27 it is strange indeed to find a consular *nobilis* holding one of the military regions in the portion of Caesar. Otherwise the earliest instances are L. Piso (*cos.* 15) and M. Crassus Frugi (14).[21]

The Valerii exhibit three more consulships in the course of the reign. First M. Valerius Appianus (12), husband of the younger Marcella.[22] He died within a few weeks of assuming the *fasces*. His son did not live long enough to reach that predictable honour, and this line ends with Valeria Messallina, the consort of Claudius Caesar. Second, Messallinus (3), the elder son of Messalla Corvinus, legate of Illyricum in AD 6. He bequeathed his *cognomen* to his brother Cotta.[23] Third, Volesus Valerius Messalla, son of Potitus, consul in AD 5. He was condemned a few years later after prosecution for criminal misdemeanour when pronconsul of Asia.[24] After whom, no more descendants of old Rufus.

It will be suitable to subjoin a Valerius who passed into another *gens*, becoming T. Quinctius Crispinus Valerianus (*suff.* AD 2).[25] Valerianus has been supposed adoptive son of T. Quinctius Crispinus Sulpicianus (*cos.* 9 BC), the ill-fated lover of Julia.[26]

The Sulpicii, another patrician house, prospered at this epoch: C. Sulpicius Galba (*suff.* 5 BC), Galus Sulpicius (4), Q. Sulpicius Camerinus (*cos.* AD 9).[27] No Galba had held the fasces since 108; and Ser. Sulpicius Rufus, the eminent jurist, came late and not easily to his consulship.[28] His son, the orator who married a sister of Corvinus, is last heard of in 35 or 34.[29] The orator's son appears to be a certain Postumius Sulpicius: a senator of praetorian rank named assistant to Messalla Corvinus when he took charge of the aqueducts in 11.[30] This man, it will be noted, carries his

---

[19] *ILS* 8964. Misinterpreted as 'zweimal' by R. Hanslik (o.c. 166). He surmises a compliment to Corvinus (here called his 'Stiefbruder'), for Corvinus had no province after his Aquitanian triumph.

[20] Thus A. E. Gordon, o.c. 42 f.

[21] Ch. IV.

[22] Ch. XI.

[23] Velleius II.112.1.

[24] *Ann.* III.68.1. For his murderous cruelty, Seneca, *De ira* II.5.5.

[25] *PIR*[1] Q 38. The adopting parent is wrongly assumed a Valerius by H. G. Gundel, *RE* XXIV.993.

[26] Thus Mommsen, followed in *PIR*[1] Q 38. Valerianus, praetor in 2 BC, became consul 'suo anno'. It is preferable to hold him a brother by adoption.

[27] None of them seems to have come to anything. The last two are only names and dates. Galba had two consular sons, the consuls of 22 and 33.

[28] A failed candidate for 62.

[29] above, p. 205.

[30] Frontinus, *De aquis* 102.

grandmother's *gentilicium* (the jurist's wife was a Postumia, of a decayed patrician house now extinct). These links between the Valerii and other patrician families excite curiosity but do little to satisfy it.

The marriages of Corvinus present an engaging problem.[31] Not, to be sure, the fable related by Jerome that in succession to Sallust he married Cicero's Terentia, who thus 'per quosdam gradus eloquentiae devoluta est.'[32] It does not need to be refuted by a mere fact, namely the son of Terentia (*suff.* 30) coeval by a year to Corvinus. The figment is relevant to the orator's second wife and relict, young Publilia. It can be segregated to advantage.

The search for the wives of Corvinus must start with his sons. The elder, Messallinus (*cos.* 3), was born in 36, so it may be assumed without discomfort. A poem of Tibullus acclaims his induction into the *quindecimviri*.[33] Which could happen to a boy *nobilis* as soon as he put on the *toga virilis*. Nothing stands against dating the poem to the year 21.

A recent theory asserts that Messallinus could not become a *quindecimvir* until he held the quaestorship, that he was born in 43 BC.[34] Why should that be? The author betrays his purpose. He wants to prolong the life of Tibullus beyond 19, with the added refinement that the pseudonym 'Lygdamus' conveys none other than the elder son of Messalla Corvinus. Which is worse than ingenious, and can only appeal to the inadvertent. Persicus, the son of Fabius Maximus, was fifteen (it can be maintained) when he took the place of his deceased parent among the *Arvales* in AD 15.[35] As so often, ingenious or frivolous dallying with the poet ignores facts and disturbs history.[36] Another pronouncement declares that Messallinus must have been born in 39.[37] Again without grounds. The abnormal favour enjoyed by this family entails a consulship 'suo anno'. Similarly for M. Aurelius Cotta Maximus, the second son, consul with the son of Messallinus in AD 20.[38] The pair kept the *fasces* for the whole twelve months, a distinction unique in the reign of Tiberius Caesar.

Twenty-two years separate the consulships of the sons of Corvinus.

---

[31] Briefly discussed in *History in Ovid* (1978), 117 ff.

[32] Jerome, *Adv. Iovin.* I. 48, cf. *CQ* XXVIII (1978), 292 f. = *RP* III (1984), 1085 f.

[33] Tibullus II.5.1.

[34] E. Bickel, *Rh. Mus* CIII (1960), 97 ff. To have Messallinus born in 43 and consul at forty suits well the 'Staatsrecht der augusteischen Zeit', so he said (ib. 102). Followed by G. Luck, *Die römische Liebeselegie* (1961), 215 f.

[35] *AE* 1947, 52.

[36] cf. above, p. 210.

[37] R. Hanslik, o.c. 134. He uses the word 'muss' and appeals to an Italian expert (Salanitro) who apparently decreed that Tibullus II.5 was written about 24. Hanslik's view has recently been adopted by J. Scheid, *Les Frères Arvales* (1975), 55, cf. 124; 126; 160.

[38] For the identity of the consul of 20 with the Cotta Messallinus of Tacitus, see below, p. 236.

Different mothers. On the standard view a Calpurnia and an Aurelia.[39] It will be expedient to tackle them in the reverse order.

In epistles to the sons of Corvinus, Ovid appeals to the memory of their father, to a friendship that went back a long way, well before the birth of Cotta. And he had saluted the infant in its cradle.[40] That is, about 14. The mother was still alive in AD 13.[41] Further, addressing Cotta towards the end of his last poem, Ovid indicates her family:

> maternos Cottas cui Messallasque paternos
> Maxime, nobilitas ingeminata dedit.[42]

Another passage, however, brings in another family on the maternal side, namely the Calpurnii (who traced their descent from Calpus, a son of Numa). Referring to the 'mores' that prove the 'nobilitas' of Cotta, he continues

> quos Volesus patrii cognoscat nominis auctor
> quos Numa materni non neget esse suos
> adiectique probent genetiva ad nomina Cottae
> si tu non esses, interitura domus.[43]

Now Valerius Maximus, the younger son of Corvinus, took through adoption the name of an Aurelius Cotta, the last of his line. That is clear. Which Cotta? M. Cotta (*pr.* ?54) is heard of for the last time as governor of Sardinia on the Pompeian side in 49.[44] For him to adopt Corvinus' younger son (born about 14) would entail a long survival.[45] Better therefore an unknown son. Choice commonly depends on an existing relationship. Hence the standard view that Messalla's wife was a sister of a Cotta (i.e. the praetor) who left his name to his nephew.

So far, acceptable. But if the mother of young Maximus was an Aurelia, how and where do Calpurnii come in? The easy solution will be to assume that M. Cotta (*pr.*?54) had married a Calpurnia. That is, the maternal grandmother of Maximus, the son of Messalla Corvinus: Ovid (quoted above) states that Calpurnii are his ancestors on the maternal side.

It is no help that another Calpurnia comes into the reckoning as the putative mother of Messallinus, the elder son, by a marriage contracted *c.* 40. Two documents are in question. First, an inscription mentioning 'Calpurnia M. f. Messallae'.[46] Calpurnii with the *praenomen* 'Marcus' are

---

[39] R. Hanslik, o.c. 134. In *PIR*[1] V 90 Dessau was strangely indecisive. He discussed only the mother of the younger son, and gave no hint of two marriages. Groag in *PIR*[2] A 1488 also confined himself to Cotta's mother.

[40] Ovid, *Ex P.* II.3.73.

[41] ib. 98.

[42] *Ex P.* IV.16.43 f.

[43] *Ex P.* III.2.105 ff.

[44] Caesar, *BC* I.30.2 f., cf. Cicero, *Ad Att.* X.16.3.

[45] A difficulty not noted by Groag in *PIR*[2] A 1485.

[46] *CIL* VI.27892 = *ILS* 5989.

not easy to come by. One might be tempted to speculate about a daughter
of M. Piso (*pr.* 44, the son of the consul of 61).[47] Better, a sister of
L. Calpurnius M. f. Bibulus, united to Corvinus by the cause of the
Republic and the Battle of Philippi.[48]

That solution is highly attractive but perhaps premature. Calpurnia
M. f. might belong to some other Messalla.[49] For Corvinus' wife the
nomenclature 'Calpurnia Corvini' would be expected. That name is in
fact registered on a tile.[50] Again, however, doubts might be conceived:
perhaps the wife of Messalla Corvinus (*cos.* 58), the great-grandson of the
orator.[51]

Certainty is baffled. Still, whatever the identity of the first wife,
Corvinus was a married man in two verifiable seasons: about 36 and about
14. Further, for that matter, Corvinus might have had more wives than
two (and perhaps a divorce when he changed sides, or in the aftermath of
Actium) before he married Aurelia, the daughter of the last Aurelius
Cotta, which might not have been long before 14.

On that occasion Corvinus opted for the plebeian *nobilitas*. His links
with several patrician families have already been noted. In closing this
rubric it may be added that, except for Marcella (married to Messalla
Appianus), no wife is known for any of the other consular Valerii of the
period, or for any direct descendant of the orator.

To proceed. Messallinus first enters history as legate of Illyricum when the
great rebellion broke out in AD 6. Tiberius had to turn back from the
invasion of Bohemia. Messallinus he sent on in advance, and Messallinus
got the worst of it in a pitched battle with the insurgents, but afterwards
was able to defeat their leader, Bato the Dalmatian, through an ambush.
Thus Dio.[52]

Velleius offers a stirring report: a victory won against great odds,
twenty thousand of the enemy being put to rout, for which exploit the
general was awarded the *ornamenta triumphalia*.[53]

Velleius was doing his best. Perhaps the performance of Messallinus was
not resplendent. Neither Velleius nor Dio record any subsequent action,
although each furnishes a full account of this long war.[54]

---

[47] For the stemma, *JRS* L (1960), 17 = *RP* (1979), 503. In that case this Calpurnia would be a
sister of M. Licinius Crassus Frugi (*cos.* 14), a Piso who (it is inferred) was adopted by M. Licinius
Crassus (*cos.* 30).

[48] above, p. 206.

[49] Thus Groag, *PIR*² C 322.

[50] Published in *Bull. Comm.* 1889, 208; H. Bloch, *HSCP* LVI–LVII (1947), no. 249.

[51] cf. the doubts of Groag in *PIR*² C 322.

[52] Dio LV.30.2.

[53] Velleius II.102.2.

[54] With names of sundry generals. Dio seems to have used a source that was also cool about the
parent of Messallinus.

Messallinus received three poetical epistles from the exile at Tomis. The first, in 11, omits the name but declares the person (*Tristia* IV.1). It opens with noble birth surpassed only by nobility of character, extols that eloquence which he inherited, 'patriae facundia linguae' (1.5), and recalls with warm gratitude how Corvinus used to encourage the poet's talent (1.29 ff.). Then the argument passes to Ovid's transgression, with a plea that Messallinus intercede with Caesar (51 ff.). The next letter, belonging to the year 12, is couched in a similar strain.[55]

Finally, *Ex Ponto* II.2. The opening poem of the book described the Pannonian triumph, celebrated on October 23, AD 12.[56] Referring to that ceremony, Ovid now brings in the entire 'Augusta domus' (2.74). Messallinus is there in the company of Tiberius and Germanicus, 'vobiscum' (2.81), and Ovid slips in a discreet allusion to the *ornamenta triumphalia* (2.89 f.).[57] He had been careful, as before, to invoke the inheritance of oratory, the 'nitor ille domesticus' (2.49); and he made appeal to the 'gratia' which Messallinus enjoys with the ruler:

principis aeterni quam tibi praestat amor. (2.48)

That was the last entreaty. No letter in the next two books. The eminent nobleman had had enough. He did not wish to be enticed into operations of intercession. And Ovid saw that it was no good. Henceforth he concentrates on the younger brother, for a time at least.

The graceful eloquence that the son of Corvinus inherited had another aspect, and highly detrimental. Tacitus was careful to bring it out.

Messallinus makes an early entrance in the *Annales*. At the first session of the Senate, when the ceremonial for the funeral of Augustus came up for debate, three men of consular rank brought forward proposals. The third, Messallinus, was out of order. The oath of allegiance to the new ruler, he said, ought to be renewed each year. Tiberius declined. Whereupon Messallinus candidly explained that his motion was meant to show public spirit and independent judgement, even at risk. As the historian adds in comment, that was the only kind of adulation that had not yet been tried.[58]

The next meeting of the high assembly, after enrolling Augustus among the gods of the Roman State, discussed the 'res publica' and the position of Tiberius Caesar (September 17). The proceedings ran into trouble and issued in fatigue. The false role enjoined in the ceremony made

---

[55] Ovid, *Ex P.* I.7. This poem contains the important notice about the dirge which Ovid composed for the funeral of Corvinus (above, p. 218).

[56] For the date, above, p. 219.

[57] Ovid has no other reference to the military prowess of Messallinus.

[58] *Ann.* I.8.4: 'ea sola species adulandi supererat'. Hardly true, if the historian had studied the reign of Caesar Augustus.

Tiberius awkward in his comportment, while certain consulars such as Asinius Gallus were less that helpful in their contribution. The scene was not edifying. One may regret that the conciliatory talents of Messallinus were not enlisted, worthy to succeed performers like Munatius Plancus or his own parent. On this occasion the thing was not properly prepared, so it appears.

Missing from the narration for six years in the sequel, the eloquent Messallinus is not found among the advocates canvassed for the defence of Cn. Piso, the legate of Syria: eight consulars are registered (*Ann.* III.11.2). But he comes out with a proposal in the aftermath. Nothing less than a golden statue to be set up in the temple of Mars Ultor (18.2). Tiberius refused to concur. Then an anticlimax. Messallinus also sponsored a vote of thanks to Tiberius and to other members of the family because Germanicus had been avenged. Which gave L. Arruntius the opportunity to intervene and ask whether the omission of Claudius (the brother of Germanicus) had been deliberate.

His next appearance the year after is his last. A motion was before the Senate that governors of provinces should not be permitted to take their wives with them. Messallinus spoke against, in mild and tactful discourse (III.34).

Tacitus in the previous year had hit upon the device of obituary notices. None, however, for the son of Messalla Corvinus. The oration did service as a conspicuous exit.

For the historian, Messallinus might usefully illustrate two associated themes: the ann als of Roman eloquence and the growth of subservience to the government. In his first missive to Messallinus Ovid acclaimed him as 'patrii candoris imago', as embodying 'patriae facundia linguae'.[59] Tacitus introduces the orator with 'ineratque imago paternae facundiae'. Perhaps an echo.[60] Or it may be only a commonplace.

At this stage in the narrative Tacitus was becoming acutely aware of a defect, of a dereliction: he needed to know more about the late Augustan years.[61] Lighting upon a peculiar episode in transactions of the Senate (D. Silanus, one of the lovers of the younger Julia, allowed to come back), Tacitus was moved, against his normal reticence, to announce a future project of some magnitude, should life be vouchsafed (III.24.3). Silanus evoked Ovid and a subversive parallel. As Tiberius Caesar stated, 'non senatus consulto, non lege pulsus'. The fancy is not idle that the historian saw the relevance to Ovid, that he may have been reading Ovid. If he lived to embark on his design, he would find instruction and delight in the *Epistulae ex Ponto*.[62]

---

[59] *Tr.* IV.4.3 ff.   [60] *Ann.* III. 34.1.   [61] cf. *Tacitus* (1958), 370.
[62] As did Gibbon, although not quite for the same reasons, cf. *History in Ovid* (1978), 225.

With Cotta Maximus, Ovid's relations were much closer. He favoured Cotta with no fewer than nine epistles (the first two not declaring his name).[63] It was not until the year 11 that he ventured an approach. The first, succeeding the initial appeal to Messallinus, is much shorter, and says very little (*Tristia* IV.5). Likewise the second (V.9), though it renders thanks to Cotta as his sole rescuer (9.19), and puts emphasis on Cotta's friendship with Caesar (9.21 f.):

O mihi dilectos inter pars prima sodales . (5.1)

The word 'sodalis' is important: it denotes equality in social intercourse. There is also an 'unswerving friendship' (5.24). The poet is not just a client, suitably deferential to an aristocratic house (and not expecting much in the way of requital for 'officia'). He had been a personal friend and companion of the young man, his junior by about thirty years. At the time of the catastrophe Cotta had not entered the Senate; but he was now married, he might hope for a son (5.27 ff.)—and was perhaps to be quaestor in 12, in the consulship of his coeval, Germanicus Caesar.[64]

The seven poems in *Ex Ponto* I–III show Ovid more appetent and expansive. He had been (it is disclosed) in the company of Cotta on the island of Elba when the news arrived of Caesar's anger (II.3.83 f.). Cotta's lineage is acclaimed as well as the 'nobilitas' of his character (III.2.104 ff.). Like his brother, Cotta inherited the gift of public speech (II.2.51; III.5.7), he has sent Ovid one of his orations (III.5.7 f.; 24), he also writes poetry (I.5.57; III.5.37 ff.).

Finally, Cotta's fervent devotion to the dynasty. He sent Ovid silver busts or statuettes of three divine personages ('caelites'), namely Augustus, Livia, Tiberius. With this embellishment of his domestic shrine Ovid can proclaim

est aliquid spectare deos et adesse putare. (II.8.9)[65]

In gratitude to Cotta as his pretext, he now passes on to entreaty of the higher beings, at some length. The last poem, however, is very short and keeps off that topic (III.8).

Book IV has no letter to Cotta. Like his brother, Cotta may at last have begun to show signs of fatigue. Ovid was now concentrating his efforts on Sex. Pompeius (*cos.* 14) and on sundry friends of Germanicus Caesar.[66] Not but that Ovid at the very end subjoins to the catalogue of Roman poets a resplendent tribute to the talents of Cotta Maximus (IV.16.41 ff.).

[63] viz. *Tr.* IV.5 and 9; *Ex P.*I.5; 9; II.3; 8; III.2; 5; 8. In the Index of *OCT* (1915) the Maximus of III.8 is assumed to be Fabius Maximus.

[64] Cotta may have been with Tiberius on the Rhine in 12 or 13, cf. the word 'sospes' in *Ex P.* III.2.3.

[65] The word 'putare' does not connote a strong belief. Observe the remark of an emperor, 'vae, puto, deus fio' (Suetonius, *Divus Vesp.* 23.4).   [66] *History in Ovid* (1978), 87 f.; 128; 156 ff.

Cotta had done nothing. The claim of 'amicitia' was not requited, it should seem. What then follows? In the year 8 Cotta had afforded Ovid some comfort, and was ready to lend material aid, if Ovid's fortune had been confiscated (*Tristia* IV.5.2ff.). At this stage at least in his life Cotta may have been a generous and amiable character—and no grounds to doubt the sincerity of his sentiments. His later comportment offers melancholy testimony of an aristocrat's subservience to power.

The consul of 20 turns up in the *Annales* as M. Aurelius and as Aurelius Cotta (III.2.3; 17.4). But a certain Cotta Messallinus had already been on show (II.32.1), and he recurs a number of times in the sequel. Borghesi pronounced them identical.[67] Grave doubts have been expressed in the recent time.[68] They can be dispelled.

Cotta Messallinus makes his entrance in 16, in a notable transaction. The suicide of the alleged conspirator Libo Drusus did not put a stay on proceedings. The Senate decreed rewards for the prosecutors; and various proposals of vengeance or thanksgiving were brought forward. The historian was careful to document the sponsors. For a good reason.[69]

Tacitus names seven persons of rank and consequence (II.32 f.). All consulars save Cotta Messallinus. What right had he to be here, if not an ex-consul? A ready answer avails: Cotta spoke as praetor-designate.[70]

Cotta's proposal was to debar the image of Libo from funeral processions. He is next heard of in 20, enjoining measures to condemn the memory of Cn. Piso, some of which were abated by the Princeps (III.17.4; 18.1). His elder brother, it will be recalled, advocated a golden statue in the temple of Mars Ultor. The sons of Corvinus were suitably alert when the chance offered to advertise that devotion to the dynasty which had annexed the term 'pietas'.[71]

Messallinus had put in a plea for the wives of provincial governors: if they transgress the husband should take the blame (III.34.4). Three years later Cotta proposed in the Senate that the husband should be held responsible for offences committed by the spouse (IV.20.4). That was a nasty epilogue to the prosecution of C. Silius, the legate of Germania Superior, which had involved his wife Sosia Galla (19.1).

Silius and Sosia were close friends of the widow of Germanicus. When,

---

[67] Accepted in *PIR*[1] A 1236, cf. the remark in V 90: 'si vere est ut esse videtur'.

[68] Like Nipperdey and others, Groag dissented, assigning separate entries: *PIR*[2] A 1487 f. (with a fairly long argumentation in the second entry). But Degrassi held them identical, *Epigraphica* VIII (1946), 38.

[69] *Ann.* II.32.2: 'quorum auctoritates adulationesque rettuli, ut sciretur vetus id in re publica malum'.

[70] A Cotta can be recognized as *praetor peregrinus* in 17 in the *Fasti Arvalium* (*Inscr. It.* XIII.1, p. 297), cf. *JRS* XLVI (1966), 18 = *Ten Studies in Tacitus* (1970), 52.

[71] cf. Ovid, *Ex P.* II.2.21 (to the elder brother): 'quaeque tua est pietas in totum nomen Iuli'.

at the beginning of 29, charges were brought against Agrippina and the eldest of her sons, Cotta Messallinus led the pack, 'cum atroci sententia' (V.3.2).

The gap in the *Annales* may cover up other specimens of loyal or reprehensible conduct before or after the catastrophe of Aelius Seianus. When next on exhibit, Cotta is in trouble, for various reasons, among them a lawsuit with L. Arruntius and M. Lepidus, about whose 'potentia' he made open complaint. He was in bad odour: 'saevissimae cuiusque sententiae auctor eoque inveterata invidia' (VI.5.1). He turned for help to Caesar, who in a despatch to the Senate expatiated on 'amicitia' of long standing, on the 'officia' rendered by Cotta. And so, as Cotta had predicted, 'me autem tuebitur Tiberiolus meus.'

So far Tacitus. In the progeny of Corvinus he has been intent to demonstrate how the gift of eloquence is debased, degenerating into adulation and servility. Not but that some aristocrats kept their honour and gained good repute, to be exhibited in sharp contrast. Before mentioning a proposal of Cotta in the Senate, he inserts an appreciation of M. Lepidus, whom the historian 'ascertains to be a man of weight and wisdom'.[72]

It was no doubt a relief for Senate and for society when Cotta Messallinus went away for a year to hold authority in Asia.[73] The date is in question, it is involved in a whole nexus of problems concerning proconsuls in the period from 35 to 41.

Tiberius for a time tried to keep to a decennial interval for Asia and Africa. The war in Africa brought perturbation to the sortition, and for other reasons tenures longer than annual also emerged. Then the ruler abrogated the system, leaving the consular proconsuls in office for six years, the praetorian for three.[74] P. Petronius (*suff.* 19) was in Asia for a sexennium, presumably 29–35, and M. Junius Silanus (*cos.* 19) in Africa.[75]

The sequence for Asia is as follows:

20/1	C. Junius Silanus (*cos.* 10)
21/2	M'. Aemilius Lepidus (11)
22/3	
?23/4	C. Fonteius Capito (12)
?24/5	Sex. Pompeius (14)
25/6	

---

[72] *Ann.* IV.20.2 (above p. 134).

[73] Attested by *IGR* IV.1508 (Sardis); *Forsch. in Ephesos* III.112, no. 22.

[74] Dio LVIII.23.5 (without any names).

[75] For proconsuls of Asia in this period see *JRS* XLV (1955), 29 f. = *Ten Studies in Tacitus* (1970), 43 f. Further, *History in Ovid* (1978), 160 f.; *ZPE* 53 (1983), 191 ff. Difficulties raised by some scholars about the tenure of M. Silanus in Africa are briefly indicated in *PIR²* J 839. Cf. above p. 191. After Silanus, C. Rubellius Blandus holds Africa in 35/6 (*IRT* 330).

26/8   M. Aemilius Lepidus (6)
28/9
29/35   P. Petronius (*suff.* 19)

One observes the exceptional seniority and tenure of Marcus Lepidus; and Sex. Pompeius might also have had a biennium.[76] What happened now and soon after tended to exclude from both provinces the men who had held the *fasces* in the four years from 15 to 18. They are no fewer than fourteen. Of that number only two are on record in the proconsulates of Asia and Africa.[77]

After prorogations occurring in 30, the thing would become flagrant in 31—and soon portentous. The motives of Tiberius Caesar need not be canvassed at this point. One of the consequences was a grievous injury done to legitimate aspirations—ten ex-consuls deprived.

Various dates have been proposed for Cotta, some of them depending on a reluctance to concede identity with the consul of 20.[78] Now the years 26–8 are excluded by the *biennium* of M. Aemilius Lepidus; and likewise 28/9, since Cotta was at Rome at the beginning of 29.[79] Nor would so short an interval from the consulship be likely. It is best to assign him the tenure 35/6, succeeding P. Petronius (*suff.* 19).[80] On a question of seniority (one can hardly speak of system in this season), let it be observed that C. Sulpicius Galba (*cos.* 22) was debarred from the sortition for 36/7.[81]

Enough having been said to the discredit of Cotta Messallinus, the historian might have waived a necrological notice in the books not extant.

In the epilogue on the latest incident (in 32) the evil aristocrat is described as 'egens ob luxum, per flagitia infamis'.[82] Cotta exemplifies those noblemen under the first dynasty whose ostentation and extravagance brought ancient houses to ruin.[83] A later age looked back with hazy admiration. Decrying present conditions, Juvenal hails Cotta as a splendid patron of letters:

> quis tibi Maecenas, quis nunc erit aut Proculeius
> aut Fabius, quis Cotta iterum, quis Lentulus alter?[84]

---

[76] The proconsulate of Sex. Pompeius should go in either 24/5 or 25/6: most scholars have put it two or three years later. C. Fonteius Capito (*cos.* 12), here presumed his immediate predecessor, was prosecuted in 25 (*Ann.* IV.36.2).

[77] cf. remarks in *Historia* XXX (1981), 196 f. = *RP* III (1984), 1357.

[78] Groag suggested 'fortasse a 22/23 vel 25/26 vel 27/28' (*PIR*[2] A 1488). Degrassi, though accepting Cotta as the consul of 20, suggested 25/6 or 27/8 (*Epigraphica* VIII (1946), 38). His tenure was put between C. Fonteius Capito (*cos.* 12) and Sex. Pompeius (*cos.* 14) by D. Magie, *Roman Rule in Asia Minor* (1950), 1581 (without indication of dates).

[79] *AE* 1934, 87 (Cos); *Ann.* V.2.2.

[80] cf. 'he might belong in 35/6', *JRS* XLV (1955), 30 = *Ten Studies in Tacitus* (1970), 44.

[81] *Ann.* VI.40.2. C.Vibius Rufinus (*suff.* 21 or 22) then acquired Asia, cf. *ZPE* 43 (1981), 374; 376 = *RP* III (1984), 1433; 1435.

[82] VI.7.1.   [83] III.55.2.   [84] Juvenal VII.94 f.

A peculiar collection. Maecenas was inevitable; Proculeius is the opulent equestrian partisan of Caesar Augustus; and Fabius is the decorative consul of 11 BC. What of Lentulus? To be sure, Gaetulicus (*cos.* 26) was a poet, but his ten years' tenure of Germania Superior (29–39) gave little scope for literary patronage;[85] and Lentulus the Augur (*cos.* 14 BC) was a notorious skinflint.[86]

In another place the satirist extols Cotta's generosity towards friends of a lower station:

> nemo petit, modicis quae mittebantur amicis
> a Seneca, quae Piso bonus, quae Cotta solebat
> largiri.[87]

Tacitus may have been writing in conscious reaction against that indulgent tradition. However that may be, the tomb of Zosimus, a freedman of Cotta Maximus, carries a notable tribute in verse. He renders thanks to the patron who gave him ample sums of money more than once and secured for his son the post of military tribune.[88]

So far the consular sons. Corvinus may have had a third son. There is a stray Messalla, *monetalis* somewhere in the middle years of the reign.[89] He baffles identification—and it matters little, so many men perishing in their early prime.

Cotta's colleague in the consulate was M. Valerius Messalla, to be identified as a son of his brother: only an item on the *Fasti*.[90] But he had a son. The following generation shows a Messalla Corvinus sharing the *fasces* with Nero in 58. Which put old men (a few) in mind of his great-grandfather, colleague of Caesar Augustus, so Tacitus avers.[91] This Corvinus took financial subsidy from Nero. Tacitus extenuates—it was a compliment to an illustrious family, and he suffered under 'innoxia paupertas'. With this consul ends the line of the Valerii Messallae.[92]

The next item brings on two other pensioners, Aurelius Cotta and Haterius Antoninus, not in good standing: they had dissipated their patrimony through high living. Haterius Antoninus (*cos.* 53) is the grandson and last descendant of the fluent and adulatory orator, of whom the historian disapproved.[93] The conduct and morals of his father, Haterius Agrippa (*cos.* 23) had been sharply condemned in the sentence that

---

[85] For his poetry see the *testimonia* in *PIR*² C 1390.
[86] Ch. XXI.
[87] Juvenal V.108 ff.
[88] *ILS* 1949 (Via Appia).
[89] *BMC R. Emp.* I. 46.
[90] There were many deaths in the early twenties.
[91] *Ann.* XIII.34.1.
[92] The shepherd 'Corvinus' in Juvenal I.208 need not be taken for a real person.
[93] Ch.XI.

precedes his last notice of Cotta Messallinus.[94] These collocations are artful
and instructive. The Aurelius Cotta may be identified as a son of Cotta
Messallinus.[95] Ovid predicted virtuous and recognizable offspring:

> sic iuvenis similisque tibi sit natus, et illum
> moribus agnoscat quilibet esse tuum.[96]

The *Annales* carry a history of Roman eloquence from the Augustan
epoch (Pollio and Messalla being recalled through their sons) down to the
author's own time, with Neronian orators whose performance he had
heard and estimated when a young aspirant. To the author of the *Dialogus*
it was a sad declension from the grace and dignity of Messalla Corvinus to
men like Eprius Marcellus and Vibius Crispus, forceful or persuasive
orators (it was conceded), but in truth only servants of the government.[97]
Oratory makes a contribution to the general theme of decline and fall.

As has been shown, only one wife of Messalla Corvinus can be identified,
an Aurelia. Nor is there any trace of the alliances contracted by his sons.
Meanwhile the line was being propagated on the female side.

The orator had at least one daughter. Her existence is deduced from
'Corvinus' in the nomenclature of a Statilius who was consul under
Claudius in 45; and he is defined by Suetonius as a grandson.[98] This Valeria
therefore married T. Statilius Taurus (*cos.* 11), the son of the great marshal
of Augustus.[99] From the match issue T. Statilius Taurus (*cos.* 44) and
Taurus Statilius Corvinus (*cos.* 45). The latter, along with a grandson of
Asinius Pollio, was involved in a conspiracy against Claudius Caesar
(in 46);[100] the former fell victim to the cupidity of Agrippina.[101]

One or other of the consular brothers may be presumed the father of
Statilia Messallina, whose husband at the time of the Pisonian conspiracy
was the consul Vestinus Atticus, as Tacitus reports.[102] More would be
heard of this lady if the text of the *Annales* did not break off at a point not
far into 66.[103] Nero, who had been one of her lovers, married Statilia in the
first half of that year.[104]

---

[94] *Ann.* VI.4.4: 'somno aut libidinosis vigiliis marcidus' etc.

[95] Though Groag in *PIR*[2] A 1486 says 'fortasse'. He suggests that this man is the Cotta of Juvenal V.109.

[96] Ovid, *Tr.* IV.5.31 f. That is, the child of a marriage contracted in 9 or 10.

[97] Tacitus, *Dial.*13.4.

[98] Suetonius, *Divus Claudius* 13.2 (the conspiracy of the grandsons of Messalla and Pollio).

[99] *PIR*[1] S 617. A sister therefore of Messalla's younger son Cotta.

[100] Suetonius, *Divus Claudius* 13.2. Dio mentions Asinius Gallus only, and states that, a small, ugly, and ridiculous person, he escaped the penalty of death (LX.27.5). No word in either author about the fate of Statilius Corvinus.

[101] *Ann.* XII.59.1.

[102] XV.68.3.

[103] That is, on a dubious hypothesis that the historian survived to complete his work.

[104] cf. *PIR*[1] S 625.

Engaging particulars are furnished by the *scholium* on Juvenal VI.434. Before marrying Vestinus, Statilia had discarded three husbands in turn. Not surprising, given the variety of her accomplishments. Tacitus would not miss her, who had an eye for the bright and the beautiful.[105]

Such was the appeal of this entrancing female that Otho, who eleven years previously had forfeited Poppaea Sabina (with no known subsequent venture in matrimony), was going to take her as his consort, so it is alleged. Her lineage at least befitted an empress. Statilia was perhaps no longer in her first youth. No bar, let it be said. One might give a thought to Milonia Caesonia, who bewitched Caligula.[106]

Indeed, Borghesi supposed that Statilia's son might be Catullus Messallinus (*cos.* 73, *suff. II* 85).[107] That would make her older than Otho (who was born in 32), and bring her close in age to Valeria Messallina. The consul of 73, by his full style L. Valerius Catullus Messallinus, is the notorious prosecutor of evil fame under Domitian, prominent (and he deserved it) at the cabinet council which held solemn debate on what was to be done with a large fish.[108] The author of the *Historiae* would have been alert to the pedigree of this Messallinus.

The other family that prolongs the descendance of Messalla Corvinus is more decorous—and more enduring. Namely the Vipstani. They emerge early in the reign of Tiberius: sudden, novel, unexplained. The Vipstani call for attention, and they respond.[109]

First, Vipstanus Gallus, a praetor of 17 dying in office, whence competition for the vacancy.[110] He may be assigned 'Lucius' for *praenomen*.[111] Second, M. Vipstanus Gallus, consul suffect in 18: only a name and a date.

The next generation brings a surprise with the *ordinarius* of 48, L. Vipstanus Poplicola.[112] He also carried 'Messalla' in his nomenclature.[113] A previous alliance with the Valerii is revealed. Let it be taken that one or other of the two Vipstani Galli had married a daughter of Corvinus' elder son (consul in 3 BC). The reign of Claudius can produce another consul of this rising family, namely the Vipstanus attested as legate of Pannonia in

---

[105] *Greece & Rome* XXVIII (1981), 41 f. = *RP* III (1984), 1366.

[106] Suetonius, *Cal.* 25.3. One of the children of the famous Vistilia (Pliny, *NH* VII.39).

[107] *PIR*[1] V 41. One would like to know more about Sex. Tedius Valerius Catullus, *suffectus* in 31 (*PIR*[1] T 38, cf. V 37).

[108] Juvenal IV.113 ff.

[109] The treatment in *RE* IXA (1961), 168 ff. is variously defective. For corrections and supplements see *Historia* XI (1962), 149 ff. = *RP* (1979), 533 ff.

[110] *Ann.* II.51.1.

[111] Two Vipstani Galli are honoured at Athens, Marcus and Lucius (*IG* II[2].4185).

[112] *PIR*[1] V 471.

[113] *AE* 1928, 98 = *SEG* IV.530 (Ephesus).

52 or 53.[114] Some uncertainty has obtained about his precise nomenclature: it can be argued that it was 'Messalla Vipstanus Gallus'.[115] Next, under Nero, a second *ordinarius*, L. Vipstanus Apronianus (*cos.* 59). That is, either an Apronius adopted by a Lucius Vipstanus, or a Vipstanus whose father had married an Apronia.[116]

The pedigree acquires value in and from the study of Latin literature. In the *Dialogus* of Cornelius Tacitus there intervenes to defend classical oratory against the moderns none other than a Vipstanus Messalla. Dignity and elegance mark his discourse, designed no doubt to recall the manner of Messalla Corvinus, even if one of the speakers had not alluded to 'maiores tui'.[117]

Tribune of a legion in 69 when the army of Moesia entered the war against Vitellius, Messalla wrote a narrative of the campaign. Tacitus used his memoir; and Messalla earns praise as 'claris maioribus, egregius ipse et qui solus ad id bellum artes bonas attulisset'.[118] Tacitus thus pays a double tribute to the friend of his youth who failed to reach the prime of eloquence—or of life. Otherwise he could not fail to stand among the *consules ordinarii* in the early eighties. Death may be surmised, perhaps in the great pestilence under Titus.[119]

His son can be recognized in the consul of 115, L. Vipstanus Messalla. And descendants of blended nomenclature can be traced for a long time thereafter. Their tribe is the 'Claudia', in which the Vipstani were enrolled.[120] The *nomen* is both rare and peculiar, and the tribe would fit an origin from Cliternia or Aequicoli in the back country behind Tibur, between the Sabines and the Marsi.[121]

Families of the patriciate exhibit diuturnity. The Valerii came out of the Sabine country, the ancestor having arrived with T. Tatius, so they claimed.[122] The Claudii also boasted the same extraneous origin, with Attus Clausus in the days of the Kings, or in the first years of the infant Republic. According to Claudius Caesar, to survive they had never had

---

[114] *CIL* III.4591 (Carnuntum). Hence consul suffect *c.* 48. Not in Degrassi, *I fasti consolari* (1952).

[115] *Gnomon* XXIX (1957), 520 = *Danubian Papers* (1971), 183. See now J. Devreker, *ZPE* 22 (1976), 203 ff.

[116] cf. Groag in *PIR*² A 972 (L. Apronius Caesianus, *cos.* 39).

[117] *Dial.* 27.1. To state that 'Tacitus' friend may be a descendant of the orator' (*Tacitus* (1958), 107) was unduly diffident.

[118] *Hist.* III.9.3.

[119] Suetonius, *Divus Titus* 8.3: 'item pestilentia quanta non temere alias'. Two other deaths interrupted the consular sequence in this illustrious family. First, C. Valerius Poplicola (son of the consul of 48), coopted into a sacerdotal college (?the *Salii*) in 63 (*CIL* VI.2002), but not heard of subsequently. Second, L. Vipstanus Poplicola Messalla (son of the consul of 115), cf. *PIR*¹ V 472.

[120] *ILS* 272 (Gabii); *CIL* XIV 2795 (Tibur).

[121] Nothing speaks for Teanum Sidicinum as suggested (though not confidently) by T. P. Wiseman, *New Men in the Roman Senate 139 B.C.–A.D. 14* (1971), 275.

[122] Dion. Hal. II.46.

recourse to adoption—an inept statement made when the father of Britannicus took in adoption a Domitius Ahenobarbus.[123]

Between Valerii and Claudii no link of propinquity happens to stand on attestation before a Claudius was adopted by a Valerius: that is, Messalla Appianus (*cos.* 12 BC). Nor, so it appears, can either house show a marriage alliance with the Fabii in the days of the Republic. These were three of the so-called 'gentes maiores' in the patriciate.[124]

Let these facts be stated for what they may be worth. In some way or another all three families came like the Aemilii into a nexus with the dynasty, and none outlasts its end. 'Saeva pax' was more deadly than civil war.

---

[123] Suetonius, *Divus Claudius* 39.2 (a specimen of his 'oblivio et inconsiderantia'). Tacitus transferred the remark to the senatorial audience: 'adnotabant periti nullam adhuc adoptionem inter patricios Claudios reperiri, eosque ab Atto Clauso continuos duravisse' (XII.25.2).

[124] Again, the Valerii under the monarchy betray no inclination towards affinity with the Aemilii or with any Cornelii.

XVIII

The Last Scipiones

One Scipio defeated Hannibal, the other destroyed Carthage, to parity of renown: 'geminos, duo fulmina belli, Scipiadas'. The first left no consular son, and the second was an Aemilius by birth, suitably furnished by Aemilius Paullus the victor of Pydna.

Aemilianus died without issue. The power and honour of the family now passed to the line of Scipio Nasica (*cos*. 191), a cousin of Africanus (and his son married a daughter of Africanus).[1] But not without hazards. In 111 death carried off P. Nasica, in the year of his consulship, and much regretted by the people of Rome. It was the great age of the Metelli (six consuls between 123 and 109), and this Scipio had acknowledged their predominance by taking for wife a daughter of Macedonicus.

His son married a daughter of L. Licinius Crassus (*cos*. 95) who was eloquent and well connected. Crassus died on the eve of the Bellum Italicum, and his son-in-law, predictable for the *fasces*, had no long survival after his praetorship (?93) and a command in Spain.[2] The match yielded two sons and two daughters. The one son, who was adopted by Crassus, left only a faint memory.[3] The other came early to notice and fame in 80, soon after he put on the toga of manhood.

Along with certain other youthful *nobiles* P. Scipio is discovered on the side of the defence when Roscius of Ameria faced prosecution.[4] He was referred to by that name, or as Scipio several times, down to the year of his decease, even though in the meantime he passed into another house when Metellus Pius, the *pontifex maximus* died in 64 or 63.[5] His official style, revealed on a decree of the Senate, became 'Q. Caecilius Q. f. Fab. Metellus Scipio'. The adoption was testamentary, and Scipio retained his rank as a patrician.[6]

Scipio's ancestry was unmatched for splendour: not only generals and

---

[1] For the stemma, *RE* IV. 1429 f.

[2] above, p. 21. Observe Cicero, *De oratore* III.8: 'luctum filiae.' By a strange mishap, the passage was not correctly interpreted by Münzer, *RA* (1920), 301, n. 1.

[3] Cicero, *Brutus* 212.

[4] *Pro Roscio Amerino* 77, cf. 149. The others are M. Messalla (*cos*. 53) and Metellus Celer (60).

[5] The variants in his naming are registered by D. R. Shackleton Bailey, *Two Studies in Roman Nomenclature* (1976), 107 f.

[6] above, p. 53. Not, as in *MRR* II. 189, a tribune of the plebs (in 59), cf. Shackleton Bailey, o.c. 98 f.

conquerors but high distinction in the arts of peace. Cicero duly puts emphasis on Crassus the orator and Scaevola the jurist.[7] In pride and ostentation Scipio paraded a whole squadron of equestrian statues on the Capitol, betraying at the same time culpable ignorance of history.[8]

Nor could he pass scrutiny for character and behaviour.[9] None the less Pompeius Magnus in his third consulship, after marrying Scipio's daughter (Cornelia, the young widow of P. Crassus), got him elected as his colleague for the second half of the year. Opportune deaths had enhanced his value, none remaining now of the Metellan consuls. Creticus (*cos.* 69), survived until 54, it is true. For the rest, L. Metellus (68) succumbed during his year of office, Celer (60) died in 59, and of Nepos (57) there is no trace subsequent to the summer of 54. And a number of other ex-consuls had recently passed away.[10]

Metellus Scipio had a further share in the fall of the Republic. On the first day of January, 49, he came out with the ultimatum to the proconsul of Gaul, and persisted, with eager support from Cato and from the consul Lentulus Crus. Without skill or success in the war (he had the centre at the battle in Thessaly), he was in command at Thapsus, redeemed for some by his words in the last emergency: 'imperator se bene habet.'[11] His coins advertised the plain and proud legend 'Scipio imp.'[12] Had Fortuna willed otherwise, Scipio or one of his line might have reached the supreme power, instead of 'imp. Caesar divi f.'

The heir to a Scipio who is also a Metellus, that was a question of concern to men of the time, and it should provoke legitimate curiosity in a later age. Scipio married an Aemilia Lepida, the daughter of Mam. Lepidus Livianus (*cos.* 77), whom he secured about the year 73 after competition with Cato his coeval, whence anger and a lasting feud.[13] A son is surmised, the youth Metellus Scipio who died at the age of eighteen.[14] Was there another, one asks.

The enquiry is arduous. In the first place it must move forward to the epoch of Augustus, to P. Cornelius P. f. P. n. Scipio, consul in 16 and

[7] *Brutus* 212. L. Crassus had married a daughter of Q. Mucius Scaevola (*cos.* 117). A tribute to eloquence and integrity was precluded by the fiction that the treatise was composed at a point in 46 before melancholy tidings arrived from Africa.
[8] *Ad. Att.* VI.1.17.
[9] At least he was present in 52 along with the tribunes at the notorious *lupanar* banquet (Val. Max. IX.1.8). On which, *Sallust* (1964), 135 f.
[10] above, p. 23.
[11] Livy, *Per.* CXIV. The source of the title is stated by Caesar, *BC* III.31.1: 'detrimentis quibusdam circa montem Amanum imperatorem se appellaverat'.
[12] Sydenham, *RRC* (1952), 175; Crawford, *RRC* I (1974), 471 f.
[13] Plutarch, *Cato* 7, cf. Münzer, *RA* 314 f.
[14] *CIL* XIV. 3483 = I². 733 (Tibur). The father owned a famous villa at Tibur (*Ad fam.* XII.2.1; *Phil.* V.19).

proconsul of Asia. Light on his identity comes from an unlikely source. The last poem of Propertius is highly anomalous. A Roman matron there speaks from beyond the grave, in solemn and moving tones: Cornelia, dying in the year her brother held the *fasces*.

Cornelia lays claim to Scipionic descent:

> si cui fama fuit per avita tropaea decori
> Afra Numantinos regna loquuntur avos.[15]

That claim (it seemed clear) certified at the same time the identity of her brother and the date of the poem.[16]

Cornelia's husband, whom she addresses, is Paullus Aemilius Lepidus. Proscribed by the Triumvirs and joining the Liberators (he secured Crete for them before the Battle of Philippi), Paullus is discovered in 36 in the company of Caesar's heir. A suffect consulate followed in 34, and before long marriage to his young bride. The two sons of Paullus and Cornelia saw the light of day soon after the Battle of Actium, perhaps in 30 and 28, so it has been conjectured.[17]

It remains to cast about for the father of P. Scipio and his sister Cornelia. A Cornelius offered, consul suffect in 38, and supposed a Publius Scipio by Borghesi, as by many in the sequel.[18] Decisive evidence has emerged to confute. First of all, the *praenomen* accrued. It was 'Lucius'.[19] Next, only a few years later, the casual find of a small inscription added the *cognomen* 'Lentulus'.[20] Hence another member of that prolific family, hitherto absent from the *Fasti* between the consul of 49 and the 'duo Lentuli' of 18.

The first document brought compensation and comfort: several new consuls in the Triumviral period, among them P. Cornelius, *suffectus* in 35. He was pounced upon with alacrity, supposed a Scipio, assumed the father of Cornelia.[21]

Curiosity might have gone on to investigate the parentage and extraction of this consul, P. Cornelius (?Scipio). Two paths offer. First, a son of Metellus Scipio (*cos.* 52), born before the father changed his name. Born, that is, to P. Scipio and Aemilia Lepida about the year 70, close in age to the girl who married P. Crassus in 55 and was annexed by Magnus three years later.

No such son is on attestation anywhere in a well-documented period of history. Yet perhaps no bar. Many young *nobiles* are absent from the

---

[15] Propertius IV.11.29 f., cf. 39 f. (corrupt).
[16] Despite doubts about his identity expressed by Groag, *PIR*[2] C 1438: 'si vere fuit'; 1475: 'fuisse vulgo putatur'.
[17] Ch. VIII (Marcus as the elder brother).
[18] cf. *PIR*[2] C 1437: 'vulgo statuitur'.
[19] On the *Fasti* of the *Vicorum Magistri*, first published in 1937. See *Inscr. It* XIII.1, p. 283.
[20] *AE* 1945, 66: 'C. Norbano L. Lentulo cos.'
[21] *Rom. Rev.* (1939), 229 n. 7, with 'perhaps'.

narration, mainly military, of the twenty years of tribulation. Most of the Lentuli lay low and escape notice; and certain aristocrats emerging as consuls before or after the War of Actium lack previous mention for allegiance or for any actions.[22]

Second, a son by adoption, who by the same token missed literary record—but not the consulate. Coins struck at Cyrene between 42 and 38 disclose a P. Lepidus, presumed quaestor or pro-quaestor.[23] He gained enregisterment as P. Aemilius P. f. Lepidus.[24] That was premature, on two counts. The filiation (it was unfortunate) does not stand on the coins.[25] Nor is the supplied *gentilicium* legitimate. None of the patrician Aemilii used 'Publius' as *praenomen*. Hence the conjecture that this man was by birth an Aemilius Lepidus who passed by adoption into another *gens*.[26] A further step would bring on a P. Cornelius as the adopting parent. And further still, identity with the P. Cornelius who became consul suffect in 35.

Complications arise. There is the Lepidus who brought Crete over to the Republican cause, generally held to be Paullus Aemilius Lepidus (*suff.* 34);[27] and, some even suppose, the P. Lepidus of the Cyrene coins might in fact be none other than Paullus.[28] All in all, it is best to waive P. Lepidus, although an alliance between Aemilii and Scipiones be plausible from past history—and from the marriage of Metellus Scipio.

To revert therefore to P. Cornelius (?Scipio), the new consul suffect of 35. On the hypothesis here adumbrated he is a son of Metellus Scipio, either by blood or (that is easier) by adoption. Thus the father of P. Cornelius P. f. P. n. Scipio (*cos.* 16), and of his sister, who can be styled 'Cornelia P. f. Paulli'.

Their mother has so far been kept out of the discussion. She is Scribonia, of the Libones, a house to which Cornelia in the poem assigns parity with the patrician Scipiones.[29] These Scribonii are an old plebeian family, only recently ennobled with her brother (*cos.* 34).[30] Furthermore, it may be noted in passing, Cornelia in her declaration claims as an ancestor Scipio Aemilianus, reinforced with an allusion to Aemilius Paullus, his father.[31] There was no link of direct descent.

With Scribonia, trouble and manifold perplexities invade the enquiry.

[22] viz. M. Messalla (*suff.* 32) and Potitus (*suff.* 29).
[23] M. Grant, *FITA* (1946), 35 f. (suggesting Cnossus); G. Perl, *Klio* LII (1970), 337 f. (Cyrene).
[24] *MRR* II. 342 ; *Supp.* (1960), 3.
[25] G. Perl, o.c. 336 n.7.
[26] Proposed in *CP* L (1955), 133 (review of *MRR*).
[27] Appian, *BC* V.2.8, cf. *PIR*² A 373.
[28] R. D. Weigel, *CP* LXXIII (1978), 42.
[29] IV.11.31 f.: 'altera maternos exaequat turba Libones/et domus est titulis utraque fulta suis'.
[30] No link to the Scribonii Curiones.
[31] IV.11.29 f.; 39 f.

This lady came first on show in abortive dynastic compacts early in the summer of 40. In sore straits after the War of Perusia, Caesar's heir turned to an alliance with Sextus Pompeius, whose fleets controlled the Italian seas. To the daughter of Pompeius he betrothed his nephew, the infant Marcellus; and for himself was constrained to accept in matrimony a sister of Scribonius Libo, who was a prominent partisan and in fact, the father-in-law of Sextus. Libo was born about the year 90, his sister, though much younger, now well past her first youth.

The marriage lasted only a year. The Caesarian leader repudiated Scribonia after she had given him a daughter, in annoyance with her 'morum perversitas', so he asserted. She was also much his senior, having run through two consular husbands, with offspring from the second, so Suetonius states: 'nuptam ante duobus consularibus, ex altero etiam matrem'.[32]

Those husbands, that is the problem. On the present hypothesis, one is discovered in P. Cornelius (?Scipio), whose son (*cos.* 16) was born about 50. But this man, it will be objected, was not an ex-consul when Scribonia contracted her third marriage.[33]

And further complications. The enquiry passes on to the Cornelii Lentuli, who took over the burial place of the Scipiones. On what plea and precisely when, that is a question.[34] The earliest avowed Lentulus to carry the Scipionic *cognomen* is the consul suffect of AD 2.[35]

The other husband was a Marcellinus, it is clear. An inscription at Rome registers the household of Scribonia and her son Cornelius Marcellinus.[36] Therefore, which Marcellinus? Borghesi was drawn to the consul of 56, Cn. Cornelius P. f. Lentulus Marcellinus, and his choice enjoyed marked favour for a long time.[37] Objection can be raised on grounds of chronology, it is true.[38] Marcellinus came late to the *fasces*.[39] Active then and eloquent (it was something of a surprise), he offered opposition to Pompeius Magnus, but is not heard of in the sequel.[40] Death may be assumed a year or two after—yet not perhaps before he took a young bride. Marcellinus was a close coeval of Magnus; and both Scribonia and Cornelia P. f. Magni thus saw the light of day in the vicinity of the year 70.

The notion cannot quite be disproved, but it might be discarded for the

---

[32] Suetonius, *Divus Aug.* 62.2.
[33] No bar. The present volume registers various lapses of the erudite biographer. Add now *Athenaeum* LXI (1983), 23.
[34] *CIL* I, p. 13 f.; I², p. 376. As Mommsen said, 'quo iure factum sit explicari nequit'.
[35] viz. P. Cornelius Cn. f. Cn. n. Lentulus Scipio (*PIR*² C 1937).
[36] *CIL* VI. 26033: 'libertorum Scriboniae Caesar/is et Corneli Marcell. f. eius'.
[37] *PIR*¹ S 220, cf. the stemma in *RE* IVA. 1,387 f.
[38] *PIR*² C 1395: 'vix est cogitandum'.
[39] G. V. Sumner, *The Orators in Cicero's Brutus* (1973), 133.
[40] *Brutus* 247; *Ad. Q. fratrem* II.5.3.

benefit of a younger Marcellinus, a son or nephew of the consul (see further below). And, on another count, the testimony of Suetonius suffers double impairment if Scribonia is blessed with children from both husbands, only one of them an ex-consul.

What the biographer says cannot be reconciled with known or verifiable facts, and the problem appears to baffle solution. Such was the declaration of the judicious Groag.[41] However, it ought not to be evaded. Groag made a tentative suggestion, operating with (P.?) Cornelius, the *suffectus* of 38. He might be a Marcellinus, adopted by a Scipio; he had two sons, assigning them different *cognomina*. Hence P. Cornelius P. f. Scipio (*cos.* 16) and the Cornelius Marcellinus of the Roman inscription.[42]

When P. Cornelius (?Scipio), now disclosed in 35, takes the place of the *suffectus* of 38 (who is L. Cornelius Lentulus), the proposal forfeits nothing. On this showing, P. Cornelius is the second husband of Scribonia. The first, earning partial redemption for Suetonius, was a man of consular rank (i.e. Marcellinus, *cos.* 56), and well on in years. Death or divorce transferred her to P. Cornelius, about her own age, on the eve of the Civil War.

It takes design as well as luck to keep clear of the Cornelii Lentuli for any time. Many of the problems that infest their stemma are trivial or antiquarian: such a plethora of nonentities.[43] The extraction of Marcellinus, the consul of 56, can no longer be deferred. He could lay a firm and undisputed claim to Scipionic descent; and he was cousin to Metellus Scipio. A single statement bears witness.[44]

Scipio Nasica (*cos.* 111) left both a son and a daughter. She married a Marcellus who had been adopted by a P. Lentulus. That is clear.[45] From the match sprang a pair of Lentuli Marcellini.[46] First Publius, sent when quaestor to take charge of Cyrenaica.[47] Second, Gnaeus, quaestor in the same season. The former lapses from record. The latter recurs as a legate of Pompeius Magnus in 67, attested as 'P. f.' on dedications set up at Cyrene.[48] A plausible theory identifies him with the Cn. Cornelius who was tribune of the plebs the year before.[49] If that is correct, his father Marcellus retained his plebeian status, the adoption therefore being

[41] Thus in *PIR*² C 1395: 'neque hanc quaestionem certe solvere licebit'.

[42] cf. his remarks in C 1395.

[43] Ch. XXI.

[44] Cicero, *De har. resp.* 22.

[45] Münzer, *RE* IV. 1390; 1597. Her husband was 'Lent. Mar. f.', a *monetalis* c. 100 (Crawford, *RRC* I (1974), 329): adopted by a P. Lentulus, cf. *Brutus* 136.

[46] See, conveniently, G. V. Sumner, o.c. 92 f., with stemma.

[47] Sallust, *Hist.* II.43, cf. E. Badian, *JRS* LV (1965), 119 f.

[48] J. Reynolds, *JRS* LII (1962), 97 ff.

[49] *De imp. Cn. Pompei* 58. Cf. *JRS* LIII (1963), 55 f. = *RP* (1979), 557 f.; G. V. Sumner, o.c. 133; D. R. Shackleton Bailey, o.c. 29, cf. 99.

testamentary, not plenary. Plebeian Lentuli in this age are a topic of some interest, notably the man who conveyed his status to the patrician P. Dolabella (*tr. pl.* 47, *cos.* 44).[50]

Cn. Lentulus Marcellinus became consul in 56. Marcellini of the next generation now engage attention. Three names stand on direct attestation,

(1) Lentulus Marcellinus, fighting as quaestor under Caesar in the campaign of 48.[51]

(2) Marcellinus, a *monetalis*, put *c*.38.[52]

(3) Cornelius Lentulus Marcellinus, praetor in 29.[53]

The *monetalis* on recent and expert dating moves back to 50, and it is convenient to assume identity with the Caesarian quaestor.[54] The praetor of 29 is elusive, not easy to fit in. There remains the quaestor, not without problems. He is generally held a son of the consul of 56. Further, he gets equipped with 'Publius' for *praenomen*.[55] With what warrant? He is assumed parent of P. Cornelius P. f. Lentulus Marcellinus, the consul of 18. And some therefore assign 'Cn. n.' to that consul.

As for the quaestor of 48, it might be advisable to suspend a decision about his *praenomen*—and also to allow for another Marcellinus in the period. Either the consul of 56 or his brother may have had more sons than one.

P. Marcellinus (*cos.* 18) is only a name on the *Fasti*. He has been held identical with the Marcellinus who was praetor in 29.[56] If so, an abnormal interval for an aristocrat—and an elderly consul. Which need not pass belief for the early epoch of the new order.[57] On the other hand, Marcellinus may be a youthful consul, at thirty-two, anticipating the resplendent sequence that leads off in 16 with P. Scipio and Domitius Ahenobarbus.

P. Marcellinus, the consul of 18, opens alarming perspectives about Cornelia, the wife of Paullus Aemilius Lepidus. A sister of P. Scipio (*cos.* 16)—but Groag conceived some dubitations.[58] A recent investigation goes from doubt to denial.[59]

As follows. The Caesarian quaestor of 48, to be assigned Publius as *praenomen*, is a son of the consul of 56. Further, identical with P. Cornelius, the *suffectus* of 35, who may be styled 'P. Cornelius (P. f. Cn. n. Lentulus

[50] Shackleton Bailey, o.c. 29 ff.
[51] Caesar, *BC* III. 62.4.
[52] Sydenham, *RRC* I.187.
[53] *CIL*. XI 7412 (near Viterbo).
[54] Crawford, *RRC* I.439.
[55] Thus *MRR* II.274: with a query in Sumner, o.c. 93, but not on his stemma (143).
[56] cf. *PIR*[2] C 1396.
[57] Observe Marcellus Aeserninus, quaestor in Spain in 48, consul in 22 (C 926).
[58] *PIR*[2] C 1438, cf. 1475.
[59] J. Scheid, *BCH* C (1976), 485 ff., with stemma.

Marcellinus)'. This consul is the second husband of Scribonia, marrying her towards the year 52, with two children, viz. P. Marcellinus (*cos.* 18) and Cornelia. P. Marcellinus may be supposed to reach the *fasces* at the age of thirty-two.

This hypothesis carries the clear advantage of simplicity. Two items, however, are dubious. First, it is not certain that the quaestor of 48 had 'Publius' as *praenomen* or was a son of Cn. Marcellinus (*cos.* 56). Second, the age of P. Marcellinus, consul in 18, is a factor of uncertainty, as indicated above. On the new hypothesis, he is assumed both identical with the praetor of 29 and a consul 'suo anno.'[60] That cannot be—and that praetor might in fact belong to the same generation as his presumed father (P. Cornelius, *suff.* 35).

Consequences would follow for Propertius. His fourth and last book presents a number of problems. Were the eleven poems set in order by the author, or by an editor? Propertius, it is the common assumption, died in 16 or not long after.

One poem avows its date, the sixth. It conveys an allusion to an event in history: 'ille paludosos memoret servire Sygambros' (6.77). In the summer of 16 Caesar Augustus went to Gaul and received, or rather confirmed, the submission of a troublesome German tribe.[61] Without warfare—but Horace was moved to predict a triumph when the ruler came back.[62] Soon seen empty, the prediction serves to date the poem.

Propertius' book terminates with the mortuary tribute to Cornelia. If she died in 18, the editor was guilty of inadvertence when placing the poem subsequent to a transaction of 16 that earned conspicuous and contemporary notoriety.

Dates or doctrines based on poetry of this age are sometimes found premature when submitted to sharp inspection; and a ready temptation solicits the subversion of conventional estimates. The decease of Tibullus is a case in point.[63] None the less, to have Cornelia die in 18, during the consulate of P. Marcellinus, will provoke some resistance.

P. Scipio the consul of 16 is rejected and left in cold isolation. There might still be a way of bringing him back, to stand as Cornelia's brother, the son of Scribonia by her marriage to P. Cornelius, consul suffect in 35.

That consul might be supposed a son by adoption of Metellus Scipio, even a Marcellinus by birth, since the inscription of Scribonia's household certifies a Marcellinus as a son of Scribonia.[64] A Marcellinus, he might well

---

[60] J. Scheid, o.c. 490.
[61] Dio LIV.20.6.
[62] *Odes* IV.2.33.
[63] above, p. 230.
[64] *CIL* VI. 26033.

prefer to drop that *cognomen* in favour of 'Scipio'.[65] Nor was it revived by P. Scipio (*cos.* 16).

Attention in the past has borne heavily on Cn. Marcellinus (*cos.* 56) and Marcellinus (*q.* 48). As has already been indicated, several sons of the consul and of his brother P. Marcellinus (quaestor in 75 or 74) may come into the reckoning when questions are asked about the parentage of P. Marcellinus P. f. and P. Scipio P. f., the consuls of 18 and 16. They may be cousins, they might even be brothers, whether by age close or distant. Identity of the *praenomen* does not exclude the latter notion.

Marcellinus, it will be recalled, is only a consular date; and he may have been fairly old. P. Scipio went on to govern Asia as proconsul. The date baffles precision: perhaps the tenure 8/7, perhaps some years later.[66]

Several children might be assigned by conjecture to P. Scipio. As follows:

(1) The Scipio who was involved in the scandal of Julia, the daughter of the Princeps, in the autumn of 2, that memorable year.[67] A grandson of 'Scribonia Caesaris', whereas Julia was a daughter.

(2) P. Cornelius Scipio, disclosed by an inscription as quaestor in Achaia in AD 1 or 2.[68] He did not survive to reach the consulate, but is notable as being in this epoch the earliest person after the consul of 16 to exhibit the two names in combination.

P. Lentulus Scipio, consul suffect in AD 2 is a cause of no small perplexity. At first sight he appears a Scipio adopted by a P. Lentulus. Yet various reasons might discountenance a son of P. Scipio, the consul of 16.

Another path opens. The Maluginenses were an ancient branch of the Scipiones, with no member attested since Scipio Maluginensis, praetor in 176. But the name revives, perhaps through artifice, in the time of Augustus with Ser. Cornelius Lentulus Maluginensis (*suff.* AD 10), who is 'Cn. f. Cn. n.'.[69] The same filiation attaches to P. Lentulus Scipio (*suff.* 2),[70] who may be regarded as his brother—until something better occurs.

The rubric is not complete without some reference to a lady with the label 'Cornelia Scipionum gentis'. The wife of L. Volusius (*suff.* AD 3) who ended his days in 56, she bore him a son in 24.[71] An inscription registers her as 'L. f.'.[72] She was probably a daughter of L. Lentulus, the *flamen Martialis*, the consul of 3 BC.[73] No Scipionic descent being plausible for this Lentulus,

---

[65] As did others in the sequel (C 1439 f.).
[66] below, p. 405.
[67] Velleius II.100.5, cf. *PIR*[2] C 1435.
[68] *AE* 1967, 458 (Messene).
[69] *PIR*[2] C 1394, cf. Ch. XXII.
[70] *PIR*[2] C 1397.
[71] Pliny, *NH.* VII.62, cf. *PIR*[2] C 1476.
[72] *CIL* XV. 7441, cf. VI.7387.
[73] Either that, or Lentulus himself was Scipionic by ancestry. Thus *PIR*[2] C 1384.

conjecture will have recourse to his wife: a daughter perhaps of P. Scipio (*cos.* 16 BC), perhaps of Marcellinus (18). Yet an Aemilia Lepida is not excluded, namely the child whom Cornelia gave to Paullus in 22, the year of his censorship:[74] if she survived to matrimony, a bride among the most desirable among the high aristocracy.[75] L. Lentulus died in Africa when proconsul.[76] This Lentulus, it is worth noting, was *consul ordinarius*, holding the *fasces* for the full twelve months, whereas Lentulus Scipio (in AD 2) was only a *suffectus*.

The last certified male descendant of the Scipiones being the Scipio Nasica whom Metellus Pius adopted, distinction soon accrued to the female line which was perpetuated through his cousin Marcellinus. The prestige of the ancient name tended to be overplayed, with appeal to Aemilianus, as in the poem of Propertius, which suitably advertises the pride of birth now renascent under the aristocratic monarchy. There were also palpable frauds. Indignation at one of them impelled old Messalla Rufus to write the history of noble families.[77]

In the last epoch of the Republic the decline of the Metelli had been sudden and dramatic, several consuls consigned to premature extinction.[78] Nor could they recover primacy. After Metellus Scipio their name recurs only once on the *Fasti*, with the consul of AD 7 in resplendent nomenclature: Q. Caecilius Q. f. M. n. Metellus Creticus Silanus. That is, a Junius Silanus (of a family more potent in the favour of the dynasty) adopted by a Metellus who escapes the notice of history.[79]

Two generations thus intervene between Q. Creticus (*cos.* 69) and the last consul of the Caecilii Metelli, and no Metellus is on record under the Triumvirate. According to Appian, a father and a son fought on different sides at Actium, the son rescuing the father from the justice of the victor.[80] The son is assumed 'Quintus M. f.'. He has been discovered in ']Caecilius M. f. M[', a proconsul of Sardinia.[81] Some hesitations arise. The proconsul might be a non-aristocratic Caecilius.[82]

---

[74] Propertius IV.11.67.

[75] Observe in passing that the name of Domitia Lepida, daughter to Ahenobarbus (*cos.* 16), is explicable. It goes back to his mother, conjectured a sister of Paullus the Censor (above, p. 166).

[76] *Inst. Iust.* II.25. Given a shortage of available consuls from recent years, Lentulus may have gone to Africa as early as AD 1.

[77] Pliny, *NH* XXXV. 8: 'cum Scipionis Pomponiani transisset atrium vidissetque adoptione testamentaria Salvittonis (hoc enim fuerat cognomen Africanorum dedecori) inrepentis Scipionum nomini.' On this person, Münzer, *RE* IV. 1505; Broughton, *MRR Supp.* (1960), 20. He is the ancestor of the aristocratic Scipiones Salvidieni Orfiti, with a consul in AD 51 (cf. *PIR²* C 1444) and long duration.

[78] Their decline is traced by T. P. Wiseman, *Latomus* XXIV (1965), 52 ff. He usefully documents unchastity in Metellae (57).

[79] Perhaps a son of C. Silanus (*cos.* 17), for whom no offspring is attested or claimed (above, p. 190). [80] Appian, *BC* IV.42.175 ff.

[81] *CIL* X. 758 (Carales), cf. *PIR²* C 62. [82] cf. *History in Ovid* (1978), 137 n. 4.

To augment complication, an unimpeachable Quintus has recently emerged, linked through blood or adoption to the Scribonii, viz. Q. Caecilius Libo Drusus.[83]

Intricate and inconclusive at several points, the present enquiry has sundry ramifications. It extends to the Lentuli, whose many branches call for further inspection.[84] It concerns the Aemilii, through the marriage of Cornelia and the destiny of her two sons. Finally, from 'Scribonia Caesaris' and her husbands emerges another nexus of problems.[85]

[83] *AE* 1964, 82, cf. below, p. 260.
[84] Ch. XXI.
[85] Ch. XIX.

XIX

Descendants of Pompeius and Sulla

Attached by allegiance and by early exploits to Sulla and to Sulla's party, Pompeius Magnus, although acquiring great commands in defiance of the Optimates, turned at the end to groups of aristocrats who for their designs needed resources he had won at their expense. The roll call of consulars on his side declares a potent coalition.[1] Next to Magnus stood Metellus Scipio and Ap. Claudius Pulcher (the son of a Metella). The Metelli had been at the core of the Sullan oligarchy—and Appius now furnished a double link with the faction of Marcus Cato.

Sundry matrimonial alliances are instructive. Sulla married a Metella, the widow of old Aemilius Scaurus, the *princeps senatus*; and Magnus, repudiating his first wife, took the stepdaughter of the Dictator. His third was Mucia, close kin to Metelli, who gave him three children. Divorcing Mucia on his return from the East, Magnus married Julia in 59. Earlier affinities revived in 52 with Cornelia, the daughter of Metellus Scipio, accruing as a splendid culmination.

Two other matches that fall in those years have attracted less attention. A casual notice in 51 discloses Gnaeus, the elder son, as a son-in-law of Ap. Claudius Pulcher.[2] His sister Pompeia, on record in 59 as betrothed, was consigned to Faustus Sulla (*q.* 54), perhaps after no long interval.[3]

No aristocratic bride fell to the lot of Sextus, the younger son, when his time and turn came, perhaps not before the beginning of the Civil War.[4] His father-in-law was L. Scribonius Libo, who first made his mark by actions in the interest of Magnus in 56.[5] After being influential in the counsels of the father, he went on to a position of predominance with the son, on whose death in 35 he transferred his allegiance, with the consulate for reward the next year.

---

[1] Cicero, *Phil.* XIII. 28 f. (above, p. 26).

[2] *Ad fam.* III.4.2. Marcus Brutus (*q.* 54) married the other daughter of Ap. Pulcher.

[3] Betrothed to a Servilius Caepio (Plutarch, *Caesar* 14 etc.).

[4] The age of Sextus has been in dispute. Thus born even earlier than 75, according to M. Hadas, *Sextus Pompey* (1930), 3 ff.; in 76 or 75 for J. Rougier, *Rev. ét. lat.* XLVII (1969), 188 ff. Against which stands the fact that in 48 the youth was not with the armies but at Mytilene, along with Cornelia (Plutarch, *Pompeius* 66).

[5] *Ad fam.* I.2.3. (in concert with Plautius Hypsaeus). Probably tribune of the plebs: not thus in *MRR* II. 209. Libo had been a *monetalis* in 62, cf. M. H. Crawford, *RRC* I (1974), 441 f. Hence born *c.*90, his sister much younger (?*c.*70).

Libo now fades from the pages of history.[6] He left two sons, neither on direct attestation but necessary links in a pedigree. The next generation is represented by L. Libo, consul in AD 16 and his brother, M. Libo Drusus, who held the praetorship in the same year.[7]

Discarded in 39, 'Scribonia Caesaris' lived on for long years, with no desire for a fourth essay in matrimony, but perhaps unobtrusively active in forming family pacts. She bore her daughter Julia company in exile to the end, and she witnessed another piece of misfortune.

In 16 Libo Drusus, indicted for an implausible conspiracy, took his own life. He fell a victim to faith in the promises of magicians and astrologers, and to conceit of ancestry. Introducing the affair, Tacitus duly notes 'proavum Pompeium, amitam Scriboniam quae quondam Augusti coniunx fuerat.'[8]

Scribonia is absent from the full and careful narration the historian insisted on furnishing. A passage in Seneca comes in for supplement. Scribonia, the 'amita' of Libo Drusus, styled a 'gravis femina', gave him courageous advice.[9] There is no call to invoke another Scribonia. Seneca, a young man at the time, was not devoid of knowledge or curiosity.

Both Seneca and Tacitus call the lady the 'amita' of Libo Drusus. She was in fact his great-aunt. The narrations of Appian and Dio are explicit: 'Scribonia Caesaris' was the sister of Libo (*cos.* 34).[10] There is no sign that both historians follow a single (and erroneous) source.

An 'avunculus' can be a great-uncle.[11] By the same token, 'amita'. Grammarians and legal writers produce the exact term 'amita magna'.[12] Normal usage discounts them. No named lady in any other Latin author carries the label of 'amita magna'.[13]

The Pompeian ascendance of Libo Drusus, that is the problem. The other Scribonia, the daughter of Libo and wife to Sex. Pompeius, is not mentioned after the year 39, when their infant daughter was betrothed to Claudius Marcellus; and that daughter lapses from knowledge four years later.[14] None the less, for reasons of genealogy, the girl Pompeia has been

---

[6] Unless he be the *arvalis* attested in 21 (*CIL* VI. 32338). Cf. above, p. 46.

[7] Or rather perhaps then praetor designate, cf. F. R. D. Goodyear on *Ann.* II.28.2.

[8] *Ann.* II.27.2. Goodyear's annotation on the ancestry (under 27.1) is defective.

[9] Seneca, *Epp.* 70.2. Surprise has been expressed that no writer registers her great age: eighty-five at the least.

[10] Appian, *BC* V. 53.222; Dio XLVIII.16.3.

[11] e.g. Augustus to Domitia Lepida (*Ann.* XII.64.2) or to Claudius Caesar (*ILS* 212: Lugdunum).

[12] e.g. 'amita magna' and 'matertera magna' in *Dig.* XXIII.2.17.

[13] The full evidence has been produced and discussed by J. Scheid, *MÉFRA* LXXXVII (1975), 349 ff. None the less, he concludes that Scribonia is not the great-aunt of Libo Drusus but his aunt. Cf. his stemma, facing p. 370. That is to say, Scribonia is not (as universally held on the evidence of Appian and Dio) the sister of the consul Libo but a daughter. The evidence is also reviewed by P. Moreau, *Mélanges Wuilleumier* (1980), 239 ff. He rejects the new thesis (ib. 244).

[14] Dio XLVIII. 38.3; XLIX.11.1.

kept alive long enough to have a husband and issue, viz. two sons and at least one daughter. Their names and extraction demanded a Libo as husband for Pompeia. An unattested son of Scribonius Libo (*cos.* 34) was therefore postulated.

This reconstruction was sponsored by scholars of repute, and it held the field for a long time.[15] An anomalous phenomenon tended to be ignored or glossed over—the second L. Scribonius Libo would be the girl's maternal uncle. The epoch defied normal morality, 'non mos, non ius', and it anticipated practices that might be current or even approved in Rome of the Caesars. Yet this union between uncle and niece strains belief as well as propriety.[16] 'Pompeia Sex. f.' should therefore be ushered out.

For Libo, the consul's son (who is a necessary postulate), a wife of Pompeian blood can be discovered without pain or effort. Faustus Sulla perished in 46. His widow, the daughter of Magnus, passed to L. Cornelius Cinna. Perhaps the praetor of 44, who was rather elderly. Better, the quaestor of that year, his homonymous son by an earlier marriage, to be identified further as L. Cornelius, consul suffect in 32.[17] From this match issued the Cinna who reached the consulate at last in AD 5 and is styled on the *Fasti Capitolini* 'Cn. Cornelius L. f. Magni Pompei n. Cinna Mag(nus)'.

Cinna Magnus had a sister called Magna, revealed by an inscription, until recently the sole testimony.[18] Hence properly '(Cornelia) Magna'. She may have preferred 'Pompeia Magna'. The *columbarium* of the Scribonii discovered on the Via Latina outside Rome yields a number of their freed slaves—and also 'Pompeia Magnae l. Aphrodisia'.[19] The hypothesis that the son of Libo married a sister of Cinna Magnus was open and attractive. The corroboration is firm and gratifying.

Another son can be detected and exploited. Beside Piso the Pontifex on the *Fasti* of 15 stands M. Livius L. f. Drusus Libo, an enigmatic figure. Not by birth a Livius, that is clear. Instead, a Scribonius Libo adopted by a Livius Drusus. Such was the view of Borghesi long ago, and the parent was to hand: M. Livius Drusus Claudianus, proscribed by the Triumvirs and taking his own life when the Republic went down at Philippi. This man, a Claudius Pulcher by birth, was the father of Livia Drusilla, who annexed the young Caesar soon after he discarded Scribonia.

The consul of 15 can serve various purposes. In the first place he illustrates testamentary adoption, with the liberties it permitted—and no law could forbid.[20] Becoming a Livius this consul as 'L. f.' retains the

---

[15] Dessau in *PIR*[1] S 214 (with stemma); Groag, *RE* XIII. 273 f. (the stemma). Hence Table V in *Rom. Rev*. This Libo (the consul's son) found no entry in *RE* IIA. 885: inadvertence, not disbelief.

[16] E. J. Weinrib, *HSCP* LXXII (1968), 249.

[17] Above, p. 30. For implausible speculation about Pompeia, F. Miltner, *RE* XXI. 2264.

[18] *ILS* 1946, cf. *PIR*[2] C 1489. 　　　　　　　　　　[19] *AE* 1964, 85.

[20] See remarks in the important paper of E. J. Weinrib, *HSCP* LXXII (1968), 247–78.

filiation. When P. Scipio Nasica passed into the Metelli, he assumed 'Q. f.', as in plenary adoption.[21]

By his link with the wife of the Princeps, Drusus Libo is a figure of social and hence political importance.[22] Yet isolated, at first sight only a consular date.[23] His distinction implies a consulate 'suo anno', as with Piso his colleague; and nothing precludes identity with the Libo on the earliest extant fragment registering the Arval Brethren, in the year 21.[24] The elderly opportunist shows no survival later than his consulship in 34.

That is not all. The nomenclature recurs with M. Scribonius Libo Drusus (*pr.* AD 16), the ostensible conspirator—whose *praenomen*, by the way, is certified by the document that advertised the detection of the 'nefaria consilia' of M. Libo.[25]

That nomenclature invites an explanation. M. Libo, it might be supposed, took over the *cognomen* 'Drusus' on the decease of his uncle, the consul of 15. Similar transferences can be adduced. Thus Aurelius Cotta becoming 'Messallinus' when his elder brother died; and P. Clodius Thrasea Paetus (it is a valid conjecture) paraded loyalty to the memory of Caecina Paetus, his wife's father.

A better solution avails. M. Libo Drusus was adopted by the consul of 15 BC. That explains the *praenomen*. His filiation might have stood either as 'M. f.' or as 'L. f.'. Better still, perhaps, the conspirator is the natural son of the consul.[26] Yet reflection will suggest that those hypotheses are not required.

To sum up, two sons for old Libo, viz. M. Livius Drusus Libo (*cos.* 15), and the postulated L. Scribonius Libo.[27] The latter, to judge by the presumed ages of his sons (the consul and the praetor of AD 16), was still among the living as late as 15. The former may not long have survived his consulship.[28]

A brief excursus now intervenes, since a recent hypothesis amalgamates the sons of old Libo.[29] The notion possesses a certain charm. One is left with the consul of 15, to marry Magna and beget two sons. The elder son, however, stands as 'L. f.' in the list of consuls prefixed to Book LVII of Cassius Dio. Some items on those rubrics can be proved incorrect.[30] But it is premature to emend a text in order to support a thesis.

---

[21] On the *s.c.* in *Ad fam.* VIII.8.5.

[22] As emphasized in *JRS* LVI (1966), 8. Cf. now *PIR*[2] L 295.

[23] Like the consuls of 18, or Messalla Appianus (*cos.* 12).

[24] *CIL* VI. 32338 (above p. 46).   [25] *CIL* I[2], p. 244 (the *Fasti* of Amiternum).

[26] That was Borghesi's view. See now J. Scheid, o.c. 366, with his stemma (facing p. 368).

[27] The firm conclusion of Weinrib, cf. the stemma (p. 274).

[28] One recalls once again two consuls dying in 12. Before long a shortage of consulars for Asia and Africa made itself felt.   [29] J. Scheid, o.c. 367, cf. 369.

[30] e.g. 'Frugi' attached to L. Piso (*cos.* 15), and 'Caecilius Nepos' or 'Rufus' for the consul of AD 17.

Evidence of another type belongs on the flank of these questions concerning identity and nomenclature. Inscriptions reveal Scribonii as patrons of Caudium in Samnium. Towers were constructed there by a L. Scribonius Libo and his homonymous son.[31] The period of the documents is not certain. If they were put about 50, the elder Libo would be the consul of 34. In that case the son is distinct from Drusus Libo (*cos.* 15), who was probably born about that time—and he is son (it may be) by an earlier marriage. Yet again, not perhaps identical with the L. Libo who married Magna, the granddaughter of Pompeius Magnus.

The folly of Libo Drusus, 'adulescens tam stolidus quam nobilis' (so Seneca labels him), did not wreck the standing or prospects of the family.[32] Various alliances came in.

The wife of his uncle (*cos.* 15 BC) is not known, but a clue leads to a daughter. In the autumn of the year 8 young Claudius (the brother of Germanicus) was compelled to renounce his betrothed because her parents came to grief (namely L. Paullus and Julia).[33] He was now aged seventeen. Before long they found him a suitable bride, but she died on the day of the wedding: Livia Medullina Camilla, descended from the dictator Camillus, so Suetonius affirms. Her father is patently M. Furius P. f. P. n. Camillus, the consul of 8, and the name Livia indicates her maternal grandfather. Camillus, it follows, had acquired for wife a daughter of M. Livius Drusus Libo (*cos.* 15 BC).[34]

Proconsul of Africa when the rebellion of Tacfarinas broke out, Camillus revived for splendour, albeit transient, the military fame of a patrician house, obscure for centuries.[35] One of his sons inherited the name of L. Arruntius. Consul with Cn. Domitius Ahenobarbus in 32, he is styled 'L. Arruntius Camillus Scribonianus.'[36] The *cognomen* advertises descent from Pompeius Magnus through Scribonii, as is made explicit on the inscription of his young son.[37] The consul of 8 had also a homonymous son who in 38 took his place among the *Arvales.*[38]

Meanwhile the Scribonii had acquired a connection with a great house

[31] *ILS* 5326, cf. 5528 (a basilica constructed at Caudium by a L. Scribonius L. f. Libo).

[32] Seneca's label is confirmed by 'alia huiusce modi stolida vana, si mollius acciperes, miseranda' (*Ann.* II.30.2). Some argue that Libo was an authentic conspirator and a serious threat. Thus R. S. Rogers, *Studies in the Reign of Tiberius* (1943), 115 ff.; B. Levick, *Tiberius the Politician* (1976), 149 ff.

[33] Suetonius, *Divus Claudius* 26.7.

[34] E. J. Weinrib, o.c. 265. He styles her 'Livia Scriboniana': a suitable accretion to prosopography.

[35] *Ann.* II.52.1; III.20.

[36] *PIR*[2] A 1140. In *Ann.* XII.52.1 his wife is 'Vibia'. Perhaps rather 'Vinicia', below, p. 278, n. 62.

[37] *ILS* 976 (Prymnessus, bilingual). Identified with the son mentioned in *Ann.* XII.52.1, cf. *PIR*[2] A 1147.

[38] *PIR*[2] F 577, cf. 574. A 'noble Camillus' is addressed in *Anth. Pal.* IV.2: either the *arvalis* admitted in 38 or a son, cf. C. Cichorius, *Römische Studien* (1922), 355; A. Cameron, *GRBs* XXI (1980), 62.

recently in sudden decline. Their *columbarium*, with the freedman M. Scribonius Storax, the *paedagogus* of Q. Caecilius Drusus Libo, brings to light an unexpected aristocrat.[39] One is moved to cast about for his parent, a Q. Metellus in the descent from Creticus. The clue is not far to seek. A Q. Metellus adopted a Junius Silanus, whence Creticus Silanus (*cos.* 7). He has been detected and accepted as the proconsul of Sardinia on an inscription.[40]

Whether or not this be the man, a Q. Metellus has to be postulated. He married a Scribonia, that is one suggestion, a sister of the two Scribonii in magistratures in 16; and Q. Caecilius Drusus Libo is his son, taking *cognomina* from the maternal grandfather.[41] The earliest specimen of that practice is furnished by Cinna Magnus (*cos.* 5).

Other explanations of the new character might be canvassed. For example, a son by adoption, like the consul Creticus Silanus. However, let it suffice to point out an indubitable link with the Metelli, even if not to be assigned much consequence—and this Caecilius Drusus Libo may well be evanescent, dying in early youth.

The count of the known and verifiable is not exhausted. One turns with relief to the Scribonia who towards the year 20 married M. Crassus Frugi, the consul of 27. This Scribonia is generally identified as a sister of L. Libo (*cos.* 16).[42] A daughter seems more likely. Libo is not on record after his consulship.

So far the Libones. Two sons and a daughter for the old man, their first consul; two sons and one daughter (or perhaps two) in the next generation.[43]

L. Arruntius can no longer suffer deferment. Holding tranquil discourse among friends in his last hours, Caesar Augustus brought up the theme of 'capax imperii' and sharply assessed the quality of three consulars: Asinius Gallus, L. Arruntius, Marcus Lepidus.[44]

In the place of Arruntius a variant version adduced the name of Cn. Piso (*cos.* 7 BC), the enemy of Germanicus Caesar. If nothing else, that item excites a suspicion that the whole anecdote was composed under the influence of subsequent transactions, and for a purpose.

Inserted by the consular annalist as annotation on two consulars who

[39] *AE* 1964, 82. Relevant to Q. Caecilius Hilarus, the freedman of 'duae Scriboniae' in *ILS* 9433. The item puzzled Dessau. The inscription (in the Fogg Museum) is discussed by H. Bloch, *HSCP* LXXXVI (1982), 141 ff.

[40] *PIR*² C 92. See however above, p. 254.

[41] Thus J. Scheid, o.c. 368, cf. the stemma facing. On his showing, be it recalled, the maternal grandfather is M. Livius Drusus Libo (*cos.* 15 BC), not the son of L. Libo (*cos.* 34).

[42] Groag in *RE* XIII. 340.

[43] And finally L. Scribonius Libo, a senator, but not of high rank, under Claudius (*CIL* VI.31545 = *ILS* 5926).

[44] *Ann.* I.13.2 f. (Ch. X).

intervened in the debate, or rather ceremony, of September 17, namely Asinius Gallus and L. Arruntius, and interrupting the exposition which resumes with two other senators (Q. Haterius and Mam. Scaurus), the anecdote is variously defective. It also presupposes information the author had not previously vouchsafed to the reader (a century later than the events).

Asinius Gallus had been explained, husband of Vipsania the daughter of Agrippa and a truculent orator, recalling the 'ferocia' of his parent. Of M. Lepidus (absent in fact in Spain) his proximity to the dynasty was decisive, a grandson of 'Scribonia Caesaris'. Arruntius remains enigmatic. The author styles him 'divitem promptum, artibus egregiis et pari fama publice'. Civil distinction, but not, as with Lepidus, experience with the armies. Lepidus and other recent consuls had won fame in Illyricum or in the German campaigns.

For all that, Arruntius is 'non indignus et, si casus daretur, ausurus'. Apart from eloquence and alert courage, resources of another kind were requisite.

The father of Arruntius (*cos.* 22 BC) was a *novus homo* and a renegade from the Pompeian cause; and Arruntius' mother and his wife both elude ascertainment. None the less, Arruntius united the Pompeian and Sullan claims to the principate, so it can be maintained.

In the year 21 L. Sulla, a 'nobilis iuvenis', incurred odium through disrespect shown to a senior senator of praetorian rank.[45] In the ensuing debate (represented as notable), kinsmen of Sulla intervened on his side, namely L. Arruntius and Mam. Aemilius Scaurus. The latter (*suff.* 21) is designated as both the uncle and the stepfather of Sulla.[46] His grandfather (*pr.* 56) had taken over Mucia, the divorced wife of Magnus, and thus became stepfather to Sextus Pompeius.

Descendants of Sulla the Dictator now enter the lists, among them some persons lost to record in the time of Augustus but necessary links between known generations.

(1) A Cornelius Sulla, son of Faustus by Pompeia, the daughter of Magnus.[47] He furnishes a father for Sulla Felix, who failed to reach the consulate but died when *frater arvalis* in AD 21.[48]

(2) Cornelia, sister of the foregoing. She is needed to elucidate the

---

[45] III.31.3.

[46] III.31.4. Sulla is probably identical with L. Sulla Felix (*cos.* 33), cf. *PIR*[2] C 1462; 1465. Scaurus had married his mother Sextia, cf. A 404. To explain the other link ('patruus') one assumes that the father of Scaurus and the grandfather (unattested) of Sulla Felix had been husbands of the same *Ignota*.

[47] The pair had two children (Appian, *BC* II.100.416).

[48] *CIL* VI. 32339c. His absence through ill health was recorded in the previous section. The decease of Sulla Felix was omitted in *PIR*[2] C 1463. For the stemma, see facing the previous page.

extraction of the depraved Aemilia Lepida, married in succession to P. Sulpicius Quirinius and Mam. Aemilius Scaurus, put on trial and condemned in 20. Of her the historian states 'super Aemiliorum decus L. Sulla et Cn. Pompeius proavi erant.'[49]

This lady's brother was M'. Aemilius Q. f. M. n. Lepidus, the consul of 11. The pedigree therefore entails conjuring up Quintus, an unattested son of M. Lepidus the Triumvir, to take in wedlock Cornelia, the daughter of Faustus and Pompeia.[50] No other expedient is worth a thought.

The problem is how and where to fit in L. Arruntius, through mother or wife—or through both. A number of combinations and permutations offer.[51]

An easy solution is to have Arruntius marry a Cornelia, an unattested sister of Sulla Felix and hence parallel in descent from Faustus and Pompeia to Manius Lepidus (*cos.* 11) and his sister.[52] A Faustus Arruntius can be extracted from the nomenclature of a freedwoman on a Roman inscription.[53] Which is welcome—presumably a short-lived son of L. Arruntius.

There is also a Paullus Arruntius, discovered in the company of Caligula when he was assassinated.[54] 'Paullus', like 'Faustus' a *cognomen* used as a *praenomen*, at once evokes descent from Aemilii Lepidi—and is taken to discountenance a marriage of Arruntius to a Cornelia, a granddaughter of Faustus Sulla and Pompeia.

Search ensues for a suitable Lepida. To disencumber the path, the father of Arruntius is now segregated, since he may have married an obscure person.[55] Yet the Arruntii were opulent and respectable, furnishing one of the virgins of Vesta in the last epoch of the Republic;[56] and, like other renegades he might have annexed a resplendent bride before or after the Battle of Actium.[57]

A brief thought goes to the daughter born to Paullus and Cornelia in 22, the year of his censorship.[58] This girl, it will be added, comes into play as a useful pawn in another genealogical reconstruction.[59] To be preferred is a second sister for Manius Lepidus (*cos.* 11), supplying the Sullan and Pompeian ancestry.[60]

[49] *Ann.* III. 22.1 (above, p. 115).
[50] cf. *PIR*[2] A 363. Q. Lepidus was probably among the living as late as 13 BC, since his daughter was to have married Lucius Caesar (born in 17).
[51] Amply discussed by E. J. Weinrib, o.c. 265 ff., with alternative stemmata (274 f.).
[52] Adopted with a query on Table V in *Rom. Rev.*   [53] *CIL* VI. 5942.
[54] Josephus, *AJ* XIX. 102.
[55] E. J. Weinrib, o.c. 272.
[56] Macrobius III.13.11 (the famous pontifical banquet).
[57] Like M. Titius (*suff.* 31), who married a Fabia (*IGR* IV. 1716).
[58] Propertius IV.11.67.
[59] i.e. as the widow of L. Lentulus (*cos.* 3 BC). Above, p. 253. If surviving, she became nubile *c.*7.
[60] Weinrib's conclusion, o.c. 269, cf. his second stemma.

Impediments occur. They are frankly confronted. Tacitus illustrates the prosecution of Aemilia Lepida with an ample narration. She was defended by her brother Manius—but not by any husband of a sister. Arruntius engages the generous interest of the historian. Arruntius, however, might have good reasons to keep clear (the lady was manifestly delinquent), hence not registered by the main source, the *Acta* of the Roman Senate.

In the next year Manius had to face an attack from Sex. Pompeius (*cos.* 14) who, alert no doubt for his own prospects, tried to debar Manius from the proconsulate of Asia, deriding him as 'socordem inopem et maioribus suis dedecorum'.[61] Again, no mention of Arruntius.

The methods of the historian come into the question. He failed to state that Sex. Pompeius was related to the dynasty.[62] Omissions sometimes excite surprise. Various explanations avail. Not only brevity, economy, and strict relevance, but ignorance. When embarking on the first hexad and urgent to break away from Caesar Augustus, Cornelius Tacitus had not devoted much study to the previous epoch.

In the *Annales* as extant, while warmly extolling the merits of the exemplary Marcus Lepidus, the author gives no sign of the Scipionic ancestry, the military fame. In this matter as in others a proper enquiry reckons with the missing Book V.

So far the claims of an Aemilia Lepida set against a Cornelia (neither lady on direct attestation). Why not both? That would account for Paullus Arruntius and Faustus Arruntius. Iterated matrimony was frequent; and the known complexities in alliances of the *nobilitas* counsel much dubitation.

The vicissitudes of the family and faction of the dynast Pompeius Magnus come into useful employ, to correct the version of the victors or undue preoccupation with the biography of the Caesars. Allies old and new in the high aristocracy or personal adherents, the party of the Republic was thinned and debilitated by lost battles in Thessaly, in Africa, in Spain, with a visible extinction of consulars.

Then Philippi, 'Romani bustum populi'. With Cassius and Brutus perished a company of young *nobiles*, several emulating by suicide the leaders, such as Livius Claudianus and Quinctilius Varus.[63] The credit of the Caesarian victory went to Marcus Antonius and abode with him, conceded by Messalla Corvinus and L. Bibulus with little hesitation or long delay. For the rest, some looked to Ahenobarbus, the admiral of the Republic, who soon made his peace with Antonius. Others went away to join Sextus Pompeius in Sicily and in the western seas.[64]

[61] *Ann.* III.32.2.   [62] Revealed only by Dio LVI.29.5.
[63] Velleius II.71. He also mentions the sons of Lucullus, Hortensius, Cato.
[64] Appian, *BC* V.2.8 f.

Many fugitives from the proscriptions and from the War of Perusia had accrued to the son of Magnus. Their ranks were diminished when the pact of Misenum was concluded in 39 with Antonius and the young Caesar. Certain Republicans now came back to Rome, among them Ti. Claudius Nero, L. Arruntius, and Sentius Saturninus.[65] Sentius was close kin to Sex. Pompeius: Libo's father had married a Sentia.[66]

The pact had no long duration, warfare soon recurring on the waters between Italy and Sicily. Sextus after his defeat in 36 fled to the eastern provinces. In the next year the generals of Antonius hunted him down and captured him in Bithynia. Before that, his last companions had given up. Seven are named, among them Libo and young Aemilius Scaurus.[67]

Nobiles who had fought for the Republic or for Magnus turned to Marcus Antonius by clear preference. In the sequel, sundry illustrious persons lapsed or seceded, the pretext for their dissidence not always honest or the duration of their allegiance confessed. The last aristocratic consular to leave was Ahenobarbus, on the eve of the conflict at Actium. He was a nephew of Marcus Cato.[68]

The prolonged sequence of wars between citizens (on another count rival parties and ambitions) brought men of birth into dire hazards. They tended to survive, and to prosper.

The gracious clemency of the victor is duly extolled in the earliest account now extant. According to Velleius, only a handful of the adversaries ('paucissimi') were put to death after Actium, and only those who refused to beg for their lives.[69] None of them is named. A later source reveals a young *nobilis*, Scribonius Curio, the stepson of Marcus Antonius.[70]

As in the story of the proscriptions, interest goes to aristocrats who survived the ordeal. Thus young Cinna, a boy at the time, the son of Pompeia by her second marriage; and Aemilius Scaurus was rescued out of regard for Mucia his mother (also the third wife of Magnus).[71]

Some renegades acquired rapid recognition for espousing the better cause. For a number of aristocrats the first decade of the new dispensation was unpropitious.[72] A submerged stratum in the *nobilitas* can be detected, for the most part only items needed to reconstruct a stemma. In the present context (Pompeian and Sullan) the following names occur:

[65] Velleius II.77.3. He also names M. Silanus and M. Titius.
[66] *ILS* 8892: 'Sentia Lib[onis]/mater Scr[iboniae]/Caes[aris'. For the stemma of the Sentii, *Historia* XIII (1964), 159 = *RP* (1979), 608. On Scheid's argument, that Scribonia was the daughter of the consul Libo, Sentia becomes his wife (o.c. 363).
[67] Appian, *BC* V. 139.579.
[68] A fact overlooked in some modern accounts.
[69] Velleius II. 86.2 (above, p. 31).
[70] Dio LI.2.5.
[71] Seneca, *De clem.* I.9.11; Dio LI.2.4 f.
[72] Ch. III.

(1) Cornelius Sulla, the son of Faustus and Pompeia, father of Sulla Felix, the *arvalis*.

(2) Q. Lepidus, son of the Triumvir, who married Cornelia, sister of the foregoing.

(3) Aemilius Scaurus, the half-brother of Sextus Pompeius. To his wife, no clue.

(4) P. Sulla. His father, elected consul for 65 with Autronius, was debarred. He had married Pompeia, the sister of Magnus, left a widow when her husband Memmius was killed in Spain, quaestor in 75.[73]

(5) L. Scribonius Libo, son of L. Libo (*cos.* 34). The husband of Magna, sister to Cinna Magnus.

This group failed to show a consul.[74] Passed over by Caesar Augustus in the first epoch of the renovated Republic, that is a ready explanation. As elsewhere, premature decease can interrupt.

The families subsist and persist, in hope of resurgence, quickly forming new alliances. And some members soon attracted the favour of the ruler.

The *novus homo* Cn. Sentius Saturninus, consul in 19, and sole consul for a part of the year, curbed disturbances in the city of Rome and earned commendation. He was a kinsman of L. Scribonius Libo (*cos.* 34). Then a son of Libo emerges as consul four years later, namely M. Livius Drusus Libo. Ephemeral perhaps, but potent in himself and significant through the link with Livia Drusilla.

When Livia's son revolted and seceded in the late summer of the year 6, the ruler faced acute problems: not only boy princes, the sons of M. Agrippa, whom he was promoting, eager and anxious, but conjoined therewith acquiescence and support from the high aristocracy.[75] There is no sign (but some might speculate) about a total discarding of Claudius Nero, with another husband for the mother of Gaius and Lucius.

Two dynastic marriages in the near sequel demand attention. About the year 4 young Julia was consigned to L. Paullus, the kinsman (and in fact nephew) of her grandmother, namely 'Scribonia Caesaris'. Further, her brother Lucius was betrothed to Aemilia Lepida, daughter of the unobtrusive Q. Lepidus, granddaughter of Sulla and Pompeius. Caesar Augustus thus annexed to his designs two lines of the patrician Aemilii Lepidi going back to the consul of 78.

Other alliances formed in the course of the decade when Claudius Nero

<hr>

[73] Orosius V.23.12. A Memmius is attested as stepson of P. Sulla in 54 (*Ad. Q. fratrem* III.3.2). P. Sulla as brother-in-law to Magnus is a fact often neglected, cf. *Sallust* (1964), 102.

[74] Nor did the ambitious Memmii after C. Memmius C. f. (*suff.* 34). An Ephesian inscription discloses him as 'C. Memmius C. f. Sullai Felicis n.' (*Wiener Anzeiger* XCIX (1963), 48 = *Inschr. Eph.* II. 403). That is, the son of C. Memmius (*pr.* 58) and Fausta. Their name crops up for the next time, and for the last, with M. Acilius Memmius Glabrio, a senator *c.* AD 16 (*ILS* 5893). In *PIR*² A 75 perhaps a son of M. Acilius Glabrio (*suff.* 33). Perhaps rather a grandson.

[75] Ch. VI.

was in eclipse. Furius Camillus (*cos.* AD 8) acquired the daughter of the consular Livius Drusus Libo. L. Arruntius (*cos.* 6) then came to confront matrimony as did Sulla Felix; and a thought might go to Creticus Silanus (*cos.* 7), who has a link with Scribonii.

Claudius Nero came back to power in the summer of 4, to resume as Ti. Caesar the second station in war or peace beside the ruler of Rome. His influence on the selection of consuls for the next decade is duly surmised and sought, with a range of variety in the estimate.[76]

The government reposed on a delicate equilibrium, in peril from the ambitions of rival groups; and every reign witnessed noblemen whom it was invidious to deny the privilege owed to birth and pedigree, whatever their capacity or allegiances. Noblemen were eager and opportunistic, retaining a mobility denied to the *novus homo*.

On the new turn in dynastic politics followed a pair of ornamental consuls, the patricians Volesus Messalla and Cinna Magnus. Caesar Augustus liked or honoured the Valerii—and the sons of Corvinus were cherished by his successor. In this instance the rulers were in for a disappointment—a cruel and murderous proconsul of Asia.

Messalla's colleague had a different fate, his name perpetuated through the ages in edifying fiction. Two versions are known, that of the historian Dio the more verbose.[77] Cinna promoted a plot, which brought Augustus into grave perplexity. Sagacious counsel, imparted at some length on the matrimonial couch, showed the way out. Augustus reasoned with the conspirator, demonstrated his folly—and awarded the consulship.

The same happy ending marks the version of Seneca, aberrant in sundry particulars, and notably because he takes the conspirator for a young man.[78] However, he furnished the ruler with a sound argument of deterrence.[79]

The source and motive of the fable is clear enough. It arose among the ignorant from the apparent paradox of a consulship for the grandson of Pompeius Magnus. But no paradox. As elsewhere, Ti. Caesar was responsive to Pompeian antecedents and loyalty to the cause of the Republic. Cinna was an old man, now about fifty.[80] It would be welcome

---

[76] Ch. VII.

[77] Dio LV. 14–22.1.

[78] Seneca, *De clem.* I.9.1 f. See the careful and economical treatment of M. T. Griffin, *Seneca* (1976), 410 f. Seneca invented the fable and Dio took it from him, according to E. Hohl, *Würzburger Jahrbücher* III (1948), 107 ff.

[79] *De clem.* I.9.10: 'cedo, si spes tuas solus impedio, Paulusne te et Fabius Maximus et Cossi et Servilii ferent?' Servilii do not belong here. The writer was moved by a prepossession in favour of Servilius Nonianus (*cos.* 35), orator and historian, and his own coeval.

[80] In *PIR*[2] C 1339 'prope sexagenarius'. Cinna was there assumed son of the praetor of 44. As likewise in *Rom. Rev.* 269. The latest stemma is supplied by G. V. Sumner, *Phoenix* XXV (1971), 369.

and significant if retardation could be proved for other *nobiles* who acceded to the *fasces* during the decade he introduced.

Honour for L. Scribonius Libo, consul in 16, was no surprise—and his brother the praetor was already a *pontifex*.[81] Though the consul fades out in the sequel, the influence of the family went on unimpaired.

Male descendants of Sulla took some time to come up. Sulla Felix, the grandson of Faustus and Pompeia, entered the Arval Brethren, it is true, a rare distinction. His name is not found among the early Tiberian consuls, though eligible well before his decease in 21 (as is shown by the age of his sons, consuls in 31 and 33).[82]

When Ti. Caesar persuaded Aelius Seianus to resign the *fasces* in May of 31, Faustus Sulla stepped into his place as colleague of the Princeps; and his brother Sulla Felix became consul with Ser. Sulpicius Galba two years later. Those phenomena illustrate the emergencies confronting the ruler. Before that, however, Faustus had been singled out for a resplendent match. Towards the year 20 died Messalla Barbatus, robbed of a predictable consulship. His widow Domitia Lepida passed to Faustus, who thus became stepfather to the infant Valeria Messallina.

Not all the members of these groups and families earned favour or approbation from Tiberius Caesar. At the session of September 17 Mam. Scaurus made a contribution after Q. Haterius. The Princeps answered old Haterius. But no words for Scaurus 'cui implacabilius irascebatur'.[83] If the historian's sharp comment looks like divination only, it is confirmed by a fact. The aristocratic Scaurus does not appear on the *Fasti* until 21—and then merely as consul suffect. Intervening in 14 in the company of consulars, he was perhaps one of the praetors.

Scaurus carries an impressive and ambiguous label: 'insignis nobilitate et orandis causis, vita probrosus'.[84] In peril in 32, he was prosecuted for treason two years later, various charges making up the count.[85] Anticipating the verdict, he took his own life, 'ut dignum veteribus Aemiliis'.

A Sulla accorded passing mention is the grandson of Pompeia, the sister of Magnus.[86] This L. Cornelius P. f. Sulla stands on high show as consul in 5 BC when the ruler decided to hold the *fasces* himself for the first time since 23. Yet only a name and a date. If he left a son, it may be the Cornelius Sulla whom along with three other senators Ti. Caesar expelled in 17, 'prodigos et ob flagitia egentes'.[87]

---

[81] Suetonius, *Tib.* 25.3.   [82] *PIR*² C 1459; 1465.

[83] *Ann.* I.13.4. No comment from F. R. D. Goodyear (1972), ad loc.   [84] VI.29.2.

[85] Among them his tragic poem, the *Atreus* (Dio LVII.24.3f.): ever a sinister and subversive theme, cf. *Tacitus* (1958), 362.   [86] above, p. 86.

[87] *Ann.* II.48.3, cf. *PIR*² C 1458. One of them was the enigmatic Appius Appianus.

The main resources of the Pompeian and Sullan nexus resided with L. Arruntius. The theme should not lose sight of Furius Camillus. In comment on his *ornamenta triumphalia* Tacitus observes 'quod Camillo ob modestiam vitae impune fuit.'[88] Whatever value be attached to the phrase, Camillus makes no further entrance to the *Annales* as extant, and he lived on for twenty years.[89] His son by adoption, Arruntius Camillus, failed to exhibit 'modestia' in his nomenclature and in his ambitions.

L. Arruntius was prominent in the Senate, with no action or attitude likely to arouse suspicion in Ti. Caesar. He incurred the enmity of Aelius Seianus, who in 31 instigated a prosecution. That was not to the liking of the ruler, and Seianus was thwarted by the intervention of Cossus Lentulus.[90]

Arruntius went on, unscathed and undiminished: in 32 Cotta Messallinus raised a complaint 'de potentia M. Lepidi ac Arruntii'.[91] But Arruntius had fallen foul of Sutorius Macro, the next Guard Prefect, and, facing prosecution early in 37 along with two other consulars on implausible allegations, he chose to end his life, not without sombre vaticinations of a worse tyranny to follow.[92]

Arruntius comes into a peculiar episode in Tiberius' management of the imperial provinces. In 23 he appointed Arruntius governor of Tarraconensis, but kept him at Rome without a successor named until ten years elapsed.[93] The transaction excites curiosity, with various explanations, some plausible and not excluding others.

The tradition that Cornelius Tacitus inherited when composing the *Historiae* incriminated the ruler: he feared Arruntius.[94] Brief reflection dismisses that notion, even without the parallel of Syria held for long years in absence by the proved loyalty of Aelius Lamia.[95]

How and when the legend arose is no mystery. Not until the second year of Claudius Caesar when the legate of Dalmatia made an armed proclamation, namely Arruntius Camillus (*cos.* 32), the son by adoption of L. Arruntius.

By the same token, Arruntius designated as 'capax imperii' in the

---

[88] II.52.5.

[89] An *arvalis*, dying in 38 (*PIR*² F 577).

[90] Dio LVIII.8.3. (without the name of Arruntius). The matter was elucidated by R. S. Rogers, *CP* XXVI (1931), 37 ff. He cited *Dig.* XLVIII.2.12: 'hos accusare non licet: legatum imperatoris ex sententia Lentuli dicta Sulla et Trione consulibus.'

[91] VI.5.1.

[92] VI.48.3, concluding with 'documento sequentia erant bene Arruntium morte usum.' The sentence was deemed an interpolation by H. Fuchs (*ed. Helv.*, 1946).

[93] In 33 the ruler castigated consulars for reluctance to take on commands, 'oblitus Arruntium, ne in Hispaniam pergeret, decimum annum iam attineri' (VI.27.2).

[94] *Hist.* II.65.3: 'ob metum'. Caesar's apprehensions are taken seriously by T. P. Wiseman, *JRS* LXXII (1982), 62.

[95] *Ann.* VI.27.2, cf. Dio LVIII.19.5 (succeeding L. Piso as *praefectus urbi* in 32.)

deathbed converse of Caesar Augustus. The anecdote declares a patent motive, not amicable to Ti. Caesar. Suetonius and Dio missed the attractive idea. They did not find it in the annalists who wrote about that period. Neither was Agrippina's petition that Tiberius accord her a husband. Cornelius Tacitus discovered it in the memoirs Agrippina's daughter indited, consigning to posterity 'vitam suam casusque suorum'.[96]

Ti. Caesar was well disposed towards descendants of Sulla and Pompeius, as is clear on abundant testimony. Another name of power accrued when Crassus Frugi married a Scribonia. That new grouping managed for some time to avoid hazard and molestation.

[96] IV.53.2 (above, p. 140).

XX

Descendants of Crassus

The sequence of dynasts whose ambition led in a straight line to the principate of Julii and Claudii is a useful device in simplified or biographical history. It goes back to the first imperial annalists, one opines. As formulated in Tacitus, the theme is variously instructive.

In the *Historiae*, repudiating the fancy that the legions at Bedriacum might have been moved to spontaneous concord, he descants on 'potentiae cupido' after the fashion and model of Sallust.[1] With a pair of names, 'dominatio' emerges: 'e plebe infima C. Marius et nobilium saevissimus Lucius Sulla.' Then 'Cn. Pompeius, occultior non melior', the next agents in the process being subsumed under the battles of Pharsalus and Philippi.

The antithesis between Marius and Sulla is conventional, the label attached to the former incorrect and misleading. Of Pompeius the estimate reflects hostility to ingenuous notions—and also Sallust's portrayal of the dynast. Next, in the exordium of *Annales*: 'non Cinnae, non Sullae longa dominatio; et Pompei Crassique potentia cito in Caesarem, Lepidi atque Antonii arma in Augustum cessere.' Passing from 'dominatio' to 'potentia' and to 'arma', the argument puts emphasis on the impermanence of the precursors, until the monarchy established firm and for ever by Augustus, 'qui cuncta . . . nomine principis sub imperium accepit.'

Other features are noteworthy. Mature judgement discards Marius. Instead, Cinna. To advantage and with propriety. Marius held no power comparable to that of Cinna, an aristocrat dominant in civil war with four consulates in a row. Again, by introducing Pompeius and Crassus together and before Caesar, the historian avoids mentioning the compact formed by the three in the months preceding Caesar's consulship; and further, with 'Lepidi atque Antonii arma' he alludes to the Triumvirate and eschews the word. The rapid exposition is a marvel of economy—and of skill.

A poet who wrote Roman history also makes a contribution. Lucan is brief and to the point:

> Sulla ferox Mariusque potens et Cinna cruentus
> Caesareaeque domus series.

---

[1] *Hist.* II.43.

Magnus could not come in that murderous sequence, and it would be wrecked by any intrusion of Crassus or the Triumvirs.[2] Crassus occurs several times, in reference to defeat and the call for revenge on the Parthians, a theme which had kept his name alive in the poets of the Augustan age, without any reprobation or malice.[3] The survival of an illustrious family lent some protection.

Posterity has been prone to contemplate Marcus Crassus with some distaste: the resources of wealth and crafty intrigue but no clear or laudable line in public policy. On a more friendly view, Crassus, intent to regain and maintain the 'dignitas' of his house (ancient plebeian *nobilitas*), extended but did not pervert methods either traditional or by now normal. This magnate may even claim redemption as a conservative statesman.[4]

Like Pompeius, his rival or intermittent ally, Crassus had been a partisan of Sulla; and like Pompeius he abode under the spell and shadow of the Metelli. With no previous link (and no distinction accruing from mother or from wife), the matches he devised for his sons furnish an indication that has not always been accorded proper value.[5] Marcus was the elder son.[6] He married a daughter of Creticus (*cos.* 69). The date would be worth knowing: perhaps in the vicinity of 63.[7] As for Publius, three campaigns in Gaul (58–6), and perhaps the age of the coveted bride, imposed a delay. She was Cornelia, daughter by an Aemilia to the last Scipio Nasica, who took over the Metellan name.

In the battle against Ariovistus, 'P. Crassus adulescens' commanded the cavalry; next, a legion, and finally a whole army corps, with which he conquered Aquitania.[8] Publius was not yet quaestor.[9] In fact, never

---

[2] Lucan IV. 822 f. The list in Silius Italicus is also instructive (XIII.853 ff.). On Marius follows Sulla: 'imperium hic primus rapiet' (858). Cinna and Crassus are absent. Pompeius and Caesar receive equable treatment, the former styled 'gratum terris Magnus caput' (862).

[3] Four times each in Propertius and Ovid. With Horace only in the indignant 'milesne Crassi coniuge barbara' (*Odes* III.5.5).

[4] The practice of converting a slice of annalistic history into a 'political biography' (such is often the title) goes on. Thus B. A. Marshall, *Crassus. A Political Biography* (1976); A. M. Ward, *Marcus Crassus and the Late Roman Republic* (1977). Compare the comment of E. Rawson, *Latomus* XLI (1982), 540: 'the subject, as reviewers have observed, is recalcitrant to the proposed treatment.'

[5] The two marriages found no mention in Gelzer's article on Crassus, *RE* XIII. 295 ff.

[6] The reverse was argued by G. V. Sumner, *The Orators in Cicero's Brutus* (1973), 159 f. Followed by B. A. Marshall, o.c. 10. For the reasons against, *Latomus* XXXIX (1980), 403 ff. = *RP* III (1984), 1220 ff.

[7] Groag suggested *c.*67 (*RE* XIII.270). In *Rom. Rev.* (1939), 22, n.1: 'presumably in the period 68–63 B.C.'.

[8] *BG* I.52.7. III.7.2; 11.3. Cf. *Historia* XXXIX (1980), 426 f. = *RP* III (1984), 1240 f. (discussing D. Brutus).

[9] His quaestorship was put in 55 by *MRR* II. 217; G. V. Sumner, o.c. 149 f. An aberrant dating, 58, was produced by A. M. Ward, o.c. 56.

quaestor.[10] After a sojourn at Rome he went to join his father in Syria during the winter of 54.

His heroic death at Carrhae evoked from Cicero warm tribute to the eloquence of an early and devoted disciple—and firm censure visited on the premature seductions of military glory that brought to ruin a partisan of Caesar.[11]

Young Publius obscures his elder brother, who as quaestor saw service with the proconsul of Gaul in 54 and 53. He is next heard of when governing the Cisalpina for Caesar in 48.[12] Decease forestalled a predictable consulship.

The son of Marcus and Metella came to the *fasces* in 30, opening the year as colleague of Caesar's heir. At first in the company of Sex. Pompeius, M. Crassus passed like other young *nobiles* to Antonius.[13] The time and occasion of his next transit evades ascertainment—as happens with others, and for a good reason, although those years are well documented.

The close coeval of Crassus, the elegant and opportunistic Messalla Corvinus, born in 64, was consul in 31. Crassus might even have been two or three years younger. The season of his father's marriage has clear relevance to the problem.[14]

The Caesarian leader was far away, prosecuting the war against his rival. Crassus his colleague held office for the first six months, with three *suffecti* following: sole consuls at Rome, but lacking substance or authority. Maecenas controlled Rome and Italy—no title, only armed power.

To the last two months belongs that peculiar transaction, the plot which Aemilius Lepidus hatched, the eldest son of the Triumvir. Maecenas dealt with it.[15] Whether Marcus Crassus was still at Rome, or had gone to Alexandria, or had already taken up his post in Macedonia, there is no means of telling. His two campaigns (29 and 28) receive an ample narration from Cassius Dio.

The Balkan lands find hardly a mention during the Triumviral period. After the pact of Brundisium (concluded in the autumn of 40) Antonius made sundry dispositions: some troops to fight the Parthini, others the Dardani (another people of the Illyrians), who constantly harassed Macedonia.[16]

---

[10] On his position in Gaul see further E. Rawson, *Latomus* XLI (1982), 545. It is there argued that he was not a *tribunus militum*.

[11] *Brutus* 282, cf. E. Rawson, o.c. 542.

[12] Appian, *BC* II. 41. 165.

[13] Dio LIII.3.4.

[14] H. Bloch has Crassus 'born about 67 at the latest' (*HSCP* LXXXVI (1982), 147: discussing *ILS* 9443).

[15] Ch. III.

[16] Appian, *BC* V.75.530.

Asinius Pollio (*cos.* 40) dealt with the Parthini, who lived in the hinterland of Dyrrhachium, not far from the shores of the Adriatic. A poet styled his triumph 'Delmaticus';[17] and erudite fantasy took Pollio to Salonae, on the coast of Dalmatia.[18] The Parthini could not lend their name, and 'Macedonicus' was ruled out for reasons other than metrical.[19]

Of the Dardanians, nothing more. And after Pollio no proconsul of Macedonia stands on direct attestation until Marcus Crassus. A thought should go to C. Cocceius Balbus (*suff.* 39), whom an inscription at Athens honours with the title of 'imperator'.[20]

Marcus Antonius would not neglect Macedonia, the basis for warfare in attack or defence against his rival—who duly turned his efforts on Dalmatia. Nothing is known. The early history of centres like Stobi and Scupi, on the frontier zone of the province, is a blank. The generals of the Triumvir had been active, it is a legitimate surmise. To the north lay Naissus, where five roads met. Naissus is late, very late, to be named anywhere in the literary record.[21] As for the Dardanian territory, it nowhere comes into the two campaigns conducted by Marcus Crassus.[22]

A host of Bastarnae surged over the Danube, more a migration than an invasion. They crossed the mountain range of Haemus, passed through the basin of Serdica and attacked the Dentheletae in the neighbourhood of Pautalia. That Thracian tribe was allied to Rome, or subject. The proconsul now took action. He marched northwards, driving out the Bastarnae, and he finally defeated them in a great battle near the Danube, in the vicinity of Ratiaria. Operations followed against Thracian tribes, among them the Bessi of the interior.

Crassus took an imperatorial salutation;[23] and the Senate duly voted a triumph.[24] That is, the war was terminated. The next year saw a renewed incursion of the Bastarnae. The proconsul seized the opportunity with alacrity, and carried the Roman arms a long way down the Danube.

A large question arises, whether the heir of Caesar, appointing a young *nobilis* proconsul of Macedonia, had in prospect campaigns of wide

---

[17] Horace, *Odes* II.1.

[18] In Vergilian scholiasts, accorded credit in the modern time by the uncritical or the ingenious. Against which, *CQ* XXXI (1937), 39 ff. = *RP* (1979), 18 ff.

[19] That Pollio in fact operated in provinces of both Triumvirs has been argued by A. B. Bosworth, *Historia* XXI (1972), 468.

[20] *IG* II². 4110.

[21] Naissus has often been assumed a legionary base in the time of Augustus or a little later. Observe e.g. A. Mócsy, *Pannonia and Upper Moesia* (1974), 44.

[22] Dio LI.23.2—27.1 (narrated under 29). For the detail, E. Groag, *RE* XIII.272 ff.; C. Patsch, 'Beiträge zur Völkerkunde von Südosteuropa V'. *Wiener S.-B.* 214, *Abh.* 1, (1932), 69 ff.; F. Papazoglu, *The Central Balkan Tribes in Pre-Roman Times* (1978), 414 ff.

[23] *IG* II². 4118 = *ILS* 8810, cf. *AE* 1928, 44 (Thespiae).

[24] Dio LI.25.2.

extension. For that task he might have chosen one of his marshals, namely Statilius Taurus, who commanded the legions on land at Actium—and who lapses from the record until despatched to wage war in northern Spain. Taurus, it may be conjectured, was the first Caesarian governor of Macedonia.[25]

And further questions. When Crassus after his first campaign was awarded a triumph, the ruler added the acclamation to his own total;[26] and, 'imp. VI' for Actium, he duly appears as 'imp. VII' on a document of the year 29.[27] To annex the acclamation of a proconsul, that was not to recur when proconsuls earned triumphs in the near sequel. The leader, who no longer carried the name and title of Triumvir, was asserting abnormal potency for his *imperium* as consul.

That was not all. In the battle against the Bastarnae Marcus Crassus killed their king with his own hands. In addition to the triumph, he put up a claim to another ceremony, to dedicate the 'spolia opima' to Jupiter Feretrius. Crassus thereby infringed the martial monopoly of the new Romulus. The ruler was not at a loss; and he could appeal to experts in legal antiquities. Crassus, it was clear, did not qualify, since he was not a consul.[28] A piece of annotation inserted by Livy brings a welcome confirmation. The Princeps, so he told the historian, had seen an ancient document in the temple of Feretrius, which proved the case.[29]

Marcus Crassus made his specious and inadmissible claim to the 'spolia opima' when returning in 28 for a triumph after the second campaign, such is the general assumption. That triumph, however, Crassus did not celebrate until July of the year 27. Despite the presumed annoyance, Caesar Augustus could not deny the honour, only retard the ceremony— and not be present himself, but departing about this time for the western provinces.

Taking or rather retaining for his 'provincia' Gaul, Spain, and Syria, the Princeps abolished proconsuls in those regions. But proconsuls, responsible now to Senate and People, continued in three armed provinces, viz. Africa, Macedonia, and Illyricum. The pretext was fair, with a kind of dyarchy, though not so in law or in fact.[30] Africa and Macedonia recalled historic rivalry and danger not far way, while Illyricum was adjunct by land to Italy. The military balance was different. Caesar Augustus

[25] *Rom. Rev.* (1939), 302. In Spain in 29, according to Dio LI.20.5: presumably succeeding Calvisius Sabinus.   [26] Denying it, 'so some say', to Crassus (Dio LI.25.2).

[27] *ILS* 881. To be assigned perhaps rather to the exploits of Cornelius Gallus. Thus E. Badian, in *Romanitas–Christianitas (Festschrift J. Straub,* 1982), 38 ff.

[28] cf. Dio LI.24.4.

[29] Livy IV.20.7. The ruler's visit to the temple probably falls several years earlier. Atticus (who died in 32) encouraged him to repair the edifice, then roofless and collapsing (Nepos, *Vita Attici* 20.3). Relevant to the survival of ancient linen fabrics—and to the veracity of Caesar's heir. For the whole incident see further *HSCP* LXIV (1959), 43 ff. = *RP* (1979), 417 ff.

[30] Once favoured, the term is now in discredit.

conceded few legions to the three public provinces. One result was continual disturbance along and beyond the borders of Macedonia.[31]

A redefinition of Caesar's powers was plain, imperative, and even desirable, perhaps enjoined by sagacious counsellors or recently acquired allies; and it was expedient to curb rival ambitions. The proconsul of Macedonia may have furnished an impulsion, grandson of the great Crassus and son of a Caecilia Metella.[32]

When Nero fell, a great *arcanum* was disclosed to the world, so they said. An emperor could be created elsewhere than at Rome. The thing was obvious from the beginning. Caesar Augustus in the first decade of his reign distrusted *nobiles* and debarred them from the high commands.[33]

M. Crassus fades from view after 27. The huge mausoleum on the Via Appia carries emblems of Gallic warfare and the name of his mother: 'Caeciliae/Q. Cretici f./Metellae Crassi'.[34] It evokes by shape and parallel the dynastic monument constructed beside the Tiber in 28—and Caecilia may have had a long survival.[35] Inscriptions from a *columbarium* yield two freedmen. One is her *argentarius*.[36] The other puts a problem: the gravestone of her doctor, Q. Caecilius Hilarus, set up by 'Caecilia duarum Scriboniarum l(iberta)'.[37] How and why a Caecilia becomes freedwoman of two Scriboniae (and which Scriboniae), that is most enigmatic.[38] The explanation lies somewhere in matrimony and inheritance. Investigation will bear in mind the new character, Q. Caecilius Drusus Libo, disclosed by the *columbarium* of the Scribonii.[39]

So far no wife for the *vir triumphalis* has been documented or is even on surmise. But for the sudden quenching of his ambitions, Marcus Crassus might have been enticed into the matrimonial stratagems of Caesar Augustus. Several nieces offered in the first years of the new dispensation.

His descendants are a question. A son or sons of Crassus might have disappeared before consular years. An item generally neglected, the daughter of a P. Licinius was interred in the family sepulchre.[40] She had been married to a man called Gallus.[41]

---

[31] Ch. XXIV.

[32] Thus H. Dessau, *Hermes* XLI (1906), 142 ff.; E. Groag, *RE* XIII. 284 f. Followed in *Rom. Rev.* 309, but discounted in *HSCP* LXIV (1959), 46 = *RP* (1979), 421. Yet the notion does not forfeit appeal, cf. P. Cartledge, *Hermathena* CXIX (1975), 36. For powerful negations see now E. Badian, o.c. 18; 25 ff.   [33] i.e. apart from Potitus Messalla (*ILS* 8964).   [34] *ILS* 881.

[35] One will also recall the mausoleum near Caieta (called Torre d'Orlando), constructed subsequent to 22 by Munatius Plancus (*ILS* 886).

[36] *ILS* 9404.   [37] *ILS* 9433.

[38] Not necessarily 'Scribonia Caesaris' and a daughter of old Libo, as suggested by H. Bloch, *HSCP* LXXXVI (1982), 148 f.   [39] *AE* 1964, 82.

[40] *CIL* VI. 21308: 'Licinia P. f. Galli'. Cf. *PIR*² L 260 (G 54 is deficient).

[41] The common *cognomen* should deter speculation. The suggestion about Cornelius Gallus (*Rom. Rev.* 310, n. 3) implies an unknown daughter of P. Crassus and Cornelia. Better, granddaughter of the consul of 30, wife to a Caninius Gallus.

The next consul is M. Licinius Crassus (*cos.* 14), sometimes supposed a son by blood. Hence problems because of ages.[42] And he might be a Piso Frugi.[43] Two epigraphic discoveries have brought clarity, disclosing 'Frugi'.[44] Standard stemmata of the Pisones therefore fall for revision.[45] Further, some notable and negative consequences touching Piso the Pontifex (*cos.* 15)—and the search for his sons.

L. Calpurnius Piso (*cos.* 133), censor and writer of annals, annexed the salubrious and pretentious *cognomen*. Two grandsons bore it in the last epoch of the Republic. They had a brother, who passed by adoption into another *gens*.

Cicero's invective against Piso Caesoninus (*cos.* 58) carried a reference to a certain M. Piso. The erudite Asconius, expounding the matter to his young sons, opined that they stood in need of enlightenment. Which he supplies, defining this Piso as consul two years after Cicero.[46] The preceptor might have added that he was an authentic Piso Frugi. In fact, 'M. Pupius M. f. Piso Frugi', as the nomenclature stands on consular *Fasti*. He had been adopted by an elderly senator of no consequence called M. Pupius, whose *gentilicium* lapses in the sequel.

A legate of Pompeius Magnus in the eastern campaigns, M. Piso was sent back to acquire the consulate.[47] His homonymous son, a partisan of Pompeius in the war with Caesar, is discovered as praetor in 44, now a friend of the consul Marcus Antonius.[48] A son of the praetor (the assumption is easy) became the son and heir of the last Crassus: M. Licinius M. f. Crassus Frugi, consul in 14 with Lentulus the Augur.

A bronze tablet shows a community in the Balearic islands contracting relations of *clientela* with M. Crassus Frugi, with his children and descendants. It carries a date in the spring of the year 10.[49] Further, the slave of a Crassus Frugi died at Tarraco.[50] The consular, it follows, was Caesar's legate governing Tarraconensis.[51] Then, in close sequence, another document disclosed him as proconsul of Africa, for the tenure 9/8.[52] That was the proper interval from the consulship, but for various reasons not always respected.

---

[42] Groag therefore had to put the parent's birth in the vicinity of 67 (*RE* XIII. 270).

[43] Thus C. Cichorius, *Römische Studien* (1922), 339 f. On evidence not valid, cf. Groag in *RE* XIII. 285.

[44] For a full exposition, *JRS* L (1960), 14 ff. = *RP* (1979), 496 ff.

[45] The new stemma is reproduced in *PIR*², *Pars* V, facing p. 40.

[46] Asconius 14.

[47] On the career of Pupius Piso, on his character and attainments, see *Class. et Med.* XVII (1956), 129 ff. = *RP* 300 ff.; *JRS* L (1960), 14 f. = *RP* 500 ff.

[48] *Phil.* III.25.   [49] *AE* 1959, 317.   [50] *CIL* II. 4364.

[51] Doubted in *PIR*² L 189 because the title does not figure on the document.

[52] *IRT* 319, showing him an augur (omitted from *PIR*² L 189). Also on the fragmentary dedication by a Syrian city, as published by M. Steinby in *L'Arca Sacra di Largo Argentina I* (1981), no. 27.

In this season the stepsons of the Princeps had the great armies in Illyricum and on the Rhine. The ruler was now eager to advertise amity with the high aristocracy, and mutual confidence. Crassus Frugi falls into line with L. Piso and Lentulus the Augur.

Like the mother, the wife of Crassus Frugi is missing. His son, the sole son known or surviving, was born about 6 BC. Consul in AD 27, he had been praetor in 24, benefiting from the mishap of Plautius Silvanus, whose place he took.[53]

Towards or about the year 20, the second Crassus Frugi took to wife a Scribonia, daughter of the consul of 16. The eldest son (it appears) was born *c.*23.[54] To whom, in ostentation of pedigree, the imprudent parent assigned the name 'Cn. Pompeius Magnus'. Caligula took it from him, declaring it not safe for the ruler that anyone should bear the name of Magnus.[55]

Claudius Caesar gave back the *cognomen,* and added much more. In the early months he gave the youth in wedlock to his daughter Antonia.[56] The paradoxical emperor whom Fate and the Guard imposed, was eager to neutralize rival claimants to the principate, or responsive to crafty counsel, and not neglecting a line that ran back to Divus Augustus. M. Junius Silanus (born in 14) was the grandson of L. Paullus and Julia. Lucius, his younger brother, is now betrothed to Octavia, the infant daughter of Claudius and Valeria Messallina. Furthermore, the Princeps, or Messallina, brought back from Tarraconensis Ap. Junius Silanus (*cos.* 28), to espouse her mother Domitia Lepida.

Ap. Silanus, of Claudian descent and holding a military province, may (or may not) have caused concern to the government.[57] Of other aristocrats, Ser. Sulpicius Galba (*cos.* 33) stood in Germania Superior, the successor of the ill-fated Lentulus Gaetulicus, and Arruntius Camillus (*cos.* 32) held Dalmatia.

An inscription brings a surprise: Crassus Frugi legate of Claudius Caesar in Mauretania and awarded the *ornamenta triumphalia.*[58] Claudius had inherited a problem from Caligula, who put to death the last ruler of that region. Not otherwise attested, the operations of the consular may have

---

[53] *Inscr. It.* XIII.1, p. 298.

[54] Quaestor to Claudius Caesar, presumably in 43 (Dio LX.21.5): benefiting from a remission of five years (5.8).

[55] Suetonius, *Cal.* 35.1.

[56] Antonia, his daughter by Aelia Paetina (A 305), presumed daughter of Sex. Aelius Catus (*cos.* 4).

[57] Emphasis is put on Silanus and other army commanders by T. P. Wiseman, *JRS* LXXII (1982), 60 ff.

[58] In *ILS* 954 the sixth line terminates with 'in M[. . .]a'. The argument for Mauretania is reaffirmed by J. Gascou, *Mélanges Boyancé* (1974), 299 ff. He assumes that Caligula made the appointment.

been more diplomatic than military, belonging at the very beginning of the reign, before the spread of insurrection called for competent generals without benefit of birth and rank.

Deriding Crassus Frugi as 'fatuus', Seneca proclaimed a further resemblance to Claudius Caesar: 'tam similem sibi quam ovo ovum'.[59] To that emperor the biographer could not deny 'auctoritas dignitasque formae', especially when seated or in repose: his legs betrayed him, in both senses.[60] Another comparison to Crassus occurs: that Piso who was the head and hollow front of the conspiracy against Nero, with the social graces and semblance of virtues, commended by a handsome presence.

Whatever his character or public repute, Crassus Frugi evaded hazard through long years, even in the last days of Tiberius Caesar when Domitius Ahenobarbus was in trouble, incriminated at the same time as L. Arruntius. The catastrophe of Lentulus Gaetulicus in the autumn of 39 passed him by. That mysterious transaction was an imbroglio in the dynasty itself, bringing exile to two princesses (Julia Agrippina and Julia Livilla) and death to young Aemilius Lepidus, whom Caligula had promised the succession.

When the Senate held debate 'de re publica' after the assassination of Caligula, one of the consuls proposed the abolition of the principate, perhaps from mixed motives. Candidates for the purple were not slow to emerge. No consular from the ancient houses is named. A certain Annius Vinicianus put up the claims of Marcus Vinicius (*cos.* 30), a man of unobtrusive virtue—and the husband of Julia Livilla.[61] Rivalry and confusion abated when soldiers of the Guard discovered Claudius lurking in the Palace.

From the conspiracy of Gaetulicus and from the eventful two days in January of 41, the name and person of Annius Vinicianus furnished a link to Arruntius Camillus. He wrote from Rome to the legate of Dalmatia, inciting him to make a proclamation.[62]

The act was abortive, the troops returning to their allegiance a few days later. Also premature, it appears. The two legions in Dalmatia, stationed not far from the coast, attracted attention from their proximity to Italy, but the imperial fleet at Ravenna controlled the sea. To achieve success, a pretender needed support or acquiescence from certain other armies.

Pannonia (three legions) furnished a base for an invader coming by land across the easy pass of the Julian Alps. The legate at this time was A. Plautius.[63] Next, the mass of legions along the Rhine, recently

---

[59] Seneca, *Apocol.* 11.2;5.

[60] *Divus Claudius* 30.1.

[61] Josephus, *AJ* XIX.251.

[62] Dio LX.15.1 f. For the conjecture that 'Vibia', the wife of Camillus (*Ann.* XII.52.1), is really a Vinicia see *Hermes* XCII (1964), 415, n. 2 = *Ten Studies in Tacitus* (1970), 99, n. 1.

[63] cf. A. R. Birley, *The Fasti of Roman Britain* (1981), 39.

augmented from eight to ten by Caligula for ambitious projects in Germany and across the Channel. Sulpicius Galba held Germania Superior, a cautious man but a potential rival.

Arruntius Camillus had friends and adherents at Rome. Next to Annius Vinicianus the most conspicuous was Caecina Paetus, a recent consul, who went to Dalmatia to join the insurgent.[64] But no descendants of Sulla and Pompeius are discovered among the partisans of Arruntius Camillus, no members of old aristocratic families.

The proclamation in Dalmatia came as a sudden menace to the dynasty.[65] The new ruler was 'nihil aeque quam timidus ac diffidens'. To illustrate which, the biographer adduces the despatch from Camillus commanding him to abdicate and retreat to the security of a private station. Whereupon Claudius sought advice from a meeting of 'principes viri'.[66]

Along with comfort for the present, they could have told him that an emperor needs 'imperatoria virtus'. Britain offered easy laurels, legions were available (the Rhine had too many), and the invasion followed in the next year.

With Claudius for a brief sojourn on the island travelled a company of the notables, some for the honour and from amity, others perhaps not safely to be left behind at Rome.[67] Among them were M. Vinicius and Sulpicius Galba; while Crassus Frugi, earning the *ornamenta* for the second time, and the youths Pompeius Magnus and L. Silanus made it a family party.

Meanwhile Valeria Messallina prosecuted her amours and her ravages, in complicity with the freedmen of the household and aided by L. Vitellius and Suillius Rufus. Beginning with Julia Livilla in 41 and Ap. Silanus (her new stepfather) the year after, the sequence of victims went on, to include in 46 the unimpeachable Marcus Vinicius (*cos. II* 45).

In the same year or early in the next came the destruction of Pompeius Magnus, in whom Messallina saw a rival to the prospects of her own son, the boy Britannicus. The widow Antonia passed to Faustus Sulla, the half-brother of Messallina.[68]

Crassus Frugi and Scribonia shared the fate of their son. The line that carried the name of Crassus had been tenuous for several generations. With four sons it now showed itself prolific.[69] On Magnus followed

[64] Pliny, *Epp.* III.16.4.
[65] The proclamation of Camillus escaped mention in V. Scramuzza, *The Emperor Claudius* (1940).   [66] Suetonius, *Divus Claudius* 35.2.
[67] *CQ* XXVII (1933), 143 = *Danubian Papers* (1971), 27 f.
[68] *PIR²* C 1464.
[69] For the stemma, *PIR²*, *Pars* V, facing p. 40. A daughter, Licinia Magna, married L. Calpurnius Piso, the consul of 57 (*ILS* 956): the grandson of Cn. Piso (*cos.* 7 BC).

M. Licinius Crassus Frugi, consul in 64: in the *Annales* of Tacitus only a date.[70]

The spring of the next year brought out the conspiracy to which C. Piso gave his name. He did nothing, and his end receives unfriendly comment that confirms his initial presentation in the narrative.[71] The plot formed in the main among Guard officers; and many Roman knights joined in. Few senators, and only one *nobilis*, namely Plautius Lateranus, inspired by hatred of Nero and by 'amor rei publicae'.[72] The catalogue of persons sent into exile offers a fine collection of nonentities.

It was the aftermath that wrought havoc among leaders in the Senate, with a train of prosecutions and deaths. The *Annales* break off with the last words of Thrasea Paetus in the spring or early summer of 66. Not long after that, Crassus Frugi met his end. The prosecutor was not, as in the case of Thrasea, a savage orator of low origins, but an ambitious and impoverished young *nobilis*, who brought to ruin two more of the eminent consulars.[73]

Nero curbed and cowed the Senate. The armies he neglected, confident in their long and fervent loyalty to the Caesars, as demonstrated in the episode of Arruntius Camillus and not in doubt since then. Instead of the artistic tour in Hellas a brief visit to the Rhine legions might have preserved a dynasty that had endured for a century.

Nero's folly brought him down—and a chain of accidents, not any plot or conspiracy. In the ensuing confusion the power lapsed to Galba, the legate of Tarraconensis, whom senile ambition had persuaded to make a bid for the purple with only one legion at his back.

In dire emergency, the new and precarious ruler adopted a son and partner. His choice would fall on some aristocrat, that was clear.[74] Passing over his own kinsman (he was a Cornelius Dolabella), Galba selected a son of Crassus Frugi and Scribonia: not Scribonianus (the third son), but his younger brother, Piso Licinianus.[75] A small boy at the time of the parental catastrophe, Licinianus was now aged thirty; and he had lived for long years in exile. Galba looked to character and integrity as well as birth.[76] Other qualities were requisite in a ruler of the world. The brief experiment showed Galba's reputation an illusion; and who could deem Licinianus 'capax imperii'?

[70] He married Sulpicia Praetextata, a daughter of Q. Sulpicius Camerinus (*suff.* 46), the last consul of the patrician Sulpicii.

[71] *Ann.* XV.59, cf. 48.   [72] XV.49.3.

[73] viz. M. Aquillius Regulus. He prosecuted both Sulpicius Camerinus (Pliny, *Epp.* I.5.6.) and Ser. Salvidienus Orfitus, the consul of 51 (*Hist.* IV.42.1).

[74] They may have speculated about P. Cornelius Asiaticus, the latest and the last of the Lentuli, who became consul in the autumn of 68 when only twenty-six or seven. Cf. *Historia* XXXI (1982), 475, and below, p. 299.   [75] *PIR*² C 300.

[76] That Galba in his 'mobilitas ingenii' (*Hist.* I.7.2) had succumbed to influences from philosophers is an engaging but hazardous notion (*Historia* XXXI (1982), 479).

Galba made a parade of severity and 'antiquus rigor'. Some of the younger *nobiles* emulated the ancient ways, with a gravity of habit and demeanour that might pass for grim and forbidding.[77] It offered protection from the perils of high society. Also a protest against the luxury of the imperial court—and against frivolous grandees like C. Piso.

Comparable to Piso Licinianus was Rubellius Plautus: 'placita maiorum colebat, habitu severo, casta et secreta domo.'[78] This exemplary young man stood in close propinquity to the dynasty, nothing less than a grandson of Tiberius Caesar.[79] In 60 Nero, inditing a friendly missive, advised Plautus to put himself beyond the reach of danger and defamation by retirement to ancestral estates in the province Asia. Two years later he was killed by a centurion.

A new counsellor had now come to potency at court, Ofonius Tigellinus. He reminded Nero of Plautus' character. Not merely 'veterum Romanorum imitamenta', but something else: 'adsumpta etiam Stoicorum adrogantia sectaque, quae turbidos et negotiorum adpetentes faciat.'[80]

The allegation is noteworthy: for the first time in the Tacitean narration the doctrines of the Stoics are impugned as a danger to the imperial government.[81] A novel factor was now emergent in the contest between the Senate and the dynasty, to be symbolized in the figure of Thrasea Paetus: not a *nobilis* but from Patavium in Transpadane Italy, a town in high repute for the ancestral virtues. Thrasea, it appears, was anything but a doctrinaire. He stood for freedom of speech and the dignity of the senatorial order. A group of friends lent support, and a family tradition of constancy.[82]

Men turned to philosophy for comfort under the impact of tyranny. Dissipation or sloth was likewise an escape; and the simulation of innocuous stupidity might be assumed as mask and protection. Some *nobiles* did not need to pretend, such as M. Silanus (*cos.* 46), a descendant of Caesar Augustus.[83] Faustus Sulla, the husband of Antonia, had a 'socors ingenium'.[84] Nero, warned by Tigellinus that he was a crafty dissembler, ordered his exile.[85] Death ensued in the year that witnessed the execution

---

[77] Thus Piso Licinianus himself, 'voltu habituque moris antiqui, et aestimatione recta severus, deterius interpretantibus tristior habebatur' (*Hist.* I.14.2).

[78] *Ann.* XIV.22.1.

[79] Blandus (*suff.* 18) had married Julia, the daughter of Drusus Caesar. For a full treatment, *AJP* CIII (1982), 62 ff.

[80] *Ann.* XIV.57.3.

[81] The next instigator is significant: Cossutianus Capito in private harangue inflaming Nero against Thrasea Paetus (XV.22).

[82] i.e. Caecina Paetus and Arria, his wife's parents.

[83] *Ann.* XIII.1.1 (the 'pecus aurea').

[84] XIII.42.1.

[85] XIV.57.3: 'simulatorem segnitiae, dum temeritati locum reperiret'.

of Rubellius Plautus: diverse by character and extraction, but equally vulnerable.

Last in the male posterity of the Dictator, Faustus Sulla owned also to a Pompeian ascendance. Other noblemen in that complex had been Cinna Magnus and Arruntius Camillus. One strain persisted with sons of Crassus Frugi and Scribonia. With the extinction of Licinianus after four days as a Caesar there remained Scribonianus, whose name and fame destroyed him the year after, in the first weeks of a new and upstart dynasty. The line went on, to arouse undeserved suspicion in the later rulers.[86]

Fate or chance awarded the principate. Men who bore the names of ancient or recent power saw usurpation in the primacy seized by Julii and Claudii and refused to surrender parity. With the prestige of Caesar Augustus they could not compete, who for his part offered conciliation. They would not tolerate a pretender from their own ranks. That was declared in the admonition issued to Cinna Magnus.[87] Danger to the Princeps had its roots in rivalry or dissidence within the 'domus regnatrix'.

With the efflux of time the new system of government grew strong and solid. To begin with, the plebs of Rome and the armies; and it extended its *clientela* everywhere. The *nobilitas* weakened and declined, clinging to privilege of birth but extruded from power and wealth by energetic and loyal *novi homines*.

Several ancient houses were entrapped in the murderous embrace of the dynasty. Rivals of the Caesars perished also. Apart from those hazards, a number of families were running out well before the aristocratic monarchy of Julii and Claudii went down in ruin.

Of the old plebeian *nobilitas*, the party of Cassius and Brutus suffered most losses in the civil wars. Although the Cassii were perpetuated, and the Domitii Ahenobarbi, no more Junii Bruti. The Junii Silani replace them, with numerous consuls; and the son adopted by the last Metellus came from their abundant stock. Six names of the plebeian *nobilitas* still adorn the *Fasti* in the reign of Tiberius.[88] All lapse and disappear except for some Calpurnii.[89]

Of the new men rising in the revolutionary wars or promoted by Caesar Augustus a number were unable to transmit for generations their ennoblement. Yet noteworthy exceptions stand out: the descendants of Asinius Pollio, the prudent Coccei, the opulent Volusii.

Tenacity and duration is exhibited in some of the patricians. Aemilii,

---

[86] In the person of Calpurnius Crassus (*PIR*[2] C 259), a son of Crassus Frugi: suspected of conspiracy under Nerva, exiled by Trajan, put to death in the first months of Hadrian.

[87] Seneca, *De clem.* I.9.10 (above, p. 286).

[88] i.e. pertaining to eleven consuls. Four of them are Junii Silani.

[89] e.g. Calpurnius Crassus (*suff.* 87) and C. Calpurnius Piso (*cos.* 111).

Fabii, and Valerii renovated their splendour, through favour of Caesar Augustus, but went out before the dynasty ended. The last Aemilius Lepidus perished in a conspiracy, no Fabius held the *fasces* after Persicus (*cos.* 34), no Valerius Messalla after the impoverished colleague of Nero (in 58). Entanglement with the Caesars was not the sole cause of decline and extinction.

Cornelii furnished a mass and variety of patricians. But even the Lentuli, prolific and cautious through the long ages, show no consul after the year 68.

XXI

Lentulus the Augur

The Cornelii advertise energy and glory in warfare waged against the Punic enemy. But the second Africanus was an Aemilius by birth, and their primacy faded before the Metelli. In the great epoch of that family, and towards its end, arose two Cornelii of ambition and power, Cinna and Sulla.

For survival, numbers matter more. Numerous in their many branches, the Lentuli perpetuated the name through the centuries.[1] Their first consul came out in 327, and sixteen follow down to Lentulus Crus, elected in the last year of the Republic. Two triumphs had been earned long ago (in 275 and 236), and then no more until recently: Lentulus Spinther (*cos.* 57), for operations against small mountain tribes in Cilicia, an honour of the kind that Cicero derided after coveting.[2]

The Lentuli tend to avoid hazard and renown, not conspicuous when the armies of the conquering Republic marched against Macedon or the Seleucid; and they escaped involvement in the vicious Spanish campaigns that engendered discord at Rome and notable prosecutions. To this epoch belongs their great man, P. Lentulus (*suff.* 162), the *princeps senatus*. When birth and wealth mobilized against C. Gracchus, old Lentulus (he was over eighty) stood in the front ranks and received a wound in the riot.[3]

A void follows in the next generation, from 130 to 72, total except for the consul of 97, who is only a date on the *Fasti*. The Bellum Italicum, with civil strife supervening, eclipses the Lentuli. Having no active part in the victory of the *nobilitas*, they soon profit by the Sullan restoration: five consulates (72 to 49).

In the meantime the unobtrusive talents of this *gens* had been in constant demand for embassies to the Greek lands, and many cities honour them as 'patroni'. At Rome, legal studies were a useful school of sophistry, but that type of law did not apply to international claims, to comfort or deceive the allies of the imperial Republic. The Romans preferred flexible terminology: 'amicitia' and 'fides'.

Though never brilliant, the attainments of the Lentuli were for political life held adequate, on the whole.[4] In his catalogue, the master of Roman

---

[1] F. Münzer, *RE* IV. 1355 ff. Broughton in *MRR* registers forty-six.
[2] *Brutus* 256: 'minuti imperatores'.   [3] *Phil.* VIII.14.
[4] cf. *Brutus* 108: 'tum etiam P. Lentulus ille princeps ad rem publicam dumtaxat quod opus esset satis habuisse eloquentiae dicitur.'

eloquence pays generous tribute to the five consuls he had known (all dead, and three by violent ends).[5] Clodianus (*cos.* 72) could not be styled 'peracutus'. Not as clever as he looked, and not fluent, yet he warmed on performance and rose to excellence. Likewise Sura (71), slow to think and slow to speak, yet he had a noble comportment, with graceful gestures, with charm and volume of voice. Marcellinus (56), always a ready speaker, showed various capacities in debate during his consulship. For Spinther (57), 'instrumenta naturae deerant'. Not any native endowment, therefore, but 'disciplina' to his credit and 'tantus animi splendor et magnitudo'. At the tail end, Lentulus Crus (49), lazy and barely to be reckoned an orator, but with a 'vox canora', and very vigorous: 'ut plena esset animi et terroris oratio'.

Cicero has done his best, even awarding praise for the quality of voice and delivery in all except Spinther. Sporadic information from other sources can offer entertaining items and some clashes of testimony. Spinther was so called because he resembled an actor of that name; and Sura had his twin in Sicily, a fisherman with the same ugly habits of speech and facial distortion.[6] As for the physique of the Lentuli, a Roman wit observed that they grew smaller and smaller: if the race went on it would disappear.[7]

Lentulus Crus, loud for action against the proconsul of Gaul, was not of much use in the sequel: a nasty fellow, flimsy, corrupt, rapacious.[8] However, the consul of the Republic found favour with the poet Lucan, who enhanced him with an oration; and Lucan even allocated to Crus the command of the left wing at the battle in Thessaly.[9]

Another piece of fiction accords better with the enduring reputation of the Lentuli. The first of their line spoke to the legions trapped by the Samnites and held out some consolation. To surrender at the cost of ignominy benefits Rome more than heroic death.[10]

Frank and free dispraisal of an aristocratic consul is seldom to be expected in Ciceronian orations. A verdict of Sallust dismisses Clodianus with a double condemnation: 'perincertum stolidior an vanior'.[11] The label would fit Lentulus Sura. This nobleman of handsome presence was heavy and torpid.[12] Also elated by oracles. He fancied himself the third Cornelius destined to hold power at Rome.[13]

---

[5] *Brutus* 234 f.; 247; 268.　　　　　　　　　　　　　　　[6] Pliny, *NH* VII.54 f.

[7] Quintilian VI.3.7: 'nascendo interiturum'.

[8] Caesar's prejudice is patent (*BC* I.4.2; III.96.1). But observe, in confirmation, Cicero, *Ad Att.* XI.6.6.

[9] Lucan V.17 ff.; VII.217 f. A Lentulus had the right wing according to Appian, *BC* II. 76.316. Hence a certain doubt. Rather perhaps Spinther. Observe that the 'Ciliciensis legio' stood on the right (Caesar, *BC* III.88.3).

[10] Livy X.4.8 ff.　　　　　　　　　　　　　　　　　　　　[11] Sallust, *Hist.* IV.I.

[12] Cicero in fact has 'P. Lentuli somnum', (*In Cat.* III.16).

[13] Sallust, *Cat.* 47.5. Sura was in fact a grandson of the *princeps senatus*.

The Lentuli were vain and arrogant—and 'Lentulitas' came into currency.[14] They betray no intellectual gifts or concern with polite letters. Despite their long frequentation with the Greek lands, no poet or philosopher is discovered in the vicinity of Lentuli; and the study of Roman law would be a burden.

Mediocrity and survival is their mark. The Lentuli lived 'senza infamia o lodo'. From that reproach, the five consuls admit a partial redemption. Active merit might be claimed for Lentulus Spinther, despite lavish laudations from the grateful Cicero;[15] and Lentulus Sura, the associate of Catilina, in fact earned infamy: 'ille patricius ... dignum moribus factisque suis exitum invenit.'[16]

In the second age of violence and tribulation, as in the first, no Lentulus is high on show. Crus and Spinther persisted on the side of Magnus and the Republic, but the family went on, annexing before long the Scipionic name. One consul stands in this period, L. Cornelius, suffect in 38, revealed not so long ago as a Lentulus.[17] But so far only a name and a date. Further, there is a chance that P. Cornelius (*suff.* 35) was a Marcellinus.[18] But seven consulships accrue in the years of peace, beginning with 'duo Lentuli', colleagues in 18. Caesar Augustus continued and surpassed Cornelius Sulla in care and provision for the ancient patriciate.

The Lentuli, the imperial even more than the Republican, are sheer delight to any who draw up the stemmata of noble families—or tedium and torment. Careful scholars confess their diffidence.[19] The latest attempt is more sanguine. It carries over to the Augustan consuls, but it omits one of the seven; and it ignores L. Lentulus (*suff.* 38).[20] This man might make a modest difference, if his identity were ascertained. Less for history, however, than for fanciers of genealogy.

That consul does not have to be equated with L. Lentulus, praetor in 44.[21] Still less with Cruscellio (the son of Crus), proscribed by the Triumvirs.[22] Another Lentulus of the time tends to be neglected, viz. the praetor Cn. Lentulus commanding a fleet in Sicilian waters.[23] One

[14] *Ad fam.* III.7.5.

[15] *Post red. in sen.* 8: 'parens ac deus nostrae vitae' etc.

[16] Sallust, *Cat.* 55.6.

[17] *AE* 1945, 66.

[18] Ch. XVIII.

[19] F. Münzer, *RE* IV. 1357; E. Groag under *PIR*² C 1379: his stemma faces p. 328.

[20] G. V. Sumner, *The Orators in Cicero's Brutus* (1973), 143 (the stemma). He states that the stemma 'is not impossible of reconstitution'. The omitted Augustan consul is Cossus Lentulus Cn. f. (*cos.* 1 BC).

[21] *Phil.* III.25. In any event, the new consul may well be a son of L. Lentulus, the *flamen Martialis* (*RE* IV. 1391) and parent of L. Lentulus L. f. (*cos.* 3 BC), who also held that priesthood.

[22] Val. Max. VI.7.3: Appian, *BC* IV. 39.164.

[23] *CIL* XI. 6058 (Urvinum). The inscription records the officer T. Marius Siculus. As Bormann assumed, the T. Marius Urbinas of Val. Max. VII.8.6; cf. A. Stein, *RE* XIV.1321 f.

hypothesis assumes identity with Cruscellio.[24] Yet perhaps not. There is every advantage in multiplying Lentuli—and avoiding premature certitudes.[25] On the present showing, the standard computation will rise by two, by a Lucius and a Gnaeus.

Problems both urgent and persistent invest the next three consuls:

18: P. Cornelius P. f. Lentulus Marcellinus (*PIR*[2] C 1396)

    Cn. Cornelius L. f. Lentulus (1378)

14: Cn. Cornelius Cn. f. Lentulus Augur (1379).

First of all, Marcellinus, who (it will be recalled) comes into the controversy about the husbands of Scribonia.[26] He is sometimes held a son of the Lentulus Marcellinus attested as quaestor in 48.[27] Identity is not ruled out. There is a question about his age. His name is discerned on a fragmentary list of the praetors of 29: 'Cornelius Lentulus Marc['.[28] A long interval therefore elapsed before he reached the *fasces*. Which is not inconceivable in the first decade of the new order. On the other hand, perhaps a different Marcellinus.[29] In any event, a praetor of 29 cannot be the son of a quaestor in 48.

Next, his colleague. For parent offers either the praetor of 44 or the consul suffect of 38 (if they are kept apart). The filiation distinguishes him from 'Cn. f.', the consul of 14, who further by good fortune is styled 'Augur' on several official documents both Latin and Greek.[30]

The narration of the *Annales* imports enduring perplexity: 'Cn. Lentulus' has five entries, 'augur Lentulus' one only. A single person or two? The matter is of high importance. It concerns the Danubian campaign conducted by a Cn. Lentulus.[31]

That campaign was assigned to the consul of 18. Such was the canonical decision, firmly stated, and it stood for a long time.[32] The Augur thus suffered diminution.

Inspection of the historian's technique might have counselled a doubt. Though capable of error about noble families now extinct, Tacitus was alert to the problems of homonyms. He used a variety of subtle devices to prevent the reader from falling into confusion about Pisones.[33] No need

---

[24] *PIR*[2] C 1389.

[25] As stated by Groag in *PIR*[2] C 1379: 'sane videntur his temporibus plures fuisse Lentuli quam qui nobis innotuerunt.'

[26] Ch. XVIII.

[27] Caesar, *BC* III. 62.4. Groag has 'fortasse' (*PIR*[2] C 1396). It is premature to assign him 'P.' for *praenomen*, as on Sumner's stemma (o.c. 143).

[28] *CIL* XI. 7412 (territory of Viterbo).

[29] above, p. 250.

[30] *RG* 10; *ILS* 5026 (the *Arvales* of AD 14); *SIG*[3] 781 (Nysa).

[31] Tacitus, *Ann.* IV.44.1; Florus II.28 f.

[32] Groag, *RE* IV. 1361 f., as previously Klebs in *PIR*[1] C 1121: duly followed in *JRS* XXIV (1934), 113 ff. = *Danubian Papers* (1971), 40 ff.

[33] *JRS* XLVI (1956), 17 ff. = *Ten Studies in Tacitus* (1970), 50 ff.

for anxiety if only one elderly Lentulus was to adorn his pages, duly introduced as 'ante alios aetate et gloria belli'.[34]

After the lapse of thirty years, a reversal was declared, though not without residual hesitation.[35] The Augur now engrossed the five items in Tacitus.[36] Hence consequences of moment. Like his colleague Marcellinus, the consul of 18 is reduced to a name and a date: Cn. Lentulus L. f. Sad but welcome, albeit not always perceived.[37]

A dedication at Delphi disclosed a quaestor of Imp. Caesar Divi f., viz. Cn. Lentulus Cn. f. Cn. n.[38] Some hold this man identical with the Augur (*cos.* 14); and further, son of Cn. Lentulus Clodianus (*pr.* 59), and grandson of his homonymous parent (*cos.* 72).[39]

The absence of the title 'Augustus' puts Caesar's quaestor in Greek lands within the limits of 30 and 28. On that showing the Augur has to wait fifteen years for his consulship. Not easy to explain or admit. Two of his presumed coevals among the *nobiles* hold the quaestorship in the period 22–19, when the ruler spent three years in the eastern provinces.[40]

Assigned to those years, the Augur would fall happily into line. The absence of 'Augustus' tells strongly against. Better, the quaestor whom Delphi honoured is not the Augur. Nor is it certain that the Augur continues the line of Clodianus. Being 'Cn. f.' he might be the son of Cn. Lentulus, attested as an admiral in the period of the Triumvirs.[41]

As consul Cn. Lentulus had for colleague Crassus Frugi, who proceeded before long to govern Tarraconensis, with four legions.[42] The augurate he may already have acquired when quite young. He was also an *arvalis*.[43] The season of his entrance to the fraternity evades precision: probably subsequent to his consulship.[44]

The central matter is Lentulus' command on the Danube, revealed by a pair of sporadic notices (in Tacitus and in Florus). It is a nexus of problems. Not only the date, but the area and definition of the command. Other

---

[34] *Ann.* I.27.1.

[35] Thus *PIR*[2] C 1378: 'pro certo diudicari nequit' (the identity of the 'vir triumphalis').

[36] *PIR*[2] C 1379: followed in *Rom. Rev.* (1939), 400.

[37] The latest commentator on *Ann.* I.27.1 (F. R. D. Goodyear, 1972) registers the problem of identity without discussion; and 'gloria belli' fails to evoke a reference to IV. 44.1.

[38] *Fouilles de Delphes* III.1.528.

[39] Groag voiced hesitation in *PIR*[2] C 1379 (twice). No sign of doubt, however, in M. Cébeillac, *Les Quaestores Principis et Candidati* (1973), 11 f. This quaestor might be the father of Cn. Lentulus Cn. f. Maluginensis (*suff.* AD 10).

[40] viz. Quinctilius Varus and Fabius Maximus (*ILS* 8812; *IG* II[2]. 4130).

[41] *CIL* XI. 6058 (Urvinum).

[42] above, p. 276.

[43] *ILS* 5026 (as president, in 14).

[44] J. Scheid, *Les Frères Arvales* (1975), 73, cf. 27. Lentulus, he suggests, took the place of L. Cornelius Cinna (*suff.* 32).

generals come in, and the condition of the literary evidence for the wars in Illyricum and the Balkans. To reach a solution, it is expedient to clear the path and find a firm line of approach.

In Illyricum a proconsul is attested in 16.[45] The next general on record is Marcus Vinicius (*suff*. 19), in 13, the last of the proconsuls or the first imperial legate.[46] Claudius Nero now took charge, conquering the Pannonians and extending the boundary of Illyricum to the river Danube (12–9). On him followed Sex. Appuleius (*cos*. 29), a nephew of the Princeps.[47] The enlarged Illyricum, with five legions, now became the central military bastion of the Empire.

Those operations had consequences for Macedonia, for Thrace, for the Moesian bank of the Danube. In three years of arduous warfare L. Piso (*cos*. 15) crushed a great insurrection in Thrace. Piso fought as 'legatus Augusti' (12–10).[48]

The question of Moesia now arises, long under dispute—because not correctly formulated. The new Balkan command began when the Macedonian legions were transferred to an imperial legate.[49] The cause and date is given by Piso's war, so it can be affirmed.

From 3 or 2 to AD 2 legates commanding 'in Thracia Macedoniaque' are disclosed: P. Vinicius (*cos*. AD 2) followed by P. Silius (*suff*. 3).[50] Praetorian legates only. The Balkan army (it may be conjectured) had for the moment given up a legion, or perhaps two, to the eastern armies.

When the Pannonians and Dalmatians rose in 6, Caecina Severus (*suff*. 1 BC), described as governor of Moesia, intervened; and again in the next year. Caecina and Plautius Silvanus (*cos*. 2 BC) then fought a battle near Sirmium.[51] This army comprised five legions: three under Caecina, two brought from Galatia, where Silvanus had suppressed a rising of the Isaurians.[52]

These prolegomena are necessary, since both the date and the definition of Lentulus' command are in question. Estimates have exhibited a wide range in time, from 13 BC to AD 11.[53] The military situation precludes the

---

[45] Dio LIV.20.1 f.; *ILS* 899 (Aenona). That is, P. Silius Nerva (*cos*. 20).

[46] Velleius II. 96.2 f. Dio puts the transference of 'Dalmatia' in 11 BC (LIV.34.4.): erroneous, like the reasons he assigns.

[47] Cassiodorus, *Chron. Min.* II.135.

[48] Ch. XXIV.

[49] *JRS* XXXV (1945), 109 f. (review of A. Stein, *Die Legaten von Moesien*, 1940).

[50] Velleius II. 101.3. Stein unfortunately omitted P. Silius from his account. The dedication to P. Vinicius at Callatis (*IGR* I. 654) now emended (*AE* 1960, 378) shows him a legate. For Sex. Aelius Catus (*cos*. 4), whose operations were noted by Strabo (VII, p. 303), uncertainty still prevails. He is perhaps best put in 9–11, cf. *History in Ovid* (1978), 69.

[51] Dio LV.29.3; 34.6, cf. Velleius II.112.4.

[52] As deduced from Dio LV.28.2 f.; *SEG* VI.646 (Attaleia).

[53] For the bibliography on Lentulus, see *JRS* XXIV (1934), 113 = *Danubian Papers* (1971) 40, with the *Addenda* (69 ff.). A. v. Premerstein stood by the late dating in *Jahreshefte* XXIX (1934), 60 ff. It persisted with J. Fitz, *RE Supp.* IX. 543.

early date—or any date anterior to the great northern campaigns and the pacification of Thrace. For the other extreme, a general twenty-five years from his consulship is not totally ruled out (although younger men were available, with experience won between 4 and 9); but Lentulus is not easy to accommodate, either in Illyricum or in Moesia. The limits can be narrowed without effort to the period 9 BC–AD 6.

The next step is to determine the command and province. Illyricum had the earliest preference, which it kept for a long time.[54] Then, in the year 1934, an ambitious attempt emerged to establish a close dating; and it was published in an ample exposition of the northern wars.[55]

The obscure decade seemed attractive, with Claudius Nero absent, Velleius not eager to advertise the exploits of other generals, and the text of Cassius Dio defective. Hence Illyricum for Cn. Lentulus, *c*.AD 1–4. There was a further advantage. Two other legates could be fitted in. First Domitius Ahenobarbus, in Illyricum before he went to Germany, where a notice in Dio attests him under AD 1.[56] In Germany M. Vinicius (*suff.* 19) followed Ahenobarbus. Likewise perhaps in Illyricum.[57] To Vinicius is attributed the acephalous *elogium* that recounts dealings with tribes beyond the middle Danube, lying between Bohemia and Transylvania.[58]

The design was to isolate Maroboduus, the ruler of the Marcommanni, on his eastern flank, separating him from the Dacians. Operations across the Danube concluded by Lentulus in the near sequel could have this place and contribution, so it was held. Finally, and most convenient, the sequence of legates between Ahenobarbus (*c*.5–2) and Messallinus (attested when the rebellion broke out in 6).[59]

The theory was elaborate and coherent—or unduly symmetrical. In the sparse and scattered fragments of Danubian history, a larger part should be conceded to nescience. Hesitation about both the date and position of Lentulus was soon expressed.[60] Indeed, the alternative was produced and firmly stated more than once: Lentulus succeeding Piso in the new Balkan command *c*.9–6 BC.[61]

To that revision not much attention was accorded.[62] Yet its reason was

---

[54] Groag, *RE* IV. 1362 (1904), cf. *PIR*² C 1379 (1936), 'probabiliter'.

[55] *JRS* XXIV (1934), 113 ff. = *Danubian Papers* (1971), 40 ff.; *CAH* X (1934), 364 ff.

[56] Dio LV.10a.2.

[57] As conjectured in *CQ* XXVII (1933), 142 ff. = *Danubian Papers* (1971), 26 ff. For other views, ib. 34 ff. (the *Addendum*). A date *c*.2 BC is now accepted by J. Fitz, *ANRW* II. 6 (1977), 546.

[58] *ILS* 8965 (Tusculum). It was claimed for Messallinus in *RE* VIIIA (1958), 161.

[59] Dio LV.29.1; Velleius II. 112.1 f.

[60] *Rom. Rev.* (1939), 400, n. 6.

[61] *Gnomon* XXIX (1957), 519 = *Danubian Papers* (1971), 181 f.; with the *Addenda* (ib. 69 f.). Further, *Akten des VI. int. Kong. für gr. u. lat Epigraphik* (1973), 596 f. Finally, *AJP* C (1979), 203 f. = *RP* III (1984), 1191.

[62] For indecisive statements about Lentulus see, for example, A. Mócsy, *Pannonia and Upper Moesia* (1974), 36 f.; 39; 43. In comment on *Ann.* IV. 44, E. Koestermann adopted without argument 10 BC, a widely favoured date. J. Scheid acceded to the dating *c*.AD 1–4 (o.c. 68).

clear and solid, and should never have been ignored. In the obituary notice on Lentulus stood the words 'triumphalia de Getis'.[63] The name of Getae indicates activities on or beyond the lower course of the Danube, below the Iron Gates. In epistles from the Pontic shore the poet Ovid, alert to various tribes, especially Getae, never uses the term 'Dacus'.

Florus, the second source for Lentulus, has 'Daci', it is true—and also Sarmatae. It is never safe to press the language of this epitomator, both careless and rhetorical. None the less, what he reports looks like police operations along the Danube with the setting up of fortified posts.[64]

The name of Lentulus should therefore perhaps be segregated from certain notices that allude to an invasion and even a subjugation of Dacia.[65]

Trouble in Thrace or an absence of the Roman army encouraged invaders from across the river, Thus in 16 BC and in AD 6.[66] The measures adopted by Lentulus may therefore follow the rebellion that Piso quelled. By the same token, a different and later date is not excluded.

Recourse therefore turns to arguments on the flank. Present in Florus, Lentulus is absent from Dio, who preserves a number of wars elsewhere lost to written recording. The gaps between 6 BC and AD 4 have been duly adduced. That is not all. This historian has certain habits. He groups the events of several years in resumptive chapters. Further, he omits facts, or betrays inadvertence, sometimes perhaps through a change of sources.

One transaction is doubly instructive. After the campaigns of the year 11, the Senate decreed a closure of Janus, which was deferred because Dacians crossed the frozen Danube and made great booty in Pannonia.[67]

Nothing is heard about Janus in the ensuing years, although it was probably closed in 8 or 7, when a period of tranquillity set in.[68] As for the Dacians, nothing appears to be done. In charge of Illyricum, Claudius Nero in 10 first went to Gaul in the company of his stepfather and then reverted to his command, dealing with Dalmatians rebellious against Roman taxation.[69] Dio at this point happens to be compressed. He passes from 11 to 10 without registering the consuls of 10, whose names turn up in the first sentence of the next book. If a change of source were surmised,

[63] *Ann.* IV.44.1. On which, *AJP* C (1979), 200 = *RP* III (1984), 1188.
[64] Florus II. 28: 'misso igitur Lentulo ultra ulteriorem reppulit ripam. citra praesidia constituta. sic tum Dacia non victa, sed summota atque dilata est.' Compare, for the Sarmatians, 'et hos per eundem Lentulum prohibere Danuvio satis fuit' (ib. 29).
[65] Thus the Dacians compelled to submit to the 'imperia populi Romani' (*RG* 30), or the Roman invasion up the valley of the Marisus, a tributary of the Tisia (Strabo VII, p. 304). Those items were assigned to the campaign of Lentulus in *PIR*² C 1379. Renewed investigation is needed.
[66] Dio LIV.20.3; LV.30.4.
[67] Dio LIV.36.2.
[68] above, p. 68. For the third closure of Janus see further *History in Ovid* (1978), 25; *AJP* C (1979), 201 f. = *RP* III (1984), 1189 f.
[69] Dio LIV.36 f. For Tiberius' actions and movements in 10 and 9, see *Phoenix* XXXIII (1979), 311 ff. = *RP* III (1984),1201 ff.

it cannot be supported by any change in tone or emphasis of the narration. Nor does the near sequel reveal anything.[70]

However that may be, nothing Danubian in Dio (apart from the campaign of Ahenobarbus) for a long lapse until AD 6, when Caecina Severus had to return to deal with Dacians and Sarmatians threatening his own area of command. Dio should have had something to report in 6 BC after the text breaks, or a year or so later. Yet he may have missed Lentulus altogether. Not inconceivable.[71]

Next, Florus. His main source for the Augustan wars was an epitome of Livy, as is demonstrated in several particulars. Livy accorded a book a year to the narration of 12–9. If in fact Lentulus in 10 or 9 followed Piso, 'in Thracia Macedoniaque', no problem. Florus, however, was able to add subsequent transactions, not deriving from Livy, such as the African war of Cossus Lentulus or the disaster of Quinctilius Varus.[72] The question is intricate, no decision valid or relevant at this point.

At the end, and on first view remote, the proconsulate of Asia. Lentulus came late, in 3/2 BC, a dozen years from his consulship.[73] Parallels avail, a consular missing his turn for the sortition because employed in the 'provincia' of Caesar. Thus Marcus Lepidus, consul in 6, still available twenty years later.[74] The colleague of Cn. Lentulus went out to Africa for the tenure 9/8.[75] Lentulus, it is conjectured, had other occupation in that season.[76]

The precise year of a military operation often baffles ascertainment. The record may get postponed in a historian's narration, as happens several times in Dio. Furthermore, the Senate may vote the *ornamenta triumphalia* either at the culminating success achieved in a war or at the termination of the mandate. Hence uncertainty by a year about Piso's war in Thrace.[77] Succeeding Piso in 10 or 9, Lentulus may have gone on for four or five years. The date and the identity of the next legate would be worth knowing. The command had taken legions from the eastern provinces. From three or four legions (one surmises) it soon fell to two.[78]

So far the Augur, on the Danube and in Asia. Nothing is known about the

---

[70] Livy terminated in 9 with Book CXLII. Aufidius Bassus (it may be conjectured) then took up the tale, cf. *Tacitus* (1958), 698.

[71] For example, Dio ignored the African campaign of Cornelius Balbus (19 BC), and the annexation of Judaea (AD 6).

[72] For the Gaetulian War, below, p. 296.   [73] *SIG*³ 781 (Nysa).

[74] *Ann.* IV.56.3 (above, p. 132).

[75] *IRT* 319 (Lepcis).

[76] *JRS* XLV (1955), 29 = *Ten Studies in Tacitus* (1970), 43.

[77] Ch. XXIV.

[78] The campaign of Quirinius against tribes of the Taurus probably belongs in 5 and 4 BC. See Ch. XXIV.

consuls of 18, save their filiation—and even that does not permit certainty about their parents. Furthermore, both consuls may have died in the near sequel.[79]

The Augur takes all. This character is not complete without some estimate of his civil attainments. On first entrance in the *Annales*, at the head of a delegation that tried to appease the mutinous legions in Pannonia, he essayed the diplomatic arts of his ancestors and incurred animosity. They threw rocks at him. Suffering a wound, Lentulus was rescued from dire peril: 'iamque lapidis ictu cruentus et exitii certus'.[80]

At the term of his existence, the septuagenarian had a brush with a prosecutor, on allegations of treason: without danger, being one of Caesar's closest friends. He died the year after (in 25).[81]

In between, three appearances in the Senate. In 16 Lentulus joined six other persons of birth and rank when ignominy was visited on the memory of an alleged conspirator. Lentulus' share in the action of public thanksgiving was to propose that no Scribonius thereafter should bear 'Drusus' for *cognomen*.[82]

The next transaction shows Lentulus the Augur blocking the plea of Maluginensis (*suff.* 10, a kinsman, but not close).[83] Maluginensis wanted the province Asia, although he was *flamen Dialis*.

Not all holders of priesthoods at Rome were anxious to interpose their sacerdotal science, although it might be advantageous, or used to damage others; and some by public utterances were shown ignorant, provoking rebuke from Ti. Caesar.[84] On this occasion the old Augur spoke not in vain. Caesar took notice, and after a discreet interval pronounced his verdict.[85]

In the same year C. Silanus (*suff.* AD 10) stood on trial before the high assembly, indicted for extortion in the governorship of Asia, with eloquent prosecutors, among them, abnormally, an ex-consul and a *nobilis*, Mam. Aemilius Scaurus.[86] The historian Tacitus has a full account. The first time (though he does not specify) that a proconsul of Asia or Africa had been prosecuted since the case of Volesus Messalla late in the previous reign.[87]

Tiberius Caesar, presiding, asked L. Piso for an opinion. With due

[79] Marcus Agrippa and two consuls died in 12.
[80] *Ann.* I.27.2.
[81] IV.29.1 (cf. Dio LVII.24.8); 44.1. He died at eighty-one, on the estimate of J. Scheid, o.c. 72. That depends on the belief that he was quaestor *c.*29 BC.
[82] II.32.1.
[83] III.39.1, cf. below, p. 297.
[84] III.64.4. (L. Apronius); VI.12.2 (Caninius Gallus).
[85] IV.71.2.
[86] On Scaurus (*suff.* 21), above, p. 267.
[87] Tiberius in fact produced his predecessor's written testimony about Volesus and the Senate's decree (III.68.1).

homage to the 'clementia principis' Piso opted for the lesser penalty. In the further procedure, Lentulus submitted an alleviation, 'adnuente Tiberio'.[88]

The transaction furnishes a hint of connivance, to the better end. The Princeps was under constraint to deprecate his authority and dissemble his intentions. Piso and Lentulus knew them; and the Augur was not merely indulging in rancorous pedantry when he spoke against the *flamen Dialis*.

Lentulus spoke out on another occasion, if credit were accorded to Tertullian. Denouncing the attire and habits of Roman women, he refers with approbation to 'Lentuli auguris consulta'.[89]

The source and validity of his information need not perplex or detain. The context gives it. Caecina Severus is brought on, warning the Senate about grave improprieties: 'matronas sine stola in publico'.

Now Caecina Severus stands on high prominence in the *Annales*, with an oration urging that wives be forbidden to accompany governors of provinces.[90] Censorious about the fair sex, Caecina said nothing about clothing. The erudite Tertullian, so it appears, enforced and expanded his recollections of the Tacitean text. He also obtruded 'augur Lentulus' from an episode a little later in the same book concerning priesthoods of the state religion.[91]

Lentulus was a diplomat, not one of the princes of eloquence. When in 20 Cn.Piso the legate of Syria faced prosecution for treason, he approached five advocates, the best of the day. They declined, but he secured three others. The catalogue is instructive, for more purposes than one. It does not include Lentulus.[92]

Nor does the historian allude to oratory when chronicling the end of Lentulus. By opportunity of their decease, Tacitus could link Lentulus and Ahenobarbus, aristocratic generals winning renown in the wars of an expansive epoch.[93] That time was now coming to engage his attention, avowed for the first time and evoked when he came upon the young nobleman who had been involved in the disgrace of Julia, the granddaughter of Caesar Augustus.[94]

Mindful of Roman eloquence and the sons of Messalla, Cornelius Tacitus when writing the Tiberian books (and averse from copying annalists) might recall, or read again, the poems of Ovid. Messallinus comes early on show in the *Annales*—and both brothers recur.

Tacitus all through assumes wealth as the substance of life and success. His tribute in epilogue on the Augur is noteworthy for benevolence: 'bene

---

[88] *Ann.* III.68.2.

[89] Tertullian, *De pallio* 4.

[90] *Ann.* III.33. Valerius Messallinus spoke against.

[91] The item tends to command credence: Thus 'anno incerto Tiberii sententiam tulit de cultu feminarum' (*PIR*² C 1379); and a *senatus consultum* is assumed (J. Scheid, o.c. 72).

[92] *Ann.* III.11.2.   [93] IV.44.   [94] III.24.

tolerata paupertas, dein magnae opes innocenter partae et modeste habitae.'[95]

The historian nowhere discloses the source of that wealth, content as is his wont with 'opes', a plain but ample word: 'pecunia' is neutral or unfriendly, 'pecuniosus' quite odious. Questions will be asked, and should have been asked. While impoverishment in seasons of confiscation and profiteers counts for virtue, the means are not manifested whereby noblemen rise to riches without loss of reputation. The Volusii stand as parallel, a family that Cornelius Tacitus knew and held in esteem.[96] Their first consul (*suff.* 12) was the 'primus adcumulator'; and when his son, the *praefectus urbi*, died early in the reign of Nero at the age of ninety-three, wealth amassed through 'bonae artes' earns celebration.[97]

By the historian's irony, Nero in a stylized response to Seneca is made to bring up the 'longa parsimonia' of Volusius.[98] The agronome Columella affords sober guidance, mentioning precepts he heard from the old consular.[99] The skilful exploitation of land, and especially of vineyards, is the answer.[100]

For Lentulus, some might import booty won in war.[101] The nomad Sarmatians had little to offer, or the Getae, often held poor and blameless, not sharing in the gold of Dacia. Agricultural Getae could be captured and sold into slavery.

The greater gains would accrue from other sources—marriage and inheritance, gifts or bequests from admiring friends of lower social rank.[102] And, before all, the 'amicitia' of the Caesars.

Seneca profited from that kind of bounty, enormously, and Seneca makes the revelation in the treatise *De beneficiis*.[103] It was to Caesar Augustus that Lentulus owed 'omnia incrementa sua'. The sum was enormous, amounting to four hundred million sesterces. Lentulus contributed only 'paupertatem sub onere nobilitatis laborantem'. Yet Lentulus was mean-spirited and ungrateful. Though 'princeps iam civitatis

---

[95] To acquire 'pecuniam magnam bono modo' was declared eighth among ten virtues in the funeral oration on a Metellus (Pliny, *NH* VII.140).

[96] *Tacitus* (1958), 302 f.

[97] *Ann.* III.30.1; XIII.30.2. The second passage runs 'cui tres et nonaginta anni spatium vivendi praecipuaeque opes bonis artibus, inoffensa tot imperatorum amicitia fuit.'
The temptation might occur to read 'praecipuaeque opes bonis artibus ⟨partae⟩'. Cf. *CQ* XXX (1980), 427 = *RP* III (1984), 1235.

[98] XIV.56.1.

[99] Columella I.7.3.

[100] An estate of the Volusii, with large barracks for slaves, has recently been discovered near Lucus Feroniae. For the inscriptions, W. Eck, *Hermes* C (1972). 461 ff.; J. Reynolds, *JRS* LXI (1971), 142 ff.

[101] Thus Groag in *PIR*[2] C 1379.

[102] However, new and unexpected evidence reveals Lentulus as 'patronus' to the *publicani* in Asia and Bithynia (*Inschr. Eph.* III.658).

[103] Seneca, *De. ben.* II.27.1 ff.

et pecunia et gratia', he kept on complaining. The service of the state had robbed him, he forfeited what he might have earned by his eloquence.

Lentulus in truth was no orator, so Seneca affirms. His performance went with his character. Sterile and constipated, 'nummos citius emittebat quam verba'.

Conflict of testimony about a Lentulus may amuse a philosophical mind. Seneca wrote from personal knowledge, and with malice. Tacitus appears incautious, under a prepossession (perhaps enhanced by the Volusii), in favour of birth and wealth, at least when credited with renown in war or political wisdom.

The Augur left no heirs, The vast fortune fell to Caesar, as a trivial anecdote happens to reveal. Tiberius in his rapacity could not wait, he accelerated the demise of Lentulus.[104]

No sons are discoverable at any time—or any marriage within conjecture. Indeed, for all seven consular Lentuli in the time of Augustus no wife is on direct attestation. As for the extraction of the Augur, it is not certain that he was a grandson of Clodianus (*cos.* 72 BC).

Brief comment can now go to the remaining consuls of the reign. Three occur in a cluster.

3 BC: L. Cornelius L. f. Lentulus (*PIR*² C 1384)

1 BC: Cossus Cornelius Cn. f. Lentulus (C 1380)

AD 2 (*suff.*): P. Cornelius Cn. f. Cn. n. Lentulus Scipio (C 1397)

The first of them, who was *flamen Martialis*, shared the *fasces* with the elder son of Messalla Corvinus, for the whole year: a distinction, since suffect consuls were a recent but enduring innovation. This Lentulus died in Africa, to be presumed proconsul.[105] Yet not perhaps in the field, though it was a season of disturbances in that region. Passienus Rufus (*cos.* 4 BC) earned the *ornamenta triumphalia*.[106] The same honour went to Cossus in AD 6 for a campaign against the Gaetuli.[107]

The campaign of Cossus happens to stand on multiple attestation, and he had a long survival.[108] The third consul leaves no trace in written history, but the line lasted for three more generations.[109] The nomenclature is significant: the first Lentulus on clear record to parade with the *cognomen* of the Scipiones; and the filiation, 'Cn. f. Cn. n.' is useful, inviting rational conjecture.[110]

---

[104] Suetonius, *Tib.* 49.1: 'metu et angore ad fastidium vitae ab eo actum'.

[105] *Inst. Just.* II.25 *praef.*, cf. *PIR*² C 1384: rejected by B. E. Thomasson. *Die Statthalter der r. Provinzen Nordafrikas* II (1960), 18, n. 19. But apparently conceded on his list in *RE, Supp.* XIII (1973), 2.   [106] Velleius II.166.2, cf. *ILS* 120; 8966.

[107] *IRT* 301 (Lepcis).   [108] Thomasson, o.c. 18 f.

[109] Down to P. Cornelius Scipio Asiaticus (*suff.* 68).

[110] A brother of Ser. Lentulus Cn.f. Maluginensis (*suff.* 10). Thus, following Cichorius, Groag in *PIR*² C 1393; 1397.

To illustrate the complications of Scipionic pedigrees it will be suitable to inspect in passing the daughter of L. Lentulus L.f. (*cos.* 3 BC). She married L. Volusius Saturninus (*suff.* AD 3)—and she is described as 'Cornelia Scipionum gentis'.[111]

The mind reverts to the Cornelia whose memory Propertius honours and transmits: the sister of P. Cornelius P. f. P. n. Scipio, the consul of 16.[112] If he is a genuine Scipio, consequences can be drawn, of some interest. P. Cornelius Lentulus Scipio (*suff.* AD 2), it might be conjectured, is his son by adoption: that is, testamentary, retaining the filiation 'Cn. f. Cn.n.' Furthermore, L. Lentulus (*cos.* 3) had a daughter of Scipionic descent, as has been shown. This Lentulus, it follows, may have married either a daughter of P. Scipio, the consul of 16, or the girl whom Cornelia bore to Paullus the Censor.

Finally, to continue with the Scipionic theme and to round off the rubric of the Augustan consuls, Ser. Cornelius Cn. f. Cn. n. Maluginensis, suffect in AD 10. He comes into a minor incident of the year 22 (noted above). Despite the restriction of his priesthood (he was *flamen Dialis*) Maluginensis put up a claim to be admitted to the sortition for the province Asia. Objection arose, in the first place from 'augur Lentulus', suitably so styled in that context.

'Maluginensis' was an ancient *cognomen*, the latest to bear it being a Scipio in 176 BC.[113] Because of their identical filiation, the *flamen Dialis* is held to be a brother of P. Lentulus Scipio (*suff.* AD 2).[114] Their parent eludes identification. Possibly Cn. Lentulus the admiral or the Cn. Lentulus who was *quaestor Caesaris* shortly after the Battle of Actium. Little profit will accrue from further speculation in those territories.

Maluginensis comes into a significant nexus. An inscription at Volsinii reveals a fact. His sister was the wife of a prefect of Egypt. That is, Seius Strabo.[115] Some now contest the attribution, it is true. The grounds are not adequate. Nor is a supporting hypothesis attractive, namely that Maluginensis and P. Lentulus Scipio were sons of Cn. Lentulus the Augur.[116]

The reign of Tiberius Caesar exhibits four more consular Lentuli.[117] First, P. Lentulus Scipio (*suff.* 24), the homonymous son of the *suffectus* of the

[111] Pliny, *NH* VII.62, cf. *PIR*² C 1476. Above, p. 252.

[112] Ch. XVIII.

[113] Cicero *De oratore* II.260. For the *cognomen*, above, p. 75.

[114] Thus *PIR*² C 1393; 1397.

[115] *ILS* 8996, cf. Ch. XXII.

[116] Argued by G. V. Sumner, *Phoenix* XIX (1965), 138 f., and adopted without query in *The Orators in Cicero's Brutus* (1973), 143.

[117] Not to mention Ser. Cornelius Ser. f. Cethegus (*cos.* 24): there was a Lentulus Cethegus (*PIR*² C 1388). The *praenomen* 'Servius' appertained to ancient Lentuli, used for the last time in the mid second century (*RE* IV. 1376 f.)

year 2. He is notable, and seems anomalous, being the earliest *nobilis* registered in command of a legion when of praetorian rank.[118]

Next, the two sons of Cossus, namely Cossus and Gnaeus, in 25 and 26. The former is only a date;[119] and so is 'P. Le[. . . . .], suffect the year after. The younger son of Cossus bore the *cognomen* of victory his parent declined—or rather was denied by a jealous government.

Gaetulicus brought the Lentuli into fame and peril: involvement with Seianus, the ten years' tenure of Germania Superior, and at the end execution for high treason, when young Lepidus perished and two sisters of Caligula were consigned to banishment.[120]

From the caution or mediocrity of the Lentuli, this man stands out for another reason, a taste for polite letters. Nine poems in the Greek Anthology carry his name. Some, it is true, are impelled to cast doubt on his authorship.[121] He also wrote in Latin, on erotic themes; and he composed a prose work, perhaps memoirs.[122]

The situation of Gaetulicus in the hazardous years 30 and 31 cannot be properly estimated if his old father be omitted, deep in the confidence of the suspicious ruler. In 31 Cossus intervened to frustrate the prosecution of the eminent L. Arruntius.[123]

Having won military glory when young, Cossus in old age exemplified the indolence of the Lentuli. Not in retirement and torpor, but when holding high office as Prefect of the City (from 33 to 36). Seneca in a sagacious appraisal puts Cossus on a level of ability with Piso the Pontifex, describing him as 'virum gravem, moderatum, sed mersum vino et madentem'. They had to carry him out of the Senate.[124]

Like Piso, he was seldom heard in the high assembly. Absent, in fact, from the *Annales*. As with Piso and others, allowance must be made for the loss of Book V. More surprising, however, no obituary notice. This historian was drawn to the deaths of Augustan consulars; and he exhibits a keen interest in the urban prefecture. Omissions therefore excite curiosity. In the year 36 the narration was dominated by different preoccupations. Tacitus might defer Cossus until Book VII.

In the next generation, two branches perpetuated the Lentuli, descendants of Cossus and of Lentulus Scipio.

---

[118] *Ann.* III. 74.2, cf. *ILS* 940 (Brixia). That command, but not that alone, retarded his access to the *fasces*. He had been praetor in 15 (*ILS* 9349).

[119] Apart from a governorship of Germania Superior, conjectured by Groag in *PIR*² C 1381.

[120] Before that affair Caligula recalled Calvisius Sabinus (*cos.* 26), the legate of Pannonia (Dio LIX.18.4). His wife was a Cornelia, presumed sister to Gaetulicus, cf. *PIR*² C 354.

[121] Not always for a good reason: 'the *cognomen* 'Gaetulicus' is not uncommon in this period', according to Gow–Page, *The Garland of Philip* I (1968), XLVIII.

[122] For the testimonia, *PIR*² C 1390.

[123] Dio LVIII.8.3, cf. above, p. 268.

[124] Seneca, *Epp.* 83.15 (cf. below, p. 345).

Savage vengeance was wrought by official act on the young children of Aelius Seianus. The sons of Gaetulicus were spared. The Caesars saw rivals or enemies in the *nobilitas*. But, aristocratic themselves, they were responsive to birth, to the adornment of the *fasces*—and to the advertising of imperial clemency.[125] One son of Gaetulicus was consul suffect in 55—which may owe something to the counsels of Seneca. In 60 a nephew shared the *fasces* with Nero. Two other sons are known and a grandson, but no more consuls.[126]

P. Scipio introduced the year 56, the colleague of Q. Volusius Saturninus (whose mother was a Scipionic Cornelia). He was the elder son of Lentulus Scipio (*suff.* 24). Finally, in the autumn of 68, P. Scipio Asiaticus, the younger son: by his father's marriage to the beautiful Poppaea.[127]

The colleague was Bellicius Natalis, from the city of Vienna in Narbonensis.[128] The pair (it is plausible) owed designation not to Nero but to Galba, reflecting the dual support behind the usurper: ancient families and the new aristocracy coming in from the Roman West.[129]

The long survival of patrician houses is an engaging theme. Their decline evokes melancholy, and sometimes derision. And a rich variety of paradox. The nearest in kin to Sulpicius Galba was a Cornelius Dolabella, the son of a niece.[130] Galba selected a Piso, who carried descent from Pompeius and Crassus.

The name of the Lentuli was kept alive in a subsequent age by a hazy tradition. They are enrolled along with the large performers in the field of late Republican eloquence by a consular orator; and a poet parades a Lentulus among munificent patrons of letters in the Augustan prime.[131]

The orator and the poet stand at the peak and culmination of the process whereby literary talent had anticipated the provincial invasion of government and the upper order. Energy and ambition in the educated class, exploiting the patronage of the Caesars, went forward from equestrian posts to produce senators, consuls, army commanders. They soon joined Italians in extruding the aristocracy of Rome.

[125] Thus Claudius Caesar on the son of the rebel Arruntius Camillus (*Ann.* XII.52.2).

[126] viz. *PIR*[2] C 1392; J 835 f. (adoption by a Junius Silanus).

[127] For this Poppaea (his second wife), *Ann.* XI.4.3. The son's *cognomen* reflects birth when the father was proconsul: in 36/7 according to *PIR*[2] C 1398. A new inscription from Lydia (noted under *Inschr. Eph.* III. 659) shows Scipio proconsul under Claudius: presumably in 41/2.

[128] *PIR*[2] B 101.

[129] cf. *Historia* XXXI (1982), 475. Scipio became consul when aged twenty-six or seven.

[130] *PIR*[2] C 1347.

[131] Tacitus, *Dial.* 37.3; Juvenal VII.95.

XXII

Kinsmen of Seianus

Men of substance and repute from the towns of Italy rose and prospered, blending with the aristocracy in a continuous process which the ruler was powerless to resist, in spite of any predilection for birth and pedigree. And without entry to the Senate, the Revolution had enhanced knights both in value and in social prestige.

The agents of the dynasts became the ministers of the Caesars. In real power, which is 'potentia', they excelled the most eminent of the consulars. To pass the comment on C. Maecenas and Sallustius Crispus did not require abnormal percipience in a historian.[1]

Maecenas married a wife from the Terentii Varrones. One of her brothers was C. Proculeius, likewise a close friend of Caesar Augustus. It is of some significance that he should find conspicuous mention in the poem which Horace dedicated to the opulent and generous Crispus.[2]

A historian was able to produce, or rather invent, an exchange of missives between Ti. Caesar and his indispensable friend.[3] In petition for the hand of a princess, Aelius Seianus looked for a precedent and found it in intentions attributed to Caesar Augustus. In response Tiberius named Proculeius and gently deprecated the notion that he had ever been fancied a suitable husband for Julia. Epilogue on that theme may adduce the son by adoption of Sallustius Crispus, who acquired Domitia, a grand-niece of Augustus.[4]

Furthermore, high posts emerged for Roman knights. First, Egypt, where the victor left as viceroy Cornelius Gallus, the poet and adventurer. His successor was Aelius Gallus, a quiet and prudent man—and, like others among the higher equestrian officials, far from alien to literary or scientific interests.[5]

Next, and before long to have primacy before Egypt, the Guard. Cassius Dio registers the innovation in 2 BC, a year of pageantry and disaster. He puts it before the ruin of Julia.[6] It should in fact be one of the consequences.[7]

---

[1] *Ann.* III. 30. Crispus is absent both from Suetonius and from Dio.

[2] *Odes* II.2. For a hypothesis that the two were related, *CQ* XXVIII (1978), 295 = *RP* III (1984), 1089.   [3] *Ann.* IV. 39 f.   [4] Ch. XII.

[5] *PIR*[2] A 189 (citing Galen for his medical competence and remedies).   [6] Dio LV.10.10.

[7] Dio sometimes groups the events of a year in an idiosyncratic fashion. Cf. *Athenaeum* LXI (1983), 9 f.; 13. About one item of 2 BC, viz. 'pater patriae', he is patently in error.

The post was modest to begin with, the first pair of prefects inconspicuous. Of Q. Ostorius Scapula, the local origin has not been ascertained.[8] His colleague P. Salvius Aper had nothing to do with the Salvii Othones from Ferentium in Etruria, whose first senator owed his place to the patronage of Livia, whose second was a consul (*suff.* 33) and close friend of her son.[9] The prefect probably came from Brixia, a rich *municipium* in Transpadane Italy.[10] No descendants are known of this Salvius, but the Ostorii show a consul early in the reign of Claudius Caesar.

After Aper and Scapula, only one prefect of the Guard is discoverable: he is said to have been held in high honour by Caesar Augustus.[11] Then comes L. Seius Strabo, one of the dignitaries who took the oath of allegiance to his successor; and in the first weeks Ti. Caesar assigned him for colleague his son, L. Aelius Seianus.[12] In the near sequel Strabo was conveniently despatched to Egypt. His tenure was brief, less than two years, as emerges from the period covered by the next prefect.[13]

Volsinii, a city of Etruria, yielded a dedication honouring Seius Strabo as commander of the Guard.[14] This city, his *patria*, furnishes a second document, acephalous.[15] A prefect of Egypt constructs public baths. Who other than Strabo? The document was welcome. It revealed the mother of the Prefect. She is Terentia A. f., a portentous name, evoking a potent nexus, high politics, and problems in sharp debate. That is, A. Terentius Varro Murena (*cos.* 23 BC), the conspirator Varro Murena (often held identical), Terentia the wife of Maecenas.[16]

Not only the mother, but the wife. She is Cosconia Gallitta, described as the daughter of a Cornelius Lentulus Maluginensis. It is no surprise that one of the high equestrian dignitaries should be senatorial by extraction or annex a wife from the ancient aristocracy. In panegyric on Aelius Seianus, Velleius alluded to his social distinction: 'principe equestris ordinis patre natum, materno vero genere clarissimas veteresque et insignes honoribus complexum familias, habentem consularis fratres, consobrinos, avunculum'.[17]

[8] The family had estates at the far end of Liguria (*Ann.* XVI. 15.1). Amiternum, the *patria* of the Sallustii, is proposed by A. M. Hanson, *ZPE* 47 (1982), 247. That paper also establishes 'Publius' as the *praenomen* of the brother, the Prefect of Egypt—who married the daughter of Sallustius Crispus, viz. Sallustia Calvina (deduced from *CIL* VI. 23601).
[9] Suetonius, *Otho* 1.
[10] cf. *ILS* 4902 (a magistrate, in 8 BC).
[11] viz. Varius Ligur (*PIR*[1] V 189, cf. 60). Observe *ILS* 171 (Alba Pompeia).
[12] *Ann.* I.7.2: 24.2.
[13] Dio (Xiphilinus) LVII. 19.6, cf. A. Stein, *Die Präfekten von Ägypten* (1950), 25 f.
[14] *CIL* XI. 2707 (fragmentary but beyond doubt).
[15] *CIL* XI. 7285 = *ILS* 8996.
[16] Ch. XXVII.
[17] Velleius II.127.3.

The relevance and corollaries of the new inscription were seen at once by the alert Cichorius; and he was able to attach two extraneous items to the stemma.[18] It will be convenient to register his reconstruction. The principal features are

(1) Cosconia Gallitta, the wife of Strabo: a sister of Ser. Lentulus Maluginensis (*suff.* 10), and also of P. Lentulus Cn. f. Scipio (*suff.* 2).[19] Her nomenclature goes back to her maternal grandfather, a Cosconius Gallus nowhere on attestation.

(2) The enigmatic L. Seius Tubero (*suff.* 18). Following Borghesi, to be taken as a son (by blood) of Strabo. It was unfortunate that Cichorius, like some scholars in the sequel, was not moved to explain the *cognomen*.

(3) Q. Junius Blaesus, consul suffect in 10, proconsul of Africa and 'vir triumphalis': styled by Tacitus three times the 'avunculus' of Aelius Seianus.[20] That is, at first sight his mother's brother. Hence a difficulty. But not insuperable since the term can denote the husband of an aunt. A useful parallel availed.[21] Blaesus, it follows, married a sister of Cosconia.

Erudite and ingenious, lucid and candid, the exposition of Cichorius enjoyed a long fortune, being endorsed by Stein and in the essential by Groag.[22] The latter scholar, it is true, added a slight embellishment. That is to say, bringing Junius Blaesus closer to his nephew Aelius Seianus: as the half-brother of his mother Cosconia instead of merely the husband of her sister.[23] Dissent was slow to find expression.

A paradox was also waiting to be declared. The more that is discovered about persons of note at Rome, the more marriages come to light or have to be postulated. Yet adepts of prosopography were shown inadvertent. Confronted with kinsmen of Aelius Seianus, they failed to invoke two wives for his parent, still less three.

It was not until the year 1955 that a hypothesis brought up an additional wife for Seius Strabo, namely an Aelia.[24] Not an Aelia Galla: that family was already accounted for by the standard assumption that L. Aelius Seianus owed his *gentilicium* to adoption by L. Aelius Gallus, the second in the sequence of prefects of Egypt.[25] Instead, an Aelia of the aristocratic Tuberones.

[18] C. Cichorius, *Hermes* **XXXIX** (1904), 461 ff.

[19] He added two consular Lentuli, viz. Cossus and P. Cornelius Scipio.

[20] *Ann.* III.35.2; 72.4; IV.26.1.

[21] Seneca, *Ad Helviam* 17.3: the husband of his aunt, i.e. C. Galerius, who in 16 succeeded Seius Strabo in Egypt.

[22] Stein, *RE* IIA (1921), 1125 f. and in *PIR*[2] A 255 (1933); Groag, *PIR*[2] C 1993 f.

[23] See the stemma in *PIR*[2] *Pars* II, facing p. 328. Adopted in *Rom. Rev.* (1939), 384, cf. Table VI; and not rejected in *Tacitus* (1958), 384 f.

[24] F. Adams, *AJP* LXXVI (1955), 70 ff. (stemma on p. 75).

[25] *PIR*[2] A 179, where he appears as 'M.(?) Aelius Gallus'. Rather 'L.', cf. A. Stein, o.c. 16 f. That he adopted Strabo's son was denied by D. Hennig, *L. Aelius Seianus* (1975), 17.

The new hypothesis was attractive.[26] It gave lodgement to L. Seius Tubero (*suff.* 18), as a half-brother to Seianus; and his stepmother was assumed sister to two Aelii, the consuls of 11 BC and AD 4 (on whom see further below). However, to fit in Seius Tubero in this fashion as a son of Seius Strabo imported a novelty. He must have kept and borne the maternal *cognomen*. Not inconceivable, and not without parallel.

Interest in the pedigree and connections of Seianus thus revived. After a short interval a radical revision was promulgated.[27] It rejected outright Strabo's marriage to an Aelia: the nomenclature of Seius Tubero is better explained as the consequence of an adoption.[28] Next, the wife of Strabo and the mother of Seianus. She is a Junia, and that for two reasons. First, Junius Blaesus (*suff.* 10) is styled 'avunculus' of Seianus. Second, Seianus' young daughter was called 'Iunilla', as disclosed by a fragment of the *Fasti Ostienses*.[29] Finally, one wife only for Seius Strabo, namely Junia. Cosconia Gallitta is to be disallowed. The inscription at Volsinii belongs not to Seius Strabo but to another Prefect of Egypt: C. Caecina Tuscus in the reign of Nero.[30]

The first two items in the revision seemed acceptable. As for the third, denying to Seius Strabo the Volsinii inscription, one careful scholar takes the case for proven.[31] Another likewise, and he goes so far as to argue that Seius Strabo was never Prefect of Egypt: he was sent there on a special mission.[32]

It is time to call a halt. Caecina Tuscus should not be allowed to pass, for all that Volsinii can show a L. Caecina, a senator of the early Augustan period.[33] Appeal was made to the *cognomen* 'Tuscus'. It does not in fact speak for one of the cities of Etruria as a man's *patria*; and it is not common in the region.[34] Rather the reverse, indicating the 'ultima origo', either remembered or asserted. The high frequency of 'Tuscus' among Spanish

[26] It was followed by R. Sealey in his detailed study, *Phoenix* XV (1961), 97 ff. See his table on p. 103. Further, approved in *Tacitus* (1958), 384, n. 4 (in reference to the two consular Aelii on the stemma proposed by F. Adams).

[27] G. V. Sumner, *Phoenix* XIX (1965), 134 ff., with table on p. 137.

[28] Sumner, o.c. 142 f. Seius Tubero was there supposed a cousin (not attested) of the consuls of 11 BC and AD 4. On that conjecture, however, the link with Seianus becomes tenuous indeed. A better solution will emerge.

[29] *FO* Vd (first published in 1931). The statements in *PIR*[2] J 738 and 853 are confused. In the latter item Junilla's mother is styled the 'altera uxor' of Seius Strabo.

[30] *PIR*[2] C 109.

[31] R. Seager, *Tiberius* (1972), 179, n. 6.

[32] D. Hennig, *L. Aelius Seianus* (1975), 7 ff. On his showing, Strabo married first an Aelia of the Tuberones, next Junia, the sister of Blaesus (ib. 15).

For the other consequences about Strabo, observe the doubt expressed by B. Levick, *Tiberius the Politician* (1976), 273: 'if he was Prefect of Egypt'.

[33] *CIL* I[2]. 2515, cf. *PIR*[2] C 96.

[34] Apart from L. Dasumius Tullius Tuscus (*suff.* 152), there is only *CIL* XI. 1810 (Saena); 7297 (Volsinii).

Romans has not escaped notice.[35] The region and city of Caecina Tuscus
therefore defies ascertainment. Transpadane Italy is not excluded.[36]

Moreover, a vital fact had been neglected. As Suetonius reports, this
man's mother was the 'nutrix' of Nero.[37] Now the Prefect of Egypt on the
inscription had for mother Terentia A. f., and he married a lady of the
patrician Cornelii. Identity with Caecina Tuscus becomes dubious—and
to be discarded forthwith.

Nothing debars Seius Strabo. Reversion to Cichorius on this point now
entails useful consequences. First, his mother Terentia keeps her
significance, and his son Seianus is the grandnephew of personages notable
in the early Augustan years. Second, Cosconia Gallitta, Strabo's wife
attested in 15 or 16, but now seen for various reasons not to be the mother
of Seianus. Third, Seianus' link with Cornelii Lentuli becomes tenuous,
being reduced to his stepmother.[38] Later on, it is worth noting, Seianus in
his ascension managed to betroth his son to a daughter of Gaetulicus.[39]

Cosconia redeemed, attention can now concentrate on the earlier wife,
or wives, of Seius Strabo. For the mother of Seianus, a Junia enjoys the
prime claim, as has been shown. In addition, an Aelia might be brought
into play. Once again, the nomenclature of L. Seius Tubero (*suff*. 18) crops
up. Adoptions tend to occur in groups already related as well as congenial.
On that notion, Tubero may be, not a son of Strabo, but adoptive: that is,
his wife's nephew. If that notion be given up, the Tuberonian connection
still acquires importance in the search for consular brothers and cousins of
Aelius Seianus.[40]

One is left with Junia, the presumed mother of Seianus. According to
Velleius, his 'maternum genus' embraced houses of high and ancient
distinction. How could that be, one is impelled to ask, since she is the sister
of the *novus homo* Q. Junius Blaesus (*suff*. 10), of unascertained parentage?
Appeal to the unattested mother of Blaesus (perhaps aristocratic, perhaps
an Aelia of the Tuberones), that seems hardly enough.

The present discussion has operated so far with two wives, or even
three. The converse was lost to sight. That is, repeated marriages of a
woman. They sometimes furnish a remarkable nexus. The prime

---

[35] Out of a total of 38, no fewer than 23 in *CIL* II, according to I. Kajanto, *The Latin Cognomina*
(1965), 188. For 'Tuscillus', *Ancient Society* XIII (1982/3), 250.

[36] Thus A. Caecina Alienus, of Vicetia (Tacitus, *Hist*. III, 8.1).

[37] Suetonius, *Nero* 35.5. She was styled 'Graeco-Oriental' by A. Momigliano in *CAH* X (1934),
727.

[38] That is, the sister of Maluginensis (*suff*. 10). Possibly a daughter, as assumed by B. Levick,
Tiberius the Politician (1977), Table D at end.

[39] *Ann*. VI. 30.2.

[40] Apart from the 'duo Blaesi,' the sons of the 'vir triumphalis' (*Ann*. VI.40.2). The elder was
suffectus in 26; and there is a fair chance that his brother held the *fasces* in 28. On which, *ZPE* 43
(1981), 373 = *RP* III (1984), 1432.

specimen is the six husbands of Vistilia in the mid–Augustan years.[41] Or again, that Plautia, nowhere named, whose three husbands link a group of families in the close vicinity of the Emperor Hadrian.[42]

Hence a second paradox in the long and intricate controversy. A solution along that line has only recently been propounded.[43] Briefly, as follows. Junia, the first wife of Seius Strabo, had previously been married to Q. Aelius Tubero, the jurist and historian, herself presumed second wife (the first was Sulpicia). Therefore, in the first instance Seius Tubero finds an explanation: Strabo adopted the stepson he acquired through marrying Junia.

Other names come in; and the Tuberones call for a brief disquisition for sundry reasons, among them the tradition of Roman jurisprudence, perpetuated less by doctrine than by men and families.

Of the Tuberones, the earliest on record are a praetor in 201 BC and a tribune in 194. It is not known in what relation they stood to other Aelii of the time, notably P. Aelius Paetus, consul in the former year, and his brother Sex. Aelius Paetus Catus, consul in 198. The latter earned fame for science of the law; and indeed Cicero employs 'Sextus Aelius' as the mark and type of a jurist.[44]

The last consulate of that line falls in 167. In that season belongs Q. Aelius Tubero, who married a daughter of the great Aemilius Paullus.[45] His son, thereby a nephew of Scipio Aemilianus, came into notoriety during the Gracchan seditions, conspicuous for frugality, integrity, and addiction to the teachings of the Stoics. No orator, rather a jurist, and failing the praetorship despite his ancestry.[46]

There is a gap in the next generation. It might be supplied by C. Aelius Tubero, the senator of praetorian rank who was rescued living from the funeral pyre.[47] Clarity resumes with L. Tubero and his son Quintus. Baffled in his prosecution of Q. Ligarius, Quintus abandoned eloquence and turned to the study of the law. With that refuge, and with the writing

[41] Pliny, *NH* VII.39. For her marriages, C. Cichorius, *Römische Studien* (1922), 429 ff.; R. Syme, *JRS* LX (1970), 27 ff. = *RP* (1979), 805 ff.

[42] For a revised stemma, *Athenaeum* XXXV (1957), 306 ff. = *RP* (1979), 325 ff. Plautia, wife to three consulars in turn, was the mother of Aelius Caesar.

[43] B. Levick, o.c. (1976), Table D. Though not supported by argument, the solution is excellent.
In comment on Velleius II.127.3, A. J. Woodman in his edition (1977) eschewed all discussion of the problems, referring merely to the papers of Sumner and Adams (in that order). Nor was *ILS* 8966 cited.

[44] Cicero, *De r.p.* III. 33: 'neque est quaerendus explanator aut interpres Sextus Aelius, nec erit alia lex Romae, alia Athenis.'

[45] *Brutus* 117. Tubero was named by Livy, who missed the relationship (XLV. 7.1; 8.8). For his frugality, Val Max. IV.3.7; Pliny, *NH* XXXIII. 142. Cf. above, p. 17.

[46] *Pro Murena* 76, cf. *Brutus* 117: 'itaque honoribus maiorum respondere non potuit'. Cicero can even style him 'nobilissima in familia . . . natus' (*De r.p.* I.31).

[47] Pliny, *NH* VII.173 (on the report of Messalla Rufus).

of archaic history for further consolation, Q. Tubero was able, like others, to pass unscathed through the age of tribulation. He survived into the years of peace: Dionysius of Halicarnassus dedicated to him a treatise on the historian Thucydides.[48]

Tubero had found a suitable wife, a Sulpicia: daughter of the great lawyer Ser. Sulpicius Rufus (*cos.* 51), who retrieved from obscurity the renown of a patrician house.[49] What Tubero could not acquire for himself accrued with his sons, Q. Tubero holding the *fasces* in 11 BC, Sex. Aelius Catus in AD 4.[50] The nomenclature he chose for the second son is instructive. It apes the consul of 198, in the intent to convey descent from him. In consonance therewith, Catus himself went on to revive the *cognomen* of these consular Aelii: he called his daughter 'Aelia Paetina'.[51]

Two consular sons. But there was also a daughter. She married L. Cassius Longinus (*suff.* AD 11), whose grandfather was a cousin of C. Cassius the tyrannicide.[52] From this match issued L. Cassius Longinus, consul in 30 with M. Vinicius for colleague (and like him soon to marry a princess). In that year, under instigation from Seianus, he denounced in the Senate Drusus (the second son of Germanicus Caesar).[53] In sharp contrast stands his brother Gaius, the suffect consul, who gave his name to a school of law. His character drew admiration from the historian Tacitus.[54]

So far relevance to the annals of Roman jurisprudence. The central theme is social history and family alliances. The two consular Aelii in the time of Augustus had a patrician mother. They are patently aristocratic, and they assert, so it appears, a consular ancestry.[55] Furthermore, like sons of the *nobiles*, Q. Tubero (*cos.* 11 BC) acquires a priesthood at an early age. He was one of the *quindecimviri* who superintended the *Ludi Saeculares*.[56] Let it be assumed that the sons of the jurist benefited from that prepossession, acceding to the *fasces* at thirty-two, or not long after.

---

[48] To the jurist, not to his consular son, cf. *PIR*[2] A 274; G. W. Bowersock, *Augustus and the Greek World* (1965), 130. Stein had preferred the son (in D 102). It was unfortunate that the father missed an entry in *PIR*[2].

[49] Tubero's marriage, and that of his daughter, are disclosed in the *Digest*. Registering C. Cassius Longinus (*suff.* 30) it states 'natus ex filia Tuberonis quae fuit neptis Servi Sulpicii' (I.2.47). Like her father, this Aelia failed to qualify for *PIR*[2]. Observe that two more daughters of the jurist are now conjectured, viz. a wife for Seius Strabo, a wife, or perhaps mother, for Junius Blaesus (*suff.* 10).

[50] *PIR*[2] A 274; 157.

[51] *PIR*[2] A 305. The second wife of Claudius, the brother of Germanicus.

[52] Thus *PIR*[2] C 502.

[53] Dio LVIII.3.8.

[54] *Ann.* XII.12.1 (in choice Sallustian language).

[55] They appear to influence writers in the sequel, in a double fashion. For Valerius Maximus, the son-in-law of Aemilius Paullus is 'Q. Tubero cognomine Catus'; and he assumed him a consul (IV.3.7). Pliny, narrating the same anecdote, about his frugality, calls him 'Catus Aelius' (*NH* XXXIII. 142). No Aelius Catus is discoverable between the consuls of 198 BC and AD 4.

[56] *ILS* 5050, l. 152.

The assumption is helpful when an estimate is sought about ages, or conjecture about marriages. To proceed therefore. Q. Tubero's birth may fall *c*.44, that of Sex. Catus *c*.30. Fourteen years separate their consular dates—which does not however preclude the same mother. Q. Tubero's sister is stated to be a daughter of Sulpicia. That fact limits her age at one end, the existence of her sons at the other. The two Cassii (consuls in AD 30), may have seen the light of day *c*.4 BC. Her own birth does not permit a close conjecture. However, hardly as much as twenty years later than that of her brother Tubero, and perhaps *c*.27.[57]

On the new and recent hypothesis, the parent survives long enough to take a second wife. The corollaries are as follows. The jurist loses Sulpicia about the year 26, contracts a marriage (with Junia), but dies not long after, leaving a son. Junia then passes to Seius Strabo. He adopts that son, who becomes L. Seius Tubero.[58] This man came to the *fasces* in AD 18, when aged about forty-two. Seius Tubero is thus older than Strabo's own son, but only by a year or two: the birth of Seianus is generally put in the period 23–20.[59]

The foregoing reconstruction, albeit hazardous, appears to be the best way to deal with the consequences issuing from the postulate of two husbands for Junia: first Aelius Tubero, then Seius Strabo. Furthermore, to Strabo has been restored the second wife, namely Cosconia Gallitta, denied by several scholars in the recent time. At the end therefore a question has to be asked. How does the reconstruction accord with the testimony of Velleius, generously equipping Seianus with 'consularis fratres, consobrinos'? At least four cousins, but only one brother, it has to be conceded. The chance subsists of a new inscription emerging to augment knowledge or import perturbations.

On October 18 of the year 31 the 'verbosa et grandis epistula' arrived from Capreae, announcing the doom of Caesar's minister and loyal friend. A few days later ensued the gruesome extinction of his children. The *Fasti Ostienses* disclose their names: Strabo, Dec. Capito Aelianus, Junilla.[60]

Junilla reflects and confirms the family name of her grandmother. Capito Aelianus comes as a surprise, but not a problem. He had been adopted. Perhaps by C. Fonteius Capito (*cos*. 12). Better, by C. Ateius Capito (*suff*. 5), the eminent and subservient jurist who terminated his

---

[57] In passing, it may be noted that the ages presumed for Aelia and for her consular sons make it unlikely that her brother Quintus (*cos*. 11 BC) was born much before 44 BC.

[58] This appears the easiest explanation of Seius Tubero. The stemma proposed by Miss Levick (Table D) gave the jurist and Junia another son, namely Sex. Aelius Catus (*cos*. AD 4). But Catus cannot be born later than 30 BC. Hence a son of Sulpicia.

[59] *Ann*. IV. 1.2: 'prima iuventa C. Caesarem, divi Augusti nepotem, sectatus'.

[60] *FO* V d.

long life in 22.[61] As for Strabo, the eldest, he is now supposed identical with a certain Aelius Gallus mentioned by Tacitus.[62]

In the near aftermath of Seianus' end Pomponius Secundus incurred danger through 'Aelii Galli amicitia'.[63] Following Borghesi, the belief obtained for a long time that Gallus was the son of Seianus, and the elder son.[64] But that belief has encountered a firm denial. Rather a relative, of some kind not specified.[65]

One reverts for guidance to L. Aelius Gallus, the adopting parent of Aelius Seianus. His parentage and extraction have failed to excite curiosity, for all that the last epoch of the Republic exhibits C. Aelius Gallus, who wrote two books on the meanings of words 'quae ad ius civile pertinent'.[66] This man earns no mention in the *Digest*, no place on the roll of jurists.[67] Yet those studious pursuits became appropriate, if he could claim kinship, even if distant or disputable, with jurisprudent Aelii. In a past age that *gens* had been notoriously prolific.[68] Gallus, it follows, may derive from an old senatorial family.[69] The Tuberones, it will be recalled, forfeited high distinction after the known and notorious grandson of Aemilius Paullus.

Aelius Gallus, the Prefect of Egypt, left no ascertained male descendants. He might have lost a son in the early Augustan years. Propertius devotes a poem to Paetus who perished at sea, on a voyage to Egypt.[70] The *cognomen* 'Paetus' is not uncommon. But, as has been shown, the Tuberones annexed it, ambitious to recall the archetypal jurist.

However that may be, the same poet, who was sparing in references to named contemporaries, brings on an Aelia Galla, whom her husband Postumus abandoned for the lure of campaigns in the Orient: Postumus is generally held identical with the senator C. Propertius Postumus.[71]

As for Aelia Galla, nothing precludes a daughter or niece of the Prefect.

---

[61] *Ann.* III.75 (the obituary notice contrasting him with another jurist, the unimpeachable Antistius Labeo).

[62] Sumner, o.c. 141: 'Aelius Gallus must be Seianus' elder son.'

[63] *Ann.* V.8.1.

[64] *PIR*[1] A 134.

[65] *PIR*[2] A 178: 'filius certe non fuit'.

[66] Gellius XVI.5.3. Cf. *RE* I. 492 f.

[67] Aelius Gallus is nowhere named by W. Kunkel, *Herkunft u. soziale Stellung der r. Juristen* (1952).

[68] Val. Max IV.4.8. He dilates upon the 'Aelia familia', sixteen of them, 'quibus una domuncula' and 'unus in agro Veiente fundus'. Hardly the old consular family, rather the frugal and virtuous Tuberones.

[69] As suggested in *History in Ovid* (1978), 101. That discussion bore upon the aristocratic Gallus in Propertius I.5.23 f. Not Cornelius Gallus, the first Prefect of Egypt, as some incautiously assume. Better perhaps a son of L. Caninius Gallus (*cos.* 37 BC).

[70] Propertius III.5. Extolling poetry and love against profit, the author alleges money as the motive for the journey.

[71] Propertius III.12; *ILS* 914 (Rome).

A brother may likewise be surmised.[72] That is, grandfather to the Aelius Gallus disclosed in the pages of Tacitus.

The historian rebuked Livia Julia, the wife of Drusus Caesar, for succumbing to the embraces of a 'municipalis adulter'. Style and drama evoke violent language.[73] Was the author insensitive to the social distinction accruing to the Roman knight on the maternal side, or even ignorant? That does not follow. About some families that died out long before his own time, Cornelius Tacitus was guilty of error or inadvertence, it is true.[74] But this careful composer tends to reserve certain facts until they become relevant. As concerns Aelius Seianus, the missing narration in Book V of the *Annales* must be reckoned with. It carried various information about persons and families. For example, the parentage of Piso the Pontifex.[75]

Seius Tubero had been named twice.[76] Q. Tubero (*cos.* 11 BC), apart from his priesthood, happens to be only a consular date: perhaps (though not for certain) failing long survival. Of Sex. Aelius Catus there is no sign subsequent to his consulship. That is, unless the conjecture be held valid that his command on the lower Danube belongs in 9–11, for a brief tenure.[77]

Ancient and reputable, the Tuberones after defeats and vicissitudes reached the consulate in the end. As with other families old or new, their dignity soon lapsed. No more consuls or even attested senators. Curiosity is aroused and baffled by L. Aelius Tubero, holding in 23 a magistracy in a Campanian town.[78]

The tale terminates with a picturesque item of a kind that the consular historian disdained. In the year 59 a lady of birth and wealth exhibited her talents as a dancer before Nero, at the festival of the *Juvenalia*: she was Aelia Catella, at the age of eighty.[79]

---

[72] C. Aelius Gallus receives a dedication at Athens (*IG* II.[2] 4117, cf., for the dating, 4181). Perhaps the author discussed above, perhaps a brother of L. Aelius Gallus, the Prefect of Egypt.

[73] *Ann.* IV.3.4: 'atque illa cui avunculus Augustus, socer Tiberius, ex Druso liberi, seque ac maiores et posteros municipali adultero foedabat.'

[74] As notably about the Antonia who married Ahenobarbus (IV.44.2; XII.64.2).

[75] cf. *Ann.* VI.10.3. Eminent aristocrats such as M. Lepidus or Cossus Lentulus should have had a mention.

[76] *Ann.* II.20.1; IV.29.1.

[77] His operations are attested only in Strabo VII, p. 303. Whether a praetorian legate or consular, *PIR*[2] A 157 leaves the question open. See *Danubian Papers* (1971), 53; 69; 71. For a tenure of the Moesian command *c.* 9–11, *History in Ovid* (1978), 69. That is, between Caecina Severus and Poppaeus Sabinus.

[78] *CIL* X.895 = *ILS* 6934 (Pompeii), cf. *PIR*[2] A 273. Aristocrats are not common in that function—and Pompeii lacked prestige. A descendant of jurists may have subsided into a life of leisure.

[79] Dio LXI. 19.2. Not old enough for Pliny's rubric which records two centenarian actresses (*NH* VII.158). Aelia Catella is assumed a daughter of Sex. Aelius Catus, hence sister of Aelia Paetina (*PIR*[2] A 289). Perhaps not, if Catus (*cos.* 4) was born *c*.30 BC.

Not Lentuli but Tuberones, that was Seianus' closest attachment to aristocratic families. A single name reveals it, Seius Tubero, whatever be the precise identity of his parent. In 24 a rash and foolish prosecutor linked him in an indictment with Lentulus the Augur, both 'intimi amici' of the ruler.[80] Lentulus was very old, dying the next year; and Seius, 'defecto corpore', is not heard of in the sequel.

The catastrophe of Seianus destroyed Junius Blaesus.[81] Five years later his sons in despair committed suicide.[82] The elder had been consul suffect in 26, and a place for the younger could be found in 28.[83]

A conjecture of a different nature may now be imported. A Junius Blaesus in the next generation boasted Antonian ancestry. On the easiest explanation, one of the 'duo Blaesi' married Domitia, the elder daughter of Ahenobarbus.[84] The match would have the approbation of Ti. Caesar. Not that he liked the Domitii: an inconspicuous marriage would help to abate their pretensions.

Ti. Caesar had been victim long since to an infatuation with his minister. In public pronouncements styling him 'socius laborum', the ruler encouraged Seianus to extend his patronage, with consulates and provinces for friends and adherents. Thus the historian Tacitus, referring to a quite early stage.[85] The poet who described the fall of Seianus duly brings out this aspect of 'potentia': 'illi summas donare curules | illum exercitibus praeponere'.[86] Whether the favourite was in fact often conceded a hand in the allocation of consulates is subject to question and strong doubt. For *nobiles* at least, many were predictable and not to be denied or even deferred by a sagacious ruler. As concerns the seven armed commands in the portion of Caesar, the practice of extended tenures had been going on for a long time. As for Syria and Tarraconensis, the consular legates were detained at Rome.[87]

One of the legates belonged to the high aristocracy. Lentulus Gaetulicus went out in 29 to Germania Superior. His son was betrothed to the infant daughter of Seianus. Gaetulicus stayed on unmolested as long as the ruler lived. Hence a peculiar anecdote.[88]

The Prefect of the Guard pursued a steady ascension. At the beginning of 29 the widow of Germanicus and Nero (the eldest son) were taken into

---

[80] *Ann.* IV.29.1.
[81] V.7.2.
[82] VI.40.2.
[83] cf. *ZPE* 43 (1981), 373 = *RP* III (1984), 1432.
[84] Ch. XII.
[85] *Ann.* IV.2.3.
[86] Juvenal X.91 f.
[87] viz. Aelius Lamia and L. Arruntius, since the year 23.
[88] *Ann.* VI.30.2 ff. (above, p. 179).

custody, Drusus in the next year. There remained Caligula and Ti. Gemellus (the son of Drusus Caesar). Boy princes again and an aged ruler—as in 2 BC, but a more alarming conjuncture. And once again, an Ahenobarbus stood in close vicinity to the succession. The old man died in 25, having previously left no trace in the *Annales* of Cornelius Tacitus.[89] The son, a grand-nephew of Caesar Augustus, married in 28 Agrippina, the eldest daughter of Germanicus.[90]

In 30 Tiberius was completing the seventy-first year of his life. He took the consulate for the next year, for the first time since 21, when he shared the *fasces* with his son. This time the colleague, by a startling and flagrant anomaly, was the Guard Prefect, no longer a minister but a regent, and soon usurping betrothal to a princess of the dynasty.[91]

In the spring of the year the ruler began to conceive doubt and hesitation, aroused at last to the logical consequence of his actions: his own supersession.[92] Vacating the consulate early in May, he compelled Seianus to do the same; and to fill his own place he appointed Faustus Sulla, the husband of Domitia Lepida (the younger sister of Ahenobarbus).[93]

Ti. Caesar was in a dire predicament. So was the high aristocracy. Many inclined towards Seianus, moved by various ambitions, by the manifest favour he engrossed, and by loyalty towards Tiberius, when even an enemy of Tiberius paid court, none other than Asinius Gallus.[94]

Of the ruler's close friends and coevals, few indeed survived. None the less, despite certain enmities, and despite the advantages he bestowed on new men, Ti. Caesar retained strong support among the *nobilitas*. The Lentuli, as usual, were cautious. Lentulus the Augur had recently ended his days, but Cossus kept the confidence of the ruler. He had intervened to block an indictment against L. Arruntius.[95]

Tiberius honoured all through an allegiance to the cause of the Republic and to the families of the vanquished. Depressed and obscure for the most part, or unobtrusive, some became perceptible in the last decade of Caesar Augustus; they formed alliances and were now gathering strength. Thus Crassus Frugi, consul in 27, the husband of a Scribonia.[96]

The long slow plot devised by Caesar against his minister and dear friend matured in sharp and savage action in October of the year 31. The next

---

[89] IV.44.1 f.

[90] IV.75 (the ominous conclusion to the book).

[91] For her identity (the widow of Drusus Caesar or her daughter) see Ch. XIII.

[92] As the ruler himself observed in sharp rebuke of a senator, a careless spendthrift: 'sero experrectus es' (Seneca, *Epp.* 122.10).

[93] *PIR*[2] C 1459.

[94] Dio LVIII.3. 1. On the political allies of Seianus see H. W. Bird, *Latomus* XXVIII (1969), 63 ff.

[95] Dio LVIII.8.3, cf. *PIR*[2] A 1330. Above, p. 268.

[96] Ch. XX.

consuls were Domitius Ahenobarbus and Arruntius Camillus. It would be worth knowing when they were designated. They might have replaced a pair that the turn of events showed undesirable. On Arruntius accrued one group in the descendance from Sulla and Pompeius.[97] In 33 the *ordinarii* are Sulla Felix (the brother of Faustus) and Ser. Sulpicius Galba.

Transmission of the power through the line of Julii and Claudii had become precarious. The boys (Caligula and Ti. Gemellus) might have no long survival. The nearest was the dreadful Ahenobarbus, 'omni parte vitae detestabilis.'[98]

The principate began in war and was maintained through matrimonial compacts, in spite of repeated deaths. Luck or accident or an armed proclamation might put it into competition again, with another ruler, of necessity from the high aristocracy. Perhaps even patrician, although few exhibited distinction or courage, apart perhaps from Lentulus Gaetulicus. Several houses had been enlisted into close alliance by Caesar Augustus. In the sequel, descendants of the great dynasts evoked sharper suspicion and fear.

[97] Ch. XIX.
[98] Suetonius, *Nero* 5.1.

XXIII

Quinctilius Varus

When Caesar Augustus set himself to revive decayed families of the ancient patriciate, the first specimen exhibited by the *Fasti* of the resplendent decade was a Quinctilius. He could even be styled 'inlustri magis quam nobili ortus familia'.[1] The comment was not unfair. In the conception of the Romans, 'nobilitas' depends on consulates. The sole and last consul of that family had been two years antecedent to the Decemvirs.

Several Quinctilii are on casual attestation during the last epoch of the Republic.[2] Not all of them are easy to sort out and attach. Three had 'Sextus' for *praenomen*. The first was a *pontifex*, present at the lavish sacerdotal banquet offered in the vicinity of the year 69 by the *flamen Martialis* Lentulus Niger.[3] No other activity finds record. Next, the praetor of 57, who went to Hispania Ulterior as proconsul. Third, the quaestor of 49, who fought on the side of Pompeius and the Republic. After the stricken field of Philippi he staged his end in pomp and dignity.[4]

Of his son Publius, as with other coeval orphans, nurture and boyhood are a blank. No relatives on either side of the family can be discovered or surmised. He emerges as one of the ruler's two quaestors, attested by a dedication on the island of Tenos.[5] In 22 Caesar Augustus set out on a peregrination of the Greek lands which lasted for three years. During that season Paullus Fabius Maximus (*cos.* 11) was likewise *quaestor Augusti*, a young aristocrat already in high favour.[6] In that post Claudius Nero (born in 42) got ahead of them, in 23, through a special dispensation.[7]

In 13 Quinctilius Varus shared the *fasces* with Claudius Nero. The consuls were brothers-in-law. Not in itself surprising, the fact has come to light recently. A papyrus reveals it, carrying a fragment of the oration delivered at the funeral of Marcus Agrippa, who died in March of the following year.[8]

[1] Velleius II.117.2.

[2] For the detail, H. G. Gundel, *RE* XXIV. 898 ff. To his stemma is attached, albeit with a query, Quinctilius Varus Cremonensis. The two adjuncts to the name occur only in scholiasts or the like. See now, discussing *Odes* I.24 (and also 18), Nisbet and Hubbard in their *Commentary* (1970).

[3] Macrobius III.13.11. For date and participants, L. R. Taylor, *AJP* LXIII (1942), 385 ff.

[4] Velleius II.71.3: 'cum se insignibus honorum velasset'.

[5] *ILS* 8812.   [6] *IG*² II.4130.

[7] Further, perhaps *quaestor Aug.*, as argued by E. Badian, *Mnem.* XXVII (1974), 160 ff. Against, D. C. Chandler, *Historia* XXVII (1978), 331 f. Cf. also B. Levick, *Tiberius the Politician* (1976), 20.

[8] *Kölner Pap.* I.10, cf. above, p. 153.

Daughters of Agrippa, that is a question—and a story. Information of unique value is furnished by the biography of Pomponius Atticus, the banker and Epicurean. Rather late in life he decided to take a wife.[9] His daughter, Caecilia Attica, saw the light of day in 51; and in 37, so it is generally held, she was consigned in matrimony to Agrippa. Old Atticus passed away in the year before the Battle of Actium, having witnessed the betrothal of an infant daughter of Agrippa to Claudius Nero.[10] The match with Vipsania was no doubt consummated soon after Nero's return from the East in 19.

No other daughters of Agrippa and Caecilia Attica are on record. One can be postulated as a bride for the orator Haterius.[11] Perhaps another for Quinctilius Varus.

Agrippa's marriage terminated in 29 or 28. A notice in Suetonius supplies a clue.[12] The freedman Caecilius Epirota gave literary instruction to Attica. Their relations being incriminated, Epirota fled to Egypt to take refuge with Cornelius Gallus. The item illustrates the perils and vicissitudes in a scholar's life—and a theme less often documented, the education of Roman matrons. Also divorce for reasons of state, not always invoking misconduct or sterility. In the year 28 Marcus Agrippa married a niece of the Princeps, namely the elder Marcella: born probably in 43.[13]

Therefore a bride can be produced for Varus, a daughter not of Attica but of Marcella—and a very recent bride. Fortune or favour did more for Varus than for Claudius Nero.[14]

There are further consequences. Aspiring to some heiress or princess, a young nobleman might have to wait until she became nubile. When Fabius Maximus received an ode from Horace, he had not yet acquired Marcia, the cousin of Caesar Augustus. But it would be an anomaly verging on folly or scandal if an ambitious *nobilis* of patrician stock eschewed until his consulship the 'decus ac robur' conferred by matrimony. For Quinctilius Varus an earlier marriage should be looked for, contracted in the vicinity of the year 23.

Evidence appeared to hand. A passage in Josephus showed a son of Varus commanding a body of troops from the army of Syria early in 4 BC.[15] Confidence was premature. Inspection of these transactions in the historian's earlier work discloses a friend of Varus, not a son.[16] Emendation

---

[9] Opulent and cherished in high society, Atticus could aspire no less than Marcus Agrippa to 'nuptiae generosarum'. He selected however a Pilia (not named by Nepos). Observe P. Peilius, a censor at ancient Cora (*CIL* I². 1509).

[10] Nepos, *Vita Attici* 19.4: 'vix annicula'.

[11] Ch. XI.

[12] Suetonius, *De gramm.* 16.

[13] Ch. XI.

[14] i.e. on the hypothesis or assumption that the bride was not a granddaughter of Pomponius Atticus (cf. above, p. 146).

[15] Josephus, *AJ* XVIII.288, cf. *PIR*¹ Q 27.   [16] *BJ* II.68.

is applied to the text. The officer was somebody else, perhaps a nephew of the governor.[17]

None the less, the assumption of an earlier wife remains valid—and baffles conjecture. A kinswoman of the Appuleii would be suitable: before the year 20 Sextus (*cos.* 29) married a sister of Varus (see below).

As will become evident, Varus' marriage to Vipsania cannot have lasted for much more than a decade from his consulship. A third wife now comes in, reinforcing the dynastic link. She was Claudia Pulchra, certainly the daughter of a niece of Augustus. That is, this time the younger Marcella.[18] Nor is the Claudian father a mystery: Messalla Appianus. This man died in 12, in the early weeks of his consulship. He left a son, an infant rather, as may be deduced through an intricate line of argument.[19] Claudia Pulchra may also have been very young, despite the age of her mother, who was born early in 39. Further, there is a chance that Messalla Appianus was not the first husband of Marcella.

On that showing, Pulchra was still in the prime of life when she succumbed to a prosecution in AD 26.[20] She bore Varus a son. An anecdote discloses his age and thus indicates (though not with precision) the season when the consular made the transition from Vipsania to Pulchra. An elderly and arrogant orator, Cestius Pius of Smyrna, administered a rebuke to young Varus, with pointed allusion to the fate of his father.[21] He was still only a boy ('praetextatus'), and he was betrothed to a daughter of Germanicus Caesar. There were three of them, Agrippina, Drusilla, Julia Livilla, born between 15 and 18. The youngest is generally taken for granted.[22] The son of Pulchra, it follows, can hardly have been born later than AD 4.

So far three wives for Quinctilius Varus. More fortunate than some of his coevals, he had several sisters, and when still a young man he made provision for them.

The first Quinctilia went to L. Nonius Asprenas, the son of a recent consul from a new family (*suff.* 36). He is styled a close friend of Caesar Augustus. Amity was put to the test when Asprenas faced indictment on a criminal charge, nothing less than poison: he gave a lavish banquet, and the guests perished, to the total of 130, so it was alleged.[23] The ruler expressed his concern in the Senate, appeared in court, but made no

---

[17] Thus W. John, *RE* XXIV. 965. He suggests a nephew of the governor, i.e. L. Nonius Asprenas (*suff.* AD 6), then serving as a military tribune.

[18] Ch. XI.

[19] i.e. Barbatus, of premature decease, the first husband of Domitia Lepida.

[20] *Ann.* IV.52 (defined as a cousin of Agrippina).

[21] Seneca, *Controv.* I.3.10: 'ista neglegentia pater tuus exercitum perdidit.'

[22] *PIR*² J 674.

[23] Pliny, *NH* XXXV. 164 etc. (above, p. 70).

statement. Asinius Pollio defended, while Cassius Severus led the prosecution, a savage orator hostile to birth and wealth. Asprenas gained an acquittal, but in any event forfeited a consulship.[24]

Next, the wife of the patrician Cornelius Dolabella. He too stood close to the Caesars. The Dictator appointed his father consul in 44: avid, pretentious and arrogant, with no sign of competence. Rather the reverse, and youthful, at an age without precedent or parallel. No writing of the time, or in the near sequel, even alludes to the anomaly. Surmise becomes legitimate.[25]

Dolabella's son turns up as a youthful nobleman in the company of Caesar's heir when Alexandria was captured: he conducted negotiations with the queen of Egypt.[26] Not heard of in the sequel, and missing the consulate, Dolabella was perhaps no longer among the living when Nonius Asprenas issued invitations to his festival. Hence one competitor the less for Quinctilius Varus and Fabius Maximus—or rather, for earlier consuls.[27]

Third, the wife of Sextus Appuleius Sex. f., the consul of 29. She came to knowledge not so long ago through a dedication set up when her husband was proconsul in Asia.[28] His extraction and person illustrate the variety and the vagaries of evidence. Suetonius was aware that the Princeps had a half-sister, namely the elder Octavia, daughter of an Ancharia.[29] The biographer's interest did not extend to her husband and her descendants. Sex. Appuleius managed to annex Octavia, himself an obscure person and not easily to be brought into connection with senatorial Appuleii, fairly numerous in this epoch. Luna is the *patria*, declared by the tombstone of his last descendant.[30]

An inscription found at Carthage offers revelations. Caesar the Dictator had adlected Appuleius among the patricians, he became a *flamen Julialis*, and at the end, after the rare honour of public obsequies, he found a resting place in the mausoleum of the Julii.[31]

His son Sextus should lead to Marcus, the consul of 20 (likewise 'Sex. f.'), at least on first inspection. That he was a younger brother, the standard

---

[24] Not identical with the *suffectus* of AD 6, as in *PIR*[1] N 93. Cf. Groag in *RE* XVI. 866 f.

[25] Like D. Brutus, not excluded as a son for Caesar, cf. *Historia* XXIX (1980), 435 = *RP* III (1984), 1248.

[26] Plutarch, *Antonius* 64. That he married a sister of Varus emerges from *Ann.* IV.66.2.

[27] That is, through age and quality. His son became consul in AD 10, therefore born not later than 24 BC.

[28] U. Weidemann, *Arch. Anzeiger* 1965, 450, whence *AE* 1966, 422.

[29] *Divus Aug.* 3.4.

[30] *ILS* 935: 'ultimo gentis suae'. The son of Sex. Appuleius (*cos.* AD 14) and Fabia Numantina.

[31] *ILS* 8963. Why at Carthage? Perhaps belonging to a public monument that honoured the *gens Augusta*.

Sex. Appuleius is detected (in 13 BC) as the old man among the four *flamines* in procession. Cf. E. Simon, *Ara Pacis Augustae* (1967), 17, with pl. 12. See above, p. 152.

acceptation denies. He is identified as M. Appuleius, quaestor in Asia in 45.[32] Hence, by the way, an elderly consul. Not an objection to be sure. Nevertheless, it is convenient (to use no stronger term) if the two consuls are taken for brothers.[33]

Of the younger man, no word subsequent to his consulship, and no wife or children discoverable. Sextus, however, had a son, who with Sex. Pompeius for colleague opened the terminal year of Caesar Augustus. The historian Dio registered the fact that both consuls were relatives of the Princeps—and Pompeius broke his leg in eager precipitance to join the funeral procession.[34] Of Sextus Pompeius, much more stands in the record.[35] His colleague may have had no long survival.[36]

Sex. Appuleius (*cos.* 29 BC), nephew to the ruler, is a character of note, not always conceded proper recognition in historical narrations or biographies. In 28 he went out to govern Spain, from which he celebrated a triumph in January of 26: the last from that country. Not long after, Sextus Appuleius is discovered as proconsul of Asia.[37] His tenure was biennial, like that of Potitus Messalla.[38] Either proconsul, or both, may therefore have covered 23 and 22, years of crisis for the new government. Finally, Appuleius was put in charge of Illyricum. A late document, but unimpeachable, attests him there in 8, hence in succession to Claudius Nero.[39] The next known legate is Domitius Ahenobarbus, the husband of Antonia.

The identity of Appuleius' wife might have been inferred from the name of his daughter, Appuleia Varilla, introduced in AD 17 as the grand-daughter of Augustus' sister.[40] A new inscription from Asia discloses her as the daughter of the proconsul.[41]

The third Quinctilia is welcome indeed. These alliances, contracted

---

[32] *PIR*[2] A 959; *MRR* II. 532; D. R. Shackleton Bailey on *Ad Att.* XII.13.2. On this man, and on other Appuleii of the time, see *Anatolian Studies . . . Buckler* (1938), 316 = *RP* (1979), 134 f.

[33] As in *Rom Rev.* (1939), 128, n. 4; 378. Adopted in the stemmata of G. V. Sumner, *Phoenix* XXV (1965), 362; U. Weidemann, o.c. (1965), 460.

[34] Dio LVI.29.5; 45.2.

[35] Ch. XXVIII. Pompeius' father, the nowhere attested son of the consul of 35, may well have had an Appuleia for wife.

[36] A 'Sex.[' was among the *Arvales* in 21 (*CIL* VI.2023b): not noted in *PIR*[2] A 962. To be identified as Sex. Appuleius in the view of J. Scheid, *Les Frères Arvales* (1975), 129. No evidence shows him still extant. Rather therefore Sex. Pompeius.

[37] On several inscriptions. One, without the title, honours his mother Octavia as sister to Augustus (*ILS* 8783: Pergamum). A recent document from Ephesus (*AE* 1966, 425) has caused some perplexity. To be assigned to Sex. Appuleius (*cos.* 14), according to F. Millar, *JRS* LVI (1966), 162. Doubt can be entertained.

[38] Revealed by an unpublished inscription from Claros: cited by U. Weidemann, o.c. 463 f.

[39] Cassiodorus, *Chron. Min.* II.135.

[40] *Ann.* II.50.1. In this affair no husband or father is mentioned,

[41] U. Weidemann, o.c. 450, whence *AE* 1966, 422.

That Varilla's mother was a Quinctilia had in fact been divined long ago by O. Hirschfeld, *Kl. Schr.* (1913), 87.

between 30 and 25 (so it may be presumed), lent support to the ascension of Varus. In due course they produced four consular nephews, viz. L. Nonius Asprenas (*suff.* AD 6), Sex. Nonius Quinctilianus (*cos.* 8), P. Cornelius Dolabella (10), Sex. Appuleius (14).

Varus acquired a priesthood before his consulship: he was either a *pontifex* or an augur.[42] Further, both Varus and Appuleius would have brought suitable adornment to that select company, the Arval Brethren.[43]

The consuls of 13 superintended public ceremonies advertising the return of the Princeps from Spain and Gaul. The event was also commemorated by the *Ara Pacis Augustae*. Furthermore, the government took decisions of moment concerning military and foreign policy. New ordinances now regulated pay for soldiers, and provision for veterans after the campaigns in prospect. The prime effort was the conquest of Illyricum, designed to round off the Empire in its central zone and win the route to the Balkan lands. It was a necessary task, begun by Agrippa before the year was out. Invasions of Germany were also to ensue.

The death of Marcus Agrippa at once brought the stepsons of the Princeps into high prominence. After the campaigns of 11 they received proconsular *imperium*. Claudius Nero had acceded to the *fasces* at the age of twenty-eight, with Drusus to enjoy the same privilege four years later. Exalting the pair, and intent on his dynastic policy, the ruler was at pains to devise honours and favours for other *nobiles*, notably those connected by blood or marriage. Several of them had a place in the processions exhibited on the *Ara Pacis*.[44]

The proconsulates of Asia and Africa stood in high prestige, and the five years' interval might be conveniently abridged. Hence youthful proconsuls. Ahenobarbus, consul in 16, went to Africa in 13;[45] and Fabius Maximus to Asia the year after his consulship.[46]

No more triumphs since 19, it is true. But aristocrats could now aspire to the *ornamenta triumphalia*, invented in 12 for the benefit of Claudius Nero. Moreover, consular commands in the 'provincia' of Caesar. Whereas hitherto the ruler had relied in the main on legates of praetorian rank, aristocratic ex-consuls now emerge, such as L. Piso (*cos.* 15) and Crassus Frugi (*cos.* 14).

Africa yielded triumphs in 22 and 19, but after the foray of Cornelius Balbus against the Garamantes in the far south, the African province lapses from record for a long space. Dio offers nothing until AD 6 when he

---

[42] *ILS* 88.
[43] Appuleius was enrolled among conjectural *Arvales* by J. Scheid, o.c. 60. But not Varus.
[44] Notably Ahenobarbus, following Drusus (Ch. XI).
[45] *ILS* 6095.
[46] Ch. XXVIII.

reports the Bellum Gaetulicum of Cossus Lentulus in a resumptive chapter, along with disturbances in other regions.[47] A similar procedure will be assumed for the missing years: for example Balkan and eastern transactions. In the interval Africa witnessed the campaign for which Passienus Rufus (*cos.* 4) earned the *ornamenta*.[48] The frontier zone, vague and vexed by the nomads, might see fighting at almost any time—and a second legion might be needed.

Between Crassus Frugi (9/8) and Cn. Piso (perhaps only three or four years subsequent to his consulship) belong three proconsuls of Africa, two of them known by the sole testimony of coins.[49] Varus is one of them. The coins, struck at the town of Acholla, display on the obverse the heads of Augustus and of two boys, on the reverse the head and the name of P. Quinctilius Varus. The boys (Gaius and Lucius) furnish a clue and suggest a date, namely the tenure 7/6. The princes came into noisy publicity in the first half of 6, with a clamour that Gaius be designated consul.[50] The Roman mob and artful agents anticipated the designs of the ruler, in premature zeal. They became open and flagrant a year later.

The tenure 7/6 therefore acquires favour.[51] The previous proconsular year is not excluded.[52] In the absence of one consul (Claudius Nero, *cos. II*), Gaius Caesar presided beside the colleague Cn. Piso at a public ceremony.[53] Which would not be lost upon an astute courtier like Quinctilius Varus.

Next, L. Volusius Q. f. Saturninus (*suff.* 12), with name and head on coins of Acholla and Hadrumetum. The Volusii were a family of old repute which had not risen above the praetorship; and Volusius for his consulship benefited from two deaths in an unhealthy year.

Volusius happens to be a first cousin of Claudius Nero, a fact not registered by any historian.[54] And something else. His wife was Nonia Polla, the sister of the Nonius Asprenas (not consular) who married a Quinctilia.[55] The son of Volusius (*suff.* AD 3) had a long survival, dying when *praefectus urbi* in the second year of Nero's reign at the age of ninety-three.[56] That fact indicates his own age, born about 60 BC, hence

---

[47] Dio LVI.28.

[48] Velleius II.116.2, cf. *ILS* 120: 'L. Passieno Rufo imperatore Africam obtinente'.

[49] M. Grant, *FITA* (1946), 228 ff.; B. E. Thomasson, *Die Statthalter der römischen Provinzen Nordafrikas von Augustus bis Diokletianus* II (1960), 13 ff. See also his summary list, *RE Supp.* XIII. 2. The coins of the three proconsuls are shown by J. M. C. Toynbee, *Roman Historical Portraits* (1978), 74 f. For the coins of Varus (four types), V. Zedelius, *Bonner Jahrbücher* CLXXXIII (1983), 469 ff.

[50] Dio LV.9.2 f.

[51] Thus Borghesi and most in the sequel, e.g. *PIR*[1] Q 27; W. John, *RE* XXIV. 909 ff.

[52] For Thomasson 'sehr wahrscheinlich' (*RE Supp.* XIII. 2). The aberrant date 4/3 was proposed by M. Grant, *FITA* (1946), 228. Cn. Piso (*cos.* 7) might belong there.

[53] Dio LV.8.3.

[54] Deduced from *Ad Att.* V.21.6, cf. *Rom. Rev.* 424.

[55] *OGIS* 468 (Pergamum).

[56] Pliny, *NH* VII.62; Tacitus, *Ann.* XIII.30.2.

coming late to the *fasces*.[57] Knowledge about the Volusii, it may be added, derives mostly from the historian Tacitus. When he decided to introduce obituary notices, the first of them was devoted to their first consul.[58]

The third proconsul of Africa is Africanus (*cos.* 10), of ostensible Scipionic descent, the younger brother of Paullus Fabius Maximus. Coins of Hadrumetum and of Hippo Diarrhytus carry his image and name, his title and priesthood.[59] But one type of the latter city has the legend 'Claudio Neroni Hippone libera'. The inference cannot be missed. No proconsul, no city would pay honour to the stepson of the Princeps subsequent to the autumn of 6 BC. Hence the tenure 6/5 can be admitted. In itself 7/6 would not be ruled out, since Claudius Nero had his second consulate in 7, with a German triumph to inaugurate it.

Taking order of seniority, the sequence would run

8/7 P. Quinctilius Varus (*cos.* 13)
7/6 L. Volusius Saturninus (*suff.* 12)
6/5 Africanus Fabius Maximus (*cos.* 11)

Attractive, but one learns to distrust regularities and patterns.[60] There are unrecognized factors. Given the shortage of ex-consuls in the period (and the claims or competence of the man) Sulpicius Quirinius (*cos.* 12) could hardly be denied either Africa or Asia. Some would opt for Asia, moved by his known posts in Galatia and in Syria. Quirinius might have been proconsul at some time between 3 BC and AD 2.

A case could be made out for Africa. A casual notice in an untidy epitomator, registering the war of Lentulus Gaetulicus against Musulamii and Gaetuli, goes on to assign to Quirinius a campaign against Garamantes and Marmaridae.[61] Garamantes may be discounted (a Virgilian allusion brought them into literary currency), but the Marmaridae are another matter, a desert tribe dwelling to the south of Cyrenaica. It does not pass belief that Augustus assigned the task to Quirinius when (or although) he was proconsul of Africa, in spite of the distance.[62]

Warfare brought Quirinius to the consulate, the first new man to be *ordinarius* since Sentius Saturninus in 19. He is styled 'impiger militiae et acribus ministeriis'.[63] One hypothesis entrusts him with troops when praetorian proconsul governing Crete and Cyrene *c.*15.[64] Another field

---

[57] Since his son was born in 38 BC.
[58] *Ann.* III.30.1. See further above, p. 116.
[59] He happens also to be recorded on a milestone (*AE* 1955, 40).
[60] The order in question was firmly advocated by B. E. Thomasson, *Eranos* LXVII (1969), 179.
[61] Florus II.31.
[62] The hypothesis of Zumpt, generally discounted.   [63] *Ann.* III.48.1.
[64] Thus, following Mommsen and Ritterling, Groag in *RE* IVA. 825 ff. A recrudescence of trouble in the Marmarica might be expected. A broken sentence in Dio gives a clue, under AD 1 (LV.10a.1). Supported by references to 'the Marmaric War' in two inscriptions at Cyrene (*OGIS* 767; *SEG* IX.63).

offers, the Balkan lands. After repelling a Sarmatian raid across the Danube, Tarius Rufus became consul suffect in 16.[65] Not long after, the Thracian Dentheletae made an incursion into Macedonia—and likewise the Scordisci.[66] When next heard of the Scordisci have become Roman allies, giving aid in 12 to Claudius Nero, during the subjugation of the Pannonian Breuci.[67] The interval had witnessed the campaign of a governor of Macedonia, taking him towards Singidunum and Sirmium: the prerequisite in any strategy for the conquest of the Save valley.

Announced (it is no paradox) by the *Ara Pacis*, the northern wars ended in 7, and peace throughout the world was duly confirmed by the closure of Janus. A domestic crisis now shook the goverment, expelling the second man in the state. In the summer of 6, Claudius Nero received the *tribunicia potestas*, and the ruler proposed to send him away on a mission to the eastern lands. Nero objected—the reasons are no mystery. Angry and pertinacious, he departed to Rhodes.

The vice-gerent would have exercised proconsular *imperium*. The selection of provincial governors therefore became sharply relevant.[68] Asinius Gallus had Asia for the tenure 6 to 5, designated by sortition early in the year, an operation that was not always left to chance. If the hand and mind of Caesar Augustus is surmised, the purpose lacked amenity. Gallus pushed to extremes the recalcitrance of his parent. A further cause for friction supervened. Gallus had married Vipsania whom Claudius Nero was constrained to discard in order to take over the widow of Agrippa.

By contrast, Quinctilius Varus might seem congenial, a mild and steady character. He was already installed in Syria by the month of September, if not earlier, succeeding Sentius Saturninus (*cos.* 19). Further Galatia should not be lost to view. The decision may already have been taken to send Quirinius there, for a military task. An astute careerist, Quirinius did not fail to pay court to the exile at Rhodes.

Caesar's legate in Syria, the choice was delicate.[69] In the first place, it called for discretion and guile. The Syrian command confronted Parthia, ostensibly a rival to the empire of the Romans. But the Parthian, in the judgement of Caesar Augustus, held no problem that defied negotiation. Never aggressive, the monarch was now in a weak position. He had recently delivered four sons as hostages to M. Titius.[70]

---

[65] Dio LIV.20.3. [66] Dio LIV.20.3 (with other campaigns under the year 16).
[67] Dio LIV.31.3. [68] Ch. VI.
[69] For the governors of Syria see Schürer, *The History of the Jewish People in the Age of Jesus Christ* I (ed. Vermes and Millar, 1973), 257 ff.
[70] Strabo XVI, p. 748. In 10 BC, so it is presumed. Under that year the *Periocha* of Livy (Book CXLI) registers peace concluded with the Parthians and the Roman standards restored. A patent confusion. Like some other writers, the compiler or his source was obsessed with the much advertised 'signa' surrendered in 20.

To the legate fell another diplomatic function. He supervised several vassal kingdoms, with princes arrogant, conceited, or insidious. The only other notice about Titius' governorship shows him on bad terms with Archelaus, the ruler of Cappadocia. A reconciliation was effected by Herod of Judaea.[71]

This governor had a long experience of men and affairs: a renegade partisan of Antonius, like his uncle, the versatile Munatius Plancus, and rewarded with a consulship, succeeding Messalla Corvinus. So far as known, Titius kept clear of involvement with the intrigues and feuds that infested the Herodian family.[72] His successor Sentius Saturninus was not so fortunate.[73] On instruction from Augustus he took part in a council at Berytus to adjudicate on the charges brought by Herod against Alexander and Aristobulus. Saturninus put in a plea for mercy, supported by his staff.[74] The procurator voted against, the large majority concurred, and the young men were condemned, without a hearing.

Saturninus had other dealings with the ruler of Judaea. Of Varus only one episode happens to be reported, the indictment of Antipater, the eldest son. This time Jerusalem was the scene. As on the earlier occasion, Herod made a long and savage denunciation; and witnesses added damaging testimony. Varus urged Antipater to offer his defence. Failing to elicit a satisfactory reply, he desisted—and Augustus had given Herod a free hand. Antipater was therefore taken into custody, and later executed: so it happened, five days before Herod made his unedifying end in the spring of the year 4.

Urgent problems arose: the testament of the ruler, which had to be ratified, and his treasures, which the procurator Sabinus wished to seize and segregate. Varus was alert. He came to Caesarea and dissuaded Sabinus. Then, disorders having broken out at Jerusalem in the festal season, he turned up with a legion and left it there when he returned to Antioch. The trouble grew and spread, provoked, it is alleged, by the conduct of Sabinus, and the garrison incurred grave danger. The governor of Syria now made his third intervention in Palestine, coming down to suppress an insurrection at the head of a large force. He brought the other two legions, and on the way he picked up fifteen hundred men at Berytus (that military colony had been founded a decade earlier).[75]

---

[71] Josephus, *AJ* XVI.270. Titius probably acceded to Syria in 13 when Agrippa departed. Cf. T. Corbishley, *JRS* XXIV (1934), 48.

[72] Accident or disproportion in Josephus should be allowed for. Archelaus was prominent in the domestic imbroglio, and it began in 12, cf. Schürer, o.c. 321 ff.

[73] For the transactions concerning Saturninus and Varus see Schürer, o.c. 323 ff.; E. M. Smallwood, *The Jews under Roman Rule* (1976), 106 ff.

[74] In the governor's *consilium* were his three sons, termed legates (*AJ* XVI.369). That is, Gaius and Gnaeus (consul and consul suffect in AD 4), and 'Lucius' (cf. *CIL* VI.9979), who disappears. A legate called Pedanius is also mentioned (*BJ* I.538): not in *RE* XIX.

[75] *BJ* II.67. Striking evidence for the military value of a *colonia*.

At Jerusalem the presence of Varus sufficed to quell the malcontents. But anarchy reigned in various parts of the country. Harsh measures of repression were needed. Thus Sepphoris was sacked, and the inhabitants enslaved. Peace was enforced. Varus' sense for order is illustrated by an engaging item—he dismissed his Arab allies, enthusiastic to excess in their looting.[76]

The historian Flavius Josephus furnishes ample narrations. In one of his writings he even elevates the 'War of Varus' to rank beside the tribulations inflicted by Pompeius and endured in his own time.[77] Otherwise it tends to be obscured by what occurred nine years later: Judaea annexed on the decease of Archelaus, the introduction of Roman taxation under the supervision of Quirinius the legate of Syria, the insurrection of Judas the Galilean 'in the days of the census'.[78]

Judas sprang to arms when Quirinius arrived.[79] An insurgent leader of the same name had previously been active in the War of Varus, seizing Sepphoris.[80] Identity has sometimes been under doubt. It may be conceded without qualms.[81]

Further, if a doublet were suspected and assumed, that shows how easily Herod's end and the annexation of Judaea might be conflated in oral tradition or in some subsequent writer. Josephus in fact passed rapidly over the uneventful decade of Archelaus the ethnarch.[82]

When action beckoned, Quinctilius Varus acted with promptitude and energy. Incautious verdicts tend to propagate a low estimate of his military experience.[83] For generals of rank and station, the Romans, it is salutary to recall, set no great store by a prolonged training in the science of war. Again, the evidence is defective. It seldom registers a military tribunate. Cn. Piso, so it appears, saw service in the Spanish campaigns of 26 and 25.[84] That was a field for other young aristocrats of his age, such as Quinctilius Varus and the two Fabii. At the same time the army had no small social value. Finally, either Africa or Syria might have justified for Varus the *ornamenta triumphalia*.

---

[76] *BJ* II.76.

[77] *Adv. Apionem* I.7.34. For the 'War of Varus' in Jewish tradition, E. M. Smallwood, o.c. 113.

[78] *Acta Apost.* V.37 (the oration of Gamaliel).   [79] *BJ* II.118, cf. 433; *AJ* XVIII.4 and 23.

[80] *BJ* II.56; *AJ* XVII. 271 (Judas the son of Hezekiah).

[81] M. Hengel, *Die Zeloten* (1961), 79 ff.; 337 f. (with the family stemma); S. Applebaum, *JRS* LXI (1971), 160.

[82] Hence no great interval fancied between the last months of King Herod and the census of Quirinius. Relevant to a problem, or rather non-problem: the Date of the Nativity. Cf. below, p. 340.

[83] e.g. C. M. Wells, *The German Policy of Augustus* (1972), 238 f.: 'only limited experience of warfare in either post'. Another writer is there cited who calls Varus 'a leading lawyer without any military qualities'.   [84] Ch. XXVI.

Varus perhaps stayed in Syria until the next year. His successor is not attested—a gap intervenes before M. Lollius arrived in 1 BC, in the company of the prince C. Caesar. Conjecture has not been lacking, some of it to dubious and to fateful effect. Something speaks for Piso the Pontifex.[85]

Silence now envelops Varus. For the reconstruction of Roman history the dark decade sets in with the momentous year 6: three gaps in the text of Cassius Dio, which, breaking off with remarks about the young princes, does not resume until the dedication of Mars Ultor in 2.

Since the return of Agrippa from the eastern provinces in 13, no word in Dio about that region, nothing about Parthia or Armenia. The historian would soon have to make good that deferment; and in due course he could hardly omit the decease of Herod and the partition of his kingdom—if not the actions of Quinctilius Varus. In 5 Caesar Augustus himself assumed the *fasces*, to lend lustre to his dynastic policy. C. Caesar now assumed the 'toga' of manhood, with the consulate when he reached the age of nineteen.

Flagrantly dynastic after the year 6, the ruler's design increased the value of the high aristocracy, and his dependence. In the past the nobles regarded the 'res publica' as their possession or convenience, with honours and emolument as the due reward for birth and ambition. They were ready to embrace the monarchy, whether friends of the absent Claudius or rivals, a few perhaps with subdued misgivings, most of them in hope and alacrity. Boy princes and a sexagenarian autocrat held out seductive prospects. Various groups and persons close to the power acquired enhancement.

When both princes perished, the ruler had to turn to Claudius Nero, who had been living in seclusion for two years after he came back from Rhodes. Germany at once claimed Ti. Caesar, and the work of conquest resumed.

Some time had passed since Drusus in his second campaign managed to reach the river Weser, in the fourth and last to march through the country as far as the Elbe in its middle course.[86] In 8 BC his brother dealt with the Sugambri: either massacre or transplantation across the Rhine. Of his operations in the following year, no detail.[87] Nor is the identity on record of the legate who took his place at the head of five legions.

---

[85] Ch. XXIV. [86] Ch. V.

[87] In Dio a brief mention (LV.8.3), nothing in Velleius. Of the previous year Velleius asserted 'peragratusque victor omnis partis Germaniae', and 'perdomuit eam' (II.97.4).

On the other hand, the legionary camp at Oberaden, on the northern flank of the Sugambri, occupied through several winters, was not given up. On Oberaden see C. M. Wells, o.c. 218 f.; S. v. Schnurbein, *RGK Bericht* LXII (1981), 5 ff.

Next Domitius Ahenobarbus, coming from the command in Illyricum. Three actions are registered of this unexpected general. First, he marched as far as the Elbe, from the direction of Raetia, so it is generally assumed, and he crossed the river; and he then assigned to the Hermunduri the territory which the Marcomanni had vacated on their migration to Bohemia.[88] Second, he constructed a causeway (the 'pontes longi') across the marshlands between the Rhine and the Ems.[89] Third, he came into conflict with the Cherusci.[90] On Ahenobarbus followed M. Vinicius (*suff.* 19), with an imperfect achievement which none the less earned the *ornamenta triumphalia*.[91]

The first campaign of Tiberius Caesar (in AD 4) reconquered certain tribes and went beyond the Weser; and part of the army spent the winter 'ad caput Lupiae fluminis'.[92] In the second a combined operation of army and fleet reached the Elbe.[93] The third was directed against Bohemia, to demolish the kingdom of Maroboduus, the ruler of the Marcomanni: by convergent strategy, Sentius Saturninus marching from Moguntiacum, Tiberius Caesar northwards from Carnuntum on the Danube. Five days short of their junction, the armies halted.

All Illyricum had risen, annulling the grand design. The rebellion of Pannonians and Dalmatians took three full years to quell. Grievances of the natives are alleged: taxation and the imposition of the levy.[94] There was something else. The original conquest of a vast area had been rapid and superficial; and the bellicose tribes of Thrace might join in, quiescent since Piso's war.

The lesson was sharp and clear. Three hundred miles from Rhine to Elbe, broken by hills and forests, by rivers and marshes, Germany had been invaded rather than subjugated; and not intersected by roads or permanent military posts.[95] A cautious and vigilant policy was enjoined—and conciliatory. On character and experience, Varus seemed the man to take the place of Sentius in 6 or 7, being a diplomat but not incapable of prompt decisions.

When Claudius Nero departed in 8 BC to hold his second consulship and his triumph, he left Germany in the state of a 'provincia paene stipendiaria'.[96] It is a question what changes had been introduced by AD 9.

---

[88] Dio LV.10a.2, cf. Tacitus, *Ann.* IV.44.2. On the vexatious problem of his march to the Elbe see K. Christ, *Chiron* VII (1977), 181 f.

[89] *Ann.* I.63.4 (the predicament of Caecina Severus on his return march in 15).

[90] Dio LV.10a.3.

[91] Velleius II.104.2 (above, p. 102).

[92] II.105.

[93] According to Velleius, the march to the Elbe was 'numquam antea spe conceptum, nedum opere tentatum' (106.2). The next sentence carries the fleet expedition, 'et eodem mira felicitate et cura ducis' etc.

[94] Dio LV.29.1.

[95] Cf. the remarks about Oberaden, above, n. 87.

[96] Velleius II.97.4.

Estimates range from a Roman province, organized as such, to an incomplete adjunct of Gallia Belgica.[97] The earliest account puts emphasis on law, justice, and arbitration.[98]

A later writer of little value, and less discernment, produces an epigram, 'saeviora armis iura'; and he has Varus attacked at the magistrate's tribunal.[99] But no source, whether sober or ornamental, affirms the imposition of Roman tribute. There is no hint in the account of Cassius Dio; and a statement in Tacitus belongs to a fervid oration.[100]

Velleius was moved to denounce the Germans. Human only by voice and shape, and a 'genus mendacio natum'.[101] Others discovered honesty and courage, recalling the primeval virtues of their own uncorrupted ancestors. That prepossession in favour of 'simplicitas' comes out in terms of general approbation or in valid episodes.[102]

Quinctilius Varus is impugned for a trusting nature and for culpable negligence. An aristocrat who had known Herod, the savage Idumaean, and the perfidious inhabitants of Syria, was easily captivated and deceived by the young prince of the Cherusci, who had seen service as an officer, who had acquired the status of a Roman knight.[103]

Search for the site of the 'clades Variana' engages the fervour of national or parochial zeal, interminably.[104] Some will be content to renounce. About the nature of the disaster, the shortest statement does least harm.

After Varus set out from his summer camp, the conspirators induced him to deviate from the normal route of return. The Roman columns were assailed when marching through wooded and marshy country, as happened in other German campaigns. Thus Drusus in danger in the defiles near the place called Arbalo, Caecina Severus while crossing the 'pontes longi'.[105] Harried and trapped, three legions were cut to pieces, and the general fell on his sword.

Germany was lost. The invasions launched by Germanicus proved a failure. The sagacity of Tiberius prevailed, and for posterity the Elbe

[97] For a firm statement, C. M. Wells, o.c. 156: 'Germany was organized as a province, except that regular taxation was apparently not yet imposed.' On the other side, D. Timpe, *Arminius-Studien* (1970), 86.

[98] Velleius II. 117.3: 'posse iure mulceri'; 4: 'iuris dictionibus agendoque pro tribunali ordine'; 118.1. 'simulantes fictas litium series'; 'ut se praetorem urbanum in foro ius dicere . . . crederet'.

[99] Florus II.30.31 ff.

[100] *Ann.* I.59.5.

[101] II.118.1. He accepted however the testimony of an elderly native who, admitted to the presence of the general, exclaimed 'hodie deos vidi' (107.2).

[102] Tacitus, *Germ.* 22.3: 'gens non astuta nec callida'. Cf. the incident of the Frisian ambassadors (*Ann.* XIV.54.3 f.)

[103] Velleius II.118.2. On which, D. Timpe, o.c. 27 ff. On the generalship of Arminius, H. v. Petrikovits, *Bonner Jahrbücher* CLXVI (1966), 175 ff.

[104] For a statement in reasonable compass see W. John, *RE* XXIV. 951 ff.

[105] Dio LV.33.3, cf. Pliny, *NH* XI.55; Tacitus, *Ann* I.63 ff. And, for that matter, Tiberius on his return march in AD 5 was ambushed—but 'magna cum clade hostium' (Velleius II.107.3).

became a name and a memory. But Illyricum had been won, the bond of central necessity.

The catastrophe meant not only the reversal of an ambitious plan of conquest that had been pursued through two decades, with optimistic forecasts dispelled. It was a blow to the personal prestige of both Augustus and Tiberius.

For a season the repute of Varus was spared or protected by the dynastic link and by his kinsmen: four nephews of consular rank. Of the two Nonii Asprenates, the elder (*suff.* 6) went out as proconsul to govern Africa, the younger (*cos.* 8) to Asia.[106] Sex. Appuleius held the *fasces* in 14, with Sex. Pompeius for colleague, another relative of the Princeps. He leaves no certain trace in the sequel. P. Dolabella (*cos.* 10) rose highest, holding Dalmatia with two legions when Augustus died. He enjoyed the favour of the new ruler, and abused it, obsequious to excess.[107]

Ti. Caesar cherished the aristocratic virtues of 'amicitia' and 'fides'. Before the late-born son of Varus came to years of manhood, he was betrothed to an infant daughter of Germanicus and Agrippina.[108]

Appuleia Varilla, however, soon came to grief, a victim of *maiestas*.[109] The scope of the law was widening. It embraced offences against ruler and dynasty, in word as well as act, and also misdemeanours by men or women who were connected with the family. Varilla was indicted on the double charge, namely injurious language and adultery. Her 'propinqui' find mention in the context of the trial. But not her brother (the consul of 14), and not her husband. His identity would be worth knowing.[110]

Next, Claudia Pulchra, the widow of Varus, although not until nine years had elapsed.[111] With her prosecution began the sequence of transactions that brought to ruin her cousin and friend Agrippina. Pulchra, so it was alleged, used poison and magic to menace the life of the Princeps. The other charge, which prevailed, was 'impudicitia': not 'adulterium', since the lady was a widow. The distinction has not been observed by all scholars in the modern time.

The next year saw an attack on 'Varum Quinctilium, divitem et Caesari propinquum'.[112] Dolabella helped with the indictment, his own cousin. Which excited pertinent observations. Mother and son, one and the same prosecutor. It was Domitius Afer. Those actions established an orator of

---

[106] The latter was retrieved from *AE* 1933, 265 (Pergamum) by U. Weidemann, *Acta Classica* III (1960), 93 ff.

[107] below, p. 424.

[108] Seneca, *Controv.* I.3.10 (above, p. 315).

[109] *Ann.* II.50 (in the year 17).

[110] An Aemilius Lepidus is conjectured an earlier husband (above, p. 126).

[111] *Ann.* IV.52.

[112] IV.66.

classic renown. Alert as ever both to *maiestas* and to the annals of Roman
eloquence, Tacitus adds suitable comment about the character of Afer,
'quoquo facinore properus clarescere'; and, eagerly anticipating an
obituary notice, he alludes to the decline of Afer's powers before
the end.[113]

On the theme of Varus, the consular historian curbed his propensity to
malice and indignation. The verdict is 'fato et vi Arminii'.[114] The role of
fate also received emphasis from Velleius, who went on to invoke the
divine power that deludes and thwarts the counsels of men.[115] That writer
duly spreads himself on personal failings of Varus, above all his torpor,
with choice vocabulary.[116] Yet the presentation is not uniformly hostile.[117]
While Varus is denied soldierly habits (and by implication, experience), he
is styled 'vir ingenio mitis, moribus quietus, ut corpore ita animo
immobilior'.[118] At first sight, the word 'immobilis' condemns. Yet not
always, or fatally.[119] On the better showing Varus is a safe and steady man,
not quite a 'stolidus', as were some aristocrats. The valedictory of Velleius
designates him 'gravem et bonae voluntatis virum'.

Varus was endowed with ample possessions. Not by inheritance, it is
clear, from the father who fell at Philippi. Velleius declares the answer, in a
sentence constructed with epithets in crude and conventional antithesis: he
plundered the opulent province of Syria.[120] Sober speculation will look to
wealth blamelessly accruing from repeated matrimony and the bounty of
Caesar.

Of intellectual gifts and pursuits, no trace is preserved. Drama and
rhetoric in ancient sources have him assiduously dispensing justice in the
wilds of Germany. That obsession engenders incautious fancies. Varus was
not a jurist. Nor is he found in the schools of declamation or in the
company of poets. If he frequented the educated class in the cities of
Phoenicia and Cilicia, he did not bring any of them back to Rome, so far as
known.

Varus had bad luck. Surviving Germany, he might have competed
with L. Piso for the post of *praefectus urbi*. Social prestige commended
Quinctilius Varus, close ties with the dynasty—and a character that
blended firmness and tact.

[113] IV.52.4, cf. XIV.19 (very brief).
[114] I.55.3.
[115] Velleius II.118.4: 'obstabant iam fata'.
[116] Not only 'segnitia' and 'socordia', but the rare 'marcor' (119.2). That word first recurs in
Celsus (medical) and in Seneca, cf. *TLL*.
[117] On his portrayal, D. Timpe, o.c. 119; 124 ff.
[118] Velleius II.117.2.
[119] cf. W. John, *RE* XXIV. 959. Further (on 120.5), A. J. Woodman in his *Commentary* on the
Tiberian chapters.
[120] Velleius II.117.2: 'quam pauper divitem ingressus dives pauperem reliquit.'

XXIV

Piso the Pontifex

Like the aristocratic Caesars, their rivals exhibit continuity, the descendants of the dynasts Sulla, Pompeius, and Crassus. They comprise a whole group. The survival or the decease of a single person made a sharp impact, and by good fortune it is sometimes recorded.

Messalla Rufus, consul in 53, lived through the wars, to witness the return of normal government. A year or two older than Caesar the Dictator, he died in 26. His colleague Domitius Calvinus was still alive in 21. At the end of the great lacuna comes Munatius Plancus, consul in 42, to be censor twenty years later. Further, Pollio and Corvinus both lasted into the closing decade of the reign. With them goes Sempronius Atratinus (*suff.* 34), who won early renown as an orator when at the age of seventeen he prosecuted Caelius Rufus. Both Atratinus and Pollio reached the eightieth year of life.[1]

Old men's memories were a precious source for historians. How far Livy had recourse to them for his Caesarian or contemporary annals is a question that baffles all surmise. A portentous survivor was Q. Haterius (*suff.* 5), a close coeval of Caesar Augustus. Dying in AD 26, he gets a curt obituary notice from Tacitus, who knew the quality of his eloquence.

Six years later died L. Piso the Pontifex, at the age of seventy-nine. The historian responds nobly, with a turn of style recalling the ancient annalists—and he was able to subjoin an artful excursus on the office of *praefectus urbi*.[2] The obituary notice further disclosed a fact of unique value, the parentage of Piso. His father was a censor, as the author had reported in an earlier passage (that is, somewhere in Book V).

The Pontifex is therefore a son of Piso Caesoninus, the excellent aristocrat whom Cicero so cleverly traduced. In 59 Caesoninus gave his daughter for wife to the consul Julius Caesar. Men of the time were not surprised to see him chosen to share the *fasces* the year after with Gabinius, a partisan of Pompeius Magnus.

The Calpurnii Pisones, with their first consul in 180, went on to success

---

[1] The death of Atratinus was registered under 21 BC by Jerome, *Chron.* p. 165 H. He was in fact succeeded as augur by P. Petronius in AD 7 (*ILS* 9338). Pollio died in 5, according to Jerome (p. 170).

[2] *Ann.* VI.10.

and duration.[3] No fewer than four consuls between 148 and 133, for example; and they are fairly numerous in the late epoch of the Republic. Apart from Caesoninus, two lines can be distinguished: Cn. Piso, quaestor in 65, who goes back to the consul of 139, and the descendants of Piso Frugi, the consular annalist (*cos.* 133).

The latter lapse or lose the Calpurnian *nomen*, their last member being taken in adoption by the grandson of Marcus Crassus and emerging as M. Crassus Frugi, consul in 14. The prestigious *cognomen* had peculiar consequences. In comment on Cicero's *In Pisonem* the learned Asconius declared that Caesoninus belonged to that family.[4] He was deceived by a verbal artifice of the orator. Furthermore, by sheer coincidence, the list of consuls attached to Book LIV of Cassius Dio assigns the *cognomen* to Piso the Pontifex (instead of Crassus, the consul of the next year). Not all scholars in the recent age have been on guard.

The other line shows consuls in the time of Augustus, viz. Cn. Piso the consul of 23 and his two sons: Gnaeus in 7, and Lucius in 1, known as 'the Augur'.[5] That was one of the devices on call to distinguish homonyms in the Roman aristocracy.[6]

Of Caesoninus, consul, proconsul of Macedonia, and censor, there is no report subsequent to the spring of the year 43, when he made his notable exertions for concord and good sense in a new civil war.[7] The late-begotten son (born in 48) may have fallen to the charge of women. A number of noble youths in this generation had been deprived of a father, some perhaps with damage, such as Claudius Nero. For others the question does not arise (lack of evidence).

Marriages lacking glamour are a topic of appeal to the serious student of Roman society. The father of Caesoninus took a municipal wife, from the old Latin colony of Placentia in northern Italy; and Caesoninus was far from being ashamed of that extraction, so Cicero exclaimed in reproach and derision.[8] In consonance therewith, it may be noted, Caesoninus' own wife belonged to a family of little consequence. Asconius was able to ascertain her identity (the daughter of Rutilius Nudus), but her mother baffled the researcher, as he confessed: 'invenire non potui'.[9]

A second marriage should be reckoned with. The son (the only son known) was junior by a quarter of a century to his sister, 'Calpurnia C. Caesaris'.

---

[3] For a brief sketch, *JRS* L (1960), 12 f. = *RP* (1979), 496 f.
[4] Asconius 4; 9 f.
[5] Ch. XXVI.
[6] For that device, and for others, *JRS* XLVI (1966), 17 f. = *Ten Studies in Tacitus* (1970), 50 f.
[7] Last heard of in *Phil.* XII.3.
[8] As quoted in Asconius 2.
[9] Asconius 9.

Through that sister the Pontifex had a link, albeit tenuous, with Caesar's heir. There is no sign of any reinforcement when the season arrived for him to look for a wife, several nieces of the Princeps becoming available not long after the War of Actium. It would be no bad thing if a young man had sense enough to resist high birth in a bride, aware of discomforts, and of danger. Arrogant women or entanglement with the dynasty brought noble houses to calamity or extinction.

Piso's wife defies all conjecture; and, as will be demonstrated, sons are not easy to certify.[10] There is only a daughter. She went to L. Nonius Asprenas, consul suffect in AD 6. The family, from Picenum, was newly ennobled—but the father of Asprenas had married one of the three sisters of Quinctilius Varus, and Varus stood in close propinquity to the dynasty, through several matrimonial alliances.[11]

From his parent the Pontifex inherited sagacity as well as cultivated tastes. The doctrines of Epicurus deprecated birth and ambition, but they did not debar the service of the 'res publica' in war or peace. Piso passed through a career of honour and splendour before he became *praefectus urbi* at the age of sixty.

The evidence is sporadic and it carries manifold perplexities.[12] Praetor in 18, so it may be assumed, Piso had probably been quaestor in 23 (the year of Claudius Nero, who benefited by a five years' remission), perhaps pro-quaestor of Caesar Augustus in Sicily and Asia the next year. His first recorded post or action shows him presiding in justice as proconsul at Mediolanum. The testimony is explicit. The orator Albucius Silo, a citizen of Novaria, protesting against the behaviour of the lictors, went on in anger to deplore the condition of Italy, 'quasi iterum in formam provinciae redigeretur'.[13]

The long zone of Transpadane Italy, extending five hundred miles from the Cottian Alps to the Julian, presented problems for the government. In 26 or 25 Terentius Varro subjugated the Salassi in Val D'Aosta.[14] His title and competence are not on record. Which is unfortunate, on several counts. In 23 or 22 M. Appuleius (*cos.* 20) constructed a building at Tridentum, by order of Caesar Augustus: he is styled 'legatus'.[15] Then, in 17 or 16, P. Silius Nerva (*cos.* 20) reduced the tribes in Val Camonica and Val Venosta.[16] He also dealt with a Pannonian raid into Istria—and was

---

[10] Ch. XXVI.
[11] Ch. XXIII.
[12] See above all the full account of Groag, *PIR*[2] C 289 (pp. 61–7). Against Mommsen, Cichorius and many others, Groag was firm that the Pontifex was not a Piso Frugi.
[13] Suetonius, *De rhet.* 6. As elsewhere, the term 'Italia' signifies Transpadana.
[14] Strabo IV, p. 206; Dio LIII.25.3 (under the year 25). Above, p. 43.
[15] *ILS* 86.
[16] Dio LIV. 20.1 f.

beyond doubt proconsul of Illyricum.[17] The next general to operate in northern Italy is Claudius Drusus, the stepson of the Princeps, in rank quaestorian.

Anomalies and variants will not arouse disquiet, unless among some adepts of constitutional law. What date shall therefore be assigned to L. Piso, holding authority as proconsul in Italia Transpadana? Perhaps a short period in 16, succeeding Silius Nerva. Better, in 14, after the conquest of the Alpine lands. That might lend some point to 'iterum' in the complaint uttered by Albucius Silo, warfare no longer excusing the presence of one who exercised *imperium*.

In 14 or 13 Illyricum was taken over into the portion of Caesar. M. Vinicius, who in 13 began under the supervision of Agrippa the Bellum Pannonicum, is to be regarded as either the last proconsul or the first of the imperial legates.[18] Cassius Dio, registering the transference of 'Dalmatia' under the year 11, is clearly in error. Coming upon the campaign of Claudius Nero against Dalmatians, he offered a tardy explanation—and false, as his language demonstrates.[19]

In that same year, as Dio reports, Lucius Piso the governor of Pamphylia was brought to Thrace to deal with a great rebellion.[20] Now Pamphylia was not a separate province. It was comprised, along with Galatia and other regions, in the kingdom which Antonius gave to Amyntas—and Augustus duly confirmed.[21] The task assigned was to subjugate tribes of the Taurus between Cilicia Tracheia and Pisidia that had defied every imperial power hitherto. In 25 the Homonadenses killed him, and Rome annexed.[22]

Amyntas inherited from Deiotarus an army trained on the Roman model. Though military colonies were now established in Pisidia and in Lycaonia, serving the ends of security, legions were still required, and were available.[23] By the year 13 a large number of time-expired soldiers had been dismissed, but the total of legions had recently risen from twenty-six to twenty-eight.[24] The time had perhaps come to complete the pacification of the mountain tribes. Hence a consular legate in Galatia-Pamphylia. A casual piece of evidence comes in, welcome but not

[17] *ILS* 899 (Aenona).

[18] Preferably the latter. Under 14 Dio records a Pannonian rebellion (LIV.24.3). Vinicius' tenure may run from 15 or 14 until 12.

[19] Dio LIV.34.4.

[20] Dio LIV.34.6. He offers a good account.

[21] As argued in *Klio* XXVII (1934), 122 ff.

[22] M. Lollius was the first governor (Eutropius VII.10.2).

[23] The legion XXII Deiotariana no doubt stayed there for as much as a decade until transferred to Egypt. A permanent garrison of 'one and probably two legions' down to AD 6 is proposed by S. Mitchell, *CQ* XXVI (1976), 307.

[24] By the incorporation of XXI Rapax and XXII Deiotariana.

indispensable. In one of the poems of Antipater of Thessalonica, Pylaemenes gives Piso a helmet.[25] Pylaemenes is a Galatian nobleman, the son of Amyntas.[26]

The Homonadenses could wait. They were left for the *novus homo* Sulpicius Quirinius (*cos.* 12). The operations, entailing the siege of their numerous *castella*, may have taken two years, perhaps 5 and 4.[27] In the latter year Syria had only three legions.[28] Quirinius' war is absent from Dio, perhaps because of the large gap in his text; but under AD 6 Dio records a recrudescence of trouble among the tribes of the Taurus. He names the Isaurians.[29] They were reduced by M. Plautius Silvanus (*cos.* 2 BC).[30] In the next year he brought his army to the Balkan lands. Five legions under the command of Plautius Silvanus and Caecina Severus fought a battle against the insurgent Pannonians in the vicinity of Sirmium.[31] From these transactions emerges a useful conclusion: consular legates governing Galatia-Pamphylia, and there may have been more than three of them.[32]

Thrace was a constant and urgent problem. When the ruler in 27 resigned three military provinces to proconsuls, he took care not to let them have large armies. The glory won by M. Crassus, the proconsul of Macedonia, was a recent annoyance.

Of the Thracian tribes the Bessi were the savagest. In 19 or 18 they rose against Rhoemetalces, uncle and guardian to the sons of Cotys. M. Lollius (*cos.* 21) had to intervene.[33] Trouble in Thrace tended to encourage the peoples beyond the Danube. L. Tarius Rufus (*suff.* 16), the successor of Lollius, repelled an incursion of Sarmatians.[34]

The Bessi again and religious fanaticism provoked the next uprising. Led by a priest, they drove Rhoemetalces to seek distant refuge in the

---

[25] *Anth. Pal.* VI.241.

[26] *OGIS* 533 (Ancyra). The relevance of Galatia as Piso's province was missed by Gow and Page, *The Garland of Philip* II (1968), 18 f., cf. 54 (on Pylaemenes).

[27] For the dating of these operations see now B. Levick, *Roman Colonies in Southern Asia Minor* (1967), 203 ff.

[28] Josephus, *BJ* II.39; *AJ* XVII.286. When the grand total had fallen to twenty-five legions Syria engrossed four.

[29] Dio LV.28.2 f. Neglected for a long time in disquisitions about Galatia and the Homonadensian War.

[30] Plautius Silvanus stood on attestation as Caesar's *legatus pro praetore* (*SEG* VI. 646: Attaleia). Cf. remarks in *JRS* XXIII (1933), 27; *Klio* XXVII (1934), 139 ff.

[31] Velleius II.112.4; Dio LV.34.6.

[32] viz. C. Marcius Censorinus (*cos.* 8), M. Servilius (AD 3), L. Volusius Saturninus (*suff.* 3). Proposed in *Akten des VI. int. Kongresses für gr.u.lat. Epigraphik 1972* (1973), 588 = *RP* III (1984), 872. Duly registered by R. K. Sherk, *ANRW* II. 7 (1980), 1036 ff.

[33] Dio LIV.20.3. Perhaps, but not certainly, as legate replacing a proconsul.

[34] Dio LIV.20.3. Indicated as Caesar's legate by the formula on *AE* 1936, 18 (near Amphipolis). Cf. *Danubian Papers* (1971), 67 f.

peninsula of Gallipoli; and they killed Rhescuporis, the son of Cotys. Piso and his legions were sorely needed.

Piso at first suffered a defeat at the hands of the Bessi, but then prevailed against them. He reduced other rebellious tribes, all of them. Finally, he dealt with a resurgence. For which exploits the Senate voted *supplicationes* and the *ornamenta triumphalia*.[35]

Such is the statement of Dio, explicit, and fairly full. It indicates three campaigns—and Velleius in fact assigns a 'triennium' to the Bellum Thracicum.[36] In the *Periocha* of Livy, Book CXL, it is registered under the year 11. That, so it may be conjectured, marks the signal victory of Piso (with award of the *ornamenta*), not his later and subsidiary operations. Hence 12–10 for Piso's 'triennium'.[37]

There is advantage in that conclusion. It correlates with another campaign. In the account of Dio, the Bessi range far and wide with impunity and another tribe harries Macedonia, the Sialetae. Where was the proconsul, one should ask.

In 12 Claudius Nero, Caesar's legate in Illyricum, conquered a large Pannonian tribe, the Breuci, who lived athwart the course of the Save. The way was now open towards Sirmium, the purpose of the campaign. To effect which, it was necessary to have another army operating from the region of Singidunum or Sirmium—as is evident, without the parallel of what occurred twenty years later in the reconquest of Illyricum. The absence of the proconsul of Macedonia explains the rebellion in Thrace and the mandate of Piso.

Piso fought his war as 'legatus Augusti', and he was empowered by 'secreta mandata', so it is stated.[38] Not an idle surmise. Instructions from the Princeps authorized Piso to deal with vassal princes, and to use the proconsul's army. No proconsul can be discovered in the sequel. A clear consequence was the new Balkan command, 'in Thracia Macedoniaque', later to acquire the name of 'Moesia'.[39]

The proconsul of Illyricum had recently been abolished. When the Senate voted Claudius Nero a triumph for the campaign of 12, the Princeps intervened, as was proper. He devised a compensation, the *ornamenta triumphalia*. It was convenient that the new award could so soon be extended to a consular legate of high birth.

The years 12 and 11 brought a notable achievement from the campaigns in Illyricum and in Germany. How far the German enterprise

[35] Dio LIV.34.7.
[36] Velleius II.98.1.
[37] As proposed in *Klio* XXVII (1934), 130—and several times in the long sequel.
[38] Seneca, *Epp.* 83.14.
[39] The problem of 'the origin of Moesia' has been much in debate—and vitiated through defects in formulation. For the plain definition see *JRS* XXXV (1945), 109 f.: discussing A. Stein, *Die Legaten von Moesien* (1940). Further, Ch. XXI (the post of Lentulus).

might be prosecuted was still perhaps a matter of some doubt. At the end of the year 11 the Senate voted that Janus should be closed.[40]

An enigmatic statement in a late author has so far been reserved and segregated. Orosius narrates with detail and names the German campaigns of Drusus (VI.21.12–17). He then advances with 'tunc etiam' to a brief notice of the African campaign of Cossus Cornelius (21.18), with an excursus ('interea') about Augustus receiving at Tarraco envoys of Indians and Scythians, and then returning to Rome after the Spanish war. The farrago continues with 'quibus etiam diebus', alluding to various wars conducted by his generals. The first item runs as follows: 'nam inter ceteros et Piso adversum Vindelicos missus est, quibus subactis victor ad Caesarem Lugdunum venit' (21.22).

This odd item calls for cautious treatment. L. Piso was proconsul in Italia Transpadana, either in 16 or in 14, it has been argued. In either year Piso might have gone to meet Augustus at Lugdunum (the ruler was absent from Rome). Not, however, victorious after a conquest of the Vindelici, beyond the Alps and beyond Piso's reach in the first of those two years, and in the second already subjugated by the campaign of the two Claudii in 15.[41]

No satisfactory explanation has been proffered.[42] Nor could any be essayed without proper attention to the sources as well as to the methods of Paulus Orosius. His main source for the Augustan campaigns is Florus.[43] Now Florus in his abridged exposition adopted a geographical order, with no thought or conception of chronology.

Florus did not omit the Thracian War of Piso. But he gives no hint of any campaign conducted by Claudius Nero. Not the Alpine War, not the operations against Pannonians and Dalmatians (12–9), not Germany (8 and 7).

Orosius, however, shows no trace of Piso's war in Thrace. But he now brings in, following Piso's mission against the Vindelici, a mention of Claudius Nero: 'Pannonios novo motu intumescentes Tiberius privignus Caesaris cruentissima caede delevit' (21.23).

Orosius goes on to record the operations against Germans, with the item of forty thousand captives (21.24). That is, the treatment of the Sugambri in 8 BC.[44] Proceeding, he cites Suetonius and conflates this

---

[40] Dio LIV.36.2.

[41] Piso's campaign has been assigned by J. Scheid to 16, the territory of the Vindelici being 'contigu à Transpadane' (*Les Frères Arvales* (1975), 78).

[42] In *PIR*² C 269 Groag, referring to the Orosius passage, wondered whether Cn. Piso might not be meant. C. M. Wells suggested L. Piso as commander of a column operating in 15, precisely (*The German Policy of Augustus* (1972), 66, n. 4.). Piso was consul in that year.

[43] He also used Suetonius—and an epitome of Livy, as is shown by comparison with Florus on the Spanish campaigns in 26 and 25. [44] Suetonius, *Tib.* 9.2.

operation, describing it as a 'maximum bellum' which demanded three years and fifteen legions (21.25). That is, the suppression of the insurrection in Illyricum (AD 6–9).[45]

Legitimate suspicions arise. Orosius ignores Piso's war in Thrace but presents him with a mission to conquer the Vindelici. On the other hand, Claudius Nero is not introduced until he deals with a resurgence of the Pannonians ('novo motu intumescentes'). Recourse will therefore be had to annalistic history, albeit scrappy. That is, Cassius Dio. In the year 10 Claudius Nero, having gone with Augustus to Gaul, was despatched to suppress a rising in Illyricum.[46] Later in the year he rejoined Augustus (who had been for most of the time in Gallia Lugdunensis), and, together with Drusus, they departed to Rome.[47]

On this showing, the victorious general who came to meet Augustus at Lugdunum is his stepson. Clearly not L. Piso from distant Thrace. As is his fashion, the hasty compiler confuses and conflates. His Piso is a vestigial remnant of the Thracian War.

Coincidence in errors can crop up. The epitomator Eutropius preceded Orosius in misinterpreting the same passage from Suetonius—although not in the same fashion.[48]

Eusebius under the year 15 transmits a mysterious notice. As translated in the Chronicle of Jerome it stands thus: 'Tiberius Vindelicos et eos qui Thraciarum confines erant Romanas provincias facit.'[49] This sentence has been the cause of elaborate theories. After his Alpine campaign Claudius Nero took up a command in the Balkan lands late in 15 or in the next year, so it was argued.[50]

A Roman advance from the side of Macedonia had certainly occurred between the years 16 and 12. In the latter year the Scordisci in northern Serbia are mentioned by Dio as now allies of the Romans. When last heard of they had been raiding Macedonia. But there is no warrant for bringing in Claudius Nero. The credit goes to an *Ignotus*, the successor of Tarius Rufus.

To conclude. The purpose of this brief excursus was to adduce a parallel, peculiar and yet not inexplicable, to Piso's conquest of the Vindelici as alleged by Orosius.[51]

---

[45] *Tib.* 16.1.   [46] Dio LIV.36.3.

[47] Dio LIV.36.4. Cf. *Phoenix* XXXIII (1979), 312 f. = *RP* III (1984), 1202 f.: discussing the ovation of Claudius Nero (Jan. 16 of the year 9).

[48] Eutropius conflated the forty thousand German captives with a war of Claudius Nero against Pannonians (VII.9). That is, unless there is a lacuna in the text.   [49] Jerome, *Chron.* p. 166 H.

[50] A. v. Premerstein, *Jahreshefte* I (1898), Beiblatt 158 ff. Followed by C. Patsch and by some other scholars. Observe now A. Mócsy, *RE Supp.* IX. 540; *Pannonia and Upper Moesia* (1974), 24. Further it 'may have been the work of Tiberius in 14–13 B.C.' (J.J. Wilkes, *Dalmatia* (1969), 61). For the reasons against, *JRS* XXIV (1934), 117 f. = *Danubian Papers* (1971), 44 f., cf. 66.

[51] Jerome took Thrace from Eusebius. Had he been alert to the error, he might have written 'Raetiarum confines'.

From a scrap of unusable evidence it will be welcome relief to turn to valid conjecture about a proconsulate. Invoking Apollo, the poet Antipater utters a prayer that he may go with Piso to Asia in his warship.[52] The goal is Asia, not Pamphylia. The patron and friend of Antipater was therefore proconsul.[53] The inference seemed clear enough. Not but that some reject Piso from the rubric.[54]

Rejection may well appear harsh and premature. In this season (*c.*8 BC) there was no plethora of ex-consuls to sharpen competition.[55] To deny Asia to a magnate like the Pontifex would add no credit or advantage to the ruler—and the known habits of this consular inclined him towards Asia.

Three documents in that province honour a L. Calpurnius Piso.[56] Perhaps the Pontifex, but perhaps the Augur (*cos.* 1 BC), who is certified as proconsul by another inscription.[57] And new discoveries accrue. Samos and Pergamum pay honour to the proconsul L. Calpurnius Piso and his wife Statilia.[58] On the first inscription both names are erased. This time, the Augur, it appears.[59] A fierce and intractable temper like that of his brother Gnaeus finally got him into trouble.[60]

Next, a governorship in Syria. At Hierapolis Castabala in Cilicia Pedias a Lucius Calpurnius Piso received a dedication, styling him 'legatus pro praetore'.[61] The region belonged to the province of Syria. Hence the hypothesis that the Pontifex was Caesar's legate in Syria, perhaps from 4 to 1.[62] The sequence in this period engages interest, for more reasons than one.[63]

L. Piso, it will be seen, occurs conveniently, to fill a lacuna after Quinctilius Varus—the end of which can be fixed by a further hypothesis. In 1 BC the prince Gaius Caesar, invested with proconsular *imperium*, was sent to the eastern lands. To him the Princeps attached M. Lollius as 'comes et rector', or 'velut moderator';[64] and when Lollius fell from favour early

---

[52] *Anth. Pal.* X.25.

[53] C. Cichorius, *Römische Studien* (1922), 326 ff.

[54] Omitted from his list by D. Magie, *Roman Rule in Asia Minor* (1950), 1581. Rejected by K. M. T. Atkinson, *Historia* VII (1958), 323 f. Groag suggested the tenure 3/2 BC (*PIR*² C 289).

[55] Of the *ordinarii* from 16 to 12, there remain as unaccounted for, Piso, M. Livius Drusus Libo (perhaps deceased), P. Sulpicius Quirinius.

[56] *IGR* IV.410 f. (Pergamum); *BCH* V (1881), 183 (Stratonicea).

[57] *ILS* 8814 (Mytilene).

[58] P. Herrmann, *Ath. Mitt.* LXXV (1960), 130, no. 30; Chr. Habicht, *Pergamon* VIII. 3 (1969), 39, no. 19. See further in Ch. XXVI.

[59] Although Habicht prefers the Pontifex (o.c. 41).

[60] Ch. XXVI.

[61] Published by Keil and Wilhelm, *Jahreshefte* XVIII (1915), *Beiblatt* 51. A governor of Syria under Agrippa, so they suggested.

[62] *Klio* XXVII (1934), 128. Hence 'nescio an' in *PIR*² C 289.

[63] Ch. XXIII. [64] Suetonius, *Tib.* 12.2; Velleius II.102.1.

in AD 2, Sulpicius Quirinius took his place as 'rector'.[65] Those terms are descriptive, indicating the function that the consular was designated to perform.[66] Without *imperium* over Syria and its legions, the guide and counsellor would be reduced to moral suasion or plain impotence. Therefore legate of Syria, so it may be contended without effort or sophistry.

On this showing, Quirinius had a short tenure of Syria, before L. Volusius Saturninus (*suff.* 12), who is attested in AD 4/5.[67] Now Quirinius was certainly governor of Syria in 6 when he annexed Judaea after the decease of the ethnarch Archelaus and carried out a census. The earlier governorship here conjectured will lack appeal for those who deny that the same man could hold a province twice. Caesar Augustus was not bound by inflexible rules in the management of his 'provincia'. That is what the item serves to illustrate—and it should not be used for ulterior purposes.[68]

A candid exposition will add that Piso's governorship is subject to caution. Homonyms abound. The Lucius Piso honoured at Hierapolis might have held authority in Pedias during the period when Ti. Caesar detained at Rome the consular legate Aelius Lamia. Compare the L. Piso attested in 25 as governor of Tarraconensis—in the absence of L. Arruntius.[69]

Before the Pontifex is accepted beyond cavil, it would be expedient to have some kind of extraneous confirmation.

Such is to hand, at least on one interpretation of the famous fragment found near Tibur.[70] With supplements that none disputes, the text stands as follows:

```
REGEM·QVA·REDACTA·IN·POTESTATEM·IMPERATORIS·CAESARIS
AVGVSTI·POPVLIQVE·ROMANI·SENATVS·DIS · IMMORTALIBVS
SVPPLICATIONESBINASOBRESPROSPERE·AB·EO · GESTA·S · ET
IPSI·ORNAMENTA·TRIVMPHALIA · DECREVIT
PRO·CONSVL·ASIAM·PROVINCIAM·OPTINVIT·LEGATVS·PRO·PRAETORE
DIVI·AVGVSTI·ITERVM·SYRIAM·ET·PHOENICEN · OPTINVIT
```

Inspected without prepossessions, the document declares three posts in order of time held by the illustrious *Ignotus*.

---

[65] Tacitus, *Ann.* III.48.1.

[66] cf. Cn. Piso, the legate of Syria, whom the Princeps in his oration styled 'adiutoremque Germanico datum a se auctore senatu' (*Ann.* III.12.1). Some might object, to be sure, that the unfortunate case of Lollius counselled a different procedure.

[67] *PIR*[1] V 660 (adducing a coin of Antioch).

[68] i.e. to support the fancy of an earlier census held in Judaea.   [69] Ch. XXVI.

[70] *CIL* XIV. 3613 = *ILS* 918. The commentary in *Inscr. It.* IV. IV.1 (1936), reproduced in 1952, was obsolete and marred by various prepossessions. The text is on exhibit in the Vatican, headed by an insertion: the name of P. Sulpicius Quirinius.

(1) Legate of Augustus, he fought a war connected in some way with a king, dead or alive, conquered a native people, and was honoured with the *ornamenta triumphalia* and the vote of two *supplicationes*.

(2) He governed Asia as proconsul.

(3) Again legate of Augustus, he governed Syria.

The *Titulus Tiburtinus* has a long and troubled history. A curt statement cutting through entanglements will suffice for present purposes. The clear approach leads through the key word 'iterum' in the last line. It indicates the sequence of posts, also something else, and vital. Standing before 'Syriam', the word goes with what precedes, namely 'legatus pro praetore/divi Augusti'. If a second governorship of Syria were being stated, the adverb 'iterum' would have to go with its verb, for this is continuous prose.

That modest truth was not promulgated until the year 1924.[71] It has not yet won general recognition.[72] Previous enquiries started from the axiom of a 'second governorship' of Syria as the third post of *Ignotus*.

A 'first governorship' was ready for ascertainment so it seemed, residing in the first post and explaining the word 'regem' with which the fragment begins. The answer was the war against the Homonadenses waged by P. Sulpicius Quirinius (*cos.* 12). Mommsen therefore produced the supplement 'bellum gessit cum gente Homonadensium/quae interfecerat Amyntam/r]egem'.[73] Quirinius was thus shown legate of Syria at some time earlier than and distinct from his governorship of AD 6 when he superintends the annexation of Judaea.

The thesis earned wide acclaim—and it was exploited with fervour from mixed motivations. If a doubt arose, it could be circumvented.

Geography dictated strategy. The Homonadenses, it is clear, could only be subjugated by an army coming from the north, from the side of Galatia. But Galatia was a province of praetorian rank, whereas the victorious general was a consular. Therefore legate of Syria.[74] As elsewhere, historians postulated a rule foreign to Roman methods of government and to the practices of Caesar Augustus. Other consular legates of Galatia awaited detection: not only L. Piso, but M. Plautius Silvanus who quelled a rising of the Isaurians.[75]

All was not lost. Quirinius might still keep the *Titulus*, with a slight change. The first post was not Syria but Galatia-Pamphylia.[76]

---

[71] E. Groag, *Jahreshefte* XXI/XXII (1924), *Beiblatt* 473 f. (citing approval in a letter from Dessau).

[72] e.g. A. N. Sherwin-White, *Roman Society and Roman Law in the New Testament* (1963), 164: '*iterum* should mean that the anonymous consular was twice legate of Syria.'

[73] Mommsen, *Res Gestae Divi Augusti*[2] (1886), 177.

[74] W. M. Ramsay, *JRS* VII (1917), 229 ff. And elsewhere. He assigned Quirinius to the period 11–7. [75] Dio LV.28.2 f.

[76] As conceded in *Rom. Rev.* (1939), 398, though a new candidate was then proposed. Quirinius continued to find firm support, e.g. H. Braunert, *Historia* VI (1957), 211.

Meanwhile, two other consulars had found advocates. First the 'vir triumphalis' Plautius Silvanus (*cos.* 2), a known proconsul of Asia (?AD 4/5), and active in Illyricum (7 to 8), but nowhere attested as governor of Syria.[77] However, the order of posts (descending) that was proposed stood in conflict with the word 'iterum'.[78] Second, M. Titius (*suff.* 31), governor of Syria *c.*10 BC. An earlier governorship was conjured up, in 20 or 19.[79] Various reasons tell decisively against.

It is a strange fact that the long controversy failed to throw up Piso the Pontifex until a late season.[80] That the *Titulus* advertised the avenging of Amyntas, dead more than twenty years earlier than the war of Sulpicius Quirinius, aroused some intermittent disquiet; and one might wonder whether, although the *ornamenta* may have become fairly common, those operations deserved two *supplicationes*.

By contrast, the three years' war in Thrace, with pitched battles against numerous and savage enemies. The insurgent Bessi had killed Rhescuporis. No author or inscription happens to accord him the regal title.[81] Whether that omission is enough to disallow Piso and revalidate Quirinius is another matter. If the document is conceded to Piso, he gains what otherwise rested on something a little short of proof: governorships in Asia (*c.*8) and in Syria (?4–1).[82]

Curiosity and equity demand a revelation at the end, to explain and deprecate the enduring preoccupation with Quirinius, governor of Syria in AD 6. It concerns a problem to which there never was an answer, the Date of the Nativity. The statements in Luke about the days of King Herod and the census of 'Cyrenios' are not easy to reconcile.[83] The problem became early apparent. The alert Tertullian came out with an answer: not the census of Quirinius but that of Sentius Saturninus.[84]

Scholars and apologists in the recent time have had recourse to

---

[77] E. Groag, o.c. 445 ff.

[78] viz. legate in Illyricum (7–9), proconsul of Asia (?6/7), legate of Syria (just before or just after 4/5). Discountenanced in *Klio* XXVII (1934), 142 f.

[79] L. R. Taylor, *JRS* XXVI (1936), 161 ff.

[80] Indicated in *Rom. Rev.* 398, n. 8. In the sequel not much heed was paid—except by Miss Levick (o.c., 1967), 209. For Piso see *Danubian Papers* (1971), 65 f., and the explicit treatment of the *Titulus Tiburtinus* in *Akten des VI. int. Kongresses für. gr. u. lat. Epigraphik* (1973), 585 ff. = *RP* III (1984), 869 ff.

[81] Observe however *PIR²* C 1553 (Cotys): 'Rhescuporis rex occisus anno ante C.11.' For the Thracian dynastic families, G. W. Bowersock, *Augustus and the Greek World* (1965), 152 ff.

[82] In Schürer, *The History of the Jewish People in the Age of Jesus Christ* I (ed. Vermes and Millar, 1973), 258 he stands as '?L. Calpurnius Piso?' Dissent by P. Herrmann and Chr. Habicht is there cited. Not but that the concluding sentence seems favourable.

[83] Luke I.5; 2.2. An explanation is propounded in the paper of 1973 (598 ff.) = *RP* III (1984), 881 f.; and cf. above, p. 324, n. 82.

[84] Tertullian, *Adv. Marcionem* IV.19: 'sed et census constat actos sub Augusto tunc in Iudaea per Sentium Saturninum apud quos genus eius inquirere potuissent.'

expedients more bold or more subtle. That is, an earlier governorship of Quirinius—and, by implication, an earlier census in Judaea.[85]

No more on that distressing topic. If the Tiburtine fragment is assigned to Piso, he acquires Syria in his career and duly joins the company of the aristocrats whom the high epoch of the renovated Republic saw not only holding the twelve *fasces* in Asia or Africa but even competing with *novi homines* in the charge of great armies.

The Syrian command had signal importance. It faced the Parthians, to whom Caesar Augustus conceded intermittent parity when advertising diplomatic success at their expense. Caesar's legate might conduct negotiations or prevent a war; and it was his function to watch over several vassal states. Above all, if a prince of the dynasty went to the eastern lands, the selection of the legate became a delicate matter. Augustus chose the smooth and crafty Lollius. On the next occasion, Ti. Caesar went to the other extreme: the intractable Cn. Piso.

C. Caesar died in February of AD 4. Ruler and government were now caught in an acute predicament: boy princes once again (or at least youthful) and the need for a regent, or a successor in the supreme power. Men of understanding or hardened intriguers found plenty to talk about in their clubs and circles; and some feared the ascension of Domitius Ahenobarbus, recently holding the great commands in Illyricum and in Germany.

Ahenobarbus was the husband of the elder Antonia. He had suitable years—and a detestable character. For Piso, his coeval, spoke a distinguished career but dynastic and domestic reasons prevailed. The son of Livia Drusilla became Ti. Caesar: his claim was reinforced by the northern wars.[86]

Since the presumed governorship of Syria, there is no hint of Piso until 13, when he acceded to the post of *praefectus urbi*, to hold it for twenty years.[87] The duration stated by Tacitus has encountered disbelief. His text was corrected to 'quindecim per annos', an alteration that enjoyed wide currency.[88] It entailed corollaries not always made apparent, namely that either the historian or a copyist made a mistake, that the critics are in

---

[85] Dismissed by Mommsen as 'homines theologi vel non theologi, sed ad instar theologorum ex vinculis sermocinantes' (o.c. 176). For a recent specimen of the second category of delinquents observe V. A. Sirago, *Principato di Augusto* (1978), 200.

[86] Ch. VII.

[87] *Ann.* VI.11.3.

[88] Thus H. Fuchs (*Ed. Helv.*, 1946). E. Koestermann repented in his second edition (Teubner, 1965). A tenure of fifteen years was assumed by E. Sacher, with no hint of doubt, in *RE* XXII. 2514; and expressly preferred by J. Crook, *Consilium Principis* (1955), 156, and by J. Scheid (o.c. 92). The notion had been strongly deprecated by Groag, *PIR*² C 289.

possession of the truth. There was a further consequence. If the innovation, the 'recens continua potestas', originated in the year 17, it was missed by the senatorial annalist, who shows a keen interest both in the office and its holders.[89]

Two authors, Pliny and Suetonius, imply, or rather assume, that Piso was not appointed before Tiberius took over the power.[90] Inspection shows mere anecdotes and testimony to be discarded without discomfort. What objections subsist?

On the decease of Augustus an oath of allegiance to the new ruler was sworn by the consuls, also by two equestrian officials, namely the *praefectus praetorio* and the *praefectus annonae*.[91] No word of the Prefect of the City.

In plain fact, the position was peculiar and anomalous (as Tacitus was careful to demonstrate in his excursus), and the *imperium* of the Prefect is not easy to define. No precedent existed. Though not an assertive character, Piso might see no reason to take the oath. Perhaps he was not at Rome but at Nola. Serene on his death-bed, the Princeps held discourse with his friends, asking how he had played out his role in the comedy of life. The occasion offered scope for subsequent revelations. The moribund ruler put up a question, which of the 'principes civitatis' might be held 'capax imperii'.

Cornelius Tacitus found the anecdote in a subsidiary source (hostile to the destined successor), and he could not resist a topic of permanent value and instruction.[92] He inserted a piece of annotation in the debate of September 17, following on the interventions of Asinius Gallus and L. Arruntius.

A pair of sporadic notices may, or may not, belong to the rubric of the last days or hours at Nola. First, Augustus found Rome a city of bricks and left it a city of marble.[93] Second, since Piso built so solidly, Augustus was encouraged to believe that Rome would last for ever.[94]

Of the functions of the prefecture, Tacitus gave a firm and ruthless definition. A consular was appointed 'qui coerceret servitia et quod civium turbidum, nisi vim metuat'. For which salutary operations, the Prefect had under his command three *cohortes urbanae*, soon increased to four. There is no sign that Piso in his long tenure was ever called upon to employ them. The Praetorian Guard sufficed. When Tiberius Caesar put out an edict, anticipating an outbreak of violence at the funeral of his predecessor, he betrayed needless anxiety and incurred ridicule.[95] The metropolis

---

[89] No need therefore to invoke the lacuna in Dio's text for the year 13.
[90] Pliny, *NH* XIV.145; Suetonius, *Tib.* 42.1.
[91] *Ann.* I.7.2.
[92] above, p. 137.
[93] Suetonius, *Divus Aug.* 28.3.
[94] Plutarch, *Apoph. Caes. Aug.* 2 (*Moralia* 208 A).   [95] *Ann.* I.8.5 f.

harboured other sources of alarm. In the next year the 'theatri licentia' erupted into a riot, soldiers of the Guard being killed and an officer wounded. The Senate took cognisance and measures of restraint were enacted.[96] Then, in 19, votaries of Jewish and Egyptian cults got into trouble.[97] A large number were expelled from the city. Senators with a taste for history might be happy to recall what Piso's father and his colleague Gabinius did to Isis and Serapis.[98]

The departure of the ruler in 26 offered an accession of authority to the *praefectus urbi*; and he gave Piso 'secreta mandata', according to Seneca.[99] However, there is no mention of Piso in any transaction, not even on that October day five years later which witnessed the ruin of Aelius Seianus. His images were cast down, his mansion burned. That was the work of the Guard and the mob, in joyous concord.

Not long before that turn of fortune, Velleius had written a handsome testimonial to Piso's comportment in his office.[100] The guardian of the city was both 'diligentissimus' and 'lenissimus'. The lavish superlatives and epigrammatic antitheses so dear to this author normally tell nothing, or instil distrust. In this instance they may perhaps be accepted. In short, the Prefect of the City kept his equilibrium all through and did nothing.[101]

Piso's independent behaviour in the Senate is extolled by Tacitus in the obituary notice: 'nullius servilis sententiae sponte auctor'. The historian vouchsafes only one specimen. When the prosecution of a proconsul of Asia was wound up, Piso pronounced for the milder penalty, not without a compliment to the ruler: 'multum de clementia principis praefatus'.[102] There is no imputation of servility. Otherwise, Tacitean allusions to imperial clemency tend to be ironical and subversive.

Tacitus was careful to register for infamy the 'sententiae' proposed by seven men of rank after the alleged conspiracy of Scribonius Libo. One name is masked by a lacuna in the text.[103] A number of scholars commend 'L. Piso'. Neither the Pontifex nor the Augur ('nobilis ac ferox vir') deserved that affront. Better, 'L. Plancus'.[104] That is, the consul of 13, whose father made the name synonymous with adulation.[105]

[96] *Ann.* I.77.
[97] II.85.4.
[98] Tertullian, *Apol.* 6.8.
[99] Seneca, *Epp.* 83.14.
[100] Velleius II.98.
[101] 'Indolence, when it is not the result of weakness and vice, is a very great virtue.' Thus Shelburne in his *Autobiography*, quoted by L. B. Namier, *England in the Age of the American Revolution* I (1930), 40.
[102] *Ann.* III.68.2.
[103] II.32.2
[104] *JRS* XLVI (1956), 18 f. = *Ten Studies in Tacitus* (1970), 51 ff.
[105] Seneca, *NQ* IV, *praef.* 5: 'Plancus, artifex ante Vitellium maximus aiebat non esse occulte nec ex dissimulato blandiendum.'

A solitary appearance, therefore. By contrast, the historian's other paragon Marcus Lepidus, who demonstrated that an aristocrat could follow the middle path between 'abrupta contumacia' and 'deforme obsequium'.[106] The *Annales* name Lepidus no fewer than seven times before recording his decease, a year after Piso.

For silence about Piso, a ready explanation avails and an argument that some may find circular. If the consular historian followed a 'single source' in much of the first hexad, it was the *Acta* of the Roman Senate. The voice of Piso was not often heard in the high assembly.[107]

Two other notable survivors from the Augustan 'viri triumphales' accede to that rubric: Domitius Ahenobarbus, not mentioned until his decease in the year 25, and Cossus Cornelius Lentulus, nowhere named.

Book V must be allowed for, most of it missing. Subsequent references show that M. Lepidus was there mentioned, likewise Aelius Lamia and L. Arruntius (in the matter of their absentee governorships of Syria and of Tarraconensis). Further, Tacitus had referred to the parentage of Piso.

Those were years of tribulation and peril, especially for enemies of Seianus. In 31 he instigated charges against Arruntius, who escaped harm, the principle being established that holders of *imperium* were not liable to prosecution. It was Cossus Lentulus who put in that plea, a confidant of Tiberius.[108] Piso may have intervened in this case, or in others. There is a chance that his grandson Nonius Asprenas (*suff.* 29) incurred danger.[109]

The temperament and sagacity of Piso found expression in quiet counsel to the ruler. When Tiberius celebrated his Pannonian triumph in October of the year 12, after eight years with the northern armies, he was aged fifty-two, but had seldom been seen in the Senate for a quarter of a century. His demeanour showed him often ill at ease or out of touch.

For preparing business, the senatorial quorum existed, and its authority was notably modified and strengthened in 13.[110] The new Princeps, however let it lapse, so it appears. He preferred to rely more on old friends.[111] The list is instructive.[112] Several, it is true, were absent in the

---

[106] *Ann.* IV.20.3.

[107] Compare the excellent Aelius Lamia. One brief notice only (IV.13.3) before his decease in 33 as Prefect of the City with the label 'genus illi decorum, vivida senectus' (VI.27.2).

Tacitean verdicts are not always reinforced in the narration. Cf., discussing the 'modestia vitae' of Furius Camillus (II.52.5), E. J. Weinrib, *HSCP* LXXII (1968), 272 f.

[108] Ch. XIX.

[109] below, p. 431. The dearth of known relatives and allies of the Pontifex will be recalled.

[110] Dio LVI.28.2 f.

[111] Suetonius may be worth quoting: 'super veteres amicos et familiares viginti sibi e numero principum civitatis deposcerat, velut consiliarios in negotiis publicis. horum vix duos anne tres incolumis praestitit' (*Tib.* 55).

[112] J. Crook, *Consilium Principis* (1955), 36: preferring however Manius Lepidus to Marcus (cf. 35).

provinces, often for inordinate periods. Others, like Piso, had not been conspicuous in the Senate. For example, the jurist Cocceius Nerva, consul suffect in 21 or 22. He is named twice only by Tacitus: when he accompanied his close friend on the journey that ended at Capreae, and when he died there in 33.[113]

Piso shared with Tiberius on addiction to strong drink. A famous 'perpotatio' of two days and two nights finds report in Pliny.[114] Suetonius adds a companion, Pomponius Flaccus (*cos.* 17), and a detail that shows up his ignorance. Tiberius, he alleges, at once rewarded them both with promotion ('confestim'), Piso to the urban prefecture, Flaccus to the governorship of Syria.[115]

Seneca purveys better entertainment. Deriding the rigid arguments used by Stoics or declaimers, the diplomat and man of the world has recourse to recent and Roman examples. Lucius Piso, he says, was drunk from the day he took the office on which depended the 'tutela urbis', yet he managed it 'diligentissime;' and he was entrusted with 'secreta mandata' on two occasions in his career. Tiberius, encouraged by this experience, gave the post to Cossus Lentulus, soaked and sunk in wine. Neither Piso nor Lentulus ever betrayed a secret.[116]

[113] *Ann.* IV.58.1; VI.26.1 f.

[114] Pliny, *NH* XIV.145 (on Piso's appointment, with the word 'credidere'). The context documents the prowess of Torquatus Novellius, a senator from Mediolanum, whose capacity extorted admiration from Tiberius, 'in senecta iam severo atque etiam saevo'.

[115] Suetonius, *Tib.* 42.1. Pomponius Flaccus got Syria when Aelius Lamia was released in 32 to become *praefectus urbi* (VI.27.2 f.).

[116] Seneca, *Epp.* 83.14 f. The sole evidence, by the way, for the urban prefecture of Cossus Lentulus.

Addendum. The bronze bust of Piso the Pontifex reproduced as frontispiece was found at Herculanum. It shows him in the season of his consulship. As a copy from the same model stands the marble head of a *togatus* in the gallery of the 'domus Augusta' at Veleia, constructed some years later, during the reign of Tiberius. For that monument, see C. Saletti, *Il ciclo statuario della Basilica di Velleia* (1968), with plate xvii, 1 and 2. Along with four inscriptions of the dynasty, the site yielded *ILS* 900: 'L. Calpurnio/L. f. Pisoni/pontif., cos.'/ . . . . . Hence, by unique fortune in Augustan iconography of senators and consuls, a firm identity: the brother (junior by a quarter of a century) of 'Calpurnia C. Caesaris.'

For a succinct statement see K. Fittchen and P. Zanker, *Katalog der r. Porträts in den Capitolinischen Museen*, etc. I (1985), 21 n. 7.

XXV

The Education of an Aristocrat

Piso's father, consul and proconsul of Macedonia, avowed Hellenic tastes. It was the custom to annex a philosopher and use him as a kind of domestic chaplain. Some selected a bearded sage whose profession or deportment might accord with Roman notions of tradition and of 'gravitas'. The familiar of Caesoninus preached the gospel of pleasure. If that were not bad enough, his patron and friend compelled him to write indecent verses.

Such is the testimony declared by Cicero in oration and invective.[1] The Epicurean he refrained from naming was Philodemus, the unimpeachable man of Gadara in the Decapolis.

How far father or family transmit political beliefs and social attitudes may arouse curiosity in any age, and it is legitimate with an aristocracy. Caesoninus was a model of good sense—if needed. Beyond doubt is his liking for Greek letters. His son the Pontifex comes into a dozen epigrams of Antipater, variously instructive, even for divining official posts; and Antipater wrote, or at least promised, an epic poem on the Thracian War.[2]

Actium and the fall of Alexandria united again the two halves of the world. The ultimate conflict did not cause much damage. Caesar's heir duly took over the 'clientela' of his rival: kings and tetrarchs and the city aristocracies. The intellectual class made a quick response, streaming to Rome, some no doubt getting places on embassies.[3] Among the earliest arrived Dionysius and Strabo. The former, an expert in rhetoric, composed treatises and embarked on a history of early Rome. Strabo chose to write a continuation of Polybius. He carried the narration into the present, terminating with the end of the Ptolemies.

Poets would not be left behind. Most in evidence is Crinagoras.[4] He had represented Mytilene on embassies to Caesar the Dictator. In 26 he went on a mission to Caesar's heir in Spain. Crinagoras remained thereafter at Rome for a number of years, operating as a court poet.[5] Other

---

[1] *In Pisonem* 68 ff.

[2] *PIR*[2] A 749, with the poems registered in C 289; Gow and Page, *The Garland of Philip* II (1968), 18 ff. In ample discourse those eminent scholars managed to eschew any reference to the articles of Groag. And Piso was called 'Frugi'.

[3] G. W. Bowersock, *Augustus and the Greek World* (1965), 122 ff.

[4] *PIR*[2] C 1580; Cichorius, *Römische Studien* (1922), 306 ff.; Gow and Page, o.c. 210 ff.

[5] His age and survival are relevant to the attribution of the poem that celebrates the exploits of a prince called 'Germanicus' (*Anth. Pal.* IX. 283). According to Gow and Page, 'insuperable

intellectuals, down to grammarians, doctors, and astrologers, found patrons and formed groups. Personal links regained continuity with the last age of the Republic.

Of philosophers, the ruler could command the most illustrious; and he employed the talents of Areus and Athenodorus in practical matters.[6] Educators were in lively demand. For her son Claudius Marcellus, Octavia was able to enlist Nestor of Tarsus, one of the Academic philosophers.[7] In fact, this lady took over the supervision of a whole kindergarten: along with the sisters of Marcellus went the two daughters she had born to Marcus Antonius, and also Iullus, the Triumvir's son.[8] As was suitable, the Porticus Octaviae, which transmits her memory, contained a choice library. The comparable monument of Livia Drusilla had classical paintings for adornment.[9]

To this rubric may be attached Julia, the daughter of Scribonia. About her mother, the record is silent between her divorce in 39 and the catastrophe of the year 2. Later evidence attests Julia's taste and wit, her addiction to polite studies and to the company of poets.[10] Her father made her take up weaving.[11] The autocrat was trying at the same time to deny the existence of a court and stem the surge of society in an elegant and prosperous age.

One of the neglected Augustan topics is the education of women. It tends to be touched upon when *hetaerae* are put under inspection, or controversies pursued about the social rank of ladies celebrated by certain poets. Enquiry often revolves in a vacuum, no allowance being made for conditions in a post-war world, which exhibited widows and the victims of desertion, divorce and spoliation among the better sort in the towns of Italy.[12]

A second topic is the disruption of family life during the twenty years of

---

objections to Drusus' (o.c. 234). Their thesis was adduced by T. D. Barnes, *JRS* LXIV (1974), 25 (discussing the first imperatorial salutation of Germanicus Caesar, in AD 13). Cichorius, acquiescing in Germanicus, had denied the authorship of Crinagoras (o.c. 307). However, nothing in fact precludes the Alpine campaign of Drusus in 15 BC.

[6] Areus followed Athenodorus as procurator in Sicily, cf. *PIR*[2] A 1035; 1288. Athenodorus in old age governed Tarsus, his native city (Strabo XIV, p. 674). If he is discovered at Petra (XVI, p. 779), that was no doubt on Caesar's business.

[7] Strabo XIV, p. 675. He succeeded Athenodorus as a city boss. A casual notice discloses Nestor the Stoic (dying at ninety-two) as the teacher of Claudius Nero (Lucian, *Macrobii* 21): named as a Stoic like the two Athenodori and others in Strabo XIV, p. 674. In *PIR*[1] N 54 the Nestores were amalgamated.

[8] Plutarch, *Antonius* 87.

[9] Ovid, *AA* I.71 f. (the solitary reference to the pictures): not registered in *PIR*[2] L 301.

[10] For the detail, *PIR*[2] J 634. Various and vivid instruction accrues from Macrobius II.5.2–9. No poem survives in her honour: or possibly one, at Thespiae in Boeotia, cf. *PIR*[2] H 192.

[11] Suetonius, *Divus Aug.* 64.2.

[12] On this theme, *History in Ovid* (1978), 202 f.

tribulation. The perils are known of the infant Claudius Nero, born in November of 42; and consequences can be drawn from deprival of his mother, whom Caesar's heir acquired early in 38, and from decease of his father when he was nine years old. Resentment towards his stepfather was sharpened in the sequel.

Not so drastic, but deserving attention, is the damage sustained by other young *nobiles* of that age group, born between the invasion of Italy and the War of Perusia. Fathers died, or were absent for long years with Antonius in the eastern lands. For example, the father of Fabius Maximus succumbed in his consulship on the last day of 45; and there is no trace of Piso Caesoninus after the spring of 43. As for Ahenobarbus, Republican and Antonian, it is probable that he never saw Rome between the summer of 44 and his consulship in 32. Important functions therefore devolved upon the mother or the guardian, upon friends of the family, freedmen, and teachers.[13]

The traditional upbringing came back with the years of peace and stability. That is, warfare, oratory, and the law. The youths Marcellus and Nero both saw service in Spain as military tribunes, in 26 and 25; and other aristocrats may be surmised. The army sometimes offered action. More often and in general, social training, acquiescence in subordination, and comradeship, but further, emulation and causes of enmity.

Public eloquence was requisite, and advertised at an early age. For Claudius Nero several cases are on record.[14] In 23 he prosecuted the conspirator Fannius Caepio (who was not present at the trial). Before that he had defended Archelaus, the ruler of Cappadocia. The eastern 'clientela' of the Claudii is a fact not to be missed.[15]

As in the previous generation, an advocate did not need much law. Nor was there an urgent call for legal experts when the prerogative of the ruler was established or modified. The government could command at need the services of the best talent; and Rome of the Caesars does not often exhibit those luminaries in opposition to the established order, either open or insidious.[16]

For most of the reign of Augustus, there is a lacuna in the line of consular jurists. Sulpicius Rufus died in 43. He left a son who failed to continue the tradition, preferring oratory, with great renown.[17] It was taken up by the pupil, the *novus homo* Alfenus Varus, who, however, is not

---

[13] The influence of old men will be variously assessed. Losing his father at an early age, Marcus Aurelius was much in the company of Annius Verus, his grandfather, and of Catilius Severus, styled 'proavus maternus' (*HA Marcus* 1.9).

[14] On which, G. W. Bowersock, o.c. 157 ff.; B. Levick, *CQ* XXI (1971), 478 ff.

[15] E. Rawson, *Historia* XXII (1973), 219 ff.; XXVI (1977), 340 ff.

[16] Antistius Labeo is hardly to be rated an exception, despite remarks of his rival (Gellius XII.12.2) or the items in Dio LIV.15.7 f.

[17] above, p. 206.

heard of after his consulship (in 39). An Aelius Tubero, belonging to a family that had links with the earliest notables in the annals of jurisprudence, survived for a time, his attention going rather to the writing of history. His son reached the consulate in 11, but leaves no trace of any legal pursuits.[18]

A certain Antistius Labeo, whose father perished at Philippi, acquired fame for independence as well as profound scholarship, hostile to innovation and standing by the old books.[19] His rival Ateius Capito became consul suffect in AD 5. His subservience, it is alleged, earned him acceleration to that honour.[20]

After a time, the contrasted pair were taken to be founders of opposing schools in legal science.[21] In the sequence, on Labeo followed Cocceius Nerva. But the successor to Capito was Masurius Sabinus, a man of obscure origin and late in acquiring even equestrian rank.[22] Law in its origins was bound up with religion, a nexus which antiquarian studies did not allow to be forgotten. Patricians kept up the old science, as witness Ap. Claudius Pulcher (*cos.* 54); while Messalla Rufus (*cos.* 53), an expert and an author, survived to witness the restoration of legal authority in the Roman state. The historian Tacitus was careful to specify the double excellence in both Capito and Nerva by an identical label.[23]

The young Claudius Nero, adherent to family tradition and averse from recent fashions, and at odds with his entourage, might well stage a retreat into sacerdotal lore. When presiding over the religion of the Roman state, Ti. Caesar was ever ready to intervene and rebuke ignorance or ritual delinquency.[24]

Whatever this man took up, he was intense and exigent.[25] Wilfully archaic in so many of his attitudes, and defending the language of the imperial people, Tiberius was given over to Greek studies. The recent age has seen many biographies, seldom with proper recognition of this passionate and

---

[18] For the Tuberones, Ch. XXII.

[19] Gellius XII.12.2. He was also interested in language and grammar (10.1).

[20] *Ann.* III.75.2. Dubious, given the presumed age of Capito. But one cannot impugn the Tacitean comment 'Capitonis obsequium dominantibus magis probabatur.'

[21] *Dig.* I.2.47.

[22] And, as Borghesi knew, from Verona—or rather from native stock in its *territorium* (*ILS* 6704: Arusnates).

[23] II.70.1; VI.26.1.

[24] VI.12.2: 'Gallo exprobrabat quod scientiarum caerimoniarumque vetus' etc. That is, Caninius Gallus (*suff.* 2 BC). Similarly, a rebuke to L. Apronius (III.66.4). Nor could he refrain from criticism of Germanicus: 'neque imperatorem auguratu et vetustissimis caerimoniis praeditum adtrectare feralia debuisse' (I.62.2).

The biographer was singularly impercipient: 'circa deos ac religiones neglegentior, quippe addictus mathematicae' (*Tib.* 69).

[25] Compare Caesar's estimate of Marcus Brutus, 'magni refert hic quid velit, sed quicquid volet valde volet' (reported by C. Matius in *Ad Att.* XIV.1.2).

permanent addiction.[26] The testimony was to hand, in a chapter of Suetonius, who, so often without insight (he was not a senator or a historian), was none the less a scholar and alert to 'curiosa' in the annals of Latin literature no less than in the behaviour of the Caesars.

A Roman aristocrat endowed with a penetrating intelligence, and with time on his hands, might have turned to Thucydides or to Polybius.[27] Tiberius went to the Alexandrian poets. Of their first glories, namely Callimachus and Apollonius, the biographer says nothing. Instead, Euphorion, Rhianus, Parthenius. Tiberius wrote poems in their honour, he had their works and their images placed in the public libraries among the 'veteres et praecipuos auctores'.[28]

The copious Rhianus wrote at least five epics on legends or legendary history.[29] Euphorion had been a favourite study at Rome in the fifties, a whole company being designated 'cantores Euphorionis'; and he was a byword for preciosity and obscurity.[30] While Euphorion and Rhianus belonged to the first generation of Alexandrian *epigoni*, Parthenius had come to recent notoriety. He brought Callimachus into currency, and he exercised a powerful influence on such poets as Cornelius Gallus and the young Virgil.[31]

By these predilections, Claudius Nero reflected the taste of the preceding generation—not alone in that, as witness the elegiac poets. Moreover, a stray fact may be noted: Crinagoras gave young Marcellus a copy of the *Hecale* of Callimachus.[32]

When in 20 the Princeps despatched his stepson on a mission to Armenia, a 'studiosa cohors' went with him. The three letters addressed by Horace betray no trace of Greek companions or of Hellenistic poetry. However that may be, the subsequent vicissitudes of Claudius Nero threw him back on his own resources, hardening and sharpening habits formed in his early education.

He needed those resources when he broke with Augustus and went away in anger to Rhodes. After five years spent in study and tranquillity, although not always at ease when trying to comport himself as an equal with citizens, Tiberius incurred danger of his life when the prince Gaius Caesar arrived in the eastern lands; but his prospects improved and the

---

[26] cf. observations in *Historia* XXIII (1974), 490 f. = *RP* III (1984), 946. For a welcome exception, B. Levick, *Tiberius the Politician* (1976), 17 ff., with supplementary comment in the review by J. P. Adams, *AJP* C (1979), 462 f.

[27] Thucydides had recently come into sudden favour, though at first through literary reasons. An item concerning Polybius casts a curious light on Marcus Brutus. Shortly before the battle in Thessaly he was occupied in making an epitome of that historian (Plutarch, *Brutus* 4).

[28] Suetonius, *Tib.* 70.

[29] R. Pfeiffer, *History of Classical Scholarship* (1968), 148 f.

[30] Cicero, *De div.* II.133: 'nimis etiam obscurus Euphorio'.

[31] W. Clausen, *GRBS* V (1964), 181 ff.

[32] *Anth. Pal.* IX. 545.

Princeps allowed him to return to Rome in the summer of AD 2, but to no place in public life. He lived for two years in total seclusion in the Gardens of Maecenas.

Nine years therefore of virtual exile. His next retreat was to last for a decade. Leaving Rome in 26, he installed himself on Capreae the next year. With him went one senator only, the consular Cocceius Nerva. For the rest, mainly exponents of 'liberalia studia', Greeks above all, 'quorum sermonibus levaretur'.[33] The poets whom Tiberius cherished showed erudition in their occupations as well as their writings. They were scholars and even librarians. Rhianos, for example, produced a notable edition of Homer.[34] Research proliferated, and with it the delight in erudite recreation or fraudulence. The Roman period brought no abatement of 'aniles fabulas' and the wilful invention of authorities.[35]

Discoursing on the idle who complain about the shortness of human life, Seneca briefly alludes to time wasted on antiquarian pursuits such as the Homeric Question: 'Graecorum iste morbus', and it has now infested the Romans.[36]

He is more explicit in the long letter that deprecates 'liberalia studia'. Homer again, research into the wanderings of Ulixes, and even the age of Hecuba, who was younger than Helen. Or again, the real mother of Aeneas. Such were the urgent preoccupations of Didymus, a scholar who filled four thousand volumes.[37]

Suetonius in a famous passage adverts with derision on Tiberius' fancy for 'historia fabularis'. He vexed his familiars with problems: Hecuba's mother, the name Achilles assumed among the maidens, what song the Sirens sang.[38] The dinner parties of a classical scholar or polymath are an exacting ordeal. With Tiberius dire peril attended. One of the 'convictores', who came prepared in advance, was expelled and driven to death.[39]

Greek art found ardent fanciers among some Romans not at all predictable. Marcus Agrippa was one of the great collectors.[40] Fashion or greed did not preclude genuine appreciation. For Tiberius, varied

---

[33] *Ann.* IV.58.1.

[34] Pfeiffer, o.c. 149.

[35] Contemning 'aniles fabulae' and 'grammaticorum commentarii', Quintilian goes on to fraud: 'adeo ut de libris totis et auctoribus, ut succurrit, mentiantur tuto' (I.8.21).

[36] Seneca, *De brevitate vitae* 13.2. He adduces Roman specimens, concluding with the question of the *pomerium* (13.8).

[37] Seneca, *Epp.* 88.6 f.; 37. On Apion (38), compare the verdict of Tiberius: 'cymbalum mundi'. Quoted by Pliny, *NH, praef.* 25.

[38] Suetonius, *Tib.* 70.3. Similar enquiries were mocked by Philippus, *Anth. Pal.* XI.321 (whether the Cyclops kept dogs); 347 (the fathers of Proteus and of Pygmalion).

The story in Plutarch fits in. After a voice made an announcement to an Egyptian steersman ('Great Pan is dead') the Emperor had him brought to Rome for questioning. Discussion ensued with 'philologi' about Pan's identity and parentage (*De defectu oraculorum* 18).

[39] Suetonius, *Tib.* 56.2.

[40] M. Reinhold, *Marcus Agrippa* (1933), 72.

documentation is available. For example, in his bedchamber on Capreae hung the painting by Parrhasius which showed Atalanta in Calydon, more than normally indulgent to Meleager;[41] and, conceiving a passion for a statue by Lysippus, he took it from the Baths of Agrippa, but had to give way before popular clamour.[42]

The grotto near Fundi, the roof of which collapsed and endangered the life of Tiberius, has supplied novel illumination. The dining chamber was adorned with large pieces of Hellenistic sculpture. They presented scenes from the Odyssey. Which encourages speculation far from idle about the Emperor's estimate of his own character and vicissitudes.[43]

A biography of the devious autocrat would not neglect casual details about drinking and eating.[44] To the end of his days Tiberius Caesar refused to listen to doctors; and when they extolled the 'nobilitas' of Surrentine wine, they got a cutting answer.[45] Other items show a taste for delicate flavours. Against the authority of the gourmet Apicius, Tiberius preferred a kind of tender cabbage;[46] in cucumbers he took a 'mira voluptas', instructing the gardeners to grow them on movable frames;[47] he had views about the wild asparagus that grew in the fields of Germany;[48] and from that country he got a supply each year of the esculent root called 'siser'.[49] Finally, fruit transmitted his name, the pears known as 'Tiberiana'.[50]

The patrician Claudii stood apart from other houses of the aristocracy. Innovators and rebellious, they courted the favour of the Roman plebs and went in for extraneous alliances. Such at least was the main line, the conspicuous Pulchri. Tiberius carried their blood through his mother's father, a Claudius adopted by Livius Drusus. The Nerones were his own direct ancestry: dull, obscure, and conventional, absent from the consular *Fasti* for nearly two centuries.

---

[41] The picture was worth a million sesterces (Pliny, *NH* XXV.69). Suetonius adds the detail 'in qua Meleagro Atalanta ore morigeratur' (*Tib.* 44.2). In an elaborate attempt to protect the reputation of the old emperor from 'le reproche d'épouvantable lubricité dont le chargent les insinuations de Suétone', Carcopino neglected the relevant passage (*Aspects mystiques de la Rome paienne* (1941), 151).

[42] Pliny, *NH* XXXIV. 69. Finally, in the last year of his life he brought from Syracuse a statue of Apollo (*Tib.* 74).

[43] As neatly supplied by A. F. Stewart, *JRS* LXVII (1977), 87 f.

[44] As emphasized in *Historia* XXIII (1974), 491 = *RP* III (1984), 947. He had probably abated on wine, cf. Pliny, *NH* XIV. 144: 'iuventa ad vinum pronior'.

[45] Pliny, *NH* XIV.64: 'generosum acetum'.

[46] XIX.137.

[47] XIX.64. In winter they were taken into glasshouses.

[48] XIX.145.

[49] XIX.90. In fact the parsnip, cf. A. C. Andrews, *CP* LIII (1958), 145 ff. Similarly J. M. André, ad loc. (Budé, 1964): 'le panais (*Pastinaca sativa*)'. The best sort grew near Gelduba, a fort on the Rhine—as Pliny could well know.

[50] XV.54. Observe also a liking for grapes smoked and pickled (XIV.16).

If the astrologer had miscalculated, other things being equal, Claudius Nero might never have left Rhodes, condemned to live out a long existence (he was very robust), or rather perhaps falling to the sword or mandate of a centurion, as happened on another island to Agrippa Postumus, the last grandson of Caesar Augustus. Posterity would faintly discern an aesthete and a military man who through arrogance and conceit failed to requite what fortune held out to the renascent *nobilitas*; and historians might not discover any reason for doing justice to his achievement in warfare, notably his conquest of Illyricum.[51]

Cornelius Tacitus, imprisoned by choice in the annals of the Roman Senate, and hampered by his point of inception, was slow to see the significance of the seven years passed at Rhodes.[52] Of Greek friends, no hint emerges until the Emperor leaves Rome. In the sequel (in Book V) mockery no doubt made play with sombre banquets and the predicament of professors. So far therefore 'les noirs loisirs du Vieillard de Capri'.[53]

Emphasis has been accorded to the Hellenic tastes of Claudius Nero. No exposition should take him for typical. Yet not wholly anomalous in his generation. There is Piso the Pontifex, and one might wonder about others, such as Fabius Maximus. The bulk of information about this epoch is heavily Roman and patriotic, and most of the interpreters concur. In so doing, they acquiesce in a breach of continuity between the Republic of the dynasts and the aristocratic monarchy of the Caesars.

Education is the clear guide, being patently Greco–Roman. Not all clues lead very far. In rhetoric Apollodorus of Pergamum taught the stepfather, whereas Claudius Nero persisted with Theodorus of Gadara, attending his lectures at Rhodes.[54] The two stood in contrast, but whether their practices diverged widely, or even their doctrines, was not apparent to experts in antiquity, from Strabo to Quintilian.[55]

About the Roman schools of declamation Annaeus Seneca compiled in old age a vast repertorium for the instruction of his sons. It is precious testimony both for social history and for trends in the development of Latin prose. Himself a tireless fancier, Seneca names a mass of speakers. Greeks were among them, yet another sign of the cultural symbiosis.[56] Also many of the new Romans from Spain, including two of the most

[51] As evident in the miserable account in Cassius Dio.
[52] *Tacitus* (1958), 695 f.
[53] So styled in Heredia's sonnet on Suetonius.
[54] According to Quintilian III.1.17. Theodorus had been his instructor in boyhood, detecting then his 'saeva ac lenta natura' (Suetonius, *Tib.* 57.1).
[55] Strabo XVI.759; Quintilian III.1.18, cf. V.13.59 f.
[56] e.g. Lesbocles and Potamon, the son of Lesbonax (*Suas.* II.15 f.). That symbiosis deepened. Direct influence of poets, Latin on Greek, is detected by G. Williams, *Change and Decline* (1978), 125 ff.

influential through precept and example, namely Porcius Latro and Junius Gallio.[57] Variegated by origin, habits, and style, the declaimers formed a noisy menagerie.

For some, declamation became a way of life, not a training for the lawcourts, where a paladin of the schools might fail miserably. It also furnished social betterment, and the chance of notoriety and promotion. Of the performers registered by Seneca, the majority are small town careerists, with few senators or sons of senators. Many of them were crude and brutal in style and argument.

None the less, men of eminent station lent encouragement. Asinius Pollio was assiduous, Messalla Corvinus less so; and, a few other senators might be found, even persistent after a consulship, such as the fluent Q. Haterius. No trace, however, of certain great orators of the early Augustan years, known from other sources. For example, Sempronius Atratinus (*suff.* 34) and C. Furnius (*cos.* 17).

Tiberius makes a solitary entrance to the pages of Seneca. Messalla asked his guest Junius Gallio what he thought of the performance of Nicetes, a *rhetor* of the 'Asianic' brand. His reply pleased Tiberius (here described as a 'Theodoreus'), and also Ovid, so his friend Gallio used to recount.[58] Ovid frequented the schools, as his poetry so patently confirms. Seneca furnishes samples of his performance, and sundry verdicts on the style.[59]

Some of the preceptors available to the young Claudius Nero deserve brief notice in passing. The earliest in repute were Rubellius Blandus and Passienus. Blandus is on record as the first Roman knight to adopt the teaching profession. Passienus acquires high praise from Seneca, named as an orator in the vicinity of Pollio and Messalla.[60] Next comes a set of four speakers, the 'tetradium', as the expert styles them. Gallio was one of them.[61]

Of the aristocrats in the age group of Claudius Nero only one makes an appearance in the schools of declamation. It is the showy and versatile Fabius Maximus. Several of that company possessed or needed the art of public speech. In the first place, Asinius Gallus: a great orator but overshadowed by his parent, such is Seneca's tribute in passing. Ample compensation avails in the narrative of Cornelius Tacitus, which designed for him a conspicuous role from the outset; and the summary of an oration is furnished.[63]

---

[57] M. T. Griffin, *JRS* LXII (1972), 1 ff.

[58] Seneca, *Suas.* III.6 f.

[59] S. F. Bonner, *Roman Declamation* (1949), 149 f.; 153 ff.

[60] Seneca, *Controv.* III, *praef.* 14.

[61] The others are Porcius Latro, Arellius Fuscus, Albucius Silo (*Controv.* X, *praef.* 13). Gallio suitably took in adoption Novatus, Seneca's eldest son.

[62] *Controv.* IV, *praef.* 4.　　　　　　　　　　　　　　　[63] *Ann.* II.33.2 f.

Next, Lentulus the Augur. The son of Seneca offers an unfriendly portrait: with enormous wealth but avaricious, and of a mean and sparse talent in oratory; and he was always complaining that the service of the state cost him time and money.[64]

In Tacitus, Lentulus is heard three times speaking to motions in the Senate, likewise Cn. Piso; Piso the Pontifex once only. Along with Ahenobarbus and Gallus those are the last of this group (sixteen consuls) still among the living when Ti. Caesar came to the power. Two of them needed no obituary notice, but three earn it, one of whom was Lentulus. The Emperor accelerated his decease, being covetous of his fortune, so Suetonius alleges.[65] Other authors disclose their close friendship.[66]

The only direct testimony to Tiberius' formation in Latin eloquence must now be stated and assessed. According to Suetonius, he took for model Messalla Corvinus, 'quem senem adulescens observaverat'.[67] If the chronology of the biographer betrays inadvertence (only twenty-two years separated the two), his comment is instructive. The young man was precious, laborious, obscure; also and in consequence tending to be better when he spoke without preparation.

Another passage contributes: Caesar Augustus censured him for the use of old-fashioned and recondite expressions.[68] Augustus set himself firmly against archaisms—and against preciosity (he blamed Maecenas on that count). His own manner in eloquence was 'elegans et temperatum'. Further, the style of his letters was easy and fluent: 'elegantia orationis . . . neque morosa neque anxia'.[69]

Again, Augustus did not bother much about spelling. The biographer is therefore moved to surprise by the report that the ruler revoked a consular legate who wrote 'ixi' for 'ipsi'.[70]

Messalla Corvinus paid exact attention to questions of spelling and of grammar. It is in this matter, rather than for that known grace and elegance of style, that Messalla found a follower in Claudius Nero, who was a purist and a pedant. In public pronouncements the Princeps avoided Greek words, and he once craved the indulgence of the Senate because he could not devise a Latin synonym.[71]

Suetonius preserves a few fragments of Tiberian discourses.[72] For

---

[64] Seneca, *De ben.* II.27.2 (above, p. 296).
[65] *Tib.* 49.1.
[66] Tacitus, *Ann.* IV.29.1; Dio LVII.24.8.
[67] *Tib.* 70.1.
[68] *Divus Aug.* 86.2: 'nec Tiberio parcit et exoletas interdum et reconditas voces aucupanti'.
[69] Gellius XV.7.3 (in comment on the letter to Gaius and Lucius).
[70] *Divus Aug.* 88. Of known legates the label would best fit Tarius Rufus.
[71] *Tib.* 71, cf. also in the anecdote concerning Pomponius Marcellus: 'sermonis Latini exactor molestissimus' (*De gramm.* 22).
[72] Especially in *Tib.* 28 f.; 67.

divining the character of this man through the style of his eloquence, a different path is open.[73]

The documentation for Augustan oratory is varied and fairly abundant, at the time and also in the sequel. By contrast, the writing of Roman history. There stands Livy, in solitary eminence between Sallust and Tacitus—and one quarter only of his work extant.[74] Livy was perhaps an isolated figure in his own age, not only through the scope and the bulk of his production, but by his life and habits.

The schools of rhetoric knew him, he wrote on that subject, and Annaeus Seneca transmits a dozen notices.[75] No anecdote discloses Livy in the company of other men of letters. Only the ruler, whose acquaintance he made perhaps as early as 29 or 28.[76] Augustus offered a comment on the later books. Livy, he said, was a 'Pompeianus'.[77] The remark cost neither anything. Then, towards the end of his long life, Livy advised Claudius, the younger brother of Germanicus, to take up history. The youth complied, finding refuge and a consolation: at the age of seventeen they made him give up his betrothed, the daughter of Paullus and Julia. He began with the assassination of Caesar the Dictator, but under deterrence from his mother and his grandmother he changed his exordium to the 'pax civilis'.[78]

The opening years of the new dispensation saw an efflorescence of history, in every type and branch. Antiquarian studies, as represented by Aelius Tubero, may soon have forfeited their appeal; and fictional narrators of the early Republic were surpassed and abolished by Livy's achievement. However, two consular annalists emerged. L. Arruntius (*cos.* 22), who had been one of the admirals at Actium, found a congenial subject in the first war against the Punic enemy, which he treated in the style of Sallust, exaggerating that manner now in fashion;[79] and Clodius Licinus (*suff.* AD 4) dealt with Rome's rise to domination in the world, taking as his point of inception the end of the second war.[80]

Recent transactions had an eager response in the reading public. The history of Asinius Pollio began with the fatal compact of the dynasts in the consulate of Metellus and Afranius. But Pollio terminated with the Battle of Philippi. The first to supply the gap were no doubt writers of memoirs,

[73] i.e. through the orations in Tacitus. Not fully exploited by H. Bardon, *Les Empereurs et les lettres latines* (1940), 112 ff.

[74] Although of significant value for the development of prose style (like Curtius Rufus), Velleius cannot claim the rank of a 'Roman historian'.

[75] Observe *Controv.* IX.2.26: 'Livius . . . aiebat'.

[76] viz. in the matter of the 'spolia opima' (IV.20.7).

[77] *Ann.* IV.34.3.

[78] Suetonius, *Divus Claudius* 41.2.

[79] Seneca, *Epp.* 114. 17 ff.

[80] On whom, *History in Ovid* (1978), 112 f.

among them Messalla and Dellius. Apologia would be perceptible, and early recognition of 'the better cause', at least in the former. The equable Dellius may not have worried. While he recounted the ambiguous record of diplomatic missions and precious detail about Antonius' invasion of Media, some of his reminiscences had value for entertainment.[81] Before long, the Caesarian and Triumviral history might pale and fade, like the much advertised glory of Actium; and the memoirs of generals and politicians engender tedium in any age, even before they excite a proper distrust. As Labienus, an orator and historian, declared, the best protection from the civil wars is to forget them.[82]

Confidence and complacency exerting their power, men were even emboldened to write contemporary annals. The elderly Livy, whose clear point of termination was in 29, precisely, went on to cover the next twenty years. Again, the senator Cremutius Cordus, who began with the year 44. He recited some of his work in the presence of Caesar Augustus.[83]

No survey however superficial should omit brief mention of Pompeius Trogus, a Narbonensian of good family who found Livy's theme lacking in perspective. Trogus composed a universal history in forty-four books. It went back all the way to the eastern empires and it accorded central prominence to the Macedonians and the kingdoms after Alexander.

This engaging character leaves no trace in his own time. Centuries were to pass before Trogus achieved recognition, honoured as one in a tetrad of classic historians.[84] The record is sparse likewise of other historians; and, as in other epochs, writers have to be allowed for whose names are lost.

From the design and structure adopted by Pompeius Trogus, some have inferred depreciation of the imperial Republic. The notion is superficial and literary.[85] It dishonours a Roman writer whose grandfather commanded cavalry of the Vocontii in campaigns of Magnus. Other presumed 'alumni' of the University now flourishing at Massilia had no quarrel either.

Irresponsible persons, 'levissimi ex Graecis', fell into invincible error when against Rome they chose to exalt the Parthians.[86] Livy administered castigation in a lengthy excursus. The eloquent patriot may be alluding to Timagenes, who bore the label 'felicitati urbis inimicus'.[87] Dissenting from

---

[81] For Dellius, *PIR*[1] D 29 (dropped in the second edition); C. B. R. Pelling, *JHS* XCIX (1979), 88. Seneca referred to 'Dellius cuius epistulae ad Cleopatram lasciuae feruntur' (*Suas.* I.7). The verb conveys a doubt about authenticity.

[82] Seneca, *Controv*. X.3.5.

[83] Suetonius, *Tib.* 61.3.

[84] *HA Aurel.* 2.1; *Probus* 2.7. Writers in that age who refer to Trogus may have known him only in Justin's abridgement.

[85] And deprecated by H. Fuchs, *Der geistige Widerstand gegen Rom* (1938), 42 f.

[86] Livy IX.18.6.

[87] Seneca, *Epp.* 91.13.

Caesar Augustus, Timagenes consigned to the flames the history he wrote in honour of the ruler of Rome.[88]

More astute and more useful was Nicolaus of Damascus. Not only a *Vita Caesaris* which terminated conveniently when Caesar's heir turned up in Italy, enrolling veterans from the legions in the summer of 44. Encouraged by his other patron, Nicolaus compiled a world history, in a hundred and forty-four books down to the year of Herod's decease. Nicolaus had been active in Herod's interest, explaining things to Caesar, many times.

In this fecund and favourable season, other writers might be surmised. For example, under Augustus or under his successor, a Greek writer of history, an *Ignotus* whom concordances between Plutarch and Appian (for the closing epoch of the Republic) might commend but not perhaps enforce.

Roman annals took their origin in the governing class, and the tradition continued for as long as the Republic remained a living memory. But history, like jurisprudence, was now invaded by men of lower station.

Asinius Pollio found fault with Livy for 'Patavinitas'.[89] The word has excited due attention and debate. It might comport, so some opined, the use of local or regional expressions.[90] Better, and comprehensive, a denial of 'urbanitas'.[91] Further, since the style is the man, there is a chance that the censorious consular did not exclude a provincial outlook.[92]

Claudius Nero might have approved a historian liable to be labelled a 'Pompeianus'. But the rich, ample, and redundant style would hardly appeal to his austere predilections, or his known manner of eloquence. Sallust is much more likely.[93] However, neither Tiberius nor other aristocrats of his generation can so far be shown to take an interest in history or in historians. Some were too frivolous—and men of sober understanding would not be drawn to romantic notions about the Roman past.

It is time to close an unremunerative rubric with the *Res Gestae* of the ruler, designed to be inscribed on bronze pillars beside the Mausoleum: a literary document in the first instance, therefore to be studied for style, structure, and strata of composition.[94]

---

[88] Seneca, *De ira* III.23.6.

[89] Quintilian I.5.56; VIII.1.12.

[90] Supported by the context of the first passage: 'taceo de Tuscis et Sabinis et Praenestinis'.

[91] K. Latte, *CP* XXXV (1940), 56. It is no good sign in a Roman historian that he should use the word 'tantisper' (*praef.* 5; I.3.1; 22.5).

[92] *Rom. Rev.* (1939), 485 f.; *HSCP* LXIV (1959), 76 = *RP* (1979), 453.

[93] For style, and for some at least of his sentiments.

[94] By conception and structure, the present volume does not comport discussion of either the *Res Gestae* or the Autobiography.

Augustus encouraged talent, and he insisted on the best. Maecenas brought him Virgil and Horace. In their company tends to be named Varius Rufus, who wrote tragedy and epic. Horace's *Letter to Augustus* offers instruction, on several counts. The taste of the times is at fault, so he undertakes to demonstrate: the public is obsessed by antiquarian studies, infatuated with the old poets (beginning with Naevius). Neat and sinuous arguments follow, and before the praise of the ruler's achievement duly emerges at the end, the vindication is declared of the modern poets, those whom Augustus cherishes, 'dilecti tibi Vergilius Variusque'.[95]

That the reading public in 13 or 12 abode under the spell of ancient or archaic writers is a piece of sly humour and wilful deception. The advocate defends the better sort of poetry. Against whom? The answer is not far to seek: the writers of love poetry in the elegiac measure.[96]

Next to Maecenas, Messalla Corvinus stands out as the patron of poets in the early Augustan years, and the centre of a circle.[97] First of all, Albius Tibullus. The curious figure of Valgius Rufus will not be omitted, named already in the company of Messalla in 35 or 34; and in the panegyric on Messalla's consulship he is acclaimed as 'aeterno propior non alter Homero'.[98] Valgius produced poems in various genres; like Messalla, he occupied himself with questions of grammar; and he even compiled a manual on botany.[99]

Valgius was a senator, Propertius and Ovid on social parity, since they belonged to the class of 'domi nobiles', the men of substance and repute in the towns of Italy. Propertius had a senator for kinsman (it is no surprise), and both Ovid and his brother embarked on the career of honours.[100] The first book of Propertius was dedicated to Volcacius Tullus, the nephew of a consul: a 'sodalis' of equal years, not a patron. Similarly, in the *Amores* of Ovid three friends enjoy the compliment of a poem. It is only at a late stage in his life that the 'magna nomina' emerge, in the poems from exile, for the reader to learn that the young man was an approved guest in the mansion of Messalla.

There was a mass of poets. Ovid in his last year registered no fewer than thirty, and others were coming on.[101] Many no doubt independent, yet one may become curious about patronage. Aristocrats should not have disdained the easy avenue to fame. Later ages looked back to a season of munificence, not merely to the proverbial name of Maecenas.[102]

---

[95] Horace, *Epp.* II.1.247.   [96] For this thesis, *History in Ovid* (1978), 174 ff.

[97] Neatly described recently by C. Davies, *Greece & Rome* XX (1973), 25 ff.

[98] Horace, *Sat.* I.10.82; *Pan. Mess.* 180.

[99] *PIR*[1] V 169. The botanical work had a 'praefatio religiosa' addressed to Augustus (Pliny, *NH* XXV.4). Valgius was rated the best translator of Theodorus (Quintilian III.1.18).

[100] Given the rarity of the name, the senator Propertius Postumus (*ILS* 914) is generally conceded as kinsman to the poet.

[101] Ovid, *Ex P.* IV.16.   [102] Juvenal VII. 94 f. (quoted above, p. 238).

Sallustius Crispus displaced Maecenas in the secret confidence of the ruler, like him alert and devious under the ostentation of easy and luxurious living. Crispus had a poem from both Horace and Crinagoras, extolling his opulence and his generosity.[103] No results are evident—and the government came into conflict with educated opinion, more than once, despite this master of statecraft.

Asinius Pollio was the first patron of Virgil as the Fourth Eclogue declares, acclaiming his consulship and a new era of peace and concord to follow from the pact of the dynasts and the marriage of Antonius and Octavia. Pollio soon lost his Virgil to Maecenas and the Caesarian cause—with, however, a vestigial remnant left in another poem in that book.[104] Pollio took to writing tragedies, then history. The sequel shows him happy to lose interest in poets, and he may not have cared to encourage younger historians.[105]

About patrons, who can tell, given the sparse evidence? There is Fabius Maximus, to be sure. One might wonder about Iullus Antonius, himself a poet, who earns an ode in the last book of Horace; or likewise Marcius Censorinus. Some of the aristocrats of that age group may have agreed with Piso the Pontifex in preferring Greek verse. In the annals of Latin poetry Piso makes a tardy entrance, being addressed on late recognition by Horace in the *Ars Poetica*.[106]

Literary clans and coteries are an alluring topic, not without its hazards. A group is defined through rivalry and enmities. Yet it may tend to be exclusive without being bound together by any kind of doctrine, from aesthetics to politics. The personal and congenial cuts across lines of division, and circles overlap.

What survives for recognition by posterity is incomplete and often deceptive, as is evident even for the epoch of Caesar Augustus. Inspection of literary circles all the way from Scipio to Symmachus furnishes instruction and a warning. The correspondence of Pliny, for all his love of fame and approbation, is exempt from the reproach of enlisting the illustrious at any cost: certain groups and types of note in high society happen to be absent.

At the palace of Messalla the young Claudius Nero might meet Ovid (his coeval to a year), various other poets, or an orator like Junius Gallio. To his tastes in Latin poetry, there stands no direct and precise testimony. Yet surmise is not wholly idle, given his erudite and Hellenistic

---

[103] *Odes* II.2; *Anth. Pal.* XVI.40.

[104] viz. *Ecl.* VIII. 6–13. It appears to be the original dedication to Pollio. Proposed however for the young Caesar by G. W. Bowersock, *HSCP* LXXV (1971), 73 ff.

[105] By a felicitous device Pollio discusses history with Livy in R. Graves, *I Claudius*.

[106] Ch. XXVI.

proclivities. A thought might go to Cornelius Gallus, who rose to be viceroy in Egypt, only to forfeit the 'amicitia' of the ruler. Gallus is named not once by Horace—but six times by Ovid, with extenuation of his offence, notably in the phrase 'si falsum est temeratae crimen amicitiae'.[107] Even a stray item might be of significance. An early action in the reign of Tiberius Caesar was the relief he accorded to the blameless impoverishment of a senator called Propertius Celer.[108] All in all, it is not likely that he was drawn to the poets who enjoyed the conspicuous favour of the government. The relations between Claudius Nero and Horace furnish various instruction.[109]

Sporadic evidence throws up a number of friends endowed with literary tastes or production. A few specimens may suffice, in the first place the 'cohors' that went to Armenia in 20 BC.[110] Then as later, high birth is not in evidence; and the aristocrat had an extensive foreign *clientela*. Julius Florus may well derive from the Gallic provinces.[111] Curiosity is aroused by Julius Marinus, who was both on Rhodes and on Capreae.[112]

Pompeius Macer has a known and eminent place, the son of Theophanes the Mytilenaean whom Magnus used as a chronicler and a political agent. Augustus appointed Macer to organize the libraries; he was also procurator of Asia; and, as Strabo states 'he is now among the foremost friends of Tiberius'.[113] The son entered the Senate, becoming praetor in 15. In 33, however, catastrophe enveloped the whole family.[114]

An inscription discloses Julius Pappus, described as a *comes* of Ti. Caesar, who put all the libraries under his charge.[115] Pappus has been identified as a son of Zoilus, one of the notables of Aphrodisias.[116]

No less than the periods of seclusion, leisure during the campaigns called for scholarly recreation and suitable companions. A pair of conjectures about the last sequence of warfare may be submitted.

First, Pomponius Graecinus, absent from Rome in the autumn of the

[107] *Am.* III.9.63 (written in 19 BC).

[108] *Ann.* I.75.3.

[109] Ch. XXVII.

[110] Horace, *Epp.* I.3; cf. 8 f.

[111] Recipient of *Epp.* I.3; II.2. A Julius Florus a little later is duly cited, 'in eloquentia Galliarum . . . princeps' (Quintilian X.3.13). That is, Tres Galliae, not Narbonensis.

[112] *Ann.* VI.10.2. First thoughts might go to Gaul, because of C. Julius Marinus, a notable of the Santones in Aquitania (*CIL* XIII. 1048 + 1074). A better identity is the ancestor of Ti. Julius Marinus (*suff.* ?101): eastern, from Berytus, as briefly indicated in *PIR*[2] J 241.

[113] Strabo XII, p. 618.

[114] *Ann.* VI.18.2. The historian fell into error about the generations intervening after Theophanes, cf. *Tacitus* (1958), 748 f., and recently, more than once. The standard view persisted, e.g. in Gow and Page, *The Garland of Philip* II (1968), 468 (on the poems of Macer).

[115] *AE* 1960, 26 (Rome).

[116] cf. remarks cited under *AE* 1969/70, 22. Rejected by J. Reynolds, *Aphrodisias and Rome* (1982), 164.

A recent accession to the rubric is L. Arruntius Hermacotas, *Fouilles de Xanthos* VII (1981), no. 64. He was a teacher of princes, presumably appointed by Tiberius.

year 8. He embraces liberal studies, 'qua sinit officium militiaeque labor'.[117]
Brother to Flaccus, the intimate friend of Tiberius Caesar and consul in 17,
Graecinus acceded to the *fasces* as suffect the year before. Second, Rufinus,
who shared in the pageantry of the Pannonian triumph in October of 12:[118]
to be identified as C. Vibius Rufinus (*suff.* 21 or 22).[119]

Like Pompeius Macer, Graecinus was honoured with a poem in the
Amores.[120] The other recipient of that distinction is the mysterious
Atticus.[121] One one theory he is the knight of high rank, Curtius Atticus,
brought to ruin on Capreae through intrigues of Aelius Seianus.[122]
Another name is worth a mention. Ovid condoles with the younger son of
Messalla on the loss of Celsus, a loyal friend.[123] Perhaps none other than
Albinovanus Celsus, a *comes* in 20 BC.[124]

Literary circles intersect, and coincidence is bound to occur. Nor do all
friendships endure without annoyance or rupture. That was evident in the
entourage of Tiberius, it came to appear normal and almost predictable.
Mishaps befell some of the 'Graeci convictores' of the touchy pedant; and
there is the case of Julius Montanus, 'tolerabilis poeta et amicitia Tiberi
notus et frigore'.[125] Above all, senators were liable to encounter harsh
rebuke for hasty presumption or neglect of the duties imposed by 'fides'
and 'amicitia'.

When a senator achieves the consulship without benefit of either birth or
'militaris industria', curiosity is legitimate and unavoidable. When
Messalla Appianus died early in 12 BC, Valgius Rufus took his place. This
man was very lucky. The influence of Corvinus may be surmised, with
support or consent not excluded from Claudius Nero, the consul of the
previous year. Next, old Haterius, suffect in 5, popular as an orator,
though neither Augustus nor his stepson liked his manner. But Haterius,
like Claudius Nero, had married a daughter of Marcus Agrippa. There is a
chance that his designation preceded the crisis in the government.

Caution is prescribed. The *Fasti* of the next year exhibit Passienus
Rufus, the first *novus homo* to be *ordinarius* since Sulpicius Quirinius in
12—and the last until Aelius Lamia in AD 3. He was the son of an excellent
speaker, it is true, but is known otherwise only as proconsul of Africa a few

[117] Ovid, *Ex. P.* I.6.10.
[118] *Ex. P.* III.4.5, cf. 64.
[119] *History in Ovid* (1978), 83ff.; *ZPE* 43 (1981), 372 ff. = *RP* III (1984), 1431 ff.
[120] *Am.* II.10.1. Macer had II.18.
[121] *Am.* I.9.
[122] *Ann.* IV.58.1; VI.10.2. Accepted by several scholars. Not, however, in *PIR*[2] A 1333; C 1609.
And one might wonder about a Julius Atticus, cf. *History in Ovid* (1978), 72.
[123] *Ex. P.* I.9.
[124] Horace, *Epp.* I.3.15 ff., cf. 8.2.
[125] Seneca, *Epp.* 122.11.

years later. An easy and valid conjecture can reach to one of the agents in his elevation.[126]

For abnormal promotions after AD 4, it is permissible to look for the influence of Ti. Caesar (adopted by Augustus at the end of June).[127] The historian Clodius Licinus now became suffect, on July 1. That Tiberius had a hand in that choice may appear unlikely. Ateius Capito in the next year is another matter. He was elderly; and if Augustus had wished to honour exceptional and acknowledged eminence in legal studies, that might have been done much earlier. Tiberius' own preferences went rather (it may be surmised) to the rival of Capito, the Republican jurist Antistius Labeo, and to his successor Cocceius Nerva. That would not in itself be a reason for deprecating Capito; and he was appointed *curator aquarum* eight years later.[128]

Clarity arrives with Lucilius Longus in 7, the only senator who shared the sojourn on Rhodes, to be recompensed at the end for his loyal devotion by a public funeral.[129] That was totally anomalous.[130] Similarly, Cocceius Nerva, who had a consulship in 21 or 22, was an intimate friend of long date, ending his days on Capreae.[131]

The modest and pleasing notion that Ti. Caesar extended his affection for liberal studies as far as recognition and reward may help to explain two consulates early in the reign, in 16 and in 18. Old Vibius Rufus had been a veteran performer in the declamation schools, but short of unmixed acclaim; and the grandfather of Rubellius Blandus was a famous teacher, the Roman knight from Tibur.

What literature may owe to a ruler or a government is a theme of permanent seduction—and a dubious enterprise. For Caesar Augustus, the tendency is to enhance, through preoccupation with the early prime. By contrast, the role of his successor is held negative or deleterious. Which is easy and obvious, since so little has survived, even of poetry.[132]

The reign was not propitious to the writing of Roman history. Of oratory one type flourished, but banefully; and the ruler gave encouragement and rewards to a number of prosecutors.

The last Augustan decade is not exempt from the general incrimination. Velleius acclaimed a happy era dawning in AD 4. Plague and famine

[126] Sallustius Crispus, who took his son in adoption.
[127] Ch. VII.
[128] Frontinus, *De aq.* 102 (above, p. 223).
[129] *Ann.* IV.15.2: 'ita, quamquam novo homini, censorium funus, effigiem apud forum Augusti'.
[130] Hence curiosity about his extraction and career. Along with Curtius Rufus (*Ann.* XI.21.2), Lucilius Longus was adduced (to illustrate Tiberius' predilection for *novi homines*) by N. Douglas in 1906 (now in *Capri*, 1930, Florence).
[131] By deliberate starvation, to the alarm of Tiberius (*Ann.* VI.26.1 f.).
[132] Except for Manilius, whose theme should have appealed to the ruler. The poem, begun when Augustus was still alive, carries an honorific reference to Rhodes (IV.763 ff.).

followed, disasters in the northern wars, discord and scandal in the dynasty. The autocrat despatched to distant exile the foremost poet. There was a graver symptom. Formal law was enlisted to indict a historian and an orator. When they prosecuted Labienus, an authentic 'Pompeianus', Cassius Severus pronounced the appropriate verdict: talent repressed when talent had become scarce.[133]

A cognate theme is the influence of education. Teachers, friends, and proclivities, much can be gathered concerning Claudius Nero. Even small and casual details are relevant, and there are constant features all through. His character, however, changed and hardened under misfortunes or rivalry in his early years, through conflict and rancour in mature manhood. When Tiberius Caesar came to the power he was fifty-four years of age; and he stated that his nature would never change.[134] He now was summoned to play out a role repugnant to his inclinations—and haunted by the memory of a ruthless taskmaster, whom in public professions he felt constrained to invoke as precedent.

When a prosecution came under debate in the high assembly it was expedient that the holder of supreme authority should conceal his purposes. With Tiberius Caesar, dissembling, from long practice and necessity, grew into a part of his nature. Political commentators in other ages have been impelled to prize dissimulation among the virtues of a prince.

If this man has appeared an enigma, it was not for want of clues in the abundant testimony. Conscious of rectitude, Tiberius paraded a powerful and forbidding front: 'horridus ac plerumque formidatus', so is he depicted.[135] 'Oderint dum probent', that was the maxim.[136] By the same token, hesitation and inner insecurity, made manifest by his 'anxium iudicium', by his tortuous procedures. Beset by manifold perplexities, the ruler stood in need of good counsellors. To his distrust as well as to his discernment Aelius Seianus appealed, who won the devotion of Tiberius through loyalty combined with signal abilities. Later history affords an engaging parallel.[137]

To comfort and sustain, Ti. Caesar also needed a doctrine, so it might seem. Books composed in the modern time are prone to enlist almost anyone under the standard of some creed or other. The historian Sallust, for example, has been reclaimed as a convert to Stoicism. That is hard on

[133] Seneca, *Controv.* X, *praef.* 7. Cassius himself was condemned, with public combustion for his writings.

[134] Suetonius, *Tib.* 67.3.

[135] *Ann.* IV.7.1. Even 'morum diritas' was brought up (*Tib.* 21.2).

[136] Suetonius, *Tib.* 59.2.

[137] viz. the ruler whom Spaniards call 'el Prudente'. One may consult G. Marañón, *Tiberio. Historia de un resentimiento* (Buenos Aires, 1939). That author, a medical man, also wrote about Philip and his favourite Antonio Pérez—who described himself as a Seianus who got away.

a man who, like Caesar the Dictator or C. Cassius, adhered to the Epicurean persuasion and acknowledged Fortuna, whose wanton caprice governs the nations.[138]

One of the faithful was Aufidius Bassus. Under a sudden onslaught of decrepitude this Epicurean faced extinction with firm courage.[139] Aufidius Bassus and Servilius Nonianus (*cos.* 35) are coupled together as annalists who covered the reign of Tiberius. For the consular, links can be discovered with friends of Thrasea Paetus.[140] That Nonianus in his writing adopted or promulgated any of their doctrines would be an idle presumption.

Stoics were robust and respectable, honoured and advertised. Thus the great Athenodorus of Tarsus; but it is not clear that Areus, whose teaching Augustus rewarded, was firm for the creed. The professor chosen to instruct the nephew of the Princeps was Nestor, not Stoic but Academic.

In the previous epoch, the doctrines of Epicurus were liable to be distorted and traduced, easy game for a clever publicist, an eloquent moralist. Silence now followed on obloquy.

The wars enhanced the appeal of tranquillity; and the Augustan peace brought back ease and luxury, and also the resumption of an 'Antonian' style of life in the educated class.[141] The language used by Horace in amiable counsel to certain friends is clear and instructive.

Some are disposed to enrol Ti. Caesar in the company of the Stoics.[142] Dignity, self-control, and obduracy against the blows of fortune, it is true. His habits contradict, and Piso the Pontifex (perhaps the best friend in a long life) would enter a caveat or a denial.

A small and neglected fact may help, the *Silloi* of Timon. It was to Tiberius that Apollonides dedicated his commentary.[143] Now Timon was an ardent supporter of Pyrrho. In parody of the *Odyssey*, the satirical author called up for censure and mockery among the nations of the dead the heroes of empty battles in the philosophic schools.[144]

Confirmation thus accrues to the diversions of Tiberius Caesar. Nero, it is on record, invited philosophers after dinner, to enjoy their wrangles.[145]

---

[138] Sallust, *Cat.* 51.25: 'quoius lubido gentibus moderatur'.

[139] Seneca, *Epp.* 30 (not mentioning the fact that he was a historian).

[140] e.g. the conjecture that his daughter married Barea Soranus (*suff.* 52). On which, *Hermes* XCII (1964), 412 f. = *Ten Studies in Tacitus* (1970), 96.

[141] See the elegant and powerful exposition of J. Griffin, *JRS* LXVI (1976), 87 ff.

[142] e.g. B. Levick, *Tiberius the Politician* (1976), 18. Nestor can be adduced (Lucian, *Macrobii* 21), but Tiberius may not have been responsive. For salubrious warnings observe now H. D. Jocelyn, 'The Ruling Class of the Roman Republic and Greek Philosophers' (*John Rylands Library Bulletin* LIX (1977), 323 ff.).   [143] Diogenes Laertius IX.12.109.

[144] On Timon see C. Wachsmuth, *Corp. poesis epicae gr. ludibundae* (1885), 8 ff.; 36 ff.; W. Nestle, *RE* VIA. 1301 ff.; A. A. Long, *Proc. Camb. Phil. Soc.* XXIV (1978), 43 ff.

[145] *Ann.* XIV.16.2.

Tiberius and Nero look forward to the great Philhellene Hadrian, the polymath whose delight it was to crush and deride the professors.[146]

At the banquets of Ti. Caesar, most of the entertainment was purveyed by professors of classical philology. There were genuine buffoons, such as 'stupidi'; and a professional 'imitator' in the Emperor's service impersonated barristers, he invented that device.[147] Tiberius indulged a savage humour and sarcasm. It was his wont to enliven serious argument with irony.[148] In short, a sceptic and a fatalist.

When Claudius Nero first attached Thrasyllus to his company, he looked to a teacher of philosophy; and Thrasyllus was a notable Platonic scholar.[149] That artful man asserted his dominance through the science of the stars, after an exacting ordeal on the cliffs at Rhodes. There is no sign that Tiberius hitherto had been a believer in astrology, still less the addict he became in the sequel.

The powerful intelligence of Tiberius impressed the historian Tacitus, but could not conquer his faith in free will. Other features entranced him. The renderings of Tiberian orations are close and congenial, revealing something of his own character; and the ultimate verdict on the style confirms. Selecting words with care, he was 'validus sensibus aut consulto ambiguus'.[150]

---

[146] *HA Hadr.* 15.10: 'professores omnium artium semper ut doctior risit, contempsit, obtrivit.'

[147] *ILS* 5225: 'Caesaris lusor/mutus argutus imitator/Ti. Caesaris Augusti, qui/primum invenit causidicos imitari'.

[148] *Ann.* VI.2.4: 'ludibria seriis permiscere solitus'.

[149] Suetonius, *Tib.* 14.4: 'quem ut sapientiae professorem contubernio admoverat'. For his Platonic studies, W. Gundel, *RE* VIA. 583 f.

[150] *Ann.* XIII.3.2.

XXVI

The Other Pisones

Education and letters made the elegant Pontifex eminently congenial to Claudius Nero. He found a more potent affinity in the contrasted temperament of a Piso from the other line, namely Gnaeus (*cos.* 7 BC), the ill-starred legate of Syria.

While exploiting all that Hellas had to give, the Romans built up their conception of the national character on opposition to the Greeks. Hence a Catonian tradition, with attitudes often crude and odious. When entering Athens in the wake of Germanicus Caesar, Piso was happy to advertise a distance from the demeanour of the philhellenic prince. A savage oration denounced the citizens for errors and failures in their past history.[1]

Asserting rank and honour in the contest for power, the Roman aristocrat made great play with 'dignitas'. The term could never be used save for approbation. Its other name is 'superbia', adherent from inveterate dispraisal to the patrician Claudii. Not that they had been oppressive towards the plebs. Rivals in the *nobilitas* had to endure affront.

In the pages of Tacitus Cn. Piso nowhere makes appeal to his 'dignitas' or to that of his family. Nor is he taxed with 'superbia'. His actions spoke. Persons of high station disdained the arts of conciliation or mere 'comitas'. Their spirit of proud independence came out as truculence: 'contumacia' or even 'ferocia'. Estimable qualities were pushed to a contrary and perverse excess. An unbending disposition might issue in harshness or cruelty towards citizen no less than foreigner. Piso is styled by Seneca 'integer a multis vitiis sed pravus, et cui placebat pro constantia rigor'.[2]

From precedents or by mimesis, families transmitted characteristic features through the generations. Thus, emulating or outdoing the patriciate, the plebeian *nobilitas* exhibits the intolerable Popillii and the stubborn Domitii, while the Cassii parade stern integrity and hostility towards personal domination.

The 'ferocissimi nobilium' perished and the new order counselled an abatement of aristocratic 'libertas' in act or word. Men of understanding now paid heed to 'obsequium', which on the better showing denotes rational deference to authority. Claudius Nero denied it when going away

---

[1] *Ann.* II.55.1 f.
[2] Seneca, *De ira* I.18.3.

to Rhodes, and Piso was 'ingenio violentus et ignarus obsequii'. Both are anachronistic, the one equipped with the 'vetere et insita Claudiae familiae superbia', while in his friend resided 'insita ferocia' bequeathed by the parent.[3]

The ancestor, consul in 139, is only a name on the *Fasti*, and the next generation leaves no trace. They emerge to brief and transient notoriety with the quaestor Cn. Piso, despatched in 65 to govern Hispania Citerior through a political intrigue—which some approved because he was a bitter enemy of Pompeius Magnus.[4]

The earliest mention of his son is a casual item that shows him when a young man conspicuous for 'libertas'. Prosecuting an adherent whom Magnus tried to protect, he boldly reviled that 'praepotens defensor'.[5] Another item, a coin, discloses Cn. Piso in Spain as 'proquaestor' to the proconsul Magnus.[6] That is, in 49. No paradox: the dynast had become a defender of the Republic.

Tacitus alludes to his allegiance and subsequent actions.[7] Piso kept loyal to the cause in Africa, and he followed Cassius and Brutus; then, permitted to return to Rome, he held aloof from the career of honours until solicited by Caesar Augustus to take a consulship.

That was in 23, after a protracted interval of retirement or recalcitrance. The year of dire emergency for the ruler thus evinced an abrupt conversion. Some may have acclaimed public spirit: to others, ambition renascent or the honourable motive of refurbishing the 'dignitas' of a family after long obscuration, with the prospect of consulships for his two sons, Gnaeus and Lucius.

Piso contracted a marriage in one aspect suitable: the daughter of a Marcus Popillius not otherwise on record.[8] Nomenclature may acknowledge the maternal ascendance in various ways. A grandson inherits 'Marcus' as *praenomen*, anomalous in Pisones. The curious will also observe that the first Gnaeus Piso shared the *fasces* in 139 with M. Popillius Laenas.

That family had fallen on evil days long since, leaving an evil report in the Roman annalists. Two brothers, consuls in 173 and 172, displayed abnormal cruelty towards natives in Liguria, matched with repeated defiance of the Senate's authority. The younger is labelled as 'asper ingenio', along with 'vultu truci'.[9] A worse specimen, but better authenticated, is the consul of 132, ruthless in persecuting adherents of Tiberius Gracchus.

---

[3] *Ann.* II.43.2. Further, Piso was 'promptus ferocibus' (78.1) and he used 'contumaces preces' (57.3).   [4] Sallust, *Cat.* 19.1 f.

[5] Val. Max. VI.2.4.

[6] Crawford, *RRC* I (1974), 463.

[7] *Ann.* II.43.

[8] *IG* VII.268; 305 (Oropus).

[9] Livy XLV.10.8. Cf. his treatment of the Syrian monarch (12.5).

A stray anecdote attributes to a Popillia M. f. a coarse and cynical aphorism, with no clue to identity.[10] The elder son of Piso and Popillia chose for wife the arrogant Munatia Plancina, whose 'nobilitas et opes' enhanced his already exorbitant pretensions, so it is stated. That *nobilitas* was in fact of the most recent, deriving from the consul of 42: perhaps her grandfather, not her father.[11] The wife or wives of the great careerist are lost to knowledge. Again, Piso's Plancina may be a second wife, to judge at least by her husband's age and that of their elder son, who became consul in AD 27.

Under prosecution and about to end his life, the legate of Syria drew up an apologia which the Princeps read out to the Senate. He asseverated a personal allegiance which went back forty-five years.[12] That indicates service as a military tribune in the Spanish campaigns of 26 and 25. His birth may be put in 44 or 43, which accords with the post of *triumvir monetalis* in 23.[13] The season for matrimony now followed, then entry to the Senate as quaestor, presumably in 19 or 18.

From 23 to the consulate in 7 there is no sign of activity or occupations. Piso may have visited the Greek lands at some time or other. He had a personal grudge against the Athenians because they refused to revoke the sentence against a client condemned for forgery by the Areopagus. Again, Piso might have been with Claudius Nero in the Alpine campaign or subsequently in Illyricum.

For the first consulate his friend had Quinctilius Varus for colleague, Piso for the second—perhaps reserved for that exceptional distinction. He reached the *fasces* a couple of years later than the 'suus annus', so it appears. And there had been sharp competition among coeval and favoured aristocrats. Bribery was alleged against the pair elected for the previous year.[14]

Next, access to the proconsulates in Asia and Africa. In this season various factors operated to abridge the five years' interval. However managed or modified, the sortition tended to come out with the satisfactory result, as later ages reveal. It was no accident that Asia fell to the Pontifex. Piso got Africa. His tenure belongs somewhere in the gap between Africanus Fabius (*cos.* 10), in 7/6 or 6/5, and Passienus Rufus (*cos.* 4).[15]

---

[10] Macrobius II.5.10, following the maxim of Julia, 'numquam enim nisi nave plena tollo vectorem.'   [11] In *PIR*[1] M 539 'filia vel neptis'.

[12] *Ann.* III.16.4. Piso got recompense in December of 14, if he is the *arvalis* chosen to replace Augustus (*CIL* VI.2023 = *ILS* 5026). There appears to be an erasure, not merely a lacuna, cf. Dessau, citing Henzen. For Groag, 'minime constat (*PIR*[2] C 287). Sulla Felix (C 1463) enjoys the preference of J. Scheid, *Les Frères Arvales* (1975), 64, cf. 119 f.

[13] That is the standard date. One might prefer 22.   [14] Dio LV.5.3.

[15] To the evidence add now *IRT* 520, which shows him a *pontifex*.

Piso may have gone to Africa as early as 4 or 3. The date acquires an adventitious value. A Cn. Piso who had been governor told Strabo that the country was like a leopard, being spotted with oases.[16] About the identity of this Piso no doubt should subsist.[17]

Strabo's information, notably in what concerned dynasties or provincial affairs in the eastern lands, tends to fade out towards 2 BC.[18] The operations of Quirinius the legate of Galatia (probably in 5 and 4) are among the most recent items.[19] Hence a useful terminus. The Geography carries sporadic particulars added on cursory revision much later, *c.*AD 19. The reference to Piso is not one of them. It occurs in the context of general and theoretical discourse, prefatory to the whole work.

The inception may be assigned without discomfort to the vicinity of 1 BC. At the outset Strabo declares that the Geography is intended for statesmen and generals;[20] and one can cite his allusion to 'the present expedition of the Romans against the Parthians'.[21] An incentive to his writing may therefore be discovered in the enterprise of Gaius Caesar.

Piso in Africa gave Seneca a text which he copiously expounded. The proconsul ordered a soldier to be executed, prematurely; and when the man was shown innocent, a centurion who intervened was also put to death. The story is recounted to exemplify 'ira' and 'furor'.[22]

Africa was not raked up at the prosecution, though it might have figured as corroborative evidence in one of the orations. That of P. Vitellius, a legate of Germanicus Caesar, was admired and remembered.[23] However, one of the advocates wanted to indict rapacity practised when Piso governed Tarraconensis: 'ambitiose avareque habitam Hispaniam'. Graver charges claimed precedence.

The date of that governorship is also a matter of some consequence. Some scholars were disposed to place it before the proconsulate.[24] Better,

---

[16] Strabo II, p. 130.

[17] Yet recourse has been had to Piso's father, in Africa in 46—commanding native cavalry (*Bell. Afr.* 3.1; 18.1). Thus W. Aly, *Strabon von Amasia* (1957), 384. Observe also 'clearly': arguing that a passage in Strabo (II, p. 131) was composed earlier than 19 BC, G. W. Bowersock, *Rome and the Greek World* (1965), 133.

[18] J. G. C. Anderson, *Anatolian Studies . . . Ramsay* (1923), 1 ff. The inconclusive remarks in *Strabon*, Vol. I. (Budé, 1969) incline towards 7 BC (the theory of E. Pais). No awareness of Anderson.

[19] Strabo XII, p. 569.

[20] Strabo I, pp. 12 f.

[21] Strabo I, p. 10: τὴν νῦν 'Ρωμαίων στρατείαν ἐπὶ Παρθυαίους. On that item follow remarks about the invasions of Germany. For parallel observe Juba, incited to write by Augustus himself for Gaius Caesar, 'ituro in Armeniam ad Parthicas Arabicasque res' (Pliny, *NH* VI.141).

[22] Seneca, *De ira* I.18.3 ff.

[23] Pliny, *NH* XI.187. Therefore presumably read by Tacitus.

[24] Registered before Africa in *PIR*[2] C 287. With 'zwischen 6 v.–12 n. Chr.', R. Hanslik was able to evade error (*RE Supp.* XII. 135). But not with L. Caninius Gallus (*suff.* 2 BC). He is put 'ca. 5/6 n. Chr.' (ib. 136). That dating ignores the war of Cossus Lentulus (?5/6).

soon after the decisive turn of events in the summer of 4 which brought employment to trusted friends of Ti. Caesar.

Certitude is now to hand. A huge monument once stood on the coast of Asturias. The inscription in large letters, without equal perhaps in all the Spains, carries the date 9/10 by the titulature of the ruler, and below, in erasure, space for 'Cn. Calpurnius Cn. f. Piso / leg. pro pr.'[25]

Piso may have enjoyed a lengthy tenure. The crisis of the northern wars caused governors to be prorogued both in 6 and in 9. The next legate of Tarraconensis on attestation is M. Lepidus, in 14. It was an envious or malicious *Ignotus* who in 20 ordained the obliteration, which was not in fact enjoined by decree of the Senate.

The geographer now comes in again. Contrary to his usual practice, Strabo furnished a full and precise statement about the garrison and administration of a consular province. Tarraconensis had three legions, two brigaded together under a single legate in the north-west, the third facing the Cantabrians. In consequence, one of the governor's three legates was set free for purely civilian tasks.[26]

This report is patently a late insertion—and it is one of the longest. The arrangement, which the author assigns to the reign of Tiberius, goes back to the year 9 when one of four legions left in garrison since 13 BC was summoned to the Rhine. No hesitation need be conceived about the source of the information accruing to a writer who had no personal interest in Spain.

Cn. Piso thus introduces a further theme, namely Strabo's Roman friends and informants.[27] Aelius Gallus holds the primacy, the Prefect with whom the scholar made a journey into Upper Egypt. With Piso, a senator and consul emerges a quarter of a century later when Strabo, once a historian, was embarking on his second work of compilation. Another may be enlisted, viz. Aelius Catus (*cos.* 4), in one of the insertions.[28] He happens to be the only general operating on or beyond Rhine and Danube to be named by Strabo.[29] That is, apart from Germanicus Caesar. The revision was able to register his triumph in 17.

About Piso the annual record of senatorial business would have something to say before he departed to Syria. First, when the high assembly was adjudicating on one of the earliest cases of *maiestas*, the Princeps impetuously exclaimed that he too proposed to cast a vote. Piso made an

---

[25] *CIL* II. 2703. On which, *Epigraphische Studien* VIII (1969), 125 ff. = *RP* (1979), 732 ff. (with a drawing on p. 732.)

[26] Strabo III, p. 166. That legate was later styled 'iuridicus'.

[27] G. W. Bowersock, *Augustus and the Greek World* (1965), 132 ff.

[28] Strabo VII, p. 303: ἔτι γὰρ ἐφ᾽ ἡμῶν Αἴλιος Κάτος etc.

[29] *History in Ovid* (1978), 101 f. Family links are there conjectured with Aelius Gallus. Cf. above, p. 309.

intervention. He confessed to the perplexity liable to ensue for a senator either way, whether the Princeps voted before or after the rest.[30] Next, after measures had been variously discussed for curbing floods of the Tiber, they concurred in the motion of Piso, 'qui nil mutandum censuerat'.[31] Third, when Tiberius announced that he would not attend a session, Piso spoke in earnest support: it was 'decorum rei publicae' if senators carried out their functions without needing the Princeps in person.[32] Piso thus got ahead of others in asserting a 'species libertatis'. Which impelled Asinius Gallus to take the contrary line.

In comment on Piso's first intervention the historian came out with a portentous pronouncement: 'manebant etiam tum vestigia morientis libertatis'. He was hasty and incautious. Piso in fact offered the Princeps an escape from an awkward situation. Nor could Caesar's friend incur offence either then or on the other occasions. As well he knew, the Princeps, himself an advocate of free speech, was eager that the Senate should play an independent role.

Piso earns credit. Other senators, astute and percipient from long practice, were not so fortunate when they sought to curry favour by playing upon the sentiments of the ruler. Thus the aged Ateius Capito, the jurist subservient as ever. Moved by public spirit and anxious devotion to the Princeps, he raised a protest, 'quasi per libertatem', only to betray his dishonesty. Caesar was not deceived.[33]

For the realities of public behaviour, another item is instructive, omitted by Tacitus but supplied by Dio, who used a different (and generally inferior) selection of annalistic material. The contrast is valuable for the transactions of 15 and 16.

After Libo Drusus had been condemned, Piso with the majority concurring opposed a motion about astrologers which had the support of Tiberius and his son Drusus. Whereupon a tribune duly interposed his veto. Such, so Dio observes, was liberty in semblance—a 'species libertatis'.[34] Respect for the 'res publica' entailed connivance and acting a part.

When Germanicus Caesar came back from the Rhine to celebrate his triumph in May of 17, frustrated, so he and others opined, of total conquest (and the sagacious ruler had done his best from the outset to dissuade the enterprise), the rank and ambitions of the prince presented a fresh annoyance. Tiberius at once decided to send him on a special mission,

---

[30] *Ann.* I.74.5.
[31] I.79.4, where some editors have inserted 'Cn.' Not needed. No other Piso had yet been mentioned.
[32] II.35.1.
[33] III.70.
[34] Dio LVII.15.9: τὸ τῆς δημοκρατίας σχῆμα.

invested with proconsular *imperium* covering the 'provinciae transmarinae'. It was no doubt expedient that the Orient should see a member of
the dynasty. Various other pretexts offered, but no urgency of any kind.

Much turned upon Caesar's legate governing Syria, with an army of
four legions, with wide powers and manifold duties. Ever and painfully in
mind of Marcus Lollius, Tiberius had to exercise his 'anxium iudicium'.
Among the consulars, smooth and pliant men were to hand such as
Munatius Plancus, the consul of 13 with an inherited aptitude for arts of
diplomacy. He had recently led the delegation chosen to negotiate with
the mutinous legionaries on the Rhine.[35]

Not good enough. The task demanded a man who, even without
benefit of active warfare, had at least held one of the military provinces.
Moreover, not to be overawed by any prince. Whereas C. Caesar was
only nineteen when assuming the *fasces* in Syria, Germanicus was aged
thirty-one when he became consul for the second time (in 18), a 'vir
triumphalis' after four years in the high command.

Tiberius looked for a resolute character and unswerving loyalty. The
old friend was the answer, although lacking any proper experience of the
eastern lands. Germany or elsewhere, Piso understood the policy of the
ruler and no doubt shared his distrust of Germanicus Caesar. Piso was
appointed to act as an 'adiutor' to the prince (Tiberius used that word).[36] In
truth to curb rather than to counsel.

Men spoke of 'secreta mandata'. They were right. The function of
Caesar's confidant and mandatory was to avert embroilment with the
Parthians, counter intrigue with Roman vassals, take a firm grip on the
legions in Syria.

In the event, Piso made haste to anticipate the arrival of Germanicus.
He put himself out to win over the troops by indulgence foreign to his
own nature and past record—and rendering him open to accusation in the
sequel. Furthermore, when Germanicus entered Armenia to enthrone a
prince at Artaxata, Piso refused to let him have any troops.

Personalities apart (with the exacerbating wives, quarrels for precedence at banquets and so on), sufficient causes of dispute resided in the
conflict of authority between the holder of proconsular *imperium* and
Caesar's legate. Their enmity broke out into open dissension. Germanicus
formally renounced 'amicitia', and Piso departed from Syria.[37] Then
Germanicus fell ill, for a second time, and died at Antioch (in October of
the year 19). Upon which, Piso turned back from his journey and tried to
regain possession of the province by armed violence.

As a result of that dereliction the legate had to face an authentic charge

---

[35] I.39.3.
[36] III.12.1.
[37] II.72.2: 'addunt plerique iussum provincia decedere.'

of high treason. Otherwise he might have withstood the allegations of poison and magic given credence by eager partisans on the staff of Germanicus, or the emotion stirred up by the advent of the mourning widow. Although credulity was rampant, the atmosphere inflamed by various rumours to the discredit of the ruler as well as his agent and friend, sober men might come to admit on reflection natural causes for the decease of a prince returning to insalubrious Syria after a summer tour in the land of Egypt.

Before the trial began, Tiberius Caesar made a judicious statement to the Senate.[38] He defined the points at issue, he drew due distinctions between the public and the personal spheres; and he firmly deprecated the excessive zeal which the friends of Germanicus persisted in advertising.

In the course of the proceedings it became clear that the Princeps was obdurate on the score of 'bellum provinciae inlatum'. Piso lost all hope at the sight of that impassive comportment: 'Tiberium sine miseratione sine ira, obstinatum clausumque vidit, ne quo adfectu perrumperetur.' He deduced no way out but suicide.

The prosecution went on. Plancina, incriminated for poisoning, had been segregated, gradually and artfully, through secret influences. Tiberius had to make an open confession, to his shame and scandal ('cum pudore et flagitio'), that he had yielded to the entreaties of his mother. Plancina was a close confidant of the Augusta.

For the rest, the consul Aurelius Cotta (i.e. Cotta Messallinus) enjoined severe and vindictive penalties. The Princeps intervened to mitigate the dishonour of a noble house, and above all to protect the sons.[39] Piso's name should stand unexpunged on the *Fasti*. Nor was M. Piso, who had been with him in Syria, to suffer relegation and forfeit his inheritance. For all that, the elder son had to change his *praenomen* from 'Gnaeus' to 'Lucius'.

The Tacitean account exhibits the author's skill in structure and emphasis, with the subtle echoes and the verbal felicities. It is also accurate and trustworthy. Recourse to the *Acta* of the Senate is patent. The oration of Tiberius Caesar looks like a close rendering. On the other hand the 'codicilli' left by Piso gave scope for sympathetic invention—'in hunc ferme modum'.[40] Piso claims the merit of a long 'obsequium'. The historian had previously styled him 'obsequii ignarus'. Further, Piso more than concedes defects of character with 'mea pravitas'.[41]

Throughout the ordeal the dour and alert Princeps kept his head, curbed

---

[38] III.12.
[39] III.18.1.
[40] III.16.2.
[41] III.16.4. Compare 'pravus' in Seneca's verdict (*De ira* I.18.3).

his tongue, and dissembled nobly. For reasons of state he had to sacrifice his friend. 'Fides' and 'amicitia' proved unavailing. That was worse than the error of judgement now shown up.

It was much more than a personal tragedy. These transactions had grave consequences for the further course of the reign. Revelations and surmise, confirming the worst suspicions about Tiberius (and about Livia), added to his unpopularity. They also sharpened his distaste for the ambiguous role of Princeps. At the beginning of the next year he seized upon a welcome pretext (Drusus Caesar as consul and the state of his own health) to go away to Campania. He prolonged his retreat for some twenty months.

Preoccupied with Germanicus Caesar, some annalists made his death a significant turning point in the reign. Cornelius Tacitus adopted a different conception: the death of Drusus four years later, the rise of Aelius Seianus. Hence two halves for his hexad.

The Pisonian affair had sundry repercussions on the writing of history. In epilogue Tacitus discussed rumour and the verbal testimony of old men, with suitable expression of caution.[42] In contrast stood his insertion of the dubious anecdote about the last hours of Caesar Augustus, naming three consulars as 'capaces imperii', viz. Asinius Gallus, M. Lepidus, L. Arruntius. One version substituted Piso for Arruntius. Not a good idea.

Tiberius Caesar kept faith with Piso, beyond the grave. The elder son acceded to the *fasces* in 27 as colleague of Crassus Frugi. He is discovered as *praefectus urbi* when the reign ended, in succession to Cossus Lentulus;[43] and he had a long life thereafter, surviving his son, the consul of 57.[44]

For Marcus Piso, no consulship. He died quite soon (there came a sequence of unhealthy seasons) or chose to lapse from the career of honours. No descendants can be certified.

One of the three advocates who undertook the defence of Cn. Piso was his brother Lucius.[45] That is, the Augur (*cos.* 1 BC). He earned a handsome presentation in two incidents of the year 16, narrated not long after the affair of Libo Drusus.[46]

Moved to anger by justice corrupted and the ruthless prosecutors, Piso announced that he would quit Rome for ever and end his days in some distant and rural retreat. The Princeps took alarm. He reasoned with Piso, gently, and urged his relatives to bring pressure. Next, Piso afforded a 'haud minus liberi doloris documentum' when he summoned to a court of

---

[42] III.16.1: 'audire me memini ex senioribus' etc.
[43] Josephus, *AJ* XVIII. 169; 235.
[44] Pliny, *Epp.* III.7.12. A comparable survivor is the jurist Cassius Longinus (*suff.* 30).
[45] *Ann.* III.11.2.
[46] II.34.

law the formidable Urgulania, deep ensconced in the confidence of the old Augusta. She refused to appear and took refuge in the Palace. Piso persisted. Tiberius in embarrassment had to intervene, which he managed with tact and restraint, and finally Urgulania was induced to pay up. As a result, so the historian concludes, 'neque Piso inglorius et Caesar maiore fama fuit.'

So far the report is amicable and promising. A change supervened. Piso did not survive unscathed. In 24 he faced prosecution for *maiestas* but died before the case came up.[47] He is introduced as 'nobilis ac ferox vir' in a passage that recapitulates the events of eight years before. According to Tacitus, the Princeps condoned Piso's pertinacity in the matter of Urgulania: 'civiliter habuit'. None the less, resentment did not abate 'in animo revolvente iras'. Curiosity waits upon an answer, as often happens when it interrogates the tortuous Caesar who hated servility—and yet feared 'libertas'.

Q. Veranius put in the indictment against the Augur.[48] Not inappropiate: one of the enemies of his brother.[49] Some of the charges were frivolous and flimsy—'sed multa cumulabantur', that is all that Tacitus saw fit to disclose. Among them may have been rapacity in a province, as in the case of his brother. Piso had been proconsul of Asia about twenty years earlier. An inscription shows his name erased, likewise that of his wife.[50] The preceding passage in the *Annales* carries a link of factional prosecutions: Sosia Galla banished, wife of a condemned governor, friends both of Germanicus and Agrippina. A decree of the Senate was passed rendering husbands responsible for provincial misdeeds of their wives.[51]

With Statilia, the Augur's wife, accrues supplement to a new family marked by success and opulence. Taurus, the marshal of Caesar's heir, acquired a consulship in 37 BC, hardly much junior to Asinius Pollio, who was born in 76 or 75. Of wife or wives, none is on record during a long life. Taurus had a son, attested as a *monetalis*, who did not reach consular years.[52] Two grandsons followed, namely T. Statilius Taurus (*cos.* AD 11) and Sisenna Statilius Taurus (16).

Such is standard doctrine.[53] It calls for close inspection. Doubt is provoked by the age of the *monetalis* and the dating of the post.[54] He should

---

[47] IV.21.

[48] The name 'Q. Granius' stood in texts since Justus Lipsius. The emendation was propounded in *JRS* XLVI (1956), 19 f. = *Ten Studies in Tacitus* (1970), 55.

[49] Named five times in connection with P. Vitellius.

[50] viz. the inscription at Samos, *Ath. Mitt.* LXXV (1960), 130, no. 30. Above, p. 337.

[51] *Ann.* IV.20.4 (on the motion of Cotta Messallinus).   [52] *PIR*[1] S 616.

[53] cf. the stemma in *PIR*[1], *Pars* III, p. 264. Reproduced by Nagl in *RE* IIIA. 2197 f.

[54] Taurus occurs along with Pulcher and Regulus on *quadrantes*, which (four colleges in number) present vexatious problems of identities as well as chronology. See now, elucidating Rubellius Blandus, *AJP* CIII (1982), 69 f. No numismatist dates Taurus and his colleagues earlier than 10 BC. Taurus (aged about twenty-two) cannot have a son consul in AD 11.

be regarded not as the father of the two consuls, but rather as an elder brother (perhaps by a different mother).

As so often happens, evidence is both sporadic and contestable. A Statilia survived into the reign of Claudius Caesar, dying at ninety-nine.[55] Either a sister or a daughter of Taurus. Further, one observes in passing, hardly to be contemplated as a wife for Piso the Pontifex.[56]

Statilia, the wife of the Augur (*cos.* 1 BC), may be identified as a daughter of Taurus born in the season of his second consulship (in 26). By the same token, sister to the two consuls. The elder is only a name, but his son, called Corvinus (*cos.* 45), indicates that he married a daughter of Messalla. The younger found mention because he possessed the town house of Cicero.[57]

In social origin and pretensions, 'Statilia L. Pisonis' was comparable to Munatia Plancina, but hardly her equal in arrogance. Sons of the match should be looked for.[58]

In the year 25 L. Piso was assassinated by a native when on a tour of duty in remote parts of Tarraconensis.[59] Not a consular, it can be asserted, but a legate of praetorian rank, acting governor when L. Arruntius was detained at Rome.[60] Given his name and family, this Piso may be assigned the senior post in the province: that is, the legate with the pair of legions.[61]

His parentage would be worth knowing. Perhaps a son of L. Piso the Pontifex (*cos.* 15 BC). If so, a son born fairly late, for he would be in near expectance of a consulship.

Homonyms in the Roman aristocracy import annoyance, and sometimes perplexity. Labels help: rank, filiation, or a priesthood. Even on official documents 'Pontifex' and 'Augur' occur, as though *cognomina*. Cornelius Tacitus was not reduced to those devices. He furnished unobtrusive guidance for the alert readers he expected but has not always found. His exposition rules out any confusion between the truculent Augur and the bland and benevolent Pontifex.[62]

The present instance carried an insight to his technique that should never have been missed. The version he preferred blamed L. Piso for harshness. The whole episode, narrated in exquisite Sallustian language, evokes past history and the great precursor.[63]

[55] Pliny, *NH* VII.158: 'Claudio principe'.

[56] As by Chr. Habicht, *Pergamon* VIII.3 (1969), 41: 'am ehesten'. He assumed that Statilia died in 54, precisely; and he chose to waive the erasure on the Samian inscription.   [57] Velleius II.14.3.

[58] A daughter has turned up on an island near the coast of Liburnia (*AE* 1949, 199). Various other Pisones had property or interests in the region, e.g. Caesoninus (ib. 205).   [59] *Ann.* IV.45.

[60] As argued in *JRS* XLVI (1956), 20 f. = *Ten Studies in Tacitus* (1970), 56 f. In *PIR*[2] C 292 this Piso had been assumed an ex-consul.

[61] Rather than the *iuridicus*, preferred by G. Alföldy, *Fasti Hispanienses* (1969), 67.

[62] cf. *JRS* XLVI (1956), 17 ff. = *Ten Studies* 50 ff.

[63] For the language, *Tacitus* (1958), 729. For the corollary to be drawn, *AJP* CI (1980), 334 = *RP* III (1984), 1227.

Spanish cavalrymen killed Cn. Piso, the quaestor of 65 BC. On one report which Sallust notes the natives refused to tolerate 'imperia eius iniusta superba crudelia'.[64] The legate L. Piso accrues to the line of those Pisones who ran true to type when they held *imperium* in Spain.[65]

A problem subsists, sons for Piso the Pontifex. They have been sought with eager pertinacity. Of some the claim was premature, to be disallowed on various grounds, notably senators who bore 'Frugi' for *cognomen*. Enquiry must even operate with Pisones nowhere on direct or named attestation.

When the Gallic rebellion broke out in 21, Acilius Aviola, the legate of Lugdunensis, intervened with decision and promptitude.[66] On the *Fasti* stands C. Calpurnius Aviola, consul suffect in 24. Identity is patent.[67] Aviola changed his name through adoption, to be presumed testamentary, by a Gaius Calpurnius. Perhaps an unknown Piso who perished before the consular age. Hesitance is prescribed. There was a C. (Calpurnius) Bibulus, aedile in 22.[68]

Next, and not even a name, the father of C. Piso, the decorative and feeble head of the conspiracy against Nero. Introducing whom, Tacitus had recourse to vague and general language: 'multas insignesque familias paterna nobilitate complexus'.[69] If the historian had chosen to specify, if at this stage in composition he had made exact investigation, the results might have been illuminating. And further, supposing the conspirator a lineal descendant of the Pontifex, this futile fellow (orator, poet, and singer) manifested a damaging declension.

An *arvalis* in 38, when the fraternity still commanded high prestige, C. Piso may have become consul early in the reign of Claudius. His parentage remains elusive. Character and habits render him not plausible as descendant of the Augur. His age excludes a son of M. Piso Cn. f. The missing parent of C. Piso might therefore raise a claim to be a son of the Pontifex.[71]

Doubts intervene. For example, C. Piso ought perhaps to have held the eponymate. Furthermore, be it recalled, the only Pisones in this epoch whose extraction is verifiable go back to Cn. Piso, the consul of 23 BC. None the less, more may exist than are documented—and even a consul.

---

[64] Sallust, *Cat.* 19.5.   [65] Therefore a son of Piso the Augur.
[66] *Ann.* III.41.1.   [67] Though not assumed such in *PIR*[2] A 47 and C 251.
[68] III.52.2.

[69] XV.48.2. Nothing can be done with the fact that his son Galerianus was a 'consobrinus' of L. Piso, the consul of 57 (*Hist.* IV.49.2).

[70] He was perhaps a son of M. Piso or a descendant of L. Piso the Augur: the opinion of Groag (*PIR*[2] C 284).

[71] A son of either the Pontifex or the Augur, according to J. Scheid, *Les Frères Arvales* (1975), 209.

A fragmentary inscription disclosed a Piso governing Dalmatia in the early years of Claudius Caesar.[72] Identity came under scrutiny. Against the Neronian conspirator stood the testimony of the *Laus Pisonis*, styling him a man of peaceful pursuits, unlike his ancestors.[73] Therefore L. Piso, the consul of 27.[74] Too eminent for Dalmatia, it might seem. He had been *praefectus urbi* and also, when proconsul of Africa, held suspect by Caligula, so it is alleged.[75] If disquiet is conceived, recourse can be had to a consular Piso otherwise unknown.[76]

There is a more alluring approach. The Pontifex was a conspicuous patron of Greek poets, in the first place Antipater of Thessalonica, who conveys clear allusions to the governorship of Galatia, the war in Thrace, the proconsulate in Asia. Apollonides of Nicaea happens to celebrate two Romans of rank, a Laelius and a Postumus, the former to be held identical with Laelius Balbus (*cos.* 6 BC), the latter with Vibius Postumus (*suff.* AD 5), who is attested as proconsul of Asia.[77]

Apollonides also produced a piece addressed to a noble youth, Gaius the son of Lucius, when he shaved his beard for the first time.[78] That is, about the age of seventeen. C. Calpurnius L. f. Piso thus emerges as the second son of the Pontifex.[79] The poem may have been written during the period when the parent was in the eastern lands (from 12 to 8 or 7).

Piso was born in 48. An early marriage contracted not long after the War of Actium and yielding two sons who assumed the toga of manhood towards the year 9 will cause no discomfort. Neither will their subsequent eclipse short of predictable consulships, given the facts of mortality and pestilence.[80]

Entertaining in itself, the quest goes beyond families and genealogy. An extraneous incentive can no longer be dissembled.

Attempts are made all the time to find a date for the poem Horace composed on the theory and practice of drama.[81] The *Ars Poetica* addresses 'Pisones' (6), defined as 'pater et iuvenes patre digni' (36).[82] The 'maior

---

[72] *ILS* 5952. [73] *Laus Pisonis* 25.

[74] Thus *PIR*[2] C 293, and those scholars who have written about legates of Dalmatia.

[75] Dio LIX.20.7. The imputation would not be a bar under Caligula's successor.

[76] See remarks in *HSCP* LXXXVII (1983), 166 f.

[77] *Anth. Pal.* IX.280; 791. Postumus had Asia for a *triennium* (*OGIS* 469: Samos). Probably from 12 to 15. [78] *Anth. Pal.* X.19.

[79] C. Cichorius, *Römische Studien* (1922), 337 ff. Not to the liking of Groag, 'id iusto fundamento caret' (C 289). But 'a fair guess' for Gow and Page, *The Garland of Philip* II (1968), 163. They affirm that the Pontifex 'had a son called Gaius'. Of which, no evidence.

[80] As stated so often in these pages. A plague during the famine years *c.*AD 6 is attested, though only by Pliny, *NH* VII.149.

[81] Doxology or bibliography cannot help. Formulation curt and clear is required.

[82] In his sparse references to the poem, Fraenkel called it 'the epistle to the sons of Piso' (*Horace* (1964), 308; 389). For the same inadvertence, *Rom. Rev.* 460, n. 5.

iuvenum' is deemed ready for essays in verse, but he has not yet written anything—'si quid tamen olim / scripseris' (386 f.). Though reaching years of discretion, he is still responsive to a father's guidance—'quamvis et voce paterna / fingeris ad rectum et per te sapis' (366 f.).

The scholiast Porphyrio adduces Lucius Piso. He is described as subsequently *praefectus urbi*, a poet himself and patron of 'studia liberalia'. Scholiasts are constrained to invent, and they come out with inept inventions. This notice commands respect. Though the scrupulous might hesitate to admit the poems, the urban prefecture is in another case. None the less, some scholars have disallowed the testimony of Porphyrio.

It need not matter. The poem speaks. It announces a Piso equipped with a pair of adolescent sons. If he is the consul of 15, that enforces a date subsequent to the *Letter to Augustus* (*Epp.* II.1) and near the end of the poet's life (he died in 8).[83]

An earlier date for the *Ars*, in 18 or 17 (after the *Letter to Florus* (II.2) and before the *Carmen Saeculare*), finds firm advocates in the recent time.[84] Not all appear to allot adequate attention to the age and identities of Roman senators old or young.

They must fall back on Cn. Piso, the consul of 23, since Pisones are the sole clear and valid criterion. His son's acquaintance with Strabo, historian and geographer, is not enough to declare a friend and patron of Latin letters liable to solicitation from Horace.

This Piso boasts two sons, to be sure (the consuls of 7 and 1). The benefit is illusory. Harsh and bitter both on subsequent performance, those men are scarcely to be redeemed by the pleasing notion that they had not yet shaped and hardened their nature in response to domestic tradition or the schooling of ambition and a career.

Finally, the elder son, to be assumed quaestor in 19 or 18. Hence a dilemma. The 'maior iuvenum' of the *Ars Poetica* had not yet approached authorship, despite precocity in young noblemen. On the other hand, innocuous pastimes suitable for an adolescent are rather late in the day for Gnaeus Piso now entering the high assembly.

In an exposition that depends upon Pisones (and is ready to waive the testimony of Porphyrio), the Pontifex wins, for all that his two sons happen not to be certified.[85] Fancies or prepossessions about the 'literary

[83] C. Cichorius, o.c. 340 f. C. O. Brink inclined to a dating 'after the years 14–13 B.C.' (*Horace on Poetry* (1963), 217). See now *Horace on Poetry* III (1982), 554 ff. He there puts emphasis on his sceptical attitude, affirming that the poem cannot be dated 'on trustworthy, that is external, criteria', whereas the internal are 'notoriously deceptive'.
[84] e.g. C. Becker, *Das Spätwerk des Horaz* (1963), 66 f. Fraenkel was curiously vague and distant, indicating 'a few years' after 20 BC (o.c. 365).
[85] A firm verdict for the Pontifex and his sons will be found in *AJP* CI (1980), 338 f. = *RP* III (1984), 1231 f. Earlier remarks made when the evidence about Pisones was put under review were not meant to publish the author's inner preference. For example, *JRS* L (1960), 20 = *RP* 508 f.

biography' of the poet occupy a due and subordinate place—and no call to enlist Horace among writers who take to theory or criticism when creative power begins to ebb.

Neither Piso benefited by an ode. The old Republican acquired sharp prominence in the year when Horace published the first three books. Instead, the consular colleague L. Sestius (I.4). The illustrious Pontifex, absent likewise from Book IV a decade later, when several of his coevals are accorded the honour, looks like a subsequent discovery or delayed recourse. Piso was back at Rome in 10 or 9, with the fresh laurels of the Thracian War.

XXVII

Nobiles in Horace

The dearth of prose enhances the poets. Horace is in no danger of being underestimated. His testimony covers a wide range, from acts and aspirations of the government to his friendship with Maecenas and his subtle comportment towards the Princeps.

A whole run of items in the first three books of the Odes evokes foreign affairs in the wide world. Few of them can claim unique or independent value. A name, a tribe, or a war appeals to erudite investigation since it may serve to furnish the date of a poem—and the passage can be quoted to lend adornment to historical narrations.[1]

The Roman public kept up a lively interest in far or fabled countries. It was stimulated by distant expeditions, Aelius Gallus on a long march towards Arabia Felix, Petronius reaching Napata in the land of the Ethiopians. Not indeed that the ruler's purpose was conquest and annexation.

Like other poets, Horace was alert to the exotic and the romantic. Hence novel and seductive names of peoples like the Geloni and the Seres.[2] Nearer to the edge of the Roman dominion, Parthia and Britannia offered scope for the military ambitions of Caesar's heir. How far the eager vaticinations of poets carried weight, or answered a clamour of public opinion, is a question that can be left to answer itself.[3]

What the Seres intend, and what Bactra, that is a cause of anxiety to Maecenas, so fantasy proclaims.[4] The Parthians were weak, torn by internal discords, so Horace casually concedes.[5] They might be mastered through the arts of diplomacy, and Britain allowed to recede. In the summer of the year 27, Caesar Augustus departed and went to the provinces of the west. His purpose was to invade the island—but he was

---

[1] Hence distortion, in general and at the expense of a large part of the long reign.

[2] Each named in Horace, as in Virgil, three times. For the Seres, see Nisbet and Hubbard in their *Commentary* on Book I (1970), on I.12.56. To which add the earliest reference (*Georgics* II.121). As for the Geloni, they were assumed close to the Roman frontier by Kiessling, *RE* VII. 1017 f. Even Strabo, so often a purveyor of the obsolete, omitted the Geloni.

[3] Evidence from poets has been exploited without due caution in recent debates about imperial policy. In the contrary sense, *History in Ovid* (1978), 48 ff.; 185 ff.

[4] *Odes* III.29.28 f.

[5] II.8.9. For the items concerning Parthia and Armenia see Nisbet and Hubbard, o.c. XXXII f. That Horace himself was eager for war and conquest is maintained by R. Seager, *Athenaeum* LVIII (1980), 103 ff.

prevented by disturbances in Spain, so a historian reports.[6] Two campaigns against Cantabri and Astures ensued, to be advertised as completing the subjugation of the peninsula.[7] The arduous task took longer. It was in fact the signal success achieved by the government in the first decade of the new dispensation.

Foreign affairs are not an urgent preoccupation with Horace or his friends. He often tells them not to worry. More benefit, and solid, can be got from what he discloses about social history. Odes and epistles mention a large number of living people, all the way from personages most eminent (not many, it is true), to a variety of friends lacking in rank or prestige. For comparison, Ovid's letters from Pontus offer, and the correspondence of Pliny. To sort out and classify the people yields appreciable and sometimes surprising results.

Too much should not be expected from the Odes, and the present enquiry bears upon the *nobiles*. Students of literature have not always been alert enough to distinctions of rank and degree. Hence common misconceptions about Horace's picture of Augustan society. Hazard comes in—and, as ever in these studies, gaps or omissions may acquire significance.

Horace devoted careful attention to order, sequence, symmetry. In Book I the patron Maecenas stands at the head, there follows a piece in which homage is paid to Caesar's heir, still suitably to be addressed as 'Caesaris ultor' in the near aftermath of Actium, and the poet Virgil has the third. Next, 'o beate Sesti' (4.14): Sestius is reminded that life is brief and transient. Then, after a short and light interlude, Marcus Agrippa makes a military and epic entrance.

The fourth poem owes its position to an extraneous fact, L. Sestius becoming consul suffect for the second half of the year 23. It was not written to honour a consul or consul designate, as might happen; and it yields no hint about public affairs. It serves to indicate the publication year of the first three books. In Sestius few saw a predictable consul. Remembered as quaestor to Marcus Brutus, he leaves no trace since then in the well-documented annals of the wars, no evidence of either proper rank or capacity for the supreme magistracy. Sestius may have been leading a

---

[6] Dio LIII.22.5; 25.2. Sometimes taken seriously, as by Nisbet and Hubbard on 'Britannos' (I.35.30). Most improbable. The ruler of Rome would not risk being cut off or bottled up in a distant island.

[7] Livy XXVIII.12.12, cf. *Odes* III.8.21 f. Mentions of Cantabri are not likely to be earlier than 26. A *curiosum* is the Concani (III.4.34), a small and remote tribe, to recur only in Silius Italicus (III.360). According to Nisbet and Hubbard, the poem 'apparently was written about 28/7' (o.c. XXXI). Cantabrians were ignored by Propertius and by Ovid.

life of tranquil leisure, like the patrician Manlius Torquatus, who was later
to receive an ode couched in a similar tone.[8]

When Sestius took over the *fasces*, replacing Caesar Augustus, he joined
as colleague another not expected consul, namely Cn. Calpurnius Piso: a
Republican previously and recalcitrant, disdaining the career of public
honours.[9] The ruler had offered him the consulate, and he accepted. The
precise time and manner of the election has not been recorded.

It was Piso who as consul received the state papers when his colleague
Augustus, grievously ill, expected not to survive. The malady of the
Princeps and anomalous consuls are far from being the only symptoms of
crisis. At the end of June the ruler modified the basis of his legal authority
in the Roman State. He gave up the consulate, held until now without a
break since 31. He kept, however, the *imperium* by which he controlled his
vast 'provincia', and it was defined as superior to that of any proconsul.

What precipitated the dramatic change is not disclosed in the sources
(such is the nature of imperial history), and sharp controversy persists. The
prosecution of a proconsul comes in, a conspiracy ensuing—and the
interpretation of a Horatian ode. Vital dates and identities remain
uncertain.[10]

It is easier for a government to defeat a conspiracy than prove its
existence; and it is expedient to cover up the clash of ambitions among
those closest to the power. Historians in the sequel may be misled by the
disjunction of related events. In 30 the vigilant Maecenas suppressed
M. Lepidus, the son of the Triumvir. That transaction is absent from the
annalistic narrative of Cassius Dio. Again, Dio relates under 26 the
catastrophe of Cornelius Gallus, the Prefect of Egypt. His disgrace belongs
earlier.[11] The historian's methods of composition sometimes contribute,
when he uses different sources, or attaches important transactions to an
item of anecdote. For example, the conspiracy of Murena and Fannius
Caepio, which he narrates under the year 22. Whether a poem of Horace
(II.10) can help to unravel the imbroglio remains to be seen.

The second book exhibits an even more artful exordium. First, Asinius
Pollio. Initial prominence goes to his history, 'motum ex Metello consule
civicum,' with a vivid evocation of theme and episodes; and Pollio's own
achievement in war and peace is extolled. Next, Sallustius Crispus,
commended for a generous use of wealth—and a reference is inserted to

---

[8] *Odes* IV. 7. By paradox Sestius turns up as consular legate governing Hispania Ulterior. On the
western coast of Callaecia stood 'tres arae Sestianae Augusto dicatae' (Pliny, *NH* IV. 111) They are
taken to commemorate the subjugation of the North-West, completed in 19. Cf. now G. Alföldy,
Fasti Hispanienses (1969), 133.
[9] *Ann.* II.43.2 (above, p. 368). In Dio only Sestius is accorded a Republican past (LIII.32.4).
[10] below, p. 387.
[11] above, p. 32.

Proculeius, 'notus in fratres animi paterni'. Proculeius was the half-brother of Terentia, the wife of Maecenas. Third, Q. Dellius, urged to keep an equal mind in adverse or in prosperous seasons.

All three exhibit a conspicuous feature in common, namely changes of side in the wars, albeit not quite with equal success and repute.[12] Another link bound them, the writing of history. The memoirs of Dellius related his diplomatic missions and included Antonius' invasion of Media. Crispus, the son by adoption of the historian, was a grandson of Sallust's sister. His original name and identity is lost to knowledge. He already stood close to the inner circle of government, so it will be surmised.[13]

In a group that unfriendly testimony could have styled renegades and profiteers, primacy belonged to Munatius Plancus with a long past behind him, the most smooth and elegant among the correspondents of Cicero. Plancus annexes one of the earliest of the odes (I.7). The poet wonders whether the veteran statesman is reposing in the cool shade of his native Tibur, or is at the wars again, 'seu te fulgentia signis/castra tenent'. Men of the time would be surprised if Caesar's heir gave military employment to Plancus after he arrived from Alexandria in the course of 32.[14] He possessed useful talents of another order.

An author needed no percipience to see that he must seclude Messalla Corvinus from this company. Dazed from the impact of the ode to Pollio, the reader on recovering would ask where his rival in oratory was to be found. He would have to wait for some time, and keep attentive. A jar of vintage wine is invoked, to come down from the shelf on command from Corvinus (III.21.7). Though soaked in doctrines, 'Socraticis madet sermonibus', Corvinus will not neglect wine—nor did old Cato. This novel presentation of the illustrious Messalla will come as a surprise to those who knew his fame and exploits from Tibullus and from the panegyrist.[15]

The three odes introducing Book II recalled the recent past. The first six in Book III, though written separately, make a compact group and are known by a conventional appellation, 'the Roman Odes'.[16] The past epoch they commend was moral, martial, and salubrious—and, while the vice and irreligion of the time is deplored, firm confidence goes to the present order. It was needed in the year 23.

---

[12] cf. Seneca, *De clem.* I.10.1: 'Sallustium et Cocceios et Dellios et totam cohortem primae admissionis ex adversariorum castris conscripsit.'

[13] The mention of Proculeius is significant. Cf., discussing the fable that the historian married Cicero's Terentia, *CQ* XXVIII (1978), 295 = *RP* III (1984), 1089.

[14] A date for the poem earlier than 30 BC is suggested by Nisbet and Hubbard, o.c. 91.

[15] The notorious drinker was Messalla the Augur, recently deceased. Cf. C. Cichorius, *Römische Studien* (1922), 235 f.

[16] For an attempt to date them (apart from the first ode) between 29 and 26, see P. Grimal, *Rev. ét. lat.* LIII (1975), 135 ff.

So far four consulars are discovered, only one of them a *nobilis*.[17] There may be one or two senators of lower degree. The poet Valgius Rufus, a member of the 'circle of Messalla', receives an ode (II.9). It leads off with the stormy Caspian and Armenia; and it exhorts him at the end to celebrate the 'nova tropaea' of 'Augustus Caesar'. Conquest is specified in ornate language,

> rigidum Niphatem
> Medumque flumen gentibus additum
> victis.[18]

The Armenian mountain stands at a certain distance from reality. More so, the curbing of the Geloni, with whom the poem ends. Niphates had been introduced into Latin poetry by Virgil, who fancied it a river.[19] Horace gently corrects his friend.

Further, Quinctius, styled 'Hirpinus', might also be a senator. He is incited not to worry about 'bellicosus Cantaber et Scythes' (II.11.1 f.). Quiet and refined dissipation is better. The Quinctii were a known and wealthy family, attested in Campania as well as in their native Samnium.[20]

A passing thought goes to Postumus, likewise reminded of the brevity of life and the need to enjoy it (II.14). Engaging perspectives appear to offer, although the *cognomen* is indistinctive. Propertius gently chides a Postumus for going away to the eastern wars and neglecting his wife, Aelia Galla.[21] The man is generally held identical with the senator Propertius Postumus. Why not also (it is suggested) with the Postumus of Horace?[22] Aelia Galla, it is noted, should be close kin to Caesar's second viceroy in Egypt.

The list is short. With the exception of Messalla it appears to include no aristocrat.[23] Horace was not anxious to solicit the eminent.[24] Later, in Book IV, only one consular has an entry. His friendship and sympathy went to younger men, endowed with social gifts and an inclination towards the Muses. Another phenomenon intervenes. Civil war and the proscriptions

[17] On the 'Varus' addressed in I.18, Nisbet and Hubbard (o.c. 227 f.) express a firm preference for the jurist P. Alfenus Varus (*suff.* 39), citing for his origin from Cremona the scholiast Porphyrio (on *Sat.* I.3.130). The admonition of E. Fraenkel deserved a mention (*Horace* (1957), 89 f.).

[18] II.9.20 ff.   [19] *Georgics* III.30.

[20] viz. C. Quinctius Valgus (*ILS* 5636: Pompeii; 5318: Aeclanum). On whom, H. Gundel, *RE* XXIV. 1103 f. Ignored by M. Schuster (ib. 1105 f.). That Horace's friend might be a brother-in-law of Pollio is suggested by Nisbet and Hubbard in their *Commentary* on Book II (1978), 168. Pollio married a daughter of a Lucius Quinctius. For the proconsul L. Quinctius Rufus, perhaps from Lanuvium, see *Historia* IV (1955), 67 f. = *RP* (1979), 287 f.

[21] Propertius III.12.

[22] Nisbet and Hubbard, o.c. 223 f. Hence an identity for the 'placens uxor' (14.21 f.). They further state that 'Postumus was a religious man and possibly even a *pontifex*' (Introd., p. 2).

[23] That is, so far. For Licinius (II.10) and for Murena, the *augur* (III.19), see below.

[24] One cannot but deprecate the notion that 'Horace's odes in general are written for *principes viri* rather than their sons' (in the introductory comments on I.26). In the year 23 there existed a mass of ex-consuls, with a whole cluster of 'viri triumphales'.

at Rome were not always murderous to the aristocracy. Many were rescued by kinsmen on the other side, by protection or by connivance. Philippi was the young men's cause, with a carnage of *nobiles*, and several families show no consul in the sequel. For others there was a gap, not filled until a generation came to manhood, emerging and exhibited in the run of consuls between 16 and 7.

The early years of the new dispensation were not propitious to birth and lineage. Normal government with annual consuls (its precise and visible declaration) returned in 28.[25] Appearances turned out to be deceptive in more ways than one. Caesar's heir continued in the *fasces*, with Marcus Agrippa for colleague, as again in the next year; and in 26 Statilius Taurus (*cos.* 37) entered on his second consulship.

In a space of five years (28–24) the government excluded eight senators from access to the consulate. Of resentment among the *nobiles* the written record betrays no trace—and confirms its inadequacy.

Alert and opportunistic in the contest between the rival dynasts, the old houses were ready to acquiesce in the monarchy, and to profit from it. Yet distaste or alarm must have been felt when the ruler, returning from Spain in 24, announced for Marcellus, his youthful nephew, a consulship to be held when he was twenty-two.

Caesar's heir depended upon army and plebs; and the military zones were in the hands of partisans no doubt proved or deemed trustworthy. At Rome an open and direct challenge either to his *imperium* or to his 'auctoritas' would not occur to the men of understanding. Accident might furnish the impulsion.

It came quite quickly. M. Primus the proconsul of Macedonia stood trial for high treason: he had waged war in Thrace without authority. Primus in that extremity alleged advice from Marcellus or from Augustus. The Princeps appeared in court, with a denial. The advocate of Primus raised objection, to be countered by the Princeps: he was there in the public interest.

Licinius Murena, who defended the proconsul, was a man of violent tongue and temper. Conceiving annoyance, he went in with a conspiracy which Fannius Caepio promoted. The criminals were detected in time, indicted, executed when trying to escape arrest. Neither his brother Proculeius could save Murena, nor Maecenas, the husband of his sister.

Such is the account of Cassius Dio, coherent and acceptable as far as it goes.[26] The historian expressed a doubt about the complicity of Murena—there were lessons in his own time and experience.

[25] Ch. III.
[26] Dio LIV.3. Introduced under the year 22 to illustrate the ruler's moderate comportment and readiness to help friends.

Licinius Murena in Dio, the conspirator is L. Murena in Velleius, Murena in Strabo, Murena and Varro Murena in Suetonius, Varro only in Seneca and in Tacitus. The variants need not be a cause of discomfort. A Varro Murena is on attestation some twenty years earlier.[27] That is, a Licinius Murena adopted by a Terentius Varro. For the conspirator the name 'Terentius' is certified through his sister, the Terentia whom Maecenas married. He is therefore a *polyonymus*.

Further problems arise of identities, of intervals in time, of the nexus of events. Welcome as it would be to decline trudging on well trodden ways or be trapped in the erudite bypaths, the present enquiry cannot have recourse to evasions. A brief clarification is imposed.[28] Not easy, and it calls for a careful order of exposition.

First therefore the consular colleague of Augustus in the year 23, disclosed by the *Fasti Capitolini*:

> A.T.[erentius A. f. . . .n. Var]ro Murena
> . . . .]est. in e.l.f.e.
> Cn. Calpu]rnius Cn. f. Cn. n. Pis[o

This consul did not resign, that would be 'abd(icavit)'. Some supplement '[in mag. damn(atus)] est.'[29] Better, as a euphemism, 'mortuus'.

Hesitation intervenes. Only the *Capitolini* exhibit A. Terentius Varro Murena. On all other lists the colleague of the ruler is Cn. Calpurnius Piso. Moreover, the condemnation of a consul in office is an enormity. Hence perhaps '[motus] est'.[30] The term lacks precedent.[31] Whichever reading be preferred, it is not clear that the agents of the government had the scruple or leisure to persuade the consul to abdicate before they killed criminals who might be declared public enemies—either before or after their execution. Public law and the proprieties will not with safety be invoked in a year when the ruler, giving up the consulship, extended the sphere of his *imperium* to a degree beyond precedent and took to himself the powers of all ten tribunes, to be interpreted in his own fashion, invulnerable because vague.

Identity of conspirator and consul, the theory commanded wide assent.[32] It permitted a tight and perhaps rapid sequence: the removal of Varro Murena, the anomalous promotion of Piso, the malady of Caesar Augustus, the change in the basis of the ruler's legal authority.

[27] As aedile in 44 (*ILS* 897: Lanuvium).
[28] For the abundant and not abating bibliography, see, e.g., G. V. Sumner, *HSCP* LXXXII (1978), 187; D. Kienast, *Augustus* (1982), 86 f.
[29] Thus Degrassi, *Inscr. It.* XIII.1, p. 59.
[30] R. Hanslik, *Rh. Mus.* XCVI (1953), 284.
[31] As does the procedure, cf. E. J. Weinrib, *Phoenix* XXII (1968), 49 f.
[32] Since *PIR*[1] T 74. For recent advocates, B. Levick, *Tiberius the Politician* (1976), 21 f.; L. J. Daly, *Historia* XXVII (1978), 83 ff.; D. Kienast, *Augustus* (1982), 86. It has been defined as the standard theory.

None the less, the amalgam can with some advantage be split and separated.[33] The Varro Murena inscribed on the *Fasti Capitolini* may never have assumed the *fasces*. Several consular lists happen to register *designati* whom death or a prosecution debarred.[34] Thus on the *Capitolini* in 108 'da]mn(atus)[est'. That entry indicates a Hortensius.

There is quite a lot to be said in favour of this view. In presents as conspirator L. Terentius Varro Murena, a presumed cousin of the failed or deceased consul-elect.[35] Neither Velleius nor Dio gave any hint of a consul brought to ruin. That could be explained, it is true, or explained away. Velleius, loyal to the government, brushed aside the enormity. As for the Greek historian in a later age, he was inadvertent. Following perhaps a source that disjoined events, he put in the next year the prosecution of M. Primus and the conspiracy of Licinius Murena.

Whichever theory be accorded preference, a concatenation of events can be sustained. There is no call to deviate. A prominent member of the Caesarian party was suppressed.[36] In the secret conflicts in the entourage of an autocrat thought moribund, Marcus Agrippa came out with power enhanced as well as authority; and Caesar's minister Maecenas begins to recede, the brother-in-law of Murena.

No necessity therefore subsists for putting the catastrophe of Varro Murena in the second half of the year, or, for that matter even later, in 22.[37] That is, unless one is prepared to invoke and exploit a Horatian ode. It addresses and counsels a man called Licinius—'rectius vives, Licini' (II.10.1).

The ancient superscription gives 'Licinius Murena'.[38] Few indeed are the scholars who hesitate to pronounce him identical with Terentia's brother. That identity, it need not be added, entails direct consequences for chronology: the conspirator still among the living in the second half of the year.[39]

---

[33] H. Dessau, *Gesch. der r. Kaiserzeit* I (1924), 50; K. M. T. Atkinson, *Historia* IX (1960), 440 ff.

[34] See the valuable contribution of M. Swan, *HSCP* LXXI (1966), 235 ff. He confessed that he was not able to supplement ']est'. In favour should be noted the fact that 23 as well as 22 was a plague year (Dio LIII.33.4).

[35] cf. the stemmata, not totally concordant, presented by K. M. T. Atkinson, o.c. 473; G. V. Sumner, o.c. 194.

[36] Velleius II.91.2: 'nam Murena sine hoc facinore potuit videri bonus.' He stated that Murena and Caepio were 'oppressi auctoritate publica'. It was in fact normally permissible to anticipate condemnation by going into voluntary exile. Compare, with emphasis on the enormity, L. J. Daly, *Klio* LV (1983), 261.

[37] Despite the powerful and subversive contribution of E. Badian in *Romanitas–Christianitas* (*Festschrift J. Straub*, 1982), 18 ff., esp. 32 f.

[38] On the inadequacies of those items see F. Klingner, *Hermes* LXX (1935), 261 ff.

[39] A copious and elaborate discussion is furnished by Nisbet and Hubbard in their *Commentary* (1978), 151–7. They incline, but not to advantage, to the highly vulnerable reconstruction of R. Hanslik, *Rh. Mus.* XCVI (1953), 282 ff. That is, several stages in the decline and fall of Murena,

Licinius, so the helpful friend urges, should not either press for deep waters or hug the shore. 'Aurea mediocritas', that is the word. It shuns alike the squalid dwelling and the invidious splendour of a palace. The tall towers fall with a heavier crash, and the lightning strikes the high peaks. Firm resolution keeps up hope in adversity, but is on guard in prosperous seasons. Bad times do not persist. Therefore,

> rebus angustis animosus atque
> fortis adpare.[40]

However, caution is expedient when the winds are favourable.

The poet enjoins avoidance of extremes. To support the identity, a valuable extraneous fact is adduced. According to Strabo, Athenaeus was implicated with Murena, put under arrest but let off, reverting to his native city with relief and a suitable quotation from Euripides.[41] Athenaeus of Seleuceia was an eminent and successful professor, of the Peripatetic School. Singularly appropriate therefore that praise of the middle path should inform a poem dedicated to a patron of the philosopher.[42]

The Licinius of the ode (if it is to be assigned a close and personal reference) seems to be under the shadow of some misfortune and to stand in need of consolation, with the advice to hope for better times. Applied to Murena, the ode is held to indicate a stage in a progressive downfall.

Wide divergences obtain among the interpreters of certain odes; and doubt arises when the character, pursuits, and social status of a recipient are either assumed to be known or to be inferred from the language. When it is a mere matter of convivial habits or a life passed in refined tranquillity, disquiet need not be felt, or hesitation about the personal relevance for example to Sestius, or to Postumus. Now Postumus must die, 'linquenda tellus et domus et placens / uxor.'[43] To draw conclusions about his marital status is illicit. The wife owes her existence to a famous passage in Lucretius.[44]

Again, the woman Licymnia, whose varied and elegant charms are depicted, vivid and lively, in an ode to Maecenas.[45] She is his wife Terentia, so the scholiast declares—and most concur. To maintain the identity, the portrayal of this Roman matron has to be explained as mainly fantasy.[46] Better, Licymnia is a *hetaera*.[47] Scholiasts are often bold or silly in their assertions.

beginning with 'he may have been driven from office early in 23', and continuing into the next year.

For criticism of this excursus, see the reviews by K. Quinn, *Phoenix* XXXIV (1980), 259; J. Griffin, *JRS* LXX (1980), 183.

[40] II.10.21 f.   [41] Strabo XIV, p. 670.
[42] Thus J. Griffin, l.c.   [43] II.14.20 f.
[44] Lucretius III.894f. Quoted by the commentators.   [45] II.12.
[46] G. Williams, *JRS* LII (1962), 38.
[47] G. Davis, *Philol.* CIX (1975), 70 ff.; Nisbet and Hubbard, o.c. 180 ff.

The tone and comportment to adopt when speaking to a person of rank invites discretion in most ages. One might wonder whether Horace is not unduly condescending towards Licinius when he both consoles and exhorts. However, that need not detain.

Some thought should have been conceded to Roman nomenclature and modes of address. In the last epoch of the Republic, the *nobilitas* prefers to drop the *gentilicium*. It was generally indistinctive. The fashion is followed by new men. Agrippa suppressed 'Vipsanius'; and Munatius Plancus, who exhibited his full nomenclature on his mausoleum, chose to be 'L. Plancus' when he set up a dedication at Rome, in 41 BC or not long after.[48]

The term 'nobilis' in the primary sense is social, not legal. Before long, usage admits the maternal line; and some indulgence might extend on the margin. In Augustan Rome, where fraud in genealogy was rife, there is no sign that recognition would be denied to a Varro Murena. Whether any Terentii, among them the polymath from Reate in the Sabine country, put up a claim to descend from the consul of 216 evades ascertainment. The Licinii Murenae, of Lanuvium in old Latium, rose in the allegiance of Sulla and, conservative in politics, established a consul in 62. That town happens to offer the inscription of a senator, A. Terentius Varro Murena.[49]

The conspirator (it will be recalled) is generally held a son or grandson of the consul L. Licinius Murena, who leaves no trace after 62.[50] His father had become a Terentius Varro. Now adoption (by the plenary act, not the mere assumption of a name) cannot annul prestige of birth, or even any privileges, so it appears, in the career of honours.[51]

Varro Murena exhibits a double opportunity, of prestige as likewise of nomenclature. Dull would a poet be and socially delinquent, if he made approach to the brother of Terentia with the appellation 'Terenti' or 'Licini'. Even were the friend of Horace a senator of praetorian family, such as a Licinius Nerva, the same holds: address by the *cognomen*. No reader other than a scholiast would fancy that his Quinctius and his Quinctilius were aristocrats.[52]

Licinius is not one of those 'qui aetatem in excelso agunt', parading on the edge of catastrophe. Licinius belongs to the middling sort, deemed by a poet to need comfort and counsel.

On this contention Licinius forfeits high rank among the famous nations of the dead where, for all that equality reigns, the disdainful expert in pedigree will issue a challenge: 'chi fur li maior tui?' No answer from the

---

[48] *ILS* 41 (Rome); 886 (near Caieta). [49] *ILS* 897.

[50] A son, on estimates that disjoin conspirator and consul. Yet either way perhaps a grandson. Nor is descent excluded from C. Licinius, the consul's brother.

[51] above, p. 52.

[52] II.11.2; I.24.5. The notable exception is 'Claudi' in *Epp.* I.8.1, helped out by 'Neronis' at the end of l. 4.

man of golden mediocrity. For present and prosaic ends, his excision is beneficial and the conspirator abides, be he Aulus or Lucius by *praenomen*.[53]

A problem subsists, how many Varrones?[54] In 26 or 25 Terentius Varro subjugated an Alpine tribe, the Salassi.[55] Next, in late June of 25, ']tius M. f. Pap. Varro', registered as one of the witnesses on a decree of the Senate.[56] Third, in 24 or 23, Varro who is Caesar's legate in Syria.[57] This Varro, praetorian legate in charge of a large army, would be worth knowing about.[58]

To round off the rubric, an ode carries the toast of 'auguris Murenae'.[59] Murena is here honoured when inducted into the college of augurs, so it is held. Further, perhaps to be assumed the same person as Varro Murena, brother-in-law of Maecenas.[60] It is time to stop, and to renounce. As the poet declared, when he raised and waived a curious topic of Raetian ethnography,

> quaerere distuli
> nec scire fas est omnia.[61]

Something can still be known, and negative phenomena have their use. Apart from Messalla Corvinus and the augur Murena, no aristocrat is certified in the three books. Horace was a client of Maecenas and he lent fervent advocacy to a programme of moral regeneration, loyally anticipating what was not enacted until the Julian laws of 18.[62] Aristocrats disliked being regimented and molested by governmental ordinances, not least when appeal was made to 'prisci mores' or Sabine frugality. That was not their authentic tradition.

If the advocates themselves were equivocal, that was nothing new, only to be expected. There was something worse. Men recalled young Lepidus,

[53] In the verdict of Kiessling–Heinze (ed. 9, 1958) the Horatian Licinius was in fact 'für uns nicht näher bestimmbar'.

[54] The familiar *cognomen* is of restricted occurrence in the upper order.

[55] Strabo IV, p. 206; Dio LIII.25.3. This Terentius Varro has generally been held identical with the consul (or consul-designate) of 23. That Strabo in a different context should present 'Murena' (XIV, p. 570) is not a safe argument for anything.

[56] viz. the *SC de Mytilenaeis* (*IGR* IV. 33 = R. K. Sherk, *RDGE* (1969), no. 26). Varro of Reate (recently deceased) should have had for tribe the 'Quirina', which is also that of the Visellii Varrones (*SIG*³ 747 = *RDGE*, no. 23).

[57] Josephus, *BJ* I. 398; *AJ* XV. 345.

[58] For identity, 'possibly a brother of Varro Murena', *Rom. Rev.* (1939), 330, n. 2, cf. 338. A case was made out for the conspirator himself (i.e. not the consul) by K. M. T. Atkinson, o.c. 469 f. Taken as proved by P. A. Brunt, *JRS* LI (1961), 234 (review of P. Sattler, *Augustus und der Senat*); E. Badian, o.c. 36, n. 45.

C. Visellius Varro found no advocate: the link to be postulated between Cicero's cousin (aedile ?59) and the *suffectus* of AD 12.

[59] III.19.10 f.

[60] Thus Kiessling–Heinze and others. On that assumption, a good argument for putting the conspiracy in 22.   [61] IV.4.21 f.

[62] A sombre and salubrious estimate of the political poems will be found in Nisbet and Hubbard, o.c. XVIII.

whom Maecenas destroyed.[63] The credit of the government was not enhanced by the fate of Murena and Caepio.

Aversion from political life had a variety of causes.[64] It can be surmised in the presumed habits and tastes of a number of Horace's friends. Interpretation is a delicate matter, the use of philosophical labels to be deprecated. None the less, many of those people look like Epicureans, Sestius to begin with, then Manlius Torquatus;[65] and there is no doubt about Varius Rufus.[66]

Horace reflects Roman society in one aspect. As has been indicated, what he says about public events and persons in the years after Actium is far from providing a complete and satisfactory picture.[67]

References abound to warfare, either now in process or ostensibly in firm prospect. Marcus Agrippa could hardly be passed over, but his past exploits call for a poet in the epic manner. That is, Varius Rufus.[68] Next in fame and next in loyalty to their leader stood Statilius Taurus. Of Taurus, no hint anywhere, and none of his old ally Calvisius Sabinus, well tried in the Caesarian allegiance.

No campaign is assigned to any named general, and none of the praetorian legates finds a mention whom Caesar Augustus used in his 'provincia'. Some of them acceded later to the consulate. M. Lollius took up an important command when a large territory, Galatia-Pamphylia, was annexed in 26 or 25.[69] Again, the excellent Marcus Vinicius winning credit on the Rhine, Tarius Rufus on the lower Danube.[70]

Many facts and names are lost.[71] By good fortune, the four legates in Tarraconensis can be recovered, from 26 to 17. First, a consular, C. Antistius Vetus (*suff.* 30 BC), serving there under Caesar Augustus. Then L. Aelius Lamia (attested in 24), C. Furnius (in 22), then the consular P. Silius Nerva (*cos.* 20).[72]

---

[63] At least for a time. According to Seneca, 'maxima laus illi tribuitur mansuetudinis' (*Epp.* 114.7). Modern writing about Horace and Maecenas tends to eschew the episode.

[64] That is, not merely disapprobation of the 'novus status' or a wilful spirit of opposition. Volcacius Tullus, the nephew of a Caesarian consul, chose to spend long years at Cyzicus (Propertius III.22.1).

[65] IV.7, cf. below, p. 396.

[66] Quintilian VI.3.78: 'L. Vario Epicurio, Caesaris amico' (where OCT prefers to read 'Varo').

[67] Observe by contrast the notion that those who received odes or epistles 'include all the greatest names of the Augustan Age' (L. P. Wilkinson, *Horace and his Lyric Poetry* (1945), 53).

[68] I.6.1. The neat equivalent of a dedication: Virgil had received the third ode. Maecenas, one notes in passing, will recount the wars of Augustus, in prose (II.12.9 ff.).

[69] Eutropius VII.10.2.

[70] Dio LIII.26.4; LIV.20.3.

[71] e.g. a praetorian command for C. Sentius Saturninus (*cos.* 19).

[72] G. Alföldy, *Fasti Hispanienses* (1969), 3 ff. In the other command (Ulterior), P. Carisius from 27 to 22, then L. Sestius (above, p. 384, n. 8). Carisius (*PIR*² C 422) won a victory in the field and also founded Emerita. Dio impugns him for luxury and cruelty (LIV.5.1).

The father of Furnius, an Antonian partisan, cropped up in 35, in eminent company along with Pollio, Messalla, and others, being addressed as 'candide Furni'.[73] Furnius reached the consulate, but not until 17. About Aelius Lamia, perplexity cannot be evaded. The matter bears on the age and rank of persons honoured with odes. It calls for a brief excursus.

In charge of Tarraconensis (and three or four legions) Lamia looks like a senior praetorian legate, born about the year 65, or perhaps earlier. His father, told to quit Rome by the consul Gabinius in 58, was a knight of weight and consequence, 'equestris ordinis princeps'.[74]

A Lamia receives three odes (I.26; 36; III.17); and he is named in one of the epistles (I.14.6), which were published in 20. The temptation was easy to hold him identical with L. Aelius Lamia (*cos.* AD 3), of later and illustrious fame as a governor of provinces and ending as *praefectus urbi* in succession to Piso the Pontifex.[75] Few were drawn to his parent, the legate in Spain. More recently, a careful and sophisticated enquiry assigned him the three odes.[76] However, a different version suggests that two odes might be assigned to the parent, one to the son (I.36).[77] The latter might also be discovered in the Lamia of an epistle, who mourns the loss of a brother:

> me quamvis Lamiae pietas et cura moratur
> fratrem maerentis, rapto de fratre dolentis
> insolabiliter.[78]

About Lamia the future consul a difficulty should have been discussed, namely his age. When a *monetalis* (about twenty or twenty-two) Lamia had for colleague a Silius, to be identified as P. Silius, later consul suffect in the same year.[79] Lamia thus stands on a double parity of age with Silius. The latter was the son of a consul, yet himself only a *suffectus*.

Lamia thus benefited not only from favour but from a privilege. An explanation avails: Lamia is one of the neo-patricians.[80] His presumed son retained that status when taken into the family of the Plautii.[81] Lamia was therefore born perhaps as late as 32 BC. And further, much too young to be the friend of Horace. One ode in question (I.26) carries a reference to the Parthian pretender Tiridates, hence falling towards the year 25.[82]

---

[73] *Sat.* I.10.86 (above, p. 205).

[74] *Ad fam.* XI.17.2.

[75] Thus *PIR²* A 200. Followed in *Rom. Rev.* (1939), 83, cf. the Index.

[76] S. Treggiari, *Phoenix* XXVII (1973), 252.

[77] Nisbet and Hubbard on I.26 (p. 301).

[78] *Epp.* I.14.6 ff. For a new and novel interpretation, E. J. Kenney, *Illinois Class. Stud.* II (1977), 229 ff. The brother did not die—he was carried off by a love affair. Weight is attached to 'insolabiliter': not serious, but a kind of parody of Lucretius III.907, where the adverb 'insatiabiliter' is satirical. The notion is attractive.

[79] *BMC R. Emp.* I.40.   [80] above, p. 52.

[81] i.e. Ti. Plautius Silvanus Aelianus, consul suffect in 45 (*ILS* 986: near Tibur). On whom, *Epigrafia e Ordine Senatorio* I (1982), 406 f.

[82] cf. Nisbet and Hubbard, o.c. XXXIII.

Another member of the family suffered neglect: Q. Aelius Lamia, a *monetalis* in the company of T. Quinctius Crispinus Sulpicianus and C. Marcius Censorinus.[83] The post is put in 20 or 19 (the others were consuls in 9 and in 8). On one hypothesis it is Q. Lamia who grieves for the loss of his brother, the recently returned legate of Tarraconensis.[84] If so, Quintus is a brother younger by more than two decades. Better, a son.[85]

As has been demonstrated, age debars Lamia (*cos.* AD 3) from the ode (I.26). It also rules out Q. Lamia (born about 42 BC).

For a friend of Horace, named four times, a single person might be deemed preferable, not two—unless the author was inadvertent. One remedy would be to conjure up a younger brother of Caesar's legate in Tarraconensis: like other friends of the poet not much concerned with warfare and government and perhaps declining to enter the Senate. On that conjecture his brother died soon after coming back from Spain in 22. So much being not known about the history, there is no point in adding the pleasing fancy that this Aelius Lamia might otherwise have ended as consul.

The family was of ancient fame, claiming for ancestor a king who founded the city of Formiae.[86] The father was brought into the Senate by Caesar the Dictator, a late entrant. It is no surprise to find the men of substance and repute from the Italian *municipia* among the poet's friends. Valgius Rufus may well be senatorial by extraction;[87] and the Samnite Quinctii, owners of large estates, had benefited from the Sullan proscriptions.[88]

Warfare in Spain is mentioned in one of the *Epistulae*, both written and published in the year 20:

> Cantaber Agrippae, Claudi virtute Neronis
> Armenius cecidit.[89]

Horace praises the achievement of Agrippa. He is also able to slip in a compliment to the stepson of the Princeps, who although conducting an army into Armenia had not fought any campaign. Young Claudius Nero is the only aristocrat to be honoured with a poem in the collection, apart from Torquatus.[90] The Manlii, a house of the patriciate renowned for pride and energy, saw their last consul in 65, and several members perished

[83] *BMC R. Emp.* I, 35 ; 175 f. Not occurring in the comments of Nisbet and Hubbard on I. 26 and 36.

[84] K. Kraft, *Jahrbuch für Numismatik und Geldgeschichte* XVI (1966), 23 ff.

[85] Thus S. Treggiari, o.c. 251: the *monetalis* dying and mourned by L. Lamia (*cos.* AD 3).

[86] III.17.1

[87] Observe 'A. Valgius, senatoris filius' (*Bell. Hisp.* 13.2).

[88] *De lege agr.* III.3, cf. 8.

[89] *Epp.* I.12.26 f.

[90] I.5.

on the side of Pompeius or for the Republic. That consul adhered to the
doctrines of Epicurus.[91] The friend of Horace is credited with eloquence,
and he may have been a poet.[92] No surprise, therefore, if Torquatus in fact
renounced the career of honours, disdaining ambition, intrigue, or subsidy
from Caesar. Thus ended the Manlii.

The collection (twenty poems) is largely devoted to friends of lower
degree, and only two of them had received odes.[93] A young man called
Lollius Maximus is addressed twice.[94] Tone and content dissuade the
notion that he might be a son of M. Lollius, the consul of the previous
year, whom the poet a little later registers when indicating his own age.[95]
The name is fairly common. Search for the father of the beautiful Lollia
Paullina thus lapses, for more reasons than one.[96]

For the aristocracy, opulent compensation arrives with a fourth book of
odes, published in the year 13. The date seems clear. One poem (the fifth)
anticipates the return of Caesar Augustus, and passages in two others
celebrate peace now obtaining to the ends of the world. The ruler came
back in the summer of 13, after three years of absence in Gaul and Spain;
and the *Ara Pacis Augustae* was begun.

Paullus Fabius Maximus and Iullus Antonius lead off, among the most
resplendent *nobiles* not yet of consular years. They are segregated and set in
high relief by the short and neutral third poem, not dedicated to any
person.

For the others, it will be expedient to desert the author's order. In the
seventh Torquatus is accorded an eloquent and majestic piece: springtime
and the seasons and human destiny, recalling the ode to Sestius. At the last,
'pulvis et umbra', and despite birth and all excellence one must go 'quo
dives Tullus et Ancus'.[97] The allusion to the kings of Rome should strike a
response from the dullest of readers. It evokes a line in Lucretius.[98] This
Manlius was also one of the Epicureans. They tend in any age to be
unobtrusive.

The next poem continues with a subtle link, the theme being the
immortality conferred by poets. It is addressed to Censorinus, another
nobilis, without any hint of family, rank or occupation. He is C. Marcius

---

[91] *De finibus* I.39.
[92] cf. 'Torquatum, immo Torquatos' in the catalogue of the eminent who composed light verse
(Pliny, *Epp.* V.3.5).
[93] viz. Iccius (*Epp.* I.12) and Quinctius (16). The list is discussed by W. Allen, *Studies in Philology*
LXVII (1970), 255 ff.
[94] *Epp.* I. 2 and 18.
[95] In 20.28, cf. E. Fraenkel, *Horace* (1957), 315. In *PIR*² J 317 no conclusion is offered.
[96] Ch. XIII. The matter is of some interest since he was widely believed to have reached a
consulship. Against which, *JRS* LVI (1966), 59.
[97] *Odes* IV.7.15.
[98] Lucretius III.1025.

Censorinus, later to share the *fasces* in 8 with Asinius Gallus—and to die when holding high office in the eastern lands.[99] The Marcii, claiming descent from a king of Rome, were the head and front of the ancient plebeian *nobilitas*, in rank almost patrician. Of the other surviving branch, the last consul was L. Marcius Philippus (*suff.* 38), who married Atia, an aunt of Caesar Augustus. Censorinus left no descendants.

So far four *nobiles*, three of them destined to be consuls and proconsuls of Asia. Next after Censorinus a consular *novus homo* benefits no less from commemoration and reinforces the theme. 'Vixere fortes ante Agamemnona multi'—but they had no poet and are dead (9.25 ff.). Horace refuses to let the efforts of Lollius succumb to oblivion through detraction. Lollius curbs rapacity and deceit, he is immune from thoughts of profit. Lollius shall be acclaimed as a consul not for one year only, but as long as just magistrates put truth and honour before expedience.

Marcus Lollius is paraded as a paragon of integrity: in default of birth, so the reader might infer, acquiring the genuine nobility of 'innocentia' and 'industria'. The portrayal evokes varying assessments.[100]

At the lowest, the bare presence of Lollius will come as a shock, to some at least. The only ex-consul in the book, and he a *novus homo*. Lollius is the great surprise, irrespective of any subsequent revelations. For the rest, a girl called Phyllis is invited to prepare a festival, and she engrosses the second half of the poem. At the centre, however, occurs Maecenas, for it is his birthday (11.19): not forgotten by his friend, but no longer to stand at the head of a poem as in the days of his power and influence.

Phyllis is the last of his loves—'non enim posthac alia calebo/femina'. Melancholy in the quinquagenarian was advertised in the opening lines of the book, harking back to 'bonae/sub regno Cinarae' (1.3 f.). Perhaps equally authentic.

A different specimen of the unverifiable is the obscure Vergilius (12.13), playfully labelled as 'iuvenum nobilium cliens' and gently rebuked for 'studium lucri'. A merchant, it appears, or perhaps rather a banker.[101]

To revert briefly to Maximus and Iullus. The first poem announces Horace's return to erotic verse. For Venus he is too old. The goddess should transfer her dominion to Paullus Maximus and hold revel in his mansion,

---

[99] Velleius II.102.1. On Censorinus see now *PIR*[2] M 222, which discusses his legateship held in the eastern lands *c.*14 BC (*AE* 1906, 1: Sinope).

[100] Noteworthy is the sympathy and enthusiasm evoked in Fraenkel, o.c. 423 ff. On Horace as a panegyrist observe Nisbet, *CR* XIX (1969), 175: 'his sincerity cannot now be determined' (reviewing E. Doblhofer, *Die Augustuspanegyrik des Horaz*).

[101] In any event, not the poet Virgil, cf. E. Fraenkel, o.c. 418. By contrast, Nisbet and Hubbard: 'probably' (o.c. 40, on I.3); and earlier, Nisbet in *CR* XVIII (1968), 56 (reviewing W. Wili, *Horaz*). Further, Ligurinus, whom the tenth ode addresses, does not belong to the present enquiry.

namque et nobilis et decens
et pro sollicitis non tacitus reis. (1.13 f.)

Maximus will make wide conquests in amorous warfare; and he will install her worship in the Alban Hills with song and dance from boys and maidens.

Theme and language indicate a bachelor. Hence a problem that not all commentators have seen. For Maximus (*cos.* 11) several reasons demand a separate treatment.[102]

The address to Iullus Antonius opens with a splendid evocation of Pindar. Modest by contrast are the efforts of Horace. Iullus is a poet and he will celebrate in proper majesty Caesar and a triumph over the Sugambri (2.33 ff.).

The German tribe furnishes a close dating. Caesar set out for Gaul in the summer of 16. But no war ensued against the Sugambri. They had made submission to Lollius and surrendered hostages.[103] Nor did Rome witness a triumph when Augustus came back after an interval of three years. Iullus, however, had a role to play, superintending as praetor birthday festivities for the ruler: horse races, combats of wild beasts, and a banquet on the Capitol.[104]

The Triumvir had two sons by Fulvia (widow in turn of P. Clodius and of Scribonius Curio). Antullus stayed with his father in the eastern lands and, barely emergent from boyhood, was put to death after the fall of Alexandria. Iullus, born in 43, was brought up at Rome by the affectionate care of Octavia, who had given Marcus Antonius two daughters.

The two brothers illustrate the new fashion of decorative or historical nomenclature. Antullus, to be regarded as a *cognomen*, not just a diminutive, recalls Anto, a son of Hercules, the ancestor of the Antonii. That family otherwise eschewed *cognomina*, as did some other houses of the recent plebeian *nobilitas*. By equipping his younger son with 'Iullus', comparable to 'Paullus' and 'Africanus' in the Fabii, Marcus Antonius advertised posthumous loyalty to Caesar the Dictator.

In the esteem of the Princeps, Iullus stood next to the two Claudii, so it is averred.[105] An early priesthood would be appropriate.[106] Consul in 10 with Africanus Fabius Maximus, and in the due sequel proconsul of Asia, Iullus gained no abatement of the rules in his career—and no chance that the Triumvir's son would command an army.

Involvement in the politics and intrigues of the dynastic group brought Iullus Antonius to ruin in 2 BC. His youthful son was sent away to the

---

[102] Ch. XXVIII.
[103] Dio LIV.20.6.
[104] Dio LIV.26.2.
[105] Plutarch, *Antonius* 87.
[106] A priesthood is mentioned but not specified (Velleius II.100.4).

university city of Massilia. He lived until AD 25, earning from the vigilant historian a necrological notice, subjoined to the decease of old Ahenobarbus, who had married his aunt.[107]

Whatever view be held of the allegations made public when Julia was disowned and disgraced, Iullus might well appear congenial as well as opportune for the role of fourth in her sequence of husbands. Of Marcella his wife, few traces survive in the records of history. When by decision of the Princeps M. Agrippa divorced Marcella, young Iullus was providentially available to take her over and reinforce the dynastic nexus.

Iullus, husband of a niece of the Princeps, and Fabius Maximus marrying Marcia, a cousin, those are facts that students of the twin poems ought not to ignore.[108]

Horace singled out Maximus and Iullus for sharp prominence. It may be convenient for the progress of the present enquiry to register certain relatives of the 'domus Augusta' who fail the compliment of an ode. Seven consulars, an impressive company:

(1) Paullus Aemilius Lepidus (*suff*. 34). His wife Cornelia (who died in 16) was the half-sister of Julia, the daughter of the Princeps.

(2) P. Cornelius Scipio (*cos*. 16), the brother of Cornelia.

(3) Sex. Appuleius (*cos*. 29). His father had married Octavia, a half-sister of Caesar Augustus.

(4) M. Appuleius (*cos*. 20), not heard of subsequent to his consulate.

(5) L. Domitius Ahenobarbus (*cos*. 16), husband of the elder Antonia.

(6) M. Messalla Appianus (*cos*. 12), husband of the younger Marcella.

(7) P. Quinctilius Varus (*cos*. 13). Early in 12 he is on attestation as a son-in-law of Marcus Agrippa.

Curiosity arises about omissions. The list is too long to reward it. Maximus and Iullus are linked not only by their propinquity to Augustus but by poetry and letters. Ahenobarbus could not qualify on that count, likewise no doubt some of the others. Nor would all of them care to be mustered together in a kind of composite portrait.[109] The family party would be the delight—or the despair—of a panegyrist. There were more enmities than rose to the surface later, or ever percolated to posterity.

The ruler for his part viewed with complacency any praise for literary or social arts accruing to young aristocrats whom he favoured and promoted. Warfare was another matter, and glory was reserved for the stepsons, fighting under his direction and auspices.

Two poems extol the Claudii, the fourth and the fourteenth. They are

---

[107] *Ann*. IV.44.3.

[108] Conforming to the discretion of the poet, Fraenkel refrained from mentioning either the wives or the dynastic link. Similarly, no identities for Maximus, Iullus, and Censorinus in C. Becker, *Das Spätwerk des Horaz* (1963), 121 ff.

[109] Ahenobarbus is discerned in the procession on the *Ara Pacis* (Ch. XII).

neatly and emphatically placed, one preceding an encomium of Augustus, the other following. The first piece is a long and elaborate victory chant after the Pindaric fashion, the younger brother introduced at the beginning of the fifth stanza, in firm style and action:

> videre Raetis bella sub Alpibus
> Drusum gerentem Vindelici. (4.17 f.)

The poem goes on to acclaim the instruction the Nerones derive from Augustus, corroborating the increment from ancestry, 'fortes creantur fortibus et bonis' (4.29), and it brings out Rome's debt to the Nerones (4.37) with a stirring recall of the victory at the river Metaurus. In conclusion, a confident prediction: 'nil Claudiae non perficient manus' (4.74).

Drusus, it will not escape notice, engrosses the action. His brother is subsumed under 'Nerones' (twice), which adheres to both: *cognomen* in the one, *praenomen* in the other.

The subsequent and shorter piece begins with Augustus, evokes the Vindelici, and proceeds at once to Drusus,

> milite nam tuo
> Drusus Genaunos, implacidum genus,
> Breunosque velocis. (14.9 ff.)

After which the 'maior Neronum' at last has his personal entry, overwhelming the Raetians and emerging 'sine clade victor' (14.14–32). For the whole achievement, the credit goes to Caesar Augustus,

> te copias, te consilium et tuos
> praebente divos. (14.33 f.)

Indeed, it was the fifteenth anniversary of the fall of Alexandria. Which enables the poet to sum up the successes achieved east and west since then, concluding with the pacification of Gaul and Spain, and

> te caede gaudentes Sygambri
> compositis venerantur armis. (14.51 f.)

In the exposition of Horace the larger and the better portion goes to the younger Claudius. He even benefits from the decorative names of three native peoples, each novel in the literature of the Latins.

Not everything is clear about the conquest of Raetia and Vindelicia, ostensibly the work of one summer. In 17 or 16 P. Silius Nerva, then proconsul of Illyricum, carried out operations against tribes in some Alpine valleys, barely escaping oblivion.[110] The final subjugation was due to the convergent strategy of two armies, one operating from northern

---

[110] Dio LIV.20.1.

Italy, the other from the upper Rhine and the region of Lake Constance.[111]

In the first poem of Horace, Drusus leads off (and he is already north of the Alps, dealing with the Vindelici). Now Drusus may in fact have been in the field earlier than Tiberius. That is the clear statement in Cassius Dio, where Drusus wins a victory near the Tridentine Alps and earns *ornamenta* giving him the status of a praetor.[112] Repelled from Italy (so Dio goes on), the Raetians attacked Gaul, so Augustus sent Tiberius against them, and both generals now operate, using a number of columns of invasion.

In assigning priority to Drusus before Tiberius, here as elsewhere, the Greek historian was perhaps deceived by his source.[113] Drusus may not have been in a position to win victories in valleys of the Alps until the Raetian tribes who held the passes had been encircled and cut off on the northern side. The matter need not be pursued further. Enough to point to a clear fact. Caesar Augustus chose to give the younger brother the command which for reasons of history and sentiment carried the higher prestige, and offered more resonant publicity. The alert Horace concurred.

A few years earlier Horace had been duly attentive with an epistle when Claudius Nero went to the eastern lands. One of the company was a certain Julius Florus, to whom in the sequel Horace sent the long missive about literary studies. The opening line runs

Flore, bono claroque fidelis amice Neroni[114]

So far, esteem and the signs of amity. It was all too easy to run into trouble, as the poet Julius Montanus found.[115] A chill may have intervened even before the publication of Book IV.

Other features in the collection were likely to irritate a touchy aristocrat. Maximus opens the book, a favourite of Augustus. Though their characters were incompatible from the outset, with occasions for the young men to meet or clash in rivalry more than once, for example if Maximus served as a military tribune in Spain in 26 and 25, or when he was Caesar's quaestor in the eastern parts. Evidence is lacking of discord before the book was published. Not long after, Maximus was proconsul of Asia. Lavish promotion of the cult of the ruler was highly distasteful to Claudius Nero; and in the period of his eclipse Augustus chose Maximus to govern Tarraconensis.

Claudius Nero had a tenacious memory, and many of his enmities took their origin from a distant past. Marcus Lollius is palmary, the reason is patent. In 16 the stepson of the Princeps, now praetor at the age of twenty-

---

[111] On these operations see now K. Christ, *Chiron* VII (1977), 171 ff.
[112] Dio LIV.23.3.
[113] Compare the treatment Dio accorded to the campaigns from 12 to 9.
[114] *Epp.* II.2.1. The earlier poem is I.3.
[115] Seneca, *Epp.* 122.11.

five, replaced the consular as legate in Gallia Comata. Lollius had suffered
a mishap in the previous year, repaired however before the Princeps
turned up, by that act inevitably to enhance the misfortune of
Lollius—while his successor went on to earn credit in the conquest of
Raetia and Vindelicia.[116]

The services of Horace were enlisted to vindicate the reputation of a
valued and veteran adherent, praising his consulship, but not touching on
warfare. The contrary estimate of Lollius could not be published for a long
time, until his disgrace in AD 2. Velleius was happy to disclose it.[117] He also
supplies a different appreciation of the Alpine campaign. That is, Claudius
Nero in the forefront, 'adiutore operis dato fratre ipsius'.[118]

Literary verdicts of Velleius also afford entertainment. Of the Augustan
poets, first 'Vergilius Rabiriusque'.[119] The latter finds a mention in Ovid as
'magnique Rabirius oris'; and Quintilian thought him worth reading, if
you have the leisure.[120] Rabirius wrote an epic on the Battle of Actium, an
august theme which several other poets modestly proclaimed beyond
their reach.

Next, and no others, 'Tibullusque et Naso'. Ovid but not Horace, the
selection should evoke surprise.[121] It is not the habit of Velleius to show
indulgence to the rejected or calamitous. The writings of Ovid had been
banned from public libraries, by the anxious and servile custodians if not
by ordinance of Caesar Augustus.

The clue leads towards the literary tastes of his successor. An exact
student of Roman ritual and of religious proprieties, Ti. Caesar may not
have condoned a superficial and frivolous performance like the *Fasti*. But
the *Metamorphoses* carried recondite erudition about legendary history,
while the *Ars Amatoria*, bold, clever, and subversive, might prove
congenial to a sceptical intelligence, a sardonic sense of humour.

[116] The 'clades Lolliana', duly enhanced by Velleius (II.97.1), and also accepted by the incautious
Tacitus (*Ann.* I.10.2), has in the modern time been taken for an incentive to Roman conquest in
Germany. Following Julius Obsequens (71), the ostensible 'clades' should belong to 17, not to 16 (as
in Dio), cf. *JRS* XXIII (1933), 17 f.

[117] Velleius II.102.1 (below, p. 431). The time had arrived long since for a modest rehabilitation
of Lollius, refusing both Velleius and the sentimental acceptance of the Horatian ode.

[118] Velleius II.95.1.

[119] Velleius II.36.3.

[120] Ovid, *Ex. P.* IV.16.5; Quintilian X.1.90.

[121] Velleius is an infallible guide to likes and dislikes of Ti. Caesar. His omission of Horace (not
always appreciated) receives strong emphasis from R. J. Goar, *Latomus* XXXV (1976), 54.

XXVIII

Fabius Maximus

It is a rare chance that brings Horace and Ovid into the same context or company.[1] In the season of the *Amores* young Ovid composed the wedding song for Fabius Maximus,

> ille ego qui duxi vestros Hymenaeon ad ignes.[2]

The conspicuous Horatian ode (IV.1) deflects Venus towards Maximus, her votary; he will march to victory over rivals in amorous warfare, 'late signa feret militiae tuae'; and he will celebrate a festival with dance and song.

The meaning and purpose of this poem has not been apparent to all commentators, although it was pointed out long ago. It is a disguised epithalamium, announcing the marriage of Fabius Maximus.[3] Hence comparable to anticipatory or concealed obituary notices in the pages of a historian.

There is something else. Maximus was probably born in 46. His father died when consul on the last day of December, 45; and there was a younger brother, Africanus (*cos.* 10). The ode was composed *c*.16, so it is generally held. There are no grounds for putting it in 11, as a compliment to the consulship of Maximus.[4]

He is paraded as a bachelor. That is peculiar, and should not have been missed. The young *nobilis* normally takes a wife in the early twenties. Maximus is close on thirty.

A problem arises. Was Maximus in fact a widower? Or perhaps, for a dynastic match, waiting until the girl became nubile? The bride of Fabius Maximus is none other than Marcia, first cousin to Caesar Augustus. Her extraction is clear. In 58, or soon after, Marcius Philippus (*cos.* 56) took over Atia, the widow of C. Octavius. Further, his son by an earlier match chose for his wife her younger sister. This Philippus, praetor in 44, perhaps

---

[1] See also *History in Ovid* (1978), Ch. VIII. The present chapter was of set purpose composed independently.

[2] *Ex. P.* I.2.131.

[3] A. T. v. S. Bradshaw, CQ XX (1970), 142 ff. As he observes, Kiessling had broached the notion in 1876. No trace of it in the ample exposition of E. Fraenkel, *Horace* (1957), 410 ff.

[4] Thus J. Carcopino, *Rencontres de l'histoire et de la littérature romaines* (1963), 136; G. Williams, *Horace. Greece & Rome. New Surveys*, No. 6 (1972), 44.

adopting for model the prudence of his father, escaped harm or notice until his suffect consulship in 38. In 33 he held a triumph from Spain; and from the booty he repaired the temple of Hercules and the Muses.[5]

Philippus is not heard of in the sequel. Marcia, the daughter of Philippus and Atia, is either a late child or, if a little older, finding in Fabius Maximus a second husband.

The 'monimenta Philippi' gave Ovid a firm and elegant conclusion to the *Fasti* on the last day of the sixth month. He could allude briefly to Atia, the 'matertera Caesaris'; and he extolled in Marcia a generous endowment,

> par animo quoque forma suo respondet. in illa
> et genus et facies ingeniumque simul.[6]

Except for members of the central dynastic nexus, the wife of Fabius Maximus is the only living person to be named in the *Fasti*. The passage was composed, it may be conjectured, in the first half of AD 4. For reasons that can be divined, Ovid went no further.[7] He was not always alert and discreet, but the turn of events in the summer imported hesitations and perplexity. The text says nothing about the princes Gaius and Lucius; and the only references to Tiberius Caesar occur in Book I, being additions which the poet made by cursory revision in the last year of his life.

Without marriage to Marcia, and before it, the scion of the patrician Fabii was singled out for high distinction. During the ruler's sojourn in the lands east of the Adriatic (22–19), Claudius Nero was charged with a mission to Armenia. Like Quinctilius Varus, Maximus is on attestation as 'quaestor Augusti', according to a fragmentary inscription at Athens.[8] For the rest, from praetor to consul, no post is at all likely. The city of Paphos happens to pay honour to Marcia, naming her husband.[9] Not a clear sign that he was proconsul of Cyprus.[10]

Born in 46, Maximus could accede to the *fasces* in 13. That year was occupied by Claudius Nero and his brother-in-law Quinctilius Varus. In the next, Messalla Appianus, with for colleague the *novus homo* Sulpicius Quirinius, who had abnormal claims, one of them being his wife Claudia, the sister of Appianus. Early in the year Appianus died.

A suffect consulate was not good enough for a Fabius. The slight

---

[5] Suetonius, *Divus Aug.* 29.5. For the edifice, L. Richardson, *AJA* LXXXI (1977), 355 ff. By mishap he assigned it to the father of Philippus, with sundry remarks in consequence (ib. 359).

[6] *Fasti* VI.804 f. The whole passage (797–812) was quoted by L. Richardson, o.c. 356: to the obscuration of Marcia. The name of the lady and her identity are also absent from the annotation of F. R. D. Goodyear on *Ann.* I.5.2.

[7] For this thesis, *History in Ovid* 30 ff.

[8] *IG* II². 4130. The title of the office is supplemented.

[9] *ILS* 8821.

[10] No *nobilis* will be found among proconsuls of Cyprus under the first dynasty. On the rank of praetorian proconsuls see the full investigation of W. Eck, *Zephyrus* XXIII/IV (1972/3), 233 ff.

retardation was soon compensated. Maximus went out at once in 10 to govern Asia, by direct mandate of Caesar. The year can now be taken as certain.[11] He remained there for a second year, as seems likely. That was the tenure of his predecessor, as emerges from a statement in Cassius Dio, not giving any name.[12] M. Vinicius occurs suitably (*suff.* 19), a trusted friend of the Princeps previously occupied in Illyricum.[13] A shortage of ex-consuls disturbed tenure or sequence as had happened much earlier, when Sex. Appuleius (*cos.* 29) and Potitus Valerius Messalla (*suff.* 29) each had a biennium.

To illustrate the careers of other ex-consuls it may be of use to append the list, from 12 to 1 BC.[14]

12/11	?M. Vinicius (*suff.* 19)
11/10	? "
10/9	Paullus Fabius Maximus (*cos.* 11)
9/8	? "
8/7	
7/6	
6/5	C. Asinius Gallus (*cos.* 8)
5/4	
4/3	
3/2	
2/1	Cn. Cornelius Lentulus (*cos.* 14).

In the five interstices are to be inserted P. Scipio (*cos.* 16), L. Piso (15), Iullus Antonius (10), C. Marcius Censorinus (8). The proconsulate of Censorinus has generally been assigned a later date (in AD 2). Not long after the end of M. Lollius in Syria occurred the decease of Censorinus, 'in iisdem provinciis'.[15] The phrase applies as well, or better, to a consular legate of Galatia.[16]

One place thus remains for an *Ignotus*.[17] The lower term, the year of Lentulus the Augur, is fixed by an inscription. For his late tenure of Asia, an explanation offers. When his year of sortition arrived, he was not available, being occupied in one of the provinces of Caesar.[18]

[11] It was assumed by Mommsen. Cf. *PIR²* F 47; and see now U. Laffi, *Studi classici ed orientali* XVI (1967), 5 ff. An aberrant dating (5/4) was proposed by M. Grant, *FITA* (1946), 387.

[12] Dio LIV.30.3.

[13] Vinicius was honoured together with Drusus on an inscription at Mylasa, still unpublished. The attribution was declared impossible by R. Hanslik, *RE* IXA. 116. Another city now discloses him. See J. Reynolds, *Aphrodisias and Rome* (1982), no. 45.

[14] There were various defects in the lists presented by D. Magie, *Roman Rule in Asia Minor* (1950), 1580 f.; K. M. T. Atkinson, *Historia* VII (1958), 324 ff.   [15] Velleius II.102.1.

[16] As conjectured in *Akten des VI. int. Kongresses für gr. u. lat. Epigraphik* (1973), 588 = *RP* III (1984), 872. Not noted in *PIR²* M 222.

[17] Sulpicius Quirinius cannot quite be ruled out, cf. above, p. 62.

[18] i.e. the Balkan command, from 10 or 9 (Ch. XXI).

Comparison with Africa suffers from the fewer names on record. As follows:[19]

9/8   M. Licinius Crassus Frugi (14)
       P. Quinctilius Varus (13)
       L. Volusius Saturninus (*suff.* 12)
       Africanus Fabius Maximus (*cos.* 10)
       Cn. Calpurnius Piso (7)

Of these, it may be noted that Varus is allotted 7/6 (just before his appointment to Syria), and Africanus 6/5.

To the activities of Maximus in Asia there stands testimony ample and effusive: the proconsul's edict and decrees of the provincial council.[20] The long letter, in an involved style, may be credited to the proconsul's authorship. Maximus enjoined the cities to change the calendar and ordain the natal day of Caesar as the inception of the year, since it announced a blessing for all mankind.

Nor was honour lacking for Maximus himself. A festival at Ilium commemorated his name.[21] That distinction, now becoming rare for proconsuls, fell to Marcius Censorinus a few years later—and it is the last.[22] Encroaching everywhere, the ruler tends to curb the honours accorded to governors as well as their authority. No more 'viri triumphales' (subsequent to Cornelius Balbus), no more cities or monuments to bear their names.

Some slight compensation has been discovered. Coins of Hierapolis in Phrygia bear the name and the head of Paullus Fabius Maximus; and then, in other cities, P. Scipio and Asinius Gallus receive the same honour.[23] Furthermore, a group of three proconsuls in Africa.[24]

It is a question, what meaning should be assigned to the phenomenon. Permission and encouragement from Caesar Augustus has been surmised. And further, so it is claimed, these proconsuls belong to a definite category, to be styled 'amici principis'.[25]

Various reasons counsel hesitation. There is a double perplexity. The phenomenon is confined to three cities in each province. Yet at the same time sporadic. No coin, for example, with heads of Piso the Pontifex or Iullus Antonius. On the other hand (and some years later) an African city

---

[19] Ch. XXIII.

[20] U. Laffi, *Studi classici ed orientali* XVI (1967), 5 ff. A convenient version of the composite texts will be found in Ehrenberg and Jones, *Documents etc.* (ed. 2, 1955), no. 98.

[21] *IGR* IV. 244.

[22] *SEG* II.549 (Mylasa).

[23] M. Grant, *FITA* (1946), 387; J. M. C. Toynbee, *Roman Historical Portraits* (1978), 74 f.

[24] viz. Quinctilius Varus, Volusius Saturninus, Africanus Fabius Maximus (Ch. XXIII).

[25] M. Grant, o.c. 229.

honours in this fashion Passienus Rufus (*cos.* 4 BC), a remarkable *novus homo*—who cannot be brought into the same company as a Fabius or a Scipio.[26]

System and policy fall short of proof. One is thrown back on accident and personality. The innovation may be due to the pretensions of Fabius Maximus and the favour he enjoyed with Caesar Augustus—by whose hand and decision he was sent to Asia, so his letter proclaimed.

In this season, the ruler had every reason to extend indulgence to the high aristocrats.[27] When Agrippa died in 12, the stepsons acquired enhancement and they proceeded to hold great military commands, with the grant of proconsular *imperium* at the end of their second campaigns. Augustus had already devised the *ornamenta triumphalia* for the benefit of Claudius Nero. It was fitting and fortunate that Piso could earn the distinction as Caesar's legate in Thrace; and in the sequel it was not denied to proconsuls of Africa, where warfare occurred from time to time.[28]

The years between 12 and 6 marked a felicitous period in the relations between the Princeps and the *nobiles*. The death of Drusus in 9 came as a blow, and it brought his brother into ever sharper prominence. Claudius Nero was needed on the Rhine. To take his place in Illyricum, the Princeps did not employ one of the aristocrats now coming on. He turned to Sex. Appuleius (*cos.* 29), his own nephew, who had held a triumph long ago. The problems of the government became acute when the Princeps and his stepson quarrelled. Various opportunities of influence and power then arose, but none of the aristocrats achieved proconsular *imperium*.[29]

Fabius Maximus next turns up at the far end of the Roman world, in north-western Spain. The people of Bracara set up an altar to Augustus on the birthday of the legate Paullus Fabius Maximus.[30] The titulature of the ruler indicates 3 BC, or the early weeks of the next year (since it omits 'pater patriae', which the Senate conferred on February 5).

The long conquest of the North-West, conducted by two separate army commands, those of Citerior and Ulterior, was completed under the supervision of Agrippa in 20 and 19. Asturia and Callaecia, at first attached to the latter, as geography and communications dictated, were transferred after a time to Citerior (i.e. Tarraconensis). The date of the change has

---

[26] ib. 139 f. Similarly in Asia M. Plautius Silvanus (*cos.* 2 BC), proconsul in AD 4/5 (ib. 388): though not his portrait head but a standing figure.

[27] As counterpart to the monarch's designs for the princes Gaius and Lucius. That was emphasized by Mommsen, *Hermes* III (1869), 272 f. = *Ges. Schriften* IV (1906), 187 f.

[28] The last was Junius Blaesus, the uncle of Seianus (*Ann.* III.72.4).

[29] Ch. VI.

[30] *ILS* 8895. He is also attested at Lucus Augusti (*CIL* II.2581). The dedication to Agrippa Postumus at Bracara (*AE* 1974, 392) will suitably be assigned to this period—and perhaps to encouragement from Maximus.

been a matter of controversy. The reason is clear—a reduction of the Spanish garrison, leading to a fusion of the two armies. The measure may be assigned without discomfort to the period 16–13 when the Princeps again visited Spain.[31] Legions were required for the campaigns in Illyricum and Germany now in prospect.

Few names of governors are discoverable, but their quality illustrates the importance of Tarraconensis. After P. Silius Nerva (*cos.* 20), legate from 19 to 17 when he went on to govern Illyricum, the first is Crassus Frugi (*cos.* 14), probably from 13 to 9.[32] Then, after Fabius Maximus, the next is Cn. Piso (*cos.* 7), attested in 9/10.[33]

It would be worth knowing how far the tenure of Maximus extended before or after 3 BC. He may have been sent to Tarraconensis three years earlier.[34] On the other hand, people at Bracara need not have taken quite so long to perceive the governor's liking for public recognition. If the ruler made the appointment in 3 BC he might well have had in mind a fairly long mandate. In August of AD 2 Lucius Caesar died at Massilia when proceeding 'ad Hispanienses exercitus.'[35] The mission, like that of his brother, would entail proconsular *imperium*. And by the same token, care in selecting the legate of Tarraconensis, to act as 'adiutor' or 'rector' to the young prince.

Either way, absent from Rome or present, Fabius Maximus became a factor of weight during the obscure decade when Claudius Nero was in eclipse. The successive predicaments of the ageing autocrat (sixty in September of 3 BC) enhanced the ambitions of sundry *nobiles*, among them the husbands of an Antonia and a Marcia. Whatever estimate Caesar Augustus formed (and kept to himself), eager speculation in clubs and salons would fasten on the theme of 'capax imperii'. Ancestry, age, and experience spoke for Maximus, and he had all the social graces. It was desirable that a 'princeps' should be 'civilis' and 'comis'. The austere Claudius Nero was uncongenial in manner, and even in deportment.[36] The claims of warfare in the north prevailed, or the tenacity of Livia Drusilla.

Despite the various pieces or aspects of information, Fabius Maximus remains a curiously isolated figure, his loyalties concentrated on devotion to the ruler. Friends and allies among his own class are not easy to

[31] G. Alföldy, *Fasti Hispanienses* (1969), 207.

[32] For Silius Nerva, *CIL* II.3414 (Carthago Nova); Crassus was proconsul of Africa for the tenure 9/8 (*IRT* 319).

[33] Ch. XXVI.

[34] Alföldy suggested 4–1 (o.c. 9).

[35] *Ann.* I.3.3. Apart from 'Hispanias petens' in Velleius (II.102.3), the sole testimony to the mandate of L. Caesar.

[36] Suetonius, *Tib.* 21.2; 68.3. Nor was the stepson compatible in physique: Augustus being short, Tiberius large of body and very tall, 'statura quae modum excederet' (68.1).

discover—or even enemies, apart from Claudius Nero whose hostility, not stated by any author, is an inference or an assumption, yet not to be gainsaid. Search is baffled for any *novus homo* owing him promotion, for any provincial clients from Spain or Asia.

Maximus acquired fame with posterity. Juvenal looked back to him as one of the generous patrons of literature, presumably because of Horace and Ovid.[37] Other signs would be welcome. In any age the services that the rich and noble render to arts and letters tend, like their talents, to be overestimated.[38]

Horace acclaimed the 'centum puer artium'. The other side of that versatility is disclosed by the famous verdict of Cassius Severus: 'quasi disertus es, quasi formosus es, quasi dives es; unum tantum es non quasi, vappa'.[39]

Whether the aptitudes of Maximus embraced philosophy, religion or astrology, there is no means of knowing. It is only perverse or frivolous erudition that tries to make him out a Pythagorean.[40] The writing of verse was a normal pastime in high society. Ovid, who was favoured with readings of his 'scripta,' nowhere specifies poetry. So far therefore an estimate of his attainments and character is not easily reached. Ovid, in allusion to the fabled descent of the Fabii, extols a frank and open nature,

> conveniens animo genus est tibi, nobile namque
> pectus et Herculeae simplicitatis habes.[41] (*Ex. P.* III. 3. 99 f.)

When 'simplicitas' is attached to Roman aristocrats, curiosity becomes legitimate.[42]

There remains the primary claim. Eloquence is celebrated by Horace and Ovid; and both use the conventional formula of ready succour to anxious clients.[48] The record happens nowhere to show him an advocate for the defence.

Maximus makes, it is true, an early appearance in the schools. Annaeus Seneca produces a short specimen of his oratory—and indeed condemns him for introducing a 'novicius morbus'.[44] The same passage reveals an unexpected fact: he once prosecuted Cassius Severus.

Cassius was a formidable adversary to take on. Seneca furnishes a full and

---

[37] Juvenal VII. 95.

[38] In the verdict of J.-F. Revel, 'ce sont eux les parasites des écrivains et des peintres et non l'inverse' (in the volume *Proust* (ed. Denoël, 1970), 95).

[39] Seneca, *Controv.* II.4.11.

[40] Thus J. Carcopino, *Rencontres etc.* (1963), 143 ff. He also adduced 'Hyginus', *De astronomia*, dedicated to a M. Fabius—arguing that the person was Fabius Maximus.

[41] *Ex. P.* III.3.99 f.

[42] below, p. 425.

[43] *Odes* IV.1.14 ('solliciti'); *Ex. P.* I.2.116 ('trepidi').

[44] *Controv.* II.4.12, cf. 11.

lively appreciation, equipped with some of that orator's own verdicts.[45] Cassius, in the phrase of Junius Gallio, at once dominated any audience. He owed more to native genius than to study; his oratory was rapid, vigorous and spirited, disdaining leisurely and lengthy exposition, and concentrated: more meaning than words. In consonance therewith, Cassius could seldom be persuaded to declaim.

Cassius was aggressive, never speaking for the defence, save to defend himself. His 'acerbitas' tends to be blamed when 'urbanitas' is praised. Thus the judicious Quintilian, who twice names Cassius in rank with Messalla and Pollio as the select and outstanding orators of the Augustan age.[46]

A speaker in the *Dialogus* of Tacitus accords a handsome testimonial. Cassius set himself against the classic models, he saw what the times demanded.[47] The speaker is Marcus Aper, the champion of the moderns. The other side is represented by Vipstanus Messalla, arguing for a more sober manner and concluding with 'non pugnat sed rixatur'.[48] This Messalla was a descendant of Corvinus, in the maternal line.

Cassius Severus was not merely a figure of note and controversy in the annals of Roman eloquence. He concerns political and social history during the last decade of the reign. To exacerbate the crisis of the northern wars supervened plague and famine at Rome, discord and scandal in the dynasty. Discontent arose, various and pervasive. One sign that persisted was the circulation of hostile pamphlets.[49] According to Suetonius in a general statement, Augustus always showed remarkable tolerance.[50] Like other writers in his own time or since, the biographer had not paid enough attention to this period.

Over-anxious or impelled by some of its secret advisers, the government went in for repressive measures. They prosecuted Labienus, a vigorous speaker who combined the virtues of the old style and the new.[51] Labienus also wrote history. His 'libertas', it is said, spared no person or class. A piece of declamation is preserved, which arraigns the rich, savagely—and with justice.[52]

A decree of the Senate consigned all the writings of Labienus to public conflagration. No matter, said Cassius Severus, for he had them all by heart.[53] Cassius in his turn came to grief. He had defamed persons of high

---

[45] *Controv.* III, *praef.* 1–7.
[46] Quintilian X.1.116; XII.10.11.
[47] *Dial.* 19.1 ff.
[48] *Dial.* 26.4.
[49] Dio LV.27.2 f. (in 6); LVI.27.1 (in 12). Punishment for their authors is mentioned only on the second occasion.
[50] *Divus Aug.* 55.
[51] Seneca, *Controv.* X, *praef.* 4 ff.
[52] *Controv.* X.4.17 f.
[53] *Controv.* X, *praef.* 8.

estate, women as well as men, and he was despatched to exile in Crete.[54]

The occasion is noteworthy. It was recalled by Tacitus in the annalistic record of the year 15. The praetor Pompeius Macer put a question to the new ruler about the law of *maiestas*.

The alert historian added pertinent annotation. Until then, he says, comment was free, only acts could be indicted. But Augustus made the change: 'primus Augustus cognitionem de famosis libellis specie legis eius tractavit'.[55] Tacitus did not need to add that the ruler, under pretext of protecting high society, protected his own person and the dynasty; and before long any criticism of 'pax et princeps' would be interpreted as an offence against the state.

To the condemnation of Cassius Severus, Seneca happens to furnish only a brief and vague allusion.[56] Students of eloquence might well wish to learn the identity of the prosecutor. Hardly one of the consular magnates, for that would be thought unseemly. Rather perhaps some careerist, who had taken Cassius as a model—and Cassius in his actions or writings had not confined his invective to the aristocracy.[57]

Himself of lowly extraction, Cassius is one of the few known speakers or writers who disparaged birth and wealth. The author of the *Dialogus* offered a temperate judgement, for and against. In the *Annales* he is hostile. In the first reference, 'libido' and 'procacia scripta'; in the second, 'sordidae originis, maleficae vitae, sed orandi validus'. The author, it is a valid conjecture, was moved by what he discovered about the baneful eloquence of the prosecutors in the days of Tiberius Caesar.

More important for history, the year when the great orator was brought to ruin. In the year 12, according to Cassius Dio: Augustus ordained that libellous pamphlets should be burned, and he punished some of the authors.[58] That is the standard date, generally found acceptable.[59]

It might not be correct. Jerome in the Chronicle under the year 32 reports the decease of Cassius Severus in the twenty-fifth year of his exile.[60] The source of Jerome is unimpeachable, namely Suetonius; but the compiler was hasty, and scribes are prone to error in numbers—as is elsewhere all too apparent, and also verifiable.

None the less, the year 8 against 12 is attractive.[61] It can be supported, though not as conveying proof, by two arguments of a diverse order.

---

[54] *Ann.* I.72.3; IV.21.3.

[55] *Ann.* I.72.3.

[56] *Controv.* X. *praef.* 7.

[57] Suetonius, *Vit.* 2.1 (allegations about the parentage of the procurator P. Vitellius).

[58] Dio LVI.27.1.

[59] *PIR*[2] C 522.

[60] Jerome, *Chron.* p. 176 H.

[61] cf. *History in Ovid* (1978), 213 f. Firm arguments were adduced by R. A. Baumann, *Impietas in Principem* (1974), 28 ff.

First, the large gap, four *folia* in the manuscript of Cassius Dio. The defeat of the Pannonian insurgents at the river Bathinus is lost. Perhaps other items, such as the decease and public funeral of Messalla Corvinus or the creation of the new post of *praefectus annonae* (the recent famine is relevant). However, given other inadequacies or omissions in that writer, caution is prescribed.

Second, the political season. Nasty and disturbed in all ways in 8, the atmosphere had abated to a certain tranquillity four years later, as was advertised by the Pannonian triumph of Ti. Caesar (in October of 12)—and as is assumed in poems of Ovid, when for that reason he regains confidence. Nothing forbids, and everything encourages, the year 8, as eminently suitable for the condemnation of deleterious characters such as Labienus and Cassius.

In the autumn of that year came the catastrophe of Paullus and Julia.[62] Convicted of adultery, the princess was sent away to a barren island. The charge brought against her husband was conspiracy. According to a Juvenalian *scholium* he was put to death for high treason.

That item is dispelled, once Julia's husband is seen to be identical with the *arvalis* 'L. [Aemilius] Paullus', who was replaced in the fraternity in May of the year 14.[63] He was kept in custody, it follows, not executed. An example of the 'clementia Caesaris', so some might opine. On a sober estimate, the Princeps had learned something from the excesses he committed nine years previously.

By good fortune, Julia's partner in adultery happens to be named, the young aristocrat D. Silanus. Caesar revoking 'amicitia', he went into exile, on a distant 'peregrinatio'. The Princeps followed sound counsel. Whereas the scandal itself could not be suppressed, a public indictment and zealous prosecutors would lead to damaging exposures of more than one type.

Another offender in that season benefited (if that is the word) from the absence of prosecution. In the apologia addressed to Caesar Augustus, and designed for publicity, Ovid came out with a firm clear statement:

> nec mea decreto damnasti facta senatus
> nec mea selecto iudice iussa fuga est.[64]

Not the Senate therefore, or any court of law. According to the edict of banishment, Ovid was 'relegatus, non exul'. None the less, the autocrat consigned the poet to a specified exile on the far edge of the Roman dominions.

Ovid's dereliction was double: 'duo crimina, carmen et error'. The first, the *Ars Amatoria*, may be summarily dismissed: erotic verses could not

---

[62] See Ch. IX—where an argument for disjoining the two banishments is registered.
[63] *CIL* VI.2023 = *ILS* 5026.   [64] *Tr.* II.131 f.

form the basis of a legal indictment. About the second, Ovid was constrained to discretion. It was known to the public, it touched and wounded the ruler; Ovid had been foolish, not criminal; he had been a witness to some misdemeanour or other.

That is, not indictable on the second charge either. The position becomes clear. Each charge, invalid by itself, was intended to reinforce the other; and further, by bringing in the *Ars Amatoria*, the rancorous autocrat tried to convey and corroborate the impression that the recent scandal was moral in its nature, not political.[65]

The calculation was rational and crafty. It failed. Ovid had to concede and confess the not to be named mistake. If the autocrat had been content with that charge, no problem: the poet could not answer back. But Caesar Augustus insisted on adding the *Ars*. His error gave his victim something to write about, a reason for living, and warfare to be waged.

The epistles in the *Tristia* eschew the names of his friends, from discretion or fear, and not to embarrass them, so Ovid proclaims more than once. In the course of the year 12 he became more confident, and with easy rapid production he polished off three books of *Epistulae ex Ponto* before the end of the next year. His friend and perhaps his publisher, a certain Brutus, is honoured with the first poem in the collection, and with the last. The second, a long piece, goes to the address of Fabius Maximus. It was composed during the winter of 12/13.[66]

Praising Fabius' skill as an advocate, Ovid urges him to apply all his eloquence to intercede with Caesar in defence of a weak case. Towards the end the plea becomes urgent and personal: the epithalamium composed for Fabius' wedding. Moreover, there is Ovid's own wife. She had been a dependant and friend of Marcia, as previously of Marcia's mother. A duty is thus incumbent: 'coniunx mea sarcina vestra est'.[67]

The tie with Marcia is also exploited in the first poem of Book III, where Ovid incites his wife to make approach to Livia. Soon after comes the second and last appeal to Fabius (III.3.), an elegant and artful piece of work. The season is described as propitious, with universal rejoicing after the triumph of Tiberius.

Ovid here brings in Livia again:

> dum domus et nati, dum mater Livia gaudet
> dum gaudes, patriae magne ducisque pater.[68]

The three poems stand in close linkage, and may have been written about the same time.

[65] This thesis is argued in *History in Ovid*, Ch. XII.
[66] *Ex. P.* I.2.26: 'quarta fatigat hiems'.
[67] I.2.145.
[68] III.3.87 f.

To bring in Livia can never have been to the liking of her husband or her son; and Fabius may well have disapproved the obtrusion of Marcia.[69] Ovid's first channel of approach lay through the sons of Messalla Corvinus, the second through Fabius Maximus. Both were now seen unprofitable, and those aristocrats receive no letters of intercession in the next book.

It was high time for Ovid to recall the admonition he once enounced to an unnamed friend: shun the 'nomina magna'.[70] None the less, he persisted, and before the end of the year 13 he turned to a patron not disclosed by any word or hint hitherto. Book IV of *Ex Ponto*, with sixteen epistles ranging in date from 13 to 16 is dedicated to Sex. Pompeius, consul in 14 with Sex. Appuleius; and he receives no fewer than four of them.[71]

Pompeius had large estates in Campania, in Sicily, and in Macedonia;[72] and, as now emerges, he had helped Ovid with funds and had enabled him to cross Thrace in safety on the way to Tomis.[73] The late recognition comes as a surprise.

Sex. Pompeius presents an entertaining item in genealogy. His grandfather, the homonymous consul of 35 BC, in fact a first cousin to Magnus, was an aged nonentity selected by the Triumvirs to adorn the *Fasti*.[74] The consul of 14 was, like his colleague, related to Caesar Augustus, so a sporadic notice attests.[75] Through which family can be only guesswork. Perhaps the Marcii.[76] Or better, the Appuleii. His father, who left no record, might have married an Appuleia.[77]

Ovid's poems indicate loyalty to the dynasty, not any relationship. But they afford a useful clue. Ovid puts emphasis on Pompeius' devotion to Germanicus. He was now approaching other friends of the prince. Those operations would hardly commend him to Ti. Caesar.

To return to Fabius Maximus, who died in the summer of 14. He receives a valedictory in a letter to Brutus later in the year. Maximus, so the reader learns with some surprise, and may well hesitate to believe, was going to intercede with Augustus when death supervened:

[69] In the poems of exile Livia is introduced by name six times (none of them, by the way, registered in the six pages of *PIR*[2] L 301). Horace was more discreet—and he never names the wife of a senator.
[70] *Tr.* III.4.4.
[71] On Pompeius, *History in Ovid*, Ch. IX.
[72] *Ex. P.* IV.15 ff. Compare the estates of his son, Seneca, *De tranq.* 11.10.
[73] *Ex. P.* IV.5.34.
[74] above, p. 30, where another derivation is cursorily noted.
[75] Dio LVI.29.5.
[76] That the consul's father married a Marcia was conjectured by R. Hanslik, *Re* XXI. 2265. That scholar was operating with 'Sex. Pompeius Cn. f.', consul suffect in 5 BC—who never existed.
[77] Hence acquiring a link with Quinctilius Varus (Ch. XXIII).

certus eras pro me, Fabiae laus, Maxime, gentis,
    numen ad Augustum supplice voce loqui.
occidis ante preces, causamque ego, Maxime, mortis
    (nec fuero tanti) me reor esse tuae.[78]

Ovid insists on blaming himself for the death of Fabius Maximus. So did the widow, in the climax of the story reported by Tacitus: the lamentation of Marcia at the funeral, 'semet incusantis quod causa exitii marito fuisset.'[79] With Maximus as sole companion, Augustus paid a visit to Agrippa Postumus, the exile on the island Planasia, and a reconciliation ensued. Maximus told his wife, she passed it on to Livia, and Augustus learned that confidence had been betrayed; and Fabius died not long after, perhaps by his own hand.

Introduced as a 'rumor' by Tacitus, the journey to Planasia has found believers here and there.[80] Indeed, a meeting of the Arval Brethren on May 14 of the year 14 is adduced for corroboration.[81] Drusus Caesar being then co-opted into the place of L. Aemilius Paullus, both Augustus and Fabius Maximus gave their votes by letter.[82] However, age and health are a safer explanation than Planasia; and five other *arvales* were absent on this occasion.

The fable may be cursorily dismissed. It has its uses, which are adventitious.[83]

First the methods of Tacitus. He overloads the innuendo, and the insertion can be condemned as inartistic since it brings into a condensed narration two personal names not mentioned already, or to recur.

Second, source criticism. The item occurs in three other sources.[84] Hence speculation, not all of it fruitful.[85] A fourth version exists, but tends to be ignored.[86]

Third, the nature of 'rumores'. Almost anything could be believed. Compare, in comment on the death of Drusus Caesar, 'quamvis fabulosa et immania'.[87]

---

[78] *Ex. P.* IV.6.9 ff.   [79] *Ann.* I.5.2.

[80] V. Gardthausen, *RE* X. 185; B. Levick, *Tiberius the Politician* (1976), 64 f.; R. A. Birch, *CQ* XXXI (1981), 456. Also, apparently, J. Carcopino, *Rencontres etc.* (1963), 122.

[81] J. Scheid, *Les Frères Arvales* (1975), 87 f.   [82] *CIL* VI.2023 = *ILS* 5026.

[83] For a fuller treatment, *History in Ovid* (1978), 149 f.

[84] Each inadequate in different ways. Thus Pliny, curt and allusive, has 'suspicio in Fabium arcanorumque proditionem', but no reference to a journey to the island (*NH* VII.150). Dio mentions it—but no names (LVI.30.1). In the verbose account of Plutarch, 'Fulvius' lets out the secret of Augustus' intentions concerning Postumus; he and his wife commit suicide together (*De garrulitate* 11, p. 508.).

[85] Thus, in comment on the Tacitean passage, F. R. D. Goodyear: 'this strange story appears to be a fairly late fabrication, based upon an earlier and more simple story, preserved in Plin. NH. 7.150 and Plut. De Garr. 11'.

[86] viz. in the *Epitome* of Pseudo-Victor, 27.1. Omitted by *PIR*[2] J 214, and by the latest commentators on Tacitus. In this brief statement Livia ascertains that Agrippa is being brought back, 'quem odio novercali in insulam relegaverat'.   [87] *Ann.* IV.11.2.

Time and ignorance might enhance. None the less, the notion of a single original source is often delusive. As concerns Fabius Maximus and the journey to Planasia, the 'prudentes' who held discourse at the funeral of Caesar Augustus might have known a full version, with corroborative detail.[88]

The fable acquires value, since it shows him influential with the ruler until the last days. Otherwise scholars are thrown back on inferences from the marriage to Marcia or the proconsulate in Asia. Obscurity envelops the counsellors of Augustus in the last decade of the reign, Ti. Caesar being detained by the northern wars for most of the time from 4 to 12. Sallustius Crispus is attested, who transmitted to a tribune of the Guard the mandate to have Agrippa Postumus executed. That is, known from Tacitus, but absent from Suetonius and Dio.

After long years of matrimony, Maximus left a late-born son: Persicus, consul in 34. In June of 15 the *Arvales* co-opted him into the place left vacant by his father's decease.[89] Taken with the year of his consulship, that date permits the inference that Persicus joined the fraternity on assuming the 'toga virilis', in the vicinity of his fifteenth birthday, hence born in 2 or 1 BC.

The novel *cognomen* reflects descent from Aemilius Paullus, who overcame Perseus, the last monarch of the Macedonians, such is the natural assumption. If he was born in 2 BC, it would be relevant to the defeat of the Persian fleet in the elaborate 'naumachia' staged to celebrate the inauguration of Mars Ultor and the Forum Augusti.

An entrance so early to the *Arvales* lacked precedent so far, but it concords with the privileges pertaining to high birth. Nor would the Princeps be able to refuse further honours to the son of a rival or an enemy. Persicus was duly invested with two priesthoods.[90] An inscription shows him proconsul in Asia. His edict directed to the Ephesians, lengthy and verbose, dealt with sundry derelictions in the cult of Artemis.[91]

Despite social eminence, Persicus missed a distinction devised by Claudius Caesar in the early years of his reign, namely the sequence of second consulates from 43 to 46. It is a notable company: L. Vitellius, a *novus homo*, had been Persicus' colleague in 34; and Asiaticus (*suff*. 35), was extraneous by origin, a Narbonensian from Vienna of the Allobroges.

When Claudius Caesar, holding the censorship with L. Vitellius in 48, announced to the Senate his decision to bring in notables from the Gallic peoples conquered by Julius Caesar, his oration, which did not eschew

---

[88] That is to say, contemporary gossip and scandal, transmitted by the annalistic sources of Pliny and Dio.

[89] *AE* 1947, 52.   [90] *ILS* 951 (Ephesus).

[91] *SEG* IV.516A. For text and discussion, F. K. Dörner, *Der Erlass des Statthalters von Asia Paullus Fabius Persicus* (Diss. Greifswald, 1935).

perverse or frivolous lines of argument, invoked 'Persicum, nobilissimum virum, amicum meum'. Gallic senators, the Emperor suggested, were no more to be deprecated than the name 'Allobrogicus' in the portrait gallery of his ancestors.[92]

The allusion is to the consul of 121. Succeeding Domitius Ahenobarbus, he completed the subjugation of Gallia Transalpina, the region later styled 'provincia nostra' or 'Narbonensis', in contrast to Tres Galliae.[93]

The malice of Claudius Caesar furnishes the latest mention of Paullus Fabius Persicus. He died not long after. No obituary notice from Cornelius Tacitus. The author was pressing forward to the end of the reign (six years compressed into Book XII of the *Annales*), and something or enough had been said about Persicus in the lost books, for entertainment or for derision.

Testimony to the Augustan aristocracy tends to be either benevolent or absent. Later writers may bring up useful details of detriment (as Suetonius on the ancestors of Nero), and the descendants became variously vulnerable.

The son of Annaeus Seneca, a close coeval of Fabius Persicus, supplies instructive comments.[94] Birth, he says prevails over merit in the career of honours. And not without reason. It is a proper tribute to the 'magnae virtutes' of ancestors. Hence the name and fame of Pompeius, commending Cinna Magnus, also Sextus Pompeius and other Pompeii; and hence Fabius Persicus, exalted by 'Verrucosi et Allobrogici et illi trecenti'.

Persicus was a man of vile habits, 'cuius osculum etiam impudici devitabant'. He was also shunned by the virtuous and exemplary Julius Graecinus, the parent of Julius Agricola, unresponsive to the Narbonensian *clientela* of the Fabii.[95]

The Fabii produce no other consul thereafter. Of Africanus (*cos.* 10 BC). the brother of Paullus, no wife or descendant is attested, and no sign of honours or activity save a priesthood and the proconsulate in Africa.

An inscription at Samos reveals a sister, Fabia Paullina.[96] She was the wife of M. Titius, proconsul of Asia *c*.34, and in 32 an admiral in the Antonian fleet.[97] The identity of his wife casts some light on the allegiance of the Fabii in the period of the Triumvirs; and it may, or may not, have some relevance to Titius' tenure of Syria at a late date, about the year 10. As was stated, it is not easy to discover political allies of Paullus Fabius Maximus.

Fabia Numantina also deserves an entry, married for a time to Sex.

---

[92] *ILS* 212.
[93] To obscure and traverse that contrast was the artful design of Claudius Caesar.
[94] Seneca, *De ben.* IV.30.
[95] *De ben.* II.21.5.
[96] *SEG* I. 383.
[97] *ILS* 891 (Miletus).

Appuleius (*cos.* AD 14). If she is the daughter of Maximus and not of Africanus, the match united two descendants of Augustus' parent C. Octavius, since Appuleius was a great-grandson of Ancharia, his first wife. Numantina set up the gravestone of her young son, styling him the last of the Appuleii.[98]

Numantina had at least one other husband, namely M. Plautius Silvanus (son of the consul of 2 BC), praetor in AD 24. Described as his former wife, she invoked sorcery against him, so it was alleged.[99] On the standard assumption, Numantina married Appuleius after divorce from Silvanus.[100]

Her husbands perhaps stand in the reverse order. There is no trace of Appuleius subsequent to his consulship.[101] Young Silvanus might have married his widow, an heiress, but not to keep her for long.

Three other descendants of the brothers Paullus and Africanus can be detected on inscriptions.

(1) Q. Fabius Allobrogicinus Maximus.[102]

(2) (Fabia) Eburna.[103] The *cognomen* is unique since the consul of 116.

(3) Fabius Numantinus, one of eight young men admitted to a sacerdotal college in the years from 59 to 64.[104] Five are patrician. Therefore a group of *Salii*, so it seemed plausible.[105] Two of the other names, however, induce perplexity. Therefore perhaps some other fraternity, such as *sodales Titii*.[106] Only one of the eight survived to reach a consulship. To the political hazards of the late Neronian years was added a great pestilence in 65.

The fancy *cognomina* of decayed Fabii appealed to Juvenal. His satire on pedigree, after the names of Corvinus and Galba, comes at once to Numantini. Then follows

> cur Allobrogicis ut magna gaudeat ara
> natus in Herculeo Fabius lare?[107]

The erudite poet duly slips in an allusion to their legendary descent, perhaps familiar to some of his readers.

Selection and invention of nomenclature is an engaging topic in fictions of any type. It crops up in an earlier poem with

> Persicus orborum lautissimus et merito iam
> suspectus tamquam ipse suas incenderit aedes.[108]

---

[98] *ILS* 935 (Luna).   [99] *Ann.* IV.22.3.   [100] *PIR*[2] A 962; F 78.

[101] above, p. 317, n. 36 (on the identity of 'Sex.[', an *arvalis* in 21).

[102] *CIL* VI.1407.

[103] Deduced from *CIL* VI.7701; 33842, cf. *PIR*[2] F 75.

[104] *CIL* VI.2002.

[105] *PIR*[2] F 49, despite Groag's initial hesitations in *RE* VI. 1831.

[106] As suggested in *Historia* XVII (1968), 80 f. = *RP* (1979), 667 f.

[107] Juvenal VIII.14 f.   [108] III.221 f.

Whether or not a wealthy Fabius ever set fire to his own house, contributing thus to the tale of scandal or eccentricity in the aristocracy, is not a question that demands an answer. Fantasy is safer.

Another ornamental name introduced the episode, the consternation provoked by the catastrophe of the edifice: 'si magna Asturici cecidit domus'.[109] The *cognomen* is appropriate to a descendant of Caesar's legate governing Tarraconensis, who in fact was active in Asturia–Callaecia. That is, if he existed.[110] Either way, the pertinent erudition of the satirist deserves acclaim.

So far *cognomina*. Already by their exorbitant *praenomina* Maximus and his brother advertised derivation from Aemilii and Scipiones. Fraudulent for Scipiones, the device was enhanced by 'Numantinus'. For all their prowess in the ancient wars, the Fabii then had no triumphal names of their own.

This family was peculiar in all manner of ways. Possessing solid claims to a princely predominance in the early epoch of the Republic, the Fabii did not bother to obtrude their name on the foundation legends.[111] In a later age they came out with three *principes senatus* in successive generations.[112]

The main line encountered hazards of perpetuation, several times.[113] The parent of Verrucosus, the famous 'Cunctator' (consul five times), is only a name. Then, in the years between the second and third wars against the Carthaginians, the Fabii verged towards extinction. Two other patrician houses came to the rescue, the Aemilii and the Servilii, furnishing sons, namely Q. Fabius Aemilianus (*cos.* 145) and Q. Fabius Servilianus (142).

Patricians have a strong tendency to intermarry. The Fabii, through pride and wilful rivalry, held aloof from alliances with Claudii and Valerii, so it appears, who like them belonged to the 'gentes maiores'. In similar fashion, reciprocal ties of marriage or adoption between Claudii and Valerii are not attested before Messalla Appianus. Allowance will be made for vagaries in the evidence. That concerns another phenomenon: few womenfolk of the Fabii in publicity, or even on record. In fact, after a sister of the Cunctator only a Fabia who was a virgin of Vesta, and that elderly Fabia who married P. Dolabella.[114]

The Fabii are absent from the war against confederate Italy and from the ensuing civil dissensions. Allobrogicus (*cos.* 121), the son of Aemilianus, had a son who turned out a notorious wastrel.[115] The next

---

[109] III.212.
[110] Groag was once disposed to recognize an authentic Fabius, bearing the two *cognomina* (*RE* VIA. 1835). In *PIR*² A 1268 stands 'fortasse'.　　　　[111] Münzer, *RE* VIA. 1742.
[112] Pliny, *NH* VII.133.　　　　　　　　[113] For their stemma, *RE* VIA. 1777 f.
[114] *RE* VIA. 1885 f. The Vestal was a half-sister of Cicero's Terentia.
[115] Cicero, *Tusc.* I.81; Val. Max. III.5.2.

generation did not find it easy to recapture their 'dignitas'. In the year 63 the *patronus* of the Allobroges comes into view, the enigmatic Q. Fabius Sanga.[116]

No word yet of Q. Fabius Maximus. In 57 he was curule aedile with Metellus Scipio. He then embarked on competition of ancestral fame, rebuilding the Fornix Fabianus, the monument of his grandfather Allobrogicus.[117] Whence the funds, that might be a question.[118] His action earned conspicuous and eloquent testimony.[119] It failed to further his prospects for a consulship.

If Maximus was setting his hopes on the proconsul of Gaul, enemies of Caesar may explain the retardation.[120] Moreover, Caesar in his predilection for patricians had other candidates: Ser. Sulpicius (at last) for 51, L. Aemilius Paullus for 50.[121] In the end, Maximus commanded in Spain an army for the Dictator, with a consulship in October of 45 and a triumph. After his decease on the penultimate day of December, silence envelopes the Fabii until the elder son emerges as quaestor to Caesar Augustus, a decade subsequent to the Battle of Actium.

Allies of the dynasty or rivals, certain houses of the patriciate, renascent after the civil wars, came to ruin in the 'cruenta pax' of the Caesars. Despite kinship through Marcia, the Fabii managed to avoid perilous entanglements, exempt from the fears of a ruler or the ambition of prosecutors. None the less, like the Valerii, they too went downhill. It was paradox and accident that a patrician, Ser. Sulpicius Galba, close coeval to Fabius Persicus, should overthrow the last emperor of the Julii and Claudii.

[116] Sallust, *Cat.*41.4.

[117] *ILS* 43. Scipio Aemilianus had a place, and Aemilius Paullus was credited with three triumphs. For competition in this season, Münzer, *Hermes* XL (1905), 94 ff.

[118] Perhaps a rich marriage.

[119] Cicero, *In Vatinium* 28: 'illis viris clarissimis, Paullis, Maximis, Africanis, quorum gloriam huius virtute renovatam non mode speramus verum etiam iam videmus.' This is the first contemporary reference to Maximus—as a friend of Vatinius.

[120] Thus Münzer, *RE* VIA. 1791.

[121] Although Paullus was not won until after his election (above, p. 106).

XXIX

Nobiles in Velleius

Warfare and despotism furnish a variety of incentives. Change accelerates in society and government, money moves about, and polite letters may derive benefit, even the writing of history—at least for a time, until subservience intervenes.

The Romans reckoned twenty years of trouble that began with Caesar's invasion of Italy and ended when Caesar's heir celebrated his triumph in August of 29. Such is the standard conception, in clear and early formulation.[1] For the study of literature, advantage can be got if the definition is modified and abridged, to yield fifteen years from the establishment of the Triumvirate down to the return of 'normal government' in 28: a period that men may find either short or long, in the estimate of different ages.[2]

Rome at last acquired a historian worthy to hold rank as a classic and stand beside the achievement of the Greeks. Sallust wrote his first essay in the year when the Republic went down at Philippi; and after a second monograph he went on to narrate the history of his own times. Sallust conforms to a familiar type: the senator in retirement composing an aggressive apologia.

Other kinds of writing were practised, in rich abundance. Banished from Senate and Forum, oratory took refuge in the schools of rhetoric; and the escape from the dreadful present, along with the seductions of the remote and the exotic, had recourse to antiquarian studies and the ancient annals. The epoch of the Kings had come back, and monarchy seemed destined to prevail.

The coinciding phenomena found expression in the ambitious project conceived by an alert and eloquent man from Patavium in Transpadane Italy. As Livy in his Preface affirmed, intense devotion to primeval Rome, to 'prisca illa', brings welcome relief from 'the tribulations which our age has for so many years endured'. The reader, he knew, was avid for that theme, 'haec nova'.[3]

Recent history carried hazard, the ashes still warm from eruptions. Yet it could be managed. When Livy reached the concluding epoch of the

---

[1] Livy, *Per.* CXXXIII: 'altero et vicesimo anno'.
[2] Tacitus, *Agr.* 3.2: 'grande mortalis aevi spatium'.
[3] Livy, *Praef.* 4 f.

Republic, a number of the dangers had abated long since, the current of opinion veering from Caesarian to Pompeian, as suited the sentiments of the better sort at Rome and in the towns of Italy no less than the convenience of the ruler. Cato became a kind of lay saint, and it was even possible to write about Cassius and Brutus, in due discretion, especially if one were not a senator.[4] The roll-call of the illustrious dead at Philippi, 'cum fracta Virtus', made an effective climax to Book CXXIV, winning approbation not from their descendants only.[5]

That book may also have ended a defined section in the vast work. The next nine were perhaps more easy. The version of the victor could be endorsed, with no indulgence shown towards the other Triumvirs, M. Lepidus and Marcus Antonius. Roman annals through the centuries rose to a culmination with the War of Actium. By that token, the author's original design was to terminate with the triple triumph in 29. That is, with Book CXXXIII.

The task was achieved, renown enough accrued, and Livy might have reposed on his laurels. But a historian has to go on. Such was the candid avowal made in one of the lost books.[6] There is no sign that Livy ever contemplated ending at any point earlier than 30 or 29.

On that showing, the last nine books are an epilogue, recounting the Republic of Caesar Augustus from 28 to 9 inclusive.[7] It broke new ground, entailed much hard work—and called for delicate treatment. How the thing was done is an engaging problem. One aspect need not baffle. Like other men of the time, Livy was able to combine without discomfort loyal enthusiasm for the new order with conservative and Republican sentiments, even if he came to conceive perplexity and some misgivings. At the lowest, his portrayal of the Roman aristocracy would be more acceptable than that of Sallust or Pollio.

The epilogue terminated with the year 9. Fortuitous, in the confident assertion of some literary scholars. Hence in handbooks the conventional phrase of the historian's decease, aged but untiring, pen in hand.

Brief reflection demolishes the facile assumption. Livy devoted a whole book to each of the four years 12–9. The campaigns in Illyricum and in Germany, conducted by the stepsons of the Princeps, must have engrossed a large part of the narration. The matter conveyed majesty and power. It recalled the conquering Republic and it corroborated the 'virtus' of the young Claudii, as already declared by Horace in two odes.

The end was tragic, Claudius Drusus perishing on the campaign that

---

[4] *Ann.* IV.34 (the oration of Cremutius Cordus, senator and historian).

[5] cf. the *Periocha* of that book. Names can be supplied from Velleius II.71.2 f.

[6] Quoted by Pliny, *NH, praef.* 16: 'satis iam sibi gloriae quaesitum, et potuisse se desidere, ni animus inquies pasceretur opere.'

[7] viz. CXXXIV–CXLII. For that conception, for the structure of the work, and for Livy's treatment of the concluding twenty years, see *HSCP* LXIV (1959), 27 ff. = *RP* (1979), 400 ff.

took the Roman arms as far as the river Elbe. But his brother's 'pietas' was a helpful motive, who went in speed to the Rhine and traversed two hundred miles of Germany in twenty-four hours.[8]

How a Roman historian expounded the exalted theme of pride and melancholy will not defy conjecture. Let Tiberius Caesar bear witness, in the edict that discouraged any excess of public grief after the funeral of Germanicus, the son of Drusus. In the past, so he declared, the Roman People had borne with fortitude the defeat of armies, generals killed, and the utter extinction of noble families: 'principes mortales, rem publicam aeternam esse'.[9]

That argument suffices. No need to insist on the obvious. Livy had to stop where he did. He cannot have intended to go on and describe the split in the government that supervened not long after and the angry secession of Claudius Nero. There is a further and positive consequence. When nine years later Claudius Nero became Ti. Caesar, the epilogue offered a safe and attractive matter.

Of the Roman annalists who recounted the reign of Caesar Augustus, none has survived; and Livy's nine books do not appear to have had much influence. For the epoch preceding, traces are perceptible in a number of later writers, including Velleius. His opuscule was dedicated to Marcus Vinicius, who assumed the *fasces* in 30. Since Velleius was born about 23 BC, it will be a manifest convenience to reckon him 'Augustan', in the dearth of contemporary prose. That plea might also be entered in favour of Valerius Maximus. He was writing about the same time as Velleius, and he drew many of his edifying 'exempla' from Livy.

In the view of Livy, the study of the past was 'salubre ac frugiferum'.[10] It imparts moral lessons both private and public—'tibi tuaeque rei publicae.' All for 'concordia', Livy deprecates the violent pride of aristocrats no less than the turbulence of demagogues; and if, following the tradition, he condemned Claudii for 'superbia', that was no cause for harm or offence.

The opuscule of Velleius is a most peculiar product. Beginning with the Trojan War, his summary expands into a panegyric of Tiberius Caesar. For present purposes, prime value goes to his portrayal of aristocrats in his own time and memory.

Some entries may merely denote agents in historical transactions. Moreover, since the author concentrates on the person of Ti. Caesar (almost to exclusion after the year 14) not all omissions are worth registering. None the less, enough emerges, coherent and revealing.

---

[8] Pliny, *NH* VIII.84.
[9] *Ann.* III.6.3.
[10] *Praef.* 10. Cf. Cicero on philosophy, 'frugifera et fructuosa' (*De off.* III.5). In the figurative sense the word is strangely rare. *TLL* next cites Pliny, *NH* XXIX.54.

Sundry members of the most ancient *nobilitas* are singled out. First of all, Messalla Corvinus, hailed as 'fulgentissimus iuvenis' when after the catastrophe at Philippi he agreed to let his life be preserved 'beneficio Caesaris', a debt which he repaid by gratitude and loyalty.[11] His elder son Messallinus cannot fail to be 'vir animo etiam quam gente nobilior'. Legate of Illyricum in the year 6, he won a resounding and memorable victory over the insurgents.[12]

The excellent M. Lepidus (*cos.* 6) also acquired distinction in those campaigns, 'vir nomini ac fortunae Caesarum proximus'; and he gets a second honorific mention, commanding the Spanish army in 14 when the legions on the Rhine and in Pannonia broke out in mutiny.[13]

P. Dolabella (*cos.* 10), then in Dalmatia, is commended for steadiness in the same emergency, although there is no evidence that either he or Lepidus had trouble with the troops. Finally, another Cornelius, one of the Lentuli, a family which in its long survival tended to avoid renown in war. Cossus wins a war in Africa and bequeaths to his son the triumphal name 'Gaetulicus'.[14]

Dolabella enjoyed credit with the ruler. He may have forfeited it in the sequel through 'absurda adulatio'. In the year 21 he proposed that the Princeps, when coming back from Campania, should celebrate an ovation. The proud Claudius made a sarcastic response, disdaining honour for a 'peregrinatio suburbana'.[15]

As for the Lentuli, Cossus was deep in the counsels of the ruler; and Gaetulicus, now legate of Germania Superior, had betrothed his daughter to a son of Aelius Seianus.

So far *nobiles* who belonged to the old patriciate. L. Piso, the Prefect of the City, could hardly fail a mention. Velleius awards space and prominence to the three years' war in Thrace. That was deserved. He goes on to extol the poise of Piso's temper, and the pursuit of elegant leisure not impairing an unobtrusive dedication to public business.[16]

Next, the amiable Marcius Censorinus (*cos.* 8 BC). In cruel emphasis on the end of Marcus Lollius, the author shoves in for contrast the grievous loss that Rome suffered when Censorinus died not long after in the same region: 'vir demerendis hominibus genitus'.[17]

Finally, the Domitii Ahenobarbi. That house had an early entry for its 'felicitas' in public honours and survival through seven generations.[18] The

---

[11] II.71.1. In fact Corvinus surrendered to Antonius.
[12] 112.1 f. Dio preserves a different version (LV.30.2).
[13] 114.5; 125.5.
[14] 116.2.
[15] *Ann.* III.47.3 f.
[16] Velleius II.98.1 ff.
[17] 102.1.
[18] 10.2: 'ut clarissima, ita artata numero felicitas'.

consul of 32 BC came into the story of the Civil Wars, first a Republican
and then for long a partisan of Antonius, whom he abandoned shortly
before the battle—not without great danger to his life, so Velleius in
extenuation asserts.[19] His son Lucius, consul in 16 BC, is also named for
praise of his character, but not there credited with any achievement in
peace or war.[20]

That consul and his son are both endowed with 'nobilissima
simplicitas'.[21] The son had recently reinforced the dynastic connection of
the Ahenobarbi. In 28 the Princeps assigned him for wife Agrippina, the
eldest daughter of Germanicus Caesar: the emphatic and concluding end
to Book IV of the *Annales*.

Attached to those Domitii, the virtue of 'simplicitas' excites curiosity
and incurs suspicion. It also appertains to P. Dolabella, 'vir simplicitatis
generosissimae'.[22]

Consulars from families of recent ennoblement qualify. Antistius Vetus
(*cos.* 6 BC), brought in early when his grandfather is mentioned, possesses
excellence to a degree, 'in quantum humana simplicitas intellegi potest'[23]
and Nerva Silianus (*cos.* AD 7), the second son of P. Silius, another
deliberate entry, is 'simplicissimus'.[24] Finally, the approved *novus homo*,
Pomponius Flaccus (*cos.* 17). He has that 'simplex virtus' that deserves
glory all the time, but never tries to snatch it. The diplomatic craft of
Flaccus was employed by Ti. Caesar in his 'prudentia', to outwit a
Thracian prince.[25]

It comes as a surprise that in his ascension 'simplicitas' does not attend
upon the modest and meritorious Seianus, 'nihil sibi vindicantem eoque
adsequentem omnia'. However, the austere but genial Seianus can be well
content with assorted gifts of nature, with 'severitas laetissima et prisca
hilaritas'.[26]

As is apparent, labels of quality are transferred from ancient lineage to the
new nobility. In the first place, Asinius Pollio, to whom the narration of
the wars could not refuse repeated mention. Velleius accords him rank
beside Messalla Corvinus: the twin glories of Augustan eloquence.[27] No
mention, however, of the history that recounted the fall of the Republic.

---

[19] 84.2. He was in fact suffering from a 'subita valetudo', and he died a few days after his transit
(Suetonius, *Nero* 3.2).

[20] 72.3.

[21] 10.2; 72.3. The consul of 54 BC earned brief mention, without epithet (50.1). In him the family
type showed with 'truci ingenio' (Suetonius, *Nero* 2.3).

[22] 125.5

[23] 43.4.

[24] 116.4 (recording his 'immatura mors').

[25] 129.1. By contrast, no mention of the great insurrection in Thrace (*Ann.* IV.46 ff.), quelled by
the legate of Moesia, the exemplary Poppaeus Sabinus.

[26] 127.3.

[27] 36.2.

A number of the new consuls came from families already in the Senate before the Republic ended. The Antistii get an early entry through C. Antistius Vetus (*suff.* 30 BC), legate in Spain; but a reference to his father had already commemorated the excellent consul of 6 BC, and also his two sons, recent consuls.[28]

P. Silius Nerva (*cos.* 20 BC) is registered by Velleius in juxtaposition to Antistius Vetus. After their actions in Spain, total peace prevailed, no trace surviving even of brigandage.[29] Intent to bring together for praise those two men, Velleius abridges history as well as distorts it. Antistius Vetus was legate under Caesar Augustus in the campaigns of 26 and 25. But the pacification of the peninsula was achieved by Agrippa in 20 and 19. Silius' governorship of Hispania Citerior falls in 19–17. In the near sequel, as proconsul of Illyricum, he prepared the conquest of the Alpine lands.[30] The credit went, as intended, to the stepsons of the Princeps. The operations of Silius (it was to be expected) are absent from Velleius. No subsequent military employment happens to be discoverable.

Sentius Saturninus, consul in 19, dealt firmly with disturbances at Rome, 'vetere consulum more ac severitate'.[31] The 'prisca severitas' of Saturninus is allowed to relax later when in AD 4, legate under Ti. Caesar on the Rhine, he is accorded a second testimonial. It enlarges on 'multiplex virtus': not only alert and vigorous in the field but in his hours of leisure 'splendidus atque hilaris'.[32]

M. Vinicius (*suff.* 19) began in 13 BC the Bellum Pannonicum, under the supervision of Marcus Agrippa.[33] Claudius Nero took up the post in the next year and prosecuted the work of conquest. Vinicius comes to notice later on, winning the *ornamenta triumphalia* for a campaign in Germany.[34]

Silius had three sons, Vinicius one, all duly acceding to consulships. Velleius supplies valuable facts arising from his own experience with the armies. He began as military tribune 'in Thracia Macedoniaque'.[35] That is, in the Balkan command set up when the Macedonian legions were taken from the proconsul at the time of Piso's war. Velleius served in succession under P. Vinicius and P. Silius: praetorian legates, the army at this time comprising only two legions. Vinicius became consul in AD 2, Silius *suffectus* in 3.

[28] 90.4; 43.4.
[29] 90.4.
[30] above, p. 400.
[31] 92.2.
[32] 105.2.
[33] 96.2.
[34] 104.2.
[35] 101.3. For the detail of his long career, G. V. Sumner, *HSCP* LXXIV (1970), 265 ff.

Velleius' narration of the great rebellion in Illyricum discloses *ornamenta triumphalia* won by two aristocrats, namely the elder son of Corvinus and M. Lepidus.[36] Reporting the final campaign, against the Dalmatians, he also notes Vibius Postumus, consul suffect in 5. That enables him to slip in a pair of ex-consuls not active in those parts, namely the *novus homo* Passienus Rufus (*cos.* 4 BC) and Cossus Lentulus (1 BC), both earning the *ornamenta* for African warfare.[37]

Further, three excellent consulars who deserved the honour but for different reasons missed it. First, L. Apronius (*suff.* 8) who was associated in the operations of Vibius Postumus. Next Aelius Lamia (*cos.* 3), described as 'vir antiquissimi moris et priscam gravitatem semper humanitate temperans'[38] (116.3). Third, the second son of old Silius, namely A. Licinius Nerva Silianus (*suff.* 7). A wholly admirable character (and, to be sure, 'simplicissimus'), he was carried off by an untimely death.[39]

Artifice is patent. Coming on the name of Apronius, the reader would know his present significance: legate in Germania Inferior while his father-in-law, Lentulus Gaetulicus, held the other army. Furthermore, the author added an anticipation of future military honours.[40] Apronius is the second in the sequence of four proconsuls who had to deal with the rebellion of Tacfarinas in Africa (from 17 to 24). But Velleius eschews a clear statement.[41]

Reasons are not far to seek. Q. Junius Blaesus (*suff.* 10) furnishes a clue. The mutinous legions in Pannonia were quelled by Blaesus, 'viro nescias utiliore in castris an meliore in toga'. Velleius subjoins the *ornamenta* he later earned as proconsul.[42]

An episode in the story of the war in Africa reveals how he acquired the post. In 21 the Princeps put forward two names: Marcus Lepidus and Junius Blaesus. Lepidus withdrew, for a motive obvious to the high assembly: Blaesus was the uncle of Aelius Seianus.[43] Further, the *ornamenta* decreed to Blaesus were a compliment to Seianus, so Tiberius proclaimed.[44] Likewise was interpreted their denial to Dolabella, 'ne Blaesi avunculi eius laus obsolesceret'.[45] Dolabella in fact terminated the war.

[36] 112.2; 115.3.

[37] 116.2. Postumus was a *novus homo*, from Larinum (*CIL* IX.730), and presumably in high favour. He had Asia as proconsul from 12 to 15 (*OGIS* 469: Samos).

[38] 116.3, mentioning subsequent posts 'in Germania Illyricoque'. They evade precision. Later legate of Syria and ending as *praefectus urbi*, Lamia enjoyed the confidence of Ti. Caesar.

[39] 116.4.   [40] 116.3.

[41] His comment on the ruler's management of that warfare is instructive: 'magni enim terroris bellum Africum et cotidiano auctu maius auspiciis eius brevi sepultum est' (129.4). There is no sign that this type of warfare (unlike a rising in Gaul) caused alarm at Rome. And 'brevi sepultum' is plain falsehood.

[42] 125.5.

[43] *Ann.* III.35.2.

[44] III.72.4.

[45] IV.26.1.

Velleius' criteria are clear. In the forefront consulars in favour with Ti. Caesar, and with the great minister. The only senator named and labelled for praise in his account of the reign subsequent to the mutinies is Pomponius Flaccus. Flaccus, it happens to be known, was a boon companion of Tiberius, sharing a two day symposium with Piso the Pontifex.[46]

Next, his own personal relations with certain families, as on attestation for Vinicii and Silii, though not with Antistii. Recent consuls become relevant: two Antistii (in 23 and 28), P. Silius Nerva (in 28). The sporadic mention of Passienus Rufus would evoke C. Sallustius Crispus Passienus (*suff.* 27), his son, whom the opulent and powerful minister of state had taken in adoption. Similarly, the *ornamenta triumphalia* of Cossus Lentulus permit an amicable reference to his son Gaetulicus, recently consul.

Selection entails omissions, some perhaps significant. One is no mystery: Paullus Fabius Maximus, an enemy of Tiberius. Having married a cousin of Augustus, Maximus counts as a rival. Likewise L. Domitius Ahenobarbus, the husband of Antonia.

Velleius names him with praise of his character, it is true, but not in any Augustan context: only in annotation on his parent.[47] Legate in Illyricum and in Germany, Ahenobarbus won abnormal glory: 'exercitu flumen Albim transgressus, longius penetrata Germania quam quisquam priorum'.[48] The alert Velleius was anxious to assert a monopoly for the 'ducum maximus', the 'perpetuus patronus Romani imperii'.[49] He was not likely to exalt the generals whom Caesar Augustus had to rely upon during the decade when Claudius Nero was off the scene. Only M. Vinicius is accorded an entry, the grandfather of his patron. No Danubian operations find record. Lentulus the Augur is absent, who, dying in 25, was linked to Ahenobarbus in the Tacitean obituary notice.

To corroborate the predilections of Velleius Paterculus it will be suitable to adduce some of the characters he presents as detrimental, for a wide variety of misdemeanours. The names brought up ancient scandals or enduring annoyance and enmities. They also illustrate subsequent vicissitudes at the time of writing, notably angry discord in the dynasty and a sequence of prosecutions. In the year 29 the widow of Germanicus Caesar was indicted, along with her eldest son. They were sent away to penal islands. Velleius permits himself a brief allusion to the shame and torment the Princeps had to suffer for their transgressions.[50] In the next

---

[46] Suetonius, *Tib.* 42.1 (above, p. 435).

[47] Velleius II.72.3.

[48] *Ann.* IV.44.2. Velleius was under no obligation to state that Drusus had reached the Elbe; but he awards the credit to Tiberius, in the campaign of AD 5 (106.3). Cf. C. M. Wells, *The German Policy of Augustus* (1972), 159. For a defence of Velleius, G. V. Sumner, *HSCP* LXXIV (1970), 273.

[49] 99.1; 120.1.   [50] 130.4.

year came the turn of Drusus, Agrippina's second son. After prosecution before the Senate he was consigned to custody in the Palace.[51]

It was now the year signalized by the consulship of Marcus Vinicius. In the course of the first six months Ti. Caesar was at last able to satisfy his grudge against Asinius Gallus. While he was dining by invitation on Capreae a decree of the Senate pronounced his arrest. Tiberius was later to allege adultery with Agrippina.[52] As concerns Velleius, while duly complimentary towards the memory of Pollio, he had no reason for mentioning Gallus at any time.

(1) The list may lead off with a famous character whose derelictions belonged to a distant past: Munatius Plancus. For posterity he is redeemed in an ode of Horace. Velleius describes lavishly his disgraceful behaviour at Alexandria before he deserted Antonius. 'Morbo proditor', and 'in omnia et omnibus venalis', and so on, it is a familiar story.[53] Attention should go to the censorship he held in 22 with Paullus Aemilius Lepidus for colleague. Both come off badly: 'cum alteri vis censoria, alteri vita deesset.'[54]

Four decades later the granddaughter brought opprobrium on the name. Plancina was the wife of Cn. Piso, the legate of Syria, indicted likewise for high treason—and, it was alleged, she had poisoned Germanicus Caesar. The intervention of Livia rescued her.

Unfriendly words about the colleague of Plancus in the censorship, that is the surprise. If the office was going to be mentioned at all, one would expect the eminent Paullus to stand in shining contrast to Munatius Plancus. He was the parent of the unimpeachable Marcus Lepidus. Perhaps the author was hasty and inadvertent. Or perhaps the authority of Lepidus was now thought to be waning through an unfortunate involvement in dynastic politics. His daughter had recently married Drusus, the son of Germanicus.

(2) A pair of conspirators. After a brief note on the conferment of the name 'Augustus', the author proceeds 'erant tamen qui hunc felicissimum statum odissent'.[55] He then names 'L. Murena et Fannius Caepio'. The former is Varro Murena. Were it not for his crime, 'potuit videri bonus'. That is, an adherent of the Caesarian party. Caepio by contrast was a Republican—'et ante hoc erat pessimus'.

(3) The five *nobiles* destroyed in the catastrophe of Julia, in the forefront the two consulars Iullus Antonius and Quinctius Sulpicianus. This item is of unique value, on many counts.[56]

---

[51] The prosecutor was L. Cassius Longinus (Dio LVIII.3.8): consul in that year, and in 33 to receive as bride Drusilla, the sister of Drusus (*Ann.* VI.17.1).

[52] *Ann.* VI.25.2.   [53] Velleius 83.1 f.

[54] 95.3.   [55] 91.2.

[56] 100.2 ff. (Ch. VI). In this context may be recalled the 'conspiracy' of young Lepidus, on lavish exposition (II.88). Also Agrippa Postumus (112.7).

(4) M. Plautius Silvanus (*cos.* 2 BC). In the second year of the great rebellion a Roman army on the march westwards from Sirmium had to face a surprise attack. There ensued a 'paene exitiabilis omnibus clades', but disaster was averted by 'Romani virtus militis', with no credit to the generals, namely the consulars Caecina Severus and Plautius Silvanus.[57]

The account is vivid and looks convincing. However, victory was won, and the army reached Siscia. Caecina went back to Moesia, but Silvanus was detained for important mandates in 8 and 9, as is shown by the full narration in Cassius Dio. Silvanus was duly accorded the *ornamenta triumphalia*.[58] He failed to qualify for Velleius' rubric, which takes in Vibius Postumus.[59]

Suspicion arises and curiosity. Caecina Severus (*suff.* 1 BC) was later legate on the Rhine under Germanicus.[60] About the family of Silvanus, two items offer for scandal. Young Claudius, forfeiting in the year 8 Aemilia Lepida, and missing through death another bride, married a daughter of the 'vir triumphalis'. Divorce followed not long after, with nasty imputations against the lady.[61] Next, a case on public notoriety in 24. The praetor M. Plautius Silvanus threw his wife out the window.[62]

As emerges from the episode, Urgulania, the praetor's mother, was a dear friend of old Livia. Arrogant and pretentious, Urgulania was a cause of annoyance to the Princeps, more than once.

The authoritarian Augusta passed away at last in 29, with reverent homage from Velleius.[63] The loss of her protection was felt by others, and by the consul Fufius Geminus, whose bitter witticisms had not spared the person of the Princeps. Like his wife, Geminus had been a favourite of Livia. In the next year he succumbed to a prosecution for treason, and his wife committed suicide.[64]

(5) Three victims of *maiestas*. They are summarily registered, with righteous indignation at the affront to Caesar.[65] First, a conspirator: 'quid hic meruit ut scelerata Drusus Libo iniret consilia?' Next, the flagrant ingratitude of C. Silius and of Cn. Piso. The former, the youngest of the consular brothers (*cos.* 13), had been a friend of Germanicus—and Piso, the enemy of the prince, was disowned and sacrificed by Tiberius Caesar. The author did not enlarge. The catastrophe of Piso was a shattering blow to Tiberius, his bad judgement shown up.

---

[57] 112.4 ff.
[58] *ILS* 921 (near Tibur).
[59] Not a person of comparable distinction.
[60] When he received the *ornamenta* (*Ann.* I.72.1). An earlier award is not beyond belief.
[61] Suetonius, *Divus Claudius* 26.2: 'ob libidinum probra et homicidii suspicionem'.
[62] *Ann.* IV.22.
[63] 130.5.
[64] *Ann.* V.2.2, cf. VI.10.1; Dio LVIII.4.5 ff.
[65] 130.3.

(6) Quinctilius Varus. That eminent and ill-starred person offered as a scapegoat—and a contrast to the military renown engrossed by Ti. Caesar.[66] A notice about Nonius Asprenas (*suff.* 6), the nephew of Varus, is subjoined to that context. Serving as legate, he brought his force of two legions down the Rhine in promptitude, to protect the winter camps. He earns firm and generous commendation. But Velleius goes on to a scandalous allegation. Some believed that Asprenas, while he rescued the living, laid hands on the property of the dead.[67] Velleius had been in a position to know, since he came to the Rhine as a legate with Tiberius early in the following year, and remained there for two years.

The notice, so foreign to the author's normal procedures, excites curiosity. The son of Asprenas, consul suffect in the second half of 29, may have run into trouble in a year made perilous for many through the ascension of Aelius Seianus. Compare the fate of Fufius Geminus, in that season of multiple hazards. By the year 31 even L. Arruntius was not secure, albeit enjoying the trust of the ruler.[68]

(7) M. Lollius (*cos.* 21 BC). Avid for money and supreme in the arts of dissembling, this fellow incurs a double charge. First, a defeat he suffered from a German incursion, with the loss of a legionary eagle.[69] That was long ago, in 17 BC. Other evidence shows that the damage was soon repaired, and the Germans made submission.[70]

The second and ultimate transgression occurred in Syria, when Lollius was 'velut moderator' to Gaius Caesar. Velleius after his service with the Balkan legions had accompanied the young prince on his journeys, and he speaks as an eye-witness. About C. Caesar, the author is discreet, yet revealing. About Lollius, the prince learned from the Parthian ruler alarming revelations of duplicity—'perfida et plena subdoli ac versuti animi consilia'.[71] A few days later Lollius died; whether or not by his own hand, the author is not in a position to say.

He could never have been in dubitation about how to portray Marcus Lollius. In the year 21 senators heard the despatch from the Princeps requesting a public funeral for Sulpicius Quirinius. Tiberius recounted the merits of that *novus homo*, with emphasis on loyal deference shown at Rhodes. Then he deviated into an attack on the memory of Lollius, the root and cause, so he proclaimed, of deleterious behaviour in Gaius Caesar.[72]

More typical than the exposure of evil men is the warm enthusiasm elicited by the virtues of the noble and eminent. As has been shown, the aristocracy enjoys a happy and favourable presentation in the odes of

---

[66] Ch. XXIII.
[67] 120.3.
[68] Dio LVIII.8.3.
[69] 97.1.
[70] above, p. 402.
[71] 102.1.
[72] *Ann.* III.48.

Horace; and in his earlier role of satirist the poet had not gone in for detraction of birth and pedigree.

The age in its prime produced an efflorescence of talent. *Nobiles* excel in oratory, and they might lend dignity and sagacity to the deliberations of the high assembly. Piso the Pontifex and Marcus Lepidus survived to convey that tradition and arouse admiration in a sombre historian. The ingenuous might have evoked Fabius Maximus.

There was another side. Arrogance and conceit, sloth or frivolity recall the last epoch of the Republic. From the tribulations of the revolutionary age the *nobiles* derived unedifying lessons of survival, and of profit. They benefited from a prosperous season. Luxury and ostentation returned. If wealth now stood in the ascendant, pride of birth acquired a notable enhancement, some old families being rescued from an obscurity of centuries, and the pursuit of public honours made easier through the patronage of Caesar Augustus.

Pliant accommodation marks the renascent *nobilitas*, for personal and family advantage. In the past the nobleman exacted deference from those below in a system that depended on consensus and *clientela*. 'Obsequium' was now transferred to the person of the ruler. Well before the reign ended it passed into subservience and adulation.

With Messalla Corvinus and other aristocrats the attitude might appear elegant, commended or covered by oratory and letters, by favour bestowed on poets both Latin and Greek. From the last epoch of the Free State some recaptured and renewed a habit of licence or dissipation that invaded the court and the dynasty, bringing calamity to the gay and frivolous even had they not been caught up in political intrigue.

In revulsion from 'non-Roman behaviour' in the recent and deplorable past, the policy of the government was pious and puritanical. It enjoined the cult of ancestral virtue and high-minded parsimony. In spite of distaste for regimentation, some members of the aristocracy were happy to conform. To despise the Greeks and practise austerity in a prosperous society was one way of advertising family tradition and allegiance to the cause of the Republic—and it set a man at a distance from the smoother opportunists.

The truculent Gnaeus Piso and his brother inherited 'ferocia' from their parent.[73] Military authority kept its appeal, and discipline to be rigorously enforced if action and glory were denied. When proconsul in Africa, Piso ostentatiously put men to death for minor offences that could have been condoned with no damage.[74]

Aristocrats could still command large armies in the province of Caesar, and some won renown in the field. No details accompany Piso's

[73] Ch. XXVI.
[74] Seneca, *De ira* I.18.3 ff. (above, p. 370).

governorship of Tarraconensis, perhaps a long tenure during the season of the northern wars. When he stood trial for high treason one of the prosecutors brought up extortion in that province.[75]

Of this character and comportment, the last exponent was the archaic Ser. Sulpicius Galba, with military credit cheaply earned and no sign of energy or decision. The historian duly applies the label of 'antiquus rigor'.[76] The ancestors were harsh and cruel: one of them rapacious in Spain[77]—and further back, the first Roman to command a fleet in the Aegean, who proposed to sell into slavery the citizens of Aegina.[78]

In epilogue and in bathos will be observed Cn. Piso, the trusted friend of Ti. Caesar. Passing through Athens on his way to Syria, he derided the ancient renown of the city and denounced its present inhabitants, 'conluviem illam nationum'.[79]

No contemporary witness arraigns the governing class. The evidence is subsequent. Much of it indeed casual or sporadic, apart from the narration of Cornelius Tacitus. Expounding year by year the confrontation between Senate and Princeps, it is coherent and damaging. As the historian went on, he came across more and more transactions that led back to the previous reign. Public funerals were one incentive. More potent the emergence of ancient discord or forgotten scandals.

The *novus homo* Annaeus Seneca was not afraid to show up the vices of *nobiles* whom the virtues of their ancestors were held to promote and protect, through social connivance. One example may suffice, Persicus the son of Fabius Maximus.[80] Still in touch with the earlier time, Seneca could have supplied many revelations.

In a later season the biographer of the Caesars sought out the personal details that the dignity of senatorial history eschewed. Ancestors of Nero might bear in their own time the conventional label of 'nobilissima simplicitas'. These Domitii (the consul of 16 BC and his son) were shown a nasty pair by scholarly research: cruel, arrogant, and intolerable.[81]

On Nero followed Ser. Sulpicius Galba, of the old patriciate. His father (*suff.* 5 BC) brought back the consulship to the family after a lapse of over a hundred years: no conspicuous talent, an ugly little man who however captured splendid or opulent brides.[82] The son likewise benefited from the favour of women, and the old Augusta liked him. The uncritical concurred. The biographer supplies a variety of particulars (including his

[75] *Ann.* III.13.1.
[76] *Hist.* I.18.3.
[77] viz. Ser. Galba (*pr.* 151): the occasion of a famous prosecution in 149.
[78] Polybius IX.42.6. Omitted by Livy.
[79] *Ann.* II.55.1.
[80] Ch. XXVIII.
[81] Suetonius, *Nero* 4 f., cf. Ch. XII.
[82] above, p. 75.

obsession with the pedigree of the Sulpicii) that bear out the condemnatory verdict of the consular historian.

If the *nobilitas* was liable as ever to sundry distempers and prone to evil habits, comfort might accrue from the 'innocentia' and the 'industria' of newer stocks. For access to a consulship, Roman tradition knew three paths: birth, achievement in warfare, excellence in the civil arts (oratory and the law). In awarding honours Tiberius Caesar conformed to that prescription.[83]

Like the nobility now resurgent, *novi homines* (rapid and scandalous by their advancement in the wars) went on to exploit the new order. Caesar's heir, distrustful of the *nobiles*, at once needed legates to command his armies; of praetorian rank for the most part, but some rising to consulships, Lollius, Vinicius, and Tarius Rufus being early specimens.

The effort of ascension left scars and blemishes on their character. Success did not always relax or embellish the practice of old-fashioned parsimony. 'Prisca severitas' served as a cover for harshness and rigour among the military, whose habits of deference induced by hierarchy in command might issue in subservience towards superiors, arrogance in dealing with others.[84]

The historian Tacitus, keen all the time to subvert conventional fancies about honest worth, furnishes a sharp delineation, singling out three Augustan consulars who neatly exemplify the promotion of *novi homines*.[85] The device is double. Their words and actions in the Senate are put on show, and obituaries confirm at no long interval. Sulpicius Quirinius rose by 'militaris industria', and by the diplomatic arts. Senators who heard the elogium were not impressed. The aged Quirinius enjoyed wealth and influence—and was much disliked. Next Q. Haterius (*suff.* 5 BC), shameless in adulation and gaining no lasting fame for his facile and Ciceronian eloquence. Finally, another old man, Ateius Capito (*suff.* AD 5), eminent for science of the law, which he degraded through undue compliance with the wishes of the government.

Others of long success and survival benefit from absence. Whereas Aemilia Lepida, when Quirinius testified against her, proceeded to raise protest by organizing a group of society ladies in the Theatre of Pompeius, her ancestor (so Tacitus records), the people of Rome rose and expelled Titius from the same edifice. Titius had killed Sextus Pompeius in Asia. Velleius was careful to bring up the episode.[86] It is a pity that he did not

---

[83] *Ann.* IV.6.2: 'nobilitatem maiorum, claritudinem militiae, inlustres domi artes spectando'.
[84] Like Curtius Rufus, the legate of Germania Superior: 'adversus superiores tristi adulatione, adrogans minoribus, inter pares difficilis' (*Ann.* XI.21.3). Not perhaps an authentic 'vir militaris'.
[85] On this trio, cf. *Tacitus* (1958), 580 f.
[86] Velleius II.79.5. Titius was a nephew of Munatius Plancus (83.2).

choose to question Tarius Rufus, the rich and harsh upstart—who acceded at an advanced age to the charge of the Roman aqueducts.[87]

The aristocratic Claudian was moved by merit and loyalty in *novi homines*—and ready to come forward in their defence. Sober discourse on his character and his policy would bring out that feature, for apologia or even for praise; and it might do no harm to adduce some of the living, if they were immune from feud and faction, safely committed to Caesar only.

The panegyrist had a more ambitious design. His excursus claims a large portion in the summary devoted to 'horum sedecim annorum opera'. It starts with Marcus Agrippa and Statilius Taurus, and reveals at the outset what the author is about by declaring the maxim 'magna negotia magnis adiutoribus egent'.[88]

A laudation follows, enlarging on the quality of Aelius Seianus, whom Tiberius Caesar has chosen as his indispensable ally and minister. After adducing parallels from the remote past for status and fame acquired by new men, and coming down to Asinius Pollio, the exposition demonstrates 'quod optimum sit esse nobilissimum' (such has ever been the Roman tradition), and reverts to Seianus at the culmination. Seianus is called to an eminent function, to aid the Princeps in his tasks, to protect him in their execution—which Senate and People understand.[89]

Praise of new men entails no depreciation of birth or lineage. Encomiasts in any age possess a normal awareness and exploit a profitable ambiguity. And indeed, social distinction adhered to Aelius Seianus, although the son of a Roman knight.[90]

The tribute of Velleius exceeds mere defence of the 'adiutor' from denigration or enmity in high society.[91] Rising through intrigue, prosecutions, and the infatuation of Ti. Caesar, Seianus was now passing beyond the station of a minister to capture that of a partner in the imperial power. Seianus in the course of the year 30 was elected consul, designated to share the *fasces* with the Princeps (his first consulship for a decade). It might be worth knowing whether that occurred before or after the author penned his words of firm approbation.

When Tiberius Caesar came at last to resipiscence and conceived distrust of his dear friend, he devised a counterplot with consummate guile. A despatch from Capreae demolished Seianus.

Aristocratic allies of the minister drew back in time, or escaped

[87] Frontinus, *De aq.* 102 (above, p. 223).   [88] 127.2.
[89] 127.4.
[90] Ch. XXII.
[91] On the other hand, positive eulogy has been questioned or even denied. Thus G. V. Sumner, *HSCP* LXXIV (1970), 293 f.: 'the historian's tone is tense, uneasy, and ambivalent'. And A. J. Woodman speaks of an 'active distaste' for the minister (*CQ* XXV (1975), 304).

molestation (like Lentulus Gaetulicus). Only one consular came to grief.[92]
Minor senators succumbed. Among them was a certain Bruttedius Niger:
introduced well in advance by Tacitus, with a hint of the fate in store for
oratorical talent when combined with hasty and inordinate ambition.[93]
Bruttedius, so it happens, had written history.[94] That Velleius was an open
and decided adherent of Aelius Seianus evades ascertainment.[95] But
laudation of the great 'adiutor' rendered a man vulnerable to eager
prosecutors, and he would need powerful protection.[96]

Valerius Maximus was more discreet—or rather, more lucky. Towards
the end of his work he was able to insert a substantial passage denouncing
Seianus, whom he addresses in language of pious horror: 'tu videlicet
efferatae barbariae immanitate truculentior habenas Romani imperii, quas
princeps parensque noster salutari dextera continent, capere potuisti?' But
the gods were vigilant, and the criminal now suffers condign punishment
in the lower world, 'si illuc receptus est'.[97]

The chance survival of a work written by a contemporary is a precious
increment. The annals of the last Augustan decade are obscure in various
aspects, despite the narration of Cassius Dio.[98] Confrontation with Velleius
is useful, since Dio exhibits inadequacies or omissions—and his main
source was hostile to Tiberius.

Velleius wrote from a unique experience of the northern wars,
continuous from 4 to 12. He was first a cavalry officer, then promoted to
senatorial rank (quaestor in 7), with service as a legate in Illyricum and on
the Rhine until he departed to share in the pageantry of the Pannonian
triumph. What he reports of his commander is convincing: constant care
for the troops and a patient strategy that avoided haste and hazard.

For the rest, distortion pervades the eloquent opuscule.[99] With
ingenuous fervour for the virtues that attend upon birth, rank, and success,

[92] viz. Junius Blaesus, cf. *Ann.* V.7.2.

[93] *Ann.* III.66.3, cf. Juvenal X. 83.

[94] Seneca, *Suas.* VI.20 f.

[95] Such a view is 'completely without foundation', according to A. J. Woodman in his
Commentary on the Tiberian chapters (1977), 247. More probably Velleius 'belonged with those
senators who were antagonised by Sejanus' (ib. 248).

[96] Observe further the prayer at the conclusion: may the gods watch over the Princeps and
designate 'successores quam serissimos, sed eos, quorum cervices tam fortiter sustinendo terrarum
orbi sufficiant quam huius suffecisse sensimus' (131.2). That Velleius meant to 'herald and promote
the claims of Vinicius to membership of the imperial house—and more' was suggested by G. V.
Sumner, o.c. 295. Not until the year 33 was Vinicius selected to marry a princess by Ti. Caesar, 'diu
quaesito' (*Ann.* VI.15.1).

[97] Val. Max. IX.11, *Ext.* 4.

[98] The same can be said of the whole reign.

[99] Few will concur in the verdict of A. Dihle: 'die panegyrische Tendenz aber führt nirgends zu
einer nachgewiesenen Entstellung der Tatsachen' (*RE* VIIIA. 646). For R. Seager, 'in all these
chapters there are perhaps only two major instances of dishonesty' (*Tiberius* (1972), 268). That is,
the claim about the Elbe (106.2) and Agrippa Postumus (112.7).

the author parades what he calls 'iustus sine mendacio candor'.[100] One of his unfailing devices is the superlative.

The Roman historians eschew it. A brief glance at Sallust or Tacitus is enough. The plain and simple 'clarus' is more powerful than 'clarissimus', which was already on the way to becoming a title. The superlative is all too often feeble and diffuse, exuding an odour of cheap rhetoric or fraudulence. Velleius comes out with specimens almost devoid of meaning. L. Piso in his comportment as Prefect of the City is at the same time both 'diligentissimus' and 'lenissimus'; and furthermore, all men must feel and proclaim 'esse mores eius vigore ac lenitate mixtissimos'.[101]

The form 'mixtissimus' is unique in Latin, so one learns (no regrets);[102] and 'fulgentissimus' is seldom attached to a person.[103] Valerius Maximus when praising his consular patron Sex. Pompeius furnishes an entertaining parallel to such manifestations: 'ut omnibus virtutibus ita humanitatis quoque laudibus instructissimus'.[104] Again, speaking of himself, he sinks to 'mea parvitas',[105] whereas Velleius has 'mediocritas mea'.[106] The language reflects the spirit of the client.

None the less, the style of Velleius has decided merits, rapid, vivid, and varied, with formulations that annex attention and tend to dwell in the memory—often to the detriment of historical understanding. Multiple devices declare an education early refined in the schools of rhetoric, belying the pleasing notion of the plain honest soldier turned author, exuberant but only through loyalty to his former commander. That exuberance is designed to convey sincerity, as is perhaps incoherence or the breathless haste ('festinatio') in which he professes to be writing.[107] Velleius may not have begun until the consulship of Vinicius was close at hand.[108]

Deceit prevails, sometimes proved, seldom exempt from suspicion. Since Velleius contradicts a number of plain facts within his own knowledge, the charge of mendacity, that might appear harsh or petulant, acquires weight and pertinence.[109]

[100] 116.5. Cf. 102.3: 'etenim semper magnae fortunae comes est adulatio.'
[101] 98.3. [102] *TLL*.
[103] 71.1 (Messalla Corvinus), cf. 64.3: 'fulgentissimo et caelesti ore' (Cicero).
[104] Val. Max. II.6.8, cf. Velleius II.94.2: 'optimis studiis maximoque ingenio instructissimo' (Drusus).
[105] Val. Max., *praef.*
[106] Velleius II. 104.3; 111.3 ('mediocritas nostra').
[107] For ways in which the term can be used see the full and careful investigation of A. J. Woodman, *CQ* XXV (1975), 279 ff. In certain instances, from Nepos (*praef.* 8) down to Jerome and the *Historia Augusta*, it looks highly conventional.
[108] Woodman, however, suggests 'the mid twenties' (o.c. 282).
[109] For that thesis, *AJP* XCIX (1978), 45 ff. = *RP* III (1984), 1090 ff. For a favourable estimate of Velleius see the papers of Sumner and Woodman here cited. Further, Sumner's review of Woodman's book in *CP* LXXIV (1979), 64 ff.

The abundant production of the Roman annalists between Livy and
Tacitus has perished. Velleius, along with Curtius Rufus, is therefore a
valuable link in the development of historical prose.[110] He is also a
precursor, announcing the destiny of history under the Caesars—adulation for the living, the dead defamed.

The predecessors of smooth Pliny in mastery of the imperial panegyric
have also perished, but the consul's 'actio gratiarum' was already
flourishing.[111] Not confined to defence of the ruler or praise of his person,
it conveyed the Senate's approbation of the 'novus status' which Velleius
knew as 'hic felicissimus status'.

[110] No cause subsists for denying identity with Q. Curtius Rufus (*suff.* 43). Cf. now J. E.
Atkinson in his *Commentary* on Books III and IV (Amsterdam, 1980), 19 ff.
[111] The earliest on attestation is the speech of Sex. Pompeius in 14 (Ovid, *Ex. P.* IV.4.35 ff.).

XXX

The Apologia for the Principate

When a government falls or an empire goes down in ruin, there is much to be explained, and explained away. First of all, by the defeated: who shall take the blame for the catastrophe? But the victorious cause may have an apologia to put in, coming from those who collaborate in the new order.

Among the Romans the perennial debate concerns the fate of the Republic, the coming of monarchy. The 'Principate', such is the convenient and unimpeachable appellation. In what ways was the 'novus status' justified and made acceptable?

The term 'propaganda' finds frequent employ in the modern time. It can apply to the period of civil strife and rival dynasts, less usefully to the years of peace and order. Distinctions will be drawn. There exists 'propaganda in vacuo', where competition is absent, the audience passive or already won over: not arts of persuasion, but the exhibition of power and beneficence.

The question arises, how far the emperors went in for propaganda, or even needed it. Caesar Augustus ordained that his 'res gestae' be inscribed on pillars of bronze outside the Mausoleum. That document carried his claim to renown, personal and unique. There is no sign that he intended it to be exhibited elsewhere than at Rome. Again, later rulers composed autobiographies—for apologia. They never put out a systematic defence of the new system of government.[1] The nearest on record is an abortive injunction that certain orations of Augustus and of Tiberius be read out in the Senate on the first day of the year.[2]

Furthermore, if propaganda, towards whom then directed? In a rapid initial survey the historian Tacitus explains the predominance achieved by Caesar Augustus, 'nullo adversante'. There was none to gainsay, not the *nobiles* or the new men, still less the provinces. From his diagnosis the author left out the Italian towns and the plebs of the city. Not without reason. The thing was obvious. The sentiments of the men of substance and repute throughout Italy could be taken for granted; and the populace of Rome lapsed happily into the *clientela* of the Caesars.

The *nobilitas* had spent money on the urban plebs. Not to buy their votes, given the electoral system, but for display.[3] Caesar conforms,

---

[1] See the discussion provoked by the paper of M. Durry in *Histoire et historiens dans l'antiquité* (Fondation Hardt, 1956), 236 ff. [2] Dio LX.10.2

[3] P. Veyne, *Le pain et le cirque* (1976), 375 ff. (on the general theme of 'évergétisme'.)

advertising benevolence through games and spectacles and cheap food. His patent function is to be a showman: as Nero in his dying words avowed, 'qualis artifex pereo'. Later and more reputable rulers knew their duty, to be generous and affable.[4] Otherwise they risked public protestations in amphitheatre or hippodrome.[5]

Legends on the coinage disclose actions or aspirations of the government, and they furnish manifold instruction to the curious enquirer. A question of general pertinence fails to be asked: who at the time could read those legends, or wanted to read them. No man of property would normally be confronted with a coin when tenants paid their rent to his agent, or any lady when fine fabrics or perfumes were purchased at her choice. Moreover, failing eyesight after the age of fifty would inhibit any curiosity among the literate.[6]

Finally, a brief word may go to the cult of the emperors. The subject has engrossed enormous attention in the course of the last sixty years or so, with a mass of erudite writing, much of it based on misconceptions or tending to propagate them. To assess causes for the fashion might furnish instruction and entertainment. However, some scholars held aloof—and a strong contrary current now becomes perceptible.[7]

Homage paid to rank and power or gratitude towards a 'saviour and benefactor', whether expressed by individuals or by a community, that was no mystery, however extravagant grew the manifestations.[8] The earliest incentives came from below, it was ungracious to repel honours, loyalty might be enlisted for useful purposes.[9] How far the rulers lent encouragement is another matter.

Therefore, if one could properly speak of 'imperial propaganda', it would go where it was superfluous. No exertions of that kind would be required to secure or stimulate conformity among the Roman plebs or the better sort in the cities abroad.[10]

Though master of the world, an emperor had to acknowledge limitations. He was not able to control opinion in the educated class, which may be roughly equated with the upper orders in Roman society:

---

[4] cf., on Trajan, Fronto p. 210 N: 'ut qui sciret populum Romanum duabus praecipue rebus, annona et spectaculis, teneri'.

[5] Z. Yavetz, *Plebs and Princeps* (1969), 101 ff.; F. Millar, *The Emperor in the Roman World* (1977), 368 ff.

[6] Tiberius at the age of fifty-four made public complaint about sight as well as health (Dio LVII.2.4).

[7] As evident in most of the symposium *Le Culte des souverains dans l'empire romain* (Foundation Hardt, 1973).

[8] It began with what Tacitus derides as 'Graeca adulatio' (*Ann.* VI.18.2). For a sane and salutary analysis, Chr. Habicht, *Gottmenschentum und griechische Städte*[2] (1970).

[9] As in the provincial *concilia*. See J. Deininger, *Die Provinziallandtage der r. Kaiserzeit* (1965).

[10] P. Veyne, o.c. 661: 'les empereurs romains ne faisaient pas plus de "propagande" que les rois de France.' He refers to the 'narcissime' of Louis Quatorze.

that is, senators and knights.[11] The Caesars of the first dynasty, although apart from Augustus they might be styled monsters, were all men of high culture and uncommon intelligence, so a sober writer in late Antiquity avers.[12] Those Caesars were in fact members of the Senate, they revered the grandeur of the old Republic—and they might conceive guilt or remorse about the position they had usurped. Tiberius Caesar disliked centralized authority and any impediment to freedom of speech. The fall of the Republic, 'multos dominata per annos', was an epic theme. If Nero had chosen it for a poem, the tone would not have been Caesarian.

Frank and open comment was not likely to be heard on the benches of the Augustan Senate, even if palliated as 'constructive criticism'. Nor did the schools of rhetoric foster independence. But a prosecution might erupt into undesirable language or revelations; and malice knew no restraint when men congregated at a club, a banquet, or a funeral.

Like sumptuary laws or state-enforced morality, a programme of indoctrination would arouse resentment and disbelief. There was a simple remedy: leave it to the educated class to devise formulations of acceptance. Willing agents were to hand, some convinced and some ingenuous, as well as the 'falsi ac festinantes'.

The apologia thus emerging was in large measure the creation of senators, and a product of tacit collusion. As a subject of study, that apologia is no doubt more attractive than 'emperor worship', yet it is none the less a shabby chapter in the 'history of ideas'; and it may prove deleterious if it diverts attention from the structure of society and the processes of imperial government.[13]

The easy and obvious recourse was the negative line: to look about and allocate the blame.[14] Governance by 'senatus populusque Romanus' succumbed under the burdens and strains imported by dominion over the nations. Yet the Republic stood invulnerable to criticism. The Roman constitution was the best that all time had known. That patent truth could be asseverated in discussion with eminent Greeks who were expert in political science.[15] It was further the best, since it issued from a superior moral code.[16] The Roman 'res publica' was both a necessary structure and a

[11] That despotism cannot equal democracy in influencing opinion was shown by Tocqueville, *La Démocratie en Amérique* II[17] (1888), 153 ff.

[12] Aurelius Victor, *De Caes.* 8.7. Caligula is not excluded. Observe the remarkable tribute in Josephus, *AJ* XIX. 208 f.

[13] Neither type is accorded undue space or esteem in the recent exemplary volume of F. Millar.

[14] For a fuller treatment than is here required see *A Roman Post-Mortem* (Todd Memorial Lecture, no. 3, Sydney, 1950) = *RP* (1979), 206 ff.   [15] Cicero, *De r.p.* I.34.

[16] *Tusc.* I.2: 'iam illa quae natura non litteris adsecuti sunt neque cum Graecia neque ulla cum gente sunt comparanda. quae enim tanta gravitas, quae tanta constantia' etc. For the relation between morality and the constitution, see Podsnap in Dickens, *Our Mutual Friend* (1865): the contrasted nation is there indicated but not named. Bagehot, *The English Constitution*, belongs to the same season (1867).

necessary habit of thought. And further, a kind of religion. It duly produced heroes and martyrs, with hagiography or hypocrisy in the sequel.

It might be open to indict the governing class, proved unequal to a proud inheritance. Sallust in his first monograph showed the way, by a deadly device. Cato, the champion of the Optimates, denounces the *nobilitas*, rapacious and corrupt, with no care for the commonwealth. Further, the historian in his diagnosis shows them incompetent: no man in that season endowed with 'ingens virtus', except Cato and Caesar.

That form of attack was debarred under the aristocratic Republic of Caesar Augustus. Sallust went on to be admired for a novel style, approved for moralistic preoccupations. The political attitude was odious and obsolete. The old families were back, protected and subsidized by Caesar's heir; and noblemen benefit from sentimental veneration in Horace and in Velleius.

However, several political leaders might be arraigned on various inculpations. Cicero failed and perished, liable to posthumous defamation from the 'adulatores praesentis potentiae'.[17] Renown of oratory could not be denied, but the style and manner went out of fashion. His political theorizing, it is true, was traditional and innocuous; and his authority might usefully have been invoked by Caesar Augustus when he 'established the State on firm foundations'.[18] There is no sign that it was done.

Cato, obstinate, conceited, and crafty, could on one count be incriminated for the outbreak of the Civil War: enlisting Pompeius Magnus to destroy the proconsul of Gaul. That charge was precluded. Cato ended as a martyr of *Libertas*, sanctified already in the near sequel. Caesar Augustus in due course came out with a firm testimonial: 'he who refuses to have the existing order changed is a good man and a good citizen.'[19]

Not Cicero or Cato therefore. The great dynasts, the 'monarchic faction-leaders', bore a heavy burden of guilt through their ambitions and their alliances. Annexing a verdict of Cato, Asinius Pollio in his history put the exordium at the fatal compact formed by the three 'principes' in the consulship of Metellus. There lay the cause and root of the crisis that broke out a decade later.

War and conquest could never be deprecated by the imperial Republic, 'princeps terrarum populus'.[20] Marcus Crassus, however, had lost a

---

[17] Quintilian XII.10.13.
[18] Quoted in Suetonius, *Divus Aug.* 28.2. Ciceronian, to be sure, cf. *Phil.* V.30 (the legitimation of Octavianus' command).
[19] Macrobius II.4.8.
[20] The term of Livy, *Praef.* 3, cf. XXIX.17.6; XXXIV.58.8.

Roman army beyond the Euphrates. Of Julius Caesar, proconsul of Gaul and dictator, there was scant mention under his son and heir—or equivocal. What was said (or not said) by Virgil and Livy brings convincing testimony.[21] Magnus by contrast, ending on the side of the legitimate government, was rehabilitated and embellished.

More recent scapegoats offered, Caesar's heir being segregated from his partners in the despotic regiment of the Triumvirs. Lepidus was consigned to ignominy or silence, but Marcus Antonius, discredited through foreign allies and the foreign woman ('nefas, Aegyptia coniunx!'), is pilloried for criminal conduct, for 'externi mores et vitia non Romana'.[22]

The style of life enhanced by Antonius did not forfeit admiration in Roman society.[23] When the glory of Actium began to fade, and the hysteria abated, the conflict could be seen in the light of a dynastic or even domestic contretemps. The daughters of Antonius, being nieces of Augustus, contributed to his matrimonial operations. Again, the nephew of Lepidus had been one of the earliest noblemen among his adherents: his two sons were marked out for preferment.

To inculpate errors of the illustrious dead was invidious, since belief in the decrees of fate or the caprice of fortune was so widely accredited. And other causes were brought to the minds of thoughtful citizens in the years of tribulation. The ancestral curse of fratricide was now working itself out, so some opined. Or better, the neglect of religion, and a long declension from ancient standards of frugality and chastity. There was no hope of redemption until the temples were rebuilt.[24]

Explanation of this order finds eager response in any age. If superficial or fraudulent, that is no bar. The defence carries a strong appeal to various emotions, and it offers exploitation for political ends. When the language is solemn and ornate, illusion or deceit can be endorsed and transmitted to distant ages.

The last epoch of the Republic, so far from decadent, bore the mark of vigour, innovation, enlightenment. Poetry and oratory bear witness—or the position of women.[25] In consonance with that rehabilitation, sharp scrutiny should be brought to bear upon the Augustan programmes of moral and social regeneration. Nothing changed in the habits of high society.[26] But it is time to turn aside from well-worn themes and essay the positive apologia.[27]

[21] *Rom. Rev.* (1939), 317 f.; *Tacitus* (1958), 432 f.
[22] Seneca, *Epp.* 83.25.
[23] J. Griffin, *JRS* LXVII (1977), 17 ff.   [24] Horace, *Odes* III.6.
[25] cf. brief remarks in *Sallust* (1964), 16 f.   [26] P. A. Brunt, *Italian Manpower* (1971), 565.
[27] This section was composed in immediate sequence to *A Roman Post-Mortem* and was used in lectures at Oxford, and elsewhere. For the complete and elegant treatment of the whole theme see J. Béranger, *Recherches sur l'aspect idéologique du principat* (1953). Further, L. Wickert, 'Princeps', *RE* XXII (1954), 2222 ff.

Though men are not always ready to acknowledge benefits or publish consolation for the loss of political freedom, those of the better sort could not disavow the advantages accruing from the new dispensation. The 'viri boni et locupletes' saw their estates mount in value, likewise their personal estimation, with easy access to the Senate; and *novi homines* from loyalty or for service rose to positions of dignity and emolument.

The high aristocrats did not need to compete any more. Birth was enough for title and claim, more potent now than in the closing age of the Republic. And, although triumphs were soon abolished, *nobiles* could still win military glory commanding armies under the mandate of Caesar.

Furthermore, old families were rescued from long obscurity to adorn the consular *Fasti*. To what solid or lasting benefit, it must often have been asked. What the *nobiles* thought about the revolutionary leader who had become their friend and benefactor was not said. Something might be divined.

As Tacitus observed of the *nobiles*, 'quanto quis servitio promptior, opibus et honoribus extollerentur'.[28] Some requited Caesar's aid with enthusiasm. Thus Fabius Maximus in Asia, enjoining that the calendar should begin with the birthday of the ruler, the event that announced glad tidings to the whole world.[29]

It suited Messalla Corvinus to put emphasis on an earlier allegiance and parade airs of independence. Had the less favourable testimony survived, it could have shown up a pretentious opportunism. The sons of Messalla were conspicuous for fervent loyalty to Augustus. Ovid's last poem to the address of Messallinus celebrates his 'pietas in totum nomen Iulum', and refers to the influence accruing to him from his devotion: 'principis aeterni . . . amor'.[30] There is more of this sort of thing to the credit (or the discredit) of the younger son, Cotta Maximus, hope in whose good offices was not so soon abandoned by the exile.

Fabius Maximus and the sons of Corvinus, those are the illustrious friends who refused succour to the victim of injustice and personal rancour. Ovid would have done well to abide by the maxim 'longe nomina magna fuge'.[31] Subservient to power, the aristocrats decline to the level of clients and flatterers. Adulation had an early beginning in Rome of the Caesars. One of the first adepts was Valerius Messallinus.[32]

In the dearth of prose extant from that epoch, poetry acquires an inordinate value. By the same token, the interpretation entails delicate

[28] *Ann.* I.2.1.

[29] Ch. XXVIII.

[30] Ovid, *Ex P.* II.2.21; 48. Augustus is likewise styled 'aeternus' in *Fasti* III.421. Eternity had been predicted of Rome by Cicero, *Pro C. Rabirio* 33; next, Livy IV.4.4.

[31] *Tr.* III.4.4.

[32] *Ann.* I.8.4.

appraisal. Poets indulge in allusions either to wars and conquests or to foreign nations (some of them very distant) that might soon feel the impact of Roman arms. Due caution has not always been observed when their language or their forecasts are adduced to explain the policy of the government, west or east.[33]

Distinctions obtain, according to the literary genre and to the time of writing. For the first fifteen years of the Augustan Principate, from 28 to 13, Horace is of prime and varied utility, whereas the elegiac poets stand apart, though by no means homogeneous.[34] There is a gap after 13, but the latest poems of Ovid come in. Not, it is true, for foreign policy, though he furnishes valuable but sporadic items concerning the lower Danube. Those poems illustrate language and habits current in Roman society, notably in respect of homage towards the dynasty.

For example, the three silver statuettes that Cotta sent to Ovid for his domestic shrine.[35] Ovid went in for appeals to Livia, likening her to Venus or to Juno.[36] The astute Horace eschewed her name. Ovid may be taken to reflect the impulsion towards undisguised monarchy made manifest by the promotion of the princes Gaius and Lucius, and not abated in the sequel, after the choice and designation of the stepson.

More sober appreciations, linking and combining republic and principate, would be found in Livy's epilogue, the nine books covering the years from 28 to 9. That epilogue terminated with a panegyric of aristocratic 'virtus' as embodied in the two Claudii, the one dying in warfare 'pro re publica', the other now the desired and destined successor.[37]

Traces of the Livian books, or at least similar sentiments, may be surmised in later writers, such as the epitomator Florus. Nor should Velleius be neglected—and four passages from the coeval Valerius Maximus may be roped in.[38]

Miscellaneous evidence therefore, and it does not amount to much. One deplores the absence of a contemporary oration, to fill the void in the laudation of power and mercy that intervenes between the *Pro Marcello* and Seneca's sermon to Nero, *De clementia*. The earliest allusion to the regular 'actio gratiarum' of a consul happens to concern Sextus Pompeius, entering office in AD 14.[39] Eloquent predecessors earlier in the reign will be assumed, such as the fluent and adulatory Q. Haterius. More to be regretted are the performances rendered at notable ceremonies by two

[33] cf. *History in Ovid* (1978), Ch. IV.
[34] Ch. XXVIII.
[35] *Ex. P.* II.8.1 ff.
[36] *Ex P.* III.1.117. For Livia as Juno, cf. *ILS* 120 (nr. Assuras, in Africa); *IGR* IV.249 (Assos).
[37] above, p. 423.
[38] Val. Max., *Praef.*; VI.1, *praef.*; VIII.13, *praef.*; IX.11, *ext.* 4.
[39] *Ex P.* IV.4.35 ff.

survivors from defeated causes: the smooth Munatius Plancus and the elegant Messalla Corvinus, the one proposing the name 'Augustus', the other 'pater patriae'.[40]

For all that, despite the silence of Augustan oratory and history, the position is not desperate. In proper caution, appeal can be made to a pair of later historians, Cornelius Tacitus and Cassius Dio. First, two speeches. Dio serves up a lengthy funeral oration delivered by Tiberius Caesar. The Roman historian disdained that device. It did not suit the structure of his opening chapters, still less his purpose. In his earlier work, however, Tacitus inserted soon after the exordium a speech on high politics. Galba, justifying his act of usurpation, develops two main lines of argument: legal authority, not despotism, and the rule of the best man, selected by adoption, not hereditary right.

Galba's exposition has been accorded much attention by scholars. The declaration is firm and clear, but it is a trap for the unwary. The author was insidious.[41]

Second, political comment. Tacitus brings on the men of understanding to pronounce their verdicts at the obsequies. Some spread themselves in censure, but others passed from apologia to an amicable assessment (albeit brief) of what the Princeps had achieved in peace and war. Dio uses a similar technique. To the oration he subjoins comment from the Romans—restricted to the favourable aspect.[42]

One item in Dio coincides with Tacitus, two others can be discovered in earlier chapters of the *Annales*.[43] A common source is thus apparent, put to different uses by the two historians. Dio, it is clear, was not following Tacitus. He went back further (that is no surprise) to one of his predecessors, an annalist who wrote under the first dynasty.

In this instance, Tacitus and Dio reproduce formulations long anterior to their own times. The opinions being unimpeachable, nay obvious enough, nothing impedes the notion that they emerged at an early season, being already in circulation not merely under the successor of Augustus but well before he died. In 2 BC the sexagenarian Princeps made dispositions for the event of his demise, which might not be far distant.[44] Whoever was charged with the laudation would not be at a loss.

The speech of Galba is in another case, it is true. Deprecation of dynastic policies would not have found public expression under Caesar's heir—but some of the maxims (it will be shown) can be put to good employ.

With this reinforcement, the argument for the Principate can proceed on its course. A short analysis will suffice, under ten heads of discourse.

[40] Words of Corvinus are quoted in Suetonius, *Divus Aug.* 58.2.
[41] On *Hist.* I. 15 f. cf. *Tacitus* (1958), 207 f.   [42] Dio LVI. 43 f.
[43] For *Ann.* I.9.5 see below, p. 448. The other items are to be found in 2.1 and 3.7. Cf. *Tacitus* (1958), 273; 690 f.   [44] above, p. 90.

First, make-believe. Awkward facts are covered up, and comfort ensues when disasters are allowed to recede from the memory. The best defence of civil strife is to forget it, so the orator Labienus said, the last member of a family in the Pompeian allegiance.[45]

The years of tribulation encouraged deceit and evasion—and an escape from the dreadful present into a sentimental past, a pastoral Arcadia or far exotic lands. Myth and romanticism persisted, with enhancement from the War of Actium.

After the great perturbations, the fabric of the commonwealth remained intact: 'eadem magistratuum vocabula', such is the subversive comment of Cornelius Tacitus. None of the dynasts had wished or intended to destroy that fabric.

Early in 28 the ruler handed over the twelve *fasces* to his colleague in the consulship. Monthly rotation of the 'insignia imperii' thus came back; and the first day of February announced the return of 'normal government'.[46] The consulate appears to regain its regular function and attributes; and no *consules suffecti* were seen for a number of years.

The old order resumed, enhanced by forms and ceremonies and by the revival of ancient rituals. As Velleius duly proclaims, 'prisca illa et antiqua rei publicae forma revocata'.[47] The only novelty he registers is the addition of two praetors. None the less, men of the time could not have refused to admit that a decisive change had intervened, not revocable.

Next, therefore, the theory of long development. Adverting on the republics of Hellas, Cato the Censor pointed out that single legislators had devised their institutions: the Roman commonwealth was created by the wisdom of many men and by the process of the ages.[48] To that theme a tribune of the plebs in the pages of Livy adds both majesty and present relevance: since Rome was established for eternal duration, and its growth knew no limits, new types of authority will become requisite. The term is precise, 'nova imperia'.[49] Indeed, it designates the form of government now installed at Rome: it went back in a straight line to the great commands over provinces and armies which the sovereign people voted to Pompeius, to Caesar—and, for that matter, to the Triumvirs.

Rome's expansion through the ages was also adduced by a pupil of Livy, none other than Claudius Caesar. He spoke in defence of a

[45] Seneca, *Controv.* X.3.5.
[46] Dio LIII.1.1, cf above, p. 1.
[47] Velleius II.89.4.
[48] Cicero, De *r.p.* II.2.
[49] Livy IV.4.4. Caesar had used 'novi generis imperia' to describe the position of Pompeius, holding for long years a great province in absence (*BC* I.85.8).

remarkable innovation—chieftains from Tres Galliae coming into the
Roman Senate. Claudius knew that any change made senators shudder.[50]

However, change can be disguised as renovation or commended as a
restoration to health and vigour.

Third, the medical metaphor. In several writers the anomalous consulship
taken by Pompeius in 52 is passed off as a 'doctor's mandate' to heal the
maladies of the commonwealth.[51] The terms 'fessae res' and 'fessum
imperium' turn up later on; and Florus describes the cessation of civil
warfare as 'aut pax fuit aut fatigatio'.[52]

The medicine administered by Pompeius was worse, it might be said,
than the disease. The therapist was 'gravior remediis quam mala erant'.[53]
An earlier practitioner, Sulla the Dictator, had in fact practised ruthless
surgery on the body politic: 'putria membra', but 'excessit medicina
modum'.[54]

The healing hand of Caesar Augustus, although firm, had been gentle,
applying only the minimum of force requisite, so the men of sober
judgement averred at the funeral: 'pauca admodum vi tractata quo ceteris
quies esset'.[55] Augustus rescued the sick man; and the ruler can be styled
'salubris princeps', or even 'salutaris'.[56]

Fourth, the need for concord and stability. It will be enough to quote the
emphatic endorsement of the 'prudentes': 'non aliud discordantis patriae
remedium quam ut ab uno regeretur'.[57] The only medicine is monarchy. A
Sallustian passage in the preface of Livy's work calls for brief comment.
Putting emphasis on the decline of 'disciplina' and of 'mores' it carries the
statement 'haec tempora quibus nec vitia nostra nec remedia pati
possumus'.[58]

The common interpretation takes 'vitia' in a narrow sense, discovering
in Propertius an allusion to an abortive piece of legislation, which
threatened to separate the poet from his mistress, precisely in 28.[59] The law
lacks other attestation. The pessimism of Livy may be wider and deeper,

---

[50] *ILS* 212 (Lugdunum): 'deprecor ne quasi novam istam rem introduci exhorrescatis'.

[51] *Pro Milone* 68; Plutarch, *Pompeius* 55; Appian, *BC* II.28.107. For a belief that Caesar was an
ἰατρός sent by Providence see Plutarch, *Comp. Dionis et Bruti* 2.

[52] Florus II.34.64.

[53] *Ann.* III.28.1, cf. Seneca on Sulla, 'qui patriam durioribus remediis quam pericula erant
sanavit' (*De ben.* V.16.13).

[54] Lucan II.141 f.

[55] *Ann.* I.9.5, cf. Dio LVI.44.2: εἰ καὶ βιαιότερόν τι . . . ἐπράχθη.

[56] Suetonius, *Divus Aug.* 42.1; *Tib.* 29.2. Cf. Dio LVI.39.2: ὥσπερ τις ἰατρὸς ἀγαθὸς κτλ. (in
the oration of Tiberius).

[57] *Ann.* I.9.4.

[58] Livy, *Praef.* 9.

[59] Propertius II.7, cf. G. Williams, *JRS* LII (1962), 33 f.; R. M. Ogilvie in his *Commentary* (1965),
28.

bearing upon the maladies of the whole community rather than on personal morals.[60]

Fifth, the imperative need for central authority. That ran contrary to the principles of Republican goverment, and also to the practice: separation of powers, not concentration in a single hand. Hortensius, a leader of the Optimates, raised protest against the *imperium* to be conferred on Pompeius by the bill of the tribune Manilius: 'ad unum tamen omnia deferri non oportere'.[61] And so, eighty years elapsing and the state transformed, Tiberius Caesar at the ceremony staged on September 17, after proclaiming 'solam divi Augusti mentem tantae molis capacem', goes on to reinforce his profession of reluctance to assume the power he already held, adding the adjuration 'non ad unum omnia deferrent'.[62]

Tiberius, in concluding his declaration, let fall the incautious notion that the burden of government might be shared with others. In the course of the discussion he reverted to it. He professed to be willing to take over 'quaecumque pars sibi mandaretur'.[63] That gave one of the consulars, Asinius Gallus, the chance to intervene with a precise and damaging interrogation—'quam partem rei publicae mandari tibi velis?' Tiberius was disconcerted, and Gallus saw that he had gone too far. His question, he said, was not designed to divide what cannot be divided, but to elicit a firm avowal from Caesar, namely 'unum esse rei publicae corpus atque unius animo regendum'.

The state regarded as an organism, that was not a novel notion. The body requires a head. And so, when the debate (if such it be called) was petering out through fatigue, Q. Haterius was moved to exclaim 'quo usque patieris, Caesar, non adesse caput rei publicae?'[64] The head existed, organic, and it could not be dissevered.[65]

Sixth, the magnitude of the Roman empire. Livy briefly indicates the problem.[66] For Florus the 'corpus imperii' could not hold together 'nisi unius praesidis nutu et quasi anima regeretur'. Torn apart by the civil wars, the 'membra' now unite.[67] It is no surprise that Galba in his oration adopts

---

[60] As argued in *HSCP* LXXIV (1959), 41 f. = *RP* (1979), 416 f.; *Sallust* (1964), 238 f.

[61] *De imp. Cn. Pompei* 52. Cf., on the position of Caesar in 46 BC, *Ad fam.* IV.9.2: 'omnia enim ad unum delata sunt'. [62] *Ann.* I.11.1.

[63] *Ann.* I.12.1. By 'pars' Tiberius surely meant role or function, cf. Suetonius, *Tib.* 25.2: 'partes sibi quas senatui liberet tuendas in re p. depoposcit'. Also, not a division of the power. That Tiberius actually mentioned and defined τρία μέρη (Dio LVII.2.4 f.) is not easy to credit.

[64] *Ann.* I.13.4.

[65] cf. Seneca, *De clem.* I.4.3: 'olim ita se induit rei publicae Caesar ut seduci alterum non possit sine utriusque pernicie.'

[66] Livy, *Praef.* 4: 'ut iam magnitudine laboret sua'.

[67] Florus II.14.6, cf. Velleius II.90.1. The 'membra' occur in a notable passage of Quintus Curtius (X.9.4).

an expedient plea—'si immensum imperii corpus stare ac librari sine rectore posset'.[68]

Various writers put emphasis on the enormous burden: 'tanta moles', 'tanta negotia', or the like.[69] The empire demands a 'rector' or a 'praeses'. Of what nature shall be his status and authority?

Seventh, not despotism. The 'prudentes' duly conclude 'non regno tamen neque dictatura sed principis nomine constitutam rem publicam.'[70] At first sight neutral, or rather prepossessing, the term 'princeps' could convey dubious connotations in the language of the late Republic—'isti principes' for leaders of the oligarchy, 'ipse princeps' for Caesar the Dictator.[71] Annexed by Caesar's heir, 'princeps' admits no questioning.

Addressing Romulus, Ovid boldly bids him make way before Augustus, 'vis tibi grata fuit: florent sub Caesare leges./tu domini nomen, principis ille tenet.'[72] Sharp antithesis is useful for orators and for publicists. Among the platitudes to be culled from the Panegyric of Pliny prime favour should go to 'scis ut sint diversa natura dominatio et principatus'.[73] Cicero in 43 BC had to defend himself from the charge of proposing 'dominatus et principatus' for the benefit of Cassius.[74] Like 'princeps', the word improved. Political terms commonly deserve and suffer debasement.

'Dux' or 'imperator' disclosed the military origins and basis of civil primacy. None the less, 'dux' could be admitted by Horace, 'dux bone'.[75] Ovid has the word no fewer than ten times (and twice in the plural, to indicate the dynasty). Nor is 'dux' restricted to contexts of conquest or of *imperium*. The ruler's attention to the repair of temples is described as 'sacrati provida cura ducis'; and the clever poet can come out with the epigram 'pacificumque ducem'.[76]

Eighth, constitutional monarchy. 'Senatus populusque' conferred the powers on the ruler. The basis of his authority was legal, hence invulnerable to attack or question. Caesar Augustus had the best lawyers on call—and the best orators.[77]

[68] *Hist.* I.16.1.

[69] J. Béranger, o.c. 175 ff. For 'tanta moles', *Ann.* I.4.3.; 11.1. Ovid has 'moles Romani nominis' (*Tr.* II.221). Horace addresses Augustus 'cum tot sustineas et tanta negotia solus' (*Epp.* II.1.1). For the language, cf. Cicero, *Pro Roscio Amerino* 22; Sallust, *Cat.* 53.2.

[70] *Ann.* I.9.5, cf. 1.1: 'nomine principis sub imperium accepit'. The latter phrase, carefully chosen, seems to lack parallel.

[71] Cicero, *Ad fam.* IX.17.3 (in 46): 'ne ipsum quidem principem scire quid futurum sit'; *De imp. Cn. Pompeii* 64: 'isti principes'.   [72] *Fasti* II.141 f.   [73] Pliny, *Pan.* 45.3.

[74] *Phil.* XI.36. Note further *De legibus* III.34: 'dominatus et potentia principum'.

[75] *Odes* IV.5.5.

[76] *Fasti* II.60; IV.408; Propertius has 'ipse . . . dux' in a context far from military (II.16.19 f.).

[77] The authorities on public law tend to be not jurists but either experts in ritual and augury or orators manipulating a 'mos maiorum'.

The summary verdict of Gibbon remains valid: 'an absolute monarchy disguised by the forms of a commonwealth'. Paraphrase will not impair the sense, namely 'absolute rule based on delegated authority'. Between Senate and Princeps there was no division of power, only of functions. The term 'dyarchy' is flawed and flaccid.

As a Roman maxim asserted, 'vis imperii valet, inania tramittuntur'.[78] Words or ceremonies can be passed over. After a brief efflux of time Seneca felt able to speak of 'principes regesque' without distinction.[79] A precise defining of Caesar's prerogative was not the problem.[80] What matters is attitudes and behaviour.

Ninth, the spirit of government. The Princeps comports himself as parent, patron, guardian. The myth of the Founder contributed, whom the Romans acclaimed 'o pater, o genitor'; and Augustus after a time duly acquired the title 'pater patriae'.

In consonance therewith, the concept of trusteeship came in. 'Patrocinium' had been applied to the dominion that the imperial Republic exercised over the nations.[81] Caesar now takes for monopoly the role of 'patronus'. His charge and care of the *res publica* and of the Empire may have been embodied in the *senatus consultum* which assigned the large *provincia* on January 16 of 27 BC.[82] Not that it was defined as any kind of legal prerogative. The word 'tutela' suitably occurs in sundry Latin writers.[83] Less in evidence was 'tutor', which would declare all too plainly that the state was in the position of a woman or a child.

A variety of other terms commends the function of guardian, protector, governor, director, president. According to Cicero, the 'wisdom of our ancestors' established the Senate as 'rei publicae custodem praesidem propugnatorem'; and statesmen are 'custodes gubernatoresque'.[84] In the beginning Romulus was 'patriae custos', likewise Marius in the more recent time.[85] So the Princeps stands on guard, like a soldier vigilant at the post of duty.[86]

For a general description, 'praeses' was also convenient. In the language

---

[78] *Ann.* XV.31.

[79] *De clem.* I.4.3: 'principes regesque et quocumque alio nomine sunt tutores status publici'.

[80] And is not, cf. P. Veyne, o.c. 616: 'les discussions des érudits sur les fondements juridiques du pouvoir impérial ont été aussi volumineuses que pauvres en résultats convaincants. Les discussions plus récentes sur ses fondements idéologiques ont été encore plus byzantines.'

[81] *De officiis* II.27.

[82] cf. φροντίς and προστασία in Dio LIII.12.1. Note also τὴν προστασίαν τῆς ἡγεμονίας in Strabo XVII, p. 840. For 'cura', 'providentia', etc., J. Béranger, o.c. 186 ff.

[83] e.g. Horace, *Odes* IV.15.43; Ovid, *Fasti* I.531. For Valerius Maximus, Tiberius is 'auctor ac tutela nostrae incolumitatis' (IX.11, *ext.* 4).

[84] *Pro Sestio* 137; *Pro C. Rabirio* 26.

[85] *In Cat.* III.24; *Post reditum* 9. The orator does not apply the term to Pompeius Magnus.

[86] Augustus is 'custos' in Horace, *Odes* IV.5.2; 15.17. For 'statio' Ovid, *Tr.* II.219—and his own words in the letter to Gaius and Lucius quoted in Gellius XV.7.3.

of the loyal town council of Pisa, Augustus is both 'custos imperii Romani' and 'praeses' of the whole world.[87] Seneca juxtaposed another term, producing 'legum praesidem civitatisque rectorem.'[88]

Hence arises the conception of rational obedience towards the ruler, as owed to a parent, a guardian, a person holding legitimate authority. 'Pietas' requires no annotation. The less emotional term is 'obsequium'.[89]

Nine types of argument or plea have been cursorily indicated. Caesar Augustus by his victory saved the state, and he welded together the imperial dominions: 'legiones provincias classis, cuncta inter se conexa'. The ruler is deemed to be endowed with the cardinal virtues, he possesses the capacity of mind and will to deal with 'tanta moles' and 'tanta negotia'.

Furthermore, Augustus held the mandate of heaven, ruling land and sea by the consensus of men and of gods.[90] The aristocracy of the intellect concurred. Of philosophers and political scientists, the most reputable were on the side of monarchy; the masters of jurisprudence preferred to stand by order and tradition; and, had the age known economic experts, they would not have gone against the interests of landed proprietors. The Pax Augusta brought not merely 'otium' but a deep calm: 'res tranquillae'.[91]

The emergence of neologisms in a period of revolution is an engaging topic of study. However, much of the political language current in the early Principate goes back to the Republic. Cicero is the main source for formulations found persuasive. Sallust also serves, not least when subversive, demonstrating how words have been perverted from their true meaning, and exposing the 'honesta nomina' that are employed to disguise operations of violence or fraud.

Both the Roman Senate and the senior statesmen (the 'principes civitatis') enjoyed an 'auctoritas' that depended on custom and status, not any 'lex' or 'potestas'. Augustus made a proud pronouncement, that he excelled all men in 'auctoritas'.[92] Which was correct: the true sources of his predominance lay outside the laws and the constitution. 'Auctoritas' enables ends to be achieved without recourse either to legal authority or to violence. It is an emanation of 'potentia'. But this is not the place to investigate or indict the Augustan 'ideology'. The tenth and last plea

---

[87] *ILS* 140.

[88] *De ira* I.6.3. In a tribune's oration in Sallust, 'praesides' are contrasted with 'domini' (*Hist.* III.48.6).

[89] For this notion, *Tacitus* (1958), 28; 547.

[90] cf. Val. Max., *Praef.* (on Tiberius): 'penes quem hominum deorumque consensus maris ac terrae regimen esse volunt'.

[91] *Ann.* I.3.7 (his sole use of the word), cf. Sallust, *Cat.* 16.5: 'tutae tranquillaeque res omnes'. Valerius Maximus commends 'tranquillitatem saeculi nostri' (VIII.13, *praef.*).

[92] *Res Gestae* 34. For 'auctoritas' as more effective than 'potestas', cf. *In Pisonem* 8.

remains, more honourable than many of the others, and it was perhaps of modest comfort to men of sombre understanding.

Tenth, therefore, the doctrine of the middle path. That is, liberty but not licence, discipline without despotism. It is declared with fervour by the Romans at the obsequies of Caesar Augustus.[93] Similarly, Galba when adopting Piso concludes with solemn admonishment: Piso will have to govern a nation that cannot put up with the extremes of either freedom or enslavement.[94]

The doctrine that obtains for the state extends to cover the senator, enjoining a useful and dignified role. Under Tiberius the situation was delicate from the outset, but not at once dangerous. The new ruler was ill at ease, hampered by the prestige of Divus Augustus or by ancient feuds and recent annoyances; and, whereas he encouraged freedom of debate, the high assembly had not enjoyed it in recent years.

Senators failed to discover edifying models in the leaders of society. Eminent noblemen set the standard in subservience. The historian Tacitus was careful to register at an early stage the 'auctoritates adulationesque' pronounced by seven men of rank in epilogue on a prosecution for high treason.[95]

His pages exhibit palmary performances. Alert and successful *novi homines* did not fall short. Thus Ateius Capito, the servile jurist, in pretence of free speech, or old Haterius proposing that a decree of the Senate be inscribed in letters of gold.[96]

That season could still show aristocrats who responded to honour and tradition. The historian is happy to commend Piso the Pontifex.[97] Above all, he was moved by Marcus Lepidus, who steered a safe course between the extremes of abrupt defiance and ignoble deference. Cornelius Tacitus was impelled by this example towards freedom of the will, against the dominance of fate and the stars.[98]

Balance and discretion were needed in Rome of the Caesars, and they were not always cheated of recompense in good fame. Tacitus had thus recounted and exhibited the career of Julius Agricola: there could still be great men under bad emperors.

Sober duty and avoidance of extremes was also desirable in the ruler. Caesar Augustus in the notorious anecdote gave the highest award to Marcus Lepidus: 'capacem sed aspernantem'.[99]

---

[93] Dio LVI.43.4.
[94] *Hist.* I.16.4: 'imperaturus es hominibus qui nec totam servitutem pati possunt nec totam libertatem'.
[95] *Ann.* II.32.1 f.
[96] III.70.2 f., cf. 75 (the obituary notice on Capito); 57.2.
[97] VI.10.3: 'nullius servilis sententiae sponte auctor'.
[98] IV.20.2.   [99] I.13.2.

Not an exhilarating prospect, the middle path, so it appears. It is the recourse of the opportunist and the careerist. The other name is compromise or collusion. Yet such is the nature of political life. It exploits ambiguities, it seeks to have the advantage both ways.

Sundry phenomena in the phraseology of different ages furnish guidance and instruction. A familiar weapon in the arsenals of deception is the oxymoron, combining a pair of elements that appeared to conflict. Thus 'democratic planning' to commend a policy, or 'centralized democracy' as a system of government.[100] It is no surprise that the Romans tried (or pretended) to effect a union between 'libertas et principatus'.[101] Their political thought, so far at least as it found expression in written memorials, was rudimentary and in a large measure predictable. It has parallel among the ingenuous in other climes.[102]

The 'middle path' rejects both the tyrant and the doctrinaire or visionary. It might therefore be endorsed as a 'useful prejudice' by persons not normally subject to illusion. Indeed, it resembles the much praised 'mixed constitution'—which, as Tacitus pointed out, is not easy to create or likely to last for any time.[103]

The history of Roman oratory demonstrated that any aspiration for a double benefit to accrue from two epochs and two political systems was a delusion. Great eloquence (that of the Republic) was not compatible with stable government. Such is the conclusion of the *Dialogus*, not without gentle irony. The ruler now holds the arbitrament, he is the wisest, and men of good sense are quick to reach unanimity.[104]

The language of Tacitus may have some relevance to the pronouncement of some unnamed sage in the recent time: 'in a true democracy there is no place for a serious difference of opinion on great issues.' The maxim clearly obtains when the issues are defined (or have been decided) by those who hold the power.

[100] The latter phrase is taken from the memoirs of N. Kruschev.
[101] The conjunction occurs in Tacitus, *Agr.* 3.1 (on Nerva).
[102] The collected speeches of a recent prime minister bore the title *Liberty and Order*.
[103] *Ann.* IV.33.1.
[104] *Dial.* 41.4.

APPENDIX: THE CONSULS

80 BC–AD 14

The prefatory matter in the Appendix to *Rom. Rev.* registered and annotated the notable accessions accruing from the *Fasti Magistrorum Vici*, first published in 1935. Here omitted. See now A. Degrassi, *Inscriptiones Italiae* XIII.I (1947). *Fasti Consulares et Triumphales*. Further, Degrassi's *I Fasti Consulares dell' Impero Romano* (1952), beginning with 30 BC.

The list now printed brings some minor improvements. And observe that L. Cornelius, consul suffect in 38, is revealed as a Lentulus (*AE* 1945, 66), that in 1939 the *suffecti* of the year 31 had been incorrectly disposed.

What follows does not pretend to be in any sense an edition of a part of the *Fasti*. It is merely an up-to-date list of consuls, designed for the convenience of the historical student. The filiation of consuls, where known, is given, for it is often a valuable clue to ready identification; and *cognomina* are added, even when they do not occur in the documents that attest the consulates of the men in question.

BC

80	L. Cornelius L. f. Sulla Felix II: Q. Caecilius Q. f. Metellus Pius
79	P. Servilius C. f. Vatia: Ap. Claudius Ap. f. Pulcher
78	M. Aemilius Q. f. Lepidus: Q. Lutatius Q. f. Catulus
77	D. Junius D. f. Brutus: Mam. Aemilius Mam. f. Lepidus Livianus
76	Cn. Octavius M. f.: C. Scribonius C. f. Curio
75	L. Octavius Cn. f.: C. Aurelius M. f. Cotta
74	L. Licinius L. f. Lucullus: M. Aurelius M. f. Cotta
73	M. Terentius M. f. Varro Lucullus: C. Cassius L. f. Longinus
72	L. Gellius L. f. Poplicola: Cn. Cornelius Cn. f. Lentulus Clodianus
71	P. Cornelius P. f. Lentulus Sura: Cn. Aufidius Orestes
70	Cn. Pompeius Cn. f. Magnus: M. Licinius P. f. Crassus
69	Q. Hortensius L. f.: Q. Caecilius C. f. Metellus Creticus
68	L. Caecilius C. f. Metellus: Q. Marcius Q. f. Rex
67	C. Calpurnius Piso: M'. Acilius M'. f. Glabrio
66	M'. Aemilius Lepidus: L. Volcacius Tullus
65	L. Aurelius M. f. Cotta: L. Manlius L. f. Torquatus
64	L. Julius L. f. Caesar: C. Marcius C. f. Figulus
63	M. Tullius M. f. Cicero: C. Antonius M. f.
62	D. Junius M. f. Silanus: L. Licinius L. f. Murena
61	M. Pupius M. f. Piso: M. Valerius M. f. Messalla (Niger)
60	Q. Caecilius Q. f. Metellus Celer: L. Afranius A. f.
59	C. Julius C. f. Caesar: M. Calpurnius C. f. Bibulus
58	L. Calpurnius L. f. Piso Caesoninus: A. Gabinius A. f.
57	P. Cornelius P. f. Lentulus Spinther: Q. Caecilius Q. f. Metellus Nepos
56	Cn. Cornelius P. f. Lentulus Marcellinus: L. Marcius L. f. Philippus
55	Cn. Pompeius Cn. f. Magnus II: M. Licinius P. f. Crassus II

54   L. Domitius Cn. f. Ahenobarbus: Ap. Claudius Ap. f. Pulcher
53   Cn. Domitius M. f. Calvinus: M. Valerius M. f. Messalla (Rufus)
52   Cn. Pompeius Cn. f. Magnus III: Q. Caecilius Q. f. Metellus Pius Scipio
51   Ser. Sulpicius Q. f. Rufus: M. Claudius M. f. Marcellus
50   L. Aemilius M. f. Paullus: C. Claudius C. f. Marcellus
49   C. Claudius M. f. Marcellus: L. Cornelius P. f. Lentulus Crus
48   C. Julius C. f. Caesar II: P. Servilius P. f. Vatia Isauricus
47   Q. Fufius Q. f. Calenus: P. Vatinius P. f.
46   C. Julius C. f. Caesar III: M. Aemilius M. f. Lepidus
45   C. Julius C. f. Caesar IV (without colleague)
         Q. Fabius Q. f. Maximus: C. Trebonius C. f.
         C. Caninius C. f. Rebilus
44   C. Julius C. f. Caesar V: M. Antonius M. f.
         P. Cornelius P. f. Dolabella
43   C. Vibius C. f. Pansa Caetronianus: A. Hirtius A. f.
         C. Julius C. f. Caesar (Octavianus): Q. Pedius (Q. f.?)
         P. Ventidius P. f.: C. Carrinas C. f.
42   M. Aemilius M. f. Lepidus II: L. Munatius L. f. Plancus
41   L. Antonius M. f.: P. Servilius P. f. Vatia Isauricus II
40   Cn. Domitius M. f. Calvinus II: C. Asinius Cn. f. Pollio
         L. Cornelius L. f. Balbus: P. Canidius P. f. (?Crassus)
39   L. Marcius L. f. Censorinus: C. Calvisius C. f. Sabinus
         C. Cocceius (Balbus): P. Alfenus P. f. Varus
38   Ap. Claudius C. f. Pulcher: C. Norbanus C. f. Flaccus
         L. Cornelius Lentulus: L. Marcius L. f. Philippus
37   M. Vipsanius L. f. Agrippa: L. Caninius L. f. Gallus
                                     T. Statilius T. f. Taurus
36   L. Gellius L. f. Poplicola: M. Cocceius Nerva
         L. Nonius (L. f. Asprenas): Marcius
35   L. Cornificius L. f.: Sex. Pompeius Sex. f.
         P. Cornelius (? P. f. Scipio): T. Peducaeus
34   M. Antonius M. f. II: L. Scribonius L. f. Libo
         L. Sempronius L. f. Atratinus: Paullus Aemilius L. f. Lepidus
         C. Memmius C. f.: M. Herennius (M. f. Picens)
33   Imp. Caesar Divi f. II: L. Volcacius L. f. Tullus
         L. Autronius P. f. Paetus: L. Flavius
         C. Fonteius C. f. Capito: M. Acilius (M'. f.?) Glabrio
         L. Vinicius M. f.: Q. Laronius
32   Cn. Domitius L. f. Ahenobarbus: C. Sosius C. f.
         L. Cornelius Cinna: M. Valerius M. f. Messalla
31   Imp. Caesar Divi f. III: M. Valerius M. f. Messalla Corvinus
                                     M. Titius L. f.
                                     Cn. Pompeius Q. f.
30   Imp. Caesar Divi f. IV: M. Licinius M. f. Crassus
                                     C. Antistius C. f. Vetus
                                     M. Tullius M. f. Cicero
                                     L. Saenius L. f. (Balbinus)

29	Imp. Caesar Divi f. V: Sex. Appuleius Sex. f.
	Potitus Valerius M. f. Messalla
28	Imp. Caesar Divi f. VI: M. Vipsanius L. f. Agrippa II
27	Imp. Caesar Divi f. VII: M. Vipsanius L. f. Agrippa III
26	Imp. Caesar Divi f. Augustus VIII: T. Statilius T. f. Taurus II
25	Imp. Caesar Divi f. Augustus IX: M. Junius M. f. Silanus
24	Imp. Caesar Divi f. Augustus X: C. Norbanus C. f. Flaccus
23	Imp. Caesar Divi f. Augustus XI: A. Terentius A. f. Varro Murena
	L. Sestius P. f. Quirinalis: Cn. Calpurnius Cn. f. Piso
22	M. Claudius M. f. Marcellus Aeserninus: L. Arruntius L. f.
21	M. Lollius M. f.: Q. Aemilius M'. f. Lepidus
20	M. Appuleius Sex. f.: P. Silius P. f. Nerva
19	C. Sentius C. f. Saturninus: Q. Lucretius Q. f. Vespillo
	M. Vinicius P. f.
18	P. Cornelius P. f. Lentulus Marcellinus: Cn. Cornelius L. f. Lentulus
17	C. Furnius C. f.: C. Junius C. f. Silanus
16	L. Domitius Cn. f. Ahenobarbus: P. Cornelius P. f. Scipio
	L. Tarius Rufus
15	M. Livius L. f. Drusus Libo: L. Calpurnius L. f. Piso (Pontifex)
14	M. Licinius M. f. Crassus Frugi: Cn. Cornelius Cn. f. Lentulus (Augur)
13	Ti. Claudius Ti. f. Nero: P. Quinctilius Sex. f. Varus
12	M. Valerius M. f. Messalla Appianus: P. Sulpicius P. f. Quirinius
	C. Valgius C. f. Rufus
	C. Caninius C. f. Rebilus: L. Volusius Q. f. Saturninus
11	Q. Aelius Q. f. Tubero: Paullus Fabius Q. f. Maximus
10	Africanus Fabius Q. f. Maximus: Iullus Antonius M. f.
9	Nero Claudius Ti. f. Drusus: T. Quinctius T. f. Crispinus Sulpicianus
8	C. Marcius L. f. Censorinus: C. Asinius C. f. Gallus
7	Ti. Claudius Ti. f. Nero II: Cn. Calpurnius Cn. f. Piso
6	D. Laelius D. f. Balbus: C. Antistius C. f. Vetus
5	Imp. Caesar Divi f. Augustus XII: L. Cornelius P. f. Sulla
	L. Vinicius L. f.
	Q. Haterius: C. Sulpicius C. f. Galba
4	C. Calvisius C. f. Sabinus: L. Passienus Rufus
	C. Caelius: Galus Sulpicius
3	L. Cornelius L. f. Lentulus: M. Valerius M. f. Messalla Messallinus
2	Imp. Caesar Divi f. Augustus XIII: M. Plautius M. f. Silvanus
	L. Caninius L. f. Gallus
	C. Fufius Geminus
	Q. Fabricius
1	Cossus Cornelius Cn. f. Lentulus: L. Calpurnius Cn. f. Piso (Augur)

A. Plautius: A. Caecina (Severus)

AD

1 C. Caesar Aug. f.: L. Aemilius Paulli f. Paullus
M. Herennius M. f. Picens

2 P. Vinicius M. f.: P. Alfenus P. f. Varus
P. Cornelius Cn. f. (Lentulus) Scipio: T. Quinctius T. f. Crispinus
Valerianus

3 L. Aelius L. f. Lamia: M. Servilius M. f.
P. Silius P. f.: L. Volusius L. f. Saturninus

4 Sex. Aelius Q. f. Catus: C. Sentius C. f. Saturninus
Cn. Sentius C. f. Saturninus: C. Clodius C. f. Licinus

5 L. Valerius Potiti f. Messalla Volesus: Cn. Cornelius L. f. Cinna Magnus
C. Vibius C. f. Postumus: C. Ateius L. f. Capito

6 M. Aemilius Paulli f. Lepidus: L. Arruntius L. f.
L. Nonius L. f. Asprenas

7 Q. Caecilius Q. f. Metellus Creticus Silanus: A. Licinius A. f. Nerva Silianus
: Lucilius Longus

8 M. Furius P. f. Camillus: Sex. Nonius L. f. Quinctilianus
L. Apronius C. f: A. Vibius C. f. Habitus

9 C. Poppaeus Q. f. Sabinus: Q. Sulpicius Q. f. Camerinus
M. Papius M. f. Mutilus: Q. Poppaeus Q. f. Secundus

10 P. Cornelius P. f. Dolabella: C. Junius C. f. Silanus
Ser. Cornelius Cn. f. Lentulus Maluginensis: Q. Junius Blaesus

11 M'. Aemilius Q. f. Lepidus: T. Statilius T. f. Taurus
L. Cassius L. f. Longinus

12 Germanicus Ti. f. Caesar: C. Fonteius C. f. Capito
C. Visellius C. f. Varro

13 C. Silius P. f. A. Caecina Largus: L. Munatius L. f. Plancus

14 Sex. Pompeius Sex. f.: Sex. Appuleius Sex. f.

BIBLIOGRAPHY

The following list comprises periodical articles and the like cited in the footnotes. It excludes books and monographs: there registered by author, title, and date.

ADAMS, F. 'The Consular Brothers of Sejanus', *AJP* LXXVI (1955), 70.

ADAMS, J. P. *AJP* C (1979), 460. Review of B. Levick, *Tiberius the Politician*.

AIGNER, H. '*M. Servilius Nonianus, cos. 35 n. Chr., ein Servilius oder ein Nonius?*', *Historia* XXI (1972), 507.

ALFÖLDY, G. 'Senatoren in der römischen Provinz Dalmatia', *Epigraphische Studien* V (1968), 99.

ALLEN, W. 'The Addressees in Horace's First Book of *Epistles*', *Studies in Philology* LXVII (1970), 255.

ANDERSON, J.G.C. 'Some Questions Bearing on the Date and Place of Composition of Strabo's *Geography*', *Anatolian Studies . . . W. M. Ramsay* (1923), 7.

ANDREWS, A. C. 'The Parsnip as a Food in the Classical Era', *CP* LIII (1958), 145.

APPLEBAUM, S. 'The Zealots. The Case for Revaluation', *JRS* LXI (1971), 156.

ATKINSON, K. M. T. 'The Governors of the Province Asia in the Reign of Augustus', *Historia* VII (1958), 300.

——— 'Constitutional and Legal Aspects of the Trials of Marcus Primus and Varro Murena', *Historia* IX (1960), 440.

BADIAN, E. 'Caepio and Norbanus', *Historia* VI (1957), 318 = *Studies in Greek and Roman History* (1964), 34.

——— 'Caesar's *Cursus* and the Intervals between Offices', *JRS* XLIX (1959), 81 = *Studies in Greek and Roman History* (1964), 140.

——— 'Waiting for Sulla', *JRS* LII (1962), 52 = *Studies in Greek and Roman History* (1964), 206.

——— 'Cato and Cyprus', *JRS* LV (1965), 110.

——— *JRS* LVII (1967), 216. Review of M. Gelzer, *Kl. Schriften*.

——— 'The Quaestorship of Tiberius Nero', *Mnem.* XXVII (1974), 160.

——— 'Notes on the *Laudatio* of Agrippa', *CJ* LXXVI (1980), 97.

——— ' "Crisis Theories" and the Beginning of the Principate', *Romanitas—Christianitas* (*Festschrift J. Straub*, 1982), 18.

BALL, R. J. 'The Structure of Tibullus I. 7', *Latomus* XXXIV (1975), 729.

BALSDON, J. P. V. D. 'The Ides of March', *Historia* VII (1958), 80.

BARNES, T. D. 'The Victories of Augustus', *JRS* LXIV (1974), 21.

——— 'Who were the Nobility of the Roman Empire?', *Phoenix* XXVIII (1974), 4.

——— 'Julia's Child', *Phoenix* XXXV (1981), 362.

BAYER, E. 'Zu den Ehen der jüngeren Marcella', *Historia* XVII (1968), 118.

BERTRANDY, F. 'Thibilis (Announa) de Juba Iᵉʳ au triumvir M. Aemilius Lepidus', *Karthago* XIX (1980), 87.

BICKEL, E. 'Die Lygdamus-Elegien', *Rh. Mus.* CIII (1960), 97.

BIRCH, R. A. 'The Settlement of 26 June A.D. 4 and its Aftermath', *CQ* XXXI (1981), 443.

BIRD, H. W. 'L. Aelius Seianus and his Political Influence', *Latomus* XXVIII (1969), 61.

BLOCH, H. 'The Funerary Inscription of the Physician of Caecilia Crassi in the Fogg Art Museum', *HSCP* LXXXVI (1982), 141.

BOSWORTH, A. B. 'Asinius Pollio and Augustus', *Historia* XXI (1972), 441.

—— 'Tacitus and Asinius Gallus', *Am. Journ. Anc. Hist.* II (1977), 173.

—— 'Augustus and August. Some Pitfalls of Historical Fiction', *HSCP* LXXXVI (1982), 151.

BOWERSOCK, G. W. 'A Date in the Eighth Eclogue', *HSCP* LXXV (1971), 73.

BRADSHAW, A. T. von S. 'Horace, *Odes* 4.1', *CQ* XX (1970), 142.

BRAUNERT, H. 'Der römische Provinzialzensus und der Schätzungsbericht des Lukas-Evangeliums', *Historia* VI (1957), 192.

BRISCOE, J. 'Supporters and Opponents of Tiberius Gracchus', *JRS* LXIV (1974), 125.

BRUNT, P. A. 'The Lex Valeria Cornelia', *JRS* LI (1961), 71.

—— *JRS* LI (1961), 234. Review of P. Sattler, *Augustus und der Senat*.

—— *JRS* LIII (1963), 170. Review of H. D. Meyer, *Die Aussenpolitik des Augustus und die augusteische Dichtung*.

—— 'Two Great Roman Landowners', *Latomus* XXXIV (1975), 619.

—— '*Nobilitas* and *Novitas*', *JRS* LXXII (1982), 7.

CADOUX, T. J. 'Sallust and Sempronia, *Humanitatis Vindex*' (*Essays in Honour of J. H. Bishop*, Armidale, 1980), 93.

CAMERON, A. 'The *Garland* of Philip', *GRBS* XXI (1980), 43.

CARCOPINO, J. 'Notes biographiques sur M. Valerius Messala Corvinus', *Rev. Phil.* LXXII (1946), 96.

CARTLEDGE, P. 'The Second Thoughts of Augustus on the *Res Publica* in 28/7 B.C.', *Hermathena* CXIX (1975), 30.

CASSOLA, F. 'I templi di Marte ultore e i ludi Martiales', *Studi . . . in memoria di Fulvio Grosso* (1981), 106.

CHANDLER, D. C. '*Quaestor Ostiensis*', *Historia* XXVII (1978), 328.

CHASTAGNOL, A. 'La Naissance de l'*Ordo Senatorius*', *MÉFRA* LXXXV (1973), 583.

—— 'La Crise de recrutement sénatorial', *Miscellanea . . . Eugenio Manni* II (1980), 465.

CHRIST, K. 'Zur augusteischen Germanienpolitik', *Chiron* VII (1977), 149.

CICHORIUS, C. 'Zur Familiengeschichte Seians', *Hermes* XXXIX (1904), 461.

—— 'Ein neuer Historiker und die Anfänge von Livius' schriftstellerischer Tätigkeit', *Römische Studien* (1922), 261.

—— 'Historisches zu den Logistorici', ib. 226.

—— 'Neues zu Krinagoras', ib. 306.

—— 'Untersuchungen zu Pomponius Secundus, d. Zur Familie des Dichters', ib. 429.

CLAUSEN, W. 'Callimachus and Latin Poetry', *GRBS* V (1964), 181.

CORBISHLEY, T. 'A Note on the Date of the Syrian Governorship of M. Titius', *JRS* XXIV (1934), 43.

CORNELL, T. J. *JRS* LXXII (1982), 203. Review of T. P. Wiseman, *Clio's Cosmetics*.

CROOK, J. '*Sponsione Provocare*. Its Place in Roman Litigation', *JRS* LXVI (1976), 132.

DALY, L. J. 'Augustus and the Murder of Varro Murena', *Klio* LXVI (1984), 157.

—— and REITER, W. L., 'The Gallus Affair and Augustus' *Lex Julia maiestatis*. A study in Historical Chronology and Causality', *Studies in Latin Literature and Roman History* I (ed. C. Deroux, 1979), 289.

DAVIES, C. 'Poetry in the Circle of Messalla', *Greece & Rome* XX (1973), 25.

DAVIS, G. 'The Persona of Licymnia. A Revaluation of Horace, *Carm.* 2.12', *Philologus* CXIX (1975), 70.

DEGRASSI, A. 'Osservazioni su alcuni consoli suffecti dell' età di Augusto e Tiberio', *Epigraphica* VII (1946), 34 = *Scritti Vari* I (1962), 559.

DESSAU, H. 'Livius und Augustus', *Hermes* XLI (1906), 142.

DEVREKER, J. 'C. Messalla Vipstanus Gallus, ou l'histoire d'un nom', *ZPE* 22 (1976), 203.

ECK, W. 'Die Familie der Volusii Saturnini in neuen Inschriften aus Lucus Feroniae', *Hermes* C (1972), 461.

—— 'Über die prätorischen Prokonsulate in der Kaiserzeit', *Zephyrus* XXIII/XXIV (1972/3), 233.

—— 'Ergänzungen zu den Fasti Consulares des 1 und 2 Jh. n. Chr.', *Historia* XXIV (1975), 324.

EHRHARDT, C. 'Messalina and the Succession to Claudius', *Antichthon* XII (1978), 51.

FERRILL, A. 'Prosopography and the Last Years of Augustus', *Historia* XX (1971), 718.

—— 'Augustus and his Daughter. A Modern Myth', *Studies in Latin Literature and Roman History* II (ed. C. Deroux, 1980), 332.

FRISCH, P. 'Zu den Elogien des Augustusforums', *ZPE* 39 (1980), 81.

FUCHS, G. 'Zur Baugeschichte der Basilica Aemilia in republikanischer Zeit', *Röm. Mitt.* LXIII (1956), 14.

GASCOU, J. 'M. Licinius Crassus Frugi, légat de Claude en Maurétanie', *Mélanges . . . Pierre Boyancé* (1974), 299.

GEIGER, J. 'The Last Servilii Caepiones of the Republic', *Ancient Society* IV (1973), 148.

GELZER, M. 'Die Nobilität der Kaiserzeit', *Hermes* L (1915), 395.

GOAR, R. J. 'Horace, Velleius Paterculus and Tiberius Caesar', *Latomus* XXXV (1976), 43.

GORDON, A. E. 'Potitus Valerius Messalla, Consul Suffect 29 B.C.', *U. of Cal. Pub. in Class. Arch.* III.2 (1954), 31.

GRAY, E. W. *CR* XIX (1969), 825. Review of Chr. Meier, *Res Publica Amissa*.

—— 'The Imperium of M. Agrippa', *ZPE* 6 (1970), 927.

GRIFFIN, J. 'Augustan Poetry and the Life of Luxury', *JRS* LXVI (1976), 87.

—— 'Propertius and Antony', *JRS* LXVII (1977), 17.

—— *JRS* LXX (1980), 182. Review of Nisbet and Hubbard's *Commentary* on Horace, *Odes*, Book II.

GRIFFIN, M. T. *'De Brevitate Vitae'*, *JRS* LII (1962), 104.

—— 'The Elder Seneca and Spain', *JRS* LXII (1972), 1.

—— 'The Tribune C. Cornelius', *JRS* LXIII (1973), 196.

GRIMAL, P. 'Les Odes romaines d'Horace et les causes de la guerre civile', *Rev. ét. lat.* LIII (1975), 135.

GROAG, E. 'Studien zur Kaisergeschichte III. Der Sturz der Julia', *Wiener Studien* XLI (1919), 74.

—— 'Prosopographische Beiträge VII. M. Plautius Silvanus', *Jahreshefte* XXI/XXII (1924), *Beiblatt* 445.

—— 'Zur senatorischen Gefolgschaft des Caesar im actischen Krieg', *Laureae Aquincenses Memoriae Valentini Kuzsinsky Dicatae* II (1941), 30.

HANSLIK, R. 'Horaz und Varro Murena', *Rh. Mus.* XCVI (1953), 282.

HANSON, A. E. 'The Copies of a Petition to the Prefect', *ZPE* 47 (1982), 233.

HARVEY, P. 'Catullus 114–115. Mentula, bonus agricola', *Historia* XXVIII (1979), 329.

HASLAM, M. W. 'Augustus' Funeral Oration for Agrippa', *CJ* LXXV (1980), 193.

HERRMANN, P. 'Inschriften aus dem Heraion von Samos', *Ath. Mitt.* LXXV (1960), 130.

HERZ, P. 'Der Aufbruch des Gaius Caesar in den Osten', *ZPE* 39 (1980), 285.

HILL, H. 'Nobilitas in the Imperial Period', *Historia* XVIII (1969), 230.

HIRSCHFELD, O. 'Die römische Staatszeitung und die Akklamationen im Senat', *Kl. Schriften* (1913), 682.

HIRST, G. M. 'Note on the Date of Livy's Birth and on the Termination of his History', *Collected Classical Papers* (1938), 12.

HOHL, E. 'Zu den Testamenten des Augustus', *Klio* XXX (1937), 323.

—— 'Ein Strafgericht Oktavians und ein Gnadenakt des Augustus', *Würzburger Jahrbücher* III (1948), 107.

HOLLADAY, A. J. 'The Election of Magistrates', *Latomus* XXXVII (1978), 874.

HOPKINS, M. K. 'The Age of Roman Girls at Marriage', *Population Studies* XVIII (1965), 309.

HUMPFREY, J. 'The Three Daughters of Agrippina Major', *Am. Journ. Anc. Hist.* IV (1979), 125.

INSTINSKY, H. U. 'Augustus und die Adoption des Tiberius', *Hermes* XCIV (1966), 324.

JOCELYN, H. D. 'The Ruling Class of the Roman Republic and Greek Philosophers', *John Rylands Library Bulletin* LIX (1977), 323.

JONES, A. H. M. 'The Elections under Augustus', *JRS* XLV (1955), 9 = *Studies in Roman Government and Law* (1960), 27.

Keil, J. and Wilhelm, A. 'Vorläufiger Bericht über eine Reise in Kilikien', *Jahreshefte* xviii (1915), *Beiblatt* 6.

Kenney, E. J. 'A Question of Taste. Horace *Epistles* 1.14.6–9', *Illinois Class. Stud.* ii (1977), 229.

Klingner, F. 'Über die Recensio der Horazhandschriften', *I. Hermes* lxx (1935), 249.

Koenen, L. 'Die "Laudatio Funebris" des Augustus für Agrippa auf einem neuen Papyrus', *ZPE* 5 (1970), 217.

Kraft, K. 'Q. Aelius L. f. Lamia, Münzmeister und Freund des Horaz', *Jahrbuch für Numismatik und Geldgeschichte* xvi (1966), 23.

Krömer, D. 'Textkritisches zu Augustus und Tiberius (Res gestae c. 34—Tac. ann. 6, 30, 3)', *ZPE* 28 (1978), 127.

Kunkel, W. 'Über die Entstehung des Senatsgerichts', *Kl. Schriften* (1974), 267.

Lacey, W. K. '*Summi fastigii vocabulum*: the Story of a Title', *JRS* lxix (1979), 28.
—— '2 b.c. and Julia's Adultery', *Antichthon* xiv (1980), 127.

Laffi, U. 'Le iscrizioni relative all' introduzione nel 9 a.c. del nuovo calendario della provincia d'Asia', *Studi classici ed orientali* xvi (1967), 5.

Last, H. M. 'Letter to N. H. Baynes', *JRS* xxxvii (1947), 152.

Latte, K. 'Livy's *Patavinitas*', *CP* (1940), 56.

Levick, B. 'The Beginning of Tiberius' Career', *CQ* xxi (1971), 478.
—— 'Tiberius' Retirement to Rhodes in 6 b.c.', *Latomus* xxxi (1972), 779.
—— 'The Fall of Julia the Younger', *Latomus* xxxv (1976), 301.
—— 'Concordia at Rome', *Scripta Nummaria Romana* (*Essays . . . C. H. V. Sutherland*, 1978), 217.
—— 'The *Senatus Consultum* from Larinum', *JRS* lxxiii (1983), 97.

Long, A. A. 'Hellenistic Philosophy. Stoics, Epicureans, Sceptics', *Proc. Camb. Phil. Soc.* xxiv (1978), 43.

Marx, F. A. 'Das Todesjahr des Redners Messalla', *Wiener Studien* xix (1897), 150.

Meier, Chr. 'Matthias Gelzers Beitrag zur Erkenntnis der Struktur von Gesellschaft und Politik der späten römischen Republik', *Matthias Gelzer und die römische Geschichte* (1977), 29.

Millar, F. 'The Emperor, the Senate and the Provinces', *JRS* lvi (1966), 156.
—— 'Triumvirate and Principate', *JRS* lxiii (1973), 50.
—— 'Emperors, Frontiers and Foreign Relations, 31 b.c. to a.d. 378', *Britannia* xiii (1982), 1.

Mitchell, J. F. 'The Torquati', *Historia* xv (1966), 23.

Mitchell, S. 'Legio VII and the Garrison of Augustan Galatia', *CQ* xxvi (1976), 298.

Momigliano, A. '*Panegyricus Messallae* and "Panegyricus Vespasiani" ', *JRS* xx (1940), 39.

Mommsen, Th. 'Die patricischen Claudiér', *Römische Forschungen* i² (1864), 285.
—— 'Zur Lebensgeschichte des jüngeren Plinius', *Hermes* iii (1869), 31 = *Ges. Schriften* iv (1906), 366.

—— 'Über die Bildnisse der römischen Proconsuln auf den Provinzialmünzen der augustischen Epoche', *Hermes* III (1969), 268 = *Ges. Schriften* IV (1906), 183.

MOREAU, P. 'De quelques termes de parenté chez Tacite', *Mélanges . . . Pierre Wuilleumier* (1980), 239.

MOTZO, B. R. 'I commentari di Agrippina madre di Nerone', *Studi Cagliaritani* I (1927), 19.

MÜNZER, F. 'Atticus als Geschichtsschreiber', *Hermes* XL (1905), 50.

—— 'Die römischen Vestalinnen bis zur Kaiserzeit', *Philologus* XCII (1937), 47; 199.

NIPPERDEY, K. 'Vorläufige Bemerkungen zu den kleinen Schriften des Tacitus III', *Rh. Mus.* XIX (1864), 270.

NISBET, R. G. M. *CR* XVIII (1968), 55. Review of W. Wili, *Horaz.*

—— *CR* XIX (1969), 173. Review of E. Doblhofer, *Die Augustuspanegyrik des Horaz.*

OLIVER, J. H. 'The Descendants of Asinius Pollio', *AJP* LXVIII (1947), 147.

PANCIERA, S. 'Ancora sui consoli dell'anno 13 d.c.', *Bull. Comm.* LXXIX (1963/4), 94.

PELLING, C. B. R. 'Plutarch's Method of Work in the Roman Lives', *JHS* XCIX (1979), 74.

PERL, G. 'Die römischen Provinzbeamten in Cyrenae und Creta zur Zeit der Republik', *Klio* LII (1970), 319.

PETRIKOVITS, H. v. 'Arminius', *Bonner Jahrbücher* CLXVI (1966), 177.

PREMERSTEIN, A. v. 'Die Anfänge der Provinz Moesien', *Jahreshefte* I (1898), *Beiblatt* 145.

—— 'Der Daker-und Germanensieger M. Vinicius (Cos. 19 v. Chr.) und sein Enkel (Cos. 30 und 45 n. Chr.)', *Jahreshefte* XXIX (1934), 60.

QUINN, K. *Phoenix* XXXIV (1980), 257. Review of Nisbet and Hubbard's *Commentary* on Horace's *Odes*, Book II.

RAMSAY, W. M. 'Studies in the Roman Province Galatia', *JRS* VII (1917), 229.

RAPSAERT-CHARLIER, M.-TH. '*Clarissima Femina*', *Rev. int. des Droits de l'Antiquité* XXVIII (1981), 189.

RAWSON, E. 'The Eastern *Clientelae* of Clodius and the Claudii', *Historia* XXII (1973), 219.

—— 'Caesar's Heritage. Hellenistic Kings and their Roman Equals', *JRS* LXV (1975), 148.

—— 'More on the *Clientelae* of the patrician Claudii', *Historia* XXVI (1977), 346.

—— '*Crassorum Funera*', *Latomus* XLI (1982), 540.

REYNOLDS, J. 'Cyrenaica, Pompey and Cn. Cornelius Lentulus Marcellinus', *JRS* LII (1962), 97.

—— 'Roman Inscriptions 1966–1970', *JRS* LXI (1971), 136.

—— 'The Origins and Beginning of Imperial Cult at Aphrodisias', *Proc. Camb. Phil. Soc.* xxvi (1980), 70.

RICHARDSON, L. 'Hercules Musarum and the Porticus Philippi in Rome', *AJA* xxxi (1977), 355.

RODGERS, R. H. '*Curatores Aquarum*', *HSCP* lxxxvi (1982), 171.

ROGERS, R. S. 'Lucius Arruntius', *CP* xxvi (1931), 31.

ROMER, F. E. 'A Numismatic Date for the Departure of C. Caesar?', *TAPA* cviii (1978), 187.

ROUGÉ, J. 'La Date de naissance de Sextus Pompée', *Rev. ét. lat.* xlvii (1969), 180.

SALMON, E. T. 'The Resurgence of the Roman Patricians *ca.* 100 B.C.', *Rev. ét lat.* xlvii *bis* (1969), 321.

SCHEID, J. 'Scribonia Caesaris et les Julio-Claudiens', *MÉFRA* lxxxvii (1975), 349.

—— 'Les Prêtres officiels sous les Julio-Claudiens', *ANRW* ii.16 (1978), 610.

—— 'Scribonia Caesaris et les Cornelii Lentuli', *BCH* c (1976), 485.

SCHMITTHENNER, W. 'Octavians militärische Unternehmungen in den Jahren 35–33 v. Chr.', *Historia* vii (1958), 189.

—— 'Augustus' spanischer Feldzug und der Kampf um den Prinzipat', *Historia* xi (1962), 29.

SCHNURBEIN, S. v. 'Untersuchungen zur Geschichte der römischen Militärlager an der Lippe', *BRGK* lxii (1981), 5.

SCOTT, K. 'The Political Propaganda of 44–30 B.C.', *Mem. Am. Ac. Rome* xi (1933), 1.

SEAGER, R. 'Neu sinas Medos equitare inultos. Horace, the Parthians and Augustan Foreign Policy', *Athenaeum* lviii (1980), 103.

SEALEY, R. 'The Political Attachments of L. Aelius Seianus', *Phoenix* xv (1961), 97.

SHERK, R. K. 'Roman Galatia. The Governors from 25 B.C. to A.D. 114', *ANRW* ii.7 (1980), 954.

SIMON, E. 'Das neugefundene Bildnis des Gaius Caesar', *Mainzer Zeitschrift* lviii (1963), 1.

SIMPSON, C. J. 'The Date of the Dedication of the Temple of Mars Ultor', *JRS* lxvii (1977), 91.

STEIN, E. 'Kleine Beiträge zur römischen Geschichte II. Zur Kontroverse über die römische Nobilität der Kaiserzeit', *Hermes* lii (1917), 564.

STEWART, A. F. 'To Entertain an Emperor. Sperlonga, Laokoon, and Tiberius at the Dinner-Table', *JRS* lxvii (1977), 76.

STRASBURGER H. 'Der Scipionenkreis', *Hermes* xciv (1966), 60 = *Studien zur alten Geschichte* II (1982), 946.

SUERBAUM, W. 'Merkwürdige Geburtstage', *Chiron* x (1980), 327.

SUMNER, G. V. 'Manius or Mamercus', *JRS* liv (1964), 41.

—— 'The Family Connections of L. Aelius Seianus', *Phoenix* xix (1965), 134.

—— 'Germanicus and Drusus Caesar', *Latomus* xxvi (1967), 413.

—— 'The Truth about Velleius Paterculus. Prolegomena', *HSCP* lxxiv (1970), 257.

—— 'The Lex Annalis under Caesar', *Phoenix* xxv (1971), 3; 357.

—— 'The Pompeii in Their Families', *Am. Journ. Anc. Hist.* II (1977), 8.

—— 'Varrones Murenae', *HSCP* LXXXII (1978), 187.

—— *CP* LXXIV (1979), 64. Review of Woodman's *Commentary* on the Tiberian chapters of Velleius.

SYME, R. 'Die Zahl der *praefecti castrorum* im Heere des Varus', *Germania* XVI (1932), 109.

—— 'M. Vinicius (*cos.* 19 B.C.)', *CQ* XXVII (1933), 142 = *Danubian Papers* (1971), 26.

—— 'Some Notes on the Legions under Augustus', *JRS* XXIII (1933), 14.

—— 'Lentulus and the Origin of Moesia', *JRS* XXIV (1934), 113 = *Danubian Papers* (1971), 40.

—— 'The Spanish War of Augustus (26–25 B.C.)', *AJP* LV (1934), 293.

—— 'Galatia and Pamphylia under Augustus. The Governorships of Piso, Quirinius and Silvanus', *Klio* XXVII (1934), 122.

—— 'Pollio, Saloninus and Salonae', *CQ* XXXI (1937), 39 = *RP* (1979), 18.

—— 'The Origin of Cornelius Gallus', *CQ* XXXII (1938), 39 = *RP* (1979), 47.

—— 'Observations on the Province of Cilicia', *Anatolian Studies . . . W. H. Buckler* (1938), 299 = *RP* (1979), 120.

—— 'Roman Senators from Dalmatia', *Serta Hoffilleriana* (Zagreb, 1940), 225 = *Danubian Papers* (1971), 110.

—— *JRS* XXXV (1945), 108. Review of A. Stein, *Die Legaten von Moesien.*

—— 'Personal Names in Annales I–VI', *JRS* XXXIX (1949), 6 = *Ten Studies in Tacitus* (1970), 58.

—— *CP* L (1955), 127. Review of T. R. S. Broughton, *The Magistrates of the Roman Republic.*

—— 'Missing Senators', *Historia* IV (1955), 52 = *RP* (1979), 271.

—— 'Marcus Lepidus, *Capax Imperii*', *JRS* XLV (1955), 22 = *Ten Studies in Tacitus* (1970), 30.

—— *JRS* XLV (1955), 155 = *RP* (1979), 260. Review of A. E. Gordon, *Potitus Valerius Messalla, Consul Suffect 29 B.C.*

—— 'Some Pisones in Tacitus', *JRS* XLVI (1956), 17 = *Ten Studies in Tacitus* (1970), 50.

—— 'Piso and Veranius in Catullus', *Class. et Med.* XVII (1956), 129 = *RP* (1979), 300.

—— 'Antonine Relatives. Ceionii and Vettuleni', *Athenaeum* XXXV (1957), 306 = *RP* (1979), 325.

—— *Gnomon* XXIX (1957), 515 = *Danubian Papers* (1971), 177. Review of W. Reidinger, *Die Statthalter des ungeteilten Pannonien und Oberpannoniens von Augustus bis Diokletian.*

—— 'Imperator Caesar. A Study in Nomenclature', *Historia* VII (1958), 172 = *RP* (1979), 361.

—— 'Sabinus the Muleteer', *Latomus* XVII (1958), 73 = *RP* (1979), 393.

—— *Gnomon* XXXI (1959), 510 = *Danubian Papers* (1971), 192. Review of A. Jagenteufel, *Die Statthalter der römischen Provinz Dalmatien von Augustus bis Diokletian.*

—— 'Livy and Augustus', *HSCP* LXIV (1959), 27 = *RP* (1979), 400.

—— 'Piso Frugi and Crassus Frugi', *JRS* L (1960), 12 = *RP* (1979), 496.

—— 'Bastards in the Roman Aristocracy', *Trans. Am. Phil. Soc.* CIV (Philadelphia, 1960), 323 = *RP* (1979), 510.
—— 'Who was Vedius Pollio?', *JRS* LI (1961), 23 = *RP* (1979), 518.
—— 'Missing Persons iii', *Historia* XI (1962), 146 = *RP* (1979), 530.
—— 'Ten Tribunes', *JRS* LIII (1963), 55 = *RP* (1979), 557.
—— 'Senators, Tribes, and Towns', *Historia* XIII (1964), 105 = *RP* (1979), 582.
—— 'The Stemma of the Sentii Saturnini', *Historia* XIII (1964), 156 = *RP* (1979), 605.
—— 'The Historian Servilius Nonianus', *Hermes* XCII (1964), 408 = *Ten Studies in Tacitus* (1970), 91.
—— 'The Consuls of A.D. 13', *JRS* LVI (1966), 55.
—— 'The Ummidii', *Historia* XVII (1968), 72 = *RP* (1979), 659.
—— 'A Governor of Tarraconensis', *Epigraphische Studien* VIII (1969), 125 = *RP* (1979), 732.
—— 'Domitius Corbulo', *JRS* LX (1970), 27 = *RP* (1979), 805.
—— 'The Conquest of North-West Spain', *Legio VII Gemina* (León, 1970), 83 = *RP* (1979), 825.
—— 'The Titulus Tiburtinus', *Akten des VI. int. Kongresses für gr. u. lat. Epigraphik 1972* (1973), 585 = *RP* III (1984), 869.
—— 'The Crisis of 2 B.C.', *Bayerische S.-B.* 1974, Heft 7 = *RP* III (1984), 912.
—— 'History or Biography. The Case of Tiberius Caesar', *Historia* XVIII (1974), 481 = *RP* III (1984), 937.
—— 'Notes on Tacitus, *Histories* III', *Antichthon* IX (1975), 61.
—— 'How Tacitus Wrote *Annals* I–III', *Historiographia Antiqua* (Louvain, 1977), 231 = *RP* III (1984), 1014.
—— 'Sallust's Wife', *CQ* XXVIII (1978), 292 = *RP* III (1984), 1085.
—— 'Mendacity in Velleius', *AJP* XCIX (1978), 45 = *RP* III (1984), 1090.
—— 'The *Pomerium* in the Historia Augusta', *Bonner HAC 1975/6* (1978), 217 = *Historia Augusta Papers* (1983), 131.
—— 'Some Imperatorial Salutations', *Phoenix* XXXIII (1979), 4 = *RP* III (1984), 1198.
—— 'Problems about Janus', *AJP* C (1979), 188 = *RP* III (1984), 1179.
—— 'The Sons of Crassus', *Latomus* XXXIX (1980), 403 = *RP* III (1984), 1220.
—— 'The Sons of Piso the Pontifex', *AJP* CI (1980), 333 = *RP* III (1984), 1226.
—— 'Minor Emendations in Pliny and Tacitus', *CQ* XXX (1980), 426 = *RP* III (1984), 1233.
—— 'No Son for Caesar?', *Historia* XXIX (1980), 422 = *RP* III (1984), 1236.
—— 'Biographers of the Caesars', *Mus. Helv.* XXXVII (1980), 104 = *RP* III (1984), 1251.
—— 'The Early Tiberian Consuls', *Historia* XXX (1981), 189 = *RP* III (1984), 1350.
—— 'Princesses and Others in Tacitus', *Greece & Rome* XXVIII (1981), 40 = *RP* III (1984), 1364.
—— 'Governors Dying in Syria', *ZPE* 41 (1981), 125 = *RP* III (1984), 1376.
—— 'A Great Orator Mislaid', *CQ* XXXI (1981), 421 = *RP* III (1984), 1415.
—— 'Vibius Rufus and Vibius Rufinus', *ZPE* 43 (1981), 365 = *RP* III (1984), 1423.

—— 'Clues to Testamentary Adoption', *Epigrafia e Ordine Senatorio* I (1982), 397.

—— 'Partisans of Galba', *Historia* XXXI (1982), 460.

—— 'The Marriage of Rubellius Blandus', *AJP* CIII (1982), 62.

—— 'Tacitus' Sources of Information', *JRS* LXXII (1982), 68.

—— 'The Year 33 in Tacitus and Dio', *Athenaeum* LXI (1983), 3.

—— 'Problems about Proconsuls of Asia', *ZPE* 53 (1983), 191.

—— 'Spaniards at Tivoli', *Ancient Society* XIII/XIV (1982/3), 241.

—— 'Lurius Varus, a Stray Consular Legate', *HSCP* LXXXVIII (1984), 105.

—— 'Neglected Children on the *Ara Pacis*', *AJA* LXXXVIII (1984), 583.

SWAN, M. 'The Consular *Fasti* of 23 B.C. and the Conspiracy of Varro Murena', *HSCP* LXXI (1966), 235.

—— 'Josephus, *A. J.* 251–252. Opposition to Gaius and Claudius', *AJP* XCI (1970), 149.

TARN, W. W. 'Alexander and the Golden Age', *JRS* XXII (1932), 135.

TAYLOR, L. R. 'M. Titius and the Syrian Command', *JRS* XXVI (1936), 161.

—— 'Caesar's Colleagues in the Pontifical College', *AJP* LXIII (1942), 385.

—— 'Trebula and the Plautii Silvani', *Mem. Am. Ac. Rome* XXIV (1956), 7.

THOMASSON, B. E. 'Verschiedenes zu den Proconsules Africae', *Eranos* LXVII (1969), 175.

—— 'Zur Verwaltungsgeschichte der römischen Provinzen Nordafrikas', *ANRW* X. 2 (1982), 3.

TIMPE, D. 'Zur Geschichte und Überlieferung der Okkupation Germaniens unter Augustus', *Saeculum* XVIII (1967), 278.

—— 'Die römische Verzicht auf die Okkupation Germaniens', *Chiron* I (1971), 267.

—— 'Zur Geschichte der Rheingrenze zwischen Caesar und Augustus', *Monumentum Chiloniense (Festschrift E. Burck,* 1975), 124.

TREGGIARI, S. 'Cicero, Horace, and Mutual Friends. Lamiae and Varrones Murenae', *Phoenix* XXVII (1973), 245.

VAN BERCHEM, D. 'Messalla ou Messalinus? Notes sur le Panégyrique de Messalla', *Mus. Helv.* II (1945), 33.

VEYNE, P. *Latomus* XXVI (1967), 723. Review of A. N. Sherwin-White, *The Letters of Pliny.*

VIDMAN, L. 'Ad Frontinum, De aq. 102', *Listy fil.* XCVI (1973), 16.

WEAVER, P. R. C. 'Dated Inscriptions of Imperial Freedmen and Slaves', *Epigraphische Studien* XI (1976), 215.

WEIDEMANN, U. 'Sex. Nonius Quinctilianus. A note on Abh. Akad. Berlin 1932, 5, 36, n.15 = AE 1933, 265', *Acta Classica* III (1960), 93.

—— 'C. Silanus, *Appia parente genitus.* A note on Tac. Ann. 3, 68, 3', *Acta Classica* VI (1963), 138.

—— 'Drei Inschriften aus Kyme', *Arch. Anzeiger* 1965, 446.

WEIGEL, R. D. 'A Note on P. Lepidus', *CP* LXXIII (1978), 42.

—— 'The Career of L. Paullus, cos. 50', *Latomus* XXVIII (1979), 637.

WEINRIB, E. J. 'The Prosecution of Roman Magistrates', *Phoenix* XXII (1968), 32.

—— 'The Family Connections of M. Livius Drusus Libo', *HSCP* LXXII (1972), 247.

WEISS, P. 'Die "Säkularspiele" der Republik, eine annalistische Fiktion? Ein Beitrag zum Verständnis der kaiserzeitlichen Ludi saeculares', *Röm. Mitt.* LXXX (1973), 205.

WIEDEMANN, T. 'The Political Background to Ovid's *Tristia 2*', *CQ* XXV (1975), 264.

WIKANDER, C. and O. 'Republican Prosopography. Some Reconsiderations', *Opuscula Romana* XII (1979), 1.

WILLIAMS, G. 'Poetry in the Moral Climate of Augustan Rome', *JRS* LII (1962), 28.

WISEMAN, T. P. 'The Mother of Livia Augusta', *Historia* XIV (1965), 333.

—— 'The Last of the Metelli', *Latomus* XXIV (1965), 52 = (revised) *Cinna the Poet* (1974), 176.

—— 'Pulcher Claudius', *HSCP* LXXIV (1968), 207.

—— 'The Census in the First Century B.C.', *JRS* LIX (1969), 59.

—— 'Legendary Genealogies in Late Republican Rome', *Greece & Rome* XXI (1974), 153.

—— 'Calpurnius Siculus and the Claudian Civil War', *JRS* LXXII (1982), 57.

WOODMAN, A. J. 'Questions of Date, Genre, and Style in Velleius. Some Literary Answers', *CQ* XXV (1975), 272.

ZEDELIUS, V. 'P. Quinctilius Varus in Achulla. Bemerkungen zum sog. Varusporträt auf Münzen aus Africa proconsularis', *Bonner Jahrbücher* CLXXXIII (1983), 469.

ZETZEL, J. E. G. 'New Light on Gaius Caesar's Eastern Campaign', *GRBS* XI (1970), 259.

Index of Persons

Of necessity the Index takes in the footnotes. The plethora of persons along with their recurrence (such as Cornelii Lentuli or the inevitable Varro Murena) caused sundry perplexities.

Emperors, their family members, and authors are registered by their standard names: authors, even of minor notoriety, benefit from typographical emphasis; and for clarity a few brief items are duplicated.

Finally, references are admitted to persons not explicitly named in the text.

Cocceius Nerva, M. (*cont.*)
  Capreae with Tiberius, 221, 345, 351; his death, 345.
COLUMELLA, cites L. Volusius, 295.
Cominius, L., obscure senator, 213.
Coponii, 44.
Coponius, Tiburtine senator, 44.
Cornelia, wife of M. Livius Drusus (*cos.* 112), 21.
Cornelia, daughter of Scipio Nasica, marries P. Crassus, 20, 271; and then Pompeius Magnus, 245 f.
Cornelia, daughter of Faustus Sulla and Pompeia, wife of Q. Lepidus, 112, 261 f.
Cornelia, grand-daughter of Faustus Sulla and Pompeia; her putative marriage, 262.
Cornelia, wife of Paullus the Censor, 29; her parentage and family, 110, 136, 246 f., 399, 250, 251, 297; her children 110 f., 136, 150 f., 167, 246, 297; in Propertius' poem, 25, 110, 246, 297.
Cornelia, wife of Norbanus Flaccus, 33.
Cornelia, wife of L. Volusius Saturninus (*suff.* AD 3), 59, 73, 297, 299; her parents and son 252 f.
Cornelia, wife of Sisenna Statilius Taurus, 73.
Cornelia, wife of Calvisius Sabinus, 298.
Cornelia, wife of T. Axius, 73.
Cornelii Lentuli, 24, 26, 50, 87, 95, 98, 246, 248 ff., 285 ff., 301 f., 304, 310 f.
Cornelli Scipiones, 16, 19, 21, 91, 103 f., 106, 108, 244 ff., 299.
Cornelius Balbus, L. (*suff.* 40), magnate from Gades, 3, 27.
Cornelius Balbus, L. (?*suff.*), nephew of the magnate, 3; proconsul of Africa 41, 45, 292, 318; his triumph 41, 62, 110, 406; his daughter's husband, 33.
CORNELIUS CELSUS, A., medical writer, 328.
Cornelius Cethegus, C., political expert, 5.
Cornelius Cethegus, Ser. (*cos.* AD 24), 297.
Cornelius Cinna, L. (*cos.* 87–84), 15, 27, 106, 284; as presented by Tacitus, 270; his daughter, 15; his widow, 36.
Cornelius Cinna, L. (*pr.* 44), 30, 266, 257.
Cornelius Cinna, L. (*suff.* 32), marries daughter of Magnus, 47, 30, 257; quaestor (in 44), 30, 47, 257; *arvalis*, 46 f., 288; his son, 47.
Cornelius Cinna Magnus, Cn. (*cos.* AD 5), 96 ff., 100; his parentage and family, 47, 64, 74, 266, 286, 257, 282; his *cognomen*, 75; spared at Actium, 100, 264; his change of allegiance, 100; his fictitious plot, 266; admonished by Augustus, 266.
Cornelius Dolabella, Cn., grand-nephew of Galba, 280, 299.

Cornelius Dolabella, P. (*suff.* 44), 27, 32, 250, 316; marries Fabia and Tullia 73, 418; favoured by Julius Caesar, 27; adopted by a plebeian Lentulus, 250; Cicero's varying attitude to him, 27; his inheritance, 33; involved in lawsuits, 69; his issue, 98, 316.
Cornelius Dolabella, P. (son of the consul at Alexandria, 44), 316.
Cornelius Dolabella, P. (*cos.* AD 10), 97; his parentage and family, 98, 316; Dalmatian command, 101, 129, 327; favoured by Tiberius, 327, 424; over-obsequious, 327 f., 424; as a prosecutor, 327; praised by Velleius, 424 f.
CORNELIUS GALLUS, C., first Prefect of Egypt, 7, 32, 143, 274, 300, 308; gives refuge to Caecilius Epirota, 36, 143, 314; his alleged crimes and downfall, 7, 32, 36, 173, 384; his arrogance, 39; mentioned six times by Ovid, 361; influenced by Parthenius, 350.
Cornelius Lentulus, Cn. Triumviral admiral, 288, 297.
Cornelius Lentulus, Cn., enigmatic quaestor, 288, 297.
Cornelius Lentulus, Cn. (*cos.* 18), 50, 258, 286 ff., 293, 405.
Cornelius Lentulus, Cn., the Augur (*cos.* 14), 5, 14, 54, 276 f., 284 ff.; his position and operations on the Danube, 61, 68, 85 f., 287 ff.; *ornamenta triumphalia*, 68; proconsul of Asia, 62, 292, 405; his mission to Pannonian legions, 293.
  An *arvalis*, 5, 288; his political actions, 193, 293, 297; friendship with Tiberius, 193, 293, 310, 355; abortively prosecuted, 310; his death, 118, 293, 296, 310 f., 355; his meanness and ingratitude, 239, 295 f., financial acumen, 72; sources of his wealth, 295; maligned by the younger Seneca, 296, 355; praised by Tacitus, 63, 295 f., 355, 428; misrepresented by Tertullian, 294; his uncertain extraction, 296; alleged sons, 297.
Cornelius Lentulus, Cossus (*cos.* 1), 87, 133, 286; *quindecimvir*, 49; his African campaign, 162, 296, 298, 320, 424, 427; *ornamenta triumphalia*, 296, 427; blocks indictment against Arruntius, 268, 298, 311; Prefect of the City, 298, 375; retains Tiberius' favour, 298, 311, 424; his sons, 68, 298 f., 424; his drunkenness and indolence, 298; lack of sources about him under Tiberius, 298, 309.
Cornelius Lentulus, Cossus (*cos.* AD 25), 298.
Cornelius Lentulus, L. (*cos.* 327), their first consul, 285.
Cornelius Lentulus, L. (*pr.* 44), 286.
Cornelius Lentulus, L. (*suff.* 38), 28, 286 f.; his nomenclature now established, 246.
Cornelius Lentulus, L. (*cos.* 3), *monetalis*, 52;

nephew of Cato, 34, 156, f. 208, 264; praised by Velleius, 424 f.

Domitius Ahenobarbus, Cn. (*cos.* AD 32), son of Antonia and *cos.* 16 BC, 141, 155 f., 166; marries Julia Agrippina, 141, 171, 311, 425; administers relief fund, 173, 192, noted as orator by the elder Seneca, 166; constructs a bath-house, 166; confused with a brother, 142, 155 f.; litigation with Domitia, 159; accused of incest with Domitia Lepida, 159; his indictment, 159, 173, 278; his death, 172, 179; detestable character, 185, 312, 433.

Domitius Ahenobarbus, L. (*cos.* 54), 54; in Pompeius' camp, 26; his death at Pharsalus, 34, 156; his wife, 58, 156; kinsmen, 25; son, 17, 58, 156; descendants, 164; his unpleasant character, 157.

Domitius Ahenobarbus, L. (*cos.* 16), 14, 54, 110, 144, 250; his parentage, 57, 113, 155, 158 f.; quaestor, 37; conduct as aedile, 157; proconsul of Africa, 62, 153, 318; legate in Illyricum and in Germany, 85, 102, 141, 280, 317, 325, 341, 428; marries elder Antonia, 37, 58, 63, 79, 113, 141, 152, 341, 428; his children, 59, 79, 141, 151 f., 155 f., 159, 163, 166 f., 425; on *Ara Pacis*, 79, 152, 166, 318, 399.

    A 'vir triumphalis', 94; as a rival to Tiberius, 131, 428; detestable and arrogant, 157; unpopular, 79, 94; his displays and sports, 72; his death and obituary, 63, 311; mentioned by Velleius, 128, 425, 428; ignored by Horace, 399.

Domitius Ahenobarbus, ?L., putative son of *cos.* 16 BC and Antonia, 142, 155 f., 167.

Domitius Calvinus, Cn. (*cos.* 53, *II* 40), 27, 54, 228; *arvalis*, 5, 46; *pontifex*, 6; strong Caesarian, 34; governor in Spain, 34; his daughter and son-in-law, 191, 193; descendants, 162.

Drusus (Nero Claudius Drusus) (*cos.* 9), 55, 318; son of Livia and Tiberius, stepson of Augustus, 37, 39; quaestor, 332; his campaigns, 65 ff., 81, 153, 354, 318, 326, 346 f., 407; promoted over Tiberius, 94, 401; his honours, 68, 78, 405; his wife, 94, 112; children, 93, 112; credited with wrong wife by Tacitus, 165; on the *Ara Pacis*, 152, 155; prominent after Agrippa's death, 318; his death, 66, 407; mentioned by Horace, 400 f.; by Livy 422 f., 445; by Velleius, 428.

Drusus Caesar, son of Tiberius (*cos.* AD 15; *II* 21), 93, 372, 375; *arvalis*, 123; favoured less than his cousin Germanicus, 94, 169; marries Livia Julia, 94, 169; his death, 24, 169, 375.

Drusus Caesar, son of Germanicus and Agrippa, 133; marries the daughter of M. Lepidus, 133, 136, 165 f.; his arrest, 133, 185, 311; prosecution and imprisonment, 429;

death, 73, 185, 415; allegedly impersonated, 195.

Drusus Libo, *see* Scribonius Libo Drusus.

Ducenius Geminus, A., proposed as *suff.* AD 54, 96.

Egnatius Rufus, demagogue, 42.

ENNIUS, his 'augusto augurio', 40.

EPICURUS; popularity of his doctrines, 74, 365.

Eprius Marcellus, T. (*suff.* AD 62), famous orator, 240.

EUPHORION, Alexandrian poet, 350.

EURIPIDES, aptly quoted by Athenaeus of Seleuceia, 390.

EUSEBIUS, on Tiberius' alleged campaign in Thrace, 336.

EUTROPIUS, misinterprets Suetonius, 336.

Fabia, Vestal Virgin, 419.

Fabia, elderly wife of P. Dolabella, 73, 419.

Fabia Eburna, 418.

Fabia Numantina, daughter of Paullus Fabius Maximus, wife of Sex. Appuleius, 59; and of M. Plautius Silvanus, 418; impugned for sorcery against Silvanus, 418; her son, the last of the Appuleii, 418.

Fabia Paullina, wife of M. Titius, 30, 73, 417.

Fabii, 12, 17, 19, 63, 76 f., 98, 157, 283, 403 ff., 419 f., two dubious Fabii in Juvenal, 418 f.

Fabius Aemilianus, Q. (*cos.* 145), 16, 419.

Fabius Maximus, Africanus (*cos.* 10), 55, 403; ?military tribune in Spain, 324; priesthood, 417; proconsul of Africa, 62, 320, 369, 417; his coins, 320, 406; his parentage, 57; nomenclature, 75, 419; a sister, 73.

Fabius Maximus Allobrogicus, Q. (*cos.* 121), 17, 156, 417; his son a wastrel, 419.

Fabius Maximus, Paullus (*cos.* 11), elder brother of Africanus, 13 f., 55, 353, 403 ff., 432; *arvalis*, 5, 60, 124, 415; ?military tribune, 324, 401; quaestor, 22, 288, 313, 401, 404, 420; proconsul of Asia, 62, 318, 401, 405 f., 416, 444; his coins, 406 f.; legate of Tarraco-mensis 86, 101, 113, 401, 407 f.; favoured by Augustus, 94, 407, 416; disliked as rival by Tiberius, 172, 401, 408 f., 428; marries Marcia, cousin of Augustus, 36, 58, 94, 153, 172, 399, 404, 416, 428; not embroiled with Julia, 112 f.; his alleged visit to Agrippa Postumus, 124, 415 f.; his death, 63, 124, 414 f.

    His parentage and family, 57, 73, 320, 403; his titles and honours, 69; nomenclature, 75; patron of poetry, 7, 360; addressed by Horace, 314, 396 ff., 401, 403, 409; by

Julia, grand-daughter of Augustus, married to Aemilius Paullus, 93, 103, 111, 142, 265; her children and grandson, 93, 111, 120, 188, 259; on the *Ara Pacis*, 152; her misbehaviour and catastrophe, 12 f., 115, 118, 168, 214; her lovers, 194, 234, 294; her punishment and exile, 120, 412.

Julia, niece of Hadrian, 167.

Julia Agrippina, *see* Agrippina the younger.

Julia Drusilla, sister of Caligula, 171, 185; marries Cassius Longinus, 136, 172, 175, 179 then M. Aemilius Lepidus, 136, 179; her alleged incest with Caligula, 186; her death and deification, 179; in Suetonius, 179.

Julia Livilla, daughter of Germanicus, 185 f.; her presumed betrothal to a son of Quinctilius Varus, 149, 315, 327; marries M. Vinicius, 171 f., 179, 278; her alleged adultery with M. Lepidus, 119, 180, 182; exiled to Pontia, 180, 278; her return, 182; accused again, 182; her exile and death, 182, 298; victim of Messallina, 279; Seneca her alleged lover, 182.

Julii, 11, 63, 75, 79, 276, 282, 316, 420.

Julius Agricola, Cn., (*suff.* AD 77), 192, 453; his father, 417.

JULIUS CAESAR, C. (*cos.* 59), marries daughter of Cinna, 15; his relations with Sulla, 15; speaks up for Catilinarians, 189; marries daughter of Piso Caesoninus, 329; his mistress, 18, 189; alleged father of M. Brutus (but perhaps of Decimus), 18; his estimate of Brutus, 349; his pact with Pompeius and Crassus, 270 f., 356, 360, 442, 447; describes Pompeius' command, 447; his proconsular campaigns and awareness of geopolitics, 64.

   Opposed by Cato, 442; by Lentulus Crus, 285; invades Italy, 421; alleged extension of *pomerium*, 68; adlects Sex. Appuleius, 316; preference for patricians, 420; proposed Dacian and Parthian campaigns, 64; plans to leave Rome, 32.

   His supremacy described by Cicero, 449; 'ipse princeps', 450; in Augustan writers, 270 f., 443; avoided by Virgil, 443; an Epicurean, 365; his lack of kinsmen, 37; adopts Octavius, 53; his will, 39; his death remembered, 39.

Julius Caesar L. (*cos.* 64), 54.

Julius Marinus, friend of Tiberius, 361.

Julius Florus, friend of Horace, 361, 401.

JULIUS FRONTINUS, SEX. (*cos. III* AD 100), *curator aquarum*, 220; his book *De aquis*, 221 f'; lacuna in the text, 224, 226.

Julius Graecinus, father of Agricola, 417.

Julius Montanus, poet, friend of Tiberius, 362, 401.

JULIUS OBSEQUENS; his dating of the *clades Lolliana*, 402.

Julius Pappus, 'comes' of Tiberius, 361.

Julius Sacerdos, Gallic nobleman, his execution, 180.

Junia, wife of Lepidus the Triumvir, 19, 107, 189; her son, 35.

Junia, wife of Servilius Isauricus, 19, 107, 189.

Junia, wife of Q. Aelius Tubero and of Seius Strabo, 305 ff.; mother of Seianus, 303 ff.

Junia Calvina, daughter of M. Silanus and Aemilia Lepida, 158, 174; last descendant of Augustus 185, 197; divorced by L. Vitellius (*suff.* 48), 174; accused of incest with her brother, 186; 'festivisssima' and 'decora' 186; allowed to return from exile, 120, 161; her survival and death, 187; death, 197.

Junia Lepida, daughter of M. Silanus and Aemilia Lepida, 158, 174 f.; wife of the jurist Cassius Longinus, 175, 192, 197; descended from Augustus, 185; prosecuted for alleged incest and magical practices, 186.

Junia Silana, her father, 175, 196; her marriage broken by Messallina, 175; her marriage to Sextius Africanus blocked by Agrippina, 160, 175; their quarrel, 160; her plot against Agrippina, 160, 185; supported by Domitia, 185; her age, 175, 196; her exile and death, 161.

Junia Tertia, wife of C. Cassius, 19, 107, 158, 189, 199.

Junia Torquata, Vestal Virgin, 193, 196.

Junii, 76, 158, 189 f.

Junii Bruti, 197, 282.

Junii Silani, 74, 162, 188 ff., 197, 199, 282, 312.

Junilla, daughter of Seianus, 303, 307 f.

Junius Bassus, derides Domitia, 161.

Junius Blaesus, legate of Lugdunensis, descended from Antonius, 144, 163, 310.

Junius Blaesus, Q. (*suff.* AD 10), *novus homo*, 100; his Pannonian command, 101, 427; proconsul of Africa, 131, 302, 427; his *ornamenta triumphalia*, 302, 304, 427; 'avunculus' of Seianus, 101, 131, 302 ff., 407, 422; involved in Seianus' fall, 163; 310, 436; his sons' suicides, 163, 304, 310; his mother and wife, 302, 304, 306; praised by Velleius, 427.

Junius Blaesus, Q. (*suff.* AD 26), his father, 163, 304; perhaps married to Domitia, 144, 163, 310; his suicide, 163, 304, 310.

Junius Blaesus (*suff?*AD 28); his father 163, 304; his suicide, 163, 394, 310.

Junius Brutus, D. (*cos.* 77), 20, 25; his wife and son, 18, 26, 198.

Antonius' will, 30, 208; his behaviour at the Egyptian court, 208; proposes name of 'Augustus', 38, 208; as censor, 41, 110, 329, 429; as a survivor, 329; elegant correspondent of Cicero, 38, 385; addressed by Horace, 385, 429; rebuked by Velleius, 214 f., 429; his mausoleum and dedication, 275, 391; drops his *gentilicium*, 391; his smooth eloquence, 38, 234, 446; his nephew M. Titius, 30, 308, 322, 434; his daughter or granddaughter, 58, 369, 429; his son, 343.

Munatius Plancus, L. (*cos.* AD 13), 97, 220, 343; leads delegation to the Rhine, 373; his father, 343.

Murena, *see* Licinius *and* Terentius Varro Murena.

Murena, addressed as augur by Horace, 392.

Murena, L., the conspirator as named by Velleius, 388. *See also* Varro Murena.

NAEVIUS, his popularity, 359.

Narcissus, imperial freedman *ab epistulis*, agent of Messallina, 165, 182.

Nero, eldest son of Germanicus and Agrippina, 94; his privileged career, 116, 348; his unfulfilled betrothal, 196; marries Julia, daughter of Drusus Caesar, 94, 116, 133, 171; her hostility, 186; his indictment, imprisonment, and death, 133, 171, 185, 237, 310 f.; reproached by Velleius, 428.

NERO, the Emperor, his ancestry, 155 ff; marriage of his parents, 171; father's decease, 179, 182; marries Octavia, 184; rejects her for Poppaea Sabina, 175; marries Statilia Messallina, 187, 240; influenced by his freedman Paris, 160 f.; has his mother arrested and murdered, 160 f.; his banquets and performances, 176, 365 f.; advertises his own clemency, 161, 192; his orations, 170; allegedly poisons his aunt Domitia, 161; exiles Sulla Felix, 281; puts down a conspiracy and quells Senate, 280; his adviser Ofonius Tigellinus, 281.

Neglects the armies, 280; his fall, 280, 275; refers to L. Volusius, 295; his attitude to the Republic, 441; his dying words, 440; suffers from Tacitus' prejudices, 185.

NERVA, the Emperor, 220; his ancestry, 223.

Nestor, Academic philosopher, teacher of Marcellus, 347.

Nestor, the Stoic, teacher of Tiberius, 347.

Nicetes, 'Asianic' *rhetor*, 354.

NICOLAUS of Damascus, historian, partisan of Herod, 358.

Nonia Polla, wife of L. Volusius Saturninus (*suff.* 12), 56; her family and son, 319 f.

Nonii Asprenates, 53, 70, 315, 318, 327, 431.

Nonius Asprenas, L. (*suff.* 36), his daughter and connections, 56.

Nonius Asprenas, L., friend of Augustus, 325; marries sister of Quinctilius Varus, 70, 315, 331; his sons, 70; prosecuted for poisoning, 70; 315; his acquittal, 316; forfeits consulship, 316; his sister and kin, 319.

Nonius Asprenas, L. (*suff.* AD 6), his parent, 70, 331; nephew of Varus, 315, 318, 331, 431; perhaps with him in Syria, 314 f.; legate in Germany, 60, 431; proconsul of Africa, 132, 327; his wife Calpurnia, 59, 331; accused of pillaging from dead, 431; confused with the homonymous friend of Augustus, 315 f.

Nonius Asprenas, L. (*suff.* AD 29), perhaps in trouble, 431.

Nonius Quinctilianus, Sex. (*cos.* AD 8), 57, 97, 318; proconsul of Asia 327.

Nonius Quinctilianus, Sex. (*suff.* AD 38), 222.

Norbanus, C. (*cos.* 83), Marian partisan, 28, 33.

Norbanus Flaccus, C. (*cos.* 38), Caesarian general, 28, 33 f.; *quindecimvir*, 48; his Spanish triumph, 33.

Norbanus Flaccus, C. (*cos.* 24), 33; possibly a *quindecimvir*, 48; his wife, 33.

Novatus, eldest son of Annaeus Seneca, adopted by Junius Gallio, 354.

Novellius Atticus, Torquatus, senatorial drinker from Mediolanum, 345.

Numa Marcius, legendary king of Rome, 212.

Numa Pompilius, legendary king, alleged ancestor of the Marcii and Calpurnii, 76.

Octavia, daughter of Octavius and Ancharia, half-sister to Augustus, 33, 316; marries Sex. Appuleius, 151; her sons, 30, 126, 151, 317, 399; granddaughter, 317.

Octavia, sister of Augustus, marries Claudius Marcellus, 141, 143; then M. Antonius, 141; her children, 36, 141 ff.; their education, 347; on the *Ara Pacis*, 152; her death, 135.

Octavia, daughter of Claudius and Messallina, betrothed to L. Silanus, 174, 181, 192, 277; but married to Nero, 184.

Octavius C. (*pr.* 61), father of Augustus, his first wife Ancharia, 316, 418; his second Atia, 193, 403.

Octavius Laenas, C. (*suff.* AD 33), *curator aquarum*, 222.

Ofonius Tigellinus, counsellor to Nero, 281.

Ollius, T., obscure husband of the first Poppaea Sabina, 178.

Orestilla, wife of Catilina, 22.

OROSIUS, on plague and fire, 22; on Augustus' Spanish campaigns, 38; on German and African campaigns, 335 f.; quotes the historian Galba, 71; quotes Tacitus, 89; uses

Propertius Celer, senator helped by Tiberius, 361.

Propertius Postumus, C., senator mentioned by Propertius, 308; probably kinsman to the poet, 359; possibly identical with Horace's 'Postumus', 386, 390.

Ptolemies, ousted by Augustus, 80.

Publilia, wife of Cicero and of Vibius Rufus, 225.

Publius Rufus, *see* Plautius Rufus.

Pulcher, Augustan *monetalis*, 376.

Pupius, M., adopts a Piso, 52, 276.

Pupius Piso Frugi, M. (*cos.* 61), Pompeian, 276; divorces Cinna's widow, 36; his adoption, 52, 276; his son and grandson, 276.

Pupius Piso Frugi, M. (*pr.* 44), his presumed son, 276.

Pylaemenes, Galatian nobleman in poem of Antipater, 333.

Pyrrho, Sceptic philosopher, 365.

Quinctilia, sister of Varus, wife of Cornelius Dolabella, 316.

Quinctilia, sister of Varus, wife of L. Nonius Asprenas, 57, 315, 331.

Quinctilia, sister of Varus, wife of Sex. Appuleius 316 ff. (*cos.* 29).

Quinctilii, 77, 98, 313.

Quinctilius Varus, Sex., *pontifex*, 313.

Quinctilius Varus, Sex. (*pr.* 57), 313.

Quinctilius Varus, Sex., perishes at Philippi, 57, 263, 313.

Quinctilius Varus, P. (*cos.* 13), 14, 54, 153, 313 ff.; his father, 57,313,328; his wives, 58, 135, 146, 149, 151, 314 f., 399; his sisters and connections, 70, 98, 315 ff., 331, 327 f., 414; four consular nephews, 318; his son, 59, 149, 315, 327; an alleged son in Josephus, 314 f.; his priesthood, 60, 318; 'quaestor Augusti', 60, 288, 313, 404; consul with Claudius Nero, 313, 318, 324, 369, 404; congenial to him, 86.

Proconsul of Africa, 62, 319 f., 406; on African coins, 319, 406; legate in Syria, 61, 86, 321 ff., 337; deals with Herod and Palestine, 322, 326 ff., dismisses Arab allies, 323; his German command, 325 f.; trapped and defeated, commits suicide, 60, 63, 292, 326; his reputation and family attacked, 327 f.

His mildness, energy, and promptitude 321, 324; no intellectual interests but a potential *praefectus urbi*, 328; his wealth, 328; his trusting nature, 326; attacked by Florus, 326; in Velleius and Tacitus, 326, 328.

Quinctilius Varus, son of Varus and Claudia

Pulchra, 59; his betrothal, 149, 315; his prosecution, 327.

Quinctilius Varus Cremonensis, 313.

Quinctia, wife of Asinius Pollio (*cos.* 40), 58.

Quinctii, 57, 77, 98, 158, 189.

Quinctii, Samnite and Campanian, 386, 395.

Quinctius Cincinnatus, L., dictator and farmer, 72.

Quinctius Crispinus, T. (*qu.* 69), 191.

Quinctius Crispinus Sulpicianus, T. (*cos.* 9), 55; his father and brother, 57, 229; *monetalis*, 395. potential proconsul, 62; involved in scandal of Julia with Iullus Antonius, 62 f., 91, 158, 429; his banishment and possible death, 158; his alleged adopted son, 229; accused of depravity by Velleius, 91.

Quinctius Crispinus Valerianus, T. (*suff.* AD 2), 95, 229; his praetorship, 158; his father and brother, 57; *arvalis*, 96.

Quinctius Flamininus (*cos.* 192), 83.

Quinctius Flamininus, T. (*cos.* 123), 57.

Quinctius Hirpinus, addressed by Horace, 386.

QUINTILIAN, his assessment of some orators, 206, 215, 353, 410; on L. Varius Rufus, 393; recommends reading of Rabirius, 402; on literary frauds, 351.

Quirinius, *see* Sulpicius Quirinius.

RABIRIUS, epic poet, 402.

Regillus, *see* Aemilius Lepidus Regillus.

Regulus, Augustan *monetalis*, 376.

Rhescuporis, King of Thrace, son of Cotys, 334, 340.

RHIANUS, Alexandrian poet and editor, 350 f.

Rhoemetalces, uncle and guardian of Thracian princes, 333 f.

'Romulus' 1, 4, 67, 98, 274, 450 f.

Roscius of Ameria, his protectors, 227, 244.

Rubellius Blandus, C., famous teacher of oratory from Tibur, 173, 225, 354, 363.

Rubellius Blandus, C. (*suff.* AD 18), *novus homo*, 51 f., 376; his Tiburtine extraction and grandfather, 173, 225, 363; quaestor, 60; his African proconsulate, 191, 237; marries Julia, daughter of Drusus Caesar, 160, 173, 182, 188, 281; his children, 160, 182, 188, 281; administers relief fund 173, 192; his ties with Tiberius, 225, 363.

Rubellius Plautus, son of Rubellius Blandus and Julia, 51, 182; accused of conspiracy, 160; advised by Nero to retire into exile, 281; his execution, 281 f.

Rutilia, wife of Piso Caesoninus, 57, 330.

Rutilius Lupus, P. (*cos.* 90), 15.

by Seius Strabo, 49, 302 ff.; his parentage, 306 f.; linked with Lentulus the Augur as friend of Tiberius, 310; in Tacitus, 309.

Sempronia, wife of D. Junius Brutus (*cos.* 77), 18; her political activity, 26, 198 f.; perhaps related to Fulvia, 26.

Sempronia, mother of M. Junius Silanus (*cos.* 25), 190.

Sempronia, perhaps an early wife of Paullus the Censor, 109.

Sempronii Gracchi, 16, 20, 91, 284.

Sempronius Atratinus, L. (*suff.* 34), orator at seventeen, 29, 354; augur 329; his origins and adoption, 29; his wife, 29; his sister's or daughter's husband, 29, 109; deserts Antonius, 109 f.; proconsul of Africa, 41, 45; his triumph, 41, 110; long-lived, 329; date of his death, 329.

Sempronius Gracchus, lover of Julia, 91, 429; his tragedies, 71, 91; mentioned by Ovid, 91.

Sempronius Gracchus, C. (*tr. pl.* 123), his opponents, 284.

Sempronius Gracchus, Ti. (*cos.* 177), his twelve children, 20.

Sempronius Gracchus, Ti. (*tr. pl.* 133), his adherents persecuted, 368.

SENECA the elder, on orators' style; Asinius Gallus, 131; Q. Haterius, 145; L. Ahenobarbus, 166; Messalla Corvinus, 215, 354; Passienus and Ovid, 354; registers small-town careerists, 354; his references to Livy, 356; on Dellius' alleged letters, 357; an anecdote about Tiberius, 354; his sparse allusion to recent events, 166, 411; the value of his compilation, 353 f.

SENECA the younger (*suff.* AD 56), *novus homo* and high-society figure, 119; 433; his alleged adultery with Julia Livilla, 119, 182; banished, 119; influences Nero, 299; his wealth, 295.

Opposes antiquarianism and liberal arts, 351; on merit against birth, 12, 417; on vices of modern *nobiles*, 74, 433; on ingratitude, 78, 295 f.; speaks of 'principes regesque', 451; of 'praeses' and 'rector' 452; his *Apocolocyntosis*, 278; *De clementia*, 445.

His appraisal of various persons, 183 f., 224, 229, 256, 259 f., 298, 355, 367, 370, 409 ff. 448; a source for certain incidents, 92, 119, 223 ff., 343; 392 f.; invents a fable, 100, 266; used by Dio, 266; his text emended, 119; in Tacitus, 170, 295.

Sentia, wife of a Scribonius Libo, 264.

Sentii, 264; their origin, 44.

Sentius Saturninus, C. (*cos.* 19), *novus homo*, 42 f., 320, 393; his family and kin, 44, 265;

quindecimvir, 48 f.; curbs disturbance in Rome, 265, 426.

Proconsul of Africa, 45, 62; legate in Syria, 85 f., 321; deals with Herod, 322; his alleged census of Judaea, 340; in Germany, 85, 101, 325, 426; his testimonial from Velleius, 426.

Sentius Saturninus, C. (*cos.* AD 4), 95, 322.

Sentius Saturninus, Cn. (*suff.* AD 4), 95, 322.

Sentius Saturninus, L., 322.

Sergii, patrician, 71, 78.

Sergius Catilina, L., his portrayal by Sallust, 12; deaths of his wife and son, 22; remarries, 22; his thwarted ambition, 78; the debate about his associates, 189.

Sergius Plautus (*pr.* AD 2), *patronus* of Urso, Stoic philosopher, 71, 78.

Servilia, niece of M. Livius Drusus, 25, 40; half-sister of M. Cato, 25; wife of M. Brutus (*tr. pl.* 83) and mother of Marcus, 25, 158, 197; marries D. Junius Silanus, 26, 189; her daughters' marriages, 19, 107, 189; mistress of Julius Caesar, 18 f., 26, 189; her political ambitions, 40, 55, 189, 198; consulted by Atticus, 199; her great-aunt Livia, 199.

Servilia, wife of the alleged conspirator Aemilius Lepidus, 35, 108.

Servilii, 40, 96, 158, 199, 266, 419.

Servilii Caepiones, 16, 77 f., 419.

Servilius, husband of an Aemilia Lepida, 147.

Servilius, M. (*cos.* AD 3), 95 f.; his nomenclature, wife, and son, 96; conjectured consular legate of Galatia–Pamphylia, 333.

Servilius, P. (*pr.* 25), depreciated by Seneca, 35.

Servilius Caepio, betrothed to the daughter of Pompeius Magnus, 255.

Servilius Caepio, Q. (*cos.* 106), 16.

Servilius Caepio, Q. (*pr.* 91), father of Servilia, 25, 158.

Servilius Caepio Brutus, Q., 53. *See* Junius Brutus, M.

Servilius Isauricus, P. (*cos.* 48; *II* 41), 27; his wife, 19, 107, 189; his presumed son, 35, 147.

Servilius Nonianus, M. (*cos.* AD 35), his parentage, 96; orator favoured by Seneca, 266; historian, 266, 365; linked with Thrasea Paetus, 365; his daughter, 365.

Servilius Vatia Isauricus, P. (*cos.* 79), 25, 54.

SERVIUS, his errors, 119.

Sestius Quirinalis, L. (*suff.* 23), *novus homo*, 41, 43; Republican, 384; quaestor of M. Brutus, 41, 383; consular legate in Spain, 384, 393; addressed by Horace, 381, 383, 390, 396; perhaps an Epicurean, 393.

Sextia, wife of Mam. Aemilius Scaurus, 261.

Sextius Africanus, T. (*suff.* AD 59), Junia Silana wants to marry him, 160, 176.

SIDONIUS APOLLINARIS, 120.

Silii, 428.

Silius, C. (*cos.* AD 13), his full nomenclature, 97; his father, 101; army commander on the Rhine, 101, 133, 236; proconsul of Asia, 176; friend of Germanicus and Agrippina, 133, 236; prosecuted by Seianus, 132 f., 176; condemned with his wife, 176, 236, 376, 430; his suicide, 132.

Silius, C., consul designate for AD 48, styled a 'nobilis', 51; taken from his wife by Messallina, 175 f.; their marriage ceremony, 184.

Silius, P. (*suff.* AD 3), 52, '*nobilis*', 95; *monetalis*, 52, 394; praetorian legate in Moesia, 101, 289, 426; his father, 52.

Silius, A. Caecina Largus, C. (*cos.* AD 13), his peculiar nomenclature, 97. See C. Silius.

Silius Nerva, P. (*cos.* 20), *novus homo*, 42; plays dice with Augustus, 72; his career and family 43 f.; his wife, 44; governor of Tarraconensis, 44, 393, 408, 426; proconsul of Illyricum, 34, 289, 332, 400, 408, 426; his Alpine operations, 78, 331 f., 400, 426; not given credit by Velleius, 426; his sons and grandsons, 52, 95, 97, 101, 425 f.

Silius Nerva, P. (*cos.* AD 28), 428.

SILIUS ITALICUS, Ti. (*cos.* AD 68), on the sequence of dynasts, 271; mentions Concani, 383; invents a Tarius, 55.

Sosia Gallia, wife of C. Silius (*cos.* AD 13), friend of Agrippina, 236; prosecuted by Seianus, 132 ff., 236, 376; her banishment, 376.

Sosius, C. (*cos.* 32), *novus homo*, *quindecimvir*, 48; partisan of Antonius, 29, 34, 207; admiral at Actium, 208 f.; spared after the defeat, 31; his triumph, 48.

Statilia, elderly lady, related to Statilius Taurus, 377.

Statilia, wife of L. Calpurnius Piso (the Augur), 337, 376 f.

Statilia Messallina, lover and then wife of Nero, 187, 240; her former husbands, 240 f.; attracts Otho, 241; her son, 241; her age, 241.

Statilii, 33, 44, 72, 78, 376 f.

Statilius Corvinus, T. (*cos.* AD 45), grandson of Messalla, 240, 377; his alleged conspiracy against Claudius, 183, 240.

Statilius Taurus, *monetalis*, his date and identity, 376 f.

Statilius Taurus, Sisenna (*cos.* AD 16), his parentage, 376 f.; his wife and daughter, 73; owns Cicero's house, 377.

Statilius Taurus, T. (*suff.* 37; *cos* II 26), *novus homo*, 27, 387, 393; Lucanian, 44; marshal, 33, 87; Antonian naval commander, 202; at Actium, 274; friend of Agrippa and Maece-

nas, 211; 'vir triumphalis', 34; proconsul of Spain, 37, and perhaps of Macedonia, 274.

Maintains his own troops at Rome, 35; supports Sentius Saturninus, 42; *praefectus urbi*, 40; his amphitheatre, 9; his children and grandson, 73, 240, 376 f.; mentioned by Velleius, 435.

Statilius Taurus, T. (*cos.* AD 11), 97; son of the marshal, 240; 376 f.; his wife and issue, 240, 377.

Statilius Taurus, T. (*cos.* AD 44), victim of Agrippina, 240.

STRABO, comes to Rome, 346; travels in Egypt with Aelius Gallus, 371; the purpose of his work, 370; its termination, 346; as a historian continues Polybius, 81, 346; his Roman informants, 371, 380; his information fades, 370; sporadic particulars and revision, 370 f.; on Augustus' division of the provinces, 8; on distances in Germany, 66; detailed information on Tarraconensis, a significant late insertion, 371; some details he provides, 66, 204, 208, 289, 361, 388, 390.

Strigones, peculiar name, 49.

SUETONIUS TRANQUILLUS, C., his personal sources of information, 102; on Augustus and his family, 118, 120 f., 172, 248 f., 316, 408, 410; on Tiberius, 82, 84, 135, 145 f., 344, 349 ff., 355 f., 449; on Caligula, 179 f., 186, 195; on Claudius, 164; on Nero and his relatives, 159, 161, 163, 417, 433 f.; on the Ahenobarbi, 156, 159, 174, 424 f.; on the children of Agrippa and Marcella, 125, 144, 147; on others, 122, 342, 355, 388, 434; quotes Messalla, 446; alert to 'curiosa', 350.

Some defects and omissions, 45, 142, 155 f., 159 f., 179 f., 248 f., 269, 355, 425; source for Juvenal scholiast, 119; for Jerome, 212, 411; for Eutropius and Orosius, 335; Heredia's sonnet on him, 353.

Suillius Rufus, P. (*suff.* ?AD 41), quaestor to Germanicus, 182; a savage prosecutor, used by Messallina, 182, 279; accuses Julia, daughter of Drusus, 182; and Valerius Asiaticus, 184.

Sulla, see Cornelius Sulla.

SULPICIA, poetess, perhaps wife of Caecilius Cornutus, 47; her parents, 47, 206.

Sulpicia, wife of a Cassius, 206.

Sulpicia, wife of Q. Aelius Tubero, 57; her father and children, 306 f.; season of her death, 307.

Sulpicia Praetextata, wife of Licinius Crassus Frugi, 280.

Sulpicii, 57, 87, 95, 158, 229, 433.

Sulpicius Camerinus, Q. (*cos.* AD 9), 97 f., 229; his cognomen, 75; perhaps the epic poet, 71.

His dealings with certain individuals: Messalla Corvinus, 100; M. Lepidus, 129; the Silani, 115, 193, 293 f.; Haterius, 146, 267; M. Lollius, 176 f., 431; Messallinus, 134, 234, 237; Cotta Maximus, 235; Scaurus, 267; Arruntius, 268; 'duo Blaesi', 163; Lentulus the Augur, 293 f., 296; Aelius Lamia, 338; Propertius Celer, 361; Cn. Piso, 60, 138, 373 f.; Piso the Pontifex, 343, 365; Piso the Augur, 375 f.; Asinius Gallus, 133, 137, 429; Sulpicius Quirinius, 177, 431; Thrasyllus, 366; Aelius Seianus, 137 f., 140, 267 f., 300, 310 ff., 364, 427, 435.

Dislikes women, 168; especially the elder Agrippina, 185 f.; but likes Antonia the younger, 169; dominated by Livia, 169; has to arrange marriages, 133, 171, 173; Julia's complaints of him, 91.

His oratory, 71, 366; studies in rhetoric, 353 ff.; his model Messalla Corvinus, 215; speeches, 348, 355 f., 366, 374, 439, 446; poetry, 350; purist and pedant, 355; powerful intelligence, 366; alleged prophecy about Galba, 172; Greek and liberal studies, 349 ff.; literary companions when abroad, 95, 350; choice preferences in Latin poetry, 360 f.; art collections, 72, 351 f.; the picture showing Atalanta, 352; interest in philosophy and astrology, 168, 366, 372; classical dinner parties, 351; 365 f.; drinker and gourmet, 345, 352; builds temple to Concordia, 78; rebuilds theatre of Pompeius, 131; ideal of free speech, 117; relief fund, 192.

Discredited in Agrippina the younger's memoirs, 140; praised by Velleius, 12, 423 ff., 428; and by Livy, 445; in Orosius, 335 f.; impresses Tacitus, 366; Dio's sources hostile to him, 139, 436; his autobiography, 140; his generation not keen historians, 358; in Horace, 361, 365 f., 391, 395, 402 ff.; probably disliked Horace, 402; in Ovid, 219, 233, 413; perhaps doesn't care for Ovid's *Fasti*, 414; his statuette, 235, 445; on *Ara Pacis*, 152; his coins, 97.

TIBULLUS, his patrons: Cornutus, 47; Messalla, 209 f., 230; his illness at Corcyra, 209; date of his death, 230, 251; in Velleius, 402.

Tigranes, ruler of Armenia, 82; succeeded by his son, 83.

TIMAGENES, anti-Roman historian, 357 f.

TIMON, of Phlius, Sceptic and satirist, 365.

Tiridates, Parthian pretender mentioned by Horace, 394.

Titius, M. (*suff.* 31), nephew of Munatius Plancus, 30; acquires Fabia Paullina, 30, 73, 417; proconsul of Asia, 417; Antonian admiral, 417; deserts Antonius, 30, 264;

informs about his will, 208; murders Sex. Pompeius, 434; as legate of in Syria, 521 f., 340; 417; receives Parthian hostages, 321; driven from theatre, 434; in Velleius, 434.

Titius Sabinus, knight, friend of Germanicus, 222.

TITUS, his alleged adultery with Domitia Longina, 187; his relevance to a tragedy, 156.

Torquatus, *see* Manlius Torquatus.

TRAJAN, on 'capax imperii', 139; on food and games, 440.

Tuberones, 305, 308, 310, 349.

Tullia, Cicero's daughter, 20.

Tullius Cicero, L. (cousin of the orator), his decease, 22.

Tullius Cicero, M. (*cos.* 63), *see* CICERO.

Tullius Cicero, M. (*suff.* 30), son of the orator, 30; governor of Syria, 33, 209; his aptitudes, 33.

Ummidius Quadratus, C. (*suff.* c. AD 40), quaestor, 60.

Ummidius Quadratus, C. (*suff.* AD 118), 58, 175.

Urgulania, mother of Plautius Silvanus, Etruscan, 73; friend of Livia Drusilla, 88, 430; prosecuted by L. Piso, 376; an annoyance to Tiberius, 430.

Valeria, fifth wife of Sulla, 36, 73, 227.

Valeria, sister of Messalla Corvinus, wife of the younger Ser. Sulpicius Rufus, 47; their poetical daughter, 47, 206.

Valeria, sister of Messalla Corvinus, wife of Q. Pedius (*suff.* 43), 206.

Valeria, daughter of Messalla Corvinus, wife of Statilius Taurus; her sons, 240.

Valeria, relative of the younger Marcella, 147.

Valeria Messallina, third wife of Claudius, 147, 174, 178, 229; her parents, 147, 164, 178 f.; her half-brother, Faustus, 164, 183, her son, 183; daughters, 277; her age, 166, 178 f.; plots against Ap. Junius Silanus, 165; her amours and allies, 279; breaks marriage of Junia Silana, 175; her victims, 182 ff., 279; her marriage ceremony with C. Silius, 184; her dominance and use of agents, 182; perhaps unfairly treated by Tacitus, 185.

Valerii, 77, 98, 158, 206 f., 216, 228, 230, 241 ff., 266, 283, 419 f.

Valerii Flacci, 25.

Valerii Laevini, 77.

Valerii Messallae, 30, 147, 158, 227 ff.

Valerius Asiaticus, D. (*suff.* AD 35, *cos II* 46), 183; his wife, 177; his alleged adultery, 178; his accusation and trial, 184; from Vienna, 416; owner of the Gardens of Lucullus, 184.

Asia, 70; prosecuted and condemned for cruelty, 193, 229, 266, 293; Tiberius' attitude to him, 100, 193.

Valerius Poplicola, C., 242. *See* (Vipstanus) Poplicola.

'Valesius', legendary rich countryman, 77.

Valgius, A., son of a senator, 395.

Valgius, Q. (*pr.* before 129), 56.

Valgius, Q., a Caesarian, 56.

VALGIUS RUFUS, C. (*suff. 12*), *novus homo*, 55 f., 153; no known proconsulate, 62; poet, grammarian, and botanist, 62, 359; his patron Messalla Corvinus, 359, 362; addressed by Horace, 386; his extraction, 395.

Varius Ligur, Guard Prefect, 301.

VARIUS RUFUS, L., Epicurean, tragedian, and epic poet, 359; addressed by Horace, 393; friend of Augustus, 393.

VARRO, polymath from Reate, his ancestry, 391, presumed tribe, 392; on *Sodales Titii* and *Arvales*, 4, 47; praises Messalla the Augur, 228.

Varro, *see* Terentius Varro.

Varrones, 392.

Varrones Murenae, 391.

Varus, *see* Quinctilius Varus.

Vatinius, P. (*cos.* 47), a friend of Fabius Maximus (*suff.* 45), 420.

Vedius Pollio, P., cruel son of a freedman, 39; agent of Augustus, 208; 'piscinarius', 72; builds a *Caesareum*, 72; his property, 72; portrayed on coins in Asia, 208; his death, 213.

VELLEIUS PATERCULUS, 421 ff.; contrasted with Sallust, 12; far from the first rank, 356; his design a panegyric of Tiberius, 12, 82, 84 f., 102, 290, 402, 423, 428, 431, 435; catalogues Augustus' achievements and 'clementia', 79, 86, 208, 264, 363; his homage to Livia Drusilla, 430; on Julia's catastrophe, 91, 429.

   On Seianus, 301, 304, 307, 425, 435 f.; promotes those in favour with Tiberius, 101, 128, 156, 205, 232, 334, 343, 424 ff., 428, 432, 435; depicts unfavourably opponents of the Principate, 35, 121, 176, 208, 214 f., 388 f., 402, 424, 429, 431; sentimental towards *nobiles*, 423 ff., 442; biased by his personal relationships, 425 f., 428; his patron, 102; his dedication to Vinicius, 423.

   Military experience, 426, 431; on the rebellion in Illyricum, 427; Varus' disaster, 328, 431; the 'clades Lolliana', 402, 424; Piso's Thracian War, 334, 424; defames the Germans, 326.

   His assessment of society, 445; on the old Republic recreated, 447; gives literary verdicts, 402, 424; his veiled language, 121; abridges, deceives, and distorts, 420, 427 f., 436 f.; his omissions, 324, 425, 428 f.; merits of his style, 437; exuberance, 437; 'festinatio', 437; carelessness, 429.

Ventidius, P. (*suff.* 43), 3, 27, 33.

VERANIUS, antiquarian writer, 6.

Veranius, Q., indicts Piso the Augur, 376.

'Verenia', primeval Vestal Virgin, 6.

Vergilius, *see* VIRGIL.

Vergilius, merchant or banker in Horace, 397.

VESPASIAN, his son's marriage, 187.

Vestinus Atticus, M. (*cos.* AD 65), husband of Statilia Messallina, 240.

'Vibia', *see* Vinicia.

Vibius Crispus, Q. (*cos. III suff.* AD 83), orator and courtier, 119, 240.

Vibius Marsus, C. (*suff.* AD 17), indicted for treason, 173.

Vibius Postumus, C. (*suff.* AD 5), *novus homo* from Larinum, 427; consular legate in Dalmatia, 100, 128, 427; proconsul of Asia, 132, 379, 427; mentioned by Velleius, 427.

Vibius Rufinus, C. (*suff.* AD 21 or 22), 225; legate under Tiberius, 100; proconsul of Asia, 238.

Vibius Rufus, C. (*suff.* AD 16), 71; elderly orator, 225, 363; perhaps *curator aquarum*, 225 f.; marries Cicero's widow Publilia, 225.

Vinicia, conjectured wife of Arruntius Camillus, 259, 278.

Vinicianus, *see* Annius Vinicianus.

Vinicii, 44, 78, 428.

Vinicius, L. (*suff.* 33), proconsul of Asia, 45.

Vinicius, L. (*suff.* 5), *monetalis*, 52; frequents Julia, 87.

Vinicius, M. (*suff.* 19), his *patria*, 44; on the Rhine, 45, 393; a *quindecimvir*, 49; begins (with Agrippa) the Bellum Pannonicum (in 13), 65, 289, 332, 405, 426; in Illyricum again, 290; in Germany, 102, 290, 325, 426; his *ornamenta triumphalia*, 325, 426.

   Proconsul of Asia, 62, 405; honoured at Mylasa and Aphrodisias, 405; friend of Augustus, 72, 405; his son and grandson, 102, 426; in Velleius, 428.

Vinicius, M. (*cos.* AD 30; *II* 45), elegant orator, 179, 429, 437; his extraction, 173; marries Julia Livilla, 172, 278, 306; administers relief fund, 173, 192; proposed as emperor, 181, 278; his discretion, 182 f., favoured by Claudius, 183; accompanies him to Britain, 279; repulses Messallina, 183; poisoned by her, 183, 279; his state funeral, 183; patron of Velleius, 423, 436; his nephew's treason, 181, 183.

TABLES

The first four tables reproduce Tables I–IV in *The Roman Revolution* (1939), modified in a few items. For the rest, to render fully intelligible a text often compressed, a long sequence became expedient; and manifold problems of selection and of presentation had to be faced. The remarks that follow may furnish guidance.

(1) Many of the stemmata printed in standard works of reference annexed authority, proper in the past but often usurped and abused by the epigonous (cf. p. 142). Fresh inspection of known evidence has entailed much revision. Only in the recent time was Piso the Pontifex liberated from the *cognomon* 'Frugi' or severed from the Crassus Frugi line (Ch. XX). The process goes on, with notable consequences, above all for the Aemilii Lepidi.

(2) Of set purpose (and for avowed reasons) the exposition accorded prime value to the ancient houses that stand conspicuous with consulships from 16 to 7 (Ch. IV). By good fortune, only ten other consuls from *gentes* of equipollent rank are elsewhere represented during the whole reign of Caesar Augustus. First, in the first decade, two Junii Silani and a Claudius Marcellus. Second, in the last twenty years, three Sulpicii, a Silanus, a Furius Camillus, a Cassius Longinus— and a Metellus, viz. Creticus Silanus (cos. AD 7), on this computation duly assigned to the adopting parentage, after the Roman fashion. They find lodgement on one table or another, with two exceptions only. The three Sulpicii are miscellaneous (two of them only names, apart from Galba's father), while Marcellus Aeserninus (cos. 22 BC) is not easy to fit in: the grandfather of the illustrious orator (praetor in AD 19), with whom the line ended (*PIR*² C 928).

(3) Given the multifarious connections in the high aristocracy, stemmata incur the risk of an intolerable extension in width. Economy and clarity enjoin divisions, as with Valerii Messallae and Junii Silani.

(4) In consequence, overlapping and much repetition. It can prove beneficent. Princesses are not just appendages to the 'domus Augusta'. They stand in their

own right. Thus the two Marcellae (Table VI); and Paullus the Censor, registered among the Aemilii (Table IV), goes on to emerge (Table V) as a personage of multiple significance in the ambiance of the dynasty.

(5) Furthermore, tables may convey sundry items of kinship not specified in text or annotation.

(6) At the same time, restrictions are imposed. Cornelii Lentuli proliferate. Not enviable or easily remunerative would be an attempt to attach the seven Augustan consuls to Lentuli of the late Republic. Not to mention their assumption of the Scipionic name (Ch. XVIII).

(7) Inferred relationships. The marriages of Scribonia (Ch. XVIII) and the aristocratic kinsfolk of Aelius Seianus (Ch. XXII) are infested with perplexities that had to be explicitly discussed. To produce stemmata carried hazards. They have been taken. But Terentii Varrones baffle (Ch. XXVII).

(8) Iterated matrimony. The more that is known about senators, the more marriages. Ladies of birth and rank conform. Domitia Lepida, the younger daughter of Ahenobarbus (cos. 16 BC), had three husbands—and conjecture evokes three for her elder sister (Ch. XII). Again, it is not certain that either Messalla Appianus or the younger Marcella, a married couple in 12 BC, had the same partner a decade previously. Other instances occur, not all attached to stemmata.

(9) On various grounds certain early marriages are surmised. There is a chance that Cornelia was not the first consort of Paullus the Censor (p. 109); and for his son Marcus (cos. AD 6) a Vipsania should be reckoned with (p. 126), anterior to the Ignota who produced Caligula's friend and coeval, the last of the line.

(10) Children, ephemeral members, or betrothals (although important) are not all put on register. But it would have come hard to deny a place (at least on Table VIII) to the son and the daughter of Ahenobarbus and Antonia who stand on the Ara Pacis (Ch. XII).

(11) Persons not directly attested as named persons are marked by italics.

They supply links not merely desirable but often necessary between generations or between allied families. Thus on prime show for descendants of Pompeius (Table XIV) and of Sulla (Table XVI). Recourse from time to time to *Ignota* both illustrates the dearth of evidence for spouses of eminent noblemen and helps the spacing of items on stemmata.

I   THE   METELLI

The family tree of the Caecilii Metelli has been compiled with the help of the tables of Münzer (*RE* III. 1229 f.; *RA* 304). Certain additions have been made, such as the family of Ap. Claudius Pulcher, the sons of Crassus, and three of the five marriages of Pompeius Magnus.

Neither this table nor some of the others that follow claim to be exhaustive, to give all collaterals or descendants. For the last Metelli see Table XVIII.

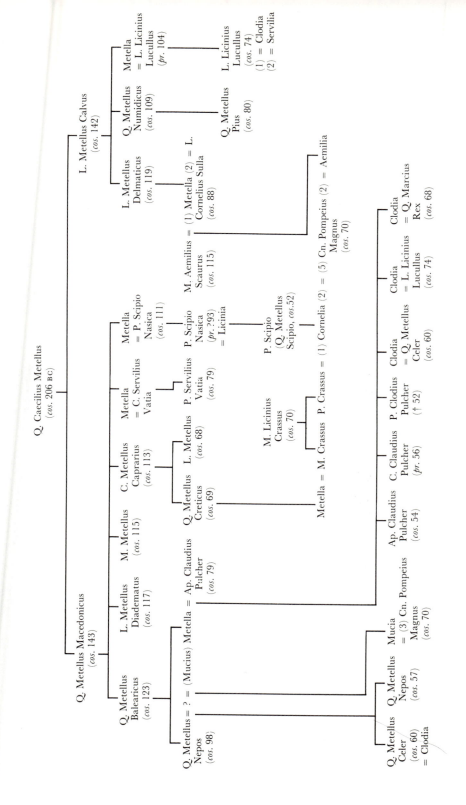

II THE KINSMEN OF CATO

This table reproduces the researches of Münzer, *RA*, 328 ff. The leading clue is provided by the two marriages of Livia, the sister of M. Livius Drusus (*tr. pl.* 91 BC). For the relationship of Catulus to the Domitii cf. Münzer, *RA*, 286 f. Here modified, thanks to E. Badian, *Studies in Greek and Roman History* (1964), 232.

The Q. Caepio who adopted Marcus Brutus is omitted. For the problems, see J. Geiger, *Ancient Society* iv (1973), 143 ff.

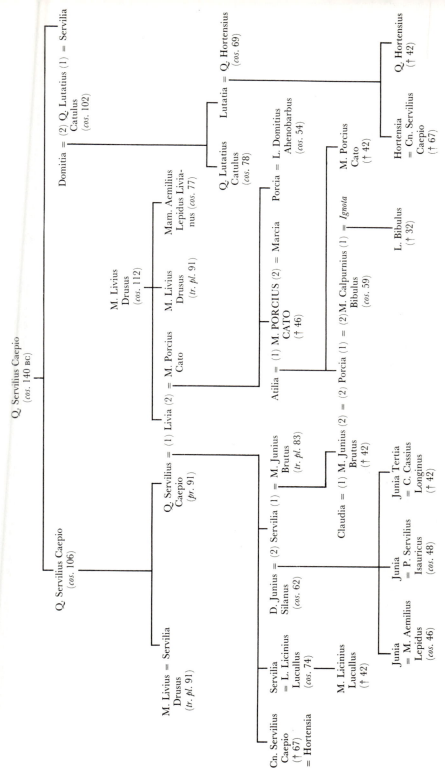

Q. Servilius Caepio
(cos. 140 BC)

Q. Servilius Caepio
(cos. 106)

Domitia = (2) Q. Lutatius (1) = Servilia
Catulus
(cos. 102)

M. Livius = Servilia
Drusus
(tr. pl. 91)

Q. Servilius = (1) Livia (2) = M. Porcius
Caepio
(pr. 91)
Cato

M. Livius
Drusus
(cos. 112)

M. Livius
Drusus
(tr. pl. 91)

Mam. Aemilius
Lepidus Livia-
nus (cos. 77)

Lutatia = Q. Hortensius
(cos. 69)

Q. Lutatius
Catulus
(cos. 78)

Porcia = L. Domitius
Ahenobarbus
(cos. 54)

Cn. Servilius
Caepio
(† 67)
= Hortensia

Servilia
= L. Licinius
Lucullus
(cos. 74)

D. Junius = (2) Servilia (1) = M. Junius
Silanus
(cos. 62)
Brutus
(tr. pl. 83)

Atilia = (1) M. PORCIUS (2) = Marcia
CATO
(† 46)

M. Porcius
Cato
(† 42)

M. Licinius
Lucullus
(† 42)

Claudia = (1) M. Junius (2) = (2) Porcia (1) = (2) M. Calpurnius (1) = Ignota
Brutus
(† 42)
Bibulus
(cos. 59)

Junia
= M. Aemilius
Lepidus
(cos. 46)

Junia
= P. Servilius
Isauricus
(cos. 48)

Junia Tertia
= C. Cassius
Longinus
(† 42)

L. Bibulus
(† 32)

Hortensia
= Cn. Servilius
Caepio
(† 67)

Q. Hortensius
(† 42)

III THE FAMILY OF AUGUSTUS

This tree, which was designed in the main to illustrate the political history and the marriage alliances during the reign of Augustus, omits certain childless matches and does not carry his descendants beyond the second generation. For much further detail see Tables IV–VIII.

It will be observed that the tree appended to PIR^2 J (*Pars* IV, 1966) covers six pages.

Account has now to be taken of the daughter of Agrippa whom Quinctilius Varus married: revealed by *Kölner Pap.* I (1976), 10 (cf. p. 146 and Table XXVI). But another accession is here added, namely Quinctilia, the wife of Sex. Appuleius (*cos.* 29 BC), from *AE* 1966, 422. For the Appuleii, Table XXVI. Finally, the bottom left side of Table III in *Rom. Rev.* was erroneous. Here amended.

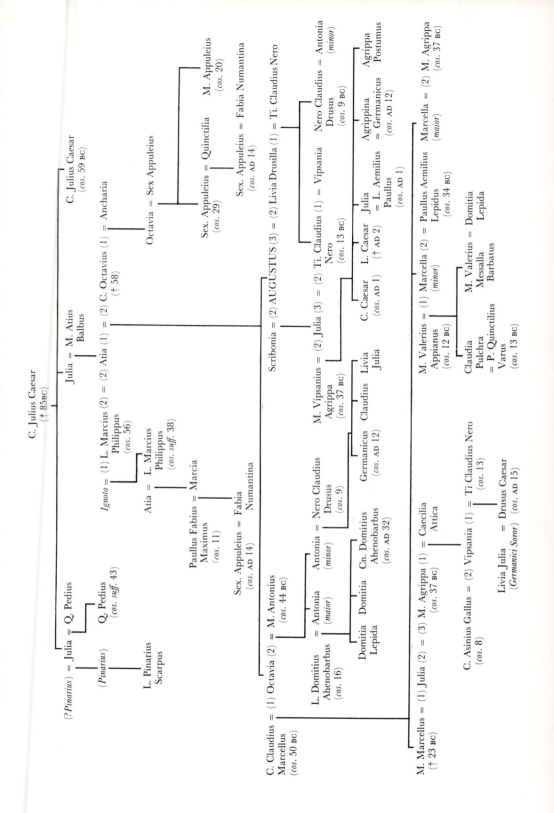

IV THE AEMILII LEPIDI

This table was taken from that of Groag (PIR^2, A, p. 57). It omits M'. Lepidus (cos. 66) and his son Quintus (cos. 21): not closely related, and no further issue. Here as elsewhere it accepts his explanation of Sullan and Pompeian ancestry in Manius Lepidus (cos. AD 11).

The redistribution of items in Tacitus that was carried out in 1955 (cf. p. 129) redeemed Marcus Lepidus (cos. AD 6) as the 'capax imperii'. Modifying PIR^2 A 363 and 369, it did not, so it happens, affect the stemma as a whole. But Paullus the arvalis (A 392) lapses. Not a son of L. Paullus (cos. AD 1) and Julia, but the man himself (Ch. IX).

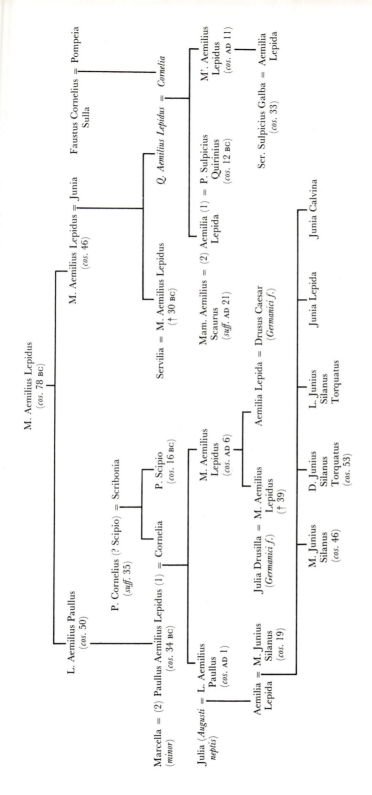

V PAULLUS THE CENSOR

This table carries conjectures either recently published or presented for the first time in the text. The relevant items or problems stand as follows.

(1) Cornelia, the Scipionic wife of Paullus. See Ch. XIX and Ch. XX.

(2) His marriage to the younger Marcella is put subsequent to the death of Messalla Appianus early in 12 (Ch. XI): not, as by others, in the short interval after the decease of Cornelia in 16. Regillus, the son of Paullus and Marcella, was quaestor to Ti. Caesar, not earlier than AD 15 (*ILS* 949: Saguntum).

(3) An early wife for Paullus can be detected, viz. a Sempronia Atratina (p. 109). Not inserted on this stemma.

(4) A postulated Aemilia Lepida, sister of Paullus and mother to L. Domitius Ahenobarbus (*cos.* 16), conveys double benefit. She explains the name of Domitia Lepida—and Paullus has his proper station, in the rear of Ahenobarbus and Antonia in the family group on the *Ara Pacis* (Ch. XII, cf. Table VIII).

(5) In the year 21 M. Lepidus (*cos.* AD 6) had young children (*Ann.* III, 35.2). An earlier marriage is to be assumed (*c.* 8 BC); and a Vipsania offers, daughter to Agrippa and Marcella (p. 125). Further, a son is conjectured, viz. the young and ephemeral M. Lepidus, who had married an Appuleia (p. 127).

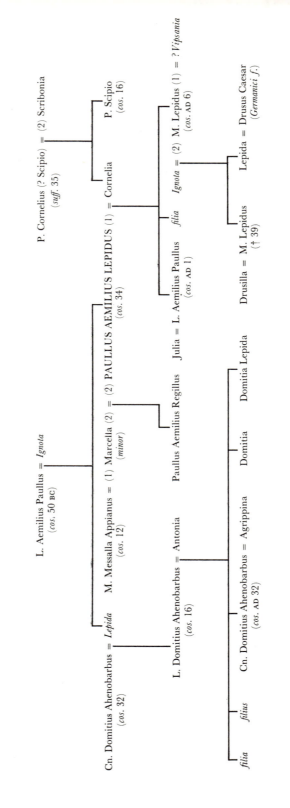

VI   THE TWO MARCELLAE

The marriages of the younger Marcella (born in 39) earn ample discussion in Ch. XI. She was consigned to Paullus the Censor soon after the death of Messalla Appianus (*cos.* 12). Previous consorts for Marcella and for Appianus cannot be excluded (p. 151), given their ages or (far from decisive) the absence of earlier born children. The approximate age of Messalla Barbatus (not surviving to a consulship) is deduced from his marriage to Domitia Lepida (p. 164). Barbatus was the first of three husbands.

In relevance to this stemma belong 'Paullus the Censor' (Table V), 'Claudii Pulchri' (VII), 'The Other Messallae' (X), 'Quinctilius Varus' (XXVI).

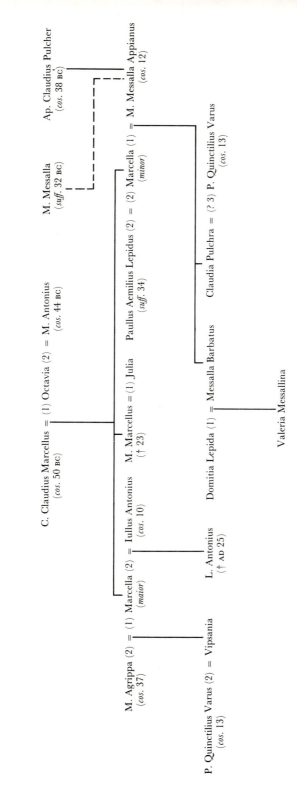

VII CLAUDII PULCHRI

Ap. Claudius Pulcher (*cos.* 54) appears on Table I, along with his two brothers and three sisters. He took in adoption the sons of his brother Gaius: whence Ap. Claudius Pulcher (*cos.* 38) and Pulcher Claudius, otherwise 'Appius minor' (*PIR*² C 983). The son of the former (mother not known) is assumed to be Messalla Appianus (*cos.* 12).

A sister has been conjectured for Appianus, to furnish Claudian ancestry for one branch of the Junii Silani (p. 194, cf. Table XIII). For Claudia Pulchra, p. 147; for the scapegrace son of P. Clodius and Fulvia, p. 149.

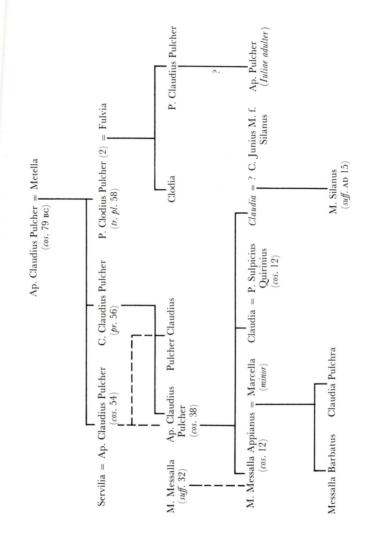

Ap. Claudius Pulcher = Metella
(cos. 79 BC)

Servilia = Ap. Claudius Pulcher   C. Claudius Pulcher   P. Clodius Pulcher (2) = Fulvia
(cos. 54)   (pr. 56)   (tr. pl. 58)

M. Messalla   Ap. Claudius   Pulcher   Claudius   Clodia   P. Claudius Pulcher
(suff. 32)   Pulcher
                   (cos. 38)

M. Messalla Appianus = Marcella   Claudia = P. Sulpicius   Claudia = ? C. Junius M. f.   Ap. Pulcher
(cos. 12)   (minor)   Quirinius   Silanus   (Iuliae adulter)
                                                 (cos. 12)

Messalla Barbatus   Claudia Pulchra   M. Silanus
                                                                                        (suff. AD 15)

VIII   THE AHENOBARBI

This table was prepared to accompany the article 'Neglected Children on the *Ara Pacis*', *AJA* LXXXVIII (1984), 583 ff. For further details, Ch. XII. The postulated Lepida brings Paullus the Censor into a closer nexus with the dynasty than earlier apparent (cf. also Table V). His sons thereby become first cousins to Ahenobarbus (*cos.* 16).

Following Messalla Barbatus, two more husbands are certified for Domitia Lepida (*PIR*[2] D 180), namely Faustus Cornelius Sulla (*suff.* 31) and Ap. Claudius Silanus (*cos.* 28), the latter son of an Appia Claudia (Table XIII).

For Domitia, the elder aunt of Nero, only one husband stands on attestation, viz. Passienus Crispus (*suff.* 27), cf. *PIR*[2] D 171. Reasoned conjecture can add two predecessors (pp. 162f.): Q. Haterius Agrippa (*cos.* 22) and Q. Junius Blaesus (*suff.* 26).

For clarity and emphasis, the marriages of the two sisters have not been attached to this stemma.

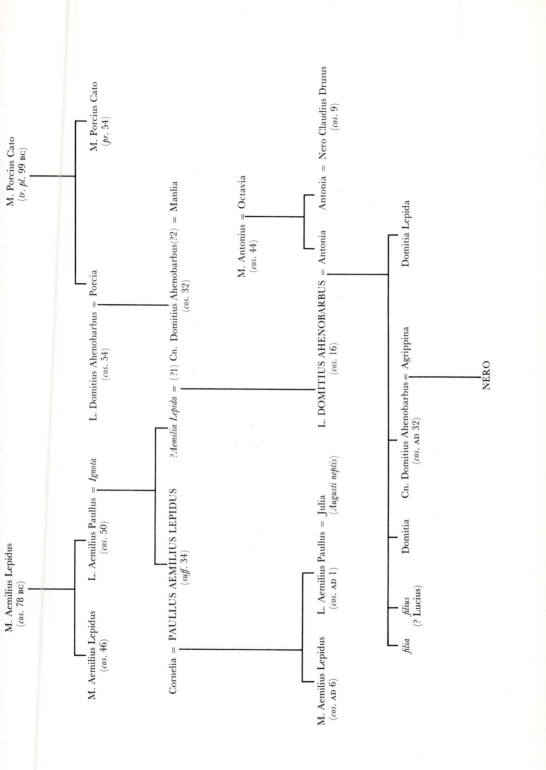

IX   MESSALLA CORVINUS

The following items of annotation may help.

(1) The stemma of the Messallae presented in *RE* VIII A, 143–6 is vulnerable and even erroneous.

(2) By marrying his first wife (not identified), the consul of 61 acquired a stepson, L. Gellius Poplicola (*cos.* 36). For problems in the evidence, Münzer, *RE* VII. 104.

(3) The arduous question of Corvinus' two marriages is discussed in Ch. XVII. Also in *History in Ovid* (1978), Ch. VII.

(4) The link with Aurelii Cottae also concerns the ancestry of Lollia Paullina (Table XI).

(5) No wife discoverable for either son of Messalla Corvinus.

(6) For Corvinus' sister, marrying the son of Ser. Sulpicius Rufus (*cos.* 51), see further 'Three Jurists' (Table XXIV).

(7) For the chance that Corvinus and L. Calpurnius Bibulus (Republican and Antonian) were closely related, see p. 232.

(8) The extraction of the Vipstani is conjectural (pp. 241 f.).

(9) Valeria, a daughter of Corvinus, was divined by Borghesi as maternal grandmother to Statilia Messallina (cf. *PIR*[1] V 160).

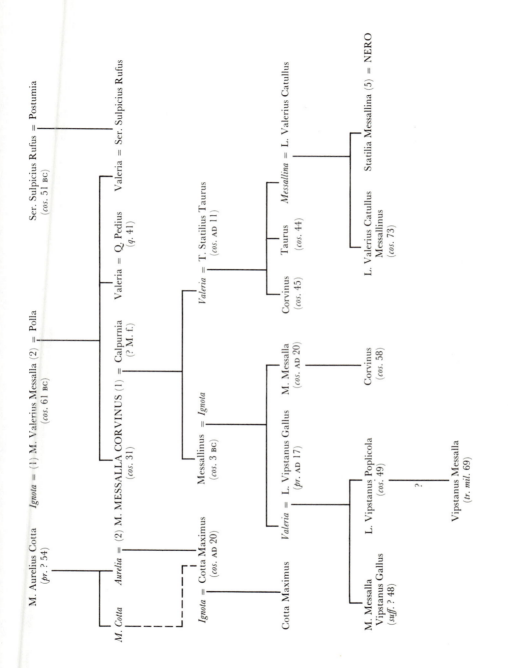

X THE OTHER MESSALLAE

From M. Valerius Messalla (*cos.* 161) to the two consuls there is only a praetor about 120 and a legate in 90. On whom, *RP* (1979), 265 f. The consul of 61 (the father of Corvinus) was 'M. f. M.'n.' (*ILS* 46). Therefore the homonym in 53 was 'M.'f.', so it was natural to assume. The patronym is now disclosed as 'Marcus' (p. 247). Hence all the more reason for nicknames, viz. 'Niger' and 'Rufus'. The latter may be more elegantly styled 'Messalla the Augur'.

This stemma links to 'The Two Marcellae' (Table VI) and to 'Claudia Pulchri' (VII).

Nothing can be done with the Messalla who was *monetalis* in a college of four about 6 BC (*BMC R.Emp.I* 46 ff.): absent, by the way, from *PIR*[1] and from *RE*. And the parentage of T. Quinctius Crispinus Valerianus (*suff.* AD 2) eludes (p. 57).

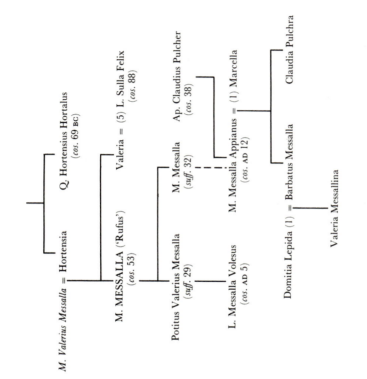

M. *Valerius Messalla* = Hortensia

Q. Hortensius Hortalus
(*cos.* 69 BC)

M. MESSALLA ('Rufus')
(*cos.* 53)

Valeria = (5) L. Sulla Felix
(*cos.* 88)

Potitus Valerius Messalla
(*suff.* 29)

M. Messalla
(*suff.* 32)

Ap. Claudius Pulcher
(*cos.* 38)

L. Messalla Volesus
(*cos.* AD 5)

M. Messalla Appianus = (1) Marcella
(*cos.* AD 12)

Domitia Lepida (1) = Barbatus Messalla

Claudia Pulchra

Valeria Messallina

Claudius Caesar declared her extraction: Lollia Paullina had for mother a sister of L. Volusius, for 'patruus magnus' Cotta Messallinus (*Ann.* XII. 22.2). The second item has caused much perplexity. Groag submitted a double hypothesis (*RE* XII. 1378). First, M. Lollius her grandfather (*cos.* 21) was by birth an Aurelius Cotta, whom a Lollius adopted. Second, the father of that Cotta went on to take in adoption the younger son of Messalla Corvinus. That is, the consul of AD 20, who assumed the *cognomen* 'Messallinus' when his elder brother died.

Various reasons tell against that construction. A different solution has been proposed, not in any great confidence (p. 178). An unattested Aurelius Cotta adopted the son of Corvinus, presumably his sister's son (Table IX). If Marcus Lollius had married another sister of that Cotta, Cotta Messallinus (*cos.* AD 20) would be a nephew to the postulated Aurelia, wife of M. Lollius and grandmother of Lollia Paullina.

Not, however, 'patruus magnus'. Although abnormally accurate, the consular historian is not inerrant about aristocratic pedigrees. For examples, *Tacitus* (1958), 748 f. He was interested in the Volusii (consuls in 87 and 92); and the grandson of Lollia Saturnina was consul suffect in 94 (for his nomenclature, *PIR*² L 320).

In *PIR*² L 328 no light is cast on 'patruus magnus'. But in L 312 a son of M. Lollius, fancied by some as a consul in AD 13, is duly deprecated. On which, p. 177.

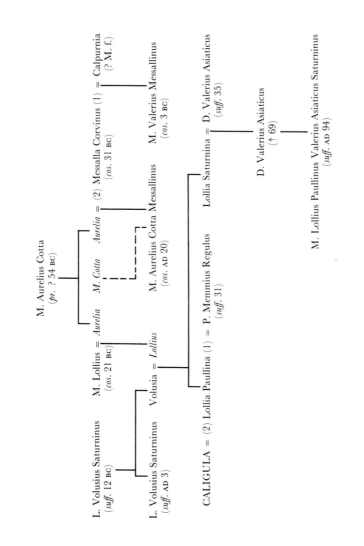

M. Aurelius Cotta
(pr. ? 54 BC)

Aurelia = (2) Messalla Corvinus (1) = Calpurnia
(cos. 31 BC)   (? M. f.)

M. Valerius Messallinus
(cos. 3 BC)

M. Cotta   Aurelia

M. Aurelius Cotta Messallinus
(cos. AD 20)

M. Lollius = Aurelia
(cos. 21 BC)

Volusia = Lollius

L. Volusius Saturninus
(suff. 12 BC)

L. Volusius Saturninus
(suff. AD 3)

CALIGULA = (2) Lollia Paullina (1) = P. Memmius Regulus
(suff. 31)

Lollia Saturnina = D. Valerius Asiaticus
(suff. 35)

D. Valerius Asiaticus
(† 69)

M. Lollius Paullinus Valerius Asiaticus Saturninus
(suff. AD 94)

XII AND XIII   JUNII SILANI

Abnormally prolific and prominent under the dynasty, this family carries many problems. On the stemma printed in *PIR*² J (p. 351), their two lines derive from M. Junius D.f. Silanus (*pr.* 77 BC). The second is there linked by a dotted line. That stemma is here adopted—and for manifest convenience divided into A and B.

A significant homonym appertains to each branch. To the first belongs M. Silanus M.f. (*cos.* AD 19), who married Aemilia Lepida (*Augusti proneptis*): proconsul of Africa for a sexennium but in the pages of Tacitus only a consular date. To the second, the eloquent M. Silanus C.f. (*suff.* AD 15), son of an Appia Claudia. His brother Decimus committed adultery with Julia (*Augusti neptis*); his daughter Junia Claudilla was given in wedlock to Caligula by Tiberius Caesar; and his presumed nephew, the consul of 28, married Domitia Lepida, her third husband. Both attachments to the dynasty proved fatal.

The mysterious C. Silanus C.f. (*cos.* 17 BC) is not here included. And, with five Junii Silani consuls between 25 BC and AD 19, the extraction can be waived of the Silanus who became Q. Caecilius Q.f. M.n. Creticus Silanus, the consul of AD 7. For whom, 'The Last Metelli' (Table XVIII).

(pr. 77 BC)

L. Silanus M. f.

Silanus

Crispina = M. Silanus M. f. (*cos.* 25 BC)

Domitia Calvina = *M. Silanus*

M. SILANUS = Aemilia Lepida (*cos.* AD 19) (*Augusti proneptis*)

L. Silanus (*suff.* AD 28)

Junia Calvina († AD 79)

Junia Lepida

L. Silanus

D. Silanus Torquatus (*cos.* 53)

M. Silanus (*cos.* 46)

L. Silanus Torquatus († AD 65)

M. Silanus D.f. (*pr.* 77)

?

C. Silanus M.f. = *Appia Claudia*

Junia Torquata (*v.V.*)

M. SILANUS C.f. (*suff.* AD 15)

Junia Silana

Junia Claudilla = CALIGULA

D. Silanus (*Iuliae adulter*)

D. Silanus Gaetulicus

M. Silanus Lutatius Catulus

C. Silanus C.f. (*cos.* AD 10)

Domitia Lepida (3) = C. Appius Junius Silanus (*cos.* 28)

M. Silanus (*suff.* ? 54)

XIV DESCENDANTS OF POMPEIUS

The stemma offered in *Rom. Rev.* (Table V) was designed primarily to illustrate alliances in the posterity of Pompeius, Sulla, Crassus. Like the products of other scholars during the last fifty years, it carried problems and uncertainties. Instead, four tables are now requisite (XIV–XVII), entailing inevitable iterations and constant recourse to Ch. XIX and Ch. XX.

Table XIV concentrates on the Scribonii Libones. They always gave, and will give, trouble in abundance. Notable benefit accrues from E. J. Weinrib, *HSCP* LXXII (1968), 274 f. Another Scribonia should perhaps be admitted, sister to L. Libo (*cos.* AD 16) and to Libo Drusus: because of the 'duae Scriboniae' of *ILS* 9433. Further, a distinct novelty: Q. Caecilius Drusus Libo (*AE* 1964, 82). On whom, see p. 260 and under 'The Last Metelli' (Table XVIII).

The descendants of Faustus Sulla and Pompeia, the daughter of Magnus, will be found on Table XVI. For the identity of the L. Cinna who married Pompeia after the death of Faustus Sulla, see p. 30.

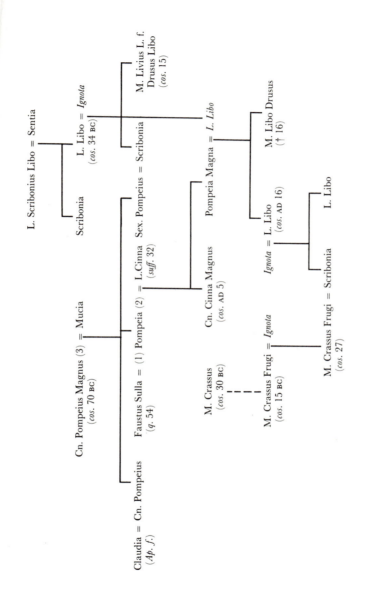

XV   M. LIVIUS DRUSUS LIBO

This character suffered general neglect: redeemed by E. J. Weinrib, *HSCP* LXXII (1968), 247 ff., cf. Ch. XIX. His reconstruction is here followed.

No wife is provided for the father of L. Arruntius (*cos.* AD 6). A conjectural Aemilia, sister to Manius Lepidus (*cos.* AD 11), furnishes a Pompeian and Sullan ascendance for Arruntius. A Cornelia had previously been surmised.

As the wife of Arruntius Camillus (*cos.* 32) a Vinicia is here conjectured (cf. p. 259) instead of the 'Vibia' of *Ann.* XII. 52.1.

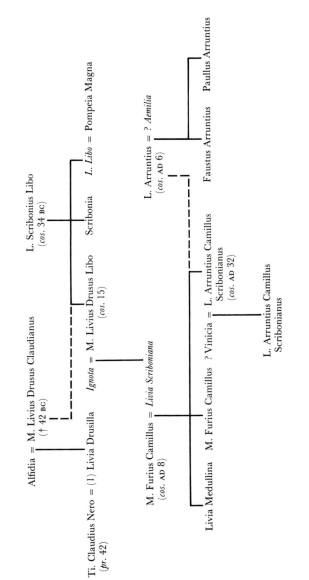

XVI DESCENDANTS OF SULLA

This stemma is taken from that of Groag (*PIR*[2] C, facing p. 362). As likewise with the Aemilii (*PIR*[2] A, p. 57). Q. Lepidus, marrying a daughter of Faustus Sulla and Pompeia (both partners nowhere attested), furnishes the ancestry of Manius Lepidus (*cos.* AD 11). For L. Arruntius (*cos.* 6) see Table XV.

As concerns Sulla Felix (*cos.* 33), an inscription found at Pisidian Antioch (*AE* 1927, 172) styles him 'gener [German]ici Caesar[is'. Perhaps a brief matrimony for Agrippina in 41, before she annexed Passienus Crispus (cf. *PIR*[2] C 1465).

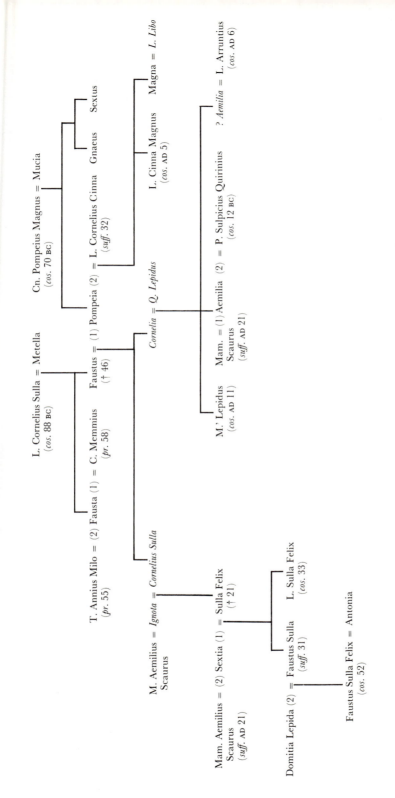

XVII DESCENDANTS OF CRASSUS

In the past confusion and error long prevailed, with manifold repercussions. Piso the Pontifex (*cos.* 15 BC) was credited with 'Frugi' for *cognomen* (on which cf. p. 330), or deemed the father of M. Crassus Frugi (*cos.* AD 27). Hence the stemma of the Calpurnii in *PIR*[2] C (facing p. 54), followed in *Rom. Rev.* Table V.

See now the revised stemma, *RP* (1979), 503. Accepted in *PIR*[2] L (facing p. 40), which also registers descendants of M. Crassus Frugi (*cos.* 64).

For a link with Libones (and with Metelli) anterior to the marriage of Crassus Frugi (*cos.* 27) and Scribonia see under 'The Last Metelli' (Table XVIII).

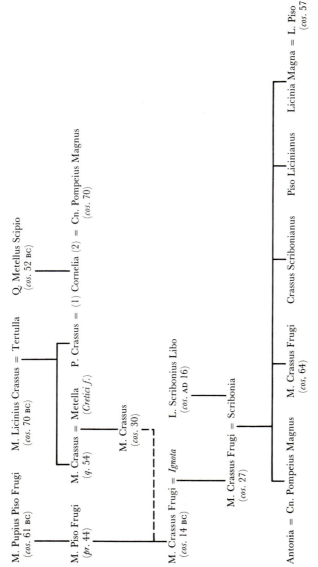

Creticus Silanus (*cos.* AD 7) was 'Q.f., M.n.'. For conjectures about Marcus and Quintus see T. P. Wiseman, *Cinna the Poet* (1974), 180, with a useful stemma of the Metelli subsequent to Macedonicus (182 f.). However, the fragmentary name of a proconsul of Sardinia (*CIL* X 758), adduced in *PIR*² C 62, is best left out of account (cf. p. 254).

Creticus is not heard of after vacating Syria in 17. A daughter was betrothed to Nero, the eldest son of Germanicus—who three years later found another bride, namely Julia, the daughter of Drusus Caesar. And the son of Creticus (C 63) could hardly have been refused a consulship by Ti. Caesar, had he survived.

A new item joins the rubric, viz. Q. Caecilius Drusus Libo. Perhaps ephemeral, and not easily added so far to any stemma (cf. p. 260 and p. 275). The inscription of M. Scribonius Storax, his *paedagogus*, revealed him (*AE* 1964, 82). Of close and cognate relevance is the dedication set up by Q. Caecilius Hilarus, freedman of 'Caecilia Crassi', along with Caecilia Eleutheris, described as freedwoman 'duarum Scriboniarum' (*ILS* 9433).

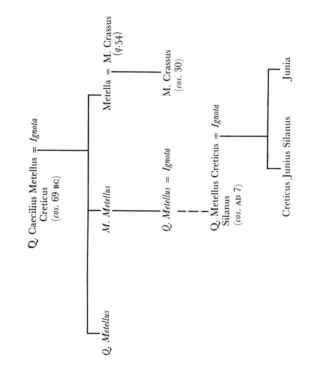

XIX   THE LAST SCIPIONES

This table serves to illustrate the pedigree of the last Scipio Nasica who, adopted by the testament of Metellus Pius, became Q. Caecilius Metellus Scipio (*cos*. 52). The extraction of his wife Aemilia (whom Cato wanted) is also exhibited. His ephemeral brother, Crassus Scipio, had been taken in adoption by L. Licinius Crassus (*cos*. 95), the maternal grandfather; and his son died at eighteen (*CIL* XIV. 3483).

Finally, it registers the Scipionic ancestry of Cn. Lentulus Marcellinus (*cos*. 56). That leads on to 'Scribonia's Marriages' (Table XX).

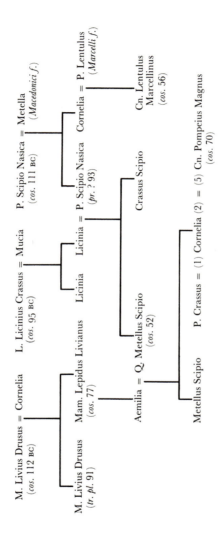

The problems are discussed to satiety in Ch. XVIII. No reason for refusing a stemma. On the contrary, it will exhibit the hazards. Curt guidance can suffice.

(1) Recording Scribonia's third venture in 40, Suetonius stated: 'nuptam antea duobus consularibus, ex altero etiam matrem' (*Divus Aug.* 62.2).

(2) For the first husband, Cn. Lentulus Marcellinus (*cos.* 56). As Dessau observed, 'collegit Borghesius' (*PIR*[1] S 220). Groag was against; and further, in a long and cautious entry (*PIR*[2] C 1395), he pronounced the problem insoluble on known evidence.

(3) The other husband eluded until the *Fasti Magistrorum Vici*, first published in 1935, disclosed a P. Cornelius, consul suffect in 35. It was not easy to reject him as a father to P. Cornelius P. f. Scipio and Cornelia, the wife of Paullus the Censor. Thus *Rom. Rev.* 229.

(4) However, this P. Cornelius (*suff.* 35) might be in fact a Lentulus Marcellinus, of Scipionic descent like the consul of 56 (cf. Table XIX).

(5) Nevertheless, Marcellinus (*cos.* 56), in the sequel of Borghesi, and P. Cornelius (? Scipio, *suff.* 35) can be taken as the successive husbands. Hence partial redemption for Suetonius. That was not the point and purpose of the investigation.

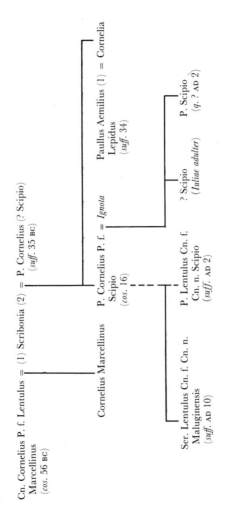

Cn. Cornelius P. f. Lentulus = (1) Scribonia (2) = P. Cornelius (? Scipio)
Marcellinus   (*suff.* 35 BC)
(*cos.* 56 BC)

Cornelius Marcellinus

P. Cornelius P. f. = *Ignota*
Scipio
(*cos.* 16)

Paullus Aemilius (1) = Cornelia
Lepidus
(*suff.* 34)

P. Lentulus Cn. f.
Cn. n. Scipio
(*suff.* AD 2)

Ser. Lentulus Cn. f. Cn. n.
Maluginensis
(*suff.* AD 10)

? Scipio
(*Iuliae adulter*)

P. Scipio
(*q.* ? AD 2)

XXI AND XXII   THE LAST LENTULI

The seven Augustan consuls were discussed in Ch. XXI ('Lentulus the Augur'); and the Marcellini duly occurred in Ch. XVIII ('The Last Scipiones'). For present purposes it was not practicable to investigate their derivation from Lentuli of the late Republic—and between 49 and 18 they show only one consul (in 38). The stemma of Münzer (*RE* IV, 1359 f.) was held 'rather inadequate and confusing' by G. V. Sumner, *The Orators in Cicero's Brutus* (1973), 142. His own version, while offering improvements, was vulnerable in certain items (notably the extraction of the Augur), and it left out L. Lentulus (*suff.* 38) and Cossus (*cos.* 1).

Instead, two selective stemmata are here presented. They are based on Groag's table (*PIR*² C, facing p. 328). However, his attachment of Maluginensis (*suff.* AD 10), adopted in *Rom. Rev.* Table VI, became obsolete long since (cf. now Table XXIII). One of the items is here omitted, viz. 'P. Le[n]tulus', consul suffect in 27: in Groag's view perhaps a grandson of old Scribonia (*PIR*² C 1387, cf. 1395).

Some may regret that no place has been found for other Cornelii of the period such as Scipiones Salvidieni Orfiti and the Dolabellae (the latter of various interest). P. Dolabella (*cos.* 10) hangs on the edge of 'Quinctilius Varus' (Table XXVI). However, the two tables show what remained of the prolific Lentuli, down to the year of Nero's end.

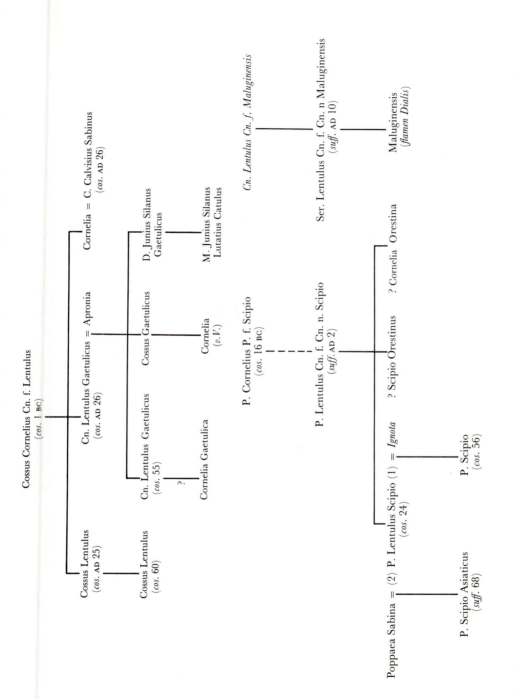

XXIII KINSMEN OF SEIANUS

Ample discussion of problems and controversy attendant since 1904 upon the emergence of *ILS* 8996 (Volsinii) is furnished in Ch. XXII. Many years elapsed before the need was seen of a wife for Seius Strabo long anterior to Cosconia Gallitta—and he may have had two in early manhood (p. 304). The thesis here accepted uses a Junia; Seianus had for maternal uncle Q. Junius Blaesus (*suff.* AD 10). Furthermore, if Junia had previously been married to Q. Aelius Tubero the jurist, Seianus acquires brothers (i.e. half-brothers), and, likewise through the Tuberones, some cousins: as postulated from Velleius II 127.3). For that family, see 'Three Jurists' (Table XXIV).

L. Seius Tubero (*suff.* AD 18) was a cause of perplexity (p. 304). On the easiest solution, a son of Q. Tubero (*cos.* 11 BC) taken in adoption by Seius Strabo. Yet perhaps a half-brother to Seianus and close to him in age. Strabo might have contracted marriages in the twenties with an Aelia as well as with a Junia.

Seianus took his *nomen* from L. Aelius Gallus, the second Prefect of Egypt, for all that some doubt and even deny. An Aelius Gallus came into the story of the year 31 (*Ann.* V. 8.1)—and that family was related to the Tuberones, so it can be argued (p. 308).

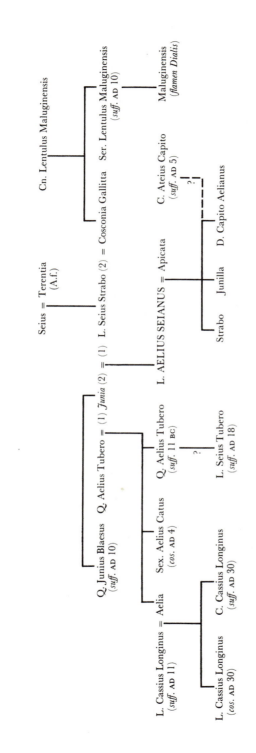

XXIV   THREE JURISTS

The following remarks supplement certain items in 'Kinsmen of Seianus' (Ch. XXII, with Table XXIII).

(1) The son of Ser. Sulpicius Rufus (*cos.* 51) being a *consobrinus* of D. Brutus, a Postumia is a desiderated mother for the latter (p. 18).

(2) The son's wife Valeria, sister to Messalla Corvinus, is mother to the poetess Sulpicia (p. 206).

(3) The three daughters of the jurist. See Münzer, *RE* IV A. 879 f.

(4) Aelii Tuberones. It is not certain that Q. Tubero (*cos.* 11 BC) and Sex. Aelius Catus (*cos.* AD 4) issue from the same wife of the jurist.

(5) L. Seius Tubero (*suff.* AD 18), is not included. On Table XXIII he appears by conjecture as a son of the consular Tubero taken in adoption by Seius Strabo.

(6) The jurist C. Cassius Longinus (*suff.* AD 30). In descent from the tribune L. Cassius Longinus an extra generation is postulated, against the suggestion in *PIR²* C 502.

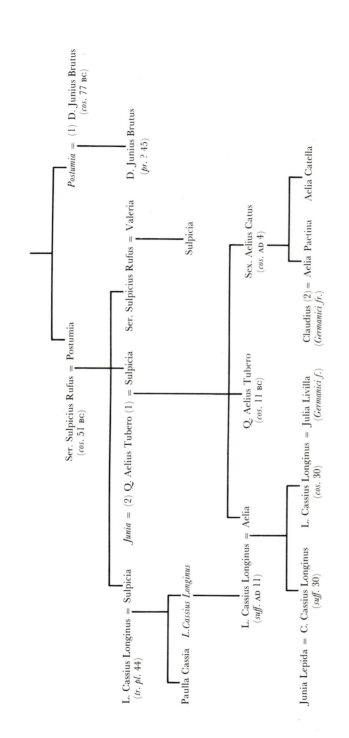

Ser. Sulpicius Rufus = Postumia = (1) D. Junius Brutus
(cos. 51 BC)   (cos. 77 BC)

D. Junius Brutus
(pr. ? 45)

Ser. Sulpicius Rufus = Valeria

Sulpicia

Junia = (2) Q. Aelius Tubero (1) = Sulpicia

Q. Aelius Tubero
(cos. 11 BC)

Sex. Aelius Catus
(cos. AD 4)

Claudius (2) = Aelia Paetina
(Germanici fr.)

Aelia Catella

L. Cassius Longinus = Sulpicia
(tr. pl. 44)

Paulla Cassia   L. Cassius Longinus

L. Cassius Longinus = Aelia
(suff. AD 11)

L. Cassius Longinus = Julia Livilla
(cos. 30)   (Germanici f.)

Junia Lepida = C. Cassius Longinus
(suff. 30)

XXV   GNAEUS PISO

Groag's *Stemma Pisonum* calls for amendment in sundry items.

(1) Piso the Pontifex (*cos.* 15 BC) forfeits any connections with M. Crassus Frugi (*cos.* AD 27), cf. Table XVII.

(2) L. Piso, killed in Spain in 25, should be transferred to the Augur (p. 378).

(3) The Pontifex retains only the daughter who married L. Nonius Asprenas (*suff.* AD 6), whence a long posterity—and the two putative sons who share with him the dedication of the *Ars Poetica*, now benefiting from strong arguments in support (p. 380).

(4) An inscription discloses a Statilia as wife to the Augur (p. 376).

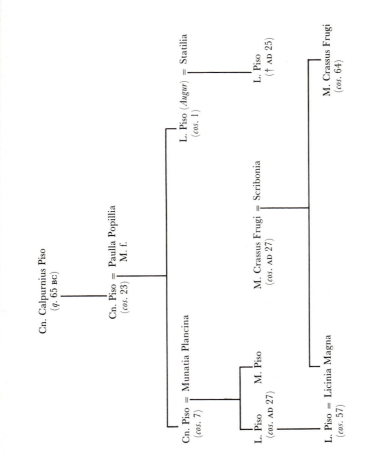

Cn. Calpurnius Piso
(*q.* 65 BC)

Cn. Piso = Paulla Popillia
(*cos.* 23)   M. f.

Cn. Piso = Munatia Plancina
(*cos.* 7)

L. Piso (*Augur*) = Statilia
(*cos.* 1)

L. Piso
(† AD 25)

M. Crassus Frugi = Scribonia
(*cos.* AD 27)

M. Crassus Frugi
(*cos.* 64)

L. Piso
(*cos.* AD 27)

M. Piso

L. Piso = Licinia Magna
(*cos.* 57)

XXVI QUINCTILIUS VARUS

Table VII in *Rom. Rev.* (cf. ib. 424) registered two sisters of Varus. One married P. Cornelius Dolabella (*PIR*² C 1345), son of the consul suffect of 44 BC. For the stemma of the Dolabellae, *PIR*² C, facing p. 318. The other married L. Nonius Asprenas, the father of the homonymous consul suffect of AD 6. For the Asprenates, see Groag's table in *RE* XVII, 870 (adding the suffect consulate in 36 of their first member).

Moreover, Table VII was able to bring in both Piso the Pontifex, whose daughter went to L. Nonius Asprenas (*suff.* AD 6) and L. Volusius Saturninus (*suff.* 12 BC), whose wife Nonia Polla (*OGIS* 468) can be identified as a sister to the Asprenates who married a Quinctilia.

Since then, no change, but a pair of noteworthy accessories. First, a third sister whom Sex. Appuleius (*cos.* 29 BC) married (*AE* 1966, 422): the Appuleii are discussed in Ch. XXIII. Second, a Vipsania attested as his wife (not perhaps the first) early in 12 BC (*Kölner Pap.* I (1976), no. 10). For convenience rather than from conviction (p. 206), she is taken to be a daughter of Marcella, not of Caecilia Attica. For Claudia Pulchra, Table VII.

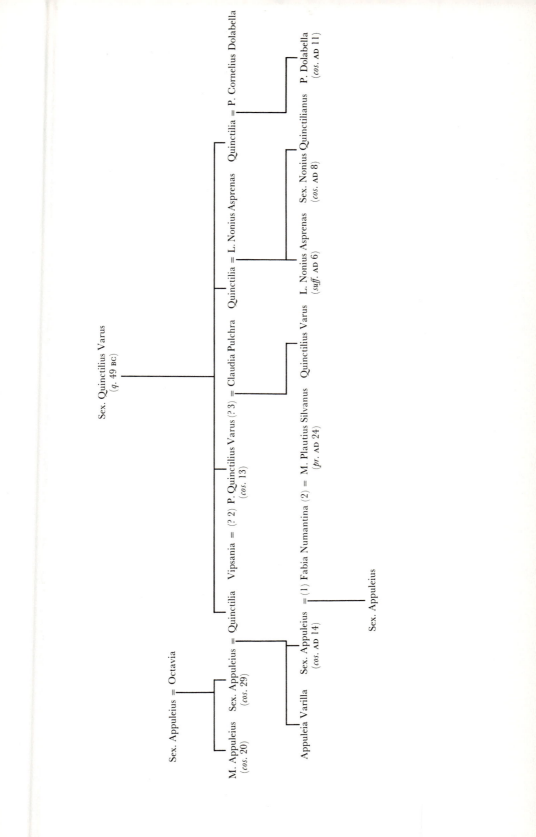

XXVII THE FABII

The table of Münzer and Groag (*RE* VI. 1777 f.) is here reproduced. For history between two wars against Carthage, observe how soon the lines lapsed both of the old Cunctator and of his rival Africanus. Two Aemilii and a Servilius Caepio had to be enlisted. Next, the gap in consulates between Allobrogicus (121) and Maximus (*suff.* 45).

As concerns the last Fabii, Numantina's husbands are put (as on Table XXVI) in an order reversing the standard acceptation (*PIR*[2] F 78; A 962). On which, p. 418. Omitted are three obscure and sporadic descendants, one of them extant under Nero (p. 418).

Apart from Marcia, the wife of Fabius Maximus, no children are on record for L. Philippus (*suff.* 38); and with Censorinus (*cos.* 8) ended the other branch of the Marcii.

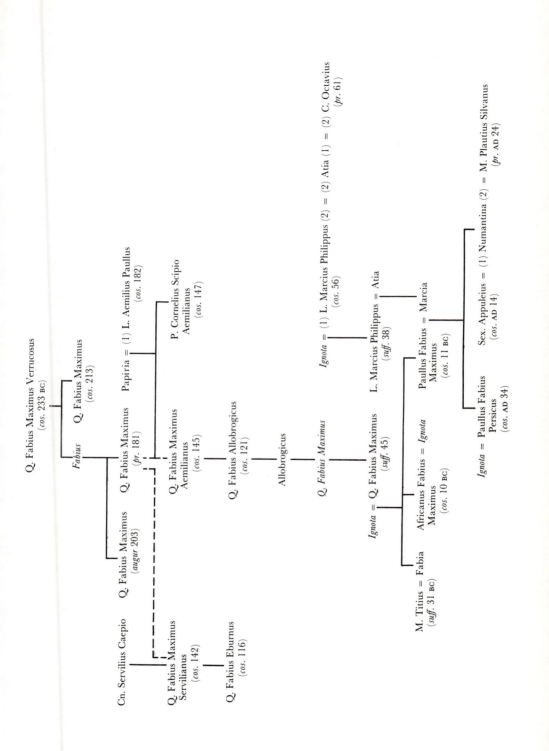

Q. Fabius Maximus Verrucosus
(cos. 233 BC)

Fabius

Q. Fabius Maximus
(cos. 213)

Q. Fabius Maximus
(augur 203)

Cn. Servilius Caepio

Q. Fabius Maximus Servilianus
(cos. 142)

Q. Fabius Maximus
(pr. 181)

Papiria = (1) L. Aemilius Paullus
(cos. 182)

P. Cornelius Scipio Aemilianus
(cos. 147)

Q. Fabius Maximus Aemilianus
(cos. 145)

Q. Fabius Eburnus
(cos. 116)

Q. Fabius Allobrogicus
(cos. 121)

Allobrogicus

Q. Fabius Maximus

M. Titius = Fabia
(suff. 31 BC)

Ignota = Q. Fabius Maximus
(suff. 45)

Africanus Fabius = Ignota
Maximus
(cos. 10 BC)

Ignota = (1) L. Marcius Philippus (2) = (2) Atia (1) = (2) C. Octavius
(cos. 56)   (pr. 61)

L. Marcius Philippus = Atia
(suff. 38)

Paullus Fabius = Marcia
Maximus
(cos. 11 BC)

Ignota = Paullus Fabius
Persicus
(cos. AD 34)

Sex. Appuleius = (1) Numantina (2) = M. Plautius Silvanus
(cos. AD 14)   (pr. AD 24)